Communications in Computer and Information Science 529

More information about this series at http://www.springer.com/series/7899

Constantine Stephanidis (Ed.)

HCI International 2015 – Posters' Extended Abstracts

International Conference, HCI International 2015
Los Angeles, CA, USA, August 2–7, 2015
Proceedings, Part II

Springer

Editor
Constantine Stephanidis
University of Crete and Foundation
for Research and Technology -
Hellas (FORTH)
Heraklion, Crete
Greece

ISSN 1865-0929 ISSN 1865-0937 (electronic)
Communications in Computer and Information Science
ISBN 978-3-319-21382-8 ISBN 978-3-319-21383-5 (eBook)
DOI 10.1007/978-3-319-21383-5

Library of Congress Control Number: 2015943372

Springer Cham Heidelberg New York Dordrecht London

Printed on acid-free paper

Springer International Publishing AG Switzerland is part of Springer Science+Business Media
(www.springer.com)

Foreword

The 17th International Conference on Human-Computer Interaction, HCI International 2015, was held in Los Angeles, CA, USA, during 2–7 August 2015. The event incorporated the 15 conferences/thematic areas listed on the following page.

A total of 4843 individuals from academia, research institutes, industry, and governmental agencies from 73 countries submitted contributions, and 1462 papers and 246 posters have been included in the proceedings. These papers address the latest research and development efforts and highlight the human aspects of design and use of computing systems. The papers thoroughly cover the entire field of Human-Computer Interaction, addressing major advances in knowledge and effective use of computers in a variety of application areas. The volumes constituting the full 28-volume set of the conference proceedings are listed on pages VII and VIII.

I would like to thank the Program Board Chairs and the members of the Program Boards of all thematic areas and affiliated conferences for their contribution to the highest scientific quality and the overall success of the HCI International 2015 conference.

This conference could not have been possible without the continuous and unwavering support and advice of the founder, Conference General Chair Emeritus and Conference Scientific Advisor, Prof. Gavriel Salvendy. For their outstanding efforts, I would like to express my appreciation to the Communications Chair and Editor of HCI International News, Dr. Abbas Moallem, and the Student Volunteer Chair, Prof. Kim-Phuong L. Vu. Finally, for their dedicated contribution towards the smooth organization of HCI International 2015, I would like to express my gratitude to Maria Pitsoulaki and George Paparoulis, General Chair Assistants.

May 2015

Constantine Stephanidis
General Chair, HCI International 2015

HCI International 2015 Thematic Areas and Affiliated Conferences

Thematic areas:

- Human-Computer Interaction (HCI 2015)
- Human Interface and the Management of Information (HIMI 2015)

Affiliated conferences:

- 12th International Conference on Engineering Psychology and Cognitive Ergonomics (EPCE 2015)
- 9th International Conference on Universal Access in Human-Computer Interaction (UAHCI 2015)
- 7th International Conference on Virtual, Augmented and Mixed Reality (VAMR 2015)
- 7th International Conference on Cross-Cultural Design (CCD 2015)
- 7th International Conference on Social Computing and Social Media (SCSM 2015)
- 9th International Conference on Augmented Cognition (AC 2015)
- 6th International Conference on Digital Human Modeling and Applications in Health, Safety, Ergonomics and Risk Management (DHM 2015)
- 4th International Conference on Design, User Experience and Usability (DUXU 2015)
- 3rd International Conference on Distributed, Ambient and Pervasive Interactions (DAPI 2015)
- 3rd International Conference on Human Aspects of Information Security, Privacy and Trust (HAS 2015)
- 2nd International Conference on HCI in Business (HCIB 2015)
- 2nd International Conference on Learning and Collaboration Technologies (LCT 2015)
- 1st International Conference on Human Aspects of IT for the Aged Population (ITAP 2015)

Conference Proceedings Volumes Full List

1. LNCS 9169, Human-Computer Interaction: Design and Evaluation (Part I), edited by Masaaki Kurosu
2. LNCS 9170, Human-Computer Interaction: Interaction Technologies (Part II), edited by Masaaki Kurosu
3. LNCS 9171, Human-Computer Interaction: Users and Contexts (Part III), edited by Masaaki Kurosu
4. LNCS 9172, Human Interface and the Management of Information: Information and Knowledge Design (Part I), edited by Sakae Yamamoto
5. LNCS 9173, Human Interface and the Management of Information: Information and Knowledge in Context (Part II), edited by Sakae Yamamoto
6. LNAI 9174, Engineering Psychology and Cognitive Ergonomics, edited by Don Harris
7. LNCS 9175, Universal Access in Human-Computer Interaction: Access to Today's Technologies (Part I), edited by Margherita Antona and Constantine Stephanidis
8. LNCS 9176, Universal Access in Human-Computer Interaction: Access to Interaction (Part II), edited by Margherita Antona and Constantine Stephanidis
9. LNCS 9177, Universal Access in Human-Computer Interaction: Access to Learning, Health and Well-Being (Part III), edited by Margherita Antona and Constantine Stephanidis
10. LNCS 9178, Universal Access in Human-Computer Interaction: Access to the Human Environment and Culture (Part IV), edited by Margherita Antona and Constantine Stephanidis
11. LNCS 9179, Virtual, Augmented and Mixed Reality, edited by Randall Shumaker and Stephanie Lackey
12. LNCS 9180, Cross-Cultural Design: Methods, Practice and Impact (Part I), edited by P.L. Patrick Rau
13. LNCS 9181, Cross-Cultural Design: Applications in Mobile Interaction, Education, Health, Transport and Cultural Heritage (Part II), edited by P.L. Patrick Rau
14. LNCS 9182, Social Computing and Social Media, edited by Gabriele Meiselwitz
15. LNAI 9183, Foundations of Augmented Cognition, edited by Dylan D. Schmorrow and Cali M. Fidopiastis
16. LNCS 9184, Digital Human Modeling and Applications in Health, Safety, Ergonomics and Risk Management: Human Modeling (Part I), edited by Vincent G. Duffy
17. LNCS 9185, Digital Human Modeling and Applications in Health, Safety, Ergonomics and Risk Management: Ergonomics and Health (Part II), edited by Vincent G. Duffy
18. LNCS 9186, Design, User Experience, and Usability: Design Discourse (Part I), edited by Aaron Marcus
19. LNCS 9187, Design, User Experience, and Usability: Users and Interactions (Part II), edited by Aaron Marcus
20. LNCS 9188, Design, User Experience, and Usability: Interactive Experience Design (Part III), edited by Aaron Marcus

21. LNCS 9189, Distributed, Ambient and Pervasive Interactions, edited by Norbert Streitz and Panos Markopoulos
22. LNCS 9190, Human Aspects of Information Security, Privacy and Trust, edited by Theo Tryfonas and Ioannis Askoxylakis
23. LNCS 9191, HCI in Business, edited by Fiona Fui-Hoon Nah and Chuan-Hoo Tan
24. LNCS 9192, Learning and Collaboration Technologies, edited by Panayiotis Zaphiris and Andri Ioannou
25. LNCS 9193, Human Aspects of IT for the Aged Population: Design for Aging (Part I), edited by Jia Zhou and Gavriel Salvendy
26. LNCS 9194, Human Aspects of IT for the Aged Population: Design for Everyday Life (Part II), edited by Jia Zhou and Gavriel Salvendy
27. CCIS 528, HCI International 2015 Posters' Extended Abstracts (Part I), edited by Constantine Stephanidis
28. CCIS 529, HCI International 2015 Posters' Extended Abstracts (Part II), edited by Constantine Stephanidis

HCI International 2015 Conference

The full list with the Program Board Chairs and the members of the Program Boards of all thematic areas and affiliated conferences is available online at:

http://www.hci.international/2015/

HCI International 2016

The 18th International Conference on Human-Computer Interaction, HCI International 2016, will be held jointly with the affiliated conferences in Toronto, Canada, at the Westin Harbour Castle Hotel, 17–22 July 2016. It will cover a broad spectrum of themes related to Human-Computer Interaction, including theoretical issues, methods, tools, processes, and case studies in HCI design, as well as novel interaction techniques, interfaces, and applications. The proceedings will be published by Springer. More information will be available on the conference website: http://2016.hci.international/.

General Chair
Prof. Constantine Stephanidis
University of Crete and ICS-FORTH
Heraklion, Crete, Greece
Email: general_chair@hcii2016.org

http://2016.hci.international/

Contents – Part II

HCI in Business and Innovation

Learning Technologies

HCI in Health

Contents – Part I

Design and Evaluation Methods, Techniques and Tools

Children in HCI

Product Design

Gesture, Gaze and Motion Detection, Modelling and Recognition

Dialogue Systems

Mobile Interaction and Smart Devices

Is Touch-based Text Input Practical for a Smartwatch?

Barbara S. Chaparro(✉), Jibo He, Colton Turner, and Kirsten Turner

Wichita State University, Wichita, KS, USA
{barbara.chaparro, jibo.he, cjturner, kxturner}@wichita.edu

Abstract. The use of smartwatches is increasing exponentially as is consumer interest. Currently, smartwatches offer the ability to read text messages, notifications, and email once they are synchronized with a smartphone. Text input, however, is limited to voice or predefined response phrases and no input keyboard is typically provided. A general consensus is that the interface of a smartwatch may be too small to implement a QWERTY keyboard. This study examined user performance and acceptance with two commercially available QWERTY keyboards, Swype and Fleksy, on a smartwatch. Contrary to the suspicion about the small screen of a smartwatch for text input, results indicate users can type accurately at speeds averaging 20–30 words per minute after brief practice, which is comparable to the typing speed of novice smartphone users.

Keywords: Smartwatch · Text input · Fleksy · Swype · Touch · Wearable

1 Introduction

Recent reports estimate over 15 million smartwatches will be sold in 2015 [1]. Experts project this number to increase to 90 million smartwatches globally in 2018 [2] and 300 million by 2020 [1]. Smartwatches let users check text messages, notifications, and emails without having to look at their phone. Responses to text notifications on smartwatches, however, are limited to voice input or a choice of predefined text responses.

The use of a small QWERTY keyboard for text entry on a smartwatch has not been implemented until recently (Samsung Gear S). Presumably this is because of the limited space for a full-size keyboard and limited touch sensitive zones given the average size of the human finger [3, 4]. Instead, many research teams have developed alternative keyboards and text input methods for such small displays. These solutions include a touch-sensitive wristband [5], touch-sensitive zooming of keys [6], round touchscreen key entry [7], panning and twist action input [8], quasi-QWERTY design [9] and a one-key QWERTY [10]. Typing performance of these alternative input methods ranges from 5–10 words per minute (WPM), along with a learning curve for new users. Text input performance with the only traditional QWERTY solution (one-key keyboard) was found to be as high as 24 WPM after 5 20-minute sessions. However, the keyboard size was 70 × 35 mm, which is approximately twice that of today's smartwatch display [10].

C. Stephanidis (Ed.): HCII 2015 Posters, Part II, CCIS 529, pp. 3–8, 2015.
DOI: 10.1007/978-3-319-21383-5_1

Funk, Sahami, Henze, and Schmidt [5] developed criteria for smartwatch text input based on the literature and their observations. The criteria include that (1) users will interact using finger input (instead of stylus) (2) the watch face will be a touchscreen (3) there will be limited dynamic feedback (4) users are likely to input short length text (5) the watch must have editing support (6) target key size must be larger than 7 mm, and (7) the watch must support some gesture-based control. Preliminary results with a new alphanumeric keyboard showed that users could learn it fairly quickly, but performance was compromised by the screen sensitivity and layout problems.

Several smartphone text input methods are available today that rely on sophisticated algorithms to predict a user's intended input. Two such systems are Swype (a trace-based input method) and Fleksy (a tap and gesture based method). Both systems use a familiar QWERTY-style keyboard and are available for Android smartphone devices, but are not yet provided on smartwatches out of the box.

2 Purpose

This study tests the feasibility of typing on a smartwatch by comparing typing performance and user satisfaction of two text input methods that use a standard QWERTY keyboard.

3 Method

3.1 Participants

Eighteen volunteers (12 Females and 6 Males) recruited from a midwestern University, ranging in age from 18 to 42 years old (M = 22.27, SD = 7.67), participated in this study. All participants were fluent English speakers, had normal or corrected-to-normal vision, owned a touch screen smartphone, and did not have any physical limitations to their hands that would prevent them from being able to text. All participants had prior typing experience on a touch screen phone. No participants had prior experience typing on a smartwatch. Participants received course credit for their participation.

3.2 Materials

A Samsung Galaxy Gear 1 smartwatch with a display size of 1.62" (41.40 mm) was used in this study. Two input methods, Swype and Fleksy, were installed on the smartwatch. Swype is a QWERTY keyboard featuring auto-correction and a trace style of text input. Unlike traditional tapping, users enter text by connecting all letters in a word with one continuous trace. When the user lifts their finger from the trace, a word-selection and auto-correction algorithm is used to select the best matching word for the trace. A space is added at the end of the word once a new trace begins. Fleksy is a point-and-tap QWERTY style keyboard featuring auto-correction and onscreen gestures to ease typing. A swipe-right gesture is used to input a space, swipe-left is used to delete, and swipe-up/down is used to scroll through suggested words.

Auditory and vibrotactile feedback were disabled on both keyboards. The order of the input methods was counterbalanced across participants. Forty randomly selected phrases from a list of 500 phrases composed by MacKenzie & Soukoreff [11] were used in the study. The phrases contained letters only (no digits, symbols, punctuation, or uppercase letters). Phrases ranged from 16 to 42 characters on both devices. Participants typed 20 phrases using each input method.

3.3 Procedure

After informed consent was obtained, participants completed a demographical survey and were trained on each input method. Participants then practiced test phrases with each input method for at least 5 min, and were allotted extra time if needed. Once they were comfortable with the input method, the experimental trials began. Phrases were displayed one at a time on a desktop computer. Participants read each phrase aloud to ensure comprehension, and verbally indicated when they started and stopped typing. Participants were asked to type as quickly and as accurately as possible and were not permitted to correct any errors. A researcher recorded task completion time using a stopwatch. Participants completed the System Usability Scale (SUS [12] and the NASA-TLX perceived workload assessment [13] after each keyboard condition. The order of input method condition was counterbalanced.

At the end, participants rated the two input methods on a 1–50 scale for preference, perceived speed and perceived accuracy. Finally, participants' hand dimensions were measured.

3.4 Dependent Variables

Typing Performance. Performance was measured by words per minute (WPM), adjusted words per minute (adjWPM), and word error rate (WER). adjWPM was calculated as WPM * WER. WER included substitution, insertion, and omission error rate.

Perceived Usability. The System Usability Scale (SUS) was used to measure participant's perceived usability of the keyboards. The SUS is an industry-standard 10-item scale with 5 response options (Strongly Disagree to Strongly Agree). The scale yields a score between 0–100, with higher score indicating higher usability.

Subjective Mental Workload. The raw NASA-TLX was used to measure participant's perceived workload of typing with each keyboard. Participants rated on a 20-point scale for mental, physical, temporal, performance, effort, and frustration.

Perceived Performance. Preference, perceived accuracy, and perceived speed with each keyboard were measured using a 50-point scale with 50 being most preferred.

4 Results

4.1 Typing Performance

A series of paired-sample t-tests were conducted to compare words per minute, adjusted words per minute and error rates across the two input methods. The first five trials were considered practice and eliminated from the analysis, leaving 15 test phrases for each method. Total error rate in addition to a breakdown by substitution, insertion, and omission errors was calculated for each keyboard at the word level. Cohen's *d* was used to measure effect size (> .8 = large) [14].

Typing speed measured by WPM revealed that participants typed faster using Swype than Fleksy, $t(17) = 5.54$, $p < .001$, Cohen's $d = 1.25$. The adjusted word per minute, which accounted for errors, produced similar results (Fig. 1). Total word error rate did not differ across keyboards, $t(17) = 1.86$, $p > .05$. The omission error rate, however, was smaller for Swype than for Fleksy, $t(17) = -2.94$, $p < .01$, Cohen's $d = 1.07$. Substitution and insertion error rates were not significantly different, $p > .05$.

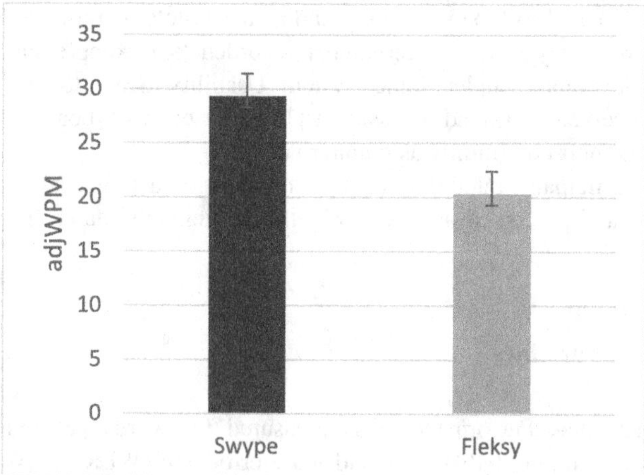

Fig. 1. Typing performance by keyboard

4.2 Subjective Measures

The perceived usability score measured by the System Usability Scale showed that participants rated Swype (M = 77.92, SD = 13.24) more usable than Fleksy (M = 46.61, SD = 17.47), t(17) = 6.21, p < .001. Fleksy was rated significantly more mentally t(17) = 3.79, p = .001 and physically demanding t(17) = 2.98, p = .008, more effortful t(17) = 4.29, p = .001 and frustrating t(17) = 5.55, p < .001 than Swype. Participants also reported that they performed worse with Fleksy than Swype, t(17) = 3.31, p = .004. Swype was perceived to be more accurate t(17) = 4.93, p < .001, faster t(17) = 5.37, p < .001, and was more preferable than Fleksy t(17) = 6.61, p < .001. The correlation between index finger width (M = 13.89 mm, SD = 1.20), which was used by all participants, and adjWPM was not significant for either keyboard, $r(17) = -0.409$, $p > .05$ for Swype and, $r(17) = -0.288$, $p > .05$ for Fleksy, which suggested that typing performance would not vary across finger width significantly.

5 Discussion

This study demonstrated that manual text input on a smartwatch is feasible and in fact, can be quite efficient. Participants were able to type an average of 29.3 WPM with Swype and 20.3 WPM with Fleksy, after correcting for errors. Total error rates were approximately 9 % for the Swype and 16 % for the Fleksy, with the majority of errors resulting from incorrect word substitutions. The typing speed on a smartwatch is comparable to the typing speed of novice smartphone users. Castellucci et al. (2011) reported that the error rate of Swype on a smartphone was 7.0 % and the entry speed was 20.9 WPM [15].

The input performance with both Swype and Fleksy was faster than most reported performance using alternative keyboards on small screen devices. This indicates that the use of the familiar QWERTY-style input is a viable method of input, despite the fact that the target key sizes (4.10 mm for Swype and 5.66 mm for Fleksy) were smaller than recommended 7 mm key size for adequate performance [5].

It can be argued that the performance difference found in this study was mainly due to a superior algorithm used to autocorrect and suggest text alternatives with Swype. While the Fleksy key size was slightly wider and taller than the Swype key size, the entire keyboard size was comparable. It is not known how much of the superior performance of the Swype was due to the tracing method rather than the traditional tap that used with Fleksy. More research must be done to isolate performance differences due to the input technique.

References

1. Siegal, J.: Smartwatch sales set to explode, expected to top 100 M within four years. BGR (2013). http://bgr.com/2013/09/27/smartwatch-sales-forecast-2020/. 27 September 2013
2. Danova, T.: Smart watch forecast: The Apple Watch Mat Lead Wrist-worn Computers to Mass Market Status., Business Insider (2014). http://www.businessinsider.com/global-smartwatch-sales-set-to-explode-2014-3. 9 September 2014
3. Raghunath, M.T., Narayanaswami, C.: User interfaces for applications on a wrist watch. Pers. Ubiquit. Comput. **6**(1), 17–30 (2002)
4. Baudisch, P., Chu, G.: Back-of-device interaction allows creating very small touch devices. In: Proceedings of the SIGCHI Conference on Human Factors in Computing Systems, pp. 1923–1932. ACM (2009)
5. Funk, M., Sahami, A., Henze, N., Schmidt, A.: Using a touch-sensitive wristband for text entry on smart watches. In: CHI 2014 Extended Abstracts on Human Factors in Computing Systems, pp. 2305–2310. ACM (2014)
6. Oney, S., Harrison, C., Ogan, A., Wiese, J.: ZoomBoard: a diminutive QWERTY soft keyboard using iterative zooming for ultra-small devices. In: Proceedings of the SIGCHI Conference on Human Factors in Computing Systems, pp. 2799–2802. ACM (2013)

7. Ashbrook, D., Lyons, K., Starner, T.: An investigation into round touchscreen wrist watch interaction. In: Proceedings of the 10th International Conference on Human Computer Interaction with Mobile Devices and Services, pp. 311–314. ACM (2008)
8. Xiao, R., Laput, G., Harrison, C.: Expanding the input expressivity of smartwatches with mechanical pan, twist, tilt and click. In: Proceedings of The 32nd Annual ACM Conference on Human Factors in Computing Systems, pp. 193–196. ACM (2014)
9. Bi, X., Smith, B.A., Zhai, S.: Quasi-qwerty soft keyboard optimization. In: Proceedings of the SIGCHI Conference on Human Factors in Computing Systems, pp. 283–286. ACM (2010)
10. Kim, S., Sohn, M., Pak, J., Lee, W.: One-key keyboard: a very small QWERTY keyboard supporting text entry for wearable computing. In: Proceedings of the 18th Australia Conference on Computer-Human Interaction: Design: Activities, Artefacts and Environments, pp. 305–308. ACM (2006)
11. MacKenzie, I.S., Soukoreff, R.W.: Phrase sets for evaluating text entry techniques. In: CHI 2003 Extended Abstracts on Human Factors in Computing Systems, pp. 754–755. ACM (2003)
12. Brooke, J.: SUS-A quick and dirty usability scale. In: Jordan, P., Thomas, B., Weerdmeester, B. (eds.) Usability Evaluation in Industry, pp. 189–194. Taylor & Francis, London (1996)
13. Hart, S.G., Staveland, L.E.: Development of NASA-TLX (Task Load Index): results of empirical and theoretical research. In: Hancock, P.A., Meshkati, N. (eds.) Human Mental Workload. North Holland Press, Amsterdam (1988)
14. Cohen, J.: Statistical Power Analysis for Behavioral Sciences. Lawrence Erlbaum, New Jersey (1988)
15. Castellucci, S.J., MacKenzie, I.S.: Gathering text entry metrics on android devices. In: CHI 2011 Extended Abstracts on Human Factors in Computing Systems, pp. 1507–1512. ACM (2011)

User Recognition and Preference of App Icon Stylization Design on the Smartphone

Chun-Ching Chen(✉)

Department of Interaction Design, National Taipei University of Technology, Taipei, Taiwan
cceugene@ntut.edu.tw

Abstract. At limited area of smartphone display, it is critical that app icon should provide good recognition and user preference. Based on the key components of an icon, this study investigated app icon design across different mobile operating systems (Apple iOS, Google Android and Windows Phone 8, with different icon design principles respectively) to understand recognition performance and user preference of different icon types. In this study, current mobile apps icons collected from app stores were characterized and examined based on different composition of "stylization" (three categories: pictorial illustration, graphic rendering and graphic symbology) and "border shape" (two categories: open and close border). The six different compositions of icons were then implemented functionally on a smartphone to test recognition time, accuracy and subjective opinion. Results show that participants prefer pictorial illustration icons, but have no significant preference on border shape. For the recognition, users perform better time on simplified stylization, but make more errors relatively. Results indicate that open border shape icon is beneficial for recognition. In conclusion, icons designed with open border shape and graphic rendering is better for users' recognition and preference on the smartphone.

Keywords: Stylization · App icon · Graphical user interface

1 Introduction

With limited display space, icons used on conventional products always take abstract pictures or symbolic illustration to represent meanings of functions in terms of semantics. Today, the advancement of high definition display and touch technology allows more graphical user interface (GUI) on devices. Designers tend to use colors and detailed graphics to make icons look splendid and attractive. This leads to an issue: are the meanings of these icons still recognizable comparing to symbolic design? In 2007, Apple released the first iPhone, which changed the role of smartphone from business to consuming use with its intuitive, user-friendly and fascinating interface. Opening a program is simply touching the icon on the screen. Apple also defined the icons applied on iOS should design with colorful, real texture and more details to create aesthetic user experience. Later Google mobile system Android also took similar way on its interface design, but with more flexibility for developers, for instances, various icon stylings versus limited icon shape on Apple iOS.

C. Stephanidis (Ed.): HCII 2015 Posters, Part II, CCIS 529, pp. 9–15, 2015.
DOI: 10.1007/978-3-319-21383-5_2

Different from the competitors, Microsoft developed its new user interface named "Modern UI" and implemented on all the mobile devices and desktop products. The design language places emphasis on typography and semantics, and creates "living tiles" to represent "sleek, quick and modern" interaction. It is clear to see that this design language takes symbology as a main part of icon design, with simple graphics, single color, tile look and dynamic feedback. The different design language from the three types of icon design raises an issue worth to investigate: what types of icon design would provide better recognition and user preference? Horton (1994) indicated that meaningful icons overcome language barriers and yield their meaning with only a quick glance, saving search time and cognitive resources [1]. At limited area of smartphone display, it is critical that app icon should provide good recognition and user preference. Based on the key components of an icon (Horton, 1994, Fig. 1), this study investigated app icon design across different mobile operating systems (Apple iOS, Google Android and Windows Phone 8, with different icon design principles respectively) to understand recognition performance and user preference of different icon types.

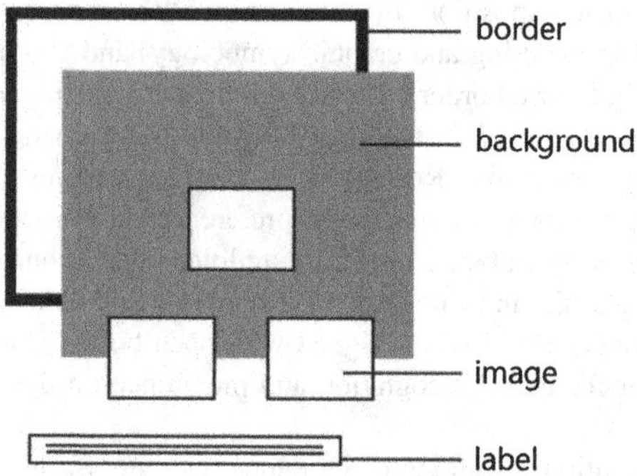

Fig. 1. Components of an icon (Horton, 1994)

2 Methods

In this study, current mobile app icons collected from app stores were characterized according to different classifications. All collected icons were then selected by experienced graphic designers for user testing. Finally, recognition time, accuracy and subjective opinion were recorded and analyzed statistically to understand the performance of different composition of icon design.

2.1 Icon Classification

Two classification principles were adopted to investigate different types of icon design. Based on the study conducted by Wang and Lin (2002) [2], this study set three categories as the "stylization" of icon graphics (pictorial illustration, graphic rendering

Table 1. Icon stylization (adopted from Wang and Lin, 2002)

Representation	Stylization	Visual elements	
		shape	Texture
Concrete	Pictorial illustration	3	3
Semi-concrete	Graphic rendering	3	2
	Graphic symbology	2	1

Ps. 3 = complicated, 2 = simplified, 1 = geometric

and graphic symbology, see Table 1 for the difference of visual elements). The other one classification principle of icon design is "border shape" (two categories: open and close border, see Table 2 for the illustration), based on current design languages of the three OSs. Therefore, in total six categories of icons were classified (Stylization*3 versus Border shape*2).

Table 2. Icon border

Border	Close	Open
Examples		
Outline	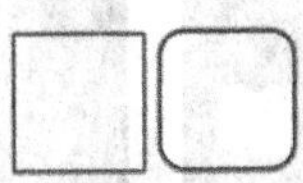	
Character	1. Icon designed in square (or with round-corner) outline, with distinct image-background combination.	1. Icon designed in free outline (could be any shape), without distinct image-background combination.
	2. Usually adopted by Apple iOS and Microsoft Modern UI.	2. Usually adopted by Google Android.

A broad search of current app icons across all mobile platforms was conducted in Jan. of 2013 to collect as many icons as possible. Three experienced graphic designers were then asked to classify collected icons according to the six categories. Finally 480 icons in 20 functions were collected, but only 96 icons in 16 functions were selected accordingly for later user testing.

2.2 Icon Recognition Experiment

A recognition experiment was then implemented to investigate performance and user preference of different composition of icons. In the experiment, as described above, the six icon categories (16 icons for each category) were implemented functionally on a smartphone. Performance and subjective opinion were recorded and analyzed statistically.

Implementation. The experiment was conducted by simulating using smartphone interface. The Samsung GALAXY SII (4.3-inch, 480 × 800 pixel display) was used for loading the program. 16 app icons was arranged in 4*4 on a single frame without background to avoid visual interference. Figure 2 shows the six categories displayed on the smartphone (three stylizations vs. two borders).

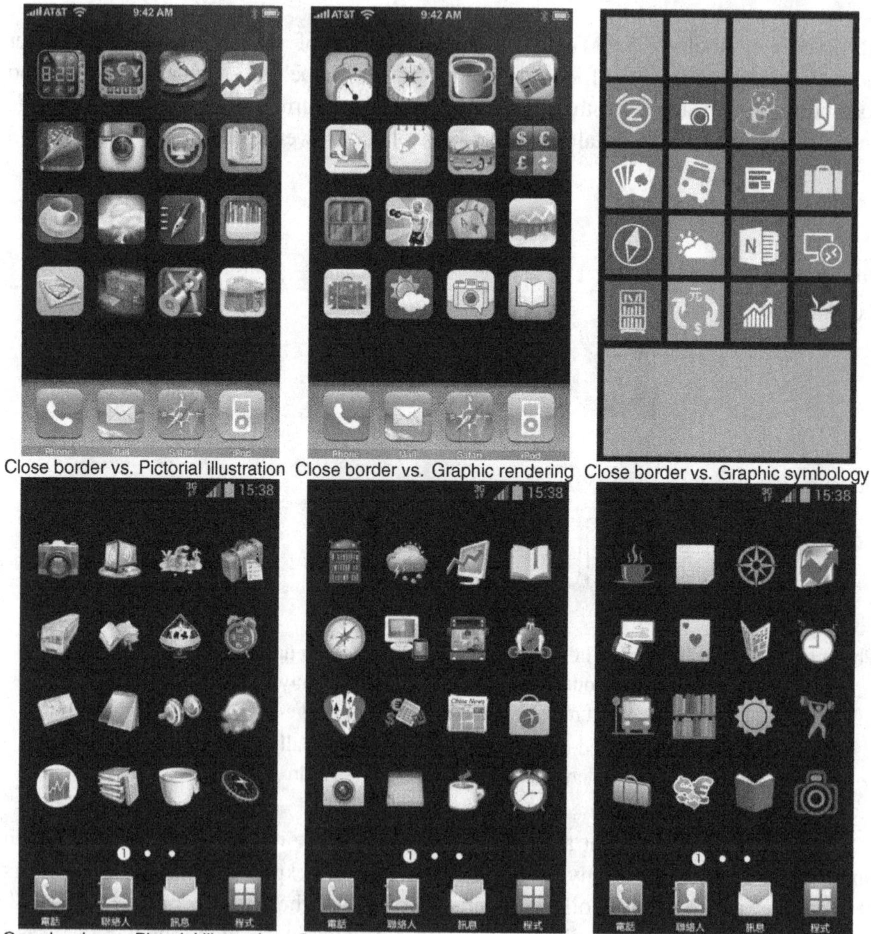

Fig. 2. Six icon categories implemented on the smartphone

Participants. 42 (16 male and 26 female, age from 20–40) smartphone users participated the experiment. All participants have at least two different mobile system using experience and without particular preference on either system.

Procedure. The six icon categories take turns randomly to display on the smartphone screen. The participant needs to select corresponded icon which function the system assigns. The system automatically records recognition time and frequency of errors. The experiment finishes after all six categories are tested. The participants are then asked to score the six categories subjectively.

Measurement. Three measures were recorded and analyzed statistically.

- Accuracy – To record if the icon was recognized correctly, through calculating frequency of errors.
- Recognition time – To record the time during the system instruction and the participant's reaction to the system.
- Preference – To calculate the score that participants gave on a 7-level Likert's Scale.

3 Results and Discussion

3.1 Accuracy

Errors found on border shape and stylization are summarized in Table 3. Results show that more errors were found on icons designed with close border comparing to open border. It is possible that open-border icons can be correctly recognized through the characteristics of different shape. For stylization, errors raise with the increase of icon simplicity.

Table 3. Errors on border shape and stylization

Classification	Border shape		Stylization		
Categories	Open	Close	Pictorial illustration	Graphic rendering	Graphic symbology
Errors	259	325	170	188	226

3.2 Recognition Time

Results show that icons designed with open border perform better than close border on recognition time. Various shapes of open-border icons may provide distinct characteristics for recognition. For stylization, significant differences were found under different border shape (as seen in Table 4). For both categories, however, icons designed with graphic rendering cost significant less recognition time than the others. This means extreme simplicity or details design on icons may not benefit recognition.

3.3 Preference

Preference of border shape and stylization are shown in Table 5. Results indicate that user has no particular preference on either border shape design. For stylization,

Table 4. The significance of recognition time on border shape and stylization

Categories	Post hoc
Border shape	
Pictorial illustration	Close > Open
Graphic rendering	Close > Open
Graphic symbology	Close > Open
Stylization	
Close	Pictorial illustration > Graphic rendering Graphic symbology > Graphic rendering
Open	Pictorial illustration > Graphic rendering > Graphic rendering

however, participants significantly prefer icons with pictorial illustration and graphic rendering to those with graphic symbology. Users may get used to colorful and detailed design icons on the smartphone.

Table 5. The preference of border shape and stylization

Categories	Significance*(p < .05)	Post hoc
Border shape		
Pictorial illustration	.497	
Graphic rendering	.197	
Graphic symbology	.050	
Stylization		
Close	.000*	Pictorial illustration, Graphic rendering > Graphic symbology
Open	.050	

4 Conclusion

In this study, it is clear to see that recognition difficulty and user preference do not perform coincidently on stylization. People prefer detailed icon design, although they are not benefited from recognition performance. Simplified icon design may improve recognition time, but cause more errors. In conclusion, the icon designed with open border shape and graphic rendering is better for users' recognition and preference on the smartphone. Graphic symbolic icon needs carefully designed in terms of semantics to increase accuracy.

Acknowledgement. Special thanks are given to Pei-Chiao Chang for her efforts on coding and conducting the experiments, and funding support from the Ministry of Science and Technology (MOST 103-2420-H-027 -002 -MY2).

References

1. Horton, W.K.: The Icon Book: Visual Symbols for Computer Systems and Documentation. Wiley, New York (1994)
2. Wang, W.Y., Lin, Y.C.: The Application of illustration stylization in retailed product packaging design. J. Des. **7**(2), 77–93 (2002). (in Chinese)

Towards Personalized Interfaces for Mobile Applications Using a Natural Text-based Interaction

Yi Ji(✉), Chek Tien Tan, and Ernest Edmonds

University of Technology, Sydney, Australia
jiyi001@homail.com,
{ChekTien.Tan,Ernest.Edmonds}@uts.edu.au

Abstract. In this paper a minimal interface for mobile application is provided that is built upon a domain specific interaction language. The domain specific interaction language provides textual interaction customization language which supports its users input any word or sentence related to the interaction that the users want to make. The textual interaction customization language supports the mobile devices users to construct a semantic and minimal interface.

Keywords: Personalized interface · Natural language · Text-based interaction · Creativity · User interface design

1 Introduction

Normally, a user interface provides a mechanism for individuals to access all the features and functionalities of their system. Without a user-oriented interface, these features and functionalities are typically inaccessible to the end user. The window-based user interface (also referred to as a graphical user interface or GUI), which is powerful for organizing the capabilities and resources available in mobile devices. It enables the user, incrementally explore and discover the capabilities of mobile devices like laptop and Mobile phone. It keeps everything in a convenient visual context, using helpful metaphors, like desktops and windows (see Fig. 1).

Unfortunately, current computer user interface and interaction have limited abilities to allow users to express themselves (Forlizzi and Battarbee 2004). Particularly, the GUI provides a menu hierarchy which is accessible via an instrument interaction (via a point device or mouse) the disadvantages for GUI is that the user is often has to repeat an endless selection cycles (using a mouse to click item) through a maze of GUI windows. As a result, the user must be able to work on a low level of interaction which means that the user is losing the ability to group a related series of basic actions into a higher level of interaction like effective communication in a semantic level (Beaudouin-Lafon 2004). Under this paradigm, there is no longer access or work with objects that are not visible or unknown to us. For instance, there are many tasks that a user must repeat it when using a GUI, such as opening certain files and activating certain controls. For such tasks, the GUI presents the user with a single logic set, implemented within the limited computer screen. In other words, current form of

C. Stephanidis (Ed.): HCII 2015 Posters, Part II, CCIS 529, pp. 16–21, 2015.
DOI: 10.1007/978-3-319-21383-5_3

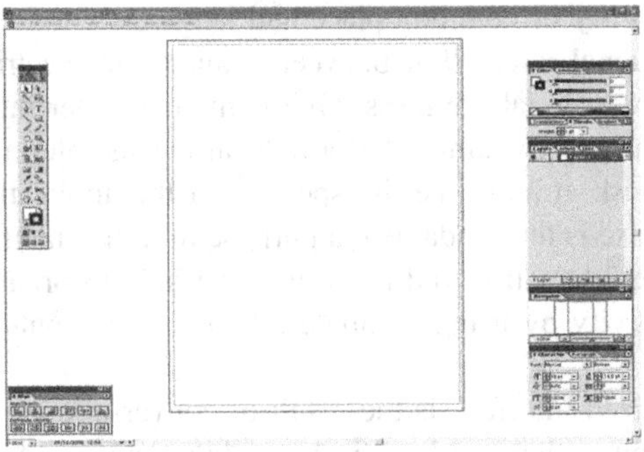

Fig. 1. Interface of Photoshop CS

interactions which is to be used to carry out human computer interactions is imbalanced and incomplete. We need to rethink about the purpose, structure of interaction and also the users' role. By investigating the human computer interaction, we can find out that the existing interfaces used in mobile equipment are mainly focusing on accessing users to complete a task or archive an object rather than supporting the user personalize his/her interactions. One example is the software entrepreneurs have developed "shortcut" utilities of various designs. Adobe Photoshop provides a shortcut to functions and processes such as opening applications and files, making menu selections, and performing multi-step operations. However, the user found it very difficult to remember all of key combination. In summary, over the years, a number of approaches and methods have been invented to deal with the problem of efficient interacting. Because of their inherent limitation, For example, instrument interactions are good at completing some fixed operation such as choosing items, dragging and moving file and so on but are unable to deal with user's individual needs from the interaction. It is clear that the current trend to rely solely on window-based user interfaces, and object-oriented interaction design method has seriously constrained a user's ability to utilize mobile device effectively.

In the following section, we provide a new type of interface that provides users with an efficient, convenient and natural way to create a personalized interface for mobile device (laptop) by utilizing human natural language. By doing so, the interface between the users and computers needs build up on a dynamic model, which represents individual user's intentions and history in order to better serve the user's needs and to eliminate unnecessary repetitive activities in an unobtrusive way.

2 Towards Personalized Interfaces

The Natural Language Processing based on an idea of concerning human communication as cooperative activity between participator (computer) and covers different aspects and levels of communication, applicable to various types of communicative activities (Allwood 1976, 2007; Allwood et al. 1992). It requires a user personalized interface to complete the conversation. To produce the user personalized interface designer need to consider how to create a conversation and make it more effective and sustainable. Mark's theory of common place and language provides a basic pattern to construct a conversational interaction between human and electrical product (Monk 2009). It requires two essential premises: One is the computer interface need to shift from a static statement to a dynamic platform. That means interface should allow the user to perform any task at any time, irrespective of the application that is currently running. Second premise is the fundamental purpose of user's interaction allows active user to understand the interaction and make the user able to organize the interface to improve their productivity by using computer. As every computer user has a unique pattern of interaction.

The user personalized interface is the result of conversational interaction between the user and the computer that can benefit the mobile device user from the following aspects: First, the personalized interface provides a way to generate effective human computer interaction by adopting the user's individual characteristics. For example, the basic acticity (completing a task by following a predefined task flow) would been transformed into a semantically format (enter semantic interaction words) that are designed to allow users to gain access to understand their perspectives and support their specific needs rather than enforcing user to complete predefined tasks or objects. We argue that the human computer interaction should become to language-based activity, and the user can define it in their personal (experience), social (using environment) and cultural context. Second, personalized interface reduce the misunderstanding between the user and the computer by provides a dynamic conversational platform. In other words, the interface allows the user to interact with the computer in a personal way rather than being a static information board. The personalized interface makes the computer response more reasonable, on a system-wide basis, to the users' input (when a user enters semantic interaction word) in any context (i.e. any level of application or operation system workplace).

Based on the above perspectives, via the domain specific interaction language and personalized interface the user can effectively control the operations of the computer.

3 Portable Drawing Application Prototype

Analogously to human-human communication, human computer interaction can also be viewed as enacting communicative acts by using a domain specific interaction language. By enhancing all of the richness and power inherent in a human language, we aim to establish a domain specific interaction language that allows the human computer interaction in a manner that is much closer to human's natural way of interaction. In particular, a user is allowed to express his/her concept to control a particular system and build a special interface. The specific interface will be changed by the terminologies the user inputted expressing unique meanings to a specific interaction context and stage of the application.

In this section, we will create a portal drawing application prototype as an example to demonstrate how to allow a user to build a personalized interface by using natural language processing. The personalized interface is generated by using a domain specific interaction language, and the language specifies high-level user interactions in three levels: syntax level, semantic level and pragmatic level.

3.1 Syntax Level

In this level, we work on generation of the user interaction domain class together with their binding to the actual application functionality or usability by using program language (in this case I use Java and OWL). Interface is the structure of the visible (or audible) forms of language. The syntax rules or grammar of a language determine the basic elements (word, sound, etc.) and the ways in which they can be combined (according to functionality or usability).

For this reason, we make use of user linguistic input in interaction design specification to carry out textual interaction customization language and produce an interface. There are two types of interaction words: Script words and Action words. Script words are utterances that can be either ordinary content words or the function title, depending on the user's intention in typing the word. Action words related to the action, which user want to operate with the system for a particular task or object. For example, to complete a task of drawing a line, a user can type a word "pen" to get pen pallet (or chose a pen from a tool bar) to draw a line; meanwhile the user allows to input a word "larger" in linguistic input window that will bring the pen size pallet on the workplace screen that access user choose a right size for the pen (see Fig. 2).

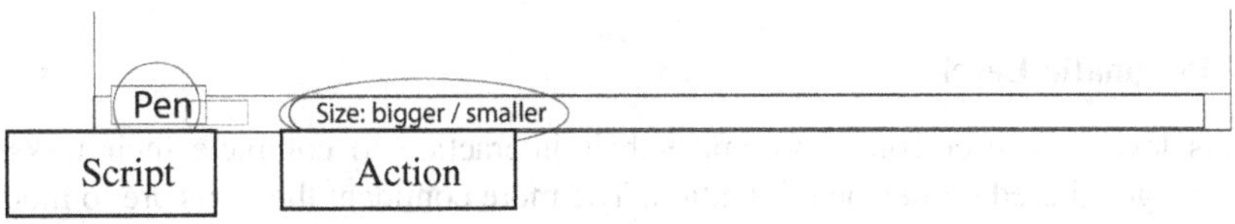

Fig. 2. Linguistic interaction bar

3.2 Semantic Level

On semantic level, users may be able to explore the systematic relation between structures in a language and a space of potential meanings. It includes the definitions of individual elements of interface (icon, menu and function) and the meaning that is generated by combining them. In this stage, the end users are going to build an individual interactive semantic image, they need to go through internalization and an externalization processes. Different users may have different classification spaces, perceptive ability and purpose of interaction, so they may have different output for the same input. It is common, users may have different language competency to specify the interface.

The textual interaction customization language allows a user utilize a Semantic Interaction Word (SIW) to operate a computer in a highly efficient way. SIW allows a user to launch applications, navigate within applications and control application functions by using textual interaction customization language rather than dragging and clicking with a pointing device such as a mouse. The textual interaction customization language is personalized by each user. In addition, the textual interaction customization language also enables a new type of interaction including function utilize organization, information retrieval, and other services to be performed by using computer. When

Fig. 3. A user personalized interface of portal drawing prototype

users go through SIW to complete a task, computer can save all information that is entered by the user, and the semantic structure of the user's workflow together composes a textual interaction customization language (Fig. 3). The user can create a specific interface to match their unique interaction needs.

3.3 Pragmatic Level

On this level, the user could systemize their interaction to complete their tasks or achieve a goal based on personal intention. The more confident the users are to modify the interface, the easier it is for the users to archive the goal they have. As a result, a concrete user semantic interface will be rendered based on how the user applying textual interaction customization language (see Fig. 4).

During the process of textual interaction, user personalized interface is guided by device profiles, application-specific style guides and the user's particular requirements. The device profiles contain device specific constraints regarding the user interface capabilities like the screen size. The user's preferences and application specific requirements guides influence the layout, selection and rendering of widgets.

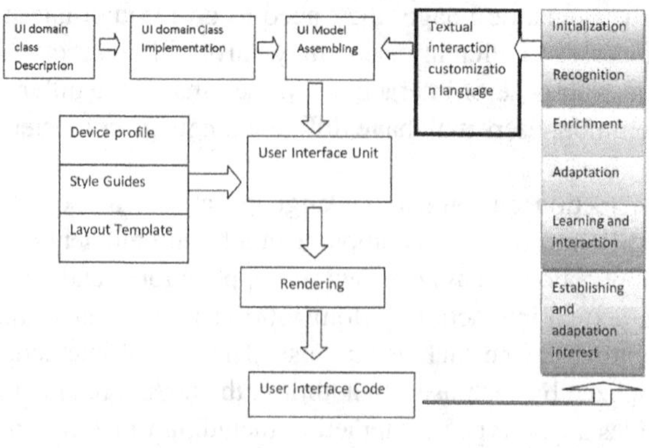

Fig. 4. The process of building a user personalized interface

4 Future Works

The future work focuses on building a Hi-Fi prototype to evaluate how the user personalized interface can optimize interaction between individual user and variety of portal devices. Moreover, we consider that the user personalized interface can be used in designing different domain specific portal device that can provide a more intuitive interaction in a manner that is simple, richer and natural than using traditional interaction design methods.

5 Conclusions

By building user personalized interface that enable us to produce most of interaction design work and making them available through natural language-based commands, and it can enhance portal device user's productivity dramatically. Moreover, user personalized interface supports a more intuitive interaction than traditional interface by improving the standard graphical user interaction (GUI) in a manner that is simple, richer and natural.

References

Allwood, J.: Linguistic communication as action and cooperation. Gothenburg monographs in linguistics, vol. 2, pp. 637–663. University of Gothenburg, Sweden (1976)

Allwood, J.: Activity Based Studies of Linguistic Interaction. University of Gothenburg, Sweden (2007)

Allwood, J., Nivre, J., Ahlsén, E.: On the semantics and pragmatics of linguistic feedback. J. of Semant. **9**(1), 1–26 (1992)

Beaudouin-Lafon, M.: Designing interaction, not interfaces. In: Proceedings of the Working Conference on Advanced Visual Interfaces, pp. 15–22. ACM (2004)

Forlizzi, J., Battarbee, K.: Understanding experience in interactive systems. In: Proceedings of the 5th Conference on Designing Interactive Systems: Processes, Practices, Methods, and Techniques, pp. 261–268. ACM (2004)

Monk, A.: Common ground in electronically mediated communication: Clark's theory of language use. In: Carroll, J.M. (ed.) HCI Models, Theories, and Frameworks: Toward a Multidisciplinary Science, pp. 265–289. Elsevier Inc., San Francisco (2009)

Can Color Tell? Smartphone LED Notification Color and Users' Perception of the Situation

Minsun Kim[1], Yongjae Kim[2], Jaeyoung Ji[1], Jiyoung Hong[2], Jinhae Coi[2], and Kwang-Hee Han[1(✉)]

[1] Cognitive Engineering Lab, Department of Psychology, Yonsei University, Seoul, Korea
{kimmin,khan}@yonsei.ac.kr, jjy0401@gmail.com
[2] UX Lab, Mobile R and D Center, LG Electronics, Seoul, Korea
ynkimk@gmail.com, {jiyoung.hong,jin.choi}@lge.com

Abstract. In this study, we investigated whether the use of LED colors that are cognitively congruent with the notification situations can help smartphone users to intuitively understand the situation. We examined whether cognitive loads placed on smartphone users differ between when single color is used and when RGB colors are jointly used to better match the situations. We predicted that participants will more quickly and correctly understand the situations when RGB colors are used than when single color is used because the use of RGB colors will improve their memory (i.e., the process of encoding and retrieval) due to the high cognitive congruency between LED colors and situations. In an experiment, we randomly assigned participants to single-color LED notification groups (i.e., red color group and white color group) and RGB color notification group and measured their cognitive loads by assessing their task performance (e.g., response time and error rate) and subjective ratings. We found no overall difference in participants' cognitive loads between groups. However, in an additional analysis, we found a significant difference exists in early rounds of experiment although the difference disappeared as participants accumulate more rounds of experiences. Our results suggest that the use of proper LED colors can help smartphone users to more effectively and efficiently understand the situations; however, the positive effect will be low for those who have more experiences of LED notification lights. We believe our study provides important implications to the study on the design of LED notification lights.

Keywords: LED notification lights · Notification situation · Cognitive load · Cognitive congruency · LED color

1 Introduction

Since smartphones provide more and more functions and information, it becomes increasingly important to design smartphone functions more effective in delivering important information to smartphone users so that they can easily and efficiently understand the situations.

LED notification lights of smartphones are a useful function which can deliver a variety of information to smartphone users, such as missed calls, incoming calls, new

C. Stephanidis (Ed.): HCII 2015 Posters, Part II, CCIS 529, pp. 22–26, 2015.
DOI: 10.1007/978-3-319-21383-5_4

text messages, and low battery. Thus, it is highly possible that smartphone users can correctly recognize the situations by glancing at the LED notification lights without necessarily activating the display. LED notification lights use different movement patterns (i.e., blink frequency) and colors to deliver different information to users. Prior research has endeavored to identify the optimal design of the movement patterns of LED lights (e.g., Chris Harrison 2012); however, relatively little research attention has been paid to how to optimize the use of colors in designing the LED notification lights.

We believe the use of color is important because people tend to have preconceived images specific to particular colors. Therefore, when a color is used in a way that does not match users' preconceived image of the color, intended information cannot be effectively delivered (Kang, 2006). Given the scant attention to the design of LED colors, however, more work is needed to know how to optimally design the colors as well as the movement patterns of the LED lights that match smartphone users' mental model.

This study aims to examine whether the cognitive loads that smartphone users experience decrease when LED notification lights match the mental model of smartphone users, i.e., high cognitive congruence between LED colors and the situations. We expect that participants will more quickly and correctly understand the situations when RGB colors are used than when single color is used because the use of RGB colors helps participants more effectively and efficiently understand the situations due to the high cognitive congruency between LED colors and situations.

2 Method

2.1 Participants

30 undergraduate students volunteered to participate in this study. All participants had normal vision and were smartphone users.

2.2 Stimuli

In a pre-test, we assessed whether it is necessary to provide LED notification lights for various situations. On the basis of the pre-test results, we identified five situations as cognitive tasks that require immediate attention from smartphone users and thus need the use of LED lights most, including missed calls/messages, *urgent* missed calls/messages, battery charging, *urgent* incoming call, and recording.

We then examined which LED color is cognitively congruent with and emotionally satisfying for each situation. Selected colors are used in RGB color condition. In single color condition, we decided to use Red color because it was most widely selected in various situations and White color because it was least widely selected.

Experimental stimuli were made by using Flash program and they were shown on monitor.

2.3 Design and Procedures

Participants were randomly assigned to three color conditions—Red, White, and RGB. We used different LED movement patterns for different cognitive tasks. Experiments consisted of learning phase and test phase.

In the learning phase, situation and corresponding LED light appeared on the screen at the same time so that participants can learn what information the LED light intends to deliver. Participants were asked to press the spacebar on keyboard to see the next screen. Learning phase was repeated twice.

In the test phase, LED light was shown on the screen for 700 ms and a situation (e.g., missed calls) was presented. For each test, we measured participants' cognitive loads by assessing their task performances (i.e., response time and error rate) and their subjective ratings. Participants were asked to answer as quickly and correctly as possible whether the situation matches the LED light by pressing "yes" key or "no" key on keyboard. We then asked participants how hard it was to answer. Participants' subjective ratings were measured using seven-point Likert scale. Tests repeated fifty times for each participant (i.e., five situations x matched/mismatched x five phases) in random order.

3 Results

We analyzed participants' response time using ANOVA, Average response times in Red color condition ($M = 1.38$) and RGB color condition ($M = 1.36$) are shorter than that in White color condition ($M = 1.44$). However, the differences are not statistically significant. (Figure 1)

Analysis by phases shows that average response times significantly decreased as the number of phases increases, $F(4{,}768) = 20.711$, $p < .05$. However, no statistically significant differences between LED stimuli were observed beyond phase 2, where the response time of RGB substantially decreases (Fig. 2).

We found the same results when we analyzed error rates and subjective ratings.

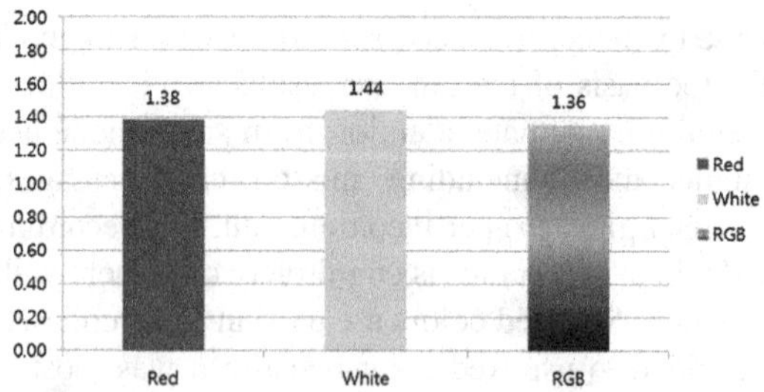

Fig. 1. Response time (sec.) of each LED color stimulus

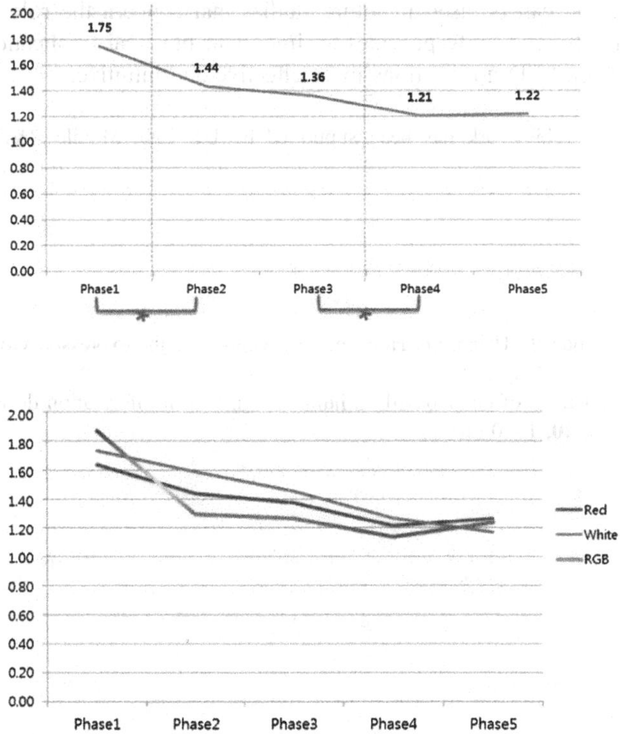

Fig. 2. Response time

4 Conclusion

This study examines how much of cognitive loads can be reduced when LED notification lights use such colors that are cognitively congruent with situations by enabling smartphone users to more intuitively understand situations. Our results suggests that, although not statistically significant, smartphone users will perceive lower cognitive loads when RGB colors—which are congruent with situations—and Red color—which has high coverage of various situations—are used than when White color—which doesn't have enough information—is used. The lack of statistical significance might be due to the fact that the number of tasks is limited to five.

Also, a phase-by-phase analysis, which is conducted to further explore the impact of learning, shows that the differences in the effects of three color conditions decrease as participants accumulate more experiences. The amount of cognitive loads that smartphone users experience in understanding situations from LED lights varies when different colors are used. However, our result suggests that the difference will start to decrease as smartphone users are exposed to LED lights.

In addition, we develop a novel evaluation method in our study which uses a series of cognitive tasks to properly measure the amount of cognitive loads reduced when colors congruent with situations are used for smartphone's LED notification lights. We believe our method can be used in future studies that concern the role of cognitive congruence. Finally, our study provides an important practical implication regarding how we can design LED notifications more effective and intuitive.

Acknowledgement. This work has been supported by UX Lab, Mobile R&D Center, LG Electronics.

References

Harrison, C., Horstman, J., Hsieh, G., Hudson, S.E.: Unlocking the expressivity of point lights. In: CHI 2012, 5–10 May 2012

Kang, S.J.: The functions of color based on human cognition in information design. J. Korean Soc. Color Stud. **20**, 1–10 (2011)

A Suggestion for a Smartphone Video Player Interface

Gyu Hong Kyung(✉)

College of Information and Communication Engineering, Sungkyunkwan University, Suwon, South Korea
georgek@skku.edu

Abstract. This paper proposes a new video player controlling application with an easy and user-friendly interface. Two existing video players, highly rated in Google Play, are analyzed. Based on the analysis, a prototype video player with an interactive interface was provided. This newly created video player that places importance on the control's button size, placement and spacing between the keys, implements control buttons that appear where the user's finger touches the display screen. To understand the usability of current video players and determine whether the new design has an impact, a survey of 51 people was conducted. The outcome revealed that the suggested video player provided the best usability for the video control. The result of this paper suggests that the proposed video player could be used as a framework for designing a user interface to enhance the usability of video players.

Keywords: Video player · Interface · Control

1 Introduction

Today's smartphone displays have become larger and wider. Control buttons are usually located at the center or lower screen, making it increasingly uncomfortable for users to operate. Media interfaces are currently made in a way that users are expected to operate the video control with both hands when devices are held horizontally. As video players strongly depend on the control buttons; the size, placement of the buttons and the spacing between them impact how convenient it is for users to operate.

The goal of this paper is to suggest a new type of video player. The paper consists of three main stages: an analysis of existing video players, a suggestion of the video player, and a survey comparing the usability of the existing video players and the prototype introduced. Both quantitative and qualitative questions were put down as a part of the survey. The quantitative method intends to produce objective and reliable data to this analysis, while qualitative method provides insight into user's viewpoints through collecting detailed data from participants. This enables the results to reflect accurate representation of individual preferences.

C. Stephanidis (Ed.): HCII 2015 Posters, Part II, CCIS 529, pp. 27–31, 2015.
DOI: 10.1007/978-3-319-21383-5_5

2 Body

MX Player and KMPlayer were selected as subjects of this study, given their high rating on Google Play. Both players have received a score of more than four marks out of five and have over 5,000,000 downloads. These applications were analyzed for the suitability as a user-friendly interface. Based on this analysis, this paper goes on to suggest a new prototype video player. For the purpose of this study, this paper defines media controls as play, pause, rewind, fast forward, skip to the previous file, and skip to the next file.

2.1 Analysis of Existing Video Players

Both MX Player and KMPlayer display their play/pause, previous and a next buttons at the bottom of their display screen. When it comes to rewinding and fast forwarding any media, these functions are operated by swiping the screen to the left or the right. To measure the sizes of the control buttons, one of LG's 5.2-inch display smartphones (LG-F320) was used. It is worth noting that phones with different display sizes have differently sized control buttons, however, for the consistency of this proposal, this study sets its standard measurements to the LG-F320 mentioned above. MX Player has rectangle control keys 22 mm in width and 8 mm in length, with no space between buttons. With regards to KMPlayer, its play/pause button is a circle with 5 mm radius, and both the previous and next buttons form rectangles of 9 mm in width and 4 mm in length. Additionally, the spacing between buttons of this media player is 9 mm.

The Analysis was conducted to investigate what makes users uncomfortable. Subjects were eight Koreans who have been using a video player application every day. The test requires the subjects to handle the functions of the video player for two minutes repeatedly. In addition, subjects were set to hold smartphone horizontally with just one hand. After the initial operation with one hand, both hands were used for the same test. After that, the survey with respect to the usability of video players was fulfilled.

The results showed that when the test subjects were asked to operate the control buttons single handed, they all answered that it was awkward with a large and wide screen. Seven subjects indicated that there was not inconvenience, concerning the test with both hands, while three subjects replied that the large screen still made them somewhat uncomfortable when reaching for control buttons. As a result of the study, I came up with the new video player design.

2.2 Suggestion of a New Video Player

Based on the analysis, a new concept for a video player was suggested where controllers would simultaneously appear on where the user's finger touches the display screen. Taking previous researches that discuss the optimal button sizes on smartphones [1, 2] into consideration, the size of the keys was set at 10 mm in width and length. In terms of the spacing between keys, the measurement of 3.17 mm was

Fig. 1. The Suggested video player

considered ideal [3]. Regarding the locations of the keys, the edge region of the screen was not of a concern on this prototype, as a study [2] observed that the edges had low subjective satisfaction and pressing performance. As regards the rewind and fast forward functions, these are embodied in swiping the screen to the left or right. Therefore, the prototype video player with an interactive interface could be conveniently controlled by one or both hands (Fig. 1).

3 Methods

3.1 Survey Design

A total of 51 Korean subjects participated in the survey. All subjects were in their 20 s and already familiar with video player applications. They have normal vision and no problem with using both their hands. In this survey, one of LG's smartphones with 5.2-inch display and Android 4.4 Kitkat (LG-F320) was used to execute six video controls from two existing video players and the new prototype, i.e., play, pause, rewind, fast forward, skip to the previous file, and skip to the next file. These were the only functions considered.

3.2 Procedures

Each subject was given written instructions on tasks and procedures at the beginning of the survey. The survey tasks were made up of two conditions; both the single handed and both handed operations. In one hand condition, subjects were asked to hold the smartphone horizontally with one hand. They were then required to operate the video players' functions repeatedly for two minutes. The first part of the experiment was then repeated on the next part with the difference of using the smartphone horizontally with both hands.

4 Results

The survey's focus was to investigate the usability of the suggested video player. In order to do so, subjects were asked about their preferable conditions when operating a video player through the smartphone and indicate preference as to which video player among the three was the most usable in each condition (Fig. 2).

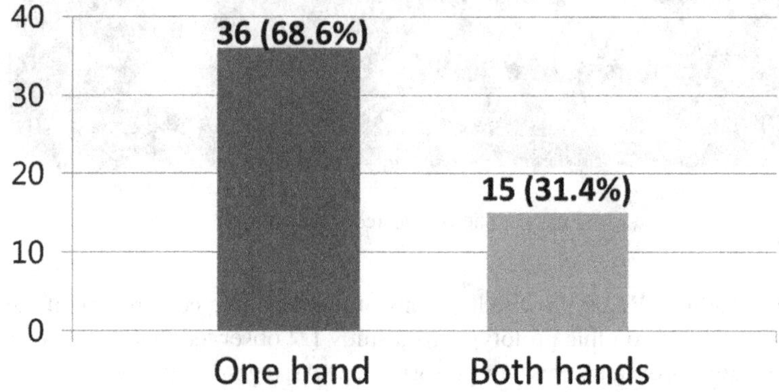

Fig. 2. The result of preferable conditions

Among 51 subjects, 36 people (68.6 %) answered that they would usually just use one hand while watching a video holding their smartphone horizontally (Fig. 3).

Under the single handed condition, 50 subjects (98 %) answered that the suggested video player is the most usable one. The reason why they chose it was due to users not being required to stretch their fingers too much and also that they can control the video player without concerning an uncomfortable hold. One attendant (2 %) responded that MX Player is the most convenient and stated that he/she feels familiar with its interface and has not felt uncomfortable (Fig. 4).

Under both hands condition, the suggested video player was chosen as the most usable video player by 33 people (64.7 %). All subjects who selected this prototype indicated that they did not have to stretch their fingers much to use the controller. 13 subjects (25.5 %) chose MX Player because they have been using it and that they

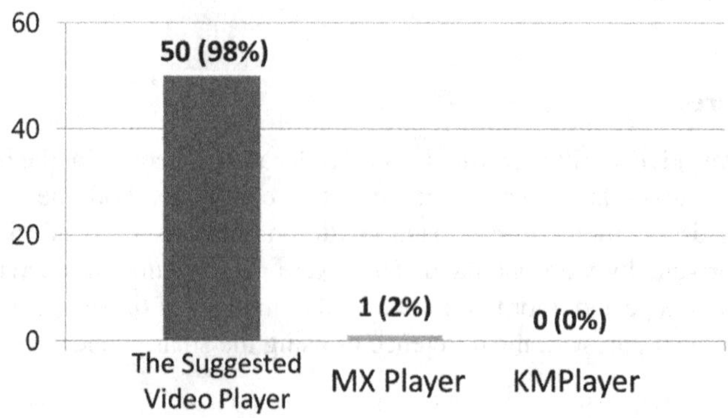

Fig. 3. The result of usable video players (one hand condition)

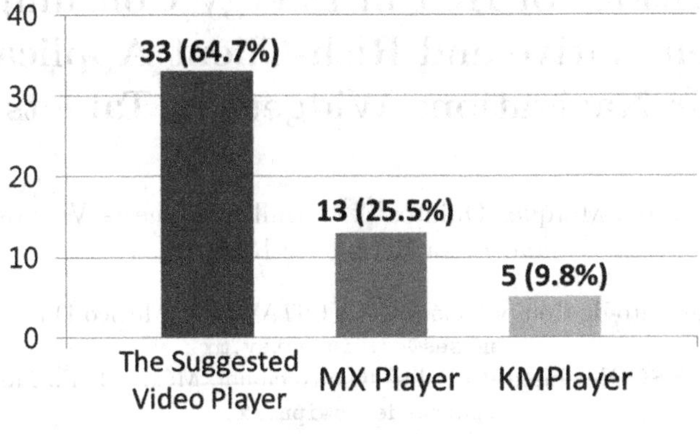

Fig. 4. The result of usable video players (both hands condition)

did not have any difficulty using it by both hands. Also, they said that MX Player's interface design looked better than the other two. 5 participants (9.8 %) picked KMPlayer and their reasons why they chose it were the same as MX Player's.

5 Conclusion

This study is an attempt to suggest a more user-centered video player interface. The study analyzed two widely known and well-reviewed video players, and compared the proposed video player with these two applications. The results showed, taken as a whole, that the proposed video player's interface is more user-friendly and convenient. In addition, as many subjects use one hand when they watch a video while holding their smartphone horizontally, this interface design would be suited for them. However, there were some indications about the design that if the design was carefully concerned, it could be a more preferable video player.

This paper principally concentrated on suggesting the video player application with an easy and user-friendly interface based on video players' main functions. Therefore, the paper could be applicable for studying interface design for other tasks of video players.

References

1. Hong, S.W., Han, S.H., Park, Y.S.: Effects of typographical factors on readability of texts on PDAs. Asian J. Ergon. **6**(2), 1–14 (2005)
2. Park, Y.S., Han, S.H.: Touch key design for one-handed thumb interaction with a mobile phone: effects of touch key size and touch key location. Int. J. Ind. Ergon. **40**(1), 68–76 (2010)
3. Mayer, C., Morandell, M., Gira, M., Sili, M., Petzold, M., Fagel, S., Schüler, C., Bobeth, J., Schmehl, S.: User interfaces for older adults. In: Stephanidis, C., Antona, M. (eds.) UAHCI 2013, Part II. LNCS, vol. 8010, pp. 142–150. Springer, Heidelberg (2013)

Implications of HCI in Energy Consumption Between Native and Rich-Client Applications for Navigations Widgets in Tablets

Ana Belem Márquez Quintos[1](✉), Amilcar Meneses Viveros[1], and Erika Hernández Rubio[2]

[1] Departamento de Computación, CINVESTAV-IPN, México D.F., Mexico
ameneses@cs.cinvestav.mx
[2] SEPI-ESCOM, Instituto Politécnico Nacional, México D.F., Mexico
ehernandezru@ipn.mx

Abstract. The mobile platforms could be classified among those using virtual machine and that not use to run native apps. A native app is developed in a specific way for an specific mobile platform. The Rich-Client Applications are structured multilayer form. Developers and users have the problem of working with the constraints of mobile devices such as the energy consumption. The developers have tried to do user-centered designs. Analyzes have been conducted to justify the feasibility of developing mobile device applications natively or rich-client. This paper presents a comparative study of navigation widget in rich-client applications against native iOS and Android applications is presented. The results presented do not make a quantitative comparison between native iOS and Android applications.

1 Introduction

The mobile platforms could be classified among those using virtual machine and that not use to run native apps. Currently, the developers mobile device performed their developments as native or Rich-Client apps to advantage the interaction that provide each platform [1,2]. This due to that apps as Fat-Client or Thin-Client not enable a interaction friendly and consume a lot resources such as process, network, memory, to name a few.

A native app is developed in a specific way for an specific mobile platform. This apps are developed with the tools provided by the platform (compilers, debuggers, profiles, among others). Furthermore, use the library and frameworks including into the architecture of the mobile platform.

The Thin-Client applications are not dependent of the mobile operating system to they work, these are easier to maintain because they do not have the application code and their functionality depends on the server. On the other hand, the Fat-Client applications have one or three layers of application code and they can operate independently of a server for a period of time. The Rich-Client

C. Stephanidis (Ed.): HCII 2015 Posters, Part II, CCIS 529, pp. 32–38, 2015.
DOI: 10.1007/978-3-319-21383-5_6

Applications are structured multilayer form. They can provide high responsiveness, they are interactive and they enrich the user experience for applications that run autonomously.

Developers and users have the problem of working with the constraints of mobile devices such as the energy consumption [3]. As a programmer, developers seeking techniques that enable the execution of applications with low energy consumption. On the other hand, users seeking to use applications that offer longer battery use, on their mobile devices [4].

The developers have tried to do user-centered designs. This generates applications that are easy to handle and therefore popular. From the point of view of resource management have focused on developments using techniques such as offloading or use of code regions that do not use a virtual machine. An interesting model is posed offloading techniques which divide a program into two parts: the part that should always run on a mobile device and that may be subject to offloading. The part that runs on the mobile device includes handling the presentation layer, its means, the set of widgets [5].

Analyzes have been conducted to justify the feasibility of developing mobile device applications natively or rich-client [1,2]. However, these analyzes have not been as concerned to establish energy consumption affects the design of native or rich-client applications. Perhaps this lack of analysis is because of the high computational complexity computing is working with mobile computation offloading techniques. However, several studies indicate that when an application is active, are the screen and render it consumes more energy [6,7]. Therefore it is necessary to study the energy behavior of the presentation layer and interaction, since this always runs on the client side, that its to say on the mobile device.

This paper presents a comparative study of navigation widget in rich-client applications against native iOS and Android applications is presented. In some mobile platforms, such as Android or Windows, the native applications are running on a virtual machine. The Rich-Client applications in Android are executed on a browser running on Dalvik. Native applications for iOS, run directly on the processor and Rich-client applications run on browsers that do not use a virtual machine.

The results presented do not make a quantitative comparison between native iOS and Android applications. The results presented do not make a quantitative comparison between native iOS and Android applications. This is because the software tools to measure the energy consumption are different in both platforms. In Android tools present consumption in Joules. In iOS tools show the level of use of the battery. Furthermore, it is expected that the energy consumption of navigation widgets is higher in Rich-Client applications. However it is interesting to know whether the behavior between environments with virtual machines (such as Android) and no virtual machine (like iOS) are similar. In addition, a literature-based and results of our experiments on the involvement of as energy consumption affects the use of the navigation widget HCI analysis is presented. This means the user behavior and the impact on the usability, effectiveness and efficiency.

2 Related Work

In recent years, programmers and engineers have developed some techniques to help make computer systems, applications and programs have good performance and low power consumption. These techniques vary depending on the device, operating system or context of use, to name a few. In general, we can see that these techniques are: schedulers , offloading, offlining, network usage, design and monitor approach.

2.1 Schedulers

This technique saves energy through proper use of multicore processors. Proper selection of the core that executes a process allows energy savings when working with non-symmetric multicore architectures. Since some not so important tasks can be left in cores of low performance and low power consumption. Another strategy prevents the migration of processes among multiple cores of a processor, so the movement of the cache is avoided and energy is saved.

Yuan et al. [8] presents a real-time scheduler energy efficient. It is mainly used to run multimedia applications, statistically cycles assigned to individual applications and runs on different speeds and times, allowing a savings of up to 72 %.

2.2 Computation Offloading

Computation offloading is a technique used primarily in applications that run on devices with limited resources. These resources are the battery, memory, processor, storage and communications. The main idea of this technique is to migrate the execution of computationally heavy tasks to other resources outside the device, such as servers.

To achieve proper use of this technique, identify the task that is subject to run out of the device. After the performance and energy to accomplish this task on the device is calculated vs time and energy it would cost to send the task to run out of the device (data transfer, transfer code, application services, use of antenna, etc.). Memory usage can also be used as a reference to see if a task is subject to be sent to run out of the device (tasks such as speech recognition or image processing are subject to these techniques).

In [9] presented a system that supports offload code fine granularity to maximize energy savings with minimal effort for the developer. This system decides, at runtime, which methods should be processed remotely to achieve greater energy savings according to the current restrictions on mobile connectivity.

In [10], the authors present a system for image retrieval based on content, which performs an intensive computation for image search. In this paper, it is decided dynamically in that moment and that is what should be sent to the server. This decision depends on the bandwidth of the wireless network, the size of all images that are needed and the number of look that requires the user. This technique achieved an energy saving of up to 45 %.

2.3 Offlining

This technique refers to the change of state of a component in a mobile device. The state change may refer to turn on or turn off some component of the device. In specific cases, such as multicore processors, can be turned on or off one multicore, or change the frequency at which they operate.

In [11], the authors propose policies according to the state in which the processor, i.e. established if the number of threads that are running exceeds the fiery core, then turn on additional cores, on the other hand, if the cores they are not in use are turned off.

2.4 Network Usage

This technique is based on the transfer and data communication across different mobile networks and uses the tail ratio to save energy.

Mital et al. [12] show that no matter the size of the data file to download, since energy is dominated by the state tail or radio. Furthermore, Looga et al. [13] propose a planner for traffic in wireless networks that performs short communication delays and combines them to form a long drive and take advantage of radio tails were generated. This planner can save up to 72 % of energy consumed by the device.

2.5 Monitoring Battery Status

This is a technique for HCI. Some authors call this technique human-battery interaction [14]. This technique allows users to monitor battery usage and also manage the use of applications on your mobile device to optimize battery consumption.

Rice et al. [15] show that in the idle state the mobile device is recommended that the 2G network is not used because it consumes more energy than 3G or wireless network.

In [4], the authors conducted a study on the attitudes and behavior of users of mobile devices. This study shows that users needed to prolong battery life. To achieve this, users tend to set the various services offered by your device, such as screen brightness, wireless network, bluetooth, among other components. However, the researchers emphasize that for users is not enough and demand more clear and detailed battery status information and energy consumption. Also, they found that users want to understand how the various applications and services affect the energy consumption of your device to learn how to control it.

2.6 Design Approach

This is a technique that allows HCI mobile consumes less power by selecting colors and content presentation application.

Several papers [11,12,16], agree that the presentation layer has a high consumption of energy and it depends on the color of the screen. Some authors have reported that use the screen in white can consume more energy than a black screen [16]. Other studies have aimed to use images in PNG format can reduce energy consumption images in other formats such as JPG or TIFF.

2.7 Impact of Energy Saving Techniques in the Components of a Mobile Device

As presented, there are different techniques applied to mobile devices to save power. To review how these strategies affect a mobile device, you should consider major hardware components of these devices, such as: Display, render system, CPU, and network. Table 1 allows to observe the impact of technical hardware component mobile.

Table 1. Energy saving techniques and their relationship with the components of a mobile device.

Techniques	Display	Render	CPU	Network
Schedulers			✓	
Offloading			✓	
Offlinig	✓	✓	✓	✓
Design	✓	✓		
Network usage				✓
Battery monitor	✓	✓	✓	✓

We can notice that Offlining approach and battery monitor could have more impact en whole device mobile. The design approach affects the display and render system. We consider this approach in our work because these components are the main consumers of energy of the mobile device in active mode [7].

3 Test and Results

To study the presentation layer, was determined using navigation widgets because these are the most used in mobile applications. The navigation widgets considered were: Fixed menu, vertical list and Page List. Also, The test system is equivalent to that of most commercial tablets. That is, with two cores and at least 512MB of RAM and touch screen. In particular, we use a Rapsberry pi b + card. This platform has a dual core processor ARM11 with 700 MHz, 512 MB RAM and OS Raspbian v3.18.

The prototypes were developed using different navigation modes to display different types of animals according to their classification. The prototypes use a navigation according to a selection of taxonomy. The prototypes have been developed for different architectures of development: (1) Native without virtual

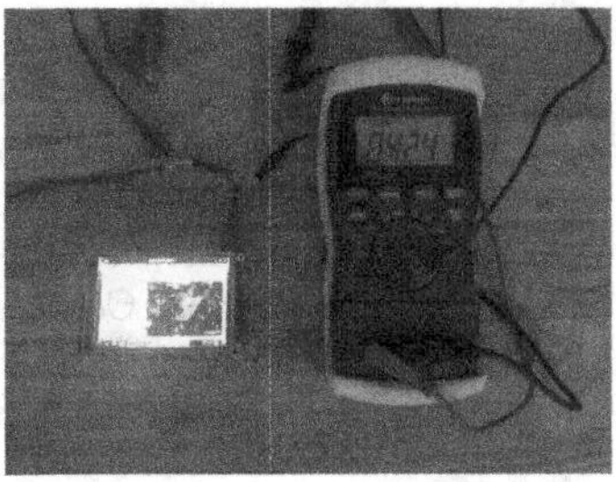

Fig. 1. Circuit to measure the power consumption of mobile device.

Table 2. Energy (Joules) widgets on prototypes

Widget	Native	Native with VM	Rich-client	Rich-client with VM
Fixed menu	0.06692	0.11827	0.41610	0.47363
Vertical list	0.06497	0.09650	0.29417	0.31088
Page	0.02230	0.03026	0.25386	0.32699

machine, (2) native with virtual machine, (3) Rich-Client in browser without VM and (4) Rich-Client in browser with virtual machine.

The prototype native application without virtual machine is programmed in QT with C ++. Native prototype application without virtual machine was programmed in Java, using the Oracle JVM. Prototypes of Rich-Client application were developed in HTML5 with Java Script. Run in browsers Epiphany and Chromium with QEMU virtual machine.

Ten tests a circuit like the one presented in Fig. 1, each prototype were performed and used to measure energy consumption. We focus on the physical measurement because the widget uses the display, render and part can be processed by the CPU. For each widget task was performed to measure specific energy consumption using each selected widget (Table 2).

4 Conclusion

There are several strategies for energy saving applications for mobile devices Table 1. In particular, the design technique affects the Display and Render system which modes are active modules that consume more energy.

According to the widgets that developed, the paging widget that less energy is consumed because is updated related to the widget content, whereas in as many widgets as work items are loaded.

The sets of widgets that use less energy are native applications, specifically QT. For Rich-Client applications energy consumption increases considerably compared to native applications, because the application is running on a browser.

As expected, the virtual machine consumes more energy than applications that do not use.

References

1. Koerber, T.: Lets talk about android-observations on competition in the field of mobile operating systems (2014). SSRN 2462393
2. Hernandez, I.M.T., Viveros, A.M., Rubio, E.H.: Analysis for the design of open applications on mobile devices. In: International Conference on Electronics, Communications and Computing (CONIELECOMP) 2013, PP. 126–131. IEEE (2013)
3. Robinson, S.: Cellphone energy gap: desperately seeking solutions. Strategy Analytics (2009)
4. Heikkinen, M.V., Nurminen, J.K., Smura, T., Hämmäinen, H.: Energy efficiency of mobile handsets: measuring user attitudes and behavior. Telematics Inform. **29**(4), 387–399 (2012)
5. Kumar, K., Liu, J., Lu, Y.H., Bhargava, B.: A survey of computation offloading for mobile systems. Mobile Netw. Appl. **18**(1), 129–140 (2013)
6. Thiagarajan, N., Aggarwal, G., Nicoara, A., Boneh, D., Singh, J.P.: Who killed my battery?: analyzing mobile browser energy consumption. In: Proceedings of the 21st International Conference on World Wide Web, pp. 41–50. ACM (2012)
7. Carroll, A., Heiser, G.: An analysis of power consumption in a smartphone. In: USENIX Annual Technical Conference, pp. 271–285 (2010)
8. Yuan, W., Nahrstedt, K.: Energy-efficient soft real-time cpu scheduling for mobile multimedia systems. ACM SIGOPS Opera. Syst. Rev. **37**(5), 149–163 (2003)
9. Cuervo, E., Balasubramanian, A., Cho, D.k., Wolman, A., Saroiu, S., Chandra, R., Bahl, P.: Maui: making smartphones last longer with code offload. In: Proceedings of the 8th International Conference on Mobile Systems, Applications, and Services, pp. 49–62. ACM (2010)
10. Hong, Y.J., Kumar, K., Lu, Y.H.: Energy efficient content-based image retrieval for mobile systems. In: IEEE International Symposium on Circuits and Systems 2009, ISCAS 2009, pp. 1673–1676. IEEE (2009)
11. Carroll, A., Heiser, G.: Unifying DVFS and offlining in mobile multicores. In: IEEE Real-Time and Embedded Technology and Applications Symposium (RTAS), Berlin, April 2014
12. Mittal, R., Kansal, A., Chandra, R.: Empowering developers to estimate app energy consumption. In: Proceedings of the 18th Annual International Conference on Mobile Computing and Networking, pp. 317–328. ACM (2012)
13. Looga, V., Xiao, Y., Ou, Z., Yla-Jaaski, A.: Exploiting traffic scheduling mechanisms to reduce transmission cost on mobile devices. In: Wireless Communications and Networking Conference (WCNC), Paris, Abril 1–4, pp. 1766–1770. IEEE (2012)
14. Rahmati, A., Zhong, L.: Human-battery interaction on mobile phones. Pervasive Mob. Comput. **5**(5), 465–477 (2009)
15. Rice, A., Hay, S.: Measuring mobile phone energy consumption for 802.11 wireless networking. Pervasive Mob. Comput. **6**(6), 593–606 (2010)
16. Perrucci, G.P., Fitzek, F.H., Widmer, J.: Survey on energy consumption entities on the smartphone platform. In: 2011 IEEE 73rd Vehicular Technology Conference (VTC Spring), Budapest, Hungary, pp. 1–6. IEEE, May 2011

Adaptive UI from Human Behavior Pattern on Small Screen Interface: Focused on Double-Swipe Interface

Hee-Seung Moon(✉) and Da Young Ju

School of Integrated Technology, Yonsei Institute of Convergence Technology, Yonsei University, Seoul, South Korea
{hsmoon121, dyju}@yonsei.ac.kr

Abstract. Recently, various smart devices are released and user's task environment is changing from desktop-sized interface to mobile device. This research proves possibility of AUI optimized for touch screen device. This paper is aimed to lead enhanced AUI with improved performance and gesture error ratio. We made experiments about users' intuitive behavior pattern on restricted interface, especially focused on double-swipe. Main contribution of this research is approach to AUI by focusing on input method from small mobile device kinds of smart watch.

Keywords: Adaptive UI · Personalization · Gesture behavior pattern · Small screen interface · Double-Swipe interface

1 Introduction

Smart device has been dramatically developed for a few years in the direction of becoming smaller. Input gesture based on tiny screen display would be limited, therefore it causes collisions between similar touch gestures. These collisions trigger user's gesture error and reduce task performance. Adaptive UI, which adapts its layout to the context of user, can be one of solutions to compensate the problem.

The aim of this paper is to suggest improved AUI with better practice time and gesture error rate based on small screen device. We made experiments about users' intuitive behavior pattern on restricted interface, especially focused on double-swipe interface with readjusting swipe threshold, considering various factors of AUI, and thereby specified guideline for designing AUI.

In the existing literature, adaptive menu, which learn user's purpose in response to item selection, has been studied primarily. Nevertheless adaptivity of interface provides better performance, AUI based on item selection often brings negative usability by showing incessant visual changes. In comparison, we focused on AUI based on input gesture, which adjust internal threshold unrecognized by user. Also, we considered novel user factors, such as satisfaction of controllability and user context, and thereby practiced more detailed approach in small screen interface.

C. Stephanidis (Ed.): HCII 2015 Posters, Part II, CCIS 529, pp. 39–44, 2015.
DOI: 10.1007/978-3-319-21383-5_7

2 Related Work

Adaptive User Interface (AUI) is defined as interface that provide immediate user assistant by learning user's actions [4]. First notion of adaptive UI was announced by Greenberg and Witten [1]. Adaptive UI applied with frequency of item usage showed better performance than static UI.

Sears and Shneiderman developed existing drop-down menu and suggested novel adaptive menu, split menu which is composed of adaptive part and functional part [3]. These adaptive menus brought positive effect on users' satisfaction and task performance. In comparison, Mitchell and Shneiderman suggested that static menu is rated better than adaptive menu altering the visual location of items both performance and satisfaction [2]. Gajos showed duplication-typed adaptive menu which don't include visual alteration had much choices from participants [5].

While importance of small screen device was emphasized, AUI was studied with focusing improvement at small screen interface. Findlater and Mcgrenere proceeded research with effect of screen size, and showed smaller sized interface can take better effect for task efficiency and satisfaction with adaptive UI [6]. Recently, researches are focused on the interactions of cause and effect with factors of adaptivity. Gajos found out accuracy and predictability of adaptive UI is related with user's satisfaction, though only accuracy influences actual performance [7].

3 Experiment I: Observing Human Behavior in Small Screen

3.1 Overview

The focus of the present paper is observing human behavior, therefore we designed UI that user can inputs double swipe gestures causing collision depending on swipe range on typical touch-based mobile phone. Two sets of experiment were considered by following factors; (1) satisfaction of recognition, (2) satisfaction of controllability. Also, user survey was followed in order to investigate human behavior.

In order to suggest gesture-based AUI, we have tried an experiment to observe general patterns of user's behavior under the condition of collision happening when two gestures are activated simultaneously. As illustrated in Fig. 1, the situation of using internal and external swipe simultaneously (double-swipe interface) was given to the participants.

Because preceding research data showed that changes coming from AUI actually decreases the usage by causing visual confusion, we then devised the experiment that detect an influence of participant's visual recognition of AUI and the actual gesture. First set included two designs; the first design of making participant aware of the AUI changes visually, and the second blueprint of making changes unnoticeable.

Also, we constructed the experiment about users' satisfaction of controllability. For clear judgment about gesture errors in terms of using UI, the experiment was progressed to see general patterns of user's reaction when unintended errors occur.

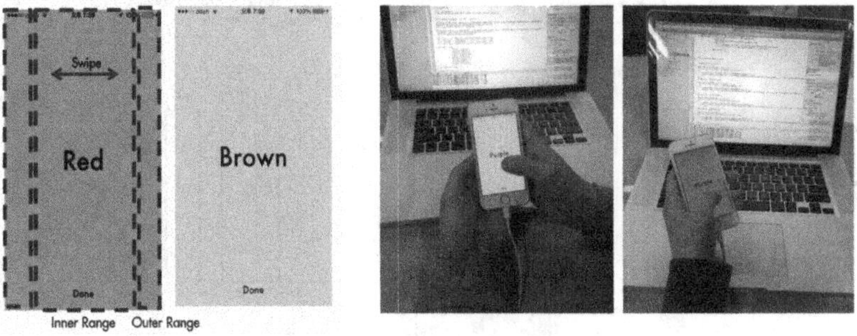

Fig. 1. Experiment I Circumstance

3.2 Methodology

Set 1: Satisfaction of Recognition. We set up four experiment environments classified with alteration method (Random/Learning) and visibility (Visible/Invisible). And accordingly, time for achieving the task was measured. In order to increase credibility, motivation was given to the participant who achieved outstanding time management, by offering additional compensation. User surveys were conducted to figure out overall satisfaction of users afterwards including measurement of users' cognitive width of threshold.

Set 2: Satisfaction of Controllability. The same method applied; motivating participants and recording time spent for accomplishing the task. Frequency of usage of particular gesture in the process was recorded as well, based on observation from prior experiment, which defined the error-response gesture. Survey was conducted after the experiment, asking participants whether their intentions and UI actually matched, and their satisfaction about the system.

3.3 Result

Set 1: Satisfaction of Recognition. 16 individuals participated (10 Males, 6 Females, age 20–29) and result is showed in Fig. 2. Some of remarkable points are that, (1) as compared with actual performance, users' satisfaction of recognition is much affected by interface, (2) invisible alteration was highly evaluated in learning condition, especially with satisfaction ($p < .1$). Various results of experiments are presented in figures.

Set 2: Satisfaction of Controllability. Samples are identical with set 1; 16 college students who are in 20 s (9 Males /7 Females). Each comparison between frequency of error-responding gestures and time efficiency, and satisfaction are analyzed on Fig. 3. Linear trend line (red) was fitted with scatterd data, each standard deviation of slope was 45.17 % (Left) and 17.76 % (Right).

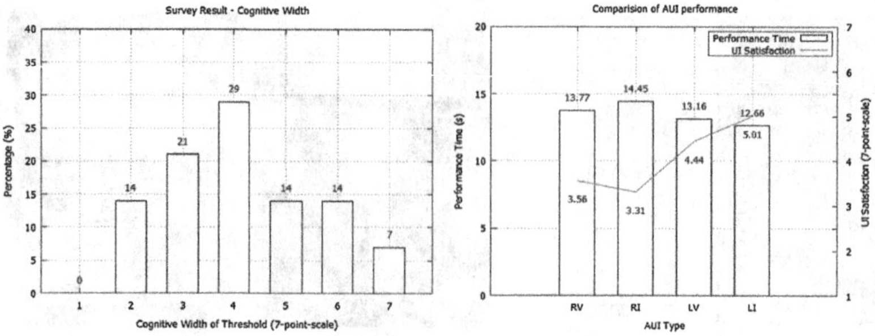

Fig. 2. Experiment I Result 1, (Left) Participants' cognitive width was examined with 7-point-scale; from Very Narrow-1 to Very Wide-7. /(Right) Comparison of four experiment group; RV(Random-Visible Threshold), RI(Random-Invisible), LV(Learning-Visible), LI (Learning-Invisible).

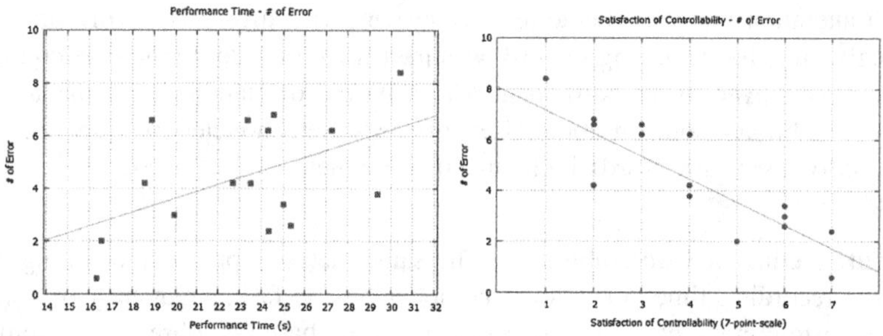

Fig. 3. Experiment I Result 2, (Left) Correlation between performance time and number of error gesture /(Right) Correlation between users' satisfaction (of controllability) and number of error gesture.

3.4 Discussion

According to the result of Set1, in the case of R (Random alteration)-group, participant showed higher efficiency when managing task when there was visual perception. In the case of L(Learning alteration)-group, there was not much differences in managing task related to visual perception, yet, their satisfaction increases when there is a visual guideline.

The more frequent usage of error-responding gesture lengthens the subtle amount of time needed for task management, which eventually result in decreasing efficiency. And as easily implied, survey also shows that the more actions participant has to take, the lower their satisfaction becomes. An interesting factor is that although the actual efficiency decreases only a little amount, participant felt greater dissatisfaction.

4 Experiment II: Applying to Tiny Screen

Tiny screen interface has been magnified as a wearable device. With limited screen size, adaptive UI still has an important role. Moreover, we attempted in-depth approach with the experiment, considering participants' using circumstance like listening music.

4.1 Methodology

We devised experimental environment like Fig. 4 (Left). Participants were lead to accomplish the task at gesture-recognizing screen (2-inch, typical watch size). Also they were instructed tasks in double-swipe interface with three kinds of main using context (Message/Music/Photo). We measured number of error for each condition, also including post-survey.

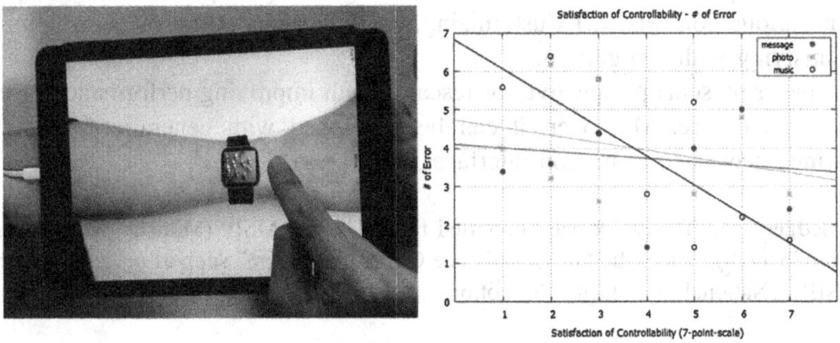

Fig. 4. (Left) Experiment II Circumstance; double-swipe interface within 2-inch screen was provided to participants /(Right) Experiment II Result; we measured correlation between satisfaction of controllability an number of error gesture within three kinds of using context (checking message, viewing photos, listening music).

4.2 Result

8 individuals (6 Males and Females, age 21–27) are participated the experiment including 5 sets of task for each condition. Result is in Fig. 4 (Right) that compared correlations between satisfaction and number of error within 3 kinds of using conditions. For each condition, linear solid lines were fitted with the data. Despite "photo" / "message" conditions are not seem to be statistically significant, within "music" condition, decreasing correlation was detected.

4.3 Discussion

One of the most notable points is that, satisfaction rapidly dropped with listening music sharper than viewing photos/messages. In order to figure out this, we found two major factors affecting context-based adaptive UI: (1) immersion in contents, (2) inherent habit of existing context. In practice, participants feels more negative usability from wrong cut-off with listening music, which has more immersion, than checking messages. It suggests that variability of AUI within using circumstance which has much immersion should be handled deliberately.

5 Conclusion

As results of various experiments, we specified several propositions with AUI. (1) Users have considerably personalized touch gesture pattern. (2) Satisfaction of recognition and controllability is affected by interface keenly, and these factors are mainly used to evaluate interface. (3) Depending on user's context, input behaviors are differentiated due to immersion, inherent habit.

Through above processes, we suggest guideline for designing AUI with three keywords. AUI on tiny screen device should focus on (1) Learning, gratifying users' personalized input pattern, (2) Context, distinguishing application of adaptation between various contexts, (3) Customizing, providing autonomy of control for user under satisfying with recognition.

This paper presents perspective for research with improving performance of users' various input device. Moreover, it can be developed with generalized input from various interfaces such as motion interface.

Acknowledgement. This work was supported in part by the MSIP (Ministry of Science, ICT and Future Planning) under the "IT Consilience Creative Program" support program supervised by the NIPA (National IT Industry Promotion Agency) (NIPA-2014-H0201-14-1002).

References

1. Greenberg, S., Witten, I.H.: Adaptive personalized interfaces—a question of viability. Behav. Inf. Technol. **4**(1), 31–45 (1985)
2. Mitchell, J., Shneiderman, B.: Dynamic versus static menus: an exploratory comparison. ACM SIGCHI Bull. **20**(4), 33–37 (1989)
3. Sears, A., Shneiderman, B.: Split menus: effectively using selection frequency to organize menus. ACM Transact. Comput.-Hum. Interact. (TOCHI) **1**(1), 27–51 (1994)
4. Liu, J., Wong, C.K., Hui, K.K.: An adaptive user interface based on personalized learning. IEEE Intell. Syst. **18**(2), 52–57 (2003)
5. Gajos, K.Z., Czerwinski, M., Tan, D. S., Weld, D.S.: Exploring the design space for adaptive graphical user interfaces. In: Proceedings of the Working Conference on Advanced Visual Interfaces, pp. 201–208 (2006)
6. Findlater, L., McGrenere, J.: Impact of screen size on performance, awareness, and user satisfaction with adaptive graphical user interfaces. In: Proceedings of the SIGCHI Conference on Human Factors in Computing Systems, pp. 1247–1256 (2008)
7. Gajos, K.Z., Everitt, K., Tan, D.S., Czerwinski, M., Weld, D.S.: Predictability and accuracy in adaptive user interfaces. In: Proceedings of the SIGCHI Conference on Human Factors in Computing Systems, pp. 1271–1274 (2008)

Hyper Panel System: Display System for Poster Layouts with Detailed Contents

Hiroshi Suzuki[1(✉)], Akira Hattori[2], Hisashi Sato[1], and Haruo Hayami[1]

[1] Kanagawa Institute of Technology, Atsugi, Japan
{hsuzuki, sato, hayami}@kanagawa-it.ac.jp
[2] Komazawa University, Setagaya, Japan
hattori@komazawa-u.ac.jp

Abstract. In this paper, we propose a hyper-panel system that can display a poster layout with detailed contents. This system combines the features of a tablet terminal, a paper-based poster, and I/O devices. We developed a peculiar device that we named the viewpoint tags. It can get axis of the devices on a paper poster by using super sonic sensor. We explain the concept of the proposed system and verify the effectiveness of this system, which was confirmed by using a prototype.

Keywords: Poster · Digital signage · Tablet PCs · Interaction · HTML5

1 Introduction

A large number of digital signage products [1, 2] that utilize large displays and replace posters of paper media, which cannot display dynamic information, have been seen in recent years. Digital signage distributes billboard information via a network, and details of such displayed information can be changed dynamically according to location or time zone. Studies have also been conducted on systems that allow the display of interactive information suitable for specific viewers [3, 4] by equipping such signage with devices such as optical cameras or touch panels, in addition to studies that conducted trials for displaying information that responds to the items and degree of interest of the viewer [5, 6]. However, such digital signage that uses large displays not only requires installation work of a large scale that increases introduction costs, but also requires substantial expense for the operation and the maintenance of the system. These signage systems are used only at some locations, such as airports, railway stations in urban areas, and large-scale commercial facilities, for precisely such reasons. Therefore, this paper proposes a Hyper Panel system, a hybrid-type digital signage system that combines tablet terminals, which are rapidly becoming popular, with paper media. This system features the ease of capturing an entire medium, a characteristic of paper media, with the convenience of having tens of thousands of people receiving information, as well as the distribution of information and the provision of interactive information, which are the advantages of digital technology, because this system combines paper media with tablet terminals. This system also provides further reduction in weight compared with digital signage systems that use large displays, and improvements are expected with regard to convenience related to installation and operation.

C. Stephanidis (Ed.): HCII 2015 Posters, Part II, CCIS 529, pp. 45–50, 2015.
DOI: 10.1007/978-3-319-21383-5_8

2 Hyper Panel System

The Hyper Panel system proposed by this paper treats content featured on a poster as hyper-link anchors that allow the interactive display of digital information from intended content on the display of a tablet terminal. Coordination with paper media that have conventionally been used as a means for displaying information is considered important. A contrivance that requires no devices, such as embedding NFC tags or placing markers on the side of the paper media, will be realized. More specifically, a user employs a special device to acquire coordinate values (viewpoint tags) of a poster in order to view digital information, such as still images and video images, on a mobile terminal in possession of the viewer, which is linked to a network.

A variety of applications can be considered for the provision of information using a poster, such as merchandise descriptions, tourist information, or navigational guide at an exhibition venue. It must be possible to set digital information in a clear manner and at arbitrary positions in order to ensure that flexible responses can be implemented to accommodate the uses or content of the posters. The configuration diagram of the system that considers such aspects is shown in Fig. 1.

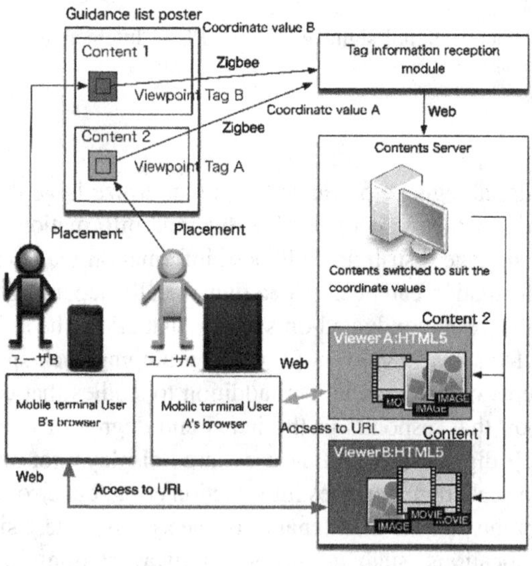

Fig. 1. The configuration diagram of Hyper Panel System

3 Prototype Implementation

A set of prototypes was implemented in order to evaluate the concept of the proposed Hyper Panel system. The implemented prototypes are not intended for actual use, but they are equipped with minimally required performance in order to evaluate the system's concept.

3.1 Viewpoint Tag

Viewpoint tags are implemented as devices for acquiring the coordinate values of the poster. Two units of Ultrasonic Range Finder are used to acquire coordinate values. Reflection plates approximately 3 cm wide are installed around the frame for mounting the poster in order to allow ultrasonic sensors to measure distances. The ultrasonic sensors are then mounted on the viewpoint tags to measure the respective distances to the frame. Let us consider the distance from the center of the tag to the left section of the frame as the X-axis, and the distance from the center of the tag to the upper section of the frame as the Y-axis, as shown in Fig. 2. A steel plate is placed under the frame, and neodymium magnets are installed on the backside of the viewpoint tags in order to secure such tags on the poster when pasted vertically. Thus, placing viewpoint tags at arbitrary locations on the displayed poster is possible, similar to placing magnets on a whiteboard.

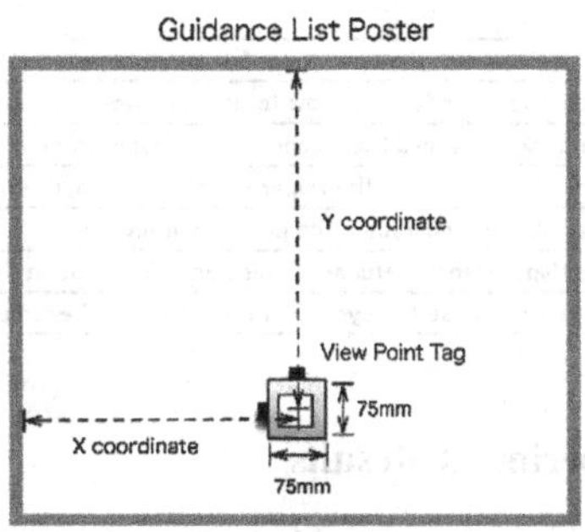

Fig. 2. Image of View Point Tag

3.2 Tag Information Reception Module

The purpose of the tag information reception module is to acquire the coordinate values of multiple viewpoint tags, and store the values in a historical database via the Web. Zigbee, a wireless communication standard, was adopted for the communication of viewpoint tags with the tag information reception module.

3.3 Viewer

The viewer for the respective viewpoint tags can be accessed by entering its URL on a browser screen. Since jQuery is used by the viewer to acquire digital information, content such as movies and static images can be switched dynamically. jPlayer [12], which supports a variety of browsers, was adopted for movie playback on the viewer. A coordinate acquisition button is located on the upper left section of the viewer screen and the position information can be updated to the latest by pressing this button.

4 Evaluation Experiment

4.1 Test Outline

An evaluation experiment for the system was conducted using the implemented prototype system and a poster. A total of 37 male and female test subjects participated in the test, ranging in age from late teens to forties. In the experiment, an examiner briefly explained how the system is used, and the test subjects were asked to place viewpoint tags on arbitrary locations on the paper in order to view the digital information. The test subjects were then asked to install viewpoint tags at arbitrary locations and view the digital information. After experimenting with the system, the test subjects were presented with a questionnaire in order to survey their responses. The survey questions are listed in Table 1.

Table 1. Quaestiones Items

Q1	Are you familiar with the operation of a smartphone?	(1)Familiar	(2)Not familiar
Q2	Were you able to understand how to use the Hyper Panel?	(5)Could understand	(1)Could not understand
Q3	Did you think you would like to operate the Hyper Panel?	(5)Agree	(1)Do not agree
Q4	Were you able to operate the Hyper Panel in the ways you wanted to?	(5)Could operate	(1)Could not operate
Q5	Were you able to understand the poster content?	(5)Could understand	(1)Could not understand
Q6	Was the Hyper Panel useful as supplemental information for the poster?	(5)Was useful	(1)Was not useful
Q7	Would you like to use the system in the future if it becomes popular?	(5)Would use	(1)Would not use

4.2 Experiment Results

The test subjects were divided into two groups, B group with proficiency in the operation of a smartphone, and A group without such proficiency, categorized based on the responses received for Question 1 of the questionnaire survey. The tabulated results are shown in Fig. 3. The combined result for score 5 (understood) and score 4 was 66.6 % for Group A with regard to system comprehension, as addressed by Question 2. On the other hand, the result for Group B was 96 %, i.e., a high degree of understanding. This leads us to believe that this system can be understood extremely well by those who are experienced with, and proficient in, smartphone operation. With regard to interest in the system as addressed by Question 3, the combined result of score 5 and score 4 was 88.9 % for Group A and 89.2 % for Group B, showing that approximately the same level of evaluation was achieved with both groups. This leads us to believe that this system evokes interest, regardless of the extent of proficiency in the operation of smartphones. With regard to system operation as addressed by Question 4, Group B evaluated the operation slightly higher than Group A. This is believed to be a reflection of the proficiency in the operation of smartphones on the results of the questionnaire. However, because over 60 % of the test subjects in Group A selected score 5 and score 4 as their response to this issue, this system is considered as one that can be operated sufficiently well even by those test subjects unfamiliar with the operation of smartphones.

With regard to poster comprehension as addressed by Question 5, there were variances among the results from Groups A and B, which is believed to indicate that the test subjects felt that details cannot be conveyed properly based on what is featured

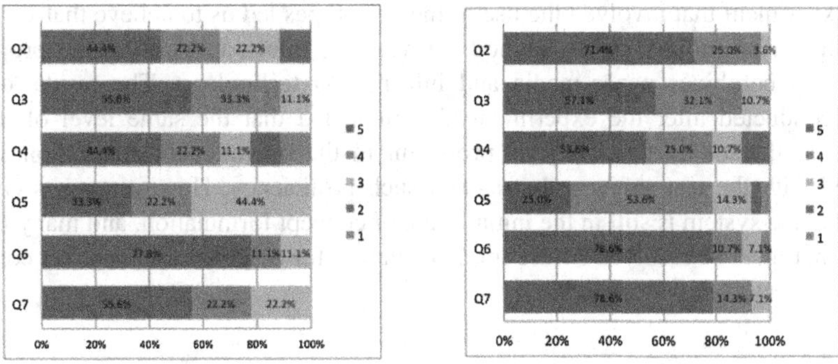

Group A(N=9) Group B(N=28)

Fig. 3. Answer ratios

on the paper of the poster alone. On the other hand, high evaluations were achieved from both Groups A and B with regard to the functions that supplement the poster, as addressed by Question 6. Such results lead us to surmise that the system complements effectively the information provided by the poster. With regard to the possibility of using the system should it become popular in the future, approximately 90 % of the test subjects in both Groups A and B indicated that they would, indeed, like to use the system. Therefore, it is evident that the test subjects were receptive to this system, those who were not proficient in the operation of smartphones, and those who were, based on the results described above.

4.3 Results and Considerations on Free Descriptions

No test subjects were bewildered by the installation of viewpoint tags or by viewing digital information, and all able to view that digital information in which they were interested by moving the viewpoint tags. In particular, the method for switching the content provided on mobile terminals by relocating the physical tags appeared to provide a fresh sensation to the test subjects, and many indicated their impression on this as being an experience they have never encountered before as a method for acquiring information. An opinion was also expressed that this system facilitates information viewing with superior perspicuity because the static images and videos related to the content featured on the poster can be viewed while simultaneously looking at the poster. This is believed to occur because of the effect generated by facilitating the simultaneous viewing of the content featured on the poster and the detailed information provided on a mobile terminal.

5 Conclusion and Future Issues

This paper proposed a Hyper Panel system that facilitates viewing digital information relevant to the layout on posters of paper medium. Furthermore, a set of prototypes for viewpoint tags and viewer was implemented based on the proposed system. The results of the experiment that involved the use of the prototypes led us to believe that we were successful in providing a new method for viewing information using the proposed system that combines paper media and information technology. The results of the survey conducted after the experiment also indicated that the same level of receptiveness as that of the test subjects proficient in the operation of smartphones was achieved with the test subjects that lacked such proficiency. However, in its current condition, the system is still in the initial stage of concept formulation, and many issues remain that must be resolved before implementation for practical use on street corners.

References

1. Florian, A., Stefan, S., Albrecht, S., Jörg, M., Nemanja, M.: How to evaluate public displays. In: PerDis 2012 Proceedings of the 2012 International Symposium on Pervasive Displays Article No. 17 (2012)
2. Uta, H., Nina, V., Kai, K., Helsinki, G., Jacucci, H., Sheelagh, C., Ernesto, A.: Large displays in urban life - from exhibition halls to media facades. In: CHIEA 2011 Extended Abstracts on Human Factors in Computing Systems, pp. 2433–2436 (2011)
3. Karen, D., Carlos, M., Andreas, S.: The search wall: tangible information searching for children in public libraries. In: TEI 2009 Proceedings of the 3rd International Conference on Tangible and Embedded Interaction, pp. 289–296 (2009)
4. John, H., Enrico, R., Nigel, D.: Real world responses to interactive gesture based public displays. In: MUM 2011 Proceedings of the 10th International Conference on Mobile and Ubiquitous Multimedia, pp. 33–39 (2011)
5. Kazuhiro, S., Ryoji, H.: An effective advertisement using Active Posters. The Special Interest Group Technical reports of IPSJ, HI, 2001(3), pp. 79–86 (2001)
6. Tamio, K., Masanori, Y., Hiroshi, W.: A composition method of situation conformity digital-signage using human position and movement. IPSJ J. **53**(2), 868–878 (2012)

Operation Sound Influence on Tablet Device Character Input Operation

Won-Seok Yang[1(✉)], Haruumi Kondo[1], and Wang-Mi Seok[2]

[1] College of Engineering and Design, Shibaura Institute of Technology, 3-9-14 Shibaura, Minato-ku, Tokyo, Japan
{yang, cyl1214}@shibaura-it.ac.jp

[2] Graduate School of Design, Okayama Prefectural University, Soja, Japan
seok@dgn.oka-pu.ac.jp

Abstract. On the other hand, because tactile feedback from the touch interface is poor, there is a lack operation it is difficult comfort see if it is running correctly problems. To solve this problem, research to improve the operability of the touch interface through auditory feedback has been conducted. On the other hand, it is clear that auditory feedback from touch interface operation in order to accelerate work is at the center of physical factors; however, not much progress in being made for research on emotions and the psychological effects of the user. In this study, we clarify the operation sound effect on the character input operation of tablet devices. From the results, we produce a tool that can examine the impact on character input operation through various operation sounds.

Keywords: Touch device · Operation sound · Feedback · POMS

1 Introduction

In recent years, tablet devices for the general public that can be used in various applications have become available from various companies; for example, Apple iPad is widely used. According to the communication usage trends survey conducted in 2013, household holdings of tablet devices increased yearly by 21.9 % from 7.2 % over 2010–2013; it is estimated that such usage will be widespread in the future [1]. One of the features of table devices that can be mentioned is their intuitive operation by touching the screen. On the other hand, because tactile feedback from the touch interface is poor, there is a lack operation it is difficult comfort see if it is running correctly problems [2].

Because of differences in the feeling operation between software and real keyboards, the former, which are often used to input characters into tablet devices, have been reported to be inconvenient [3]. To solve this problem, research to improve the operability of the touch interface through auditory feedback has been conducted. On the other hand, it is clear that auditory feedback from touch interface operation in order to accelerate work is at the center of physical factors; however, not much progress in being made for research on emotions and the psychological effects of the user [4].

Therefore, to input characters input into tablet devices, investigating the effects of auditory feedback on user emotions is necessary [5].

C. Stephanidis (Ed.): HCII 2015 Posters, Part II, CCIS 529, pp. 51–56, 2015.
DOI: 10.1007/978-3-319-21383-5_9

In this study, we clarify the operation sound effect on the character input operation of tablet devices. From the results, we produce a tool that can examine the impact on character input operation through various operation sounds.

2 The Aim of Research

This study aimed to clarify the effects of operation sounds on text (character)-input operations on a tablet terminal. From the results, we created a tool that can investigate the effects of various operation sounds on text (character)-input operations.

Feedback at Text input times. In many cases, one relies on visual and auditory feedback when inputting characters on a tablet terminal. As visual feedback, in general use is a color change of the key touched on the software keyboard, or a "pop-up" of the character corresponding to the touched key, etc. This enables users to confirm whether or not the inputted character is the desired character (Fig. 1). As auditory feedback, an actual keyboard is mimicked, and a analogous sound effect is generated to give the sense that a key was pressed (below, "operation sounds").

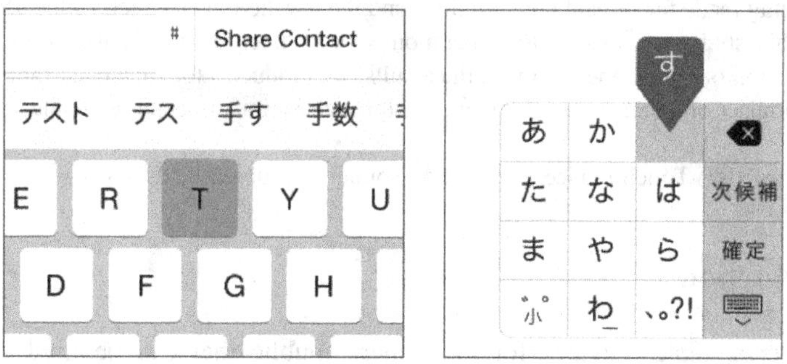

Fig. 1. Visual feedback on a software keyboard

3 Research Method

We surveyed research regarding auditory feedback with a touch panel, and hypothesized that operation sounds had effects on the operability of the touch panel. We then investigated the effects that the presence or absence of sounds had on character-input operations on a tablet terminal.

4 Effects on Character-Input Operations of the Presence or Absence of Sounds

We had subjects input designated text using a tablet terminal, and surveyed subjects before and after the test as to what effects the presence or absence of operating sounds had on changes in feeling (mood), subjective evaluations, and working speeds (Fig. 2). As the tablet terminal, we used the iPad mini 2 made by Apple Inc.

Fig. 2. Experimental Scenes of character input using a Tablet Device

4.1 Research Plan

Subjects were 12 university students familiar with keyboard operations due to daily use of a smartphone or tablet terminals, and either right-handed or ambidextrous.

1. The test was explained to the subjects.
2. Subjects performed the POMS (Profile of Mood States) survey prior to the test.
3. Subjects were asked to use a tablet terminal to input designated texts. Flick input was used as the input method. Subjects were in a standing position, and input processes were recorded by filming with video (a camera was attached to respective subject's head).
4. The POMS survey was administered to subjects after the test. Subjects were also asked to write their subjective evaluations on a questionnaire paper. Using the above-described process, for each individual subject, the test was performed twice (2 times; once in a state where operation sounds were generated on the tablet terminal ("with operation sounds" state), and once when no such operation sounds occurred ("without operation sounds" state)). As identical texts were used in the second test, to ensure that no differences occurred due to subject learning levels (proficiency), the order in which each subject had either operation sounds or no operation sounds was made random, and the second test was given after the space of three or more days from the first test. Subjects were not informed of the change in the state of operation sounds on the tablet for the second test. Two texts were used for input: the "*Iroha*" song (the Japanese "alphabet song") and the "*Torinaku*" song ("The Birds are Singing") (Fig. 3).

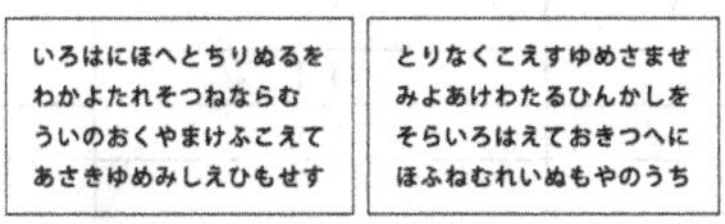

Fig. 3. Texts used left: the "*Iroha*" song, right: the "*Torinaku*" song

4.2 Research Results

1. Changes in feeling (mood). Analysis of variance was performed regarding changes in feeling (mood) pre- to post-test. The results showed that, in the "with operation sounds" state, no significant differences appeared for any of the six (6) scales

(Table 1). Meanwhile, in the "without operation sounds" state, the p value of "A feeling of vitality/energy" was 0.042 ($p < 0.5$), thus a significant decline (Table 2).

2. Subjective evaluations. Analysis of variance was performed regarding subjective evaluations of the respective "with operation sounds" and "without operation sounds" states. The results showed that the p value of "the difficulty level of inputting the texts" was 0.096 ($p < 0.1$), confirming marginal significance (Table 3). In other words, the results showed that, in regards to the difficulty level of inputted texts, the "with operation sounds" state had a trend of "feeling easier". Also, although no significant difference appeared for the other categories, a decline was seen in all scores.
3. Working speeds. In the tests, measurements were made of time taken for character input, and mean values were calculated. The results were as follows: "with operation sounds" state, 100.6 s; "without operation sounds" state, 105.3 s. The result of a t-test showed no significant difference. No significant differences occurred in the subjective evaluations of identical question categories. Thus, both quantitatively and qualitatively, the presence or absence of operation sounds had no effect on working speeds.

Table 1. Changes in feeling (mood): "With operation sounds" state

	Measurements before the Experiments	Measurements after the Experiments	Comparison of Measurements before and after the Experiments (P<0.05)
T-A	3.2	3.2	n.s.
D	2.0	1.1	n.s.
A-H	2.0	0.4	n.s.
V	4.4	4.3	n.s.
F	3.7	2.4	n.s.
C	6.0	4.8	n.s.

Table 2. Changes in feeling (mood): "Without operation sounds" state

	Measurements before the Experiments	Measurements after the Experiments	Comparison of Measurements before and after the Experiments (P<0.05)
T-A	4.2	3.6	n.s.
D	2.1	1.1	n.s.
A-H	1.5	0.1	n.s.
V	5.6	2.3	P<0.05
F	4.3	1.9	n.s.
C	6.5	5.5	n.s.

4.3 Considerations

The above-described results show how the presence or absence of operation sounds impact text-inputting operations on a tablet terminal. In a state where operation sounds

Table 3. Subjective evaluations in "with/without operation sounds" states

Question	sound	No sound	Comparison of Measurements sound and no sound the Experiments (P<0.05)
Amount of character input	2.8	3.2	n.s.
Time of character input	3.0	3.3	n.s.
Tub-flick of reaction	3.1	3.2	n.s.
Difficulty of the sentence	2.7	3.3	P<0.1
Weight of the tablet device	3.1	2.9	n.s.

are present, surely a sense of security regarding operations is obtained from the auditory feedback, helping to control any decline in the sense of vitality one has when engaging in operations. Thus, operation sounds are thought to have the effect of maintaining vitality when performing text-inputting operations. As for time required for text-inputs, the presence or absence of operation sounds had no effects. Meanwhile, in prior research, it was shown that when touch-panel devices were operated, the state where auditory feedback is provided had reduced input times [5]. Thus, further investigation is required, including by increasing the numbers of subjects, examining differing input contents, etc.

5 A Tool for Investigating the Effects of Operation Sounds on Text (Character)-Input Operations

We learned from this study that operation sounds serve to maintain the vitality/energy of users, and that with operation sounds, even large amounts of text inputting can be performed without feeling boredom. We also considered that the recent increased daily use of tablet terminals for email, uploads to social network systems (SNS), etc., entails increased character (text)-inputs, meaning that the effects of operation sound differences are important. Thus, based on the results obtained from this study, we made a tool for investigating the effects of a variety of different operation sounds on character (text)-input (Fig. 4).

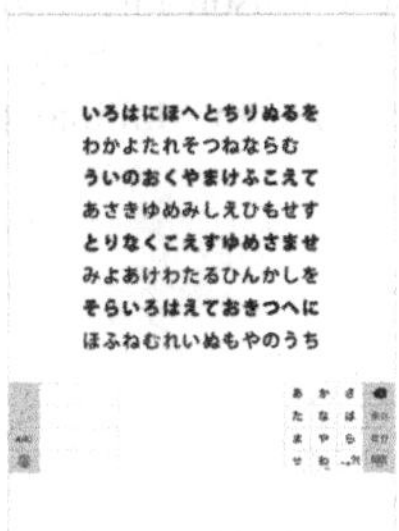

Fig. 4. Prototype image of tool

6 Conclusion

To clarify the effects of operation sounds on character (text)-input operations on tablet terminals, we surveyed such effects on test subjects' changes in feeling, subjective evaluations, working speeds, and working styles. As for changes of feeling, results showed that the "with operation sounds" state served to dampen reductions of "vitality" (energy) in users. Among the subjective evaluations, in regards to "difficulty of inputting text," the "with operation sounds" state tended to be felt as easier for text inputs. As for time required for text (character)-inputs, the presence or absence of operation sounds had no effects in our study. However, in prior research, cases have been reported where the existence of operation sounds resulted in reduced input times. Thus, further investigation is required with differing test environment arrangements. A further note is that no test subjects became aware that a change had occurred in the operation sounds state during the test period. We think that this is due to the fact that although people perceive operation sounds with their senses, it is done unconsciously. From our test results, we learned that operation sounds do have an effect on character-input operations. We also believed that study is required regarding how changes in operation sounds impact character-input operations. This time, we were unable to change operation sounds for the tablet terminals used, so we searched for an application that would permit a tablet to serve as a test device having operation-sound changing functions; to our knowledge, as of the current point in time, no such application existed. We thus believed that to enable smoother testing in future surveys of effects due to operations sounds on tablet terminals, a more suitable test device was required; we therefore created a tool for investigating the effects of a variety of operation sounds on character-input operations.

References

1. Ministry of Internal Affairs and Communications : Communication trends use survey 2013 (2014)
2. Hasegawa, A., Hasegawa, S., Kanda, T., Omori, M., Miyao, M.: Characteristics of displays of e-Book terminals on text readbility. In: IDW 2011, pp. 1131–1134, Nagoya, Japan (2011)
3. Logicool: Investigation of tablet terminal actual use (2014)
4. Asako, K., Hideyuki, O., Fumihisa, S., Hideyuki, T.: A study for presentation of tactile sensation with sound feedback to touch sensor, Information Processing Society of Japan, vol. 68, pp. 9–16, 6 September 2007
5. Tatsuno, J.: Evaluation of Touch Panel with Multimodal Interaction, University of KINKI, vol. 2, pp. 83–88 (2011)

Social Media

Virtually Augmented Social Skills Training

Kevin Ambrose(✉)

Educational Psychology, Graduate Center, CUNY,
365 5th avenue, 3rd floor, Room 3206, New York, NY 10016, USA
kambrose@gc.cuny.edu

Abstract. This poster will detail a pilot study conducted at the City University of New York assessing the usability of a virtual environment for teenagers. In this study, the PI sought to test the viability of social skills measures for this population, find glitches in the code of tasks built into the virtual environment, and seek feedback from participants on improvements to be made to the intervention. The results of this study will aid in the creation of a social skills intervention designed for individuals with autism spectrum disorders.

Keywords: Second life · Virtual environments · Autism · Social skills

1 Virtual Environment and Social Skills Training Needs

Virtual Environments (VEs) allow for the creation of realistic 3d representations of real world environments which can be interacted with and explored in real time (Cobb et al., 2002). In addition, there are virtual environments that specialize in supporting interactions between large masses of users known as collaborative virtual environments (CVE) and those specializing in supporting interactions between smaller groups or individual users referred to as single-user virtual environments (SVE). Within virtual environments, human representations are employed and controlled by the user. An avatar is a human representation within the VE that represents an actual human, while an agent is a human representation within the VE that represents only a computer algorithm. Virtual environments may be especially suited for training individuals with disabilities in skills that cannot be effectively practiced safely in real life scenarios because of the detrimental outcomes associated with failure in the expression of the targeted skill. For example, VEs have been used to train individuals in skills including crossing the street, grocery shopping, and banking.

An ideal SST intervention identified by Parsons and Mitchell (2002) includes: repetition of the target skill or task; rote learning of social rules; fading of prompts over time; verbal instruction/explanation of the social skill; a consideration of how one's behavior impacts others (i.e. understanding other minds); practice of skills in realistic settings; the ability to practice the skill across contexts; role-play of target behaviors; accessibility and ease of use for schools and teachers; and affordability for home and school environments. Virtual environments have the capability of meeting all of these recommendations.

Autism is a complex developmental disability that involves impairments in social interaction; communication; and restrictive or repetitive behaviors, activities, or

C. Stephanidis (Ed.): HCII 2015 Posters, Part II, CCIS 529, pp. 59–64, 2015.
DOI: 10.1007/978-3-319-21383-5_10

interests (American Psychiatric Association 2000). Autism, or Autistic Disorder, is one of a group of Autism Spectrum Disorders (ASDs), a category that also includes Pervasive Developmental Disorder Not Otherwise Specified (PDD-NOS) and Asperger's syndrome (AS). According to information from the Center for Disease Control and Prevention, it is estimated that 1 in 68 children in the U.S. have an Autism Spectrum Disorder (http://www.cdc.gov/ncbddd/autism/data.html).

Virtual environments meet the recommendations of McConnell (2002) and they can be manipulated to enhance social skills training for individuals with autism. The virtual world can capture the child's perceptions and fantasies to help confront distorted thoughts as well as problematic behaviors (Smokowki and Hartung 2003). For example, a program to teach children how to interact with a bully would be able to make a bully appear to grow bigger if the input from the user was negative or have the bully shrink in size as the learner uses appropriate ways of communicating with the bully.

2 Pilot Study

A pilot study was conducted with eight participants at the Children's Interactive Learning and Development (CHILD) Lab in the City University of New York (CUNY) Graduate Center. The intent of the study was to assess the usability of Second Life for individuals ages 13–18 as a tool for learning social skills. In addition, the principal investigator (PI) sought to test the viability of social skills measures with this population, find and correct glitches or bugs in the virtual environment, and seek feedback from participants on improvements to be made to the intervention.

2.1 Participants

Healthy subjects between the ages of 13–18 were recruited using CUNY Institutional Review Board (IRB) approved flyers and snowball sampling methods. The Principal Investigator (PI) obtained informed consent and parental consent forms from all eight participants recruited. Subjects were 7 males and 1 female ranging in age from 13–17. The mean age of the participants was 15.5. Subjects were named Ryan, Raymond, Glendon, Christopher, Evan, Rehat, Jerry, and Hannah. All subjects were native English speakers who attended New York City public schools.

2.2 Materials

The materials used for this study were the Social Skills Improvement System (SSIS) Student Rating Scales (13–18) by Gresham and Elliot (2008) and an Apple desktop computer running a multi-user, online virtual reality environment created by Linden Labs called Second Life (SL).

3 Procedures

Subjects participated in this pilot study at the CHILD Lab located in the CUNY Graduate Center. Upon entering the lab for the experiment, the PI explained to each subject that the purpose of the study was to assess their social skills and their ability to complete social skills tasks in a virtual environment called Second Life. In one individual session, subjects completed the SSIS and then were assigned an avatar to use in Second Life. The subjects were restricted to the property of Southern Tier Health Link New York (STHLNY), a nonprofit electronic medical records advocacy group that the PI had partnered with. The PI guided the subject through the basics of how to move and chat in Second Life and when the subjects were comfortable moving around the virtual environment, they were asked to begin the Virtually Augmented Social Skills Training VASST) tasks at a school building on STHLNY's simulation or sim within Second Life designed and built by the PI.

For the pilot study, the VASST program consisted of four tasks. Each task began with a participant clicking on a red box within the virtual school which opened up a dialog menu from which the participant chose the task. Each red box had only one task and one level of the task. When the task was completed successfully, a dialog script told the participant that they made the correct choice and they must click on a blue box to teleport to the next task.

In Task 1, participants were asked to click on one of two computer based agents that they would approach for friendship. Subjects were told by a dialog menu that Person1 was friendly and had many friends, while Person 2 was not friendly and had very few friends. Participants were given the option of choosing a hint. The hint told them that it was best to choose someone friendly as a potential friend.

In Task 2, participants were asked to decide how they would introduce themselves to a potential friend and were given the option of choosing a hint. One introduction read, "Hi my name is______, what is your name?" and the other introduction read, "What are you doing here?" The hint told the participant that it was best to choose an introduction that introduced themselves and asked the potential friend something about themselves.

For Task 3, participants had to choose the best response to a situation in which they were being threatened by a bully. One response available read, "Tell the bully to stop bothering you" and the other response read, "Ask for help from a teacher, a friend, or the school security guard". If they choose the former response, they were given feedback which said, "A bully may not stop bothering you if you tell them to. There is a better solution. Please try again". The hint told them that it would be best to contact school personnel when dealing with bullies.

For Task 4, participants were asked to choose a coping statement to give to someone who was bullied. One statement read, "I feel sad that you were bullied. I know that you are hurting now, but I hope that you remember that things will get better" and the other statement said, "Looks like you got picked on because you have no friends." The hint in this task told the participant to choose a statement that would address the individual's feelings and make them feel better.

Before each task, the participant was asked how they would act in real life in the situation described in the task. After each task, the participant was asked to explain the choice they made. Participants were given a $10 Amazon.com gift card for participating and they were also asked to voluntarily provide feedback on a short, online survey.

4 Results

All participants completed the SSIS and were able to complete all of the VASST tasks. The SSIS measured social skills, problem behaviors, and academic competence. Sex based norms were used as social skills have been found to develop at different rates for males and females. Christopher received a SSIS Social Skills Scale Standard Score of 96 (Confidence Interval, 89–103) placing him in the average range. Christopher's SSIS Problem Behaviors Scale Standard Score was 128 (Confidence Interval, 122–134) which placed him in the above average range. Glendon received a SSIS Social Skills Scale Standard Score of 104 (Confidence Interval, 97–111) placing him in the average range. Glendon's SSIS Problem Behavior Scale Standard Score was 110 (Confidence interval 104–116) which placed him in the average range. Evan received a SSIS Social Skills Scale Standard Score of 90 (Confidence Interval 83–97) placing him in the average range. Evan's SSIS Problem Behavior Scale Standard Score was 87 (Confidence Interval 81–95) which placed him in the average range. Raymond received a SSIS Social Skills Scale Standard Score of 92 (Confidence Interval 85–99) placing him in the average range. Raymond's SSIS Problem Behavior Scale Standard Score was 104 (Confidence Interval 98–110) which placed him in the average range. Jerry received a SSIS Social Skills Scale Standard Score of 107 (Confidence Interval 100–114) placing him in the average range. Jerry's SSIS Problem Behavior Scale Standard Score was 108 (Confidence Interval 102–114) which placed him in the average range. Ryan received a SSIS Social Skills Scale Standard Score of 93 (Confidence Interval 86–100) which was in the average range. Ryan's SSIS Problem Behavior Scale Standard Score was 101 (Confidence Interval 95–107) which placed him in the average range. Rehat received a SSIS Social Skills Scale Standard Score of 96 (Confidence Interval 89–103) which was in the average range. Rehat's SSIS Problem Behaviors Scale Standard Score was 92 (Confidence Interval 86–98), placing him in the average range. Finally, Hannah's SSIS Social Skills Scale Standard Score was 92 (Confidence Interval 86–98) which was in the average range. Hannah received a SSIS Problem Behaviors Scale Standard Score of 89 (Confidence Interval 82–96) which was in the average range.

A correct response on each VASST task was scored as 1 point. Only the individual's first response was recorded for scoring purposes. While only the individual's first response was used for scoring purposes, all participants were required to choose the correct response before advancing to the next task. The highest possible total score for all tasks was 4 points. Christopher, Glendon, and Evan had VASST scores of 4 points. Jerry, Ryan, and Hannah had VASST scores of 3 points. Raymond and Rehat had VASST scores of 2 points. Sixty-two and a half percent of participants completed Task 1 correctly, 87.5 % completed task two correctly, 62.5 % of participants completed Task 3 correctly, and 100 % of participants completed Task 4 correctly. Participants demonstrated learning while completing the tasks. For example, Ryan answered that he would "fight someone who tried to bully him" before completing Task 3, but chose a solution for the task that was non-confrontational and involved school personnel to resolve the issue. If they failed on their first attempt, participants were able to make the appropriate response for each task by using the "hint" feature.

5 Conclusion and Discussion

This usability study was successful in confirming that participants would view the virtual environment as a simulation of the real world, participants would be able to navigate and complete tasks in the virtual environment, and participants would learn to use information from the virtual environment coupled with their real world experience to make decisions for the VASST social skills tasks. In addition, participants in this pilot study made suggestions for improvements in the design and implementation of the virtual environment and were able to uncover glitches with scripting that the PI was able to correct.

From participant suggestions as well as witnessing participants complete the VASST tasks, a number of enhancements will be made to the virtual environment. For example, the SSIS Intervention Guide will be used to create personalized interventions for participants based off of data gathered from their SSIS Rating Scales self-report answers. These interventions will be made into additional VASST tasks and the current VASST tasks will have 3 additional levels of complexity for the situations they depict. Lastly, as suggested by multiple participants, the computer based agents, or NPCs, will be animated using a newly available "puppeteering" feature in Second Life. This will allow the participants to be more engaged with the tasks as well as witness vignettes of each VASST task rather than just reading about what each task entails. Using animations should also reduce the cognitive load of understanding each task. This research has the potential to positively impact the lives of many individuals who below average and well below average social skills. Further study must be done with a high-functioning autism population to determine if the intervention will lead to an increase in social functioning. This research is of paramount importance to the field of educational psychology as the findings of future research will further the understanding of virtually augmented training methods as well as their efficacy with an ASD population. Moreover future research may offer a method of preventing some of the detrimental social and emotional effects of victimization. Lastly, as the push for the use of educational technology heightens, future VASST research will give educators and psychologists an intervention to use that can be replicated at low or minimal cost and benefit a host of individuals.

References

American Psychiatric Association (2000). Diagnostic and statistical manual of mental disorders (4th edn., text rev.). doi:10.1176/appi.books.978089042334

Center for Disease Control and Prevention Autism spectrum disorders: Treatment (2009). http://www.cdc.gov/ncbddd/autism/data.html

Cobb, S., Beardon, L., Eastgate, R., Glover, T., Kerr, S., Neale, H., Parsons, S., Benford, S., Hopkins, E., Mitchell, P., Reynard, G., Wilson, J.: Applied virtual environments to support learning of social interaction skills in users with Asperger's Syndrome. Digit. Creat. **13**(1), 11 (2002)

Elliot, S., Gresham, F.: Social Skills Improvement System, NCS Pearson Inc

McConnell, S.R.: Interventions to facilitate social interaction for young children with autism: review of available research and recommendations for educational intervention and future research. J. Autism Dev. Disord. **32**(5), 351–372 (2002). doi:10.1023/A:1020537805154

Parsons, S., Mitchell, P.: The potential of virtual reality in social skills training for people with autistic spectrum disorders. J. Intell. Disabil. Res. **46**(5), 430–443 (2002). doi:10.1046/j.1365-2788.2002.00425.x

Smokowski, P.R., Hartung, K.: Computer simulation and virtual reality: enhancing the practice of school social work. J. Technol. Hum. Serv. **21**(1/2), 5 (2003)

Acceptance and Quality Perception of Social Network Standard and Non-Standard Services in Different Cultures

Katsiaryna S. Baran(✉) and Wolfgang G. Stock

Department of Information Science, Heinrich Heine University Düsseldorf, Düsseldorf, Germany
Katsiaryna.Baran@hhu.de

Abstract. Language and culture play important roles in social computing and social media research. Due to network effects, on national or regional social network service (SNS) markets there is only one "standard," which is broadly accepted by the users. Sometimes users additionally check out another SNS (a "non-standard") but do not or only rarely use it after adoption. For typical evaluation dimensions of perceived quality (ease of use, usefulness, trust, fun) and dimensions of acceptance (adoption, use, impact, diffusion) we analyze the importance of the evaluation dimensions and the correlations between all dimension for both, the standard and a non-standard SNS as well as for two cultures, namely Russia and Germany. In our study, the SNS standards are Facebook in Germany and Vkontakte in Russia, the non-standards are Vkontakte in Germany and Facebook in Russia.

Keywords: Social network services · TAM · UTAUT · ISE · Perceived quality · Acceptance · Facebook · Vkontakte · Standard · Culture

1 Introduction

Along the last decade, social network services (SNSs) became popular in nearly all parts of the world. With Boyd and Ellison [3], we define SNSs as Web services allowing users to construct profiles, to connect with other users, and to view other profiles on the service. Due to network effects, we are able to identify exactly one SNS player, which became "standard" on a national information market [16]. For example, in the U.S. the standard SNS nowadays is Facebook, while in Russia and neighboring countries Vkontakte is very popular [1].

Why are SNSs that popular? What drives successful SNSs [13]? In the literature of information services acceptance we bank on well-established models such as the Technology Acceptance Model (TAM) [6], the Unified Theory of Acceptance and Use of Technology (UTAUT) [23] and the Information Service Evaluation Model (ISE) [20], which in turn is a modified version of the DeLone/McLean [7] and the Jennex/Olfman [11] model. Some of the models are applied to describe the success of SNSs. Most authors use modified (i.e., enriched) versions of TAM [4, 5, 10, 12–15, 17, 22] or (to a lesser extent) UTAUT [9, 19].

C. Stephanidis (Ed.): HCII 2015 Posters, Part II, CCIS 529, pp. 65–70, 2015.
DOI: 10.1007/978-3-319-21383-5_11

Our theoretical base is the ISE model [20]. We are going to study both, the importance of the dimensions of ISE for the users as well as the correlations between indicators of perceived quality and indicators of acceptance of SNSs. Additionally, we study SNSs across cultures and countries [18, 21]. For two countries (Russia and Germany), we analyze perceived quality and acceptance of SNSs for both, the actual standard and another (known and used) service. Our research questions (RQ) are: Are there differences of the perceived quality values and the acceptance values between the standard SNS and the non-standard SNS (RQ 1)? How do all dimensions of SNSs' perceived quality and SNSs' acceptance correlate? Are there differences in the correlation values between the standard and the non-standard (RQ 2)? Our exemplary SNSs are Facebook [8] and Vkontakte [1].

Under what conditions is IT accepted and used? Davis' empirical surveys [6] lead to two dimensions of perceived quality, namely perceived usefulness and perceived ease of use. In the further development of technology acceptance models, it is shown that additional dimensions join in determining the usage of information systems. On the one hand, there is the trust that users have in a system, and on the other hand, the fun that users experience when using a system [20]. Our literature study yields that all four dimensions of perceived quality (ease of use, usefulness, trust, and fun) were applied in nearly all studies of SNS success.

We consider information acceptance as a concept consisting of the four aspects of adoption, usage, impact and diffusion of an information service [2, 20]. If the "right" person in an appropriate situation meets the "right" service, she or he will adopt this service for the first time. Adoption does not mean use. One can adopt a service and stop to use it or use it only rarely. And one can adopt it and use it permanently. In the case of use it is possible that the user's information behavior will change. This aspect we will call "impact." Finally, an information service will diffuse into a society, when many people use it and it has impact on their information behavior. Diffusion is a typical phenomenon of network economics following the principle of "success breeds success." The more users an information service is able to attract the more the value of the service will increase. More valuable services will attract further users, etc. Other authors call the diffusion dimension "perceived connectedness" [21], "perceived critical mass" [22], "network externalities" [26] or "perceived social capital" [4, 5].

2 Method

The participants of this study were current SNS users in Russia (Moscow) and in Düsseldorf (Germany). Empirical data was collected by a questionnaire and additionally by in-depth qualitative interviews in February and March 2014. Our test persons were students from Lomonosov Moscow State University (N = 54) and students from Heinrich Heine University Düsseldorf (N = 27). A total of 81 test persons finished the questionnaire and the interview. All Russian participants had a Vkontakte account and used it frequently; all Russian students had also a Facebook account, but most of them did not use it actively. German students had a Facebook account and used it very actively. They did not have a Vkontakte account. So our test persons were instructed to create it for this study and used it actively about one month. All test

Table 1. Importance of quality and acceptance dimensions for the standard (Vkontakte/Russia: N = 54; Facebook/Germany: N = 27; Scale: 1 to 10) and the non-standard (Facebook/Russia: N = 54; Vkontakte/Germany: N = 27; Scale: 1 to 10).

	Vkontakte Russia Mean (SD)	Facebook Germany Mean (SD)	*Vkontakte Germany Mean (SD)*	*Facebook Russia Mean (SD)*
Ease of use	**9.13 (0.94)**	**7.91 (1.32)**	*7.82 (1.61)*	*4.95 (2.47)*
Usefulness	**3.93 (2.02)**	**5.67 (1.65)**	*4.38 (1.40)*	*2.49 (1.82)*
Trust	**6.38 (2.52)**	**5.90 (2.24)**	*3.83 (2.14)*	*2.46 (2.01)*
Fun	**5.77 (2.39)**	**4.80 (1.95)**	*3.73 (1.94)*	*2.59 (1.84)*
Adoption	**7.98 (2.76)**	**7.33 (2.65)**	*4.41 (2.99)*	*2.57 (2.53)*
Use	**7.47 (2.06)**	**7.05 (1.70)**	*2.98 (1.59)*	*2.13 (1.70)*
Impact	**5.17 (2.64)**	**4.89 (2.12)**	*2.32 (1.52)*	*1.76 (1.53)*
Diffusion	**6.95 (2.65)**	**6.26 (2.41)**	*4.19 (2.70)*	*3.87 (3.08)*

Bold: standard; italics: non-standard; SD: standard deviation.

persons were familiar with both SNSs. The questionnaire included 50 items. On a scale between 1 (not at all) and 10 (highly applying), every test person had to estimate the importance of an indicator for his/her SNS behavior for both services. Besides the language all questions were identical. We calculated the mean values for the two analyzed standards and the two non-standards as well as additionally the correlations (Pearson, two-sided) for all pairs of dimensions.

3 Results

In Table 1 we see the mean importance values of the studied eight dimensions for the standard SNSs and for the non-standard SNSs. For the both standard SNSs, the values are (more or less) similar. But the differences between the values for the national standard and the non-standard are, for nearly all dimensions, huge.

In Tables 2.1 and 2.2 we present the correlations between the eight dimensions for the standard and for the non-standard SNSs. A very important dimension is the SNS's use. Use correlates independently from standard or non-standard positively with all other dimensions. Remarkable correlations for the Russian standard (Table 2.1) are between use and trust (+0.54***), use and fun (+0.55***), use and adoption (+0.55***) as well as use and impact (+0.70***). The more the standard SNS in Russia is used, the more it is perceived as trustworthy and funny (and vice versa).

In Russia, there is a high interdependence between use and impact: the more a user applies an SNS the more his or her information behavior has changed. For the German standard SNS (Table 2.2), use is highly correlated with impact (+0.53**; similar to Russia), but here use is also highly correlated with diffusion (+0.61**). The more diffusion is perceived the more the SNS is used (and—of course—vice versa).

Especially for Germany (standard and non-standard) we observe high correlations of diffusion with fun (standard: +0.68***; non-standard: +0.74***) and with impact

Table 2.1. Russian standard (Vkontakte) vs. Russian non-standard (Facebook) by Russian SNS users (n = 54)

	Ease of use	Usefulness	Trust	Fun	Adoption	Use	Impact	Diffusion
Ease of use	1							
Usefulness	+0.12 +0.15	1						
Trust	+0.27* +0.20	+0.38** +0.40**	1					
Fun	+0.02 +0.32*	+0.44** +0.78***	+0.61*** +0.50***	1				
Adoption	+0.19 +0.30*	+0.13 +0.29*	+0.41** +0.42**	+0.31* +0.49***	1			
Use	+0.17 +0.32*	+0.33* +0.40**	+0.54*** +0.52***	+0.55*** +0.64***	+0.55*** +0.75***	1		
Impact	+0.21 +0.22	+0.34* +0.19	+0.54*** +0.30*	+0.65*** +0.52***	+0.38** +0.41**	+0.70*** +0.59***	1	
Diffusion	+0.13 +0.17	-0.10 -0.06	+0.17 +0.21	+0.14 +0.09	+0.26* +0.23	+0.34* +0.09	+0.25* +0.11	1

Bold: standard; italics: non-standard; *: p < 0.05; **: p < 0.01; ***: p < 0.001; all other: not significant.

Table 2.2. German standard (Facebook) vs. German non-standard (Vkontakte) by German SNS users (n = 27)

	Ease of use	Usefulness	Trust	Fun	Adoption	Use	Impact	D.
Ease of use	1							
Usefulness	+0.35* +0.44*	1						
Trust	+0.40* +0.43*	+0.77*** +0.63***	1					
Fun	+0.28 +0.57**	+0.59** +0.53**	+0.68*** +0.67***	1				
Adoption	+0.22 +0.43*	+0.36* +0.38*	+0.54** +0.62**	+0.35* +0.49*	1			
Use	+0.30 +0.59**	+0.40* +0.33*	+0.43* +0.59**	+0.35* +0.50**	+0.38* +0.66***	1		
Impact	+0.45* +0.45*	+0.37* +0.48*	+0.48* +0.69***	+0.53** +0.57**	+0.47* +0.62**	+0.53** +0.78***	1	
Diffusion	+0.24 +0.54**	+0.39* +0.35*	+0.41* +0.41*	+0.68*** +0.74***	+0.42* +0.46*	+0.61** +0.51**	+0.79*** +0.59**	1

Bold: standard; italics: non-standard; *: p < 0.05; **: p < 0.01; ***: p < 0.001; all other: not significant.

(standard: +0.79***; non-standard: +0.59**). For Russian users, the correlations of diffusion (for the standard as well as for the non-standard) are not that high. For some correlations, there are huge differences between the standard and the non-standard SNS. E.g., the correlation value of fun and ease of use is not very high or around zero in Germany (+0.28) and in Russia (+0.02) for the standard, but is moderately high for the non-standard (Germany: +0.57**; Russia: +0.32*). However, for other correlations, there hardly are differences between the national standard and the non-standard, but between the studied countries (Russia versus Germany) as, for example, the mentioned differences of the correlations of diffusion.

4 Discussion

What is new in this study? To our knowledge, this is the first study on social network services (SNSs) which incorporates the difference between a standard service (which is broadly accepted and used in a country or region due to network effects) and the non-standard services (other services, which are thoroughly known, but not or only rarely used in the same country or region). There are clear differences in the mean values of perceived quality and acceptance between the respective information services. While here (RQ 1) is a decisive result, this holds not true for the correlations between the single dimensions (RQ 2). For some correlation values we find remarkable differences between the standard SNS and the non-standard SNS (e.g., fun and ease of use). But for most correlations, we are not able to present such clear differences between the standard and the non-standard SNS. There are also clear similar patterns inside one culture (Russia versus Germany), e.g., all correlations of diffusion—independently from the standard/non-standard dichotomy. Here, obviously the cultural environment plays an important role.

References

1. Baran, K.S., Stock, W.G.: Facebook has been smacked down. The Russian special way of SNSs: Vkontakte as a case study. In: Proceedings of the 2nd European Conference on Social Media (ECSM 2015), 9–10 July 2015, Porto, Portugal (2015)
2. Baran, K.S., Stock, W.G.: Acceptance and quality perceptions of social network services in cultural context: Vkontakte as a case study. In: Proceedings of the 9th International Multi-Conference on Society, Cybernetics and Informatics (IMSCI 2015), 12–15 July 2015, Orlando, Florida, USA (2015)
3. Boyd, D.M., Ellison, N.B.: Social network sites: definition, history, and scholarship. J. Comput. Mediated Commun. **13**(1), 210–230 (2007)
4. Choi, G., Chung, H.: Elaborating the technology acceptance model with social pressure and social benefits for social networking sites (SNSs). Proc. Am. Soc. Inf. Sci. Technol. **49**, 1–3 (2012)
5. Choi, G., Chung, H.: Applying the technology acceptance model to social networking sites (SNS): impact of subjective norm and social capital on the acceptance of SNS. Int. J. Hum. Comput. Interact. **29**(10), 619–628 (2013)
6. Davis, F.D.: Perceived usefulness, perceived ease of use, and user acceptance of information technology. MIS Q. **13**(3), 319–340 (1989)
7. DeLone, W.H., McLean, E.R.: The DeLone and McLean model of information systems success. a ten-year update. J. Manag. Inf. Syst. **19**(4), 9–30 (2003)
8. Facebook: Our Mission (2014). http://newsroom.fb.com/company-info
9. Gruzd, A., Staves, K., Wilk, A.: Connected scholars: examining the role of social media in research practices of faculty using the UTAUT model. Comput. Hum. Behav. **28**(6), 2340–2350 (2012)
10. Jih, D., Zhou, M.-M.: A study on the user acceptance model of SNS websites based TAM. In: Proceedings of the 19th International Conference on Industrial Engineering and Engineering Management: Assistive Technology of Industrial Engineering, pp. 1409–1420. Springer, Berlin (2013)

11. Jennex, M.E., Olfman, L.: A model of knowledge management success. Int. J. Knowl. Manag. **2**(3), 51–68 (2006)
12. Kwon, O., Wen, Y.: An empirical study of the factors affecting social network service use. Comput. Hum. Behav. **26**(2), 254–263 (2010)
13. Kwon, S.J., Park, E., Kim, K.I.: What drives successful social networking services? A comparative analysis of user acceptance of Facebook and Twitter. Soc. Sci. J. **51**(4), 534–544 (2014)
14. Leng, G.S., Lada, S., Muhammad, M.Z., Ibrahim, A.A.H.A., Amboala, T.: An exploration of social networking sites (SNS) adoption in Malaysia using technology acceptance model (TAM), theory of planned behavior (TPB) and intrinsic motivation. J. Internet Bank. Commer. **16**(2), 1–27 (2011)
15. Lin, K.-Y., Lu, H.-P.: Why people use social networking sites: an empirical study integrating network externalities and motivation theory. Comput. Hum. Behav. **27**(3), 1152–1161 (2011)
16. Linde, F., Stock, W.G.: Information Markets: A Strategic Guideline for the I-Commerce. De Gruyter Saur, Berlin (2011)
17. Rauniar, R., Rawski, G., Yang, J., Johnson, B.: Technology acceptance model (TAM) and social media usage: an empirical study on Facebook. J. Enterp. Inf. Manag. **27**(1), 6–30 (2014)
18. Rohn, U.: Social networking sites across cultures and countries: Proximity and network effects. Qual. Res. Rep. Commun. **14**(1), 28–34 (2013)
19. Salim, B.: An application of UTAUT model for acceptance of social media in Egypt: a statistical study. Int. J. Inf. Sci. **2**(6), 92–105 (2012)
20. Schumann, L., Stock, W.G.: The Information Service Evaluation (ISE) model. Webology 11 (1), article 115 (2014)
21. Shin, D.-H.: Analysis of online social networks: a cross-national study. Online Inf. Rev. **34** (2), 473–495 (2010)
22. Sledgianowski, D., Kulviwat, S.: Using social network sites: the effects of playfulness, critical mass and trust in a hedonic context. J. Comput. Inf. Syst. **49**(4), 74–83 (2009)
23. Venkatesh, V., Morris, M.G., Davis, G.B., Davis, F.D.: User acceptance of information technology: toward a unified view. MIS Q. **27**(3), 425–478 (2003)

Between the Profiles: Another such Bias. Technology Acceptance Studies on Social Network Services

Katsiaryna S. Baran(✉) and Wolfgang G. Stock

Department of Information Science, Heinrich Heine University Düsseldorf, Düsseldorf, Germany
Katsiaryna.Baran@hhu.de

Abstract. Unfortunately, social science surveys are often confronted with biases. Due to network effects, on network markets, e.g. on markets of Social Network Services (as Facebook), only one company, the "standard," dominates a local (or even the global) market. Common models of evaluation and acceptance of information systems (as variants of the Technology Acceptance Model, TAM) capture systems' quality on dimensions of perceived ease of use, perceived usefulness, trust, and fun. In an empirical investigation on different user groups, we found that the users were not able to present unbiased quality estimations of "their" standard system and other, non-standard systems. They were captured in their standard, leading to the conception of the "standard-dependent user blindness" (SDUB). So users' quality statements on information systems on network markets are a highly vulnerable area of surveys.

Keywords: Technology acceptance model (TAM) · Social network service (SNS) · Survey · Bias · Standard-dependent user blindness (SDUB) · Facebook · Vkontakte

1 Introduction

To capture user experience with information systems and to perform qualitative and quantitative measurement and evaluation tasks, social sciences as well as computer science (including HCI research) often make use of surveys [14, 19]. All known common models of technology acceptance and information system evaluation bank on user statements. The Technology Acceptance Model (TAM) [5] and its successors, e.g. TAM 2 [21], the Unified Theory of Acceptance and Use of Technology (UTAUT) [22], the Model of Adoption of Technology in Households (MATH) [4], TAM 3 [20], the DeLone and McLean model [6, 7], the Jennex and Olfman model [10] or the Information Service Evaluation Model (ISE) [16] try to measure information systems' quality on dimensions such as perceived ease of use, perceived usefulness, trust, and fun. All those dimensions are constructs. Are the constructs valid? Studies based on the TAM model family always work with user surveys. Are the surveys valid and reliable?

During the course over the last years, Social Network Services (SNSs) became very popular all over the world [2]. The diffusion of services on information markets such

C. Stephanidis (Ed.): HCII 2015 Posters, Part II, CCIS 529, pp. 71–77, 2015.
DOI: 10.1007/978-3-319-21383-5_12

like Facebook or Vkontakte is a typical phenomenon of network economics following the principle of "success breeds success". The more users an information service is able to attract the more the value of the service will increase. More valuable services will attract further users. If an information service passes the critical mass of users, network effects will start [11]. When such a critical mass of users is achieved, we typically observe a steep increase in users and usage [17]. Each user that enters the network imposes a positive externality since she or he increases the value of the system. This leads to positive feedback loops for direct network effects (more users—more valuable service—any more users) and indirect network effects (more complementary products —more valuable service—any more complementary products) and in the end to one standard in a certain region [13, 17]. The value of being a member of a SNS does not depend in the main on the objective characteristics of an SNS but on the number of other people that are using the same SNS ("to keep in touch with old and current friends" [8]). The important feature is that "users are suppliers of content as well as consumers of content" [8]. The presence of network effects implies that positive feedback effects are working for the largest network; the strong becomes stronger and the weak becomes weaker. This, in turn, implies—in terms of the Swedish pop group ABBA— that "the winner takes it all, the looser standing small" [1]. Due to these network effects, we are able to identify exactly one SNS player, which became standard on a national information market.

In Germany, we could observe a struggle between studiVZ, a German SNS, and Facebook; and the winner was and is: Facebook [2]. In Russia, there was a struggle between Odnoklassniki (which was the first mover) and Vkontakte, while Facebook never played a major role. The winner in Russia is Vkontakte [12, 18]. So both SNSs, Facebook and Vkontakte, are not first movers in Germany (it was studiVZ) and in Russia (here it was Odnoklassniki), but they became the standard on the SNSs' national market. Facebook achieved a critical mass of German users and is able to keep its dominant position as well as Vkontakte did it in Russia [23].

Here, our research question arises: Under such conditions, are users able to give an unbiased view on the information quality dimensions of "their" standard SNS and (perhaps even better) other SNSs, which is needed for studies based on TAM and related models? The "classical" view of TAM-like studies is the analysis of the influences of indicators of perceived information system quality (as ease of use, usefulness, trust, and fun) on the acceptance of the information systems. In Fig. 1, this is the direction from the left-hand side of the model to the right-hand side. In our research, we also change the direction and ask for the influences of the acceptance indicators (in our studies [3], we work with the four dimensions of adoption, use, impact, and diffusion) on the perceived quality indicators. Our research problem lies in the direction from the right to the left in Fig. 1. How does the user's acceptance of one single information system influence her or his perception of the ease of use, the usefulness, the trust, and the fun of this system? Under the conditions of a standard (as in SNS markets), how does the user's acceptance of the standard influence the quality perceptions of the standard system and of further non-standard information systems? Hence, in this work we propose the following hypothesis:

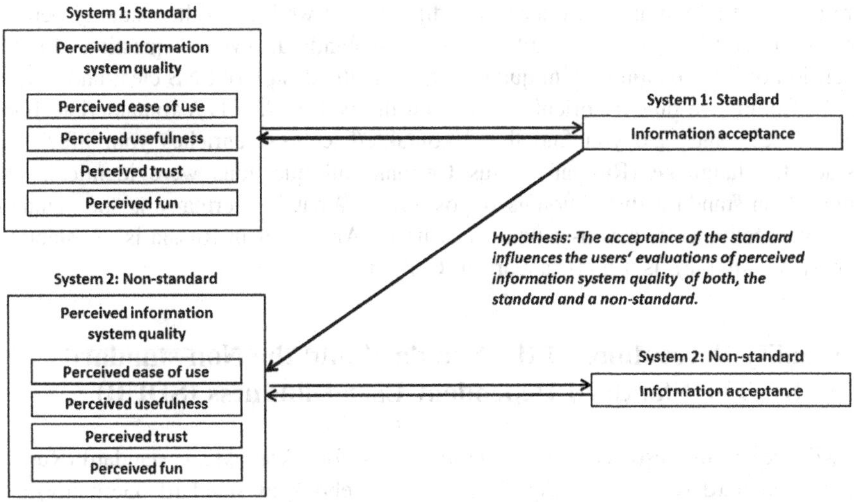

Fig. 1. Research model

The user perceptions of the quality of a SNS are strongly influenced by the standard SNS. The "winner-takes-it-all" situation makes its users "blind" to give an unbiased quality perception of "their" (standard) SNS and of other (perhaps even better) SNSs.

2 Research Method

Facebook achieved a critical mass of German users and is able to keep its dominant position in Germany as well as Vkontakte did it in Russia. We tested our hypothesis on two case studies, namely Vkontakte and Facebook. The target respondents of this study were current SNS users in Moscow, Russia, and Düsseldorf, Germany. Empirical data for this study was collected by a questionnaire in February and March 2014. Our test persons were Russian students from Lomonosov Moscow State University (N = 54) and German students from Heinrich Heine University Düsseldorf (N = 27). The surveys took place at both universities. We conducted the study among those user groups, because both social network sites, Facebook and Vkontakte, are initially targeting at students but later welcoming everyone [18]. A total of 81 test persons finished the questionnaire. Among these SNS users, 61.1 % were female and 38.9 % were male. Most of the test persons were between 18 and 28 years old. A large proportion of Russian participants has a Vkontakte account and use Vkontakte frequently; all Russian students have also a Facebook account, but most of them do not use it actively. German students have a Facebook account and use it very actively, but they did not have a Vkontakte account. So our test persons were instructed to create it for this study and used it actively about one month. All test persons were familiar with both SNSs.

The questionnaire included 50 items. On a scale between 1 (not at all) and 10 (highly applying), every test person had to estimate the importance of an indicator for his or her SNS behavior for both services, Facebook and Vkontakte. Our test persons were asked on adoption, use, impact and diffusion as well as on their quality perceptions for both SNSs, the standard and the non-standard. Typical questions for the dimension of information system quality were: "Is the design of SNS clear and easy to use?," "Could you quickly orient yourself on the website?," "Is Vkontakte/Facebook easy to use?" and "Do you find that Vkontakte/Facebook enriches your life?" etc. Besides the language (Russian versus German) all questions were identical. The standard/non-standard distinction is oppositional. What in Germany is the standard (namely Facebook), is a non-standard in Russia. And what in Russia is the standard (namely Vkontakte), is a non-standard in Germany.

3 Quality Perceptions of the Standard and the Non-standard SNSs: The Standard Dependent User Blindness (SDUB)

We will present the results of our two case studies, for Vkontakte as standard (Russia) and non-standard (Germany) (Fig. 2) and for Facebook as standard (Germany) and non-standard (Russia) (Fig. 3). For all indicators of information systems' quality our Russian and German participants chose their favorite SNS—Russian users favor Vkontakte over Facebook and German users favor Facebook over Vkontakte. Almost all values are twice as high for the standard. Keep in mind that there were identical questions and identical systems to evaluate! The only difference is in the user group with its specific standard. Additionally, the differences between the standard SNS and the non-standard SNS are statistically very significant for nearly all indicators apart from usefulness of the Russian standard (Vkontakte).

For perceived ease of use, the difference between the evaluation of the standard and the non-standard users is 1.31 points (**) for the case study of Vkontakte and even 2.96

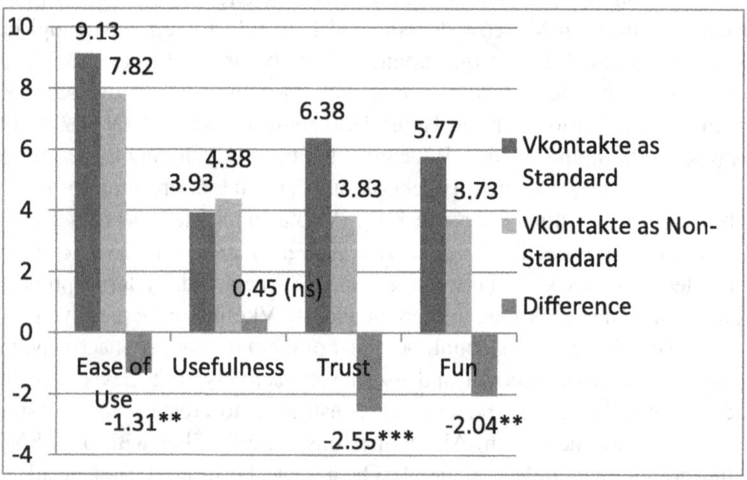

Fig. 2. Quality perceptions for standard and non-standard SNSs. Case study 1: Vkontakte ns: not significant; **: p < 0.01; ***: p < 0.001 ***: p < 0.001

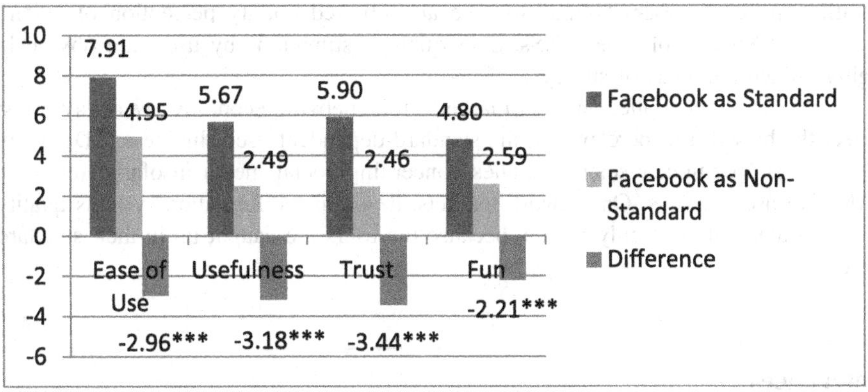

Fig. 3. Quality perceptions for standard and non-standard SNSs. Case study 2: Facebook

points (***) for the other case study of Facebook. The standard is more easy to use for its common users.

The case study of Vkontakte does not lead to statistically significant differences for the TAM dimension of usefulness. But the Facebook case study shows a great difference of 3.18 points (***). For Facebook standard users this SNS is more than twice as useful as for non-standard users (5.67 points in contrast to 2.49 points).

Perceived trust shows extreme differences for both case studies. The difference for case study 1 (Vkontakte) is 2.55 points (***), while the difference for the Facebook case study is 3.44 points (***). The standard's users do trust "their" SNS and trust to a much lesser extend other SNSs.

For perceived fun both case studies exhibit great differences between the standard and non-standard users. The Vkontakte study amounts to a difference of 2.04 points (**) and the Facebook case to a difference of 2.21 points (***). All users have much more fun with "their" standard than with a non-standard SNS.

It is obvious that identical questions on the same SNSs lead to completely different answers in dependence of the affinity of the users' standard SNS. Our research hypothesis could be clearly confirmed. The users were not able to give an unbiased quality perception on SNSs. We will call this bias on SNS markets the "standard-dependent user blindness" (SDUB) [3]. This bias seems not to be a known bias (such as the similar bias of social desirability [9]), but a new method bias [15].

4 Conclusion

Considering the wide distribution of TAM-like studies in the social sciences, computer science and information systems research as well as the great importance of SNSs nowadays, the results of our study on the conditions of the system quality perceptions are extremely interesting and also new. This study discovered that users perceive the quality of a SNS dependent on their standard SNS in favor of their standard system and in disadvantage of the non-standard information systems. The "winner-takes-it-all" situation makes its users "blind" to give an unbiased quality perception of "their" (standard) SNS and of other SNSs. SNS quality estimations by users are obviously highly vulnerable areas of surveys.

If such an effect applies on other markets of the network economy, we always must expect the biased user perceptions, the standard-dependent user-blindness (SDUB), in all social and computer science studies concerning social media insofar it relies on TAM-like user surveys. On network markets, describing information systems quality by user statements is highly biased, because the users are caught up in their standard system.

References

1. Anderson, B., Ulvaeus, B.: The winner takes it all/ABBA. Polar Music (1980)
2. Baran, K.S., Fietkiewicz, K.J., Stock, W.G.: Monopolies on social network services (SNS) markets and competition law. In: F. Pehar, C. Schlögl (Eds.), Re:inventing Information Science in the Networked Society. Proceedings of the 14th International Symposium of Information Science, Hülsbusch, Boizenburg, Germany (2015)
3. Baran, K.S., Stock, W.G.: Interdependencies between acceptance and quality perceptions of social network services: the standard-dependent user blindness. In: Proceedings of the 9th International Multi-Conference on Society, Cybernetics and Informatics (IMSCI 2015), 12–15 July 2015, Orlando (2015)
4. Brown, S.A., Venkatesh, V.: Model of adoption of technology in households: a baseline model test and extension incorporating household life cycle. MIS Q. **29**(3), 399–426 (2005)
5. Davis, F.D.: Perceived usefulness, perceived ease of use, and user acceptance of information technology. MIS Q. **13**(3), 319–340 (1989)
6. DeLone, W.H., McLean, E.R.: Information systems success. the quest for the dependent variable. Inf. Syst. Res. **3**(1), 60–95 (1992)
7. DeLone, W.H., McLean, E.R.: The DeLone and McLean model of information systems success. a ten-year update. J. Manage. Inf. Syst. **19**(4), 9–30 (2003)
8. Fjell, K., Foros, Ø., Steen, F.: The Economics of Social Networks: The Winner Takes it All? Institute for Research in Economics and Business Administration (SNF Working Paper; 42/10), Bergen, Norway (2010)
9. Furnham, A.: Response bias, social desirability and dissimulation. Personality Individ. Differ. **7**(3), 385–400 (1986)
10. Jennex, M.E., Olfman, L.: A model of knowledge management success. Int. J. Knowl. Manage. **2**(3), 51–68 (2006)
11. Katz, M.L., Shapiro, C.: Systems competition and network effects. J. Econ. Perspect. **8**(2), 93–115 (1994)
12. Khveshchanka, S., Suter, L.: Vergleichende Analyse von profilbasierten sozialen Netzwerken aus Russland (Vkontakte), Deutschland (StudiVZ) und den USA (Facebook). Inf. Wiss. Prax. **61**(2), 71–76 (2010)
13. Linde, F., Stock, W.G.: Information Markets A Strategic Guideline for the I-Commerce. De Gruyter Saur, Berlin, New York (2011)
14. Müller, H., Sedley, A., Ferrall-Nunge, E.: Survey research in HCI. In: Olsen, J., Kellogg, W. (eds.) Ways of Knowing in HCI Research, pp. 229–266. Springer, New York (2014)

15. Podsakoff, P.M., MacKenzie, S.B., Podsakoff, N.P.: Sources of method bias in social science research and recommendations on how to control it. Annu. Rev. Psychol. **63**, 539–569 (2012)
16. Schumann, L., Stock, W.G.: The Information Service Evaluation (ISE) model. Webology, 11(1), Article 115 (2014)
17. Shapiro, C., Varian, H.R.: Information Rules: A Strategic Guide to the Network Economy. Harvard Business School, Cambridge (1998)
18. Sikorska, O.: Facebook vs. Vkontakte: Kampf der Titanen auf dem russischen Markt (2013). http://allFacebook.de
19. Stern, M.J., Bilgen, I., Dillman, D.A.: The state of survey methodology: challenges, dilemmas, and new frontiers in the era of the tailored design. Field Methods **26**(3), 284–301 (2014)
20. Venkatesh, V., Bala, H.: Technology acceptance model 3 and a research agenda on interventions. Decis. Sci. **39**(2), 273–315 (2008)
21. Venkatesh, V., Davis, F.D.: A theoretical extension of the technology acceptance model: four longitudinal field studies. Manage. Sci. **46**(2), 186–204 (2000)
22. Venkatesh, V., Morris, M.G., Davis, G.B., Davis, F.D.: User acceptance of information technology: toward a unified view. MIS Q. **27**(3), 425–478 (2003)
23. Winkels, M.: The Global Social Network Landscape:A Country-by-Country Guide to Social Network Usage. eMarketer, New York (2013)

The Proteus Effect: Influence of Avatar Appearance on Social Interaction in Virtual Environments

Yulong Bian[1], Chao Zhou[2], Yu Tian[1], Peng Wang[1], and Fengqiang Gao[1(✉)]

[1] School of Psychology, Shandong Normal University, Jinan 250014, China
gaofq_11@163.com
[2] College of Psychology, Liaoning Normal University, Dalian 116029, China

Abstract. In virtual interactions, avatars can affect people's perceptions, attitudes, and behaviors consciously or unconsciously, which is known as the Proteus effect. The study created a new paradigm of "virtual scenario simulation" to investigate the impact of avatars on social behavior in different social interaction contexts. Experiment 1 investigated the impact of avatars on social participation level in participating-social-interaction contexts. Experiment 2 extended the work to maintaining-interaction context. Results showed that: (1) both situational factor (social interaction contexts) and individual factor (shyness level) could affect the occurrence of the Proteus effect. (2) The Proteus effects were moderated by the social interaction contexts. (3) In the maintaining-interaction context, the Proteus effects were moderated by the level of shyness.

Keywords: Proteus effect · Virtual environment · Avatar · Shyness · Social interaction

1 Introduction

Originally, the Proteus effect means that when given a role, individual tends to behave in line with the characteristic of the role. Yee and Bailenson [1] defined the Proteus effect in virtual world: In general, users make inferences about their expected dispositions from their avatar's appearance and then conform to the expected attitudes and behavior. Avatar cues are linked with particular images, those can prime social stereotypes. In other words, perception of avatar is the start point of Proteus effects.

Previous work has preliminarily demonstrated that features of avatar have large implications on social influence [2,3,4]. Nevertheless, the Proteus effect in virtual social environment needs to be supported by more empirical researches.

For explaining the mechanism of this effect, one theoretical framework is proposed based on self-perception theory, which argued that an observation of avatar's appearance led participants to make inferences about their disposition that in turn led to changes in behavior [5,6]. It is difficult to find that the situational factors are ignored by existing empirical research and theoretical construction. Therefore, it is necessary to investigate the influence of situational factors on the Proteus effect.

C. Stephanidis (Ed.): HCII 2015 Posters, Part II, CCIS 529, pp. 78–83, 2015.
DOI: 10.1007/978-3-319-21383-5_13

In addition to situational factors, individual differences are also ignored. Taking into account the specificity of shyness in virtual environment, it interests us in this study. Shy individuals tend to be more self-focused than non-shy individuals [7,8]. Thus, low-shy individuals are more likely to reference avatar cues than high-shy individuals in virtual environment. Above all, Proteus effect is possible moderated by shyness level.

In the current work, we were interested in exploring how avatars can affect how we interact with other people. Referencing the division of social context by Wang, we divided the social context to participating-interaction context and maintaining-interaction context. Two experiments would be conducted in this study.

2 Experiment 1 Proteus Effect in Participating-Interaction Context

2.1 Hypotheses

Hypothesis 1 (H1): Participants employing avatars with high attractiveness will display higher social participation level.
Hypothesis 2 (H2): The Proteus effect will be moderated by shyness levels.

2.2 Methods

Participants. Total 247 undergraduates were recruited and measured shyness level, then 46 high-shy and 46 low-shy participants were selected to participant experiment.

Design. The experiment involved a 2 attractiveness (high/low) × 2 shyness (high/low) two-factor between-subject design. Participants were randomly assigned to an avatar with attractive or unattractive appearance of his or her own gender.

Materials. Avatars and virtual scenarios. The study created a new paradigm of "virtual scenario simulation" to further understand the Proteus effect. The avatars and virtual scenarios were modeled using a video game "The Sims 3". Creating two sets of avatars with high or low attractiveness (see Fig. 1). Constructing 4 virtual social scenarios reflecting participating- interaction context. For different groups, the scenario depicted the same setting. The only variation was the employed avatars (Fig. 2).

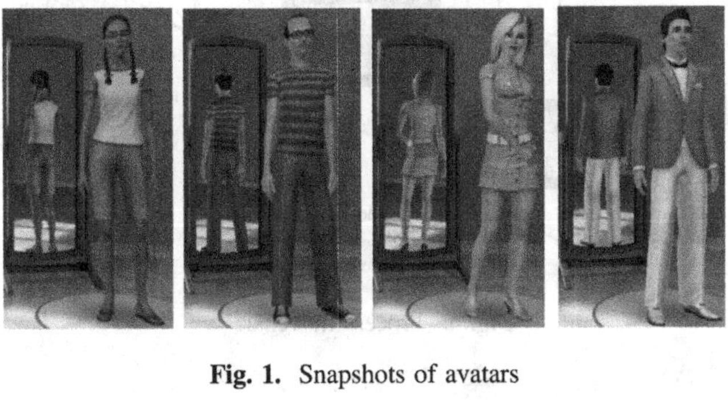

Fig. 1. Snapshots of avatars

Fig. 2. Virtual scenario in different avatar conditions

Measure. A question assessing social participation level would be depicted in the end of each scenario, and participants select the description in line with his/her behavior (Fig. 3).

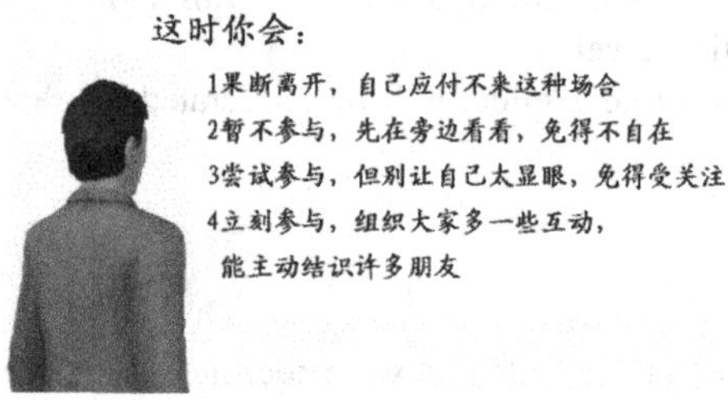

这时你会：
1果断离开，自己应付不来这种场合
2暂不参与，先在旁边看看，免得不自在
3尝试参与，但别让自己太显眼，免得受关注
4立刻参与，组织大家多一些互动，
能主动结识许多朋友

Fig. 3. Reaction interface example

Procedure. Experimental process is shown in Fig. 4.

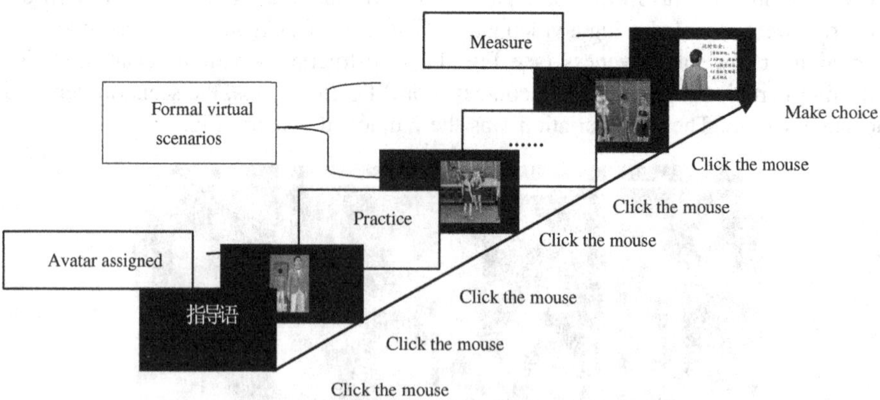

Fig. 4. Process flowchart

2.3 Results

A one way ANOVA was conducted and results showed a significant main effect of attractiveness condition, F (1, 88) = 13.06, p = 0.001, η_P^2 = 0.129. Participants employing avatars with high attractiveness (M = 3.20, SD = 0.53) were significantly more likely to participate in virtual social interaction than participants employing avatars with low attractiveness (M = 2.82, SD = 0.50), which supported H1. The main effect of shyness condition was marginally significant, F (1, 88) = 3.85, p = 0.053, η_P^2 = 0.042. Low-shy participants (M = 3.11, SD = 0.55) were more likely to participate in virtual social interaction than high-shy participants (M = 2.90, SD = 0.52).

The interaction was not significant, F (1, 88) = 0.52, p = 0.472, which indicated the moderating effect of shyness was not significant. The reason may be that the situation strengthen the attention and reference to avatar, which influenced both high-shy and low-shy individuals. If that is the case, the moderating effect will be found when eliminating the additional influence of situation.

3 Experiment 2 Proteus Effect in Maintaining-Interaction Context

3.1 Hypotheses

If the situation changed, the effects found in experiment 1 may be different.
Hypothesis 1 (H1): There will be no significant main effect of avatar attractiveness.
Hypothesis 2 (H2): The effect of avatar attractiveness on social performance will be moderated by shyness.

3.2 Methods

Participants. Participants were same with experiment1.

Design and Procedure. The experiment involved another 2 × 2 two-factor between-subject design. The procedure was same as experiment 1.

Materials. Avatars and virtual scenarios. Avatars are same as experiment 1. Constructing virtual social scenarios reflecting maintaining-interaction context, the form of those is same with experiment 1.

Dependent Measure. Two items(Cronbach's alpha = 0.847) assessing social performance level would be depicted in the end of each virtual scenario, and participants evaluated the behavior description on Likert 9 -point scale.

Item 1: Your behavior will be: uncommunicative 1 2 3 4 5 6 7 8 9 communicative
Item 2: Your behavior will also be: colorless 12 3 4 5 6 7 8 9 humorous

3.3 Results

A one way ANOVA was conducted, results didn't found the main effect of attractiveness condition, F (1.88) = 3.08, p = 0.083, which was different with result in experiment1, but supported H1.

There was significant main effect of shyness condition, F (1, 88) = 4.35, $p = 0.040 < 0.05$, $\eta_P^2 = 0.047$. Low-shy participants (M = 12.50, SD = 2.91) were significant more likely to participate in virtual social interaction than high-shy participants (M = 11.27, SD = 2.90).

The interaction was marginally significant, F (1.88) = 3.55, $p = 0.063, \eta_P^2 = 0.039$. To clarify the significant interaction effect, we conducted follow-up analyses of simple main effects and found that low shy participants in attractive avatar condition (M = 13.58, SD = 3.05) achieved higher posttest scores than in un attractive avatar condition (M = 11.42, SD = 2.37), $F(1,89) = 6.38$, $p < 0.05$. For high shy participants, the analyze was non-significant, F (1, 89) = 0.01, $p > 0.05$. These results indicated the moderating effect of shyness was significant, which supported H2.

4 General Discussions

The current study conducted two experiments to investigate the Proteus effect in virtual social interaction contexts, and investigate the effect of situational factor and Individual differences on Proteus effect.

In present study, the effects of avatar attractiveness were moderated by social contexts. The appearance of avatar can affect a person's confidence [1,4], so individuals behaved depend on avatar in participating- interaction context. But in maintaining-interaction context, the social performances were most depended on actual social skills instead of appearance, which decreased the attention to self-presentation [9].

Shyness moderated the Proteus effect in experiment 2. Shy individuals tend to bemore self-focused than non-shy individuals [7,8], there is a tendency for shy individuals to attribute reactions to stable internal rather than unstable internal or external causes [10]. Thus, low-shy individuals are more likely to reference self-presentations in virtual environment. That was the reason why the social performances of high-shy individuals were significantly affected by the avatar cues.

According to the self-perception theoretical framework [11], when entering into the virtual environment, the perceptions to avatar lead to Proteus effect. Nevertheless, Proteus effect is also influenced by situation and shyness. We explained the moderating effects of social contexts and shyness levels in an extend self-perception framework based on current results (see Fig. 5).

One limitation of this study is that we examined this effect with avatars of different races with each other, but participants are all from china. So, although we have controlled their differences on attractiveness, it remained an open question as to whether the race differences would cause interference. An additional limitation is that the virtual environments are lack of ideal interactivity—specifically that avatars can't directly express the behavior that users really want to express. Future work should solve these

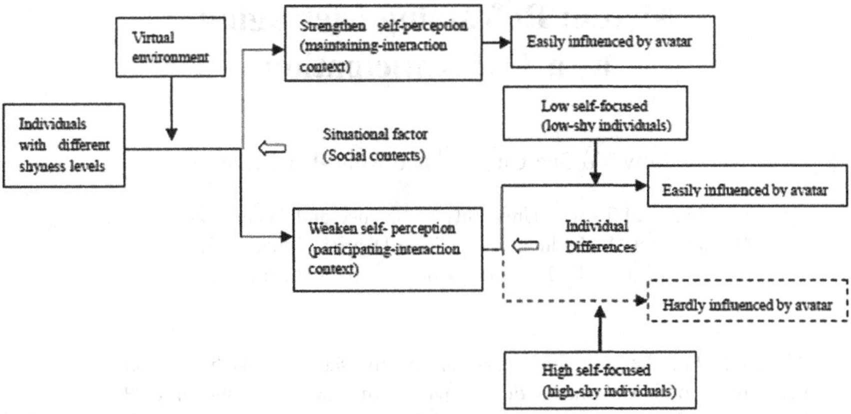

Fig. 5. Self-perception theoretical framework based on current work

issues. Overall, the results of current study would be beneficial to the field of virtual reality and virtual psychology.

References

1. Yee, N., Bailenson, J.N.: The Proteus effect: the effect of transformed self-representation on behavior. J. Hum. Commun. Res. **33**, 271–290 (2007)
2. Bailenson, J.: Transformed social interaction in collaborative virtual environments. In: Messaris, P., Humphreys, L. (eds.) Digital Media: Transformations in Human Communication, pp. 255–264. Peter Lang, New York (2006)
3. Yee, N., Bailenson, J.N., Ducheneaut, N.: The Proteus effect: implications of transformed digital self-representation on online and offline behavior. J. Commun. Res. **36**(2), 285–312 (2009)
4. Brien, L.O.: An investigation into how avatar appearance can affect interactions in a virtual world. J. Soc. Humanistic Comput. **1**(2), 192–200 (2009)
5. Peña, J., Hancock, J.T., Merola, N.A.: The priming effects of avatars in virtual settings. J. Commun. Res. **9**, 1–19 (2009)
6. Frank, M., Gilovich, T.: The dark side of self and social perception: black uniforms and aggression in professional sports. J. Pers. Soc. Psychol. **54**, 74–85 (1988)
7. Alm, C.: The role of shyness and self-focused attention for attribution of reactions in social situations to internal and external causes. J. Scand. J. Psychol. **48**, 519–527 (2007)
8. Schmidt, L.A., Fox, N.A.: Individual differences in young adults' shyness and sociability: personality and health correlates. J. Pers. Individ. Differ. **19**(4), 455–462 (1995)
9. Schlenker, B.R., Leary, M.R.: Social anxiety and self-presentation: a conceptualization and model. J. Psychol. Bull. **92**(3), 641–669 (1982)
10. Alm, C., Lindberg, E.: Attributions of shyness-resembling behaviors by shy and non-shy individuals. J. Pers. Individ. Differ. **27**(3), 575–585 (1999)
11. Bian, Y.L., Zhou, C., Gao, F.Q.: The Proteus effect: a new perspective on virtual world study. J. Psychol. Sci. **37**(1), 232–239 (2014)

Mettle: Reframing Messaging as a Felt Anticipation

Amy Yo Sue Chen(✉) and Rung-Huei Liang

National Taiwan University of Science and Technology,
No. 43, Sect. 4, Keelung Road, Daan District, Taipei 106, Taiwan
{M10110301,liang}@mail.ntust.edu.tw

Abstract. For the past few years, instant messaging (IM) has become the mainstream of social media due to its convenience and efficiency. People, however, tend to exchange message rapidly without further thinking and caring about others or environments. Hence, we develop a non-instant messaging (non-IM) model where anticipation is naturally born. To find design opportunities, we put design probing into practice and found out an emotional expression problem, and that there were still other meaningful perceptions. As a result, we made a prototype of our preliminary concepts aiming to articulate anticipation and sense of place. After the interview with users, we made an adjustment in proposed design to meet users' needs. The whole working process was done with Research through Design (RtD) method. Our work targets at optimizing this dialogical research so that everyone can create and share their personal felt experiences easier via Mettle.

Keywords: Experience design · Anticipation · Non-instant messaging · Sense of place · Emotional communication

1 Introduction

During the last decade, instant messaging (IM) has become the mainstream of social media due to its convenience and efficiency. Nardi et al. asserts that instant messaging effectively supports informal communication tasks such as quick questions, clarification, coordination, scheduling and keeping in touch with important others. These tasks usually involve rapid exchange of information [1]. In fact, there are still other meaningful reasons why people need messaging. For instance, people may want to know news, which creature it is on the flower, how to surf, why Apple is so successful, when dinosaur was extinct, how to do everyday tasks, and all kinds of treasure knowledge in this world, and most importantly, people yearn for understanding others exactly as they desire to be understood. However, not everyone can express his or her thoughts appropriately. We sometimes start an endless fight due to weak communication skills. Common solution to communication problems is to give each other some time. With time, it is easier to calm down, to cast their mind back to the event as a detached third party, to introspect, and to figure out how to say things right. In this case, we may say that slow way is more efficient in emotional expression than fast way is. Hence, we think about applying slow technology concept to messaging, which emphasizes on

C. Stephanidis (Ed.): HCII 2015 Posters, Part II, CCIS 529, pp. 84–90, 2015.
DOI: 10.1007/978-3-319-21383-5_14

reflection instead of function [2]. In Fig. 1, the sending point and the receiving point in IM almost overlap at the same place on the timeline. We then separate them, as Fig. 2 shows, to avoid the immediate pressure in communication. The distance between the two temporal phrases can be seen as the effort of messaging.

Fig. 1. The sending point and the receiving point in instant messaging.

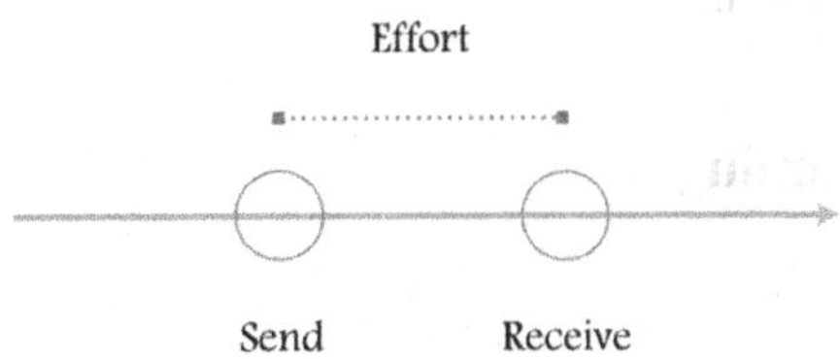

Fig. 2. The distance can be seen as effort in slow messaging.

With this effort, the whole transmitting process is limited. Since digital limitation seems to bring great possibility in designing new forms and functions as Pierce mentioned in Counterfunctional Things [3], we look forward to exploring interesting effort type in slow messaging.

Our research did a pilot test to observe people's impression on current slow messaging, and used prototypes to explore proper effort type and enter the cycle of learning, adjusting, and testing just for proposing a non-instant messaging (non-IM) model that may make people easier to express their thoughts bravely and clearly with lower pressure.

2 Case Study

FutureMe is a website for users to write e-mails to future self. It is inferred that people have their own emotion such as anticipation, passion, and fear. Furthermore, some public letters not only weave great stories in personal life but also inspire other people. Briefly, FutureMe provides a meaningful way for people to cast and review their imagination of life with the self-to-self feature in slow messaging. A similar case to FutureMe is a mobile application called Slow Message. It allows one to send emails to whomever you want. It arrives in a few days, weeks, months, or even years approximately. By quickly defining a loose timeframe to receive a message, one might be surprised by this message on an unexpected time in the future. In sum, Slow Message offers a self-to-others platform for people to send slow messages. Another case comes to be a popular website in Europe, BookCrossing. Aiming to connect people through books, this website sets up an online library to share with entire world. Readers can follow the Label - Share - Follow steps to send a book to the wild for others to hunt, and track its current position along with new owners' feedback. By means of the sharing organism, books are vitalized and readers get more involved in sharing precious knowledge or reflective stories. The connection between people and books, in this case, emphasizes the sharing instead of the ownership. It turns out that BookCrossing gives an interesting delivering ways in slow messaging due to people's affection towards tangible object and physical environment.

Cases above show the current image of slow messaging and their influence on people. Especially in FutureMe and SlowMessage, we see that anticipation plays a good role in slow messaging. According to the definition of anticipation in Technology as Experience [4], anticipation comes into existence right after the sending moment, and goes dead once the receiving moment is met. The two cases let anticipation be the primary topic of this research.

3 Exploratory Framing

3.1 Focusing

In order to find out other design opportunities, we used cultural probes as Gaver proposes [5] and took FutureMe and BookCrossing as tools to test the interaction experiences in slow messaging.

3.2 Probing

The experiment is held in Taipei, Taiwan. There are 20 participants (9 male, 11 female) aged from 20 to 60 in this probing. They use mobile phones and computers every day, and come from different background.

In this probing, participants first need to read one public letter on the FutureMe website, and then write a letter to future self. Next, they have to prepare one book and do the Label - Share - Follow steps on BookCrossing. Material kit, which is actually an online note in Evernote, is prepared for them to record their feelings and thoughts whenever and wherever they want, and synchronize the note to us when they think the content is ready.

Participants were asked to answer the overall probing questions about their background and current use of IM on the online questionnaire. The content of one-to-one interview depends on the questionnaire outcome, the records from the material kit, and the personal experiences about messaging. They can specifically share their experiences.

3.3 Results

- All the participants are frequent users of smart phone and computer. Under this circumstance, their opinion that current IM ways cannot preserve some buffer zone for communication is very encouraging to our research.

- The statistical graph generated from the questionnaire shows that FutureMe is more interesting and enjoyable, but it is not as much interactive as the traditional E-mail is. On the other hand, BookCrossing supplies a surprising way of book exchanging, but they still prefer to go to the traditional library since the functionality is more reliable.
- Some of them were impatient at the beginning of writing the letters to future self. Not until they became more concentrated could they realize the peace and importance of facing themselves.
- Participants shared rich experiences in messaging, such as postcards sent in journey, personal diary, notes passed in class, time capsule, and the secret sign on the bulletin board in train station.
- All the participants are looking forward to further development of messaging.

3.4 Lessons Learned

Although IM enables us to communicate immediately without spatial limitation, it cannot satisfy all human needs of communication. That is, it is not empty within sending and receiving moments. Beside anticipation, subjects passionately talked about some feelings towards certain places in their personal experiences in messaging. Sense of place stands for the beliefs about the connection between self and place, or feelings toward the place [6]. As a result, our secondary topic turns out to be sense of place, and the preliminary goal targets at articulating one messaging way, which promotes anticipation and sense of place.

4 Prototype

A prototype of mobile application named Mettle was prepared for user study. Instead of website, mobile application provides a closer relationship with people, gets users location easily, and interacts with users anytime and anywhere.

4.1 System Description

Literally, Mettle is a combination of message and shuttle. In the application, the embodied message, mettle, takes off from senders' location (start point), flies along a path, and lands at receivers' location (destination point) in a constant speed. As we can see in Fig. 3, the messaging acts like a carrier pigeon flying on the map. Intuitively, we remain the non-IM feature that messaging needs an effort to reach destination to create anticipation. In other words, it requires a certain period of time for the delivery of mettles. The countdown time of the hour glass and the advancing mettles are to dynamically notify users about the remaining time and distance. After the mettle has reached the destination, users can review those received silent messages from Inbox. In order to stimulate sense of place, the whole message's journey is visualized on map. When users see the moving messages, it supplies the locational information to

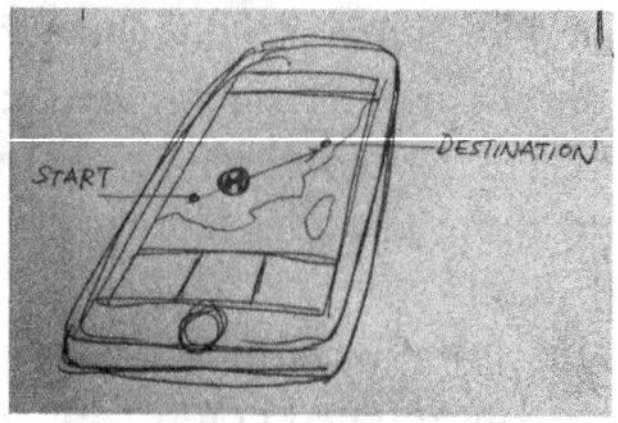

Fig. 3. Prototype of mettle

users imagination. On the other hand, each mettle may contain text, photo, video, and audio at the same time, so that receiver is capable of catching all kinds of features of certain place.

There is a noticeable absence of research dealing with the topic of exchanges in time and space. Hence, with Gamification [7] and In Situ Design [8] concepts, we trickily allow receivers to choose whether they want to wait until mettle arrives or to steal it by moving closer to it within an area called theft radius.

4.2 Preliminary User Study

To investigate the needs of users, we interviewed people with different backgrounds, and used the sketching prototype to introduce our idea. One of the feedbacks is that anticipation usually fades out as time goes by. On the other hand, theft radius game is not appealing to users as long as the threshold of the action is too high to achieve.

4.3 Interaction Adjustment

Although sense of place plays an important role in felt experience that locations and the places' impression on users are considered as anchors of the messaging, users do not perceive significant meaning in connecting places to slow messaging. To fill the gap of our research and users' desire, we target to goals that the weak anticipation part in messaging needs to be activated, and that providing a more reasonable way to get involved in the messaging should solve the frustrating problem in theft radius.

In addition to the functions in prototype, we redesigned two new ideas to make an adjustment of the interactive mechanism in order to optimize anticipation (See Fig. 4). First, Dunn et al. have discussed about the experiential quality in spending money in psychological view [9]. Since consumers would be happier if they buy many small pleasures instead of few big ones, we tried to make messages divided into tiny parts, and distribute them on various locations, which is meaningful for users on map. This design not only provides more anchors but also gives some reminders of the messaging process. Second, instead of linear pace, the mettles should slow down whenever they are near senders or receivers so that the possibilities of stealing are enhanced.

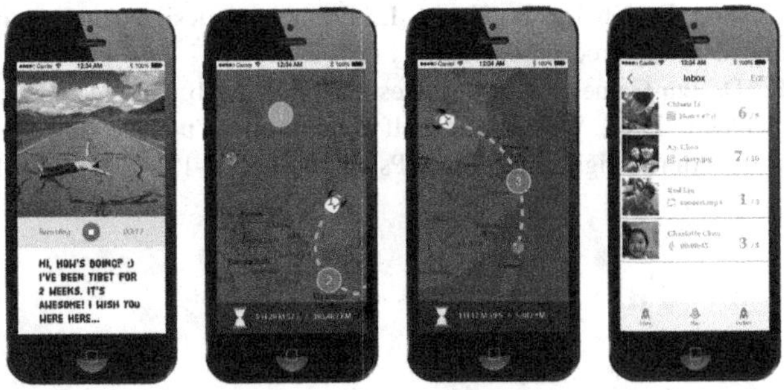

Fig. 4. Proposed Design of Mettle. One mettle starts from sender's location (red point). It goes along touchpoints and finally arrives at receiver's location (blue point) (Color figure online).

5 Discussion and Conclusion

Mettle is done with the hope that this non-IM application provides a disruptive solution to the emotional expression problem of IM. We predict that the future interview results would show that it crafts a more practical sense to imagine, expect, and remember experiences. Mettle could also be applied to other fields such as tourism, LBS games, spatio-tempral storytelling, and education. In this research, we use a dialogical method as Wright and McCarthy propose in Technology as Experience, and dedicate to qualitative research in experience design. Comparing to FutureMe and BookCrossing, Mettle reveals a possibility that anticipation can co-exist in time and space, and, furthermore, be exchanged within the two domains. The more users participate in, the more they gain. With the belief that place is a reminder of memories and time is a catalyst, we hope to continue adjusting the proposed design and optimize this dialogical research so that everyone can easily create and share their personal felt experiences via Mettle.

References

1. Nardi, B.A., Whittaker, S., Bradner, E.: Interaction and outeraction: instant messaging in action. In: Proceedings 2000 ACM Conference Computer Supported Cooperative Work, pp. 79–88 (2000)
2. Hallnäs, L., Redström, J.: Slow technology–designing for reflection. Pers. Ubiquit. Comput. **5**, 201–212 (2001)
3. Pierce, J., Paulos, E.: Counterfunctional Things: Exploring Possibilities in Designing Digital Limitations **1**, 375–384 (2014)
4. McCarthy, J., Wright, P.: Technology as experience. Interactions **11**, 42–43 (2004)
5. Gaver, B., Dunne, T., Pacenti, E.: Design: cultural probes. Interactions **6**, 21–29 (1999). doi:10.1145/291224.291235
6. Jorgensen, B., Stedman, R.: Sense of place as an attitude: lakeshore owners attitudes toward their properties. J. Environ. Psychol. **21**, 233–248 (2001)

7. Deterding, S., Dixon, D., Khaled, R., Nacke, L.: From game design elements to gamefulness: defining gamification. In: Proceedings 15th… (2011)
8. Kristiansen, E.: Design Games for In-Situ Design. Int. J. Mob. Hum. Comput. (2013)
9. Dunn, E.W., Gilbert, D.T., Wilson, T.D.: If money doesn't make you happy, then you probably aren't spending it right. J. Consum. Psychol. **21**, 115–125 (2011). doi:10.1016/j.jcps.2011.02.002

Social Media Use and Impact on Interpersonal Communication

Yerika Jimenez[1(✉)] and Patricia Morreale[2]

[1] Department of Computer and Information Science and Engineering, University of Florida, 412 Newwell Drive, Gainesville, FL 32611, USA
jimenyer@ufl.edu

[2] Department of Computer Science, Kean University, 1000 Morris Ave, Union, NJ 07083, USA
pmorreal@kean.edu

Abstract. This research paper presents the findings of a research project that investigated how young adult interpersonal communications have changed since using social media. Specifically, the research focused on determining if using social media had a beneficial or an adverse effect on the development of interaction and communication skills of young adults. Results from interviews reveal a negative impact in young adult communications and social skills. In this paper young adult preferences in social media are also explored, to answer the question: Does social media usage affect the development of interaction and communication skills for young adults and set a basis for future adult communication behaviors?

Keywords: Social media · Social interaction · Interpersonal communications · Young adults

1 Introduction

Human interaction has changed drastically in the last 20 years, not only due to the introduction of the Internet, but also from social media and online communities. These social media options and communities have grown from being simply used to communicate on a private network into a strong culture that almost all individuals are using to communicate with others all over the world. We will concentrate on the impact that social media has on human communication and interaction among young adults, primarily college students. In today's society, powerful social media platforms such as Myspace, Facebook, Twitter, Instagram (IG), and Pinterest have been the result of an evolution that is changing how humans communicate with each other. The big question we asked ourselves was how much has social media really impacted the way that humans communicate and interact with each other, and if so, how significant is the change of interpersonal interaction among young adults in the United States today?

The motivation behind this research has been personal experience with interaction and communication with friends and family; it had become difficult, sometimes even rare, to have a one-on-one conversation with them, without having them glancing at or interacting with their phone. Has social interaction changed since the introduction of

C. Stephanidis (Ed.): HCII 2015 Posters, Part II, CCIS 529, pp. 91–96, 2015.
DOI: 10.1007/978-3-319-21383-5_15

advanced technology and primarily social media? In correlation with the research data collected in this study, it was concluded that many participants' personal communication has decreased due social media influence encouraging them to have online conversations, as opposed to face-to-face, in-person conversations.

2 Related Work

The question of how social media affects social and human interaction in our society is being actively researched and studied. A literature review highlights the positive and negative aspects of social media interaction, as researchers battle to understand the current and future effects of social media interaction. A study done by Keith Oatley, an emeritus professor of cognitive psychology at the University of Toronto, suggests that the brain may interpret digital interaction in the same manner as in-person interaction, while others maintain that differences are growing between how we perceive one another online as opposed to in reality [1]. This means that young adults can interpret online communication as being real one-on-one communication because the brain will process that information as a reality. Another study revealed that online interaction helps with the ability to relate to others, tolerate differing viewpoints, and express thoughts and feeling in a healthy way [2, 3]. Moreover a study executed by the National Institutes of Health found that youths with strong, positive face-to-face relationships may be those most frequently using social media as an additional venue to interact with their peers [4].

In contrast, research reveals that individuals with many friends may appear to be focusing too much on Facebook, making friends out of desperation rather than popularity, spending a great deal of time on their computer ostensibly trying to make connections in a computer-mediated environment where they feel more comfortable rather than in face-to-face social interaction [5]. Moreover, a study among college freshman revealed that social media prevents people from being social and networking in person [6].

3 Experimental Design

This research study was divided into two parts during the academic year 2013–2014. Part one, conducted during fall semester 2013, had the purpose of understanding how and why young adults use their mobile devices, as well as how the students describe and identify with their mobile devices. This was done by distributing an online survey to several Kean University student communities: various majors, fraternity and sorority groups, sports groups, etc. The data revealed that users primarily used their mobile devices for social media and entertainment purposes. The surveyed individuals indicated that they mainly accessed mobile apps like Facebook, Pinterest, Twitter, and Instagram, to communicate, interact, and share many parts of their daily life with their friends and peers.

Based on the data collected during part one, a different approach and purpose was used for part two, with the goal being to understand how social media activities shape the communication skills of individuals and reflects their attitudes, attention, interests, and activities. Additionally, research included how young adult communication needs change through the use of different social media platforms, and if a pattern can be predicted from the users' behavior on the social media platforms. Part two of this research was conducted by having 30 one-on-one interviews with young adults who are college students. During this interview key questions were asked in order to understand if there is a significant amount of interpersonal interaction between users and their peers. Interpersonal interaction is a communication process that involves the exchange of information, feelings and meaning by means of verbal or non-verbal messages. For the purposes of this paper, only the data collected during spring 2014 is presented.

4 Data Collection

Through interviews, accurate results of the interaction of young adults with social media were collected. These interviews involved 30 one-on-one conversations with Kean University students. Having one-on-one interviews with participants allowed for individual results, first responses from the participant, without permitting responses being skewed or influenced by other participants, such as might occur in group interviews. It also allows users to give truthful answers, in contrast to an online or paper survey, as they might have second thoughts about an answer and change it. The one-on-one interviews consisted of ten open-ended questions, which were aimed to answer, and ultimately determine, how social media interaction involuntarily influences, positively or negatively, an individual's attitude, attention, interests, and social/personal activities. The largest motive behind the questions was to determine how individual communication skills, formally and informally, have changed from interacting with various social media platforms. The interviews, along with being recorded on paper, were also video and audio-recorded. The average time for each interview was between two to ten minutes. These interviews were held in quiet labs and during off-times, so that the responses could be given and recorded clearly and without distraction (Fig. 1). A total of 19 females and 11 males participated, with ages ranging from 19 to 28 years old.

Fig. 1. Female participant during one-on-one interview

After conducting the interviews and analyzing the data collected, it was determined that the age when participants, both male and female, first began to use social media ranged between 9 to 17 years. It was found that, generally, males began to use social media around the age of 13, whereas females started around the age of 12. The average age for males starting to use social media is about 12.909 with a standard deviation of 2.343. For females, the average age is 12.263 with a standard deviation of 1.627. From this, we can determine that males generally begin to use social media around the age of 13, whereas females begin around the age of 12.

After determining the average age of when participants started using social media, it was necessary to find which social media platforms they had as a basis; meaning which social media platform they first used. MySpace was the first social media used by twenty-three participants, followed by Facebook with three users, and Mi Gente by only one user, with two participants not using social media at all. It was interesting to find that all of the participants who started using Myspace migrated to Facebook. The reasoning provided was that "everyone [they knew] started to use Facebook." According to the participants, Facebook was "more interactive" and was "extremely easy to use." The participants also stated that Myspace was becoming suitable for a younger user base, and it got boring because they needed to keep changing their profile backgrounds and modifying their top friends, which caused rifts or "popularity issues" between friends. After finding out which platform they started from, it was also essential to find out which platform they currently use. However, one platform that seemed to be used by all participants to keep up-to-date with their friends and acquaintances was Instagram, a picture and video-based social media platform. Another surprising finding was that many users did not use Pinterest at all, or had not even heard of the platform. After determining which social media platforms the users migrated to, it was essential to identify what caused the users to move from one platform to another. What are the merits of a certain platform that caused the users to migrate to it, and what are the drawbacks of another platform that caused users to migrate from it or simply not use it all?

4.1 Social Interaction Changes

For some participants social interaction had a chance for a positive outcome, while others viewed it in a more negative aspect. The participants were asked if their social interactions have changed since they were first exposed to social media (Table 1). One participant stated that "it is easier to just look at a social media page to see how friends and family are doing rather than have a one-on-one interaction." As for people's attitudes, they would rather comment or "like" a picture than stop and have a quick conversation. On the other hand, another participant felt that social media helped them when talking and expressing opinions on topics that they generally would not have discussed in person. Moreover, the participants are aware of the actions and thing that they are doing but continue to do it because they feel comfortable and did not desire to have one-on-one interactions with people.

The participants were also asked to explain how social media changed their communication and interactions during the years of using social media (Table 2). The data shows that participants interact less in person because they are relating more via

Table 1. Social interaction change

Has your social interaction changed since your first exposure to social media?
Participant x: "I have been interacting more on social media to see how my friends and family are doing. It easier to see their status and pictures than actually call them or have a face-to-face conversation". "Personally I think that people's attitudes have changed because when people see you around school they act like they do not know you. But online they like all your pictures and comment."
Participant x1: "It made me more open with people – I feel comfortable sharing information and discussing topics that I wouldn't have mentioned in person. "
Participant x2: "Using social media makes it easy to start a conversation. However, most of the time you will never have the same conversation because people are scared of actually saying something face to face. Online, you do not have to deal with the stress of seeing that other person's gestures or body language."
Participant x3: "I text 24/7 and I ignore people around me while I am texting. Sometimes I cannot control myself"

Table 2. Communication and interaction changed

How has your communication changed since social media?
Participant x: I interact less, because I can simply see that everyone is doing good by looking at their online pictures and status.
Participant x1: It made me more cautious – afraid to put my personal information up.
Participant x2: My communication is the same. However, people have changed a lot. The internet creates their popularity, but they walk around and act like they now know you but they cannot say hi and act like they do not know you. If people don't not learn how to separate the two (reality vs. social media) then there will not be any more one-to-one interaction between people
Participant x3: Yes, I look at their pictures and I try to understand them just by their pictures- without speaking to them. In other words, I judging by looking

online pictures and status. For other participants, it made them more cautious and even afraid of putting any personal information online because it might cause problems or rifts in their life. On the contrary, some participants stated that their communication and interaction is the same; however, they were able to see how it had changed for the people that are around them. A participant stated that "internet/social media is a power tool that allows people to be whatever they want and in a way it creates popularity, but once again they walk around acting like they do not know you and 'like' your pictures the next day."

5 Discussion

The data illustrated in this paper shows how much the introduction and usage of social media has impacted the interaction and communication of young adults. The future of interaction and communication was also presented as a possibility, if the current trend continues with young adults and social media or online communities. This raises the notion of possibly not having any social, in-person interaction and having all communication or interaction online and virtually with all family and friends.

6 Conclusion

Referring back to the question asked during the introduction: how much has social media impacted the way we communicate and interact with each other? After reviewing all the findings, seeing the relationship individuals have with their mobile phones, and comparing social media platforms, it is clear that many young adults have an emotional attachment with their mobile device and want interaction that is quick and to the point, with minimal "in-person" contact. Many young adults prefer to use their mobile device to send a text message or interact via social media. This is due to their comfort level being higher while posting via social media applications, as opposed to in-person interaction. To successfully and accurately answer the question: yes, social media has had a very positive and negative effect on the way we communicate and interact with each other. However, how effective is this method of "virtual" communication and interaction in the real world?

References

1. Paul, A.: Your Brain on Fiction. The New York Times, 17 March 2012. http://www.nytimes.com/2012/03/18/opinion/sunday/the-neuroscience-of-your-brain-on-fiction.html?pagewanted=all&_r=0. Accessed 26 April 2014
2. Burleson, B.R.: The experience and effects of emotional support: what the study of cultural and gender differences can tell us about close relationships, emotion, and interpersonal communication. Pers. Relat. **10**, 1–23 (2003)
3. Hinduja, S., Patchin, J.: Personal information of adolescents on the internet: a quantitative content analysis of myspace. J. Adolesc. **31**, 125–146 (2007)
4. Hare, A.L., Mikami, A., Szwedo, Y., Allen, D., Evans, M.: Adolescent peer relationships and behavior problems predict young adults' communication on social networking websites. Dev. Psychol. **46**, 46–56 (2010)
5. Orr, R.R., Simmering, M., Orr, E., Sisic, M., Ross, C.: The influence of shyness on the use of facebook in an undergraduate sample. Cyber Psychol. Behav. **12**, 337–340 (2007)
6. Tong, S.T., Van Der Heide, B., Langwell, L., Walther, J.B.: Too much of a good thing? The relationship between number of friends and interpersonal impressions on facebook. J. Comput. Mediated Commun. **13**, 531–549 (2008)

Emotional Selling on Social Media: The 'Punctum' of Personality and Photographs

S.M.S. Mustafah, H. Khalid(✉), and A.S. Ismail

Putra Business School, Seri Kembangan, Malaysia
{sheikh.mbal3,azrin.mbal3}@grad.putrabs.edu.my,
haliyana@putrabs.edu.my

Abstract. Instagram marks a shift in operation from a collection of in situ photography towards a mode of engagement for small home-based businesses to promote their products. We unfold two significant aspects that influence customer engagement on Instagram: photographs and personality. Photographs with 'punctum' often capture users' attention and engage them. Findings from this study also suggest that negative emotions influence user engagement through provocation, sarcasm, and frustration, but do not necessarily promote buying behavior.

1 Introduction

This paper presents a case study of an entrepreneur who uses social media for her home-based baking business. The study utilized a qualitative research methodology to understand the experience, values, and ideas related to the effectiveness of social media to the home-based business operation. Different qualitative tools were exploited to ensure the validity of the findings. In this exploratory study, we unfold two important factors that influence user engagement on Instagram and thereby help business growth. These two factors are photographs and personality of the seller. Specifically, this paper explains the type of photographs that most effectively captures user attention and the kind of personality that may engage customers.

On Instagram, photographs play a major role in capturing customers' attention. Apart from photographs, the merchant's personality is a brand by itself. Although these factors are very important in social media marketing, especially on Instagram, to our knowledge there is hardly any research done on this topic. It is also our belief that much less attention has been given to date to research on Instagram compared to Facebook [1], Twitter [2] and blogs [3]. Thus, our research hopes to fill this gap in the literature.

In contrast to previous studies conducted on Instagram [4, 5], our research employed the case study method as the main approach. A case study provides careful insight and rich information on the issue being studied. In this study, we focused on a small home-based baker who uses social media applications to market her products and services. For the purpose of this paper presentation, the entrepreneur's name is under a pseudonym.

The owner, Nancy, holds a postgraduate degree in Corporate Communication and worked in the industry for three years upon graduating. However, the corporate sector

C. Stephanidis (Ed.): HCII 2015 Posters, Part II, CCIS 529, pp. 97–102, 2015.
DOI: 10.1007/978-3-319-21383-5_16

did not give her much satisfaction, which led to her decision to quit her job and run her own business. The business, which began with chocolate-making, has progressed successfully to baking, pastry making, and culinary training. Most of her classes are conducted at her residence. Prior to using Instagram and Facebook for her business, she was an avid blogger who wrote about interesting places she had visited. Her blog was also used as a space to promote her products and services to her followers. Now, Nancy uses various social media platforms, including Facebook, her blog, Twitter, and Instagram, to promote her business and build relationships with her customers.

2 Background of Study

According to Barthes [6], photographs have two different effects on the viewer: 'studium' and 'punctum'. A 'studium', or informational and aesthetic value, is available to anyone. However, a 'punctum', which is a shock, thrill or emotion elicited by the photograph, is specific to the individual. A photograph that touches a viewer's heart and influences his or her action is said to have a 'punctum' on the viewer.

In business, photographs are used to communicate ideas, beliefs, and feelings associated with products and services. For example, photographs in the tourism industry are used as representations of destinations [7]. In HCI, many studies on photographs have focused on different subjects such as self-presentation [8], community building [9], preserving heritage [10] and photo-sharing for the elderly [11].

Apart from photographs, the personality of a seller could influence user engagement and buyer purchasing behavior. Seller personality is important for initiating trust and building long-term relationships [12]. A seller's personality on social media is expressed through his or her interaction with others in the space and through self-representation in his or her photographs. The emotions that sellers portray here have multifaceted impacts. Emotions influence strategic decisions [13], shape buyer-seller interaction [14], and help both parties achieve their objectives [15]. In business, there is a reciprocal linkage between positive emotions and business gain [12]. On the contrary, it is also true that negative emotions influence user engagement with certain brands through provocation, sarcasm and frustration, but do not necessarily promote buying behavior.

3 Research Methodology

This research focuses on a case study of a small home-based business. The tools for data collection include an in-depth interview with the business owner, online observation of the owner's social media pages, and content analysis of photographs posted, comments published, and "likes" given on these social media pages. The interview method was selected as the primary tool due to its proven ability to investigate issues in depth. Discovery of an individual's personality and how he or she thinks and feels about a topic can be explored during an interview. The merchant's interaction on Instagram was observed for a period of three months. Photos posted, comments published and "likes" given over this duration were quantified and analysed.

4 Findings

This section presents findings based on our interview, online observations, and content analysis.

4.1 Photographs on Instagram

Nancy started her Instagram account in November 2013. Prior to that, she had utilized two Facebook accounts to promote her products. However, her inconsistency in posting had made Facebook an ineffective tool for marketing. She found Instagram to be more user friendly and very responsive. Within five months of registering on Instagram, she had 2383 followers with a total of 503 pictures posted. During our 3-month online observation period, Nancy posted 50 photos and received 256 comments. We used this total as our sample for content analysis.

Fifty-eight percent (58 %) of the photos posted during the 3-month period were about her products. The rest of the photos were about her personal activities. Nancy took great efforts in presenting her photographs on Instagram. Figure 1 below shows an image of her dessert product with various hues and tones, such as yellow pastry, red strawberry, and dark chocolate, which immediately make this an enticing image. The addition of the dark chocolate on the white cream (punctum) draws more attention from the viewer and may increase the temptation to buy.

[redacted]

Fig. 1. Enticing photo of product

In comparing the two types of photos posted by Nancy, the audience appears to value photos of products more than photos of personal activities. This is established from the "likes" and comments received for each post. There are around 28 to 67 "likes" for photos that show products, which is higher than the range of 13 to 53 "likes" obtained for personal activity photos posted on the account. Photos of products also engaged more comments. We divided the comments received into 4 categories as shown in Fig. 2 below:

Ninety-three (93) out of the 256 comments received for her photos discussed business information and solicited explanations. Various types of comment contributors voiced out inquiries or requested clarification on business information. Some of the

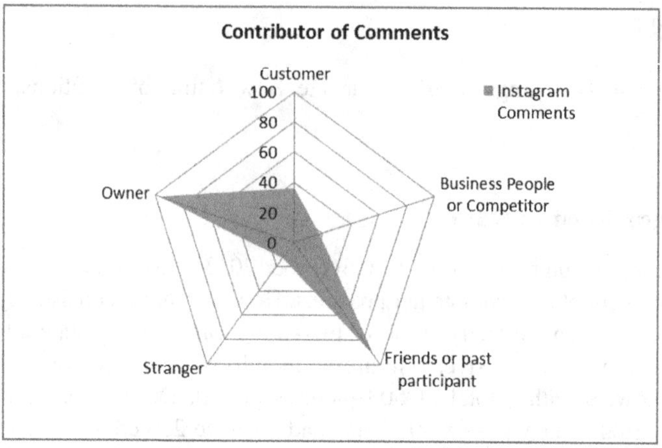

Fig. 2. Contributor of comments

inquiries involved booking orders of the product or baking class schedules. For every order requested by the audience, the owner diverts the order to a private phone number for in-depth discussions. Meanwhile, 60 out of the 256 comments discussed motivation and support to the business.

The highest contributor of comments was the owner herself, showing that engagement with content can solicit good feedback for businesses. Customers can freely interact with the owner to clarify any piece of information. Also, the engagement of friends or previous customers who shared their baking class experiences and product appearances is an indicator that the business receives good support from the audience.

4.2 Personality

Based on our interview session and online observation, Nancy appears to be an extrovert with an outspoken and firm personality. She takes punctuality seriously in her business, avoids being bias, and maintains pre- and post-support for her clients at all times. It is interesting to observe how she spends a lot of time building her business image through her personality. Descriptions or captions that she writes to accompany her photographs on Instagram are not just about the products but also include ramblings on her customers' and students' attitudes, as shown in an example below:

"One thing you should know about online students, some of them are really too pushy, lazy to google up and expect I'm gonna be the one who provide everything. Even lazy to scroll up....Stop saying I have an easy job"- Instagram, April 2014.

Sometimes, she shares her feelings in her personal Facebook account about certain incidents between her and her customers, as exemplified in Fig. 3 below:

Expressing her negative emotions on Instagram or Facebook could escalate to a vicious relationship with her customers. Although this is true, based on our findings, there are some customers who admire her courage and honesty in expressing her feelings. Being oneself is very important in engaging customers to one's business. Contrary to traditional marketing styles where negatives vibes are hidden to avoid

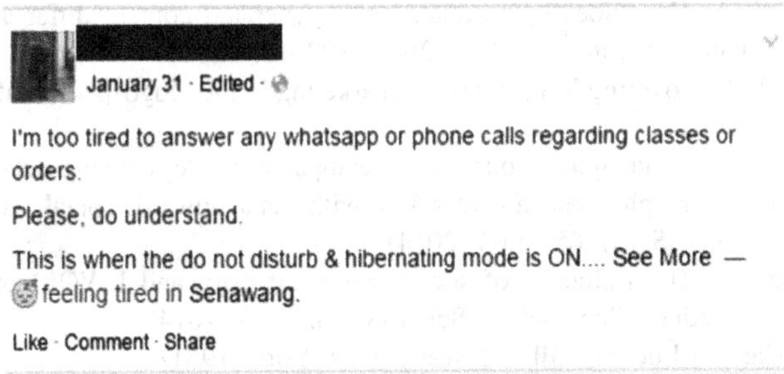
[redacted]
January 31 · Edited ·
I'm too tired to answer any whatsapp or phone calls regarding classes or orders.
Please, do understand.
This is when the do not disturb & hibernating mode is ON.... See More —
feeling tired in Senawang.
Like · Comment · Share

Fig. 3. Expressing feelings in personal Facebook account

unfavorable consequences with customers, being transparent with one's feelings could actually attract customers in social media. On this platform, business owners are not just selling products, but are also marketing their personalities. Anger, frustration, joy, and happiness give multidimensional impacts to customers when these emotions are translated into comments, posts and photographs. People who admire this type of personality and attitude will become loyal customers, while those who feel badly affected will move away.

5 Conclusion

Businesses that use social media in their marketing mix know the importance of user engagement to their posts. User engagement could help build a long lasting relationship with customers. At the time of writing this paper, Instagram is yet to have its own user engagement formula. Although statistical revelations of user engagement are important, the factors influencing these numbers are also significant. In this exploratory study, we have revealed two important factors that engage users: photographs and personality of the seller.

For home-based business owners, photographs are choreographed in different angles, filtered, enchanted with wordings, and published to the public using their mobile phones or digital cameras. The photographs are posted over regular intervals hoping to gather as many views as possible and promote sales. Photographs in social media have shifted our expectations of images and everyday aesthetic [16]. The ephemeral of photographs in social media is different; they are about realism, urbanization, attention to detail, and creativity. In this study too, the business owner showed her solid determination to promote her items by constantly improving her marketing style and choosing different platforms to draw the attention of the social media community. Her bubbly personality, coupled with her talent to evoke both positive and negative feelings through her photos and wordings, have managed to captivate and charm many loyal supporters, thus bringing her competitors to shame.

References

1. Gambao, A.M., Goncalves, H.M.: Customers loyalty through social networks: lessons from Zara on Facebook. Bus. Horiz. **57**(6), 709–717 (2014)

2. Smith, N.S., et al.: How does brand-related user-generated content differ across youtube, facebook, and twitter? J. Interact. Mark. **26**(2), 102–113 (2012)
3. Lin, C.Y., et al.: Discovering influencers for marketing in the blogosphere. Inf. Sci. **181**(23), 5143–5515 (2011)
4. Howard, D., et al.: Managing your social campaign strategy using facebook, twitter, instagram, youtube & pinterest: an interview with dana howard, social media marketing manager. Bus. Horiz. **57**(5), 657–665 (2014)
5. Thoumrugreje, A.: The influence of social media intensity and EWOM on conspicuous consumption. Procedia – Soc. Behav. Sci. **148**(25), 7–15 (2014)
6. Barthes, R.: Camera Lucida. Hill and Wang, New York (1981)
7. Kim, H., Stepchenkova, S.: Effect of tourist photographs on attitudes towards destination: manifest and latent content. Tourism Manage. **49**, 29–41 (2015)
8. Van House, N.: Collocated photo sharing, story-telling, and the performance of self. Int. J. Hum.-Comput. Stud. **67**(12), 1073–1086 (2009)
9. Khalid, H., Dix, A.: The experience of photologging: global mechanisms and local interactions. Pers. Ubiquit. Comput. **14**(3), 209–226 (2010)
10. De Kadt, C. et al.: Revisiting district six: a case study of digital heritage reconstruction from archival photographs. In: Proceedings of the 6th International Conference on Computer Graphics, Virtual Reality, Visualisation and Interaction in Africa. ACM, February 2009
11. Apted, T et al. Tabletop sharing of digital photographs for the elderly. In: Proceedings of the SIGCHI Conference on Human Factors in Computing Systems. ACM, April 2006
12. Anderson, P.L., Kumar, R.: Emotions, trust and relationship development in business relationships: a conceptual model for buyer-seller dyad. Ind. Mark. Manage. **35**, 522–535 (2006). Elsevier, July 2005
13. Ben Ze'Ev, A.: The Subtlety of Emotions, Psycologuy. MIT Press, Cambridge (2001). www.psycprints.ecs.soton.ac.uk/archive/00000136/
14. Carnevale, P.J., Isen, A.: The influence of positive affect and visual access on the discovery of integrative solutions in bilateral negotiations. Organ. Behav. Hum. Decis. Process. **37**, 1–13 (1986)
15. Greenhalgh, L., Chapman, D.I.: Negotiator relationships: construct measurement and demonstration of their impact on the process and outcomes of negotiation. Group Decis. Negot. **7**(6), 465–489 (1998)
16. Murray, S.: Digital images, everyday aesthatic. J. Vis. Cult. **7**(2), 14 (2008)

Towards the Easy Analysis of Mass Media Audience Reaction on Social Networks via Discursive Category Tools

Stefanie Niklander[1(✉)], Ricardo Soto[2,3,4], and Broderick Crawford[2,5,6]

[1] Universidad Adolfo Ibañez, Santiago, Chile
stefanie.niklander@uai.cl
[2] Pontificia Universidad Católica de Valparaíso, Valparaíso, Chile
{ricardo.soto,broderick.crawford}@ucv.cl
[3] Universidad Autónoma de Chile, Santiago, Chile
[4] Universidad Cientifica del Sur, Lima, Perú
[5] Universidad Central de Chile, Santiago, Chile
[6] Universidad San Sebastián, Santiago, Chile

Abstract. The Mass Media involves information and communication products targeted to a wide audience. Today such communications products are also available on Internet where people can react to a given information by posting critics, congratulations, opinions or whatever they want via social networks. Such reactions are considered valuable information for instance to government and companies. However, this information is hard to automatically process as people commonly use ironies, stereotypes, metaphors expressed in informal writing plenty of chat abbreviations, emoticons, and slang words. In this paper, we illustrate how tools based on discursive categories can be used to analyze such reactions and thus to process and understand the information behind them.

Keywords: Social networks · Discourse category tools · Mass media

1 Introduction

The Mass Media involves information and communication products targeted to a wide audience such as television, radio, and newspapers. Today such communications products are also available on Internet where people can react to a given information by posting critics, congratulations, opinions or whatever they want via social networks such as Facebook and Twitter. Such reactions are considered valuable information for instance to government and companies that intend to receive useful feedback from people in regard to a given event, product, or concern. However, this information is hard to automatically process as people commonly use ironies, stereotypes, metaphors expressed in informal writing plenty of chat abbreviations, emoticons, and slang words. In this paper, we illustrate how tools based on discursive categories can be used to process such reactions and thus to understand the information behind them.

C. Stephanidis (Ed.): HCII 2015 Posters, Part II, CCIS 529, pp. 103–106, 2015.
DOI: 10.1007/978-3-319-21383-5_17

The discursive categories are words or sentences previously defined by the researcher that will allow an exhaustive analysis of the media. We employ two classic discursive categories, namely visibility and invisibility [4]. The visibility focuses on the form in which a given information is presented to the audience, while invisibility observes the form in which the information is hidden to the audience. We present interesting results where the use of these discursive categories allows us to easily process the social network information in order to provide clear feedback.

2 Results and Discussion

In this work we want to know what are the reactions of the public against the texts produced by the Mass Media in order to get the keys to understanding the behavior of people. This focuses on finding different ways of thinking and different ways to decode the messages from the audience. The importance of this research lies mainly in that as Bourdieu [1] argues, all audience studies are focused on marketing and commercial issues and there is no concern to understand the reaction to the messages. Analyzing the reactions of the audience with respect to a new, is to study the emissions that are actually built by the speakers. Garreton [2] points out the importance of analyzing the discourses generated by society, denoted them as "an important clue" to categorize the views of this society. From our standpoint, the language is not considered only a mean to express and reflect our beliefs and opinions, but also an element that participates in the construction of social reality.

In this work, we study the reactions of the public against an article published on December 16, 2013 in the Chilean newspaper called "La Tercera". The topic is related to the presidential candidate Michelle Bachelet. In this regard, we note what topics the readers make visible and invisible through their comments on each of the analyzed news. In total, we analyze 10 news about the Chilean candidate and the 55 posted comments that contained these publications. We observed that public opinion is manifested by speeches full of stigmatization which heavily impacts on the division of Chilean society, producing a polarization of political discourses. This results in a invisibility of social problems that really affect the country and a visibility of the topics that are irrelevant for country development. We identified that the comments analyzed in the "La Tercera" newspaper are built around the following topics:

1. Visibility of physical characteristics of Michelle Bachelet. On several occasions the public was limited to mention that from March 2014 the country would be governed by a fat woman, therefore the physical characteristics of the president are visible, trivializing the most important fact, which is the election of a new president. We emphasize that all comments highlighting the aesthetic characteristics of the president are posted by her opponents.
2. Visibility of low intellectual capacity of Michelle Bachelet. The comments that referred to the limited capabilities of Bachelet to govern the country are repeatedly posted. It is constantly stated that a person who does not

handle the four arithmetic operations cannot govern a nation. As in previous thematics, these comments are posted by Bachelet's opponents. However, unlike in previous cases, Bachelet's supporters counter-argued that she has already demonstrated the intellectual capacity to assume the presidency.

3. Visibility of low morale of the political sector of Michelle Bachelet. Unlike previous topics, this axis does not refer specifically to Bachelet, but to people forming his political sector. Public opinion tends to comment on these news that leftist politicians are thieves and they steal again as they did in the previous government.

In summary, we see that comments make visible the topics having no direct connection with the published news, and only tend to criticize or defend, as appropriate, to politicians of a certain political sector. Therefore, we note that there is an allusion to the passions as part of the political argument. In addition, and as argued by Chantal Mouffe [3], it is evident that all comments on the social network are built from the antagonism us/they. Depending on the political sector that the public tends to defend, they are characterized themselves as workers, honest and intellectually superior, while the opposite side is characterized as unemployed, corrupted and with low intellectual capacity. People attempt to highlight positive features from their political side and deliver negative characteristics to their opposite party. In relation to the topics that the public make invisible when expressing their opinion, we find that people rarely tend to discuss aspects of the news published, therefore, the allocated space is freely used by readers to comment and mainly to insult the protagonist of the news. There is no critical arguments, but only comments with irrelevant content. Therefore we observe an absence of a real social criticism on the arguments of each comment, where people is limited to criticize or laud from an emotional standpoint.

3 Conclusions

In this paper, we have illustrated how the discursive categories visibility/invisibility can be used to process the people reactions on internet through posted comments with respect to a given information. In particular, we have taken a set of news with their corresponding comments related to the Chilean presidential elections. After applying the above categories, we could show that, at least in the news from our corpus, the public does not react, on most occasions in relation to the topics discussed in texts, but rather tends to comment situations or issues unrelated to the information provided. For instance in this case study, Michelle Bachelet is grossly disqualified by people from the opposite political side making repeated references to their body and intellectual capacity. This is worrying as the next President of the Republic is analyzed only by its aesthetic characteristics, without highlighting any approach or criticizing his previous or current government program. We believe this situation is manifested mainly because Michelle Bachelet is a woman, because if someone of the opposite sex had the same aesthetic characteristics, public opinion will not be focused on that.

As future work we expect to analyze new social phenomena using these same categories as well as to automatize this process to easily explore analogous social behaviors on social networks.

Acknowledgements. Ricardo Soto is supported by Grant CONICYT/FONDECYT/INICIACION/11130459 and Broderick Crawford is supported by Grant CONICYT/FONDECYT/REGULAR/1140897.

References

1. Bourdieu, P.: Capital Cultural, escuela y espacio social. Siglo XXI Editores, México (1997)
2. Garreton, M.: The Postpinochetismo A Democratic Society Chile. Prometheus (2007)
3. Moufle, C.: En torno a lo político. Fondo de cultura económica, Buenos Aires (2007)
4. Whitty, G., Rowe, G., Aggleton, P.: Discourse in Cross-Curricular Contexts: limits to empowerment. Int.Stud. Sociol. Educ. **4**(1), 25–42 (1994)

A Proposal of an SNS to Support Individual Practices in a Voluntary Community

Kohei Otake[1(✉)], Masashi Komuro[2], Yoshihisa Shinozawa[1], Tomofumi Uetake[3], and Akito Sakurai[1]

[1] School of Science for Open and Environmental Systems, Keio University, 3-14-1 Hiyoshi, Kohoku-ku, Yokohama-shi, Kanagawa-ken 223-8522, Japan
otake_kohei@keio.jp, {shino, sakurai}@ae.keio.ac.jp
[2] Komuro Consulting Group, 1-30-15, Shibuya-ku, Tokyo 151-0053, Japan
ceo@komuroconsulting.com
[3] School of Business Administration, Senshu University, 2-1-1 Higashimita Tama-ku, Kawasaki-shi, Kanagawa-ken 214-8580, Japan
uetake@isc.senshu-u.ac.jp

Abstract. Widespread popularization of social networking services (SNSs) prompted, for example, a voluntary community such as an orchestra club of a university to use an SNS to support their activities. However, it is not all-purpose and lacks functions to improve members' individual skills. Appropriate practice is a great help but we hardly find functions to motivate practices by, for instance, mutual evaluation, members' advice, and creating competing environment. In this paper, we focus on members' individual practices in an orchestra club and propose a SNS to foster and maintain their motivations to practice based on the analysis result of current conditions. As the first step of the system development, this paper introduces design of a prototype system and the results of a preliminary evaluation.

Keywords: Social networking service · Gamification · Voluntary community

1 Introduction

Recently, the number of voluntary communities such as local communities and university club activities are increasing. In these communities, such as orchestra clubs of a university, there are various types of members and there is usually little time to meet and practice together. Therefore, it is usually difficult to improve members' skill and motivation without their individual activities. Under this situation, most of these communities use SNSs. However, existing SNS offers few functions to support their individual activities, it is usually difficult to improve their skill [1–4].

In our past research, we proposed an SNS for voluntary communities using the concept of gamification [1]. We implemented the SNS for the orchestra club of Senshu University and showed the effectiveness of our SNS. However, we also found that it was still needed to support their individual activities based on the analysis of their current conditions.

C. Stephanidis (Ed.): HCII 2015 Posters, Part II, CCIS 529, pp. 107–112, 2015.
DOI: 10.1007/978-3-319-21383-5_18

2 Purpose of This Study

In this study, we purposed to implement new functions in the SNS to support members' individual practices in a voluntary community. We focus on the gamification methods since these methods can maintain and improve their motivation [5].

3 Analysis of the Current Conditions

First, we targeted the Senshu University orchestra club and analyzed the current conditions of their individual activities. Based on this analysis, we classified their activities into the following three types.

- Communication activity

– To share information with other members. This activity will be a starting point of Collaboration activity and Competition activity.

- Collaboration activity

– To share their individual practices with other members. This activity will be a starting point of Communication activity and Competition activity.

- Competition activity

– To compete for the outcome of their individual practices with other members. This activity will be a starting point of Communication activity and Collaboration activity.

4 Proposal of an SNS to Support Individual Activities

We proposed three functions to support above three types of activities by applying a concept of gamification. The functions we proposed were as follows.

1. Communication Bulletin Board to support Communication activity
2. Feedback System to support Collaboration activity
3. Ranking System to support Competition activity

4.1 Communication Bulletin Board to Support Communication Activity

First, we make a few topics that are often discussed when they practice with each other (e.g. a difficult part during practices, a set piece, etc.) in the Communication Bulletin Board. Additionally, users can post new topics that they would like to discuss. Users can post comments on these topics freely. It is possible to set a restriction on a topic so that only specific users can participate. Users can easily share information with other members by using this function. Moreover, users can create topics related to Collaboration activity and Competition activity thus facilitating those activities.

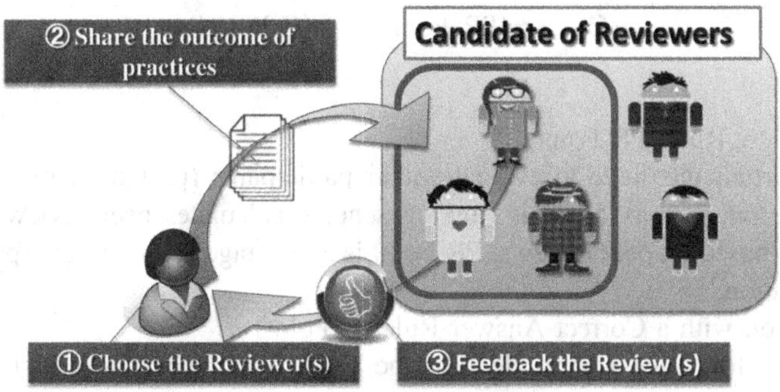

Fig. 1. Feedback System

4.2 Feedback System to Support Collaboration Activity

Figure 1 shows a rough sketch of Feedback System to support Collaboration activity.

A user who would like to seek advice can share his/her outcome of practices with the other user(s) (Reviewer(s)) who are chosen by the user. The reviewers evaluate his/her outcome of practices and give feed back to the user. The feedback contents are recorded in the user's account, and it is possible to check them anytime. By using this function, the user can practice collaboratively with other users. Moreover, users can conduct easily Communication activity and Competition activity related to the feedback content.

4.3 Ranking System to Support Competition Activity

Figure 2 shows a sketch of Ranking System to support Competition activity.

Users can participate in a competition by submitting outcomes of their practices. Ranking system calculates the competition score (CS) of their submitted outcomes as follows by using following two evaluation rules. α and β are weights.

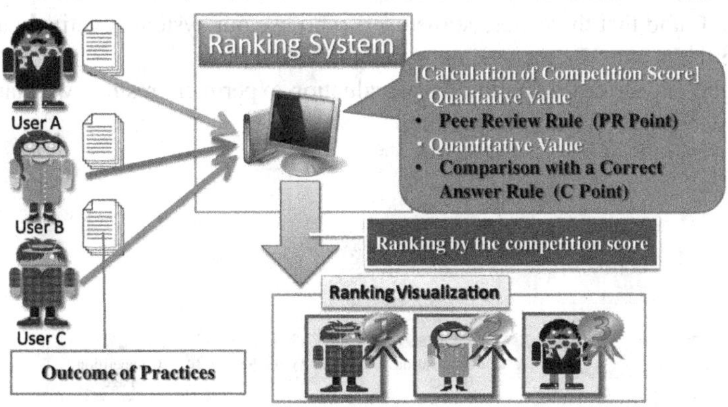

Fig. 2. Ranking System

$$CS = \alpha\,(\text{PR Point}) + \beta\,(\text{C Point}) \quad (1)$$

- Peer Review Rule (PR Point)
  - All participants have to evaluate other participants (peer review) at five-point scale (min 1, max 5). This ranking scheme calculates peer review point (PR Point) based on peer reviews. PR Point is an average score of other participants' evaluation.
- Comparison with a Correct Answer Rule (C Point)
  - Best performance is provided for the music for the practice. In this ranking scheme, our system calculates comparative point (C point) based on comparing the best performance with the outcome of the user's practices. Comparative point is a product of the concordance rate and β.

Participants are ranked based on the competition score (CS). Top 3 participants are exhibited on the competition page. By using this function, it becomes possible for the users to compete easily with other members. Moreover, users can conduct easily Communication activity and Collaboration activity based on these results.

5 Prototype System

To test the feasibility of our proposal, we made a prototype system. Screen hierarchy and screenshots of our prototype system are shown below (Figs. 3, 4).

6 Preliminary Evaluation of the Prototype System

To evaluate our system, we conducted the following experiment for 3 weeks.

- Target: Keio piano club
  - 12 students (men 6, women 6), level: intermediate

As a result, we found that there were some users who use our system aggressively, but we also found that there were some users who use our system negatively and there were some users who do not use our system (Table 1).

Through analysis of this preliminary evaluation experiment results, we clarified the following two points for improvement.

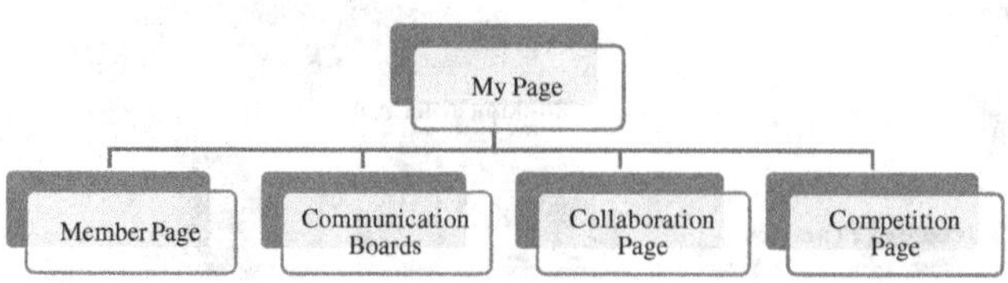

Fig. 3. Screen hierarchy of our prototype system

"My page"

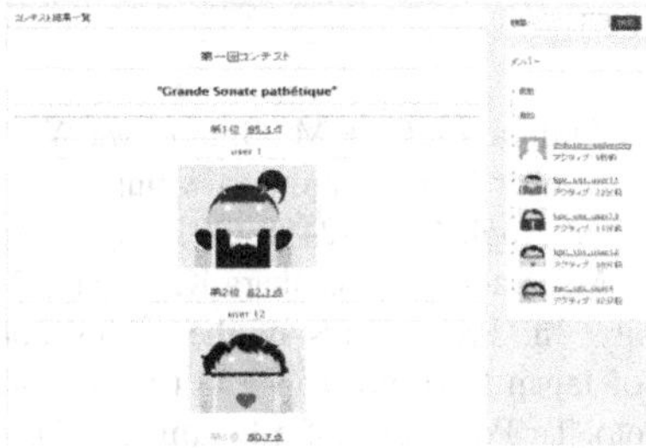

"Competition page"

Fig. 4. Screenshots of our prototype system

Table 1. The type of the users

Use aggressively (Share the practice time, practice type…)	42 %
Use negatively (Just seeing)	25 %
Not use	33 %

- Improvement of the rate of utilization of our system
  - It is necessary to provide easy interface for the beginners of the system. We think that it will be effective to use methods which are used in social games. For example, at the beginning of the game, users' avatars, where the avatars are graphical representation of the users and are chosen by them, keep their levels which are easily increased at the start, so that users can easily realize the growth of characters in the game.
- Improvement of the sharing rate of the information
  - Some members did not share information. It is necessary to provide a new function which makes it possible to express information such as practice hour and contents easily.

However, there is no negative opinion about a concept of our proposal.

7 Conclusion and Future Works

In this paper, we proposed new functions to motivate members' individual practices in a voluntary community. We proposed three functions to support the three types (Communication, Collaboration and Competition) of activities based on the analysis of their current conditions. To examine feasibility of our proposal, we implemented a prototype system and conducted a preliminary evaluation.

Through the practical use of our prototype system, we clarified two points for improvement. However, there is no negative opinion about a concept of our proposal.

In our future works, we revise the prototype system and evaluate it in actual uses.

References

1. Otake, K., Sumita, R., Oka, M., Shinozawa, Y., Uetake, T., Sakurai, A.: A proposal of SNS to improve member's motivation in voluntary community using gamification. Int. J. Adv. Comput. Sci. Appl. **6**(1), 82–88 (2015)
2. Yano, Y., Muramoto, Y., Kitahara K., Okubo, M.: A proposal of SNS for activation physical community. In: Proceedings of the 75th National Convention of Information Processing Society of Japan IPSJ, pp. 153–154 (2013). In Japanese
3. Matsumoto, T.: Possibility of e-Learning by using Gamification. Japan. Soc. Inf. Syst. Educ. **27**(3), 34–40 (2012). (in Japanese)
4. Sabetto, T., Kotani, M.: Utilizing the enterprise social network for knowledge management. J. Inf. Sci. Technol. Assoc. **62**(7), 296–301 (2012)
5. Moise, D.: The use of gamification in events marketing. Int. J. Econ. Practices Theor. **4**(2), 185–190 (2014)

Providing Tools to Enable Information Audit in Social Networks

Alexandre Pinheiro[1(✉)], Claudia Cappelli[1], and Cristiano Maciel[2]

[1] Universidade Federal do Estado do Rio de Janeiro - UNIRIO, Rio de Janeiro, Brazil
{alexandre.pinheiro,claudia.cappelli}@uniriotec.br
[2] Universidade Federal de Mato Grosso - UFMT, Cuiabá, Mato Grosso, Brazil
cmaciel@ufmt.br

Abstract. In the moment that social networks arise as a new source of information, we also started to concern about the information shared in this environment. It is difficult to users of social networks to distinguish the accuracy of the information spreaded. The combination of auditability features and research directions in human-computer interaction area will guide the development of tools for evaluating information. We present prototypes of tools that once available, will allow users to decide about the credibility of information that they access and share.

Keywords: Auditability · Social networks · User tools

1 Introduction

In a scenario where the Internet has established itself as an environment where we can make complex researches, query a huge amount of databases and search for information, the social networks have become a choice of information source. Social networks are able to generate great impact on a particular subject, regardless of the provenance of information, whether from official sources or simple user status update. This kind of system provides first-hand data, but one pressing problem is to distinguish true information from misinformation and rumors. In many cases, social media data is user generated and can be biased, inaccurate, and subjective [1].

Many users are not ready to determine the credibility of online information. Given this statement it is essential to encourage the development of people skills to make content evaluation on the Internet, however how people seek information and the types of information they seek is a complex interplay between characteristics of the information seeker, the properties of the information they are looking for, and the systems in which they seek information [2]. Considering the behavior and characteristics of the users plus the information that they face as variables, we focused on developing tools for social networks intended to support verification of content.

The aim of our work is to analyze, build mechanisms and subsequently make the operationalization of auditability characteristics as tools for information validation, using references from interaction design, in order to obtain better usability in such systems. Successful tools for community generated content need to address the lack of

C. Stephanidis (Ed.): HCII 2015 Posters, Part II, CCIS 529, pp. 113–117, 2015.
DOI: 10.1007/978-3-319-21383-5_19

transparency [3]. To create such tools we applied concepts of transparency on information systems headed up by the provision of audit capacity of spreaded content. In other hand we aligned this theme with Human-Computer Interaction (HCI) research guidelines.

This article is based in an exploratory approach and is structured as follows: In the Sect. 2 we present our analysis about the non-functional requirements related to a catalog of information auditability in social networks and the HCI foundations to build tools based on these requirements. Some of the suggestions of tools, main purpose of this study are explained and presented as prototypes in the Sect. 3. The conclusion of this article, citing the next stages of work is available in Sect. 4.

2 Auditability and Human-Computer Interaction

2.1 A Catalog to Define Auditability Characteristics

To promote the information audit in social networks we need to deal with non-functional requirements (NFR). The identification and proper expression of NFRs are essential to the understanding and reasoning of the impacts of further design decisions [4]. To set these NFRs we can use a catalog [5].

The Catalog of Transparency developed by Cappelli [6] is a pillar for this research, especially as regards the characteristic of auditability and its definition. Auditability is defined as the ability to examine carefully for accuracy with the intent of verification [7]. This characteristic is identified through the assessment of practices that implement explanation, traceability, verifiability, validity and controllability of information. We use these definitions as a starting point to formulate a catalog for information auditability characteristics in social networks.

2.2 Relating HCI Definitions and Auditability Characteristics

After define auditability characteristics, the next step of this work consists in specify a set of operationalizations and implementation mechanisms that can implement these characteristics um software. To identify them we applied the foundations and practices of HCI area.

To help us with the challenge of listing non-functional requirements related to auditability, turning it on tools for evaluation of information by users, we focused our research on a literature review related to experience in the use and interaction with web interfaces, in the construction of quality systems and in recommendations for best practices defined by international standards [8]. After this step we reached, in a first approach, 15 characteristics that can be explored in order to minimize the problems of the lack of auditability of information in social networks. These characteristics are: accountability, adaptability, availability, clarity, completeness, composability, controllability, correctness, decomposability, dependability, extensibility, traceability, uniformity, validity and verifiability. The implementation of some of these characteristics will be reported in Sect. 3 of this article.

According to Baranauskas [9], the HCI research is based on the belief that we have people using interactive systems. These interactive systems should be designed following requirements, capacity and user preferences for an interaction with usability. People do not have to change to suit the system, the system must be rather designed to suit their requirements. We need to develop tools that besides providing the audit capacity of information need to be adapted to any kind of user. Some researches [10] found that users judgments were based on two basic criteria: the characteristics of the information "objects" that they found online and the characteristics of the source of online information. The characteristics of the information objects that participants were concerned about included the type of information object, its content, its presentation and its structure.

After a review of numerous models (created by many authors) of evaluation information, Metzger [11] proposed in an article a common checklist to credibility assessment. In this way the tools that follow the suggestions of the checklist would be able to help social network users acquire the skills needed to find credible online information and to evaluate existing theoretical models and user-based strategies of credibility assessment. Table 1 shows the relation of some functional requirements based on HCI guidance and the auditability characteristics.

Table 1. Relationship between HCI based items and the Catalog of Auditability

Checklist item	NFR characteristic(s)
Presence of date stamp	Verifiability; traceability
Source citations	Dependability; traceability
Author qualifications	Verifiability
Seals from trusted third parties	Composability
Sponsorship by reputable organizations	Composability; traceability
Professional and consistent design	Uniformity
Easy navigation, well-organized	Uniformity
Absence of broken links	Availability; traceability
Notification/presence of review process	Validity
Domain name and URL	Traceability
Ability to verify claims elsewhere	Verifiability
Comprehensiveness of information provided	Correctness; clarity

3 Reviewing Tools Prototypes

Using Fig. 1 as a guide we can see the number of items that we will cover in this prototype. In the tooltip 1 we bring as a requirement, a feature that permits the user to assign other profiles to verify the user's reputation and online social presence. In this example we use LinkedIn, because it is a social network for job search and is essential that the users are presented as they really are. This feature enhances the positioning information produced by the users and is related to the composability, which describes the gathering of more data from other partitions adding it to the existing information and traceability.

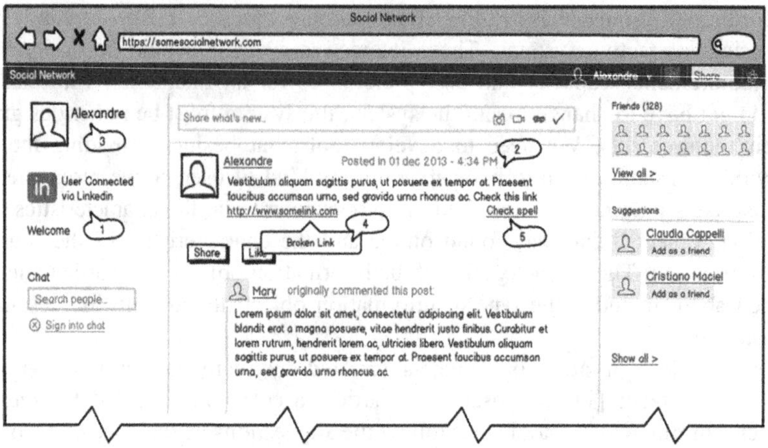

Fig. 1. A social network with several prototypes of suggested tools

It is indispensable that all shared information is marked with a timestamp as shown in the tooltip 2. The existence of this option shows whether the information is current and contextualizes the users when they check information. For the verifiability is desirable that the information has a date and time, so we can use as a filter to legitimize that content and traces it. The user qualifications as information producer can be considered as a reference by other users. The tooltip 3 shows the importance of having a social network account with complete register and profile image. The dissemination of information on social networks is enhanced by sharing of external links. Track these links can give us tips on the information contained in these destinations and guide users about what they can find. The availability of the link is another item considered on our list (tooltip 4) because with no data available for analysis we do not have content and cannot trace related information. The tooltip 5 deals with the correctness and clarity of information. Well written, clear and concise information show the concern and commitment of the source. Provide tools such as spell checking will help users to improve the information that they are producing. The main functional requirement related to the prototypes will be the capacity to alert a user when information on social network contains any hint of misinformation based on NFR concepts that we mapped.

4 Conclusion

In this work we present some guidelines for development of interfaces with tools that support transparency and auditability in social networks. We visited the concepts in the HCI area to help us with this approach. The directions of this work focus in a way to take advantage of different forms of social networks, seeking their auditability. Our next steps are: continuing the analysis of the operationalizations and mechanisms and a tool construction implementing the prototype. Before develop the tool we will check these prototypes using Nielsen Heuristics [12]. Another suggestion for the prototypes review is submit them to the approach of five traditional evaluation criteria: authority, accuracy, objectivity, currency, and coverage. These criteria have their origins in the world of print, but are universal criteria that need to be addressed regardless of the information being evaluated [13].

References

1. Abbasi, M.-A., Liu, H.: Measuring user credibility in social media. In: Greenberg, A.M., Kennedy, W.G., Bos, N.D. (eds.) SBP 2013. LNCS, vol. 7812, pp. 441–448. Springer, Heidelberg (2013)
2. Lampe, C., Vitak, J., Gray, R., Ellison, N.: Perceptions of facebook's value as an information source. In: Proceedings of the SIGCHI Conference on Human Factors in Computing Systems, pp. 3195–3204. ACM (2012)
3. Chi, E.H.: The social web: research and opportunities. IEEE Comput. **41**(9), 88–91 (2008). http://dx.doi.org/10.1109/MC.2008.401
4. Cysneiros, L.M.: Evaluating the effectiveness of using catalogues to elicit non-functional requirements. In: WER, pp. 107–115 (2007)
5. Chung, L., Nixon, B.A., Yu, E., Mylopoulos, J.: Non-Functional Requirements in Software Engineering. International Series in Software Engineering, vol. 5, Springer, Heidelberg (2000). http://dx.doi.org/10.1007/978-1-4615-5269-7
6. Cappelli, C.: An Approach for Business Processes Transparency Using Aspects. Dissertation, Pontifícia Universidade Católica do Rio de Janeiro (2009)
7. Leite, J.C., Cappelli, C.: Software transparency. Bus. Inf. Syst. Eng. **2**(3), 127–139 (2010)
8. Pinheiro, A., Cappelli, C., Maciel, C.: Increasing information auditability for social network users. In: Yamamoto, S. (ed.) HCI 2014, Part I. LNCS, vol. 8521, pp. 536–547. Springer, Heidelberg (2014)
9. Da Rocha, H.V., Baranauskas, M.: Design e avaliação de interfaces humano-computador. Unicamp (2003)
10. Rieh, S.: Judgment of information quality and cognitive authority in the web. J. Am. Soc. Inf. Sci. Technol. **53**(2), 145–161 (2002)
11. Metzger, M.J.: Making sense of credibility on the web: models for evaluating online information and recommendations for future research. J. Am. Soc. Inf. Sci. Technol. **58**(13), 2078–2091 (2007)
12. Nielsen, J.: Heuristic evaluation. In: Nielsen, J., Mack, R.L. (eds.) Usability Inspection Methods, vol. 17, Issue 1, pp. 25–62. Wiley, New York (1994)
13. Tate, M.A.: Web Wisdom: How to Evaluate and Create Information Quality on the Web. CRC Press, Boca Raton (2009)

A Longitudinal Field Study on Kiss Mediation Interface for Long Distance Relationships

Elham Saadatian[1](✉), Hooman Samani[2], and Ryohei Nakatsu[1]

[1] Keio-NUS CUTE Center, Interactive and Digital Media Institute, Singapore, Singapore
{elham,idmnr}@nus.edu.sg

[2] Department of Electrical Engineering, NTUP, Taipei, Taiwan
hooman@mail.ntpu.edu.tw

Abstract. In this paper we present a longitudinal field study of "kiss messaging interface" designed and developed for people in long distance relationships (LDRs). Mediators of intimacy are a novel class of telecommunication systems that enable people in LDR to express affection and intimacy despite being non co-located. To better understand how people experience these interfaces in the realistic and outside the lab environment, and how they blend in the users context, longitudinal field studies are required. To address the need of studying the mediators of intimacy in their natural usage context, a longitudinal field study is performed and design insights are explored under actual daily contexts over a three-weeks period. Also the study on the mediator of kiss technological probe, provided us with the user expectations from the mediators of the kiss which could also contribute towards the design of other similar technologies.

Keywords: User experience · Telepresence · Affective computing

1 Introduction

Technologies designed and tested only in laboratories commonly fail when they are deployed to the market and used in their natural setting. This issue is more likely to happen in ubiquitous computing technologies, since they are more closely tied to their context [2]. It could be due to some influencing factors such as, interruptions, noises, and multitasking, that could influence on the users' performance during the evaluation, which are not considered in laboratory tests. Besides differences between people's expected behaviors and their actual behavior in the complexity of real settings could be another reason for such failures. Moreover, issues such as privacy and adoption can only be evaluated in an environment where people live out their normal lives [5].

The issue of privacy is specially more prominent in testing technologies that are designed for the purpose of intimate communication. However, despite the private nature of intimate communications, and significance of field study in

C. Stephanidis (Ed.): HCII 2015 Posters, Part II, CCIS 529, pp. 118–122, 2015.
DOI: 10.1007/978-3-319-21383-5_20

design of the prototypes, they are rarely evaluated in their natural usage context. This may be due to challenges of the field evaluation of such interfaces such as robustness of the prototypes, costs and time needed for reproducing multiple prototypes, and challenges of finding participants in long distance relationships (LDR) who agree to participate in such demanding social experiment and generally complications of data collection methods of field studies.

To explore the design space for mediators of the intimacy for couples in LDR, a three weeks field study is performed and design insights are explored within their natural usage contexts. The above mentioned objective is achieved by iterative design and development of an embodied media for mediating kisses within four main iterations and finally an evaluation in the real usage context. The development progressed from concept generation and evaluation to physical properties, and then to the interface properties which are detailed in our previous studies [3,4].

The kiss messaging system is composed of a couple of interfaces consist of touch sensors and haptic actuators. Each device is paired with another and the amount of force and shape of the kiss by the user is sensed and communicated to another device and is emulated using actuators. Figure 1 shows the kiss messaging technological probe used in a longitudinal field study.

Fig. 1. Kiss messaging technological probe in usage

2 Methodology

To perform the longitudinal field study a sample of 10 LDR people (N = 20) with a mean age of 26.4 years (SD = 4.60) and age range between 20 to 35 was recruited. The demographic information about the participants is detailed in Table 1.

Table 1. Demographic information of ten participant couples in the longitudinal field study

ID	Age (F, M)	Place of residence	Relationship duration in months	Intimacy level	Visit/year
C1	20, 23	Sweden, Malaysia	19	Committed, share financial responsibilities	1
C2	21, 21	Taiwan, Singapore	17	Serious	1
C3	25, 27	Spain, Singapore	22	Committed, share financial responsibilities	2
C4	35, 34	Serilanka, Singapore	15	Committed	3
C5	34, 26	UK, Turkey	3	casual	1
C6	29, 28	Japan, Netherland	10	Committed	1
C7	30, 28	Iran, Singapore	24	Engaged	1
C8	22, 27	Malaysia, Singapore	20	Serious	12
C9	20, 25	Australia, UK	24	Serious	2
C10	24, 29	China, Singapore	22	Committed	3

Then a set of Kiss messaging prototype and diary books were posted to them to log their daily experiences. The diary was also included qualitative open-ended questions, which gave hint to couples to narrate their daily usage and experiences with the kiss messaging prototype as a mediator of the intimacy. It helped participants to elaborate more subjective and unexpected experiences through verbal story telling. Other formats of logging, such as pictures, audio records or even video, were advised as a complementary to the text-based diary.

The user interactions with the device were also logged in this system as an objective measure. It could measure frequency of use, times and duration of each usage and synchronous or asynchronous interaction. The experiment was followed by a half an hour post-interview and debriefing session which was done within one week from the end of the experiment.

3 Results and Discussion

The interview data were recorded and transcribed. The interview data together with diaries were coded and analyzed by mining the key themes, and classifying them to infer patterns and similarities by looking at repeated categories. In total 397 experience diaries were collected and analyzed based on qualitative content analysis method. Content analysis is chosen since in our study coding categories

Table 2. Content analysis results in the familiarization phase in the first three days

Category	Theme	Examples
Positive reactions (N = 28)	Aesthetic (N=10)	This is so cute
	Joy of co-experience (N = 6)	Enjoyed configuring the system together
	Serendipity (N = 12)	The unexpected sound of the motors made them laugh
Negative reactions (N = 15)	Cultural reaction (N = 15)	Initially felt guilty using Kissenger

will be inferred directly from the text data [1]. We applied open and axial coding to transform the collected data into quantitative data.

In the open coding the words corresponding to the users perceived and desired experiences were selected. The choice of words were decided based on the participants' words with the aim of defining main themes without any predefined class. As a result, 40 loosely related codes refering to about 650 instances of the data emerged. Afterwards, axial coding was done. In this stage open codes with commonalities were put together and classified into 10 main categories referring to features such as: appearance, functionality, intuitiveness, etc.

According to the inferred temporal pattern and the collected semantic data, the 10 themes were distributed in 2 main adoption phases of familiarization and incorporation. Familiarization reflects to the first experiences that were due to the intense emotional reaction to a new technology which decreased drastically after three days of usage. The incorporation phase reflected on the data that showed users have accepted the interface and incorporated it in their daily life.

Table 2 summarizes the results of familiarization phase:

Table 3 summarizes the content analysis results in the incorporation phase.

Table 3. Content analysis results in the incorporation phase

Category	Theme	Subclass
Positive reactions (N = 64)	Temporal usability (N = 22)	Functionality (N = 7)
		Intuitiveness and ease (N = 15)
	Affectivity (N = 42)	Shape and appearance (N = 9)
		Joy of co-experience (N = 15)
		Uniqueness (N = 10)
		Multisensory connection (N = 8)
Negative reactions (N = 73)	Temporal usability (N = 42)	Privacy (N = 8)
	Affectivity (N = 31)	Naturalness (N = 10)

Table 4. Suggested improvements during the interview

Theme	N	Explanation
Initiations	6	Facilitating natural way of initiation such as eye contact
Portability	10	Smaller or wearable designs such as accessories
Usability in public	7	A design that does not attract the attention of outsiders
Association	4	A relation between remote partner and the kissenger appearance
Realness of lips	7	Use of soft or skin-like material
Delays	5	Delays should be minimized as much as possible

An analysis of the post-experiment interviews, indicated that at least 15 out of 20 participants found that Kissenger could potentially improve their communication habits. They reflected this indirectly in terms of physical connections, private channel, expressiveness and enjoyment. Also four of the couples asked if they could keep Kissenger and use it in the future.We also were interested to know what changes the participants prefer to be done in Kissenger. The results of the suggested improvements are classified in Table 4

Our field study suggested the possibility of meaningfulness of the Kiss messaging interface in the daily life of the remote couples. The field study has highlighted potential design pitfalls and user requirements that designers should consider when making similar devices. We hope that this kind of field studies will facilitate participatory design for remote couples to get involve in technology design.

Acknowledgement. This research is supported by the National Research Foundation, Prime Minister's Office, Singapore under its International Research Centre @ Singapore Funding Initiative and administered by the Interactive &Digital Media Programme Office.

References

1. Hsieh, H.F., Shannon, S.E.: Three approaches to qualitative content analysis. Qual. Health Res. **15**(9), 1277–1288 (2005). (Sage Publications)
2. Intille, S.S., Tapia, E.M., Rondoni, J., Beaudin, J.S., Kukla, C., Agarwal, S., Bao, L., Larson, K.: Tools for studying behavior and technology in natural settings. In: Dey, A.K., Schmidt, A., McCarthy, J.F. (eds.) UbiComp 2003. LNCS, vol. 2864, pp. 157–174. Springer, Heidelberg (2003)
3. Saadatian, E., Samani, H., Parsani, R., Pandey, A.V., Li, J., Tejada, L., Cheok, A.D., Nakatsu, R.: Mediating intimacy in long-distance relationships using kiss messaging. Int. J. Hum. Comput. Stud. **72**(10–11), 746 (2014)
4. Samani, H.A., Parsani, R., Rodriguez, L.T., Saadatian, E., Dissanayake, K.H., Cheok, A.D.: Kissenger: design of a kiss transmission device. In: Proceedings of the Designing Interactive Systems Conference, pp. 48–57. ACM (2012)
5. Visser, T., Vastenburg, M., Keyson, D.: Snowglobe: the development of a prototype awareness system for longitudinal field studies. In: Proceedings of the 8th ACM Conference on Designing Interactive Systems, pp. 426–429. ACM (2010)

Trust Towards Social Media in Emergencies: A Perspective of Professional Emergency Personnel in Europe

Hermann Szymczak(✉), Pinar Kuecuekbalaban, Daniela Knuth, and Silke Schmidt

Institut für Psychologie Lehrstuhl Gesundheit und Prävention, Ernst-Moritz-Arndt Universität Greifswald, Robert-Blum-Street 13, 17487 Greifswald, Germany
szymczakh@uni-greifswald.de

Abstract. Research shows that people increasingly rely on social media in emergencies and disaster situations. This is not surprising, considering how social media and mobile social computing have become an integral part of daily life for many people. As a consequence, authorities responding to emergencies are often expected to make use of social media as well, e.g. to monitor information related to specific incidents on social networks such as Twitter, or respond to requests made on such platforms. To gain a better understanding of this subject, we investigated the perspective of professional emergency personnel. Specifically, we asked members of various PSOs (Public Safety Organizations) from eight different countries in Europe (n = 1.223) about their view on using social media in the context of emergencies. The present study was conducted as part of the SOTERIA project (Online and Mobile Communications for Emergencies), a multinational project funded by the European Commission. Our data shows that members of PSOs themselves would trust information provided on social media significantly less than they expect the public to trust information on social media during emergencies. With the exception of Poland, this difference occurred across countries and might indicate an inclination of PSOs to consider social media as a tool to broadcast information rather than to collect information. As a practical consequence, a possible bidirectional exchange of information between the public and PSOs might be hampered by this attitude and valuable information not taken into consideration.

Keywords: Crisis communication · Europe · Disaster · Emergency · Social media · Trust

1 Introduction

Social media and mobile online communication have long become an integral part of our lives. In many countries, a permanent availability of mobile internet enables more and more people to stay connected around the clock.

Understandably, social media have also become a topic in emergency management, as people increasingly rely on social media in the context of emergencies, e.g. to gather

C. Stephanidis (Ed.): HCII 2015 Posters, Part II, CCIS 529, pp. 123–128, 2015.
DOI: 10.1007/978-3-319-21383-5_21

information, to request help from officials, to exchange information with others, and to coordinate people and resources (Lindsay, 2010). Social media are also used for mutual social support by affected citizen (Neubaum, Rösner, Rosenthal-von der Pütten, & Krämer, 2014).

Whereas civilians are using social media willingly as a(n) (additional) tool for handling emergency situations, Public Safety Organizations (PSOs) are often "reluctant to use these media, or even have regulations prohibiting their use, because they do not feel that they are secure and trustworthy" (Hiltz, Gonzalez, & Van de Walle, 2012, p.1). One of the main reasons for this reluctance lies in the inherent participative nature of these media, as everyone can possibly post anything. This opportunity for participation also enables the propagation of false information (e.g. Mendoza, Poblete, & Castillo, 2010; Rains, Brunner, Oman 2015).

However, despite the risk of false information, one problem arising from the discrepancy of social media use by citizens and PSOs is the possibility that crucial information might be missed or ignored. Therefore, it is important to investigate the hesitation PSOs display towards the incorporation of social media into their official emergency response.

2 Research Question

We hypothesized, that this reluctance may in part be caused by a lack of trust towards these media as a source of information by emergency personnel.

There is a difference between *using information* and *disseminating information* through social media. Members of PSOs should be less trusting towards information provided by the general public for two reasons. First, they face more responsibility and should, therefore, handle information more scrutinizing. Second, receiving information is associated with a lack of control, as almost everyone could post everything via social media such as Facebook or Twitter (Rains, Brunner, and Oman, 2015). Furthermore, the amount of information generated through social media use during emergencies is often overwhelming (Hiltz & Plotnick, 2013), making it difficult for emergency personnel to act on any information without being able to obtain a thorough overview over all the information.

On the other hand, PSOs should assume civilians to be more trusting towards emergency relevant information provided on social media as they do not have this professional responsibility and can engage in more informal emergency communication in a peer-to-peer fashion (see e.g. Sutton, Palen, & Shklovski, 2008). Therefore, one might assume PSOs attribute a more trusting stance to the public.

Hypotheses. PSOs show less trust towards social media in emergency situations than they expect the public to show towards these channels as an information source.

3 Methods

3.1 Participants

Age and Nationality. Active PSO personnel from eight different European countries (Finland, France, Germany, Republic of Ireland, Norway, Poland, Portugal, U.K.) were recruited for this study (n = 1223). The sample was predominantly male (84.5 %) with a mean age of M = 37 years (SD = 11.2 years).

Organizational Membership. Participants were members of different PSOs, including firefighters (39.2 %), the Red Cross (30.1 %), emergency medical services/paramedics (22.5 %), civil defence organizations (9.7 %), and police (6.7 %). Multiple answers were possible.

Paid or Voluntarily Members. Respondents were either paid members of a PSO (40.6 %) or members on a voluntary base (49.0 %) or both (9.1 %), 1.4 % of answers were missing.

3.2 Materials and Procedures

Procedure. The items analyzed for this study were part of a larger questionnaire distributed as part of SOTERIA, a project by the European Commission. The questionnaire was initially developed based on a literature review by the German SOTERIA partners from the University of Greifswald (in German language), and pre-tested with a cognitive debriefing task with seven German participants.

In a next step, the questionnaire was translated into English, Finnish, French, Polish, Norwegian and Portuguese by the respective SOTERIA partners. Finally, the questionnaire was distributed as online survey within all of the eight partner countries. Each country disseminated the survey to members of several PSOs.

The whole SOTERIA questionnaire consisted of about 50 questions covering a broad range of topics related to the use of social media in the context of emergencies. For this study, specific items concerning trust were analyzed, tapping on the attitude of PSO personnel towards the trustworthiness of social media channels in emergencies and their view of how they think the general public would trust social media in such cases.

Trust Ratings. Trust towards specific online media can be conceptualized and measured distinctively (Beldad, de Jong, & Steehouder, 2010; Schultz, Utz, & Göritz, 2011; Wang & Emurian, 2005). For this research, we investigated trust towards social media in emergency situations.

In order to get a measure of trust towards social media, participants were asked about three different social media channels, namely Facebook, Twitter, and YouTube. Our aim was to include a heterogeneous group of social media with a social networking site, a microblog and a video sharing platform (Kaplan & Haenlein, 2010).

Trust Towards Social Media (Trust Self). In order to obtain a reliable measure of trust towards social media, respondents were asked to answer the following question for each of the three channels mentioned above: "If the general public were to use the following channels to provide information during an event, how much would you trust this information?" Answers ranged between 1 ("not at all") and 5 ("very much"). Therefore, respondents rated their trust towards information provided by the public via social media for the three different channels.

The three items were tested for unidimensionality/internal consistency (Cronbach's $\alpha = .775$) and subsequently aggregated to obtain a single sum score for "trust towards social media" ($M = 6.65$, $SD = 2.66$).

Assumed Trust Towards Social Media (Assumed Trust Public). The second measure "assumed trust towards social media" was calculated in a similar fashion, using participants answers to the question "In your opinion, how much does the general public trust information from the following channels during an event?" on a 5-point Likert Scale for three items (Facebook, Twitter, YouTube).

A subsequent test for internal consistency revealed a sufficient high Cronbach's α ($\alpha = .811$) to assume unidimensionality and compute a single sum score ($M = 8.68$, $SD = 2.91$).

4 Results

A repeated measures t-test was conducted. Results show that on average respondents trust social media in emergency situations ($M = 6.68$, $SD = 2.66$) significantly less than they expect the general public to trust them ($M = 8.68$, $SD = 2.91$), $t(1222) = -23.96$, $p < .001$. Calculating the effect size, a medium effect of Cohen's $d = 0.68$ (Cohen, 1988) was found.

5 Discussion

Our data confirms the hypothesis of a "trust-gap" between the extent to which PSOs trust social media and the extent to which PSOs assume the public to trust social media. Above and beyond, this gap seem to be substantial, as the medium effect size indicates.

Although the sample consisted of PSOs from eight different European countries, Germany (37.7 %), France (21.1 %), and Norway (20.6 %) predominated. Therefore, one has to be cautious with generalizations.

Separate analyses for each country revealed significant effects for every country, with the exception of Poland, $t(16) = -.52$, $p = .61$. However, the Polish sample consisted of only $n = 17$ (1.4 % of total the sample) and the non-significant t-test might be due to this small sample size. A descriptive difference in the Polish sample of 0.35 between *trust towards social media* ($M = 6.94$, $SD = 2.86$) and *assumed trust of social media* ($M = 7.29$, $SD = 2.54$) indicates a trend in conformity with our hypothesis.

More research is needed to illuminate the actual trust of the general public towards social media in emergency situations. Our research only takes into account the PSOs perspective. To get the full picture, the citizen perspective has to be analyzed as well. For instance, it is important to investigate how much citizens assume PSOs to trust social media.

6 Conclusion

Our findings indicate that members of PSOs encounter citizen-generated information on social media in emergency situations rather cautious. On the other hand, they assume civilians to trust these media more.

According to our data, using social media as a mean for distributing information to the public in a top-down fashion should be more acceptable for PSO members. Assuming that people really trust social media to a fair extent even in emergencies, organizations should use social media deliberately as an additional broadcasting tool.

The question is how social media could be incorporated into the official emergency response not only as a tool for information distribution, but also as a "backchannel" (R. S. Hiltz et al., 2012; Sutton et al., 2008) for PSOs to communicate with the public. Clear guidelines and rules are needed to utilize these communication tools as a source of information for PSOs.

References

Beldad, A., de Jong, M., Steehouder, M.: How shall I trust the faceless and the intangible? A literature review on the antecedents of online trust. Comput. Hum. Behav. **26**(5), 857–869 (2010). doi:10.1016/j.chb.2010.03.013

Cohen, J.: Statistical Power Analysis for the Behavioral Sciences. Routledge Academic, New York (1988)

Hiltz, R.S., Gonzalez, J.J., Van de Walle, B.: Assessing and improving the trustworthiness of social media for emergency management: a literature review. In: Norwegian Information Security Conference (2012)

Hiltz, S.R., Plotnick, L.: Dealing with information overload when using social media for emergency management: emerging solutions. In: Proceedings of the 10th International ISCRAM Conference, pp. 823–827 (2013)

Kaplan, A.M., Haenlein, M.: Users of the world, unite! The challenges and opportunities of social media. Bus. Horiz. **53**(1), 59–68 (2010). doi:10.1016/j.bushor.2009.09.003

Lindsay, B.R.: Social media and disasters: current uses, future options, and policy considerations. J. Curr. Issues Media Telecommun. **2**(4), 287–297 (2010)

Mendoza, M., Poblete, B., Castillo, C.: Twitter under crisis: can we trust what we RT? Workshop Soc. Media Analytics **9**, 71–79 (2010). doi:10.1145/1964858.1964869

Neubaum, G., Rösner, L., Rosenthal-von der Pütten, A.M., Krämer, N.C.: Psychosocial functions of social media usage in a disaster situation: a multi-methodological approach. Comput. Hum. Behav. **34**, 28–38 (2014). doi:10.1016/j.chb.2014.01.021

Rains, S.A., Brunner, S.R., Oman, K.: Social media and risk communiction. In: Cho, H., Reimer, T., McComas, K.A. (eds.) The SAGEHandbook of Risk Communication, pp. 229–239. SAGE Publications, London (2015)

Schultz, F., Utz, S., Göritz, A.: Is the medium the message? Perceptions of and reactions to crisis communication via twitter, blogs and traditional media. Public Relat. Rev. **37**(1), 20–27 (2011). doi:10.1016/j.pubrev.2010.12.001

Sutton, J., Palen, L., Shklovski, I.: Backchannels on the front lines: emergent uses of social media in the 2007 southern california wildfires. In: Proceedings of the 5th International ISCRAM Conference, pp. 1–9 (2008)

Wang, Y.D., Emurian, H.H.: An overview of online trust: concepts, elements, and implications. Comput. Hum. Behav. **21**(1), 105–125 (2005). doi:10.1016/j.chb.2003.11.008

HCI in Business and Innovation

Creativity in Agile Software Development Methods

Broderick Crawford[1,2,3](✉), Kathleen Crawford[1], Ricardo Soto[1,4,5], and Claudio León de la Barra[1]

[1] Pontificia Universidad Católica de Valparaíso, Valparaíso, Chile
{broderick.crawford,ricardo.soto,claudio.leondelabarra}@ucv.cl
kathleen.crawford.a@mail.pucv.cl
[2] Universidad Central de Chile, Santiago, Chile
[3] Universidad San Sebastián, Santiago, Chile
[4] Universidad Autónoma de Chile, Santiago, Chile
[5] Universidad Cientifica del Sur, Lima, Peru

Abstract. Creativity is an inherent aspect to the development of new products, therefore a critical capacity for software development. Indicators to measure creativity are grouped into two main areas: (1) those related to the creative result itself and its quality (including novelty and usefulness) and (2) those related to the creative team itself (considering indicators such as individual and group satisfaction, development of cognitive skills, group interaction, ...). From this perspective, the aim of this work is to introduce some ideas for assesing the creativity of software products.

Keywords: Creativity · Software engineering · Measures of creativity

1 Introduction

Psychology and Computer Science are growing in a interdisciplinary relationship mainly because human and social factors are very important in software engineering. The development of new software products requires the generation of novel and useful ideas. Software is developed for people and by people [9]. However, most of software engineering research is technical and does not emphasize the human and social aspects [2,3].

By other hand, the traditional development process of new products has been recently criticized in [10], pointing out that fundamental creative aspects are not considered at all and as a consequence this development is not useful, viable or innovative. In this context, it is interesting to study the assesing of creativity in software products, being of particular interest to consider how is done it by the agilists.

Agilists value working software, it is more valuable than comprehensive documentation. Agile teams write code first and then document as needed. They deliver working software often and their progress is best measured by using the

C. Stephanidis (Ed.): HCII 2015 Posters, Part II, CCIS 529, pp. 131–135, 2015.
DOI: 10.1007/978-3-319-21383-5_22

software. This represents a shift in the traditional software development paradigm and is best suited for the actual economy, releasing software at any time the market demands [4,5].

Since human creativity is thought as the source to resolve complex problem or create innovative products, one possibility to improve the software development process is to design a process which can stimulate and measure the creativity of the developers and its products. There are few studies reported on the importance of creativity in software development teams. In a few publications the importance of creativity has been investigated in all the phases of software development process [1,7,8] and mostly focused in the requirements engineering [13,15,17].

Nevertheless, the use of techniques to foster creativity in requirements engineering is still shortly investigated. Moreover, in some studies requirements engineering is not recognized as a creative process in all the cases [12]. We think that analysts, designers, programmers, testers, managers, entrepreneurs, users, researchers and other stakeholders involved in sofware development need to be creative.

Clearly, creativity is related with a wide spectrum of business, it is crucial for designing better products, it initiates innovations and aids in problem solving allowing an organization to survive. But it is often difficult to measure the creativity.

A method for assessing the degree of creativity is necessary to help select the most creative products. We are working (based in the study in [19]) in a method that can help identify the degree of creativity in software products. We intend to be able to assess not only whether a product is creative or not, but also how much creative it is. At first, in this paper we try to ilustrate what is meant by creativity, and what its current measures are, and how adequate these are in software industry.

2 Definition of Creativity

In a recent comprehensive survey of the definitions of creativity [18], Sarkar and Chakrabarti analyzed over 160 definitions proposing a common definition of creativity, as follows: "Creativity occurs through a process by which an agent uses its ability to generate ideas, solutions or products that are novel and valuable". Value, in the context of software products, take on the meaning of utility or usefulness.

Similar views of creativity have also been expressed by other researchers. Furthermore, in [18] they propose measures for creativity manifesting that creativity should be measured directly in terms of novelty and usefulness of the results.

Then, according to the above definition, assessing creativity therefore requires assessment of novelty and usefulness. At the following, some definitions and assesing methods for novelty, usefulness, and creativity are briefly presented.

2.1 Defining, Measuring and Assessing the Novelty of Products

"Novel" are those things that are "new" to all people. "Novelty" is the quality of being new and fresh and interesting [14]. Novelty comprises both new (something that has been recently created) and original (the first one made, it is not a copy).

Different researchers proposed methods for measuring novelty [16,20], mainly focus on the identification of novelty of products and not on their degree of novelty. One way of assessing novelty of a product, is to compare the characteristics of that product with those of other products.

Methods that can be used to decompose a product into its characteristic components or features are suitable for supporting this assessment. A widely used model is the Function–Behaviour–Structure (FBS) model, different works on FBS models illustrates its value for classifying product-characteristics [6]. In relation to apply FBS to software engineering, although initially the authors did not have software in mind when developing their framework, in [11] the authors map software engineering to FBS, representing software engineering artifacts and practices using the Rational Unified Process.

Function, behaviour and structure in FBS model are defined as follows:

- Function: descriptions of what a system does: it is intentional and at a higher level of abstraction than behaviour.
- Behaviour: descriptions of how a system does its function. This is generally at a lower level of abstraction than function.
- Structure: it is described by the elements and interfaces with which the system is constructed.

It is noted that product-characteristics can be employed to ascertain the relative degree of novelty of products and the FBS model can be used for determining novelty of software products.

2.2 Defining, Measuring and Assessing the Usefulness of Products

The common definition of usefulness is "the quality of having utility and especially practical worth or applicability". Others definitions consider usefulness in terms of "utility" in terms of appropriateness and social value.

In order to study the methods for assessing product usefulness, we were unable to find in the literature direct measure for usefulness. When a product may be perceived as useful?. It is the actual use of the product and its results that validate its usefulness. Then, the usefulness of a product should be measured by its actual use. In relation with the importance of use or level of importance, it depends on the impact of the product on the lives of its users. Some products are indispensable, while others are not. Accordingly, it is possible identify different levels of usefulness of a product.

Then, a method for assessing the usefulness of products should consider the importance of usage, popularity of usage, and rate of use as criteria for assessing overall usefulness.

2.3 Assessing the Creativity of Products

Considering that novelty and usefulness of products should be consider as the main influences on creativity, it is necessary to express creativity as a function of these two factors. Basically, any expression that try to measure creativity should consider it as the product of these two factors: novelty and usefulness.

3 Conclusions

It was exposed that according to the definition of creativity, it should be measured directly in terms of novelty and usefulness of the results. Then, assessing creativity requires assessment of novelty and usefulness. Some methods for assess novelty, usefulness, and creativity were briefly presented. It is clear that a better formalization of these influences is an area of research in developing.

Acknowledgments. Broderick Crawford is supported by Grant CONICYT/FONDECYT/REGULAR/1140897. Ricardo Soto is supported by Grant CONICYT/FONDECYT/INICIACION/11130459.

References

1. Crawford, B., de la Barra, C.L.: Enhancing creativity in agile software teams. In: Concas, G., Damiani, E., Scotto, M., Succi, G. (eds.) XP 2007. LNCS, vol. 4536, pp. 161–162. Springer, Heidelberg (2007)
2. Crawford, B., Soto, R., de la Barra, C.L., Crawford, K., Olguín, E.: Agile software teams can use conflict to create a better products. In: Stephanidis [21], pp. 24–29 (2014)
3. Crawford, B., Soto, R., de la Barra, C.L., Crawford, K., Olguín, E.: The influence of emotions on productivity in software engineering. In: Stephanidis [21], pp. 307–310 (2014)
4. de la Barra, C.L., Crawford, B.: Fostering creativity thinking in agile software development. In: Holzinger, A. (ed.) USAB 2007. LNCS, vol. 4799, pp. 415–426. Springer, Heidelberg (2007)
5. de la Barra, C.L., Crawford, B., Soto, R., Misra, S., Monfroy, E.: Agile software development: it is about knowledge management and creativity. In: Murgante, B., Misra, S., Carlini, M., Torre, C.M., Nguyen, H.-Q., Taniar, D., Apduhan, B.O., Gervasi, O. (eds.) ICCSA 2013, Part III. LNCS, vol. 7973, pp. 98–113. Springer, Heidelberg (2013)
6. Gero, J.S., Kannengiesser, U.: The situated function–behaviour–structure framework. Des. Stud. **25**(4), 373–391 (2004)
7. Glass, R.L.: Software Creativity. Prentice-Hall Inc., Upper Saddle River (1995)
8. Gu, M., Tong, X.: Towards hypotheses on creativity in software development. In: Bomarius, F., Iida, H. (eds.) PROFES 2004. LNCS, vol. 3009, pp. 47–61. Springer, Heidelberg (2004)
9. John, M., Maurer, F., Tessem, B.: Human and social factors of software engineering: workshop summary. SIGSOFT Softw. Eng. Notes **30**(4), 1–6 (2005)

10. Kotler, P., TríasdeBes, F.: Marketing Lateral. Editorial Pearson/Prentice Hall, Spain (2004)
11. Kruchten, P.: Casting software design in the function-behavior-structure framework. IEEE Softw. **22**(2), 52–58 (2005)
12. Maiden, N., Gizikis, A., Robertson, S.: Provoking creativity: imagine what your requirements could be like. IEEE Softw. **21**(5), 68–75 (2004)
13. Maiden, N., Robertson, S.: Integrating creativity into requirements processes: experiences with an air traffic management system. In: 13th IEEE International Conference on Requirements Engineering (RE 2005), 29 August–2 September 2005, Paris, France, pp. 105–116. IEEE Computer Society (2005)
14. Makins, M.: Collins English Dictionary. HarperCollins, Glasgow (1991)
15. Mich, L., Anesi, C., Berry, D.M.: Applying a pragmatics-based creativity-fostering technique to requirements elicitation. Requir. Eng. **10**(4), 262–275 (2005)
16. Piffer, D.: Can creativity be measured? An attempt to clarify the notion of creativity and general directions for future research. Think. Skills Creativity **7**(3), 258–264 (2012)
17. Robertson, J.: Requirements analysts must also be inventors. IEEE Softw. **22**(1), 48–50 (2005)
18. Sarkar, P., Chakrabarti, A.: Studying engineering design creativity-developing a common definition and associated measures (2008)
19. Sarkar, P., Chakrabarti, A.: Assessing design creativity. Des. Stud. **32**(4), 348–383 (2011)
20. Shah, J.J., Smith, S.M., Vargas-Hernandez, N.: Metrics for measuring ideation effectiveness. Des. Stud. **24**(2), 111–134 (2003)
21. Stephanidis, C. (ed.): HCI 2014, Part I. CCIS, vol. 434. Springer, Heidelberg (2014)

Use of Quality Management Principles in the Shaping of Work Environment

Adam Górny(✉)

Faculty of Management Engineering, Poznan University of Technology, 11 Strzelecka St., 60-965, Poznan, Poland
adam.gorny@put.poznan.pl

Abstract. Adherence to the systemic approach to improving working conditions is increasingly becoming a central prerequisite for the successful operation of business organizations. By adopting systemic principles to improve the quality of working conditions, organizations gain access to effective tools for eliminating hazards and strenuousness and consequently acquire the ability to grow and improve themselves [8]. Any measures adopted within that framework are undertaken in recognition of the roles and tasks of employees seen as the internal clients of specific processes. In this paper showed important conditions, ensured effectiveness of work conditions improve by the systemic approach. In particular, reference was made to capabilities, which impacted on improving conditions of work. This activities was related to the principles of quality management system.

Keywords: Quality management · Work environment · Management principles

1 Introduction

A key prerequisite for the safe and efficient performance of work in a business organization is to check whether the working environment meets legislative requirements in all of its parameters. Any potential violations should be seen as distortions that warrant modifications. In their self-improvement efforts, enterprises should recognize the commitment to change the working environment as a priority consideration [9].

The working environment can be described by reference to characteristics which enable organizations to keep the space in which humans operate free of hazards and strenuousness [6]. Such characteristics additionally define ways in which occupational activities can be carried out efficiently. The man, with his qualifications as well as it is professional preparation particularly essential conditioning factor and effective management led of economic activity. Its role in the meaning displays across character of human factors, often determining internal and the external possibilities the development of enterprise [5]. Their agreement to be treated as one of essential criteria of effectiveness opinion of laded processes, which are defining from expectations the external customers (the buyers of articles and the services) and internal (the workers of the enterprise).

C. Stephanidis (Ed.): HCII 2015 Posters, Part II, CCIS 529, pp. 136–142, 2015.
DOI: 10.1007/978-3-319-21383-5_23

Additionally, factors characterizing the working environment, indirectly define ways in which occupational activities can be carried out efficiently.

2 Preconditions for the Systemic Improvement of Working Environment

Organizations which discover inconsistencies between parameters of the working environment and the criteria defining the desirable characteristics of the space in which humans operate need to respond by identifying improvement measures and defining their scopes [13]. Such responses are particularly critical where working environment assessments and improvements rely on elements of the process approach. It requires [4]:

- disclosure all conducted in business activities as the processes,
- determine a sequence of processes and its interactions,
- determine the conditions of ensure course effectiveness of the processes, including a guarantee possibility of their control,
- provide the resources needed for the processes operation,
- monitoring and analyzing processes, and in the situations occurring deviations from the desired state, the introduction of improvement activities.

In such an approach, the working environment is seen as an internal process, or a part thereof, carried out to ensure compliance with prescribed working conditions. In shaping the working environment seen as conditions for the completion of an internal process to meet quality engineering guidelines, organizations may adopt quality management principles, methods and tools, which are instrumental in improving processes and their parts. The idea of this approach is shown in Fig. 1.

The implementation of quality management principles required to provide the resources and conditions to enable their practical application. As a particularly important resource can point out the knowledge possessed by the staff responsible for the execution of processes or access to this knowledge, combined with its ability to collect and process. In day-to-day practice, quality improvement principles, methods and tools allow organizations to effectively improve their working environments. The work environment is to be seen as critical for business outcomes (the outcomes of manufacturing or service provision operations). Organizations which fail to recognize work environment needs often end up having to pay the price as they lose market positions and their competitive advantage [4]. Further, a competitiveness analysis calls for consideration of the availability of production factors. The key criteria for competitiveness which constitute means of production include the human factor, described as the productive value of employees, and the social capital defined by the role a business organization plays in its social environment. This is particularly significant for ensuring effective operation in realms which require continuous improvement. It is also helpful in satisfying the growing demands of stakeholders.

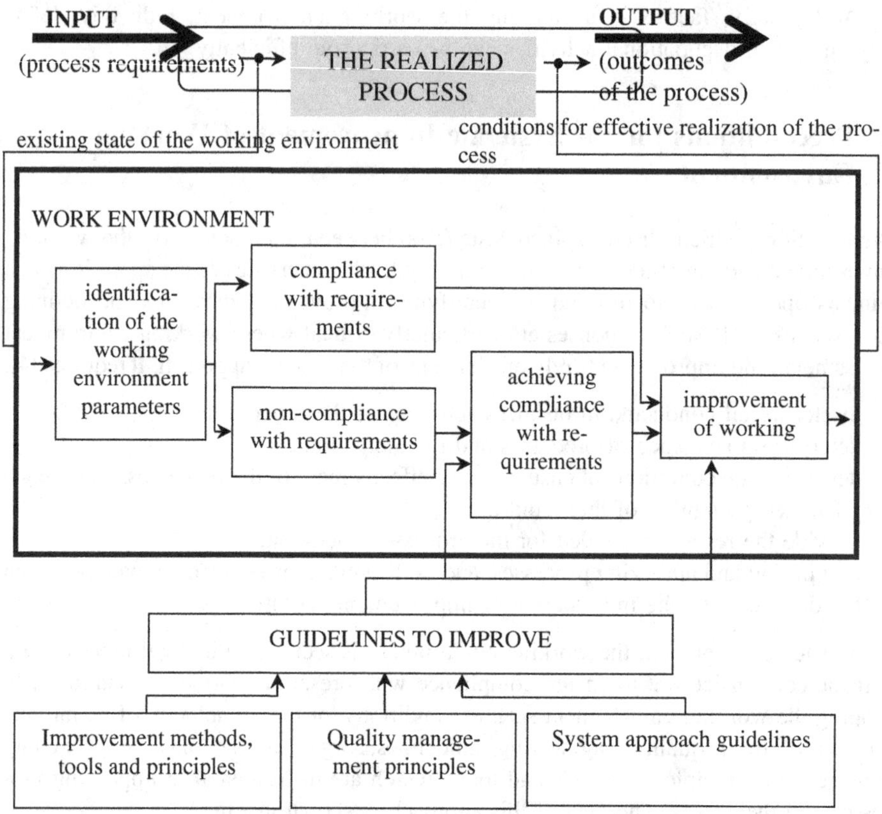

Fig. 1. Essence of inclusion principles, tools and methods supporting the quality management to improve the work environment.

3 Guidelines for Application the System Principles

In formulating the above management guidelines and putting them into practice, it is vital to account for the specific nature of the working environment to which the requirements pertain. The work environment is a central component of a business organization's management system and plays a pivotal role in enabling it to achieve desired economic benefits [4, 7]. Any measures undertaken by business organizations are designed to mitigate or eliminate hazards and strain affecting the workers.

In shaping the working environment by the principles of systemic management, organizations should rely on quality management guidelines. Such guidelines apply to [2, 11, 14]:

- **customer orientation** – the customer being the internal customer of processes; customer orientation makes it necessary to identify and fulfil customer needs and assess customer satisfaction by undertaking specific measures,

- **leadership** – leadership requires the formulation of a mission statement and a statement of vision for growth; such a mission and vision need to be sold to employees; proper ways and means also need to be found to achieve strategic and operational goals,
- **commitment** – commitment is the central prerequisite for high quality performance; it combines motivation, organization culture, communication and teamwork,
- **process approach** – in the process approach, customer demands are seen as a function of performance in the process chain designed to satisfy customer needs and expectations,
- **systemic approach** – this approach is based on the perception of a company's outcomes produced as a synergy of all benefits derived from carrying out processes in the company,
- **continuous improvement** – continuous improvement contributes to the resolution of any identified issues and involves projects designed to benefit the organization and its customers through e.g. performance improvement,
- **dedication to decision-making** – such a dedication requires the regular gathering of information, its immediate processing, notification of any findings to appropriate parties and their use as a basis for informed decision-making,
- **partner relationships with suppliers** – the relationships are based on information exchange, assessments and checks of supplier qualifications and on the use of additional verification criteria while recognizing the specific nature of each requirement.

Examples of actions, allowing to shape the work environment associated with the principles of quality management system are presented in Table 1. Usage the system of quality management principles on improving requires attention to the recipient of actions, i.e. workers as an important resource of business.

Man treated is as a resource. It is characterized by the ability to effectively carry out the tasks of the company. Worker form part of a system which combines all aspects of an organization's performance as seen from the viewpoint of an internal customer of its internal processes. Therefore, an organization's operational effectiveness hinges ultimately on the efficiency of its processes which in turn depend on the conditions, working conditions included, in which such processes are performed [1]. In its very essence, the systemic approach brings all of the tasks carried out by an enterprise into a chain of mutually interrelated links (or processes) which, in order to work effectively, must meet the criteria of the process approach. Contemporary management concepts recognize the need to place particular emphasis on the human factor. People in organizations must be perceived as opportunities rather than threats. This is of particular significance in view of the skills and competencies which make some workers irreplaceable. Companies which lose such key personnel may pay a very high price [4]. However, such workers will be unable to perform efficiently in changing environments unless proper conditions are ensured to accommodate them in their company.

Table 1. Examples of taken measures related with the working environment, joined with the principles of quality management system.

Quality management principles	Examples of actions
Customer focus	- identification of environmental requirements, ensuring the proper functioning employee in the workplace,
	- adjustment of working environment to the needs of employees,
	- assessment of the compliance a work environment with employees expect,
	- take into account assessment the conditions of work (feasibility tasks)
Leadership	- inclusion in mission and vision of enterprise development issues shaping the work environment,
	- the working environment description contains issues for strategic and operational development of the company,
	- providing the necessary means to achieve the objectives of enterprise development, containing issues of the working environment
Involvement of people	- recognized by all, including the management, motivation to take action to improve conditions of work
	- shaping corporate culture, addressing the issues of the working environment (safety culture),
	- shaping the working environment, providing free of hazards and nuisance communications,
	- the use of teamwork in shaping the work environment
Process approach	- the processes implemented issues related to the shaping of the environment work,
	- method of processes implementation take into account the needs and expectations of employees,
	- method of process realization takes into account to minimize adverse environmental impacts of work,
	- evaluation criteria of processes include the environmental for their implementation,
	- assessment the possibility of process improvement issues concerning the development of the working environment
System approach to management	- work environment is treated as an integral part of the management system in firm,
	- in the assessment of the organization takes into account the requirements associated with the formation of work environment,
	- shaping environmental effects are important part of the benefits arising from the implementation of the principles of system management

(*Continued*)

Table 1. (*Continued*)

Quality management principles	Examples of actions
Continual improvement	- during the improvement of implemented measures, regard the measures improving of work environment, - non-compliance with the requirements and expectations of the environment are the cause of improving work processes conducted, - improving the work environment is treated as a way to obtain benefits for the organization and its customers and for the internal customers of processes
Factual approach to decision-making	- parameters describing the work environment are collected in a systematic way, - collect the information are necessary to make tangible decisions include parameters describing the work environment, - parameters describing the work environment are considered as an important element assessing the merits of actions undertaken improvement
Mutually beneficial Supplier relationship	- evaluation and verification of suppliers takes into account that they meet the criteria the work environment describing, - a information describing the work environment are immediately communicated to all interested

4 Conclusions

In improving the environmental performance of the tasks is reasonable to apply the tools, methods and, above all, the principles of quality management. Concurrently, by improving the working environment, enterprises support their employees in performing their work thereby promoting the growth of their organizations. Such efforts may be seen as progress towards strengthening the companies' employee-orientation [3, 10, 12]. The measures make businesses safer and benefit them tangibly.

In order to benefit from the deployment of a management system in any field of an organization's operations, a number of primary as well as secondary factors need to be considered. This guarantees the achievement of the company's desired outcomes. An analysis of preconditions for the effectiveness of a quality management system shows that it is next to impossible to adopt a proper approach to client satisfaction if work environment issues are left out of the equation. In prospect, companies which adopt such management principles gain the ability to rationally select concepts (such as lean management, reengineering, benchmarking, just-in-time deliveries) thereby supporting organization management. As a consequence, they are in a position to improve their operations in keeping with TQM guidelines and are inspired to continually enhance their performance.

References

1. Butlewski, M., Misztal, A., Ciulu, R.: Non-financial factors of job satisfaction in the development of a safety culture based on examples from poland and romania. In: Duffy, V.G. (ed.) DHM 2014. LNCS, vol. 8529, pp. 577–587. Springer, Heidelberg (2014)
2. EN ISO 9004: Managing For the Sustained of an Organization – A Quality Management Approach. European Committee for Standardization, Brussels (2009)
3. Gołaś, H., Mazur, A.: Macroergonomic aspects of a quality management system. In: Jasiak, A. (ed.) Macroergonomic Paradigms of Management, pp. 161–170. Poznan University of Technology, Poznan (2008)
4. Górny, A.: Czynnik ludzki w systemowym zarządzaniu jakością. In: Sikora, T. (ed.) Zarządzanie jakością - doskonalenie organizacji, vol. 1, pp. 350–366. Uniwersytet Ekonomiczny, Krakow (2010)
5. Górny, A.: Human factor and ergonomics in essential requirements for the operation of technical equipment. In: Stephanidis, C. (ed.) HCI 2014, Part II. CCIS, vol. 435, pp. 449–454. Springer, Heidelberg (2014)
6. Górny, A.: Occupational Risk in Improving the Quality of Working Conditions. In: Vink, P. (ed.) Advances in Social and Organizational Factors, pp. 267–276. AHFE Conference, Poznań (2014)
7. Górny, A.: The elements of work environment in the improvement process of quality management system structure. In: Karwowski, W., Salvendy, G. (eds.) Advances in Human Factors, Ergonomics And Safety In Manufacturing And Service Industries, pp. 599–606. Taylor and Francis Group, Boca Raton (2011)
8. Górny, A.: The use of Ishikawa diagram in occupational accidents analysis. In: Arezes, P., et al. (eds.) Proceedings of International Symposium on Occupational Safety and Hygiene (SHO2013), pp. 162–163. Sociedade Portuguesa de Seguranca e Higiene Occupacionais, Guimaraes (2013)
9. Górny, A.: Zarządzanie Ryzykiem Zawodowym. Wydawnictwo Politechniki Poznańskiej, Poznań (2011)
10. Mazur, A.: Shaping quality of work conditions. In: Dahlke, G., Górny, A. (eds.) Health Protection And Ergonomics For Human Live Quality Formation, pp. 31–44. Publishing House of Poznan University of Technology, Poznan (2009)
11. Misztal, A.: Eight quality management principles - practical context. In: Borucki, A., Pacholski, L. (eds.) Some Problems And Methods Of Ergonomics And Quality Management, pp. 125–135. Wydawnictwo Politechniki Poznańskiej, Poznań (2010)
12. Mrugalska, B.: Environmental disturbances in robust machinery design. In: Arezes, P., et al. (eds.) Occupational Safety and Hygiene, pp. 229–236. CRC Press, Taylor & Francis, London (2013)
13. Mrugalska, B., Nazir, S., Tytyk, E., Øvergård, K.I.: Process safety control for occupational accident prevention. In: Arezes, P.M., et al. (eds.) Occupational Safety and Hygiene III, pp. 365–369. Taylor and Francis Group, London (2015)
14. ISO: Quality Management Principles. ISO Central Secretariat, Geneva (2012)

NEC's Approach to Social Value Design

Izumi Kohno(✉), Masahiro Nishikawa, Takaya Fukumoto, and Takashi Matsuda

NEC Corporation, Tokyo, Japan
kohno@ay.jp.nec.com, m-nishikawa@cd.jp.nec.com,
t-fukumoto@ah.jp.nec.com, t-matsuda@cj.jp.nec.com

Abstract. NEC's Social Value design (SVD) depicts an abundant future for people and society through the provision of solutions that use advanced technology. SVD is studied from the two perspectives of the "User Experience" and the "Social Experience," and provides society and our business customers with "Innovation". We use human-centered design and design thinking to enforce SVD. We introduce our solutions and systems as achieved results of SVD approach.

1 Introduction

Social Value Design (SVD) is a NEC's design concept (Fig. 1). SVD sketches a vision of the future from the perspective of the individual and society, and then completes the picture by designing and providing the businesses of our customers with relevant new value. As our Information Society advances and various IT systems become widespread and complex, the demand for ease of operational use also rises, and there are increasing expectations for a more comfortable experience. In order to respond to such needs, it is vital to view systems and services from a human perspective and adopt a "User Experience" approach that enhances the value for people.

In addition, the creation of a vision for a city and the solution of various social issues using ICT necessitate the drafting of the image of the society that we would like

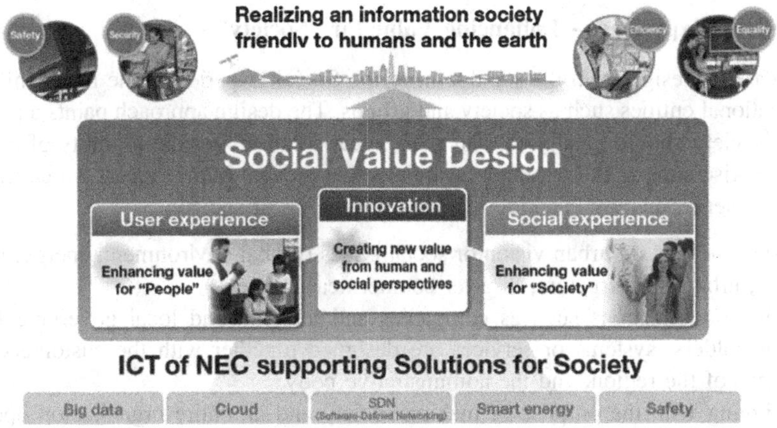

Fig. 1. Social value design

C. Stephanidis (Ed.): HCII 2015 Posters, Part II, CCIS 529, pp. 143–148, 2015.
DOI: 10.1007/978-3-319-21383-5_24

to create, not only from the perspective of the individual person but also from standpoint of organized entities such as nations, corporations and even neighborhood associations. Answering these needs requires what we at NEC call the "Social Experience" approach to studying the issues - a way of thinking that seeks answers that will enhance the value of systems and services from the perspective of society at large.

However, the individual's desire for ease and comfort is often in conflict with the organization's pursuit of efficiency. The comfort of the individual is at odds with global environmental issues. These are few examples of why it is difficult to grasp and resolve issues from the perspective of both the individual and society.

In order for the life desired by an individual to mesh with the concept of a richer society overall, it is necessary to sketch a vision for the future that can be shared by both the individual and society. Consideration of the solution methodology based on a balanced perspective that draws on the standpoints of both the individual and society will lead to the creation of innovation.

2 Three Component of Social Value Design

2.1 User Experience - Enhancing Value for "People" -

In enhancement of the User Experience, design focuses on the users and operators of systems and services, and seeks to make the operation of systems and devices easy, efficient and comfortable, and provides equality of access irrespective of the user's nationality, abilities or other attributes.

- Producing designs which make complex systems and services easy to use and understand.
- Designing so that as many people as possible can use the product in various environments and conditions. (Universal design)
- Designing emotion and experience.

2.2 Social Experience - Enhancing Value for "Society" -

In the case of design from the standpoint of the Social Experience, the focus shifts to organizational entities such as society and groups. The design approach paints a picture of how society should ideally be, and seeks ideal solutions for the plurality of people who comprise society - for example, solutions that prevent human errors which trigger social problems, thereby enabling the smooth running of society.

- Design focused on urban vision or social issues (global environment, energy, food, water, urban infrastructure, disaster countermeasures, etc.).
- Taking organizations such as companies and national and local governments as stake holders, systems or services are designed together with the customers, the citizens of the region, and the administrative body.
- Designing with the purpose of making society and an entire organization operate efficiently and smoothly without any problems.

2.3 Innovation - Creating New Value from Human and Social Perspectives –

Innovation grasps the points in contention between the individual and society perspectives, and that creates new value that strikes a balance between both viewpoints. Innovation takes highly advanced technologies and links them to value for the individual and society, which in turn changes the way we live and work for the better.

- Designing the vision and concept of the society or business.
- Designing a new life style or work style.
- Designing services or product ideas not yet in existence.

3 Means for Realizing Social Value Design

The realization of SVD requires a change in the way that we traditionally approach the development of products and services. We use human-centered design (HCD) and design thinking to enforce SVD. HCD is the philosophy of making things according to the user instead of first producing something and then thinking about the user. Design thinking is an approach used in business for the purpose of creating something new such as market creation, business models and new services. While the approach conceived by IDEO, a US design consultancy and a leading proponent of Design thinking, places importance on concept generation and visualization in a five-step methodology of understanding, observation, visualization, evaluation and refinement/implementation that employ tools such as "fieldwork","prototyping", "user testing", and "brainstorming", the design thinking process is essentially the same as that for HCD. People related the system or service form a team, and design and development is carried out with HCD/design thinking process (Fig. 2).

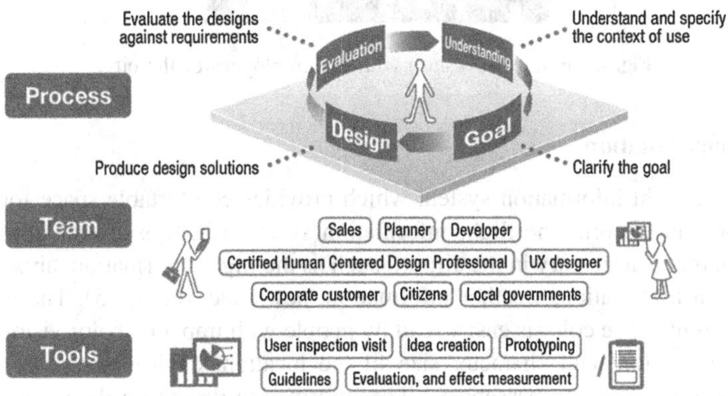

Fig. 2. Means for realizing social value design

4 Examples of Social Value Design

4.1 Vison for City in 2030

We created a vision for the city, Tigre Argentina, in 2030 and a plan of how this can be achieved through ICT (Fig. 3). For creating the vision, designers actually visited Tigre and conducted workshop with city employees (Fig. 4), then we created a scenario of how Tigre could be experienced in 2030 so as to convey our image of the future in an easy to understand way.

Fig. 3. Examples of vision for the city in 2030.

Fig. 4. Future workshop with the employees of the city.

4.2 Airport Solution

We created a flight information system which provides comfortable space for various people using an airport. The flight information system displays in real time various information that is necessary in the airport, such as the flight information, airport access transportation information, weather information, news, etc. (Figure 5). The board has high accessibility. The color is easily read by people with impaired color vision and the elderly, and the font and character size fit the location, environment, and distance between the board and the passengers. The information design on the board also has high usability. The information is laid out to correspond with how important it is, so passengers can quickly find the information they need.

Fig. 5. Flight information board

Fig. 6. Evaluation using the actual display panel.

Designers specified the context of use by observing various information boards at several airports and train stations and then determined which user interface design concept to use. They developed several prototypes and evaluated them iteratively during the project execution. They carried out evaluation and verification of visibility and comprehensibility using the actual display panels (Fig. 6).

4.3 Multi-Function Compact ATM

The multi-function compact ATM (Automated Teller Machine) co-developed by the NEC Group in cooperation with Seven Bank, Ltd. is designed to function as an integral part of a new-style infrastructure that facilitates a variety of contemporary lifestyles. It provides people with access to ATMs in their neighborhood 24 h a day. The ATM is designed so that as many people as possible can use the product in various environments and conditions for universal design (Fig. 7). It provides voice guidance for people with impaired vision and installing an operation display, an interphone and input buttons at lower positions on the ATM for people with wheel chairs. The letters on the screen were enlarged and the sentences shortened to enhance readability for everyone.

Designers carried out user test for current system to understand and specify the context of use, and clarified the goal. Several types of prototype such as screen image,

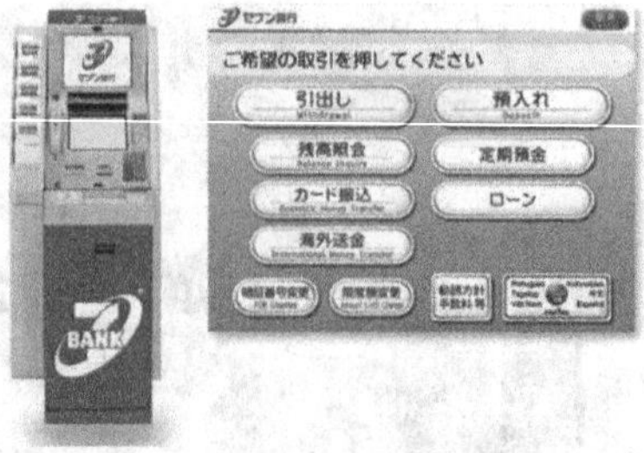

Fig. 7. Multi-function compact ATM

Fig. 8. Evaluation by people with impaired vision.

paper prototype, or hardware mock-up were used for design and evaluation. Universal design checks were executed each developing process, for example evaluation by people with impaired vision was executed to obtain the required level of accessibility (Fig. 8).

5 Conclusion

We are using Social Value Design to create solutions for society that provide advanced social infrastructure to the world. In this paper, we introduced, a vision for the city in 2030, a flight information board and a multi-function compact ATM using various methods such as observation, workshop, prototyping, user testing, and information sharing, and the end result was enhancing "User Experience", "Social Experience", and creating "Innovation".

Assessment of Business Analytics Trust Through Examination of Personal IT Use

Benjamin Larson(✉) and Casey Cegielski

Department of Aviation and Supply Chain Management, Auburn University, 405 W. Magnolia Ave, Auburn, AL 36849, USA
{bzl0011, cegieca}@auburn.edu

Abstract. IT consumerization has brought social media (SM) and personal mobile devices into many workplaces. This has prompted researchers to examine the benefits and risks of this trend. However, little research has examined how personal experiences with technology such as social media may affect decision making on the job. This study examines the potential impact of individuals' trusting beliefs (competence, benevolence, and integrity) regarding algorithms and social media communities (SMC) on initial trust in SM-based business analytics (BA), as well as on relative advantage over non-SM based BA. Study results suggested that the initial trust was influenced by the belief in the competency of personal algorithms as well as trust in SMC. It also indicates that increased trust in SMC influences relative advantage. Implications and suggestions for further research are discussed.

Keywords: Trust · Business analytics · Big data · Consumerization · Social media

1 Introduction

The use of technology designed first for use by consumers in a corporate environment, also known as IT consumerization, has been increasingly impactful upon organizations and their information systems (IS). Consumerization concepts, such as Shadow IT and "bring your own device," bring to the workplace benefits as well as risks, spurring research interest. However, little research has examined how personal experiences with technology such as social media may affect decision making on the job. in this paper we examine the potential impact of individuals' trusting beliefs (competence, benevolence, and integrity) [1, 4, 7] regarding personal algorithms and social media communities (SMC) on initial trust in social media (SM) based business analytics (BA), as well as how trust in SMC relates to relative advantage [2] of non-SM based BA.

2 Theoretical Foundation

Trust is important because it can be viewed as helping individuals overcome perceptions of uncertainty [7]. Individual trust in technology such as ecommerce has been a focus of many researchers [1, 4, 7]. One of the ways in which trust can be measured is

C. Stephanidis (Ed.): HCII 2015 Posters, Part II, CCIS 529, pp. 149–153, 2015.
DOI: 10.1007/978-3-319-21383-5_25

by examining the trusting beliefs of the trustor, the individual who is placing trust, on the trustee, who or what that is being trusted [1, 4, 7]. While many beliefs have been studied the three most common are *competence* which is the belief in the ability of the trustor to perform the task, *benevolence* which is the belief that the trustor is not trying to take advantage of the trustee, and *integrity* which is the belief that the trustor will perform the task [1, 4, 7]. There is no standard as to how to measure these beliefs are represented in research, and they have been measured as a single construct or separate beliefs [1, 4, 7, 9].

There are various potential antecedents to trusting beliefs including institution based trust which includes situation normality [1, 4, 7]. In examining the concept of IT consumerization, we are examining how an employee perceives the use of something that they already have familiarity with. We argue that employees' personal exposure to technologies beginning to be used at work in recent years is similar to consumers' perceived normality of the general internet in the past. One of the ways in which perceived normality was measured was also by examining the trusting beliefs in the institution such as the internet [7]. In looking at SM based BA the institutions that we want to evaluate are two technologies – the algorithms or the instructions written for a computer to solve a problem, and the SMC from which the data will be collected. By examining the personal trust in these two technologies we hope to evaluate whether the user develop trust in SM-based BA and whether the personal exposure makes the user perceive a relative advantage in SM-based BA versus non SM-based BA.

Relative advantage is perceived to be a strong predictor of adoption of new technologies [2]. While Algorithms are common to both SM and non-SM based BAs, one difference is in the user's perceived ability of the communication channels to provide the right information [2]. In this way trust in the SMC can be viewed as a potential antecedent to a relative advantage of SM-based BA versus non SM-based BA. Therefore we predict the following hypotheses:

H1: Increased trusting belief in Algorithms will lead to trust in SM-based BA.
H2: Increased trusting belief in SMC will lead to trust in SM-based BA.
H3: Increased trusting belief in SMBA will lead to a trust relative advantage of SM-based BA.
H4: Increased trusting belief in SMC will lead to a trust relative advantage of SM-based BA.

3 Methods

Survey data were collected from students (n = 186) at a public university. The students were asked to complete an online questionnaire designed to capture the trusting beliefs trust relative advantage as well as to record the demographic information. In addition, the students were also questioned about whether they would choose to use SM-based BA in a situation in which there was a higher risk and higher reward for using SM-based BA than using non-SM-based BA. The students were all users of SM with 98.5 % using SM daily. The students were predominantly undergrads (89.8 %) and consisted of 48.4 % females. The majority of students favored the use of SM-based BA (80.6 %).

The data was analyzed using covariance-based structural equation modeling (CB-SEM). Alternative models were examined as to whether it was best to represent the trusting beliefs as individual constructs or mediated through a single variable measuring trust.

4 Results

Results from a confirmatory factor analysis suggested that all items loaded significantly on their respective constructs, and that all factor loadings were statistically significant and met the common threshold of 0.5 [5]. Average variance extracted (AVE) was found to be greater than .5 and all construct composite reliabilities were above .6, suggesting construct validity [3] for the measurement instrument (see Table 1). Factor correlations were found to all be below the recommended threshold of .85, suggesting discriminant validity [6]. A Harmon's Single Factor Test was conducted, showing a single factor explained less than half of the variance in the data, suggesting no common method bias. Results from the structural and measurement model evaluation suggest adequate model fit [6] (see Table 2).

Results suggested a statistically significant effect of trust in SMC ($\beta = .36$ $p < .001$) and the belief in algorithm competence ($\beta = .461$ $p < .001$) on trust in SM-based BA, supporting H2 and partially supporting H1, respectively (see Fig. 1). However, the trusting beliefs of benevolence ($\beta = .022$ $p = .967$) and integrity ($\beta = .130$ $p = .209$) of algorithms do not impact trust in SM-based BA, suggesting competence is the key factor in generating SM-based BA. Trust in SM-based BA had a statistically significant relationship with relative advantage ($\beta = .575$ $p < .001$), supporting H3. Also, trust in SMC had a statistically significant relationship with relative advantage ($\beta = .304$ $p < .001$), supporting H4 and suggesting initial individual bias based upon personal experiences or familiarity with social media.

Table 1. Construct reliability

	CR	AVE	AC	AB	AI	SMC	SMBA	RA
AC	0.88	0.70	**0.84**					
AB	0.82	0.60	0.73	**0.78**				
AI	0.80	0.58	0.71	0.75	**0.76**			
SMC	0.87	0.69	0.47	0.55	0.51	**0.83**		
SMBA	0.89	0.73	0.74	0.65	0.66	0.65	**0.86**	
RA	0.89	0.73	0.56	0.61	0.50	0.67	0.77	**0.85**

Note: N = 186; CR: composite construct reliabilities; The Square root of AVEs are presented on the diagonal in bold. AC= Algorithm Competence, AB= Algorithm Benevolence, AI = Algorithm Integrity, SMC= Trust in the SMC, SMBA= Trust in SM-based BA, RA= Relative Advantage.

Table 2. Fit indexes

	Measurement Model	Structural Model
Chi-square	791.81	795.75
DF	414.00	417.00
Chi-square/DF	1.91	1.91
CFI	0.91	0.91
PCFI	0.81	0.81
NFI	0.82	0.82
RMSEA (90% C.I.)	0.07 (.063, .078)	0.07 (.063, .077)

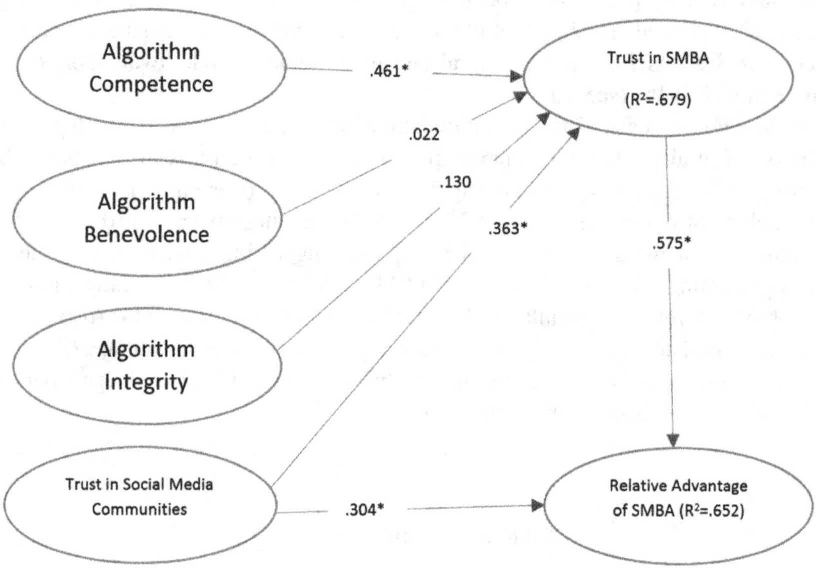

Fig. 1. Path analysis with standardized betas

5 Conclusions

Business analytics is an increasingly important field of study, and we have access to a variety of data that are not economical to be manually analyzed. Meanwhile, we see algorithms and analytics increasingly in our private lives as consumers see product recommendations as they shop online and use social networking sites. We asked if this personal exposure to analytics affected how we would trust business analytics in the workplace. The results show that trust formed through personal exposure does change initial perception and indicate that as a user's trust in SMC increases, so does the relative advantage of using that data in absence of contrary information.

As business and personal technology continues to blend together there needs to be a greater understanding of not only how cognitive trust but also emotional trust in our personal use of systems will affect individuals at the workplace. As organizations begin to utilize new information sources to make decisions this increased trust lead managers to make decisions in the face of uncertainty. Workload as well as task complexity can heavily influence the extent to which automation and information systems are used [8]. The volume and variety of big data seems to dictate the use of algorithms but how they are initial constructed and modified may depend on the level of trust of the managers in the face of a new and uncertain technology.

References

1. Bhattacherjee, A.: Individual trust in online firms: scale development and initial test. J. Manage. Inform. Syst. **19**(1), 211–242 (2002)
2. Choudhury, V., Karahanna, E.: The relative advantage of electronic channels: a multidimensional view. MIS Q. **32**(1), 179–200 (2008)
3. Fornell, C., Larcker, D.F.: Evaluating structural equation models with unobservable variables and measurement error. J. Mark. Res. **18**(1), 39–50 (1981)
4. Gefen, D., Karahanna, E., Straub, D.W.: Trust and TAM in online shopping: an integrated model. MIS Q. **27**(1), 51–90 (2003)
5. Hair, J.F., Anderson, R.E., Tatham, R.L., Black, W.C.: Multivariate Data: Analysis with Readings. Prentice-Hall, Upper Saddle River (2010)
6. Kline, R.B.: Principles and Practices of Structural Equation Modeling, 2nd edn. Guilford Press, New York (2005)
7. McKnight, D.H., Choudhury, V., Kacmar, C.: Developing and validating trust measures for e-commerce: an integrative typology. Inform. Syst. Res. **13**(3), 334–359 (2002)
8. Parasuraman, R., Riley, V.: Humans and automation: use, misuse, disuse, abuse. human factors. J. Hum. Factors Ergon. Soc. **39**(2), 230–253 (1997)
9. Pavlou, P.A., Dimoka, A.: The nature and role of feedback text comments in online marketplaces: implications for trust building, price premiums, and seller differentiation. Inform. Syst. Res. **17**(4), 392–414 (2006)

Leadership in Agile Software Development Methods

Claudio León de la Barra[1], Sergio Galdames[1], Broderick Crawford[1,2,3](✉), Ricardo Soto[1,4,5], and Kathleen Crawford[1]

[1] Pontificia Universidad Católica de Valparaíso, Valparaíso, Chile
claudio.leondelabarra@ucv.cl, sergiogaldames@gmail.com, broderick.crawford@ucv.cl, ricardo.soto@ucv.cl, kathleen.crawford.a@mail.pucv.cl
[2] Universidad Central de Chile, Santiago, Chile
[3] Universidad San Sebastián, Santiago, Chile
[4] Universidad Autónoma de Chile, Santiago, Chile
[5] Universidad Cientifica del Sur, Lima, Peru

Abstract. There is a common agreement that Leadership is represented by two main ideas: direction and influence. The first related to the knowledge of where the organization should be oriented and the second with the capacity to mobilize others towards that direction. Recent research has rejected these assumptions, stating emphatically that the power of organizations and teams are not in these mythical figures (as the super leader), but in the knowledge shared by all its members. Thus, finding the right direction and success on the path undertaken shall not rest in the hands of one person, but in the capabilities of the entire group.
This paper analyses how this approach to leadership can be observed in software development teams, specifically through agilists methods (Extreme Programming).

Keywords: Software development · Extreme programming · Leadership · Distributed leadership

1 The Definition of Leadership

It is extremely difficult to describe a unique definition to leadership. According with Thomson [16], not only leadership has multiple definition but also the number of definitions grows every year. Among the diverse 'labels' are "transformational, transactional, strategic, charismatic, paternalistic, bureaucratic, situational, operational, participatory, democratic, helpful, autocratic, laissez-faire, cash or evolutionary" [16]. Similarly, Husband [10] recognize in the mid-eighties, the plurality on the construct but expressed that all definition could be organized in three distinct clusters: "task - relationship; centralization - decentralization and power - influence" (p. 103). In other words leaders deal with performance and people; distribution and concentration of responsibilities; the capacity to lead others.

C. Stephanidis (Ed.): HCII 2015 Posters, Part II, CCIS 529, pp. 154–158, 2015.
DOI: 10.1007/978-3-319-21383-5_26

Moreover, the work of Leithwood, Day, Sammons, Harris, and Hopkins [12] tried to identify the core elements of effective leadership. Their findings suggest that all leadership definitions has at least to commons characteristics, all implies direction and influence. This means that 'a leader' exercise these two skills: setting the direction, goal, target or objective, and pushing others forward to that specific place. Therefore, leadership become a central capacity in any team or organization characterized by environmental change, rapid adaptation and flexibility [15]. In simply words, while we have a hard time trying to find a definitive definition for leadership, it connects with a wide range of concepts related with organizational change and adaptation, in which there is an important contribution of social forces and peoples behaviours [9].

Considering that leadership is mostly a construct related with the motivation and mobilization of people, recent studies have recognized the relevance of adopting a distributed approach [17]. This idea, abandon the romantic notion of one heroic leader who usually was born with the ability to lead others. On the contrary, leadership appears as a skill that not only can be develop by training, but also can be shared by different individuals or even groups within the organization. Additionally, the distributed approach related closely with turbulent context and rapid change, in which different individuals could emerge in different organizational moments or challenges, accordingly with their specifics skills.

Likewise, the benefits of distributed leadership has been extensively documented [13,14]. The evidence suggest that organizations who embrace this approach foster organizational learning, team work motivations and the sustainability of changing process. Understand leadership as distributed practices, also means to understand that all the people inside the organization or team can exercise power, set a direction and generate influence in others. From an organizational perspective, this perspective encourage the specialization and differentiation of the members, in order to prepare them for their eventual 'lead moment'.

Accordingly, distributed leadership is highly relevant for teams conformation. However, the distributed approach is not guaranty of success at least other conditions are put in place first. As the evidences suggest, teams only work effectively when its members perceive psychological safety, clear goals and shared meaning [5,11]. The study of Ashauer and Macan [1] identified how team performance could be highly explained by the role and practices of the leaders in trying to generate trust and collaboration. In these teams is encouraged the challenging of the professional and personal belief, therefore allowing new knowledge and change to be introduced. Similarly, the research of Cardno [6], identified that one of the most common enemies of team learning was 'fear to be ashamed by others'. This means that in many cases, people do not share their ideas freely, concerned by the opinions of their peers. Therefore, leaders main role in those situations is to ensure people are comfortable enough to share, listen and contribute to others, fostering adaptation and team growth.

2 Leadership in Software Developing Teams

Generally, leadership in software developing teams and particularly through agilistic methods are strongly influenced by a distributed approach to leadership [3,4]. In these teams, 'directions and influence' can be observed when the team is aiming to develop and implement a new software. Specifically, for Extreme Programming, XP [2,7,8], the main characteristic of this method is the teamwork, that includes managers, costumers and developers. All of them work as part of the team dedicated to deliver quality software, and as result the software usually accomplish customer needs when it is needed. XP implements a simple and effective work development style as groupware and XP points out to improve a software project in four essential ways: communication, simplicity, feedback, and courage. These roles constitute in XP, a series of twelve practices: planner game, 40 hours a week, small deliveries, metaphors, on site customer, tests, simple design, coding standards, refactoring, pair programming, collective property, continuous integration, just open the rules and open work areas.

In Extreme Programming the roles are seven: the Customer, who writes the requirements and functional tests; the Programmer, who kept the code as simple as possible and helps the client to write functional tests; the Tester, who runs the functional tests; the Tracker, who tracks the estimates made by the team; the Coach, who is responsible for the overall process; the Consultant, who has specific expertise and, finally, the Manager, who is a link between the client and the programmers.

In terms of responsibilities, the Programmer is accountable for the outcome of the main project: the application system. This role writes source code for the software system under development. The Customer is the person who tells the programmer what to program. The programmer knows how to program. The customer knows what to program. The Tester is responsible to run the project repeatedly to create an update picture of the project state, besides, this role help customers to select and write functional tests. The Tracker is the ones who keep track of all the numbers in a project. This role is close to the reliability of the team. The person that plays this role knows all the records and facts of the project, and should be able to tell the team, when the next iteration is finish as planned. The Coach is the person responsible for the development process to work as a whole. The coach notices when the team is getting "off track and bring it "back on track. To do this, the coach must have experience with XP. The Consultant, is the person who has an expertise to processes a knowledge that the XP team needs as an additional special knowledge, so, they "hire a consultant who possesses this knowledge. The consultant transfers this knowledge to the team members, allowing them to solve the problem on their own. The Big Boss or Manager needs to know all the technical details and states of the project and know if any intervention is needed to have a successful project.

In particular, leadership is strongly connected with the total definition of the problem, the collection and analysis of the information, the development of solutions, and the facilitation of process and activities.

- The collection of information related to a problem in XP is made by the Client him-self, who has the first contact with the software development team. It Is not limited awareness of the problem that the client declare, but also aims to ensure, at all times, the collection of the necessary information to define and even redefine the problem.
- In XP, the Client and the Manager of the team, work together to define the problem and look for the possible solutions.
- The function of transforming the information, create new relations, and consequently generate interesting solutions, is the Programmer. In XP methodology he/she is in charge of the analysis, design and programming of software.
- In XP, the person who clarifies and evaluates the new ideas, in terms of its feasibility, is the Tester and the Tracker.
- In XP, the responsibility to make the definitive selection of the solutions is the Tracker and the Client.
- The person who has to implement the selected ideas (the working software) would be the Client, including the processes and procedures that this role implies.
- The Facilitator is the person that helps the team. This role is represented in XP to the coach.
- The role to help the team to work would be equivalent to the role of the consultant in XP.

3 Conclusion

The roles in XP are characterized by high professional interaction among its members and the respective client. As was presented previously, a distributed approach to leadership is best suited in teams like these who are mostly working with finding and gathering information, analysing and interpreting data, and taking decisions to improve working condition.

However, future studies should put more attention in the role of the manager or Big Boss, considering that the current data is to slim yet for such an important role in XP teams.

Acknowledgments. Broderick Crawford is supported by Grant CONICYT / FONDECYT / REGULAR / 1140897. Ricardo Soto is supported by Grant CONICYT / FONDECYT / INICIACION / 11130459.

References

1. Ashauer, S.A., Macan, T.: How can leaders foster team learning? Effects of leader-assigned mastery and performance goals and psychological safety. J. Psychol. **147**(6), 541–561 (2013)
2. Beck, K.: Extreme Programming Explained: Embrace Change. Addison-Wesley Longman Publishing Co., Boston (2000)
3. Beck, K.: Agile alliance (2001). http://agilemanifesto.org

4. Beck, K., Beedle, M., Bennekum, A.V., Cockburn, A., Cunningham, W., Fowler, M., Grenning, J., Highsmith, J., Hunt, A., Jeffries, R., Kern, J., Marick, B., Martin, R.C., Mellor, S., Schwaber, K., Sutherland, J., Thomas, D.: Manifesto for agile software development (2001). http://agilemanifesto.org
5. Bush, T., Glover, D.: Distributed leadership in action: leading high-performing leadership teams in english schools. School Leadersh. Manage. **32**(1), 21–36 (2012)
6. Cardno, C.: Team learning: Opportunities and challenges for school leaders. School Leadersh. Manage. **22**(2), 211–223 (2002)
7. Crawford, B., de la Barra, C.L.: Enhancing creativity in agile software teams. In: Concas, G., Damiani, E., Scotto, M., Succi, G. (eds.) XP 2007. LNCS, vol. 4536, pp. 161–162. Springer, Heidelberg (2007)
8. Crawford, B., de la Barra, C.L., Soto, R., Dorochesi, M., Monfroy, E.: The role of knowledge management in agile software development. In: Stephanidis, C. (ed.) HCII 2013, Part I. CCIS, vol. 373, pp. 17–21. Springer, Heidelberg (2013)
9. Dinham, S.: How schools get moving and keep improving: leadership for teacher learning, student success and school renewal. Aust. J. Educ. **51**(3), 263–275 (2007)
10. Husband, R.L.: Toward a grounded typology of organizational leadership behavior. Q. J. Speech **71**(1), 103–118 (1985)
11. Lahtero, T.J., Kuusilehto-Awale, L.: Realisation of strategic leadership in leadership teams work as experienced by the leadership team members of basic education schools. School Leadersh. Manage. **33**(5), 457–472 (2013)
12. Leithwood, K., Day, C., Sammons, P., Harris, A., Hopkins, D.: Successful School Leadership What It Is and How It Influences Pupil Learning. University of Nottingham, Nottingham (2006)
13. Mascall, B.: Shifting sands of leadership in theory and practice. J. Educ. Adm. Hist. **39**(1), 49–62 (2007)
14. Melville, W., Jones, D., Campbell, T.: Distributed leadership with the aim of "reculturing": a departmental case study. School Leadersh. Manage. **34**(3), 237–254 (2013)
15. Starr, K.: Principals and the politics of resistance to change. Educ. Manage. Adm. Leadersh. **39**(6), 646–660 (2011)
16. Thomson, P.: Creative leadership: a new category or more of the same? J. Educ. Adm. Hist. **43**(3), 249–272 (2011)
17. Wilkinson, J., Olin, A., Lund, T., Stjernstrm, E.: Understanding leading as travelling practices. School Leadersh. Manage. **33**(3), 224–239 (2013)

Interactive Tool to Find Focal Spots in Human Computer Interfaces in eCommerce

eCommerce Consumer Analytics Tool (eCCAT)

VenkataSwamy Martha, Zhenrui Wang, Angela Jiang(✉), and Sam Varghese

@WalmartLabs, Sunnyvale, CA 94086, USA
{vmartha, zwang, ajiang0, svarghese}@walmartlabs.com

Abstract. eCommerce is one of the popular electronic services available in the vast Internet world. eCommerce endpoints, also called eCommerce websites, in general, are a composition of several web pages. Within eCommerce endpoints, there exist specific web page types that are abnormal in their consumption of information and user behavior called focal spots. Finding a focal spot is key for understanding and improving the human interaction interface on eCommerce endpoints. In order to make business decisions concerning these focal spots, decision analytics teams are employed to identify focal spots with abnormal consumer perception and to address areas in which to expand business. We propose a methodology for transforming user activity data into useful business analytics to find focal spots if any. In this work, we developed a prototype of a one-stop solution for non-technical users to understand customer response analysis on a given eCommerce endpoint. The proposed system, 'eCommerce Consumer Analytics Tool (eCCAT)', consists of a data extraction and automated analysis component and a visualization component. The interactive tool further provides a way to find a page in the eCommerce endpoint with an extreme key performance indicator.

1 Introduction

eCommerce is one of the most important and predominant channels in the retail world today. Like traditional physical retail, eCommerce is faced with several of the same crucial components concerning delivery: supply chain, shopping experience, assortment, point of sale, etc. However, unlike its physical counterpart, eCommerce is exposed as the nexus of multiple customer touch points, simultaneously servicing search, evaluation, and purchase use cases [1]. As a result, the eCommerce experience must accommodate and solve for not only an array of usage situations but also of cognitive styles at a large scale.

This paper attacks the problem of identifying areas within the eCommerce experience that are crucial to financial outcomes and therefore the success of the platform

Disclaimer: The views expressed in this article are solely those of the authors and do not necessarily reflect the official policies or positions of their employers.

C. Stephanidis (Ed.): HCII 2015 Posters, Part II, CCIS 529, pp. 159–163, 2015.
DOI: 10.1007/978-3-319-21383-5_27

through a visual analytics system called eCommerce Consumer Analytics Tool (eC-CAT). The effectiveness of analytical reports is highly dependent on human computer interaction widgets and effective data visualization [2]. In particular to demonstrate the system capabilities, we employ reports in which a key performance indicator, such as revenue participation, conversion rate and traffic of each page type in an eCommerce endpoint, is visualized in a user interface that can easily be consumed without in-depth context of the eCommerce website map or any formal training of the system [3].

2 Focal Spots

A website or endpoint on the Internet is a collection of webpages. eCommerce endpoints, when generalized, follow a pattern of webpage types: 1. Home Page, 2. Product Listing Pages, 3. Product Description Pages, 4. Cart Page, and 5. Checkout Page. We are interested in page types that are abnormal in their user behavior and information consumption called focal spots that pose a direct impact on business results. Among these page types, Product Listing Pages (PLPs) are notably profuse in their informational content and sensitivity to user cognitive styles [4]. Because PLPs are a class of display methods for information retrieval and recommendations, they are instrumental in serving the multitude of information needs. We focus on understanding the user experience of these focal spots, covering a holistic set of factors including user interface, content served, timing performance, etc. Furthermore, focal spots themselves are comprised of multiple web pages. These focal spot pages can be analyzed in a similar methodology where pages that are abnormal in their user behavior or performance called focal points are identified and serve as specific, actionable areas for improvement. The impact of user experience at these focal points can be either positive or negative.

3 Data Collection and Processing

Customer feedback and data is collected from eCommerce end points using web beacons which have been used for many analytics purposes including understanding the behavior of customers. Web beacons are API calls that carry log data made in the client browser with the beacon server as the other end point of the call. Each web beacon turns into a log record in the log server where the beacon server stores the received data over the call. A log record represents an activity performed by a client or an activity record. Some of the key attributes in activity records that are crucial in analysis are timestamp, session identifier activity type, and activity parameters to name a few. Sessionization is one of the foremost steps in analysis of activity records. Sessionization segments all the activity records into groups, each group representing a session. 'Session' is a broad term used to represent a time slot constrained by specific parameters. Widely used sessionization algorithms split activities by 30 min of inactivity with a session identifier [5]. Further analysis into a session leads to an understanding of the dynamics of each activity in the session. For example, both a page view and a click are activities that determine the performance of a page. Connecting activities within a session based on navigational patterns turns each session into a set of activity networks. There is a path from each node in an activity network to a network node that represents conversion. A page in a given website is said to be converted if and only if there is a path from the network node representing the page to the conversion page.

Once sessionization of activity records is complete, multiple types of analyses can be carried out to discover important business insights. A report can be generated by counting the number of times a page is viewed, the number of times the page is converted, the number of times the page is driving traffic to other pages in the endpoint and other metrics and aggregated to analyze the performance of a given focal spot. The set of metrics upon which focal spots and their respective constituent pages are evaluated are considered key performance indicators (KPIs) which are directly associated with business impact. Each page within the focal spots can then be sorted in order of a certain metric, for example conversion, to identify the pages with the worst performance. We define these distinct pages as focal points, and they represent specific opportunities for improvement.

4 eCommerce Consumer Analytics Tool (eCCAT)

Data visualization is crucial to understanding any domain's performance over time and the key components that contribute to the advancement of that domain [6]. The eCommerce Consumer Analytics Tool (eCCAT) pairs this domain data visualization with display interaction to allow decision makers, regardless of formal training or in-depth knowledge of the domain map, to understand the performance of the endpoint, its focal spots, and take direct actions on focal points. We choose to elevate focal spots out of all pages within the eCommerce endpoint to create maximally informative visual analytics to eliminate information overload without compromising utility. Business problems are frequently evaluated on a comparative basis, which can be either broad or specific, encompass confirmatory or exploratory analysis, and serve several use cases from reporting to specific problem solving. The complexity and variety of these problems makes visual analytics fundamental in fine-tuning the decision-making process [7]. To accommodate for these possibilities, we created an interactive visual interface with automated data analysis that is agnostic to cognitive styles while retaining a level of intuitiveness from problem-solving heuristics that is consistent with making business decisions.

As shown in Figs. 1 and 2, the eCCAT incorporates three main styles of data visualization: 1. Relative contribution, 2. Time series, and 3. Tabular data. Each visualization provides information that is key to making a decision and is augmented with interactive devices that allow the decision maker to segment information by various dimensions such as time aggregated on, KPI metric, and focal spot on the fly.

As a result, the eCCAT is used as a problem-solving partner, answering questions (explicit or implicit) posed by the decision maker who supplements the information with his or her domain specific knowledge. The supplement of visual analytics to the business domain, regardless of specificity of function, can lead to advances in the domain itself through effective decision making and improved understanding [8].

Fig. 1. Relative contribution of focal spots and tabular display of key focal points and its KPIs

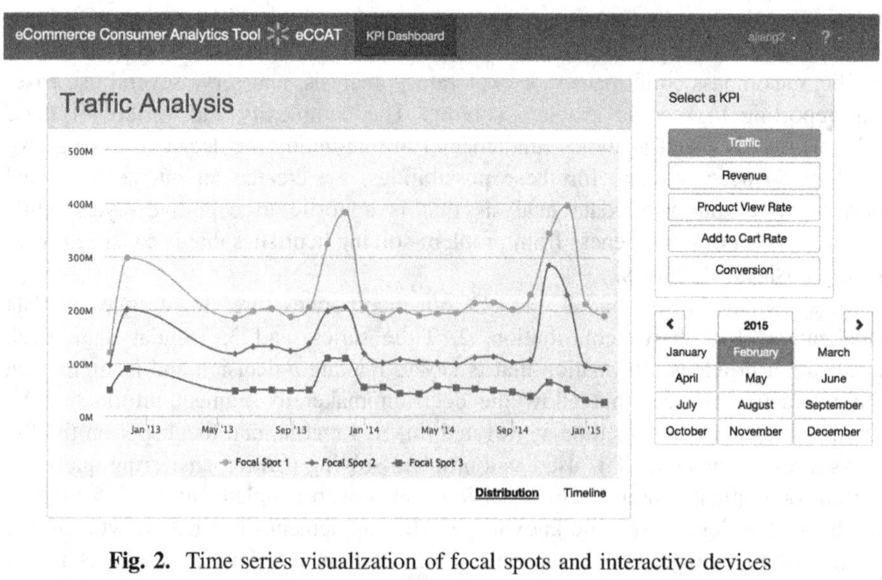

Fig. 2. Time series visualization of focal spots and interactive devices

5 Conclusion

eCommerce plays a vital role in the retail industry. This paper proposed a mechanism to identify focal spots in an eCommerce platform called eCCAT. The eCCAT system incorporated analysis of data derived from sessionization of user activity records obtained from web beacons. Aggregation and time series of key performance indicators allowed us to generate analysis of focal spots. A visual analytics interface replete with interactive devices and data visualization, agnostic to cognitive problem solving styles, was created to surface information about focal spots directly to decision makers.

For future work, a statistical time series model could be built to monitor the change in a KPI metric to discover focal points automatically. Particularly, the metric within a specified time window can be used in fitting a time series model (e.g. autoregressive integrated moving average model). When a model that fits data well is found, a one-step prediction interval is constructed. The new observation will be compared with the predicted interval to determine whether the value is significantly different (in the statistical sense) from the underlying structure of historical data. If such difference is found, a focal point is discovered and attention should be paid to dive deeper into the time point of change to determine the cause of change (especially for negative ones), e.g. data logging errors, site issues, external factors, etc. Finally, as new observation becomes available, the model is fitted again with the time window slid forward to cover new data. This 'fit-predict-slide' cycle repeats as new data arrive since site performance itself will change as a result of new features deployed.

References

1. Joines, J.L., Scherer, C.W., Scheufele, D.A.: Exploring motivations for consumer web use and their implications for e-commerce. J. Consum. Mark. **20**(2), 90–108 (2003)
2. Waldegg, P.B., Scrivener, S.A.R.: Designing interfaces for culturally diverse users. In: Proceedings of Sixth Australian Conference on Computer-Human Interaction 1996, pp. 316–317, 24–27 Nov 1996
3. Purchase, H.C.: The effects of graph layout. In: Proceedings 1998 Australasian Computer Human Interaction Conference, pp. 80–86, 30 Nov–4 Dec 1998
4. Kinley, K., Tjondronegoro, D., Partridge, H.: Web searching interaction model based on user cognitive styles. In: Proceedings of the 22nd Conference of the Computer-Human Interaction Special Interest Group of Australia on Computer-Human Interaction, pp. 340–343. ACM, New York (2010)
5. Spiliopoulou, M., Mobasher, B., Berendt, B., Nakagawa, M.: A framework for the evaluation of session reconstruction heuristics in web-usage analysis. INFORMS J. Comput. **15**, 171–190 (2003)
6. Chen, C.: Searching for intellectual turning points: progressive knowledge domain visualization. Proc. Natl. Acad. Sci. USA **101**(suppl.), 5303–5310 (2004)
7. Keim, D.A., Mansmann, F., Thomas, J.: Visual analytics: how much visualization and how much analytics? ACM SIGKDD Explor. Newslett. **11**(2), 5–8 (2010)
8. Munzner, T., Johnson, C., Moorhead, R., Pfister, H., Rheingans, P., Yoo, T.S.: NIH-NSF visualization research challenges report summary. IEEE Comput. Graph. Appl. **26**(2), 20–24 (2006). doi:10.1109/MCG.2006.44

Usability Evaluation of an M-Commerce System Using Proxy Users

Gabriela Novak[1(✉)] and Lars Lundberg[2]

[1] Ericsson AB, Ölandsgatan 1, SE-371 23 Karlskrona, Sweden
gabriela.novak@ericsson.com
[2] Department of Computer Science and Engineering,
Blekinge Institute of Technology, SE-37971 Karlskrona, Sweden
lars.lundberg@bth.se

Abstract. We have done a usability evaluation of a mobile commerce system developed by Ericsson in Sweden. The main market for the system is in developing countries in Africa. Consequently, there is a geographical distance between the developers and the users, and it is difficult to involve actual users in usability tests. Because of this, a team of solution architects that work with the product was used as proxies for the actual users in the usability test. When the test was completed, a group of actual users came to Sweden to attend a course. In order to get additional input to the usability evaluation, the usability test was repeated with the actual users. The results from the two groups were very similar, and our conclusion is that the proxy user group was a good alternative to actual users.

Keywords: Proxy users · Surrogate users · Usability testing · Mobile commerce

1 Introduction

We consider a system for mobile commerce (M-Commerce). M-Commerce systems make it possible to perform bank style transactions through mobile phones. The M-Commerce market is growing rapidly in developing countries in Africa. The Swedish branch of the Ericsson telecommunication company is developing an M-Commerce system called Ericsson Wallet Platform (EWP).

Due to globalization and outsourcing, it is becoming increasingly common to have a considerable distance between the developers and the actual users. In this case, the long geographical distance between the site of development (Sweden) and the context of use (Africa) is a problem. The solution architects [14] (SA-team) are collecting requirements for the EWP at customer sites. Such information gathering is capturing contextual information and provides a basis for later evaluation activities [1].

Various studies within the banking and payments sector have shown the importance of context of use [2, 3, 16]. Due to the geographical distance, the SA-team from the integration department in Sweden replaces the actual users in this usability test. We will

C. Stephanidis (Ed.): HCII 2015 Posters, Part II, CCIS 529, pp. 164–169, 2015.
DOI: 10.1007/978-3-319-21383-5_28

therefore refer to the SA-team as proxy users (proxy users are sometimes referred to as surrogate users [15]). Our usability test approach is thus based on the idea that the SA-team's insight and customer understanding brings the actual users' needs to the EWP development in Sweden.

When the usability test was completed, a group of actual users came to Sweden to attend a course. In order to get additional input, the usability test was repeated with the group of actual users. It turned out that the results from both usability tests (with the SA-team and actual users, respectively) were very similar.

2 Background

There are a number of definitions of usability [4–6]. Testing with real users is the most fundamental usability evaluation method. Our focus is to investigate if proxy users can be used to overcome the fact that there is a long distance between the development site (Sweden) and the place where the system is used (Africa). Some alternative approaches to proxy users are Personas [7, 11] and Focus groups [4]. Focus groups can be subjected to remote testing, with the use of video conferencing and other forms of electronic networks, which is an inexpensive way of conducting usability testing.

In remote usability testing user research can be conducted with participants in their natural environment with the use of modern technology like screen sharing or online remote usability services. The problems with remote usability testing include restricted or no view of the participants body language, and technical difficulties due to the distance and network capacity.

3 Usability Test of the EWP

There are a number of stakeholders in EWP. These stakeholders include consumers, agents, merchants, and customer care. EWP has a number of interfaces and the object of our usability testing is the graphical user interface that supports the work of customer care agents, financial controllers and compliance officers.

Our usability test combined a set of tasks with the application of the think aloud protocol [12, 13]. During the tasks we measured completion time and number of errors. Interviews were conducted with the test participants and a questionnaire was designed in order to steer the interviews. We used semi-structured interviews [8]. The usability test consisted of the following steps:

- test preparation
- test participant selection
- task definition – the test cases performed
- test execution.

The steps described in detail are in the subsections below.

3.1 Test Preparation

The test began with a brief description of tasks, techniques used to collect data, and the aim of the usability test. This was presented to each participant. After the test participants completed the tasks and the times to complete the tasks were measured and recorded, the interview process began.

3.2 Test Participants

According to Nielsen, the optimal number of testers for a usability test is 5; with adding more users the same findings are observed and not much new is discovered [17]. The five test participants in the usability test were selected among the SA-team, as one of their job duties is collecting requirements for system adjustments and configuration, requirements that expand the system in order to support specific tasks discovered as potentially beneficial in the EWP solution. In order to do their job, the SA-team at Ericsson is required to visit customer sites and gather information. The main purpose of the solution architect role is converting the requirements into an architecture and design that will become a blueprint of the solution [14].

The interface used for this usability test is used by customer care personnel at a mobile network operator (MNO). When the usability test with the SA-team was completed, a group of four actual users from Africa came to Sweden in order to attend an educational course. This gave us a good opportunity to repeat the usability test with these actual users.

3.3 Task Definition

We selected 4 tasks for the usability test and the SA-team reviewed the relevance of the selection:

1. Transfer of funds. An amount of 10 EUR to be transferred between account holder A and account holder B.
2. Edit account holder information. The user is to search for an account holder and edit the account holder information – in this case update of the street number in the address field.
3. View transaction history. The user is to search for an account holder and for the specific account holder select view historical data and view vouchers.
4. Four-eye principle. The four-eye principle is a process that prevents users from performing certain operations in a single step. An approval is required by another user, for example a supervisor.

3.4 Test Execution

The usability test was conducted at Ericsson, Sweden. The participants received individual invitations to the usability test session via the Outlook tool and team rooms were booked for the session in order to prevent possible interruptions and distractions. Participants used the evaluator's laptop, in order to access the environment containing the latest EWP installation with the interface.

4 Test Results

All five participants from the SA-team completed the test in less than 20 min. The number of errors per participant did not exceed 3 and the time spent to support the participants was between 1 and 4 min.

The four actual users completed the usability test in 11–16 min, i.e., they needed approximately the same time as the SA-team proxy users. They all needed 1–2 min support; the minimum number of errors was 0 and the maximum number of errors was 4. Again, approximately the same values as for the SA-team.

The first task proved to be challenging, since four of the SA-team as well as all actual users needed support. The main problem was that the interface was not self-explanatory as to where to find the transfer option. The time to complete the task was approximately the same for the SA-team members and the actual users. The participants, SA-team as well as actual users, expressed the need for revising the terms used for actions and an inconsistency with input fields was noted as well.

The second test case was completed with minor support provided to the first two actual users. Some improvement suggestions were also noted from both groups of users (SA-team and actual users): a search button should be present, a going back button should be added and a system message of successful edit should be displayed.

As a part of account holder management, a view of transaction and voucher history is presented and this is the focus of the third test case. Usability issues were detected since not all SA-team participants knew where to start and the interface not being self-explanatory was highlighted again. Both groups thought that the display of transaction history was hard to understand, and suggestions of explanation of the colours used in the table were recorded. One actual user also expressed the need to make the data in the transaction history exportable as a PDF file.

The enforcement of the four-eye principle is a very common part of tasks within the financial industry, due to the possibility of errors or misuses. It consists of special permissions in order for some actions to be approved by a supervisor. The fourth test case concerns the four-eye principle. This task proved to be the most confusing one for the SA-team as well as for the actual users and many improvement possibilities were detected, such as approval history, information of pending approval tasks being displayed for all users, and more logical positioning of the approval action.

Our tests showed that we got (almost) the same comments and improvement suggestions from the SA-team and the actual users. Also, the number of errors as well as the time and support needed were similar for both groups.

5 Discussion and Related Work

Two examples of successful usability engineering projects with no or limited access to actual users are the Information Map Studio (IMS) at the SAS institute, and the Nokia Communicator (N9000) mobile device.

IMS is an application that enables a technical user to create a business view of data that are relevant to analytical needs of business users which use reporting tools. The project had no established customer base. Initial testing of the original design showed a significant amount of usability issues. After the identified issues were fixed, a second iteration with a follow up usability test was conducted. The results of the test showed that the IMS application had made usability gains on every aspect of the user interface. The first iteration of testing included SAS employees who had experience with IMS (see pages 112–134 in [9]).

At Nokia, usability tests are used to evaluate the flow of tasks that have been found critical for mobile devices. They faced a challenge with a new product and there were no real users to conduct the testing. Due to the competitive market, the device was not to be shown to the people outside of the development team. During the development, different methods were used to discover potential problems (usage scenarios, focus groups) and user testing was conducted after the product was released to the public. Users were given the device for some weeks and were asked to report positive and negative features. The results confirmed the developer's concerns about the effects of consistency with other similar applications that run on desktop machines (see pages 464–474 in [10]).

In both cases discussed above, the unavailability of real users was an obstacle. While the approaches to usability testing were different, the usability on the products was eventually improved using proxy users.

While using proxies has its benefits, there are limitations to consider as well [15], e.g., the proxy users may know the product too well or have been too involved in the design.

6 Conclusions and Future Work

We have done a usability test that used solution architects as proxies for the actual users of the interface to the M-Commerce system. The results using the proxies and the actual users were very similar; the same usability issues were identified and the proxy users and the actual users needed approximately the same support and the same time to complete the tasks. The conclusion from our study is therefore that proxy users can be an alternative when the actual users are not easily accessible due to geographical distance or other reasons. Previous reported projects at SAS and Nokia support this conclusion [9, 10].

This method can be further developed and applied in different parts of the EWP solution, since this study targeted only one interface and one specific group of users. We will extend this study in two ways: we will conduct usability tests for other interfaces of M-Commerce, and we will also investigate if it is possible to use other groups than solution architects as proxy users.

References

1. Maguire, M.: Methods to support human centered design. Int. J. Hum. Comput. Stud. **55**(4), 587–634 (2001)
2. Maguire, M.: Context of use within usability activities. Int. J. Hum. Comput. Stud. **55**(4), 453–483 (2001)

3. Zollet, R., Back, A.: Website usability for internet banking. In: Proceedings of 23rd Bled eConference. Slovenia (2010)
4. Nielsen, J.: Usability Engineering. Elseiver, Amsterdam (1993). ISBN 9780125184069
5. Shneiderman, B.: Universal usability, association for computing machinery. Commun. ACM **43**, 84–91 (2000)
6. ISO/IEC, ISO 9241-11: Ergonomic requirements for office with visual display terminals (VDTs). Part 11 Guidance on usability, ISO/IEC 9241-11:1998 (E) (1998)
7. Pruitt, J., Grudin, J.: Personas: practice and theory. In: Proceedings of the 2003 Conference on Designing for User Experiences, DUX 2003 (2003)
8. Wilson, C.: Interview Techniques for UX Practitioners: A User-Centered Design Method, Semi-Structured Interviews. Newnes, London (2013). ISBN 978-0-12-410450-1
9. Sherman, P.: Usability Success Stories: How Organizations Improve by Making Easier to Use Software and Websites. Gower, London (2007)
10. Preece, J., Rogers, Y., Sharp, H.: Interaction Design: Beyond Human-Computer Interaction. Wiley, New York (2002). ISBN 0471492787
11. Putkey, T.,: Personas in user experience. http://thecontentwrangler.com/2011/08/23/personas-in-user-experience/
12. Van Den Haak, M.J., De Jong, M.D.T., Schellens, P.J.: Retrospective vs. concurrent think-aloud protocols: testing the usability of an online library catalogue. Behav. Inf. Technol. **22**(5), 339–351 (2003)
13. Think-aloud and cooperative evaluation. http://www.cs.bham.ac.uk/~rxb/HTML_text/hci/Schedule/Evaluate-2.html
14. Bogue, R.,: Anatomy of a software development role: solution architect. http://www.developer.com/mgmt/article.php/3504496/Anatomy-of-a-Software-Development-Role-Solution-Architect.htm
15. Travis, D.: Usability testing with hard-to-find participants. http://www.userfocus.co.uk/articles/surrogates.html
16. Venkatesh, V., Ramesh, V., Massey, A.P.: Understanding usability in mobile commerce. Commun. ACM **46**(12), 53–56 (2003)
17. Nielsen, J.: Why you only need to test with 5 users. http://www.nngroup.com/articles/why-you-only-need-to-test-with-5-users/

Current State of HCI Practice in the Estonian Software Development Industry

Abiodun Ogunyemi[1(✉)], David Lamas[1], Hegle Sarapuu[2], and Isaias Barreto da Rosa[3]

[1] Institute of Informatics, Tallinn University, Narva mnt 29, 10120 Tallinn, Estonia
{abnogn, david.lamas}@tlu.ee

[2] Trinidad Consulting OÜ, Teaduspargi 8, 12618 Tallinn, Estonia
hegle.sarapuu@trinidad.ee

[3] ECOWAS Commission, Niger House, Area 1, Abuja, Nigeria
isaiasbr@gmail.com

Abstract. The information society is expected to use information technologies extensively. This expectation often results to pressure on the software industry to develop rapidly, software systems to provide e-services to the society. Unfortunately, many unusable systems are developed and deployed to the society in the process. In Estonia, more than 90 % of the inhabitants use IT for various activities, and most government and business services are delivered through the Internet. Further, the field of human-computer interaction (HCI) is still very young, and Tallinn University, remains the only institution in the Baltic zone, running a programme (masters) in HCI. This study presents the preliminary results of a recently conducted online survey on the extent of uptake of HCI practices. The outcomes of the study show that awareness and knowledge of HCI are still very low in the Estonian software industry.

Keywords: HCI · Human-centred design · User experience · Human-centred software engineering

1 Introduction

A major reason for unusable software products is often the lack of knowledge of HCI practices, needed for the production of successful software [1]. Unfortunately, the information society suffers from the consequences of this considerable lack [10].

The transition of the society from the industrial age to knowledge, suggests that information technologies will become pervasive. Although HCI has been an important issue for software organizations over time, its practice and other aspects such as usability, user experience (UX), and human-centred design (HCD), remain at a low rate of uptake in most software industries of different regions of the World [10, 14]. For example, in Eastern Europe and, in Russia in particular, although there is "a significant number of experts who day by day perform routine usability activities under orders of the developed Russian software industry, and the quality of their work meets the commonly accepted standards", there is no indication for the industry to boast of

C. Stephanidis (Ed.): HCII 2015 Posters, Part II, CCIS 529, pp. 170–175, 2015.
DOI: 10.1007/978-3-319-21383-5_29

greater achievements in the HCI aspects [4, p. 22]. In some other developed countries such as the US, government regulations make it mandatory that software product development complies with certain HCI standards [3]. There are very scarce studies in Estonia, however, to describe the state of HCI practice in the local software industry. This research aimed to determine the extent of HCI awareness, and perceptions of usability, and UX, and approaches to human-centred design practice in the Estonian software industry.

In the next section, we provide an overview of the Estonian software industry. Next, we present our method, provide our results, and finally, we discuss and provide the implications from our study.

2 The Estonian Software Industry

Software development is concentrated in the IT departments of the banking sector in Estonia. The software divisions of Hansabank (now Swedbank), and Uhispank (now SEB), were once regarded as informal leaders in the software industry [2]. These banks developed in-house banking applications to support automated teller machines (ATMs), mobile and internet banking services, thereby reducing operational costs of running several branch offices [2, 6]. Thus, "the fast development of the Estonian banking sector and the high-tech solutions elaborated by the banks' own product development departments have reinforced their need for quality software, and trustworthy and secure products, thus having also positive effects on generating innovative solutions" [9, p. 8].

The Institute of Cybernetics, Tallinn, used to be where Estonians' software expertise was developed during the Soviet days. Unfortunately, sustainability was lost and potential threats for business development, innovation and growth were the consequence [2]. A study by Kalvet, [8] revealed that "compared to the Estonian ICT manufacturing industry, which is largely consolidated, heavily export-intensive and based on foreign capital, the Estonian software industry is different. The number of companies in the sector is very high, production volumes and exports are low and specialization is still not established" (p. 7). Dutta, [6], reiterated the need for Estonia's participation in the global software market when he warns, "in-house innovations may never leave the "house"". The author gave an insight that most applications developed by the private companies such as the banking sector are tailored to sectional needs to gain a competitive edge in the local market. The author summed up by suggesting that Estonia would need to "package and sell its innovative ICT services abroad" in order to be recognized as a global e-leader.

A strategy proposed by Savisaar, [12] "to ensure the development of innovative products and services", is to intensify "co-operation between research institutions and entrepreneurs". The author reasons that such cooperation would cause a re-orientation for practitioners from low value-added ventures to production of higher added value activities. The concern would therefore, be, how these proposals could be achieved without considerations for the HCI dimensions, such as user values, and design practice. This study stems from the need to diffuse HCI values, and practice in the

Estonian software industry, in order to promote the development of software products that deliver user and market values rapidly.

3 Method

The research online survey questionnaire was designed based on the literature review of HCI-Software Engineering integration. As HCI is relatively new in Estonia, we rely on existing literature, to draw our questions, and conduct a quantitative exploratory investigation of the Estonian software industry. The questionnaire contained both closed-ended multiple choice and open-ended questions. Some questions allow multiple answers. The descriptive statistics and visualization techniques were used to analyse the closed-ended questions, and thematic analysis was used for the open-ended questions. The purposive sampling approach [13] was used to invite organizations to participate in the survey. The emailing addresses of twenty-seven Information Technology and Software Services companies were obtained and these companies were invited automatically.

We partnered with an IT service company (Trinidad Consulting OÜ), which specializes in HCI consulting services. The company helped in inviting organisations, which carry out some form of software development. These organisations are found in the government, banking, and telecommunications, among others. The Developers Club, Estonia, was as well partnered with, and members were invited through their emailing list. The survey was deployed using the 'LimeSurvey' open source survey facility. The questionnaire was designed in such a way that some questions would only appear if the answer to a preceding question is relevant to the one proceeding it. Some questions also allowed multiple options and some do not. The survey ran from June 1st, 2014 to 30 September 2014. A total of one hundred and seventeen invites were sent and sixty-two organisations participated, bringing the response rate to 53 %. However, only thirty-two responses were complete and useful for the analysis. Incomplete responses were discarded.

4 Results

The outcomes of the study show that awareness and knowledge of HCI are very low in the Estonian software industry. Majority of the respondents (82 %), have between one and ten years of experience in their main roles, and this suggests that there could be more young professionals in the Estonian software industry. Nineteen organizations, out of thirty-two, are aware of HCI practices, and the rest are not.

The software development cultures in the thirty-two organizations remain largely SCRUM, waterfall, lean, and extreme programming respectively.

In Fig. 1, we see that the proportion of practitioners involved with HCI roles such as usability and UX is very low compared to other roles such as software engineers, programmers, and project managers. A study by Venturi, [14] shows a similar trend.

Further, the organisations report that they select own employees for usability testing. Thirteen organizations do not prioritize usability, and only five, always do. As

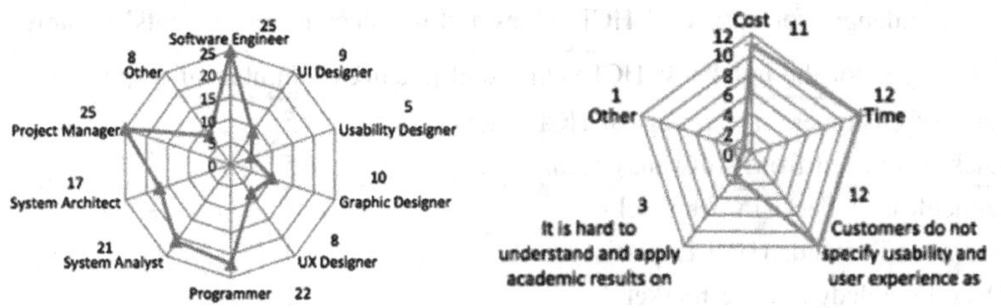

Fig. 1. Software teams' roles in respondents' organizations and reasons for lack of priority for usability testing.

it can be seen also from Fig. 1, the major reasons provided by the organizations is cost and time, for lack of priority for usability testing (Multiple options was allowed). The result is consistent with the findings of Ardito et al., [1] and Bygstad et al., [5].

Regarding how the respondents perceived UX, the results in Fig. 2 suggest that the organisations surveyed may not understand fully, the distinction between usability and user experience. The finding on UX perceptions is similar to the work of Wechsung et al., [15].

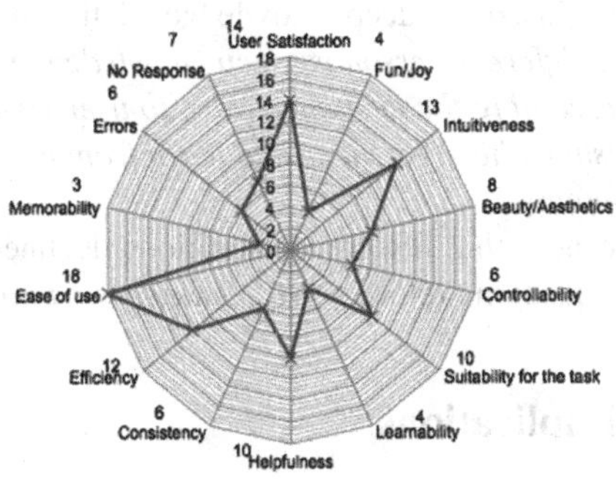

Fig. 2. How the respondents perceived UX values

In terms of human-centred design (HCD) practice, the major principle being followed by the twenty-five of the organizations is the understanding of users, tasks and environments. Other principles, as specified in the ISO 9241-210 framework [7], appear to be less prioritized.

The results from the analysis of the open-ended questions are captured into Table 1. The answers were provided by twenty-five, out of the thirty-two respondents.

A major challenge indicated by the respondents is the lack of HCI awareness by the customers. One respondent remarked: "*Customers have no idea of the background of ICT development and how big part HCI has in it. For them it seems just like non-material, additional cost*". Similarly, another respondent reiterates: "*I think not. I think it is mostly up to the customer and they do not focus too much on usability requirements*". However, these respondents suggest to: "*Raise overall awareness*

Table 1. Challenges for uptake of HCI values and practices in respondents' organisations

Challenges for the uptake of HCI values and practices	Number of respondents
Lack of customers' awareness of HCI practices	5
Lack of interest from software organisations	15
Difficult to collect UX feedbacks	1
Resource demands (HCI Expertise)	3
Deep knowledge of the market	1

regarding HCI values inside the organization and among partners. Make following HCI values obligatory in certain public procurement procedures". Another suggestion is: "*Quantifying the cost of bad usability or bad HCI in general".*

On user feedbacks, one respondent indicates: "*How to efficiently get user feedback? For example, we use in design phase user testing with max three persons. When they feel UX OK or good, still afterwards in masses*". The respondent suggests a solution: "*There should be balance between continuous user testing with many users AND efficient use of time and money. It has to be found in every project :)".*

On resource demands, one respondent indicates: "*Mainly resource challenges as there are very few UX experts available".* This respondent, however, believes it is up to the university to address this need: "*We have addressed the need to universities*".

Finally, the challenge posed on deep knowledge of the market, is the need "*to locate and understand the different personas; deep knowledge of the market (about the users on the market); overcoming the customer view, to user view".* On what could be done, a suggestion is to "*show the differences and learn from example projects that are developed within the company".*

It is sad, however, to note that fifteen organisations declined to share their challenges. One of these organisations retorts: "*No challenges as no interest*".

5 Discussion and Implications

The outcomes of the study present a mixed reaction. On the one hand, awareness and knowledge of HCI are still very low among the organizations surveyed. For example, fifteen organizations declined to share their challenges, and it could be difficult to investigate level of HCI practice in this set of organizations. On the other hand, there is an indication that HCI practice could succeed in some of the organizations surveyed. This set of organizations, however, appears to be limited by insufficient HCI expertise, especially, in UX, and human-centred design aspects.

Another major concern emerging from our results is that of lack of awareness of HCI practices in the customers' organisations. Some issues with customers' organisations include reluctance to allow end users participate in software projects, perception that HCI is time consuming and a general lack of prioritization of non-functional requirements [11].

Overall, when compared to other Eastern European countries such as Denmark, Finland, Norway, and Iceland, the fundamental issue still remains the lack of priority for certain HCI aspects such as usability and UX. Thus, the results obtained are similar to those by Venturi, [14] and Wechsung et al., [15]. This study as well shows an indication for the need to diffuse HCI awareness in customers' organisations.

The lessons derived from this study provide some implications. For the researchers, there is a need to promote HCI by looking more closely into software methodologies and adoption cultures of the software industry, and increasing both customers, and users' awareness of the importance of HCI dimensions. Short-term training programmes could be organized to mitigate the shortage of HCI expertise in the industry. Practitioners also need to include HCI topics in their events and programmes. Finally, client organizations and Tender offices need to make HCI values such as usability, and user experience mandatory in their requirements.

Acknowledgments. This study was supported by the European Social Fund in the framework of the DoRa programme. The DoRa programme is carried out by Archimedes Foundation.

References

1. Ardito, C., Buono, P., Caivano, D., Costabile, M.R., Lanzilotti, R.: Investigating and promoting UX practice in industry: an experimental study. Int. J. Hum. Comput. Stud. **72**(6), 542–551 (2014)
2. Best, M.H., Bradley, J.: Analysis of Estonian Business Structure and Competitiveness: Present Situation and Future Development Challenges. Tallinn (2006)
3. Buie, E.: HCI standards: a mixed blessing. Interactions **6**, 36–41 (1999)
4. Burmistrov, I.: A new destination for offshore usability. Interactions **13**, 22–24 (2006)
5. Bygstad, B., Ghinea, G., Brevik, E.: Software development methods and usability: perspectives from a survey in the software industry in Norway. Interact. Comput. **20**(3), 375–385 (2008)
6. Dutta, S.: Estonia: A Sustainable Success in Networked Readiness? (2006)
7. ISO: ergonomics of human-system interaction - part 210: human-centred design for interactive systems. ISO 9241-210:2010, pp. 1–32. ISO (2010)
8. Kalvet, T.: The Estonian ICT Manufacturing and Software Industry: Current State and Future Outlook. Poliitikauuringute Keskus Praxis, Tallinn (2004)
9. Kalvet, T., Tiits, M.: Drivers, degree and patterns of the integration of the Estonian ICT sector into the global innovation networks (2012)
10. Majid, R.A., Noor, N., Adilah, W., Adnan, W., Mansor, S.: Users' frustration and HCI in the software development life cycle. Int. J. Inf. Process. Manag. **2**(1), 23–39 (2011)
11. Ogunyemi, A., Lamas, D.: Interplay between human-computer interaction and software engineering. In: Proceedings of the 9th Iberian Conference on Information Systems and Technologies, pp. 1–10. IEEE Xplore, Barcelona (2014)
12. Savisaar, E.: Estonian information society strategy 2013. Tallinn (2006)
13. Tongco, M.D.C.: Purposive sampling as a tool for informant selection. Ethnobot. Res. Appl. **5**, 147–158 (2007)
14. Venturi, G., Troost, J.: Survey on the UCD integration in the industry. In: Proceedings of the Third NordiCHI Conference, pp. 449–452 (2004)
15. Wechsung, I. Naumann, R., Schleicher, R.: Views on usability and user experience: from theory and practice. In: Proceedings of the NordiCHI 2008 Conference, pp. 1–4. ACM, Lund (2008)

How Non-Technological Innovation Reinforces the Effect of Technological Innovation on Firm Performance?: An Empirical Study of Korean Manufacturing Industry

Hyun-Sun Ryu[1(✉)] and Jung Lee[2]

[1] Korea University, Seoul, Republic of Korea
hamkkai@gmail.com
[2] KIMEP University, Almaty, Kazakhstan
junglee@kimep.kz

Abstract. By using empirical data collected from 870 manufacturing firms in Korea, the present study investigates the relationships between technological innovation (i.e., product and process innovations) and non-technological innovations (i.e., organizational and marketing innovations) and its overall innovation success with innovation initiatives. We highlight the business value of non-technological innovations by proposing its moderating effect on innovation success. We then argue that technological innovation exhibits a strong impact on innovation success only when non-technological innovations adequately strain the relationship between them. This study enhances the understanding of innovation in organizations by showing that the effective interaction between technological and non-technological innovations helps firms succeed in innovations and enhance firm performance.

Keywords: Innovation · Technological innovation · Non-technological innovation · Innovation success · Firm performance

1 Introduction

Innovation plays a central role in economic growth. Schumpeter [8] argued that economic development is driven by innovation through a dynamic process in which new technologies replace the old process, which labeled "create destruction." Firm innovation mainly aims to enhance firm performance by reducing costs and improving productivity; thus, it is the core factor for sustaining business. Firms can gain their competitive advantage and improve their performance through innovation activities to develop new products and new processes [10]. These activities of firms generally indicate technological innovations [7].

Despite shifting the value area of firms from technological to non-technological area, most firms still focus on technological innovations. However, only technological innovations are not sufficient to understanding innovation activities of firms because the innovations include technological activities (e.g., introducing and developing new technologies) as well as non-technological activities (e.g., re-establishing business

C. Stephanidis (Ed.): HCII 2015 Posters, Part II, CCIS 529, pp. 176–182, 2015.
DOI: 10.1007/978-3-319-21383-5_30

strategies, changing in organizational method, and external network and marketing) [1]. Thus, firms should understand the relationship between technological and non-technological innovation when they conduct innovation activities. Therefore, this study aims to analyze the relationship between technological and non-technological innovation from a balanced approach. Our finding shows that the role of non-technological innovation is significant in determining the innovation success and enhancing firm performance.

2 Theoretical Development

Developing new product and new process can enhance productivity and gain competitive advantage of firms [2]. Technological innovation is linked to new product and process innovation, resulting in giving new value and improving existing value to customers. Additionally, firms can also increase customer satisfactions through product differentiation by re-establishing the business strategies and organizational method and by developing new market method. Based on this concept, this study defines the scope of innovation as four types of innovation, namely, product, process, organizational, and marketing innovations, which can encompass a wide range of changes in a firm's innovative activities.

2.1 Technological Innovation

Technological innovation consists of product and process innovations. Product (goods or services) innovation has been identified to be the market introduction of either new or significantly improved goods and services [9]. Product innovation includes new or significantly improved good and services in terms of technological specifications, components and materials, incorporated software, user friendliness, and other functional characteristics. Moreover, process innovation indicates the introduction of new or significant improved methods such as production processes, supporting activities for production process, logistics, delivery and distribution methods for goods or services [9], leading to decrease costs, increase product quality and market share. Thus, firms can gain a competitive advantage that improves customers' satisfactions through process innovation, resulting in achieving innovation success. Production innovation always accompanies with process innovation and they positively influence innovation success. Thus, the hypothesis is the following:

H1-Technological innovation has a positive effect on innovation success.

2.2 Non-technological Innovation

Organizational and marketing innovations are consisted of non-technological innovation. Organizational innovation is a new organizational method in enterprise's business practices (including knowledge management), workplace organization, or external relations that have not been previously used by an enterprise [9]. Organizational innovation includes organizational structure, learning process, and adaption to changes in technology and the environment [5]. A firm's organizational structure can affect the efficiency of innovation activities, with some structures better suited to particular environments [5]. A greater degree of organizational integration may improve the co-ordination, planning, and implementation of innovation strategies. In addition, the demand of new products may depend not only on product quality and characteristics but also on their social characteristics and image [4]. Marketing theories focus on implementing marketing practices, such as Marketing Mix Model [6]. Marketing innovation is the implementation of a new marketing concept or strategy that differs significantly from enterprise's existing marketing methods [9]. Marketing innovations focus on better addressing customer needs, opening up new markets, or newly positioning a firm's product on the market. Hence, our hypothesis is the following:

H2- Non-technological innovation has a positive effect on innovation success.

Organizational innovation is closely related to process innovation. Creating new development department or sales department, as well as reorganizing workflow and external network to improve the productivity and quality are examples of process innovation. Moreover, marketing innovation is also associated with product innovation. As new products needed to be introduced via a new marketing method, firms are required to accept new marketing methods to increase productivity and product quality. For this reason, technological innovation can positively influence innovation success with non-technological innovation. Thus, we proposed the following hypotheses:

H3-The effect of technological innovation on innovation success will be positively moderated by non-technological innovation.
H4-Innovation success has a positive effect on firm performance.

3 Research Methodology

3.1 Development of Measures

The survey respondents were randomly selected form entire population of manufacturing firms based on the 2008 Korea Innovation Survey (http://kis.stepi.re.kr). To develop the measurement instruments, four items such as product, process, organizational, and marketing innovations were measured on yes–no questions and the other item such as innovation success were on a five-point Likert scale from "extremely low" to "extremely high." A survey item concerning firm performance was measured as factual data using sales growth from 2005 to 2007. In case of yes–no questions, the measurement instrument should be merged to one dummy variable because the nominal scale was difficult to use in this analysis. Finally, we employed 5 constructs and 16 items as measures in this study (a full list of the items is available upon request).

3.2 Sample and Data Collection

For our empirical analysis, the 2008 Korea Innovation Survey was used. The survey only focused on manufacturing firms. Hence, respondents who had implemented at least one innovation in the reference period 2005 to 2007 were asked to respond to the whole questionnaire. The questionnaires were distributed to 3081 firms and 1432 responses were finally received. The complete case approach applied was the missing data imputation method. Finally, 870 responses were found useful for this study with a usable response rate of 28.24 %. The respondent characteristics in terms of number of employees, total sales revenue, and R&D budget are summarized in Table 1.

Table 1. Characteristics of the sample

Employee (#)	Freq. (%)	Revenue ($)	Freq. (%)	R&D budget (%)	Freq. (%)
<100	368(42.3)	< 50 mil.	186(21.4)	<1.0	226(30.6)
100 ~ 500	307(35.3)	50 ~ 100 mil.	86(9.9)	1.1 ~ 5.0	385(44.3)
500 ~ 1,000	117(13.4)	100 ~ 500 mil.	223(25.6)	5.1 ~ 10.0	129(14.8)
1,000 ~ 3,000	56(6.4)	500 ~ 1,000 mil.	94(10.8)	10.1 ~ 15.0	34(3.9)
3,000<	22(2.4)	1,000 mil. <	281(32.3)	15.1<	56(6.5)
Total	870(100)	Total	870(100)	Total	870(100)

4 Analysis and Results

4.1 Measurement Model

Convergent validity was assessed by looking at the composite reliability (CR) and average variance extracted (AVE) from the measures. Table 2 shows that the obtained CR values ranged from 0.75 to 0.87, which exceeded the threshold value of 0.7. The AVE ranged from 0.37 to 0.86 [3], which was above the acceptable value of 0.5 A score of 0.5 indicates an acceptable level for the average variance extracted by a measure [3]. Results showed that the average variances extracted by measures ranged from 0.37 to 0.86, which were above the acceptable value. All measures except ORI are significant on their path loading as the level of 0.01. Table 3 shows that the square root of the average variance extracted for each construct was greater than the correlations between it and all other constructs (detailed results of measurement model test are available upon request). These results explain that measurement models were strongly supported by the data gathered, thus requiring further analysis.

4.2 Structural Model

With adequate measurement models, the proposed hypotheses are tested with PLS. Figure 1 shows the results of PLS structural model including the path loadings, t-values of the paths, and R-square. Among the four hypotheses, three are significant.

Table 2. Results of PLS measurement model

Construct	Item	CR	AVE	Loading	t-value
Tech. innovation (TI)	PDI	0.75	0.52	0.9529	3.7355
	PRI			0.5687	2.5717
Non-Tech. innovation (NTI)	ORI	0.87	0.86	0.0122	0.5324
	MKI			1.3143	49.2481
Tech.Innov. * Non-Tech. Innov. (TI*NTI)	PDIORI	0.87	0.63	0.7960	58.6032
	PDIMKI			0.7845	43.4375
	PRIORI			0.7387	34.2293
	PRIMKI			0.8417	71.0944
Innovation success (INS)	INS1	0.80	0.67	0.5874	21.2143
	INS 2			0.5882	19.6908
	INS 3			0.2015	3.9321
	INS 4			0.2373	4.8457
	INS 5			0.6874	31.6320
	INS 6			0.6942	31.4541
	INS 7			0.7544	36.6935
	INS 8			0.8441	40.1499
Performance (FP)	FP	1.0	1.0	1.0000	0.0000

Table 3. Correlations between constructs

Construct	TI	NTI	TI*NTI	INS	FP
TI	***0.787***	–	–	–	–
NTI	−0.031	***0.927***	–	–	–
TI*NTI	−0.090	−0.417	***0.794***	–	–
INS	−0.039	−0.336	0.714	***0.698***	–
FP	−0.057	−0.026	0.056	0.072	***1.000***

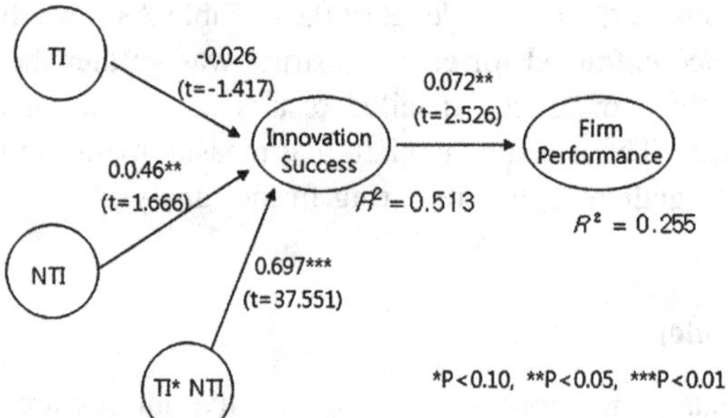

Fig. 1. Result of PLS structural model

Technological innovation exhibited no significant effect on innovation success. However, non-technological innovation was significantly related to innovation success. Non-technological innovations can positively influence innovation success with technological innovation. It means that the effect of both technological and non-technological innovations is more synergistic than that of each innovation.

5 Discussions and Implications

A negative relationship between technological innovation and innovation success is observed in this study although technological innovation has been considered as an important factor for innovation activities. It means that technological innovation does not guarantee innovation success. Therefore, a firm should strategically conduct technological innovation and focus on establishing the positive relationship between them. Furthermore, our result implies that the non-technological innovation is a critical factor for superior innovation success. Firm should consider non-technological innovations, especially marketing innovation, to achieve innovation success and it may function as a significant differentiator of firm performance. This study increases our understanding that the leveraging effect of non-technological innovation (organizational and marketing innovation) in facilitating the relationship between technological innovation (product and process innovation) and innovation success. The technological innovation with non-technological innovation results in high innovation success, leading to superior firm performance. Hence, establishing an accompanying model between technological and non-technological innovations would help manufacturing firms to succeed in innovation and enhance their firm performance. Future research should be expected to determine the relationship between sub-innovations (i.e., product-organization, product-marketing, process-organization, and process-marketing innovations). Additionally, we limited this study to only manufacturing firms. Therefore, future research should extend the scope of service firms to explore more relevant effect of innovation.

References

1. Armbruster, H., Bikfalvi, A., Kinkel, S., Lay, G.: Organizational innovation: the challenge of measuring non-technical innovation in large-scale surveys. Technovation **28**(10), 644–657 (2008)
2. Brynjolfsson, E., Hitt, L.M.: Beyond computation: Information technology, organizational transformation and business performance. J. Econ. Persp. **14**(4), 23–48 (2000)
3. Fornell, C., Larcker, D.F.: Structural equation models with unobservable variables and measurement errors. J. Mark. Res. **18**(2), 39–50 (1981)
4. Hunt, S.D.: Marketing Theory: The Philosophy of Marketing Science. Richard D. Irwin Inc, New York (1983)
5. Lam, A.: Organizational Innovation. The Oxford Handbook of Innovation. Oxford University Press, Oxford (2005)

6. Perreault, W.D., McCarthy, E.J.: Basic Marketing: A Global Managerial Approach. McGraw-Hill, New York (2005)
7. Raymond, L., St-Pierre, J.: R&D as a determinant of innovation in manufacturing SMEs: an attempt at empirical clarification. Technovation **30**(1), 48–56 (2010)
8. Schumpeter, J.: The Theory of Economic Development. Harvard University Press, Cambridge (1934)
9. Tanaka, N., Glaude, M., Gualt, F.: Oslo Manual: Guidelines for Collecting and Interpreting Innovation Data. OECD, Paris (2005)
10. Wang, C., Lu, I., Chen, C.: Evaluating firm technological innovation capability under uncertainty. Technovation **28**(6), 349–363 (2008)

Innovation Lessons: Implications of Nikola Tesla's Life for Today's Engineers, Scientists, and Technology Designers

Maximus Schmorrow[1] and Dylan Schmorrow[2](✉)

[1] Cunningham Park Elementary School, Vienna, VA, USA
maxschmorrow@gmail.com
[2] Soar Technology Inc., Ann Arbor, MI, USA
dylan.schmorrow@soartech.com

Abstract. Nikola Tesla was one of the greatest inventors of all time. His life was full of interesting twists and turns. He is most famous for inventing the Alternating Current motor, Tesla Coil, and the Bladeless Turbine, to name a few. Other inventors inspired him, such as, Thomas Edison and George Westinghouse. His trust in the people that inspired him eventually impacted him negatively. Nikola Tesla made mind-blowing discoveries and inventions that are still used today. His first break-through was creating a rotating magnetic field to make an Alternating Current without having to use a commutator. He also invented the Tesla Coil, which was able to produce a high voltage of electricity for transporting the electricity farther distances. These coils can be seen at the tops of electrical poles that hold electrical wires and cables sometimes for miles. Tesla's final invention was the bladeless turbine, able to produce energy using fluids, gases and centripetal force. His most popular invention was the Alternating Current motor, which did not use a dynamo or a commutator, but the rotating magnetic field. This would prove to be one of Tesla's greatest contributions. This paper examines the life of Nikola Tesla and document the ups and downs he faced while becoming one of the greatest inventors of all times. Although there have been many attempts to extract ubiquitous lessons learned from his life, this paper is unique in it's international focus (i.e., impact on North American innovation from European thought leadership) and serves as a mechanism for discussing the implications for HCI (i.e., process, design and social interactions). It also provides specific innovation lessons from his life and provides a summary of the implications of these lessons for 21st century engineers, scientists and technology designers.

Keywords: Innovation · Engineers · Scientists · Tesla · Invention · Discovery · Inventors · Lessons learned · HCI · Systems design · Technology · Designers · Implications

1 Introduction

Nikola Tesla was one of the greatest inventors of all time [1]. His life was full of interesting twists and turns. He is most famous for inventing the Alternating Current motor, Tesla Coil, and the Bladeless Turbine, to name a few [2–5]. Other inventors

C. Stephanidis (Ed.): HCII 2015 Posters, Part II, CCIS 529, pp. 183–186, 2015.
DOI: 10.1007/978-3-319-21383-5_31

inspired him, such as, Thomas Edison and George Westinghouse. His trust in the people that inspired him eventually impacted him negatively [6].

Nikola Tesla was born on July 10,1856 in a small town called Smiljan where Croatia is located today. His father, Milutin, was a minister and his mother, Djouka, stayed on the farm selling products they made and grew. When Tesla was a young boy, he caught Cholera and spent his time reading his father's Mark Twain novels. Nikola had four siblings: Dane (Dah-nay), Angelina, Milka, and Marica. Dane was their parent's pride and joy, until he was thrown of their horse and passed because of the injuries. Nikola couldn't make or build anything without his parents mourning over Dane's passing. This made him want to become an inventor so his parents would be proud [7].

In 1875, Nikola Tesla enrolled in the Polytechnic Institute located in Graz, Austria. He was planning on to be a mathematics professor, so he studied arithmetic, geometry, calculus, theoretical and experimental physics, analytical chemistry, mineralogy, machinery construction, botany, wave theory, optics, French, and English. Nikola studied more than twenty hours a day and changed his major to engineering. After he returned from school, his father urged him not to go a second year because of his unhealthy study habits. He went back for a second year, and a Gramme dynamo, patented by a Belgian engineer, was sent to his physics class. Tesla suspected that the dynamo could work without a commutator, but his physics teacher proved him wrong and for the rest of the class explained how impossible that is. This triggered a spark that made Tesla determined to prove his professor wrong [8].

For four years Tesla tried to create alternating current without a dynamo or a commutator. During that time, his friend Anthony Szigeti was hired as Tesla's assistant. Anthony was a former classmate and good friend of Nikola. They would go on walks, thinking of ways to design the alternating current motor. On one walk Nikola froze with the answer to the question. As Szigeti helped him down to a bench, Tesla explained how the motor worked with a rotating magnetic field. Since constantly rotating, it was able to alternate without a commutator. While Tesla had all the information, he needed to get the money to do it [1].

The first person Tesla went to was Thomas Edison. Tesla and Edison entered a deal that Tesla agreed to fix all Edison's electrical issues he had and perfect the light bulb, for fifty thousand dollars. After a year, Tesla came back with all the electrical issues gone and the light bulb perfected. When he asked Edison for payment as agreed, Edison was shocked, and all he said was, "You don't understand our American humor." Tesla was angry and quit even though Edison offered him a raise to stay [9]. Soon after, Nikola Tesla met Alfred Brown and they created a company called Tesla Electric Company, where Brown provided Tesla with a lab to work in. In this lab, they were able to develop many of the inventions that Tesla is known for to include the Tesla Coil and the Alternating Current Motor [9].

2 Inventions and Challenges

Nikola Tesla made mind-blowing discoveries and inventions that are still used today. His first break-through was creating a rotating magnetic field to make an Alternating Current without having to use a commutator [4]. He also invented the Tesla Coil, which was able to produce a high voltage of electricity for transporting the electricity farther distances. These coils can be seen at the tops of electrical poles that hold electrical wires and cables sometimes for miles. Tesla's final invention was the bladeless turbine, able to produce energy using fluids, gases and centripetal force. His most popular invention was the Alternating Current motor, which did not use a dynamo or a commutator, but the rotating magnetic field. This would prove to be one of Tesla's greatest contributions [4]. Alternating Current and Direct Current had many differences though. Direct Current is a way of transporting electricity that can only flow one direction and it's voltage can not be changed. Alternating Current is the natural flow of electricity and can change the amount of voltage it is transporting. Alternating Current is more efficient because it can transport electricity for further distances and doesn't need a power plant every mile [1].

Nikola Tesla led a life full of ups and downs. On one hand, he was famous for his inventions and his discoveries and was able to work alongside many other world famous inventors. On the other hand, he did not make wise business decisions. For example, he did not enter into a written contract with Thomas Edison. Edison ended up cheating him out of payment that they had verbally agreed to. Also, George Westinghouse took advantage of Tesla by taking ownership of Tesla's many patents and inventions. Although, Tesla was brilliant and famous due to all the discoveries he made, Nikola died on January 8, 1943 penniless and alone. He deserves more recognition for his scientific contributions to our world [1, 6, 8, 9].

3 Innovation Lessons and Implications for HCI

Although there have been many attempts to extract ubiquitous lessons learned from his life, Barbara Eldredge summarizes these succinctly in five general lessons [10]. Her lessons included: (1) when someone tells you it can't be done, do it anyway; (2) take risks, they always make you stronger; (3) learn from failure, success will follow; (4) don't stop, use past achievement to propel future progress; (5) time can always turn crazy ideas into genius innovations. However, other innovation lessons can be derived from examining Nikola Tesla's life. John Buescher examined innovation and technology in the 19th century [11] and identified two key technological innovations that profoundly altered life in Europe. They were steam and electricity. These technological innovations dramatically expanded the power of humans and animal strength as well as simple tools. Much of the foundational thinking that led to these innovations originated in Europe and subsequently had a profound impact on the rapid growth in North American. In many ways Nickola Tesla's on life story showcases the impact on North American innovation from European thought leadership. In the 21st century many still see the profound impact of European thinking on North American innovation. A current example is the European Commission's 2020 Initiative, Digital Agenda for Europe. In this example policies focused on the socio-economic impact of open innovation is helping promote long-term sustainability as well as creating new products and services [12]. Thought leadership in Europe not only has a direct impact on the European economy and society, but it also impacts North American innovation profoundly in a similar way Nikola Telsa's efforts impacted North America.

4 Conclusion

In this paper, we advocate that Nikola Tesla was one of the greatest inventors of all time. We also suggest that his trust in the people that inspired him eventually impacted him negatively. However, he made mind-blowing discoveries and inventions that are still used today and his innovations transformed North American. There are many lessons to be derived by examining the life of Nikola Tesla. There are lessons for the individual innovator and there are lessons that help foster an understanding of the role of European thought leadership on North American innovation. Understanding the implications of these lessons benefit 21st century engineers, scientists and technology designers. The story of Nikola Tesla's life provides a role model innovator to model oneself on as well as providing an example of how thinking on one continent can impact innovation on another continent.

References

1. Aldrich, L.: Nikola Tesla and the Taming of Electricity. Morgan Reynolds Inc., Greensboro (2005)
2. Tesla, N.: Apparatus for Transmitting Electrical Energy. U.S. Patent No. 1,119,732 (1914)
3. Tesla, N.: Art of Transmitting Electrical Energy Through the Natural Mediums. U.S. Patent No. 787,412 (1905)
4. Tesla, N.: A new system of alternate current motors and transformers. AIEE Trans. **5**, 305–327 (1888)
5. Tesla, N.: Turbine. U.S. Patent No. 1,061,206 (1931)
6. Seifer, M.: Wizard: The Life and Times of Nikola Tesla. Citadel Press, New York (1998)
7. Tesla, N.: My Inventions. The Philovox (2006)
8. Rhees, D.: Electricity – The greatest of all doctors: an introduction to high frequency oscillators for electro-therapeutic and other purposes. Proc. IEEE **87**(7), 1277–1281 (1999)
9. O'Neill, J.: Prodigal Genius: The Life of Nikola Tesla. Book Tree, San Diego (2007)
10. Eldredge, B.: Lessons From Tesla. http://realart.com/thought-lab/lessons-from-tesla. Accessed 8 April 2015
11. Buescher, J.: Innovation and Technology in the 19th Century. http://teachinghistory.org/history-content/ask-a-historian/24470
12. European Commission: Digital Agenda For Europe. http://ec.europa.eu/digital-agenda/en/news/socio-economic-impact-open-innovation-20

The Importance of Using Gestalt and Grid in Building Brands

João Carlos Riccó Plácido da Silva(✉), Luis Carlos Paschoarelli, and José Carlos Plácido da Silva

PPGDesign, Universidade Estadual Paulista, Bauru, Brazil
joaocarlos_placido@hotmail.com,
{paschoarelli,placido}@faac.unesp.br

Abstract. The lack of a targeted projetual method has hindered the new professionals in developing new brands. The use of specific techniques of graphical validating enables the reduction of concordance errors in a graphic mark. This study demonstrates the importance of two techniques of visual theory that assist the development of projects in this area. Being evaluated in already existing brands on the market, which proves the most important items in this graphic development process, demonstrating because they are effective.

Keywords: Brands · Gestalt · Grid · Projetual method

1 Introduction

Daily we are approached by a lot of information available in various means of dissemination, such as the news, advertisements, sounds, videos, printed materials, digital media, the internet and others. This exaggerated amount of information it generates a negative influence on companies using such means to convey their products. The printed pieces or transmitted in various media available today, are usually charged or abuse of colors to draw the attention of users, using the maximum that is that the more flashy such parts, the greater the chances of being noticed.

Therefore, it is always a great challenge for the graphic designer create and develop visual identities for institutions whether public or private, since the brand has to convey ideas, intentions and the market it serves. Develop a brand design, which enables easy understanding for all, is not an easy mission, for it must take into consideration that probably the repertoire of knowledge and values of users is large and unknown, so imagine the specific knowledge of colors, gestalt and grid that translate the meaning of the action that you want to communicate.

The human cognitive system is characterized by the treatment of symbolic information, that is, human beings create and develop images through mental models or representations of reality, which can be models or aspects of reality [1]. In this sense, cognitive system is the term used to refer to structured and formal representations grounded in psychology theories.

The informational ergonomics is widely used in research linking signaling sites and the recognition and understanding of the signs and displays information. The human

C. Stephanidis (Ed.): HCII 2015 Posters, Part II, CCIS 529, pp. 187–191, 2015.
DOI: 10.1007/978-3-319-21383-5_32

structure and information processing are the main methods used to understand and organize functionality studies and understanding of warnings signs [2].

This study seeks to demonstrate two techniques that can help the development of brands, which are the Gestalt and the Grid construction, making an analysis projects have been finalized and implemented, seeking to check the most important laws and confirm the help of constructive mesh.

2 Marca

The brand is the symbolic representation of an institution or product, something that can be identified immediately, as a symbol, an icon or a word. It consists of a sensible sign, i.e. a joint verbal information with visual information, a linguistic sign used to designate, verbalize, write and internalize an institution, so that it is close and identifiable to the user [3].

The measure that competition has created an infinity of companies in the same industry, we realized the need to seek an emotional connection between companies and customers, making those irreplaceable, since that aims to a lasting relationship. A brand is strong when just standing out in a crowded market for the same products or services. People fall in love by the marks, trust them and believe in the superiority they convey. The way they are perceived affect its fixation, or not, by users [4].

This term, brand, is often used to refer to a particular object, as an institution, a service or a product, a name, a word mark, images, concepts that distinguish this object, or service, or the object itself. When this term is used, commonly being referred to a graphical representation within the scope and jurisdiction of the graphic design professional who works with the graphic design of a symbol or logo, either individually or in combination [5].

3 Gestalt

The studies related to Gestalt began in the late nineteenth century in Austria and Germany, with the results of studies of perception, also known as Psychology of Form, Gestalt Psychology or Gestalt. They considered the psychological phenomena, as a standalone set, indivisible and linked together in their design, planning and internal law, which are independent of individual perception and formulate their own laws of human perception.

For Arnheim [6], visual perception is organized through the establishment of full and central standards in understanding some laws. This pattern can be structured in the internal sense, part of this image, so that the appearance of any part depends on a greater or lesser extent, and within the structure, which, in turn, is influenced by the nature of its parts. The act of seen these relationships is a more effective way to establish these differences and establish a set of perceptual tensions that ultimately highlight contrasting elements within the impact. From this premise, the comparisons between contrast, similarity, proximity-age, among others, share the study of mental comparisons and relationship with the existing one.

Studies have shown the brain as a dynamic system that provides an in-teração between the elements that are submitted to it at any given time, using principles of perceptual organization, such as proximity, continu-aged, like, segregation, filling, unit, simplicity and figure-ground. With this enabled state that the brain has its own operating principles, in order to self-organize stimuli received through the senses, such as touch, I found are, hearing, taste and smell.

According to the principles of Gestalt, there are eight main aspects in per-perception of objects and shapes: Unit, Segregation, Unification, Lock, Continu-age, Proximity, Similarity and prägnanz Form [7].

4 Grid

The development of constructive meshes or grids was as experimental counter basic artists of the twentieth century, such as the works of Piet Mondrian whose abstract structures inspired this system. The grid has a proposal to get the visual elements and orders them to a more cohesive composition layout. Basically the grid is a constructive mesh with several rectangles that are used to sort the graphics. This technique is applied after the definition of the type of project and the target audience to which it is intended, that is, after the concept already developed entirely, so the content determines the grid structure [8].

To ensure consistent positioning of the individual elements, which constitute the tag, develops a grid that ensures reproduction and application of the mark at any support and their requisites for more consistent visual perception. The grid, mesh construction or construction of grids, in essence, are exactly the same, however, there are several ways of working with this tool, for example: Editorials grids, the grids for web and grids used in construction symbols, logos, pictograms - these, the best known and called constructive meshes or building grids.

This technique aids in clarity, organization and ease of distinction between different information in the brand, both at the time of development, as after the completion helping the user to better understand the image that is presented there. There are a number grid structures, but the most used for the development mark is modular, which allows finer control of the work and is composed of a combination of columns that can organize content space in small portions.

5 Analyze

In order to demonstrate the importance of gestalt and the grid, were captured in the Brazilian market a total of 50 brands that were subjected to a form of analysis that made it possible to check the attributes of the gestalt and as the grid influences the pregnancy of the way this presents to the user.

In the analysis a standard grid mesh was inserted in all brands to check the composition and organization of the visual elements. It was determined a dimensional standard setting it always in the middle both upper and lateral brand analyzes of thus becomes possible to verify the existence output lines or visual elements that do not fit the overall composition of the brand and is classified as existing or not. This way we could question whether it has been used a grid in the development of the project, or if this was respected.

Analyzing the composition, it is possible to see how the whole first mark evaluating the amount of color available to it and then measuring the level of pregnancy of the form, which is another Gestalt laws. Thus it is possible to analyze the whole mark, or more symbol logo, which binds to visual ergonomics items discussed in typography. Regarding the pregnancy of the way, it was decided by an analysis bar, like the one made in the typography, where an increasing scale in the part one {1} has been taken by very bad and the five {5} was used for great.

In gestalt, the first three laws are list that appears in the symbol of the brand, it is already integrated it or just typography. Colors, quantified - the different colors that appear also expressed as percentages. The symbol observe if there was one or not and if it was integrated into the set, also expressed as a percentage. Finally the pregnance shape in percentage. In Gestalt, the laws that prevail in relation to the symbols of the marks are in descending order closure, similarity, unity, unification and continuity, segregation and proximity (Table 1).

Table 1. Brand analysis results by gestalt and grid construction

Brand analysis results by gestalt and grid construction						
Unification	Unity	Similarity	Closure	Continuity	Proximity	Segregation
25	19	27	37	19	10	13
Pregnance form					Total	
1	2	3	4	5	150	
0	0	2	24	74		

In the table above, you can see the comparative result of all brands obtained and analyzed. The overall results presented here are of utmost importance to understand how is treated the relevance of each item of the brand for its development. In Gestalt, the laws that prevail in relation to the symbols of the marks are in descending order closure, similarity, unity, unity and continuity, segregation and proximity. In pregnance form, is demonstrated that 74 % were considered of great understanding and fixation of the mark, they were concerned that use of the grid, as they showed an Locks, and to organize the elements in order to facilitate the understanding and organize visual reading.

6 Conclusive Notes

The market needs has become the designer work a more arduous and quick task, reducing project time some steps are left out causing simple mistakes that can result in an incomprehensible design or misunderstood by the end user. Studies about the development should have the objective of facilitating and assisting new professionals with the aid of technical development and validation of such graphic designs, that is, set the client briefing connection and the end user.

The analysis shows that brands that reach high points regarding the pregnancy of the form used the grid to organize the forms present in the brand so as not to allow the observer looking exhaust drawing below. The use of "Lock" and "Unification", Gestalt items that appear in more regarding Gestalt analysis, shows the concern that there are no elements more than necessary for the understanding of the way, being less used the "segregation" since this creates intuit elements than necessary in understanding mark.

The techniques of Gestalt and the building grid, when applied to developed-ment marks, assist in the correct use of spaces and forms which enables the reduction of errors in the completion and submission of the project. New workers can be guided by specific methods and image correction techniques, so there is greater precision in project development, correcting and directing the attributes that the client expects to spend for the user.

References

1. Cybis, W.A., Betiol, A.H., Faust, R.: Ergonomia e Usabilidade – Conhecimentos, Métodos e Aplicações. Novatec Editora, São Paulo (2007)
2. Wogalter, M.S. Dejoy, D.M., Laughery, K.R.: Organizing theoretical framework: a consolidated communication-human information processing (C-HIP) model. In: Wogalter M.S., Dejoy D.M., Laughery, K.R. (eds.) Warning and Risk Communication. Taylor & Francis, Abington (1999)
3. Costa, J.A.: Imagem da Marca, Um Fenômeno Social. Editora Rosari, São Paulo (2008)
4. Wheller, A.: Design de Identidade da Marca. Editora Bookman, Porto Alegre (2009)
5. Peón, M.L.: Sistemas de Identidade Visual. Editora 2AB, Rio de Janeiro (2008)
6. Arnheim, R.: Arte & percepção Visual: Uma Psicologia da Visão Criadora. Pioneira, 13 ed., São Paulo (2000)
7. Gomes Filho, J.: Gestalt do Objeto: Sistema de Leitura Visual da Forma. Escrituras Editora, São Paulo (2000)
8. Tondreau, B.: Criar Grids: 100 Fundamentos de Layout. Tradução Luciano Cardinali. Editora Blucher, São Paulo (2009)

Change of Government R&D in HCI Categories in Korea

Seung-Kyu Yi(✉)

Office of Strategic Foresight, Korea Institute of S&T Evaluation and Planning (KISTEP), Seoul, South Korea
skyist@kistep.re.kr

Abstract. As the convergence between machine/electronics and humanities/biology is increasing, HCI is expected to become a significant trend in terms of both technology and socio-economy in the future. The aim of this paper is to briefly illustrate the growing importance of government R&D in Korea as a high R&D intensity country. The R&D spending scale of HCI was examined from 2009 until 2013. In addition, changes of the research characteristics were analyzed in terms of different indices, such as research and experimental development stages, the type of research-conducting agent, a classification in terms of 6 kinds of technologies (6T), and socio-economic objectives of research. In this study, HCI related categories were carefully selected using the Korean national classification system of science and technology. Through empirical evidence, this study will provide practical implications for future HCI technologies in terms of government R&D strategy.

Keywords: Korea · Government R&D · S&T classification system · R&D spending on HCI

1 Introduction

HCI (Human Computer Interaction) is increasing in importance from a social view as well as a technological view. This is partly due to its representative role in fusion research. Fusion research is a prominent characteristic of advanced science technology. While "humans" and "computers" were seen as very distant from each other, fusion research examines the interactions between these two spheres. In its initial stage fusion research focused mainly on the combination and connection of fairly similar areas. As fusion research became more mature, however, it started to also examine the combinations of and connections between very different areas. As a result, research in HCI areas that were characterized by a high level of qualitative difficulty became more and more active – signifying an increase in the standard of fusion research. From a social point of view, HCI's importance can be explained through its relevance to future trends which are evoked by technological and social change. Among the recent key-trends that impact the future "IoT (Internet of Things)" and "Hyper-connected Society" are the most prominently mentioned. HCI has connected two spheres that were traditionally cut off from each other, humans and machines, and recognized the impact that they have on each other. Thus, it can be said that HCI is a core element of future society.

C. Stephanidis (Ed.): HCII 2015 Posters, Part II, CCIS 529, pp. 192–197, 2015.
DOI: 10.1007/978-3-319-21383-5_33

The importance of fusion research in Korea's national research and development policies is steadily increasing. In 2008, the Korean government introduced "Fundamental plans for the development of national fusion technology ('09–'13)". In 2014, it took another step by creating the "Fusion technology strategy for realizing a creative economy ('14–'18)". Considering that fusion research is a prominent field, Korea's investments in HCI research and development can be expected to have increased after 2009. The "Fundamental plans for the development of national fusion technology ('09–'13)" actually included the strengthening of support fusion technology and humanities/culture/arts etc. as one main strategy. Moreover, it is likely that also the research characteristics have changed in a way that the research and development has sped up and the research contents reflect the needs of society.

2 Approach

In order to examine the change of HCI in Korea's national research and development, research spending scale and characteristics of HCI processes at the starting point of the "Fundamental plans for the development of national fusion technology ('09–'13)" in 2009 were compared to those related to the national research and development undertaking in 2013. Data is annually provided by the Ministry of Science, ICT and Future Planning in their "Governmental R&D survey and analysis" and was also used for the purpose of this study. This data includes the contents and research funds as well as other diverse information about all national research and development processes. While in 2009, the number of research subjects amounted to 39,565, by 2013 it had risen to 50.865. The Korean national standard classification system on science and technology was used to find out which of these subjects were related to HCI. This classification system is organized into 6 fields, 33 categories, 369 divisions and 2,899 sections. Categories that were related to "Humans" and "Computers" were analyzed one by one and those that contained research subjects related to HCI were selected. As can be seen in the table below, 7 categories were found to be related to "Humans", and 2 categories were selected for their relation to "Computers" (Table 1).

Table 1. HCI related categories from the Korean national standard classification system on S&T

Field		category
Human	H. Humanities	HA. History/Archeology
		HB. Philosophy/Religion
		HC. Linguistics
		HD. Literature
		HE. Culture/Arts/Sports
	O. Human Science and Technologies	OA. Brain Sciences
		OB. Cognitive/Emotion & Sensibility Sciences
Computer	E. Engineering	ED. Electricity and Electronics
		EE. Information/Communication

The importance of HCI and its change in characteristics was analyzed by comparing HCI research from 2013 to the selected subjects from 2009. To assess HCI's importance the scale of research funds was analyzed. Furthermore, the rate of increase of all national research and development undertakings as well as that of HCI related funds were compared. Certain studies also analyzed the degree of research maturity, the performance, the technological field, and the research objective. The table below summarizes the relevant indices and contents (Table 2).

Table 2. List of Indices analyzed

View	Index	Contents
Importance	R&D Spending	Governmental R&D
Technological Maturity	R&D Stage	Basic research/ Applied research / Experimental development
	Technology life cycle	Introduction / Growth / Maturity / Decline
Actor	Type of research-conducting agent	University / Industry / GRI ; Government Related Institute
Technological field	Classification in terms of 6 kinds of technologies (6T)	IT (information) / BT (biology) / NT (nano) / CT (culture) / ET (environment) / ST (space)
Purpose	Socio-economic objective	13 categories in Public sector and 20 categories in industry

3 Results

3.1 Importance in Governmental R&D: R&D Spending

The result of comparing analysis shows that research in HCI categories increased more than 4 times faster than entire government R&D during a five-year period. Especially growth rate of research spending of HCI is 2 times higher than that of the entire multi-disciplinary research. This means importance of HCI is growing in government R&D and technologies in the future (Table 3).

Table 3. Comparing R&D spending on HCI categories (2009 vs 2013)

(USD, Million $)*	2009	2013	CAGR(%)
R&D in HCI categories	6.70	24.02	**37.62**
Multi-disciplinary R&D	1,486.16	2,994.32	**19.14**
Government R&D	11,337.03	15,445.92	**8.04**

*adapted annual average exchange rate in 2013 year (Korea Won (KW) to USD)

3.2 Characteristics of R&D

The result of comparison analysis in terms of technological maturity shows that relative ratio of the basic research subject increased by about 30 %. Also research in the "other stage" which means unclassified or across multi stage increased by 32.5 % and relative ratio of research in the introduction and growth stage decreased but still accounted for over 90 % except for "other stage". This means new research of complex technologies across different TLC stage increased (Table 4).

Table 4. Comparing ratio of research subjects in HCI categories by R&D stage and TLC (2009 vs 2013)

R&D stage	2009	2013	comparison	TLC stage	2009	2013	comparison
Basic research	40.9%	70.4%	**29.5% ↑**	**Introduction**	65.9%	50.9%	15.0% ↓
Applied research	34.1%	13.9%	20.2% ↓	**Growth**	29.5%	11.1%	18.4% ↓
Experimental development	25.0%	13.9%	11.1% ↓	**Maturity**	-	0.9%	0.9% ↑
Other	-	1.8%	1.8% ↑	**Decline**	-	-	-
				Other	4.5%	37%	**32.5% ↑**

The result of comparison analysis in terms of actor shows that relative ratio of research by university decreased, but still highest, and relative ratio of research by industry increased. This means diversity of agent conducting HCI R&D increased (Table 5).

Table 5. Comparing research-conducting agent of R&D on HCI categories (2009 vs 2013)

Conducting agent	2009	2013	comparison
University	70.1%	43.2%	**26.9% ↓**
GRI	22.1%	19.0%	**3.1% ↓**
Industry	5.7%	16.7%	**11.0% ↑**
Other	2.1%	21.0%	**18.9% ↑**

The result of comparison analysis in terms of technological field, namely 6T, shows that research in field of IT (Information tech.) decreased and CT (Culture tech.) increased (Table 6).

The result of comparison analysis in terms of research purpose shows that diversity of purpose of HCI R&D increased from 6 kinds in 2009 to 9 kinds in 2013. Ratio of research for industrial purpose was maintained highest. Among research for "industrial production and technology", main industries are "Electronic components, computer, video, sound and communication equipment (15.9 %('09) → 19.4 %('13)), "Publishing,

Table 6. Comparing technological field of R&D on HCI categories (2009 vs 2013)

6T	2009	2013	comparison	6T	2009	2013	comparison
BT	11.4%	10.2%	1.2% ↓	**CT**	18.2%	27.8%	**9.6% ↑**
IT	65.9%	54.6%	11.3% ↓	**ET, ST**	-		
NT	-	1.9%	1.9% ↑	**Other**	4.5%	5.6%	1.1% ↑

Table 7. Comparing socio-economic objective of R&D on HCI categories (2009 vs 2013)

Socio-economic objective of R&D	2009	2013	Comparison
Exploration and exploitation of the Earth	-	-	-
Environment	-	-	-
Exploration and exploitation of space	-	-	-
Transport, telecommunication and other infrastructures	-	0.9	0.9% ↑
Energy	-	-	-
Health	13.6	4.6	9.0% ↓
Agriculture	4.5	-	4.5% ↓
Education	-	0.9	0.9% ↑
Culture, recreation, religion and mass media	4.5	6.5	2.0% ↑
Political and social systems, structures and processes	-	3.7	3.7% ↑
General advancement of knowledge	11.4	5.6	5.8% ↓
Defense	-	-	-
Other public purpose	2.3	12.0	9.7% ↑
Industrial production and technology	63.7	63.0	0.7% ↓
Other Industrial purpose	-	2.8	2.8% ↑

video, broadcast communications and information services (18.2 % → 18.5 %)", "Professional scientific and technical services (6.8 % → 3.9 %)", "Arts, sports and recreation related services (4.5 % → 2.8 %)", "Medical, precision and optical instruments and watches (6.8 % → 2.8 %). Also, "Healthcare and social welfare services (2.8 % in '13)", "Education services (1.9 % in '13)", "Vehicles and transport equipment (0.9 % in '13) are newly emerged purposes (Table 7).

4 Conclusion

The change in scale of HCI related research has increased HCI's importance in Korea's national research and development and will strengthen HCI's role in future. It also provides implications for the further promotion of policies. Considering the high growth rate of the scale of HCI research funds, it becomes clear that HCI's relative importance to Korea's national research and development will increase rapidly.

Especially relative ratio of basic research as well as new and complex research carried out by universities as well as industries has been high or increased. This means that the base of research systems have been strengthen and that it is very probably that HCI research will consistently be expanded. As a consequence, policies that efficiently create and spread research outcomes have become essential. This further means that the CT area among 6T has gained great relative importance among the characteristics of the main technological field. As regards the economic and social objectives of research, this study showed that the objectives of the public sector as well as the industrial sector are becoming more and more diversified. These changes demonstrate that there's a possibility for HCI to become widely used in society which farther means that it is important to establish a legal framework, and introduce policies to develop the infrastructure that is needed for such a development. Last but not least, from an industrial perspective it is necessary to persistently work on the needed system and monitor the environmental changes of industries that have emerged as main fields of application.

References

1. National S&T Commission. Governmental R&D survey and analysis in FY2009 (written in Korean), Oct 2010
2. The Ministry of Science, ICT and Future Planning. Governmental R&D survey and analysis in FY2013, Aug 2014
3. National Science and Technology Information Service. http://www.ntis.go.kr

Learning Technologies

Usability of Mobile Applications in Saudi Higher Education: An Exploratory Study

Nada Al-Wabil(✉)

Department of Information Technology,
Institute of Public Administration, Riyadh, Saudi Arabia
wabiln@ipa.edu.sa

Abstract. This paper reports on a comprehensive survey of mobile applications offered by higher education institutions in Saudi Arabia. In this study, we examine the accessibility, User Experience (UX) design, and usability of services offered by these applications. In recent years, research has shown growing trends in mobile application adoption and usage in the context of higher education in Saudi Arabia. Evidence from the local context suggests that mobile applications have potential to increase retention of students, enhance teaching and learning, and facilitate the provision of services. Our understanding of mobile application services offered by public and private higher education institutions in Saudi Arabia is inadequate. Therefore, we present a synthesis of mobile applications and a categorization of types, platforms, target users, and examine their usability. The study included mobile applications and services offered by twenty six public universities and nine private universities. Design implications of our usability review for these mobile applications that are offered by higher education institutes for students, faculty and administration are discussed.

Keywords: E-Learning · Mobile applications · Arabic interface · Saudi Arabia

1 Introduction

Recent advances in mobile technologies have accelerated the adoption of technology in higher education. Evidence, from the local context of Saudi Arabia, suggests that mobile applications have potential to increase retention of students [1], enhance teaching and learning [1–3], [5] and in the provision of services [4]. While HCI research has examined design considerations of Arabic interfaces for systems in higher education, our understanding of design consideration for mobile application services offered by public and private higher education institutions in Saudi Arabia is inadequate.

Universities in Saudi Arabia have evolved [18] from Umm Al-Qura University opening in Makkah al-Mukarramah in 1949, making it the first higher educational institution in the Kingdom of Saudi Arabia, to 35 universities in 2015 [15, 18]. The students' population growth has risen in 2014 to more than 1,300,000 students [17]. The faculty population in Saudi higher education institutions grew to more than 64,000 faculty members in 2014 [17]. Technology services for users in the context of higher

C. Stephanidis (Ed.): HCII 2015 Posters, Part II, CCIS 529, pp. 201–205, 2015.
DOI: 10.1007/978-3-319-21383-5_34

education institutions evolved from traditional web-based registration and enquiry services, to navigation apps indicating innovation in providing services for academic populations. IT infrastructure is also rapidly developing which extends the opportunity for more service accommodation, and integration [10, 19].

This paper reports on a comprehensive survey of mobile applications offered by higher education institutions in Saudi Arabia. In this study, we present a synthesis of mobile applications and a categorization of types, platforms, target users, and examine their usability. We examine the availability, accessibility, User Experience (UX) design, and usability of services offered by these applications.

The paper is structured as follows. The following section describes the diffusion of mobile applications in higher education. Section 3 investigates the usability and accessibility of these apps by surveying the literature reporting on applications in the context of study. We conclude in Sect. 4 with a summary of insights gained from the exploratory study and directions for future research.

2 Diffusion of Mobile Applications in Public and Private Universities in Saudi Arabia: Case Study

In this study, we examined the mobile applications available on iOS and Android platforms for 35 universities in Saudi Arabia. Preliminary findings show that public universities have the lead in providing mobile applications when compared to private universities in Saudi Arabia as evident in Tables 1 and 2. Notably, some applications are available online for institution-specific services (e.g. course-related services or educational technology applications for specific courses) but were not linked to the institution and thus were not included in the list.

Table 1. Overview of mobile applications in public universities

University name	iOS apps	Android apps
King Abdullah University of Science and Technology	2	2
Umm Al-Qura University	1	3
Islamic University	2	2
Al-Imam Mohammad Ibn Saud Islamic University	2	4
King Saud University	9	17
King Abdulaziz University	3	16
King Fahd University of Petroleum and Minerals	2	2
King Faisal University	2	9
King Khalid University	5	6
Qassim University	3	3
Taibah University	2	4
Taif University	0	2
University of Ha'il	1	1
Jazan University	1	1

(Continued)

Table 1. (*Continued*)

University name	iOS apps	Android apps
Al Jouf University	1	1
Al Baha University	0	2
University of Tabuk	3	3
Najran University	0	2
Northern Borders University	1	7
Princess Nora bint Abdulrahman University	1	6
King Saud bin Abdulaziz University for Health Sciences	0	2
University of Dammam	1	3
Shagra University	0	0
Salman Bin Abdulaziz University	1	5
Almajmaah University	2	2
Saudi Electronic University	0	3

Table 2. Overview of mobile applications in private universities

University name	iOS apps	Android apps
Prince Sultan University	0	0
Effat University	1	1
Arab Open University	2	2
University of Buisness and Technology	0	1
Fahad Bin Sultan University	0	0
Prince Mohammad Bin Fahd University	0	1
Alfaisal University	1	1
Al Yamamah University	3	3
Dar Al Uloom University	0	1

As shown in Table 2, private universities have been lagging behind in terms of applications offered by the institutions. The emphasis is often more on teaching than research and development in private institutions, in addition to the fact that student and faculty populations of private institutions is smaller when compared to the public universities in this context of study.

While the majority of the mobile applications, that are available in the public domain, provide services related to the administrative and learning contexts of higher education institutions, some applications were designed for specific research contexts.

3 Mobile Applications: Design Considerations

Research on examining usability and accessibility in the context of higher education services have investigated visual design, user acceptance, and compliance with standards [13, 14]. In the Arab region, the issues of cultural design aspects relevant for usability and accessibility have been reported in recent years [9, 11–13]. However, these interfaces were not in the context of systems developed for users in higher education apart from the university website usability survey of [13]. Within the context of Saudi Arabia, very few studies have examined interfaces and mobile services [7, 8, 16] and even fewer in the context of higher education. For example, the usability evaluation study of [6] examined e-government and reported the lack of accessibility compliance. Overall, the research examining higher education is relatively scarce. One example is a recent study examining website design in universities [15]; however the review did not focus on mobile applications which have specific design requirements that are not yet examined and more work needs to be done in this area. Design considerations for these apps is beyond visual design considerations but actually extends to the functionality and utility provided for an academic population on the go. Design considerations specific to the local context are alignment for bilingual interfaces and socio-cultural factors.

4 Conclusion

Trends and challenges in the provision of technology-enabled learning and technology-facilitated services in higher education are increasingly highlighted to address the issues hindering diffusion of innovations in higher education. Mobile technologies designed for teaching, learning, services and research resources that reside in the public domain of higher education institutions have impact on the momentum of technology integration in the contexts of education. The preliminary findings reported in this study, indicate patterns of diffusion of mobile application in the contexts of learning and services in higher education. Further work examines the specific usability and accessibility issues in the design of these mobile application with a focus on the socio-cultural factors in the interaction design for these applications in our local context.

References

1. Al-Fahad, F.: Students' attitudes and perceptions towards the effectiveness of mobile learning in King Saud University. Turkish Online J. Educ. Technol. TOJET **8**(2) Article 10 (2009)
2. AlMegren, A.: Status of e-learning at several major universities in Saudi Arabia. In: Proceedings of World Conference on e-Learning in Corporate, Government, Healthcare, and Higher Education 2011, pp. 1022–1028. AACE, Chesapeake, VA (2011)
3. Al-Harbi, K.: e-Learning in the Saudi tertiary education: potential and challenges. J. Appl. Comput. Inform. **9**(1), 31–46 (2011)
4. Alshwaier, A., Youssef, A., Emam, A.: A new trend for e-learning in KSA using educational clouds. Adv. Comput. Int. J. (ACIJ) **3**(1), 81–97 (2012)
5. Nassoura, A.: Students acceptance of mobile learning for higher education in Saudi Arabia. Int. J. Learn. Manag. Syst. **1**(1), 1–9 (2013)

6. Al-Faries, A., Al-Khalifa, H.S., Al-Razgan, M.S., Al-Duwais, M.: Evaluating the accessibility and usability of top Saudi e-government services. In: Janowski, T., Holm, J., Estevez, E. (eds.) Proceedings of the 7th International Conference on Theory and Practice of Electronic Governance (ICEGOV 2013), pp. 60–63. ACM, New York (2013)
7. Al-Nuaim, H.: An evaluation framework for Saudi e-government. J. e-Gov. Stud. Best Pract. **2011**, 12 (2011). doi:10.5171/2011.820912, Article ID 820912
8. AL-Zuabi, H.F., AL-Shaikhli, I.F.: Evaluation of usability problems of labor portal in Saudi Arabia. Int. J. Adv. Comput. Sci. Inf. Technol. (IJACSIT) **2**(1), 14–25 (2013)
9. Marcus, A., Gould, E., Wigham, L.: Culture-centered design: culture audit of screen designs for educational software in Saudi Arabia. In: Patrick Rau, P.L. (ed.) IDGD 2011. LNCS, vol. 6775, pp. 85–93. Springer, Heidelberg (2011)
10. Abdallah, S., Albadri, F.: A perspective on ICT diffusion in the Arab region. In: Abdallah, S., Albadri, F. (eds.) ICT Acceptance, Investment and Organization: Cultural Practices and Values in the Arab World, pp. 1–15. Information Science Reference, Hershey (2011)
11. Khashman, N., Ménard, E.: A study of cultural reflection in Egyptian government websites. In: Marcus, A. (ed.) DUXU 2014, Part II. LNCS, vol. 8518, pp. 139–147. Springer, Heidelberg (2014)
12. Khashman, N., Large, A.: Measuring cultural markers in Arabic government websites using Hofstede's cultural dimensions. In: Marcus, A. (ed.) HCII 2011 and DUXU 2011, Part II. LNCS, vol. 6770, pp. 431–439. Springer, Heidelberg (2011)
13. Marcus, A., Hamoodi, S.: The impact of culture on the design of Arabic websites. In: Aykin, N. (ed.) IDGD 2009. LNCS, vol. 5623, pp. 386–394. Springer, Heidelberg (2009)
14. Alotaibi, M.B.: Assessing the usability of university websites in Saudi Arabia: a heuristic evaluation approach. In: Proceedings of the 2013 10th International Conference on Information Technology: New Generations (ITNG 2013), pp. 138–142. IEEE Computer Society, Washington, D.C. doi:10.1109/ITNG.2013.26. http://dx.doi.org/10.1109/ITNG.2013.26 (2013)
15. MOHE: Academic institutions in Saudi Arabia: a statistical report. http://statistics.mohe.gov.sa/DCFiles/Universities-Guide.pdf
16. Alotaibi, M.B.: Determinants of mobile service acceptance in Saudi Arabia: a revised UTAUT model. Int. J. E-Services Mob. Appl. **5**(3), 43–61 (2013). doi:10.4018/jesma.2013070103 http://dx.doi.org/10.4018/jesma.2013070103
17. MOE: Universities Statistics. http://he.moe.gov.sa/AR/MINISTRY/DEPUTY-MINISTRY-FOR-PLANNING-AND-INFORMATION-AFFAIRS/HESC/UNIVERSITIES-STATISTICS/Pages/default.aspx
18. MOHE: Saudi Arabian Universities. http://mohe.gov.sa/en/Ministry/General-administration-for-Public-relations/BooksList/book8eng.pdf
19. CITC: ICT Indicators Report, End of Q2 2014. http://www.citc.gov.sa/English/Reportsandstudies/Indicators/Indicators%20of%20Communications%20and%20Information%20Techn/ICT%20Indicators%202014%20-%20Q2%20-%20Analysis%20Report_Final.pdf

On-the-fly Notes: Instructor to Student Transfer of In-Class Produced Notes

Nancy Alajarmeh(✉)

Department of Computer and Information Technology,
Tafila Technical University, Tafila 179-16110, Jordan
najarmeh@ttu.edu.jo

Abstract. This paper introduces a system that utilizes the capabilities of smart devices to create and transfer in-class made notes to the cloud in a real time manner. This system comes as an extension to the services made by traditional Learning Management Systems (LMS). The described system, used alone or joined with any LMS, facilitates immediate sharing and access to the notes produced in-class and it allows students to view these notes later at their convenience.

Keywords: E-learning · Education · Instruction · Class notes · Smart devices · Learning management systems · Blended instruction

1 Introduction

The popularity and widespread of handheld smart devices, along with the recent reliability and affordable prices of wireless networks, made the utilization of these resources in education a wise act [2]. The reliance on technology in education emerged because of the need to obtain flexible content that is easier to produce, demonstrate, transform, share, access, and reproduce [1]. The emergence of what is called "e-learning" applications has dramatically contributed to education and this gives justification to those governments, in many parts of the world, that monitor to a wide extent the spreading of e-learning resources [2, 6].

The spread of e-learning in the past twenty years is evident. With a growth rate exceeded the expectations in 2013, the growing market of e-learning for the next few years is estimated to even increase by 7.6 % growth rate contributing a revenue of $51.5 billion by the year 2016 [2].

In a large research context, e-learning has proven efficiency in achieving quality results within short time [2, 4]. A massive research work has concluded an equivalent efficiency of online platforms as a medium to deliver instruction compared to traditional methods known from centuries [1]. These promising findings have been appealing to researchers to expand in the e-learning field.

1.1 Learning Management Systems

Recent trends in education have emphasized both web-based (i.e., pure e-learning) instruction and blended (i.e., hybrid) instruction [5]. Hybrid instruction, relying on both

C. Stephanidis (Ed.): HCII 2015 Posters, Part II, CCIS 529, pp. 206–211, 2015.
DOI: 10.1007/978-3-319-21383-5_35

traditional and web-based instruction, has evidently exceeded the advantages gained from each of its major components when taken alone. A significant contribution that came to support blended instruction is the advent of LMSs, also referred to as online learning platforms or Virtual Learning Environments (VLE), to which the success of e-learning is accredited [4].

An LMS is web-based software that manages learning resources and their users: instructors and learners. LMSs support in-class teaching by facilitating the creation, delivery and management of learning resources [3, 5]. Tracking the learner's performance is provided by LMSs via different means, such as online auto-assessment and scores recording. Today, LMSs are widely used in thousands of universities and institutions around the world for making courses and related learning resources available at the learner's best convenience, known as "anywhere anytime" access, and for promoting collaboration among learners and their instructors [5].

While LMSs are widely used nowadays, they are still at a primitive stage of utilization in terms of the availability of informal class instruction, for example extra explanations written on board. Several studies revealed limitation in the LMS capabilities of content creation (i.e., transfer of verbal and hand-written instruction that take place in class) [3]. Interestingly, issues such as capability of integration with external systems are relatively gaining higher significance than adding new features to any LMS [3]. The described system in this paper aims at facilitating in-class creation of notes and real-time transfer of those notes to the cloud. The notes are kept either by utilizing the capabilities of the existing (i.e., used) LMS or by giving each instructor a space to which the notes are uploaded and shared with students.

2 Bring Your Own Device

The era we live in is characterized as high in tech and smart devices. The world is now shifting towards what is called "Bring Your Own Device" (BYOD) [2]. BYOD outlines a trend in which individuals carry their own mobile devices, mainly capable smart phones and tablets, to wherever they go for productivity. Such trend, in conjunction with cloud services, exhibits flexibility in terms of remote accessing and accomplishing tasks. This trend covers a wide range of daily applications such as access to media, entertainment, social networks and education.

The advent of BYOD trend is attributed to the affordable prices of hand-held smart devices and the available cloud services. The new generations of smart devices are getting very popular with high demand from all age categories of users. Consequently, this trend is expected to result in less Personal Computers (PC) and more hand held smart devices. To support this argument, it has been reported that the number of PCs is expected to shrink from 28.7 % in 2013 into 13 % in 2017 [2]. In the meantime, the spread of tablets is expected to increase from 11.8 % in the year 2013 to reach 16.5 % by the year 2017 [2]. A recent study has shown that the time spent on smart mobile apps has exceeded the time spent on web browsing. Numbers have revealed tablets to be the mostly used mobile device among the K-12 sector [2].

2.1 Teaching in the BYOD Era

Teaching methods have been improving along years. Not only teaching styles but also the forms information delivered to students have always varied from time to time. While for many recent years professors in universities have relied on PCs inside classes to present their material, it is time to follow the BYOD trend and switch to more convenient and light-weight smart devices for instruction.

Hand-held smart devices such as large-screen smart phones and tablets support the use of digital pens (i.e., stylus) for interaction and user input. These portable devices can be used in presenting information as shown in Fig. 1, and thus instructors may rely in explaining the material on using them instead of the commonly used whiteboards. Smart devices facilitate two important tasks: recording and sharing information being presented to students in class. By using these smart devices, the content presented in class is recorded and archived for students' use at their convenience.

3 On-the-fly Notes Design

On-the-fly Notes system, introduced in this paper, aims at facilitating real-time transfer of the notes produced in class by instructors. The system utilizes either large-screen smart phones or tablets to create notes while instructing. Simultaneously, the notes are viewed on a larger board using a projector as shown in Fig. 1. These notes, captured as snapshots, are immediately transferred to the cloud, where students can always access anytime and anywhere.

Apart from being a medium to produce, demonstrate, share, and reproduce notes, On-the-fly Notes has more to offer. On the one hand, students will not need to write notes after their instructors. This will eliminate the distraction and loss of valuable instructed notes that occur when a student tries to coordinate between following the presented notes and writing them on a notebook. On the other hand, On-the-fly Notes saves a backup for class notes. This backup can be accessed anytime from anywhere by both instructors and students.

The On-the-fly Notes system comprises two modules: a web application and an android application. The android application is mainly used by instructors. The instructor dashboard in the android application contains three main components for each class (i.e., subject) he/she teaches: Books, Note Board, and LineDrive. The Books component, shown in Fig. 2, refers to the books and supplemental material that belong to the subject. The content of this component is uploaded by the instructor.

The Note Board component, shown in Fig. 3, refers to the white space given to the instructor as a whiteboard for making notes in class. The Note Board is projected on screen to students in the class time as seen in Fig. 4. The same content viewed on screen is captured as snapshots and transferred to the On-the-fly Notes cloud or to the used LMS. Students enrolled in that subject can access this content at their convenience. The LineDrive refers to the captured snapshots produced in class using the Note Board component. The LineDrive can be seen as a notebook of the instructor notes. The instructor has full control to modify the content by adding or deleting certain snapshots. The LineDrive and the Books components are what students can access for

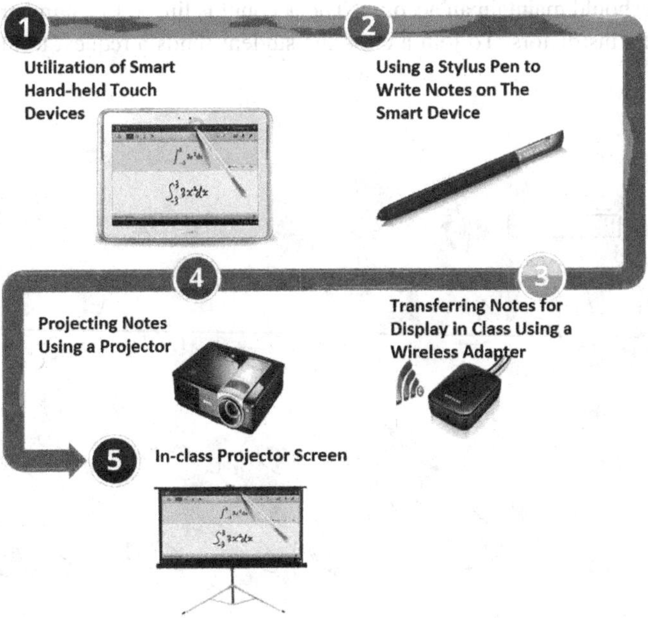

Fig. 1. The hardware needed to utilize a hand-held device for in-class instruction

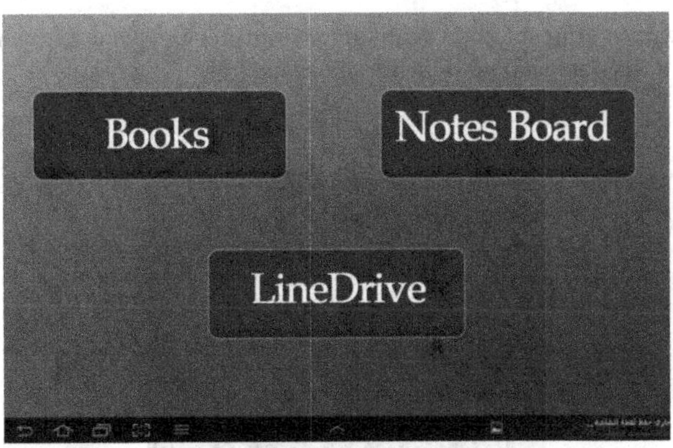

Fig. 2. The android application for instructors has three components: books, notes board, and linedrive.

each subject they are enrolled in. Access to these components can be using the android application or the web application.

The web application module of the On-the-fly Notes system can be used by both instructors and students. The instructor account can be set up to send all generated snapshots to an LMS. The instructor can manage all subject resources using his/her account through the web application. Students use the web application for joining subjects and accessing resources uploaded by instructors for those subjects.

Each student should maintain an account. The account is linked to a number of subjects taught by their instructors. To join a class the student sends a request to the instructor account.

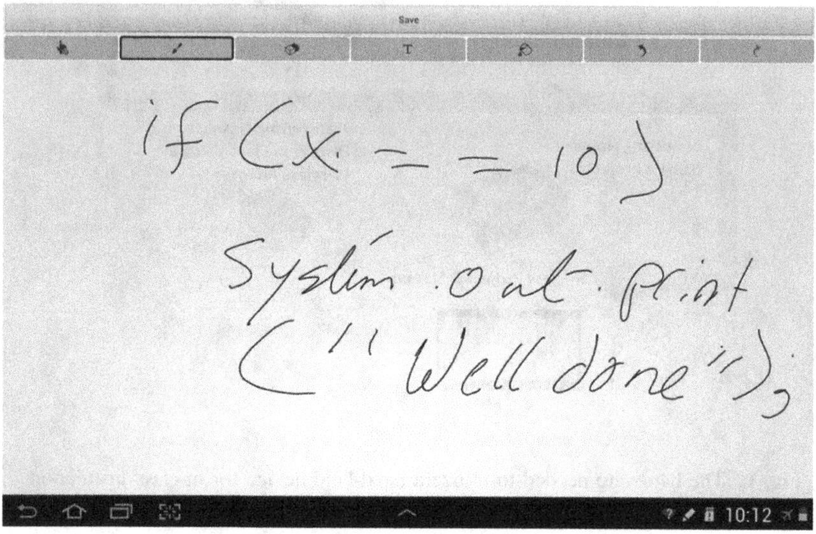

Fig. 3 A script written using the notes board in the instructor android application. This script is then captured as a snapshot and transferred to the cloud.

Fig. 4. Using the note board for in-class instruction and projecting its content on screen

References

1. Randall, B., Sweetin, J., Steinbeiser, D.: Learning Management System Feasibility Study Part II of the Open Source Collaborative Moodle Assessment Report (2010)
2. E-Learning Market Trends and Forecast 2014-2016 Report. Docebo (2014). http://www.docebo.com/landing/learning-management-system/elearning-market-trends-and-forecast-2014-2016-docebo-report.php
3. Martin, F.: Blackboard as the learning management system of a computer literacy course. MERLOT J. Online Learn. Teach. **4**(2), 138–145 (2008)
4. Paulsen, M.F.: Experiences with learning management systems in 113 European Institutions. Educ. Technol. Soc. **6**(4), 134–148 (2003). http://ifets.ieee.org/periodical/6_4/13.pdf
5. Smits, D., De Bra, P.: GALE: a highly extensible adaptive hypermedia engine. In: Proceedings of ACM-CHH, pp. 63–72 (2011)
6. Wells P., Fieger, P., deLange, P.: Integrating a virtual learning environment into a second year accounting course: determinants of overall student perception. In: Proceedings of the AAA Annual Meeting, San Francisco (2005)

Facebook as a Learning Tool in Formal Learning Process

Alaeddin M.H. Alawawdeh(✉) and Stewart James Kowalski

Department of Computer and Media Technology, Gjøvik University College, Gjøvik, Norway
alaeddin.a@gmail.com, stewart.kowalski@hig.no

Abstract. Social networks and the huge number of users in worldwide offer great social and business potential. In this research, we aim to find the required features in social networks (Facebook) to enhance it as learning tool. Firstly, we observed the exist Facebook features that can be used in the learning process in comparison with the LMS (Fronter). Afterwards, we propose some required feature in Facebook based on the experiment that we ran on students. Those students had been studying Introduction to Information Security course in the second year of bachelor degree in our university.

Keywords: Facebook · eLearning · Learning tools · Formal learning process

1 Introduction

Learning can be seen as a constructive process where learners build understanding through acquiring knowledge on a scaffolding of meaning [1]. The learning process can occur in three main modes: formal, non-formal and informal learning. Formal learning is an organized learning process through institutions like universities. This type of learning is a systematic process follows the institute regulations and rules, it can be online or offline. The students have to pass an evaluation process to be reward a certification. The learning and the knowledge is restricted to specific subjects through the learning process. Non-formal learning is a learning process organized by a social group. The learning mode is planned and is usually the result of voluntary participation. Informal learning is an unorganized learning process directed and controlled by the learner [2, 3]. In our research, we are focusing on the formal learning mode.

Christopher Whitty and Rachid Anane propose a framework to enhance student engagement with the community through non-formal learning [4]. They used social networks to encourage students to share types of knowledge within the learning process. They implement the framework in a social network to facilitate the social interaction and collaboration between the learners, which gives the possibility for the learner who control his learning process to explore topics outside restricted Learning Management System (LMS) structures.

Other researchers have published work in progress papers about merging social network with LMS's. In the paper published by Caminero et al. "Work in progress: Extending an LMS with social capabilities: Integrating Moodle into Facebook." [5], the

C. Stephanidis (Ed.): HCII 2015 Posters, Part II, CCIS 529, pp. 212–217, 2015.
DOI: 10.1007/978-3-319-21383-5_36

authors proposed the integration of the most used social network (Facebook) with open source learning management system (Moodle) [6, 7]. They are targeting courses, which had distanced learners. Their aim was to increase the social communication between the students to improve the learning process. The authors created an application to give the students the ability to access Moodle through Facebook, also they developed a web service in Moodle accessed by Facebook and used for their ease of implementations. As this is a work in progress paper data is still being collected.

Dabbagh and Kitsantas published the paper "Personal Learning Environments, social media, and self-regulated learning: A natural formula for connecting formal and informal learning." [8]. In this study, they provide a pedagogical framework for using social media to create personal learning environments (PLE) that support students through their regulated learning. That framework contains three levels. The second level is a social interaction and collaboration, where they ask the instructor to encourage students to participate and collaborate in activities through the learning process. They are aiming to encourage the students to self-regulated learning process targeting to help students find a new and better strategies for formal learning.

The above research gives indicators of the potential for using Facebook in formal learning to improve the learning process and communication/connection between students, teacher and the subject materials. In our research, we are seeking to check which features are needed in Facebook to make it usable as a learning tool with or without LMS in the formal learning process.

The rest of the paper is organized as follows. Section 2 describes our with Facebook. Section 3 gives an analysis of the results. Lastly, Sect. 4 concludes the paper.

2 Experiment Setup

This experiment was directed to bachelor degree students who are studying an information security course at our university. They were using both Facebook and an LMS (Fronter) in the course. The professor of the course Nils K. Svendsen created a Facebook group for the course. Firstly, we observed the students interactions and participations with the Facebook group and the LMS during the 10 week course. Afterwards, we published a questionnaire for the students and we collected the data.

3 Result and Analysis

We found that the most of students joined the Facebook group in the same moment they saw the name of the group in the first lecture. In total 87 students or more than 70 % of the total student body interact with Facebook course groups through the duration of the course (Fig. 1).

The questionnaire contained six questions concerning the students' interaction with the LMS (Fronter) and with the Facebook group during the course. Figures 2 and 3 show students' appreciation and use of Facebook compared to Fronter using a Likert scale of 1 to 5 with 5 for strongly agree and 1 for strongly disagreeing with the statement in the questionnaire.

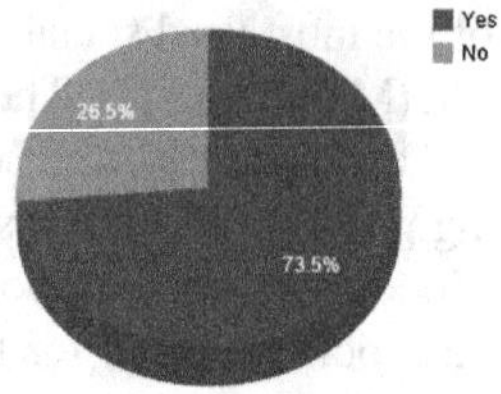

Fig. 1. Students' interaction in the Facebook group of Information security course

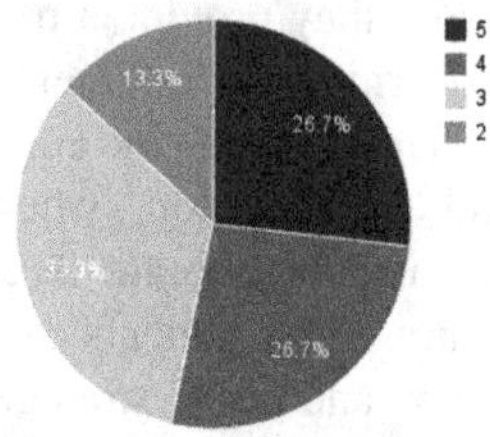

Fig. 2. Facebook easier than Fronter

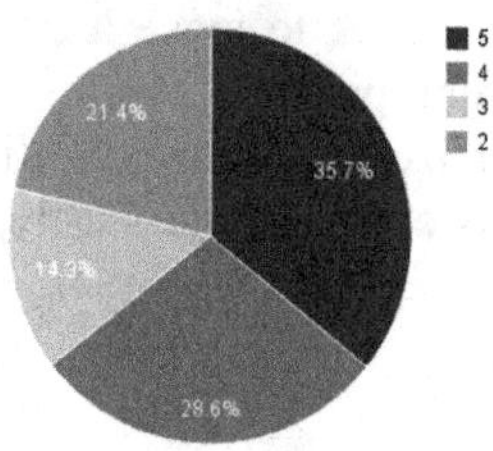

Fig. 3. Facebook better for notification than Fronter.

Figure 4 shows which platform the student used to submit work in the course. Most of the students used LMS (Fronter) to submit. Figure 5 shows that the most of the students did not find it ease submitting tasks in Facebook. The fifth question was about the ease to return and review topics/files through the course using Facebook vs Fronter? As seen in Fig. 6, more than 70 % of the students used Fronter to return and review the course files.

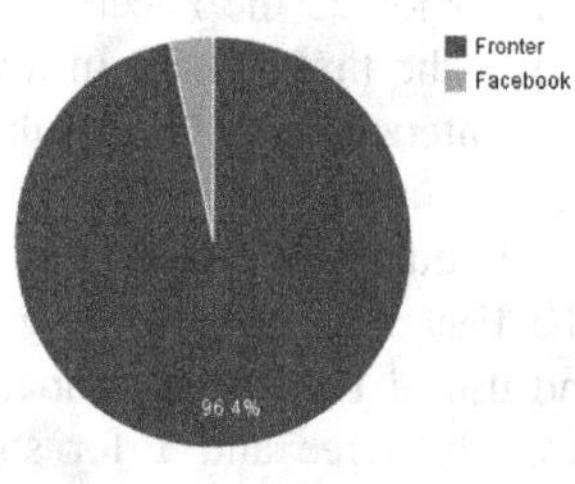

Fig. 4. Which platform to submit.

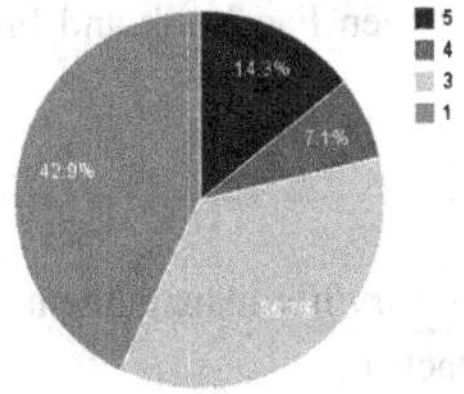

Fig. 5. Facebook easy to submit.

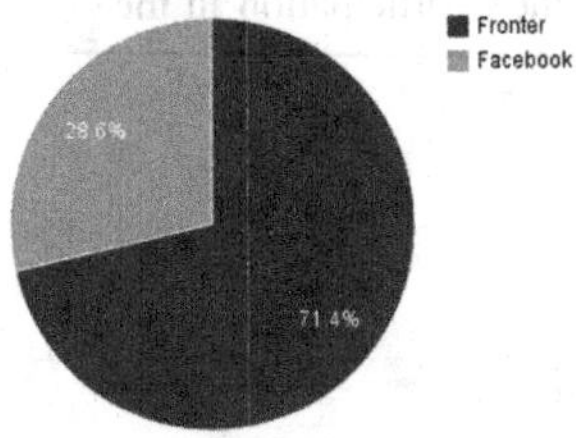

Fig. 6. Return/Review material

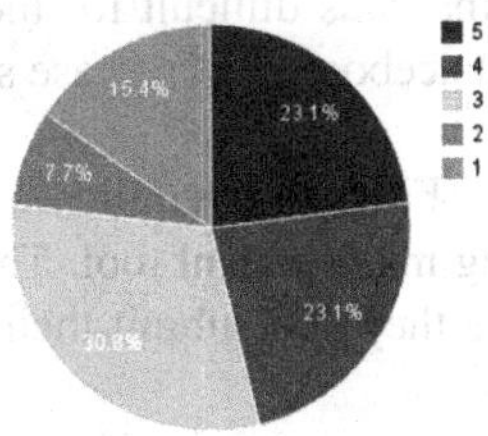

Fig. 7. Facebook vs Fronter easy of use

Question six is: Do you use Facebook more than Fronter forum during the course? Figure 7 shows that it was easier for more than 75 present of the students to use Facebook to discuss and subject matter of the course than the Fronter forum.

Table 1 below is a preliminary list comparing Facebook and Fronter features that can be used to enhance the learning Interaction communication process.

4 Conclusion

This action research has studied the use of Facebook as learning tools and compared it to a traditional learning management system (Fronter). Based on this case study, we found that most of student were more interested to use Facebook to get notifications about the course. Also, they were more often used and preferred Facebook as a forum to discuss the tasks and exercises in the course.

Table 1. Comparison between Facebook and Fronter LMS capabilities

Action	LMS (Fronter)	Facebook
Transfer files to and from teacher	Yes	Yes
Organizing transferred files/file repository/file management	Yes	No
Students receiving tasks from the teacher	Yes	Yes
Giving online exams for students controlled by some period	Yes	No
Forum: capability of having a discussion about appropriate topic	Yes	Yes
Capability of evaluating the student's participation in the forum	Yes	Yes
Evaluate students' exams	Yes	No
Evaluating tasks/homeworks	Yes	Yes
Chat control	Yes	Yes
Check users online	Yes	Yes
Check user participation percentage	Yes	No

In general, we found that Facebook was easier and faster for the students to deal with the course through the learning process, but from analyzing the answer of questions 3, 4 and 5 we found that was difficult for the students to submit tasks and manage course files through the Facebook. In this case study the student found Fronter the easiest method to do that.

The previous results indicate Facebook requires a better and easier file transfer system if is to be used as learning management tool. This feature will help students to deal with clear file system where they can submit their tasks and submit work to the instructor easier.

References

1. Lin, B., Hsieh, C.: Web-based teaching and learner control: a research review. Comput. Educ. **37**(3), 377–386 (2001)
2. Colletta, N.J.: Formal, nonformal, and informal education. Int. Encyclopaedia Adult Educ. Training **2**, 22–27 (1996)
3. Coombs, P.H., Prosser, R.C., Ahmed, M.: New Paths to Learning: For Rural Children and Youth. International Council for Educational Development, New York (1973)
4. Whitty, C., Anane, R.: Social network enhancement for non-formal learning. In: 47th Hawaii International Conference on System Sciences (HICSS), 2014, pp. 1645–1654. IEEE (2014)
5. Caminero, A.C., Ros, S., Robles-Gomez, A., Tobarra, L., Hernandez, R., Pastor, R., Rodriguez-Artacho, M., Cristobal, E.S., Martin, S., Tawfik, M.: Work in progress: extending a LMS with social capabilities: integrating moodle into Facebook. In: Frontiers in Education Conference (FIE), 2012, pp. 1–2. IEEE (2012)
6. Madge, C., Meek, J., Wellens, J., Hooley, T.: Facebook, social integration and informal learning at university: 'it is more for socialising and talking to friends about work than for actually doing work'. Learn. Media Technol. **34**(2), 141–155 (2009)

7. Moodle: https://moodle.org/. Accessed 07 Nov 2014
8. Dabbagh, N., Kitsantas, A.: Personal learning environments, social media, and self-regulated learning: a natural formula for connecting formal and informal learning. Internet High. Educ. **15**(1), 3–8 (2012)

The Use of Facebook as an Assisting Tool in Teaching Computer Science Courses

Anwar Alhenshiri(✉) and Hoda Badesh

Faculty of Information Technology, Misurata University, Misurata, Libya
{anwar, hoda}@alhenshiri.net

Abstract. This paper describes the results of a study in which two Facebook pages were investigated as assisting tools in teaching two computer science courses. The intention was to measure the importance of utilizing a social networks widely used by students for improving the engagement factor of students with the course content. The results of the study showed that students although use Facebook for social purposes such as exchanging messages, their use of the course pages was of less significance. Students, although followed the pages as expected, their engagement was only for the purpose of seeking announcements or questions listed by the instructor, i.e. they used the page as a bulletin board.

Keywords: Social network · Facebook · Students · Learning · Education · Engagement · Human factors

1 Introduction

The primary use of Facebook, which is a widely-recognized social network that started in 2004, is communicating with family and friends through the exchange of messages and pictures. As of October 30, 2013, Facebook was ranked first in social networks in terms of globally monthly active users (1.5 billion MUAs) according to Ballve (2013). Hence, this research is aimed at exploiting Facebook's perceived effectiveness in improving the engagement factor with course material taught to computer science students.

It is estimated that more than 90 % of undergraduate students use Facebook for sorority events and socializing (Shih 2010). Prior to investigating the use of Facebook for educational purposes, research emphasized the concept of collaboration though social networks. In other words, how one can find answers to questions within the setting of the social network which includes family, friends, and colleagues and their further connections. Research has found that Facebook—as a social network—can widely participate effectively in collaborative activities (Selwyn 2009).

Facebook has several tools that allow for posting information and pictures. It also allows for attaching different kinds of files within groups. Moreover, it has the capabilities of commenting on posts and on comments with text, pictures, videos, and hyperlinks. In addition, Facebook allows users to chat textually and via communication. Therefore, exploring those tools to improve how students become more engaged with course material motivated the research discussed in this paper.

C. Stephanidis (Ed.): HCII 2015 Posters, Part II, CCIS 529, pp. 218–223, 2015.
DOI: 10.1007/978-3-319-21383-5_37

The research questions is: does Facebook improve the engagement of students with the course content? And is there a difference between the cases of graduate and undergraduate students given the age gap between the two groups? The remainder of the paper is structured as follows. Section 2 highlights some research work related to the topic of choice. Section 3 discusses the research methodology. Section 4 explains some of the results of the study. Section 5 provides a brief discussion of the results and concludes the paper.

2 Related Work

The rapid growth of Web 2.0 has had deep effect on education. Learning outside the classroom is becoming more and more important with the dominance of social networks. Students could share ideas, exchange questions and information, and interact with their teachers over the internet via social networks such as Facebook. Several studies including Shih (2010) have shown that using online tools in education has become crucial to exceed the limits of the classroom walls.

Earlier studies focused on the debate of whether social networks are advantageous or not to the education environment. For example, the study in Selwyn (2009) showed that Facebook can be seen to provide a 'ready space' for use in education. Robiyer et al. (2010) compared the likelihood of using Facebook for educational purposes by students and by faculty members. Their study showed that, in 2010, students were more accepting to the idea of using Facebook to assist the classroom while teachers were more likely to use traditional methods such as email.

Later, the focus shifted to the possibilities of actually using Facebook in the education process. For example, the study discussed in Shih (2013) showed that students within community groups on Facebook are very confident to share information regarding their class. Moreover, the study discussed in Kayri and Çakır (2013) showed that Facebook provides continuity of learning by eliminating the need for repetition by teachers. In addition, the study in Bicen (2013) showed that Facebook along with other Web 2.0 tools can have a positive effect on the students' learning skills. It encouraged not only the students' team work via sharing course material but also teachers to organize activities that could not be done in real life.

According to educatorstechnology.com, Facebook has several advantages if used properly in educating students. For example, Facebook has a friendly and inviting environment that helps students engage with the material and participate in the subjects discussed in class. Their everyday use of Facebook helps to make students more comfortable with its use in learning. Furthermore, Facebook can facilitate collaboration and improve discussions.

To explore those advantages and to further highlight the possible usefulness of a widely used social network such that of Facebook, the study in this paper explores the benefits of Facebook in assisting with teaching computer science courses. It also compares the cases of graduate and undergraduate students.

3 Methodology

The research is mainly a study in which two Facebook pages were created by the principal investigator who is also the instructor of two computer science courses. The first is a third-year computer science course (operating systems (OS)), and the second is a graduate computer science course (advanced topics in databases (DB)). The instructor created the two pages as community pages. Both the students and the instructor could post on the timelines of the pages.

The instructor announced each page during the first class and all students in the class joined the pages to receive information and interact with the page by (liking) it. The number of students in the OS class was 46 and the number of the students in the DB class was 14. It is worth noting that all students joined their designated pages. The pages were active during the Fall Semester of 2014–2015 (Sept 2014 to January-2015). The instructor informed the students that the following will be posted to the Facebook pages:

1. Announcements regarding class time changes and exam times.
2. Information regarding assignments and homework.
3. Information regarding projects required for the class.
4. Questions that need to be discussed and answered.
5. Links to websites that would help students with the courses.

Two questionnaires were given to students. The first was a generic pre-study survey given to a sample of students in the Faculty of Information Technology in Misurata University. The second was a post-study survey that questioned students in both classes after having used the two pages during the semester.

The activities of the instructor included maintaining the page and providing posts to students. Those posts included: (1) information to students about the course material, (2) questions to students to discuss and answer online, (3) homework and assignments to bring to class, and (4) different kinds of announcements regarding quizzes, exams, and the like. The instructor collected information such as post reach, post likes, and comments by students on daily basis.

The students in both classes were asked to follow the corresponding course page. There activities involved: (1) posting on the page, (2) liking posts, (3) commenting on posts, and (4) answering questions. They also asked questions about: information, other questions, and announcements posted by the instructor. Students commented on each other's comments and answers as well.

4 Study Results

The study investigated aspects regarding the interactions between students and the page content, the type of content that interested students the most, and the difference between graduate and undergraduate computer science students in dealing with Facebook pages used in education. The study also measured the effectiveness of the structure of each page and the distribution of content over the semester timeline. However, in terms of human-computer interaction, the results discussed in this paper will concern: the students' engagement with the pages, the type of content that interested students most, and the difference between graduate and undergraduate computer science students with respect to interacting with social networks for learning, given that there is an age gap between the two groups.

4.1 Pre-study Questionnaire

The pre-study questionnaire asked students about their use of Facebook in general and in socialization. It also questioned about the use of Facebook in reading scientific material. Participants were also asked about the possible uses of Facebook in discussions and forums in addition to using Facebook pages for course exercises. Most students (57 out of 60) indicated that they use Facebook in socialization and to read scientific material. With regard to the use of Facebook pages in course exercises, most students (50 out of 60) welcomed the idea and showed interest in following Facebook pages related to courses they study.

4.2 Students' Engagement

To measure the students' engagement with each Facebook page, the study investigated two kinds of posts. The first is posts on the page by the instructor and the second is students' posts. With each type of post, the study recorded whether each post was a question, a piece of information (text, image or video), or an announcement. The investigation involved the number of likes per each type of post, the number of comments by students, and the post reach. Table 1 shows the results.

Table 1. Students' engagement with the Facebook pages

Page	Posted by	Type of Post	Count	Likes	Comments	Avg. Post Reach
The OS page	instructor	Question	7	22	12	41
		Information	4	28	1	38
		Announcement	14	104	44	41
	students	Question	4	12	0	31
		Information	1	2	0	23
		Answers	11	24	0	0
The DB Page	instructor	Question	5	16	18	30
		Information	8	30	6	16
		Announcement	10	29	6	16
	students	Question	3	3	5	12
		Information	5	1	8	23
		Answer	7	12	4	22

As shown in Table 1, students were more interested in what the teacher posted on the page. In the case of the undergraduate course, they only posted about half of the questions the instructor posted (7 vs. 4). They posted fewer pieces of information (4 vs. 1). The cases of the graduate course was very similar. Students provided fewer questions and fewer informational posts. However, graduate students had more comments on the instructor's question and informational posts than undergraduate students (18(5) vs. 12(7)) who had more comments on announcements made available by the instructor (44 vs. 6).

There was a weak correlation between the number of likes and the number of comments in both course pages (using Pearson Product $r = 0.48$ in the OS course, $r = -0.08$ in the DB course) Having higher likes (mean = 6 likes per post in the OS case) than comments (mean = 2 comments per post in the OS case) indicates, although not directly, that students were less interactive and more likely followers of the page. Similar results were recorded with the DB course page.

4.3 Interaction Based on Post Types

By taking a second look at Table 1, one notices that students in both classes focused on questions and information posted by the instructor instead of having discussions by commenting on each other's posts. Announcements by the teacher had the highest numbers of likes in both classes (104 and 29). This may indicate that students considered the page as an online bulletin board.

4.4 Graduate vs. Undergraduate Courses

By comparing the cases of graduate and undergraduate students, the results show that similar interests were recorded. Both groups focused on the same kind of posts in terms of likes and comments they provided. Both pages had very few posts by students. In the case of the graduate course page, the student posts and questions had more consideration by other students with no significant difference when compared to the case of the undergraduate course page.

4.5 Post-study Questionnaire

This questionnaire was posted online to those who used the Facebook page in each of the two courses. The survey can be located at the following link and it was open for two days for students to complete (Link[1]). The result showed that the highest percentage of students used the page to read the teacher's questions (47 %, 28 out of 60). None of the participants was interested in following their classmates' answers to questions. Most participants (88 %) found the teacher's questions and the information posted on the page useful. Also, 88 % of the participants thought the instructor was the most

[1] https://www.surveymonkey.com/s/8G7PWFF.

important source of information on the page. With a significant difference ($z = 2.9$, $p < 0.004$), 63 % (38/60) of the participants indicated the page improved their understanding of the course material while 37 % (22/60) did not. Two of the participants thought the page could have more inviting posts and more questions.

5 Discussion and Conclusion

This research is preliminary and there are further results that could not be presented in this paper due to space limits. As shown in the results provided above, students are more likely to use Facebook with a course as a bulletin board to get the teacher's announcements quickly. Furthermore, they focus on questions more than information since questions may appear on exams as they think and so indicated in the post-study survey.

The results of the study also showed that graduate students are more likely to use Facebook to exchange information and participate in discussions. This is reflected by their interaction activities on the posts provided by both the instructor and each other. Further research may look into the type of information that can be posted on Facebook pages used in education. The type of information may play a significant role in how students follow and interact with pages related to courses they study.

References

Ballve, M. (2013). http://www.businessinsider.com/the-worlds-largest-social-networks-2013-12, Business Insider. Accessed 2 Feb 2015

Bicen, H., Uzunboylu, H.: The use of social networking sites in education: a case study of Facebook. J. Univ. Comput. Sci. **19**(5), 658–671 (2013)

Kayri, M., Çakır, O.: An applied study on educational use of Facebook as a web 2.0 tool: the sample lesson of computer networks and communication. J. Comput. Sci. Inf. Technol. (IJCSIT) **2**(4), 48–57 (2013)

Robiyer, M.D., McDaniel, M., Webb, M., Herman, J., Witty, J.V.: Findings on Facebook in higher education: a comparison of college faculty and student uses and perceptions of social networking sites. Internet High. Educ. **10**, 134–140 (2010)

Selwyn, N.: Faceworking: exploring students' education-related use of Facebook. Learn. Media Technol. **34**(2), 157–174 (2009)

Shih, R.C.: Effect of using Facebook to assist English for business communication course instruction. TOJET **12**(1), 52–59 (2013)

The Current Use of Cell Phone in Education

Elham Alsadoon[1(✉)] and Hamadah Alsadoon[2]

[1] King Saud University, Riyadh, Saudi Arabia
ealsadoon@ksu.edu.sa
[2] AlBaha University, Al Baha, Saudi Arabia
hhalsadoon@hotmail.com

Abstract. This study aimed to explore the current use of cell phones in education among Saudi students in Saudi universities and how students perceive such use. Data was collected from 237 students at King Saud University. Descriptive analysis was used to analyze the data. A T-test for independent groups was used to examine whether there was a significant difference between males and females in their perception of using cell phones in education. Findings suggested that students have a positive attitude toward the use of cell phones in education. The most accepted use was for sending notification to students through a system provided by King Saud University. This electronic system allows instructors to easily send any SMS or email to their students. The use of cell phone applications came in the second rank of using cell phones in education. Students have already experienced the benefits of having these applications handy wherever they go.

Keywords: Cell phone · Mobile learning · E-learning · Higher education

1 Introduction

Mobile devices have spread rapidly all around the world and have become more commonly used than computers [1]. These digital technologies have been part of the daily life of today's students. The technological environment they live in has created a generation called 'digital natives' with a different way of thinking and of processing information from past generation [2]. This type of learner is characterized as "digitally literate, always on, mobile, experimental and community oriented" [2] (p. 3). This phenomenon has prompted educational institutions to adjust their educational services to the current trend of providing mobile learning [1].

Providing today's learners with the educational resources that they expect, such as mobile learning, is a pedagogical need [3]. Mobile learning, or m-learning, as defined by [4] is "learning that happens across locations, or that takes advantage of learning opportunities offered by portable technologies" (p. 51). Mobile learning "is quickly becoming the preferred method for learning on today's college campuses" [3] (p. 1) and mobile applications have become common methods to deliver learning [5]. Mobile learning attracted educators "because mobile devices are portable, ubiquitous, easily accessible and used by many people" [1] (p. 202). The study aims to explore the ways in which Saudi students might use cell phones in education.

C. Stephanidis (Ed.): HCII 2015 Posters, Part II, CCIS 529, pp. 224–229, 2015.
DOI: 10.1007/978-3-319-21383-5_38

2 Significant of the Study

"Middle East is considered as a second fastest growing region after US and Canada in mobile and telecommunication adoption. The two countries which are considered as the biggest mobile markets within the region are, Saudi Arabia and Iran" [6] (p. 787). Regardless of gender, socioeconomic status, or age, the college students in Saudi Arabia own and carry cell phones with them everywhere [7]. The widespread use of cell phones in the Saudi society, directed the educators' attention to the potential that these tools have in delivering learning. Efforts to utilize the cell phones for educational purposes have been the concern of parties involved in educational processes [8, 9]. Few studies have been conducted to examine students' attitudes toward the use of cell phones in the higher education in Saudi universities [7, 10]. However, the use of cell phones in Saudi universities is still in its trial level and there is a need to explore the current use of cell phones in higher education and investigate the best practices of such uses.

3 Using Cell Phones in Education

Educators should consider the power of these cell phones and their potential as learning tools for digital natives who grew up carrying these devices with them all the time and not to fight these tools their students have already adopted in their lives [11]. Cell phones are powerful education tools that can capture digital natives' attention so they can engage in learning [1]. Using cell phones for educational purposes has been the subject of studies in recent years [1, 8, 9]. Literature revealed many features that distinguish cell phones from other technologies. The following section presents the most cited features of cell phones and the advantages of using them in learning.

Cell phones are ubiquitous. Ubiquitous refers to "on-demand computing power with which users can access computing technologies whenever and wherever they are needed" [12] (p. 174). While not all students own laptops or MP3s and PDAs [7, 13, 14] almost all college level students have a cell phone, which means that they are already prepared with the needed equipment for mobile learning [15, 16]. The use of these devices provides just-in-time learning, which is a learning that can be delivered when and where it is needed [17].

Cell phones are inexpensive, which is an important feature of cell phones making it a practical tool for learning. Cell phones are cheaper than computers, so they can be less expensive tools to provide Internet access [8]. The cost and flexibility are the best features to motivate students to use cell phones in learning [18]. Because cell phones are affordable, many students buy the newest and advanced models that provide them with many services, tools, and applications that benefit them in their everyday life. The expensive, powerful educational tools that were once only available on expensive computers are now available on inexpensive mobile devices [19]. Therefore, these devices have the potential to empower the learning environment. The low cost of cell phones puts advanced features of technology in students' hands. These days, cell phones have different features such as "voice, short messaging service (SMS), graphics, user-controlled operating systems, downloadables, browsers, camera functions (still and video), and geopositioning" [11] (p. 4).

Another advantage of cell phones is that they support and facilitate sharing in many ways. Cell phones' users can share information by calling or exchanging text messages or multimedia messages. Students can share information on the Internet if they have Internet access from their cell phones by using emails or blogs. Cell phones facilitate sharing educational materials and support collaborative learning [20]. Cell phones bring new channels for interaction between learners and teachers and among learners themselves [8]. Time that might otherwise be wasted can now provide benefits because mobile learning provides the opportunity for anyone to be a lifelong learner [20].

Another feature of mobile phones that opens the door to access unlimited learning resources is their capability to access the Internet. The ability of the cell phone to connect to the network wirelessly provides new means for learners to access their classes without coming to the classroom and for the teachers to change the idea of the classroom [21]. "Wireless networks and mobile communications coupled with personal computing devices present new means for students to access classroom information and communicate with peers and teachers" [21] (p. 2). Moreover, the Internet access helps in delivering learning to rural areas [13]. The use of a mobile device and a wireless connection provides all students in the group with equal opportunities to use the technology to achieve the task [22].

The use of text messages is another feature of cell phones. It is one of the cell phone's functions that are used most often. Students use their cell phones more for sending and receiving messages and less for accessing the web [15]. Short messages system was a great tool to exchange information between students [19]. The use of text messages solves the problems of large class size and the shyness of students that prevents them from participating or asking questions [18]. A study of the impact of using text messages on students' learning of English vocabulary found that students enjoy learning language using their mobiles, and they reported that it was easy for them to recall the terms they received on their cell phones [14]. Another study compared the processes of learning words by sending them to students by phones to one group and emailing them by using electronic mail to the other group and found that students' learning through phones was better [15]. Students prefer SMS and MMS because they are immediate and convenient, and more importantly they feel what they receive through them is more personal [24].

The use of mobile devices in a classroom can reduce the time spent on doing tedious work; as a result, it frees the teacher's time to work on instructional tasks such as guiding the students [22]. Mobile devices "help professors with organizing courses, and managing research materials and information. Traditionally, professors have spent a lot of time with paperwork related to students' assignments, exams, and grading" [24] (p. 90). Mobile learning can solves some of the problems of traditional education such as the problem of a large class that limits the interaction between teachers and learners, motivation of the multitasking generation, and time to answer students' questions [23].

Another problem in the traditional classroom can be solved by using mobile phones is limited computers in the classroom [22]. Only students skilled in terms of using the technology work on these computers. The use of mobile devices allows all students to work on the task and exchange their ideas and provide all students in the group with equal opportunities to use the technology to achieve the task [22]. The use of mobile phones allows teachers to overcome the barrier that prevents them from teaching creativity [25]. Teaching creativity, which involves media production, requires access to appropriate technology. The widespread use of cell phones among students permits using them as a learning tool to support the use of creative activity. Using mobile devices in learning supports the learning beyond the classroom; increases the independence of learners; and supports teaching students with disabilities [20].

4 Methodology

This study is an attempt to explore the current use of cell phones in the educational system in Saudi Arabia from the perspective of Saudi students. Data were collected through a self-developed questionnaire consisting of four parts: demographic, close-ended, open-ended, and comments. The questionnaire was piloted and improved to reach an acceptable level of reliability. It was sent via email to the participants who were selected randomly to represent students at the College of Education at King Saud University. 237 participants completed the survey. The response rate was 41 % (237/580).

5 Results

The study found that the majority (97 %) of the participants own laptops and almost all of them own a cell phones (99.6 %). The use of cell phones as a tool to check grades and schedules, to browse the Internet in the classroom where no Internet service is provided, and to exchange information among students gained more agreement than the idea of using them as tool to deliver knowledge.

The two ways of using cell phones in education that received the largest student agreement to were using cell phones to notify students about coming events and using cell phone applications such as translators and calculators. These were the most-mentioned applications of a cell phone by students as revealed by the open-ended questions. On the other hand, using cell phones to provide quizzes was not used and not perceived as a practical use of cell phones in education.

Results indicated that Saudi students perceived the cell phone as a tool to play educational games or education audio materials but such use was occasional. The use of cell phones to deliver context-aware information was used but rarely too. Participants' attitudes were positive toward the ways that they had already experienced, such as receiving notifications or using cell phone applications. Students have also played media on their cell phones, or browsed the class webpage and their attitudes toward such uses were positive. Reading from a cell phone screen was rare. With the spread of smartphones, more users used them to access their emails. It is no wonder some students stated that they have used their cell phones to learn English. The availability of cell phone applications designed to teach English at low cost facilitates learning the language.

References

1. Keskin, N., Metcalf, D.: The current perspectives, theories and practices of mobile learning. TOJET Turk. Online J. Educ. Technol. **10**(2), 202–208 (2011). http://www.arabnews.com/saudiarabia/article406075.ece
2. Cobcroft, R., Towers, S., Smith, J., Axel, B.: Mobile learning in review: opportunities and challenges for learners, teachers, and institutions. In: Proceedings of the Online Learning and Teaching Conference, Brisbane, 26 Sept 2006. Accessed 10 May 2010. https://olt.qut.edu.au/udf/OLT2006/gen/static/papers/Cobcroft_OLT2006_paper.pdf (2006)
3. McCombs, S., Liu, Y.: Channeling the channel: can iPad meet the needs of today's m-learner. In: Koehler, M., Mishra, P. (eds.) Proceedings of Society for Information Technology & Teacher Education International Conference 2011, pp. 522–526. AACE, Chesapeake (2011)
4. Chuang, K.: Mobile technologies enhance the E-learning opportunity. Am. J. Bus. Educ. **2** (9), 49–53 (2009)
5. Khaddage, F., Knezek, G.: Device independent mobile applications for teaching and learning: Challenges, barriers and limitations. In: Barton, S. et al. (eds.) Proceedings of Global Learn Asia Pacific 2011, pp. 1–7 (2011). AACE. http://www.editlib.org/p/37143
6. Al Hosni, N., Ali, S., Ashrafi, R.: The key success factors to mobile commerce for Arab countries in Middle East. In: iiWAS'2010 - The 12th International Conference on Information Integration and Web-based Applications and Services, Paris, pp. 787–790, 8–10 Nov 2010
7. Al-Fahad, F.N.: Students' attitudes and perceptions towards the effectiveness of mobile learning in King Saud University, Saudi Arabia. Turk. Online J. Educ. Technol. **8**(2) (2009). Accessed on 15 April 2010. http://www.tojet.net/volumes/v8i2.pdf#page=112
8. Pietrzyk, C., Semich, G., Graham, J., Cellante, D.: Mobile technology in education. In: Koehler, M., Mishra, P. (eds.) Proceedings of Society for Information Technology & Teacher Education International Conference 2011, pp. 640–650. AACE, Chesapeake (2011)
9. Scctt, K., Kitchings, S., Burn, D., Koulisa, M., Campbell, D., Phelps, M.: Wherever, whenever learning in medicine: interactive mobile case-based project. In: Proceedings Ascilite Sydney 2010 (2010)
10. Alharthi, M.: The use of SMS in learning. In: Paper Presented at the 7th International Conference of the Use of Internet in Learning. Egypt. 7 Oct 2008 (2008)
11. Prensky, M.: Listen to the natives. Educational Leadership **63**(4), 8–13. Accessed 14 Dec 2010 (2005). http://www.siprep.org/prodev/documents/Prensky.pdf
12. Peng, H., Su, Y., Chou, C., Tsai, C.: Ubiquitous knowledge construction: mobile learning re-defined and a conceptual framework. Innovations Educ. Teach. Int. **46**(2), 171–183 (2009)
13. Pettit, J., Kukulska-Hulme, A.: Going with the grain: mobile devices in practice. Australas. J. Educ. Technol. **23**(1), 17–33 (2007)
14. Cavus, N., Ibrahim, D.: M-learning: an experiment in using SMS to support learning new English language words. Br. J. Educ. Technol. **40**(1), 78–91 (2009). doi:10.1111/j.1467-8535.2007.00801.x
15. Thornton, P., Houser, C.: Using mobile phones in English education in Japan. J. Comput. Assist. Learn. **21**(3), 217–228 (2005). doi:10.1111/j.1365-2729.2005.00129.x
16. Franklin, T.: Mobile learning: at the tipping point. TOJET Turk. Online J. Educ. Technol. **10** (4), 261–275 (2011)

17. Gay, G., Rieger, R., Bennington, T.: Using mobile computing to enhance field study. In: Koschmann, T., Hall, R., Miyake, N. (eds.) CSCL 2: Carrying Forward the Conversation. Erlbaum, London (2002)
18. Patten, B., Arnedillo Sanchez, I., Tangney, B.: Designing collaborative, constructionist and contextual applications for handheld devices. Comput. Educ. **46**, 294–308 (2006)
19. Roschelle, J.: Unlocking the learning value of wireless mobile devices. J. Comput. Assist. Learn. **19**(3), 260–272 (2003)
20. Hayes, P., Joyce, D., Pathak, P.: Ubiquitous learning - an application of mobile technology in education. In: Cantoni, L., McLoughlin, C. (eds.) Proceedings of World Conference on Educational Multimedia, Hypermedia and Telecommunications 2004, pp. 1811–1816. AACE, Chesapeake (2004)
21. Wentzel, P., Lammeren, R., Molendijk, M., Bruin, S., Wagtendonk, A.: Using mobile technology to enhance students' educational experiences, EDUCAUSE, 2005 (2006). http://net.educause.edu/ir/library/pdf/ers0502/cs/ecs0502.pdf. Accessed 16 Dec 2010
22. Liu, T., Wang, H., Liang, T., Chan, T., Ko, H., Yang, J.: Wireless and mobile technologies to enhance teaching and learning. J. Comput. Assist. Learn. **19**, 371–382 (2003)
23. Al-khamaysah et al.: Suggested that mobile learning could solve the problem of a large class that limits the interaction between teachers and learners, motivation of the multitasking generation, and time to answer students' questions (2007)
24. Kim, S.H., Mims, C., Holmes, K.P.: An introduction to current trends and benefits of mobile wireless technology use in higher education. AACE J. **14**(1), 77–100 (2006)
25. McGreen, N., Arnedillo Sanchez, I.: Mobile phones: Creative learning tools. In: Isaias, P., Borg, C., Kommers, P., Bonanno, P. (eds.) Mobile Learning 2005, pp. 241–245 (2005b). Malta: International Association for Development of the Information Society Press. Accessed 15 Dec 2010. http://www.iadis.net/dl/final_uploads/200506C014.pdf

The Instructional Model Framework of Undergraduate Industrial Design Core Course

Wenzhi Chen(✉)

Department of Industrial Design, College of Management,
Chang Gung University, 333 Kwei-Shan, Tao-Yuan, Taiwan, R.O.C.
wenzhi@mail.cgu.edu.tw

Abstract. Design is a powerful weapon for companies, and it is important to educate excellent designers for industry. The purpose of this study was to explore instructional design and to develop an instructional model for undergraduate industrial design core (studio) courses. The study was divided into two phases. First, 18 instructors were interviewed to collect qualitative data to formulate a framework of the instructional model. Then, a survey was conducted with a questionnaire designed according the framework and references to collect quantitative data to verify the model. The questionnaire was sent to 245 industrial design instructors, and 105 were returned. Finally, an instruction model for industrial design core course was formulated. The information provided in this study can deepen the understanding of instructional planning and provide a reference for teaching in design education.

Keywords: Industrial design · Design education · Instruction model · Teaching problems

1 Introduction

Design education has emphasized practice since the Bauhaus era, and studio pedagogy is the primary teaching method, especially in the industrial design domain [1, 2]; however, there are still many unanswered questions regarding studio pedagogy [3]. The core course of industrial design education focuses on teaching students to integrate the skills and knowledge learned from surrounding courses, training in design thinking, analysis, synthesis abilities, and accumulating design experience.

The studio is the primary and most used pedagogy of the core course in industrial design education. But how do the instructors plan, design, implement, and evaluate the core courses to achieve their education aims? The purpose of this study is to explore and formulate the instructional modes of undergraduate industrial design core course to increase the understanding of the design education.

C. Stephanidis (Ed.): HCII 2015 Posters, Part II, CCIS 529, pp. 230–234, 2015.
DOI: 10.1007/978-3-319-21383-5_39

2 Literature Review

2.1 Instructional Model

Instructional design is a system of procedures for developing education and training programs in a consistent and reliable fashion [4]. The goal is to make learning more efficient and effective and less difficult [5]. This new approach emphasizes thinking as the aim of education, and the curriculum should focus on increasing the human process of the acquisition of knowledge, skills, and attitudes. It also focuses on the contract between learners and teachers, time instruction, subject matter, and learning environments [6]. Some scholars regard instruction design and design as the same. Both deal with an ill-defined problem, so the process of the instruction design is similar to the design process [7].

Several processes and models have been developed. The process of the instruction design usually contains the phrases, "analyze", "design", "develop", "implement", and "evaluate", commonly called "ADDIE" [4]. Morrison et al. [5] propose a model in which the functions should include instructional problems, resources, objectives, strategies, delivery, learner characteristics, content sequencing, task analysis, and evaluation instruments. The ADDIE process [4] and the functions of the instruction design proposed by Morrison et al. [5] can be referenced for creating the instructional model of industrial design core course.

2.2 Instruction of Undergraduate Industrial Design Studio

The aim of industrial design education is training students to be professional designers. The curriculum of design education is consists of four categories: (1) fundamental courses that develop the design formation; (2) technology-based courses that provide the scientific formation of design; (3) artistic courses that strengthen the base of design and expression; (4) design studio courses, which are a synthesis of the previous three categories. Design studio courses constitute the most important part of design education [8].

Many researchers discuss and explore studio teaching. For instance, Zehner, Forsyth [9] propose guidelines for curriculum development and indicate the key indicators of effective studio teaching. Attoe and Mugerauer [10] explore excellent studio teaching in architecture. But how is studio instruction designed? It is worth exploring formulated instructional models to increase understanding of the studio teaching.

3 Method

A two-phase study was designed to explore the planning, implementation, and evaluation of the undergraduate industrial design core course. First, an interview was conducted to collect the qualitative data. Eighteen industrial design instructors from eight universities participated in the interviews. The main questions of the interview included how instructors plan, implement, and review their courses. Each interview took about one hour; the content was transcript, then analyzed using the qualitative data analysis and research software, ATLAS.ti A framework of the instructional model was formulated according the data.

In the second phase, a questionnaire was design according the framework and related references. The 245 questionnaires were sent to 24 universities, and 105 were returned (a return rate of 42.86 %). The analysis used the SPSS statistical software package. First, the descriptive statistics were computed, and the analysis of variance were used to detect significant differences among variables. Finally, the instructional model was verified and modified.

4 Results

The instructional model framework of industrial design core course was formulated according the interview data. The general instruction design process includes 5 phases as "analysis", "design", "develop", "implement", and "evaluate". According the interview data, we simplify the process into 3 phases as "plan", "implement", and "evaluate".

To verify the instructional model framework of undergraduate industrial design core course, a survey was conducted to collect the quantitative data. The framework of the instructional model was modified according the results of the survey. The model was constructed by simplifying the instruction design process and the grade years. The framework of the model presented as Fig. 1.

In the plan phase, there were six elements: objectives, factors that should be considered, studio model, project attributes, project numbers, and project scale. The teaching objectives were changed with years; the number and importance of objectives were increased with grade. The first year course emphases the abilities of aesthetic and

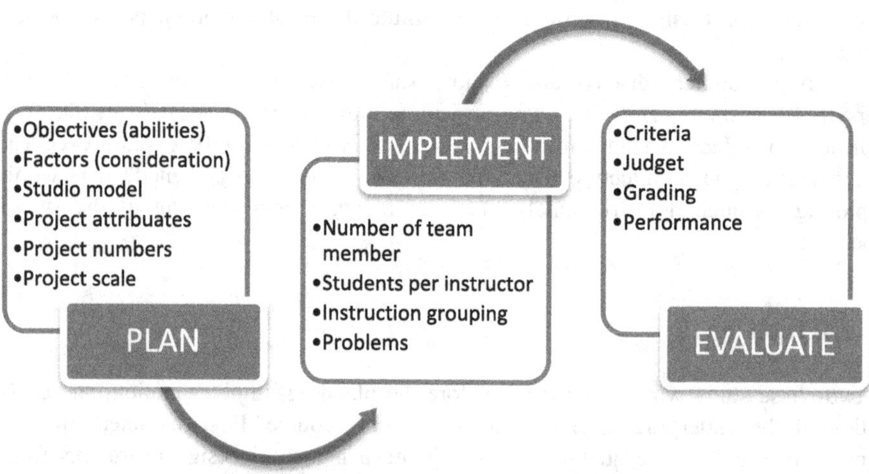

Fig. 1. The framework of industrial design core course instructional model

form, drawing and presentation, and design humanities. The second year focus is on computer-aided design and engineering design. The third and fourth years ask the students to practice the abilities that professional designer should be equipped with, including product planning and development, marketing and business, computer-aided design, aesthetic and form, engineering design, drawing and presentation, and design humanities. The factors that should be considered when designing instruction include: the objectives of course and the department, the projects and assignments, the attributes of students and instructors, and project management. The pedagogy of the studio should be different each year. The workshop pedagogy is most suitable for the first and second year courses. The third and forth year courses focus on the cross-disciplinary pedagogy. The first and second year projects focus on the arousal of imagination and creativity on a smaller scale. The third and fourth year projects have a larger scale and focus on design practice, practice and exploration of theories, and specific topics.

There are four elements in the implementation phase: the number of team members, the number of students each instructor should teach, the grouping method, and the problems instructors face. The ideal number of team members is two to three students per team. The best ratio of student to instructor decreases each year, from 11–20 (first year) to 1–10 (fourth year). The students should be grouped differently and change instructors for each project in 1–3 year in order to experience different types of design and teaching styles. But the instructor should be fixed in the fourth year course to implement graduate design projects. The main problems in the implementation phase were related to students and instructors. The problems of students include: students rely too much on the Internet, they possess an insufficient ability to analyse, they experience excessive external incentives, have bad learning attitudes, poor observation skills, insufficient design experience, and poor basic design skills. The main problems of instructors are the heavy loading of the administrative duties and teaching.

In the evaluation phase, the main approaches to evaluate the performance of the course are the final presentation and exhibition in the end of the project or semester. The judge of the first year was the course instructor, but scholars and experts from outside the campus can be invited for the 2–4 year courses. The criteria of the first year course focuses on creativity, innovation, form, and aesthetic. The second year emphasizes personal ability and performance. The criteria for the 3–4 year are more severe; the criteria includes integrity and design quality, form and aesthetic, creativity and innovation, design process, and personal ability and performance.

5 Concluding Remarks

The purpose of this study was to develop an instructional model and explore the instructional problems of core (studio) courses of undergraduate industrial design programs. Finally, the instruction model for industrial design core course was proposed. The information provided in this study can deepen the understanding of the instructional planning and provide a reference for teaching in design education.

Acknowledgments. This research was funded by the Ministry of Science and Technology of Taiwan under grant numbers NSC 101-2410-H-182-018 and NSC 102-2410-H-182-016. Thanks are extended to all participants and research assistants for their contributions to these projects.

References

1. Schön, D.A.: Educating the Reflective Practitioner. Jossey-Bass, San Francisco (1987)
2. Reimer, Y.J., Douglas, S.A.: Teaching HCI design with studio approach. Comput. Sci. Educ. **13**(3), 191–205 (2003)
3. Ochsner, J.K.: Behind the mask: a psychoanalytic perspective on interaction in the design studio. J. Architectural Educ. **53**(4), 194–206 (2000)
4. Gustafson, K.L., Branch, R.M.: What is instructional design. In: Reiser, R., Dempsey, J.V. (eds.) Trends and issues in instructional design and technology, pp. 16–25. Allyn & Bacon, New York (2002)
5. Morrison, G.R., et al.: Designing Effective Instruction, 6th edn. Wiley, New York (2010)
6. Alzand, W.: Instruction design and educational quality. Procedia Soc. Behav. Sci. **2**(2), 4074–4081 (2010)
7. Jonassen, D.H.: Instructional design as design problem solving: an iterative process. Educ. Technol. **48**(3), 21–26 (2008)
8. Demirbas, O.O., Demirkan, H.: Learning styles of design students and the relationship of academic performance and gender in design education. Learn. Instr. **17**(3), 345–359 (2007)
9. Zehner, R., et al.: Optimising studio outcomes: guidelines for curriculum development from the Australian studio teaching project. In: 2nd International Conference on Design Education. Connected, Sydney (2010)
10. Attoe, W., Mugerauer, R.: Excellent studio teaching in architecture. Stud. High. Edu. **16**(1), 41–50 (1991)

Developing Simple Tools for Measuring and Evaluating Students' Works with a Smartphone

Ryota Fukutani(✉), Akinobu Ando, Shota Itagaki, and Hiraku Abiko

Miyagi University of Education, 149 Aramaki-Aoba Aoba-ku, Sendai, Japan
{ryotafukutani, itagaki.shota}@gmail.com,
{andy, abiko}@staff.miyakyo-u.ac.jp

Abstract. In this study, we developed a simple set of tools for a teacher to efficiently and easily evaluate and measure the accuracy of the result of students' craft works. This tool is developed for running on a smartphone, and has three functions; 1. Measuring the flatness of surfaces, 2. Measuring the accuracy of connected parts, and 3. Taking photos of the working process and final result. The result of the evaluation is sent to LMS (Learning Management System) and stored. It works as a part of an integrated management system. Despite only having three functions, this tool can solve chronic problems and drastically reduce the workload for general Japanese teachers. Without this tool, one teacher is solely accountable for checking and evaluating a vast number of students' works in a very short period of time.

Keywords: Smartphone · Technology education · LMS (Learning Management System) · Evaluation of flatness of material surface · Evaluation of joint angle

1 Introduction

Japanese teachers are required to manage many kinds of school affairs. They must not only teach classes but must also guide students, manage club activities, organize committees, prepare teaching materials for the next class, and conduct evaluations. Generally, there is only one teacher who teaches the Technology Education class in a given school. Therefore, the teacher is expected to check and evaluate all of the students' craft works. A typical class in Japan consists of about 28 students on average [1]. Additionally, it is assumed that there is an average of five classes in a grade, and three grades in a school. This means the teacher needs to manage the results of 420 students in a short period. Moreover, even if the teacher only checks five parts; e.g., two parts of the angle and three parts of the flatness of a craft work as shown in Fig. 1, it means that the teacher has 2100 points to check and remark. A teacher usually only evaluates craft works by observation and records findings on a sheet. However, this traditional way takes a long time and it is difficult for the teacher to remain consistent. In addition, non-digitized data is not compatible with the LMS. Moreover, inaccuracy is a prevalent issue with this method. If there are tools that could more

C. Stephanidis (Ed.): HCII 2015 Posters, Part II, CCIS 529, pp. 235–240, 2015.
DOI: 10.1007/978-3-319-21383-5_40

accurately record the interface between results of students' works and a teacher's evaluation, these problem would be solved. Therefore, this research aimed to develop new tools for an application where a teacher is able to evaluate and record students' craft works with more accuracy, efficiency, and ease. We decided to use only a general smartphone, which was equipped with some basic sensors. Considering the application will be used daily, it was necessary to choose a common device for our application.

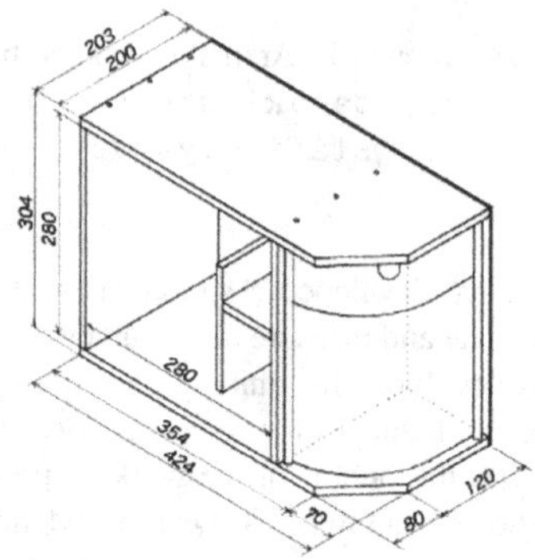

Fig. 1. Example of a design drawing [2]

As we mentioned earlier, a Technology Education teacher tends to be very busy because he/she is required to objectively rate students' works in addition to preparing materials and so on outside classes. It takes a teacher a very long time to evaluate the result of a lot of students' works (Fig. 2), plus it requires his/her sense of touch and sight.

Fig. 2. A sample of situation that there are a lot of students' craft works made in a Technology Education class.

In recent years, in Japan, there are a lot of parents who are highly concerned with the quality of education in schools. Teachers are often requested by students' parents to provide student grades and evaluations. If teachers have the resources to provide objective data, they can be relieved from bearing the accountability to provide explanations. Nowadays, smartphones are frequently used for various purposes in our everyday life. In 2007, it was proposed in the educational field that a teacher could record students' score and remarks by using a cellular phone [3]. However, it was just the input device and it did not have measuring and evaluation functions. It was not until recently that the use of smartphones was implemented to manage a student's skill practice. In this study, our research questions are as follows; 1. Can our new application for a smartphone accurately measure students' craft works? 2. How can the application make a teacher's evaluation and workload accurate, efficient, and easy?

In this paper, our purpose is to develop a simple new tool for measuring and evaluating, which can work on a smartphone to reduce a teacher's workload and allow him or her to check students' craft works more easily and efficiently.

2 Outline of Our Method

2.1 Outline of Our Approach

Figure 3 shows an outline of our approach. Our developed tool consists of three functions. The first is a function of measuring angles, the second is a function of measuring flatness and contortion, and the third is a function of taking photos. These three simple functions are assembled as an integrated system.

For measuring angles or flatness, we used three axes angle sensors and gyro sensors. This application is developed for general Android devices. The measured data and evaluated results are immediately sent to the LMS server, which we already developed [4]. The data and result are stored in the LMS database, thus teachers can access a student's learning history anytime.

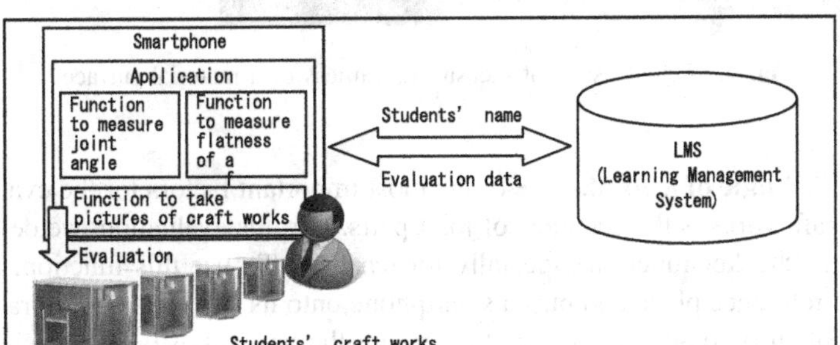

Fig. 3. Outline of our approach

2.2 Description of Functions

Both of these applications have a result view and data export function in CSV file format. Additionally, a teacher can see the rank of an evaluation as S, A, B, C, and D.

Approach 1. Flatness of Material Surface. In addition to checking if the angle is proper or not, it is also important to measure the flatness of the surface. This is especially important for cutting wood pieces with a saw. It is difficult for a beginner student to cut down correctly without any unexpected roughness. The flatness is measured by mounting a smartphone with an attachment made with a 3D printer slide on a surface that a teacher wants to evaluate. By sliding on a surface, our application measures the volume of the vibrations by using three axes acceleration sensors (Fig. 4).

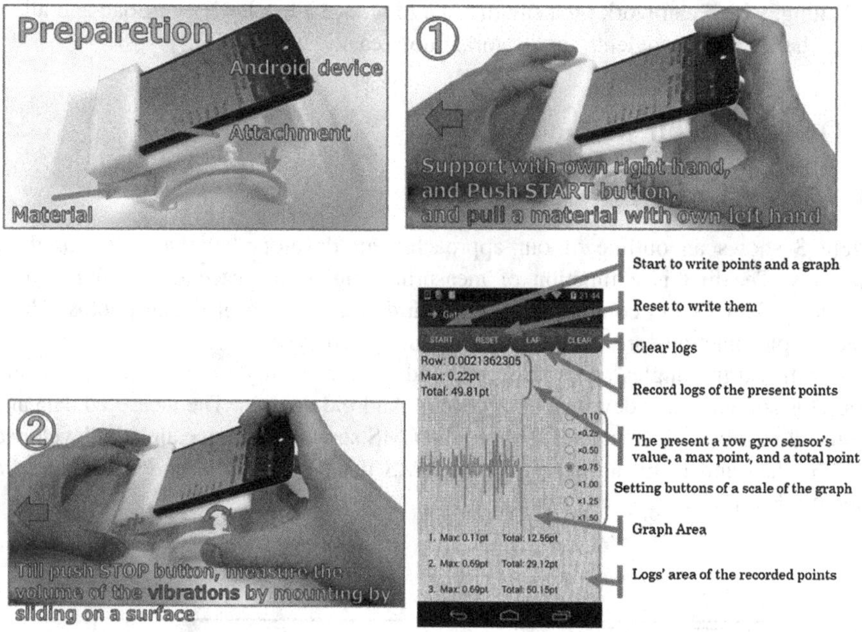

Fig. 4. Actual usage of measuring flatness of a material surface

Approach 2. Angle of a Joint. One of the most important factors for the evaluation of students' craft works is the accuracy of joint parts. For this evaluation, we developed a simple angle checker function especially for teachers. To use this function, a teacher decides the reference plane and puts a smartphone onto its surface as a calibrator. Next, a teacher puts it onto another surface to measure the angle. Lastly, the teacher should just touch the next button to save the data and proceed to the student evaluation (Fig. 5).

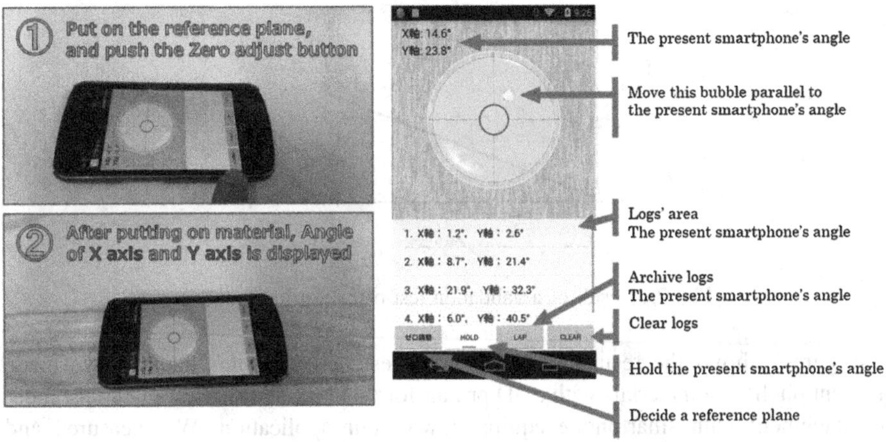

Fig. 5. Actual usage of measuring joint angle

Approach 3. Taking Photos. When a teacher should check students' achievement, it is important to record the condition of their works. Our third function is to take photos using a camera built in a smartphone and to store them in the LMS server. Using this function would help a teacher remember or recall it visually and correctly.

2.3 Validation of Our Application

Figure 6 shows the result of validation tests of measuring angle of X axis and Y axis. Using the absolute flat surface in our laboratory, a smartphone equipped with our application was put on the surface for calibration. We measured and recognized a gap between the values measured by our application and the optimal 45 degree, 90 degree measurement. As a result, there was some gap, which we fixed with correction processing.

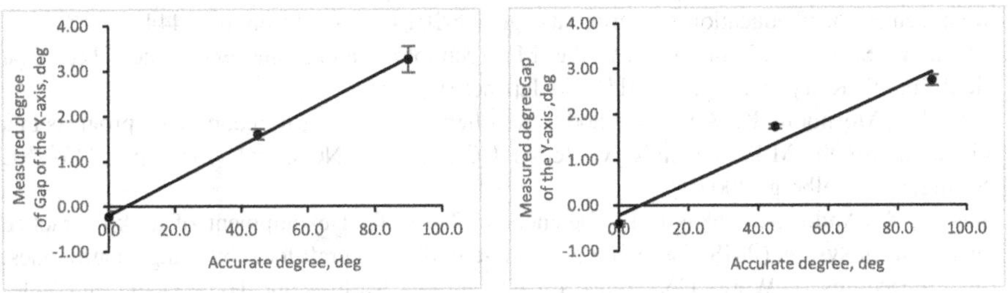

Fig. 6. Results of validation tests of measuring angle of X axis and Y axis

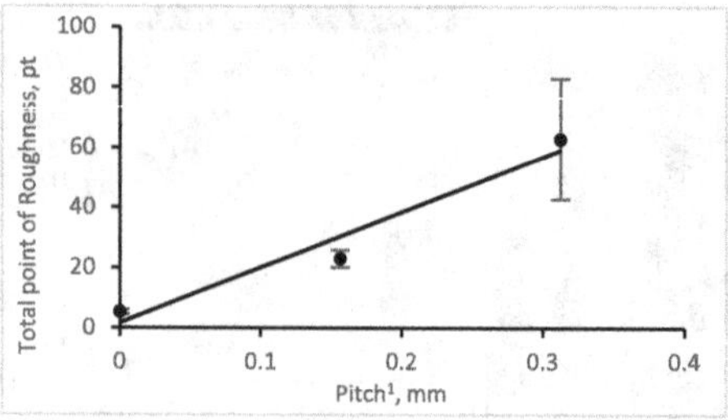

Fig. 7. Result of a validation test of measuring flatness

Figure 7 shows the results of a validation test that measures flatness. We made different pitch[1] test materials with a 3D printer for this test. We slid test materials under an attachment with smartphone equipped with our application. We measured and recognized a gap between the values measured by our application. As a result, it became clear that our tool can simply evaluate efficiently.

3 Conclusion

In this study, we developed a new simple application using a smartphone especially for a technology education teacher. The application consists of three functions; 1. Measuring flatness, 2. Measuring angle, 3. Taking photos. It is expected to reduce a teacher's workload because a teacher can check and evaluate students' craft works easily, effectively and accurately and store the evaluation data on the LMS. Our objective is not only to use this as a test run, but to eventually put it into valid practice.

Acknowledgement. This work was supported by KAKENHI (24730721, 2450169, and 22531009).

References

1. Education at a Glance 2014 | OECD READ edition. http://www.keepeek.com/Digital-Asset-Management/oecd/education/education-at-a-glance-2014_eag-2014-en#page444
2. Mada, Y., Sioiri, M., Tsuruta, A., Otake, M.: Technology and Home Economics [Technical field], p. 49. Kairyudo, Japan (2011). (in Japanese)
3. Ando, A., Morimoto, K.: A new method for teachers and students to record daily progress in a class. In: Smith, M.J., Salvendy, G. (eds.) HCII 2007. LNCS, vol. 4558, pp. 245–251. Springer, Heidelberg (2007)
4. Itagaki, S., Ando, A., Takaku, T., Takeno, H., Torii, T.: Development of a skill practice management system (PMS) for learning Japanese traditional craft tools by using smartphones. In: Proceedings of World Conference on Educational Multimedia, Hypermedia and Telecommunications, pp. 1001–1009. Chesapeake, Tampere (2014)

[1] Pitch means a distance from a top to next top of the roughness are same shapes.

A Content-Based Approach for Supporting Teachers in Discovering Dependency Relationships Between Instructional Units in Distance Learning Environments

Fabio Gasparetti(✉), Carla Limongelli, and Filippo Sciarrone

Roma Tre University, Via Della Vasca Navale 79, 00146 Rome, Italy
{gaspare,limongel,sciarro}@dia.uniroma3.it

Abstract. eLearning courses are usually built in such a way that training resources are organized for making the learning process effective. In most cases, the top-level learning objective will have prerequisites which must be satisfied. Those prerequisites should be formally identified by a hierarchy of dependencies built accordingly. We evaluate a series of hypotheses for understanding the feasibility of automating this task by means of a general-purpose content-based approach that exploits semantic analysis techniques.

Keywords: Sequencing · Distance learning · Semantic analysis

1 Introduction

Research on Course sequencing aims to automatically produce a personalized sequence of didactic material and activities on the basis of each student's needs and preferences [3].

Still, with advances in science and technology a wide range of technological options are available to the teachers, and distance education offers us big opportunities in comparison with traditional classroom instruction, reaching a wider student audience, meeting the needs of students who are unable to attend on-campus classes and linking students from different social, cultural, economic, and experiential backgrounds. Nevertheless, teaching and learning at a distance is as effective as traditional instruction when the employed learning material, method and technologies are appropriate to the instructional tasks.

Standalone instructional units (or *learning objects*), where each unit covers a single learning point in its entirety, and large online repositories (e.g., Connexion[1] and Ariadne[2]) simplify the educators to share, manage and use educational resources. Additional resources can also be retrieved by selectively crawling the web [9]. Once a subset of these objects have been selected, instructional designers

[1] http://cnx.org.
[2] http://www.ariadne-eu.org.

C. Stephanidis (Ed.): HCII 2015 Posters, Part II, CCIS 529, pp. 241–246, 2015.
DOI: 10.1007/978-3-319-21383-5_41

must decide the sequence in which learners will accomplish these objectives. It is not a trivial task and involves a variety of skills.

The mutual-dependency relationship between the content of the learning object and the context into which it is being placed determines whether or not the object "fit" into that context [4,7,8]. The correct concatenation or *sequencing* of contextualized educational resources develops the required meaningful distance learning course.

The position paper reports an original general-purpose content-based approach for assisting teachers in defining *prerequisite* relationships between text-based learning objects and, at the same time, providing a list of valid sequences of learning objects that satisfy them. Semantic analysis techniques identify relevant Wikipedia concepts mentioned in each learning object. After this annotation step, by tapping the vast semi-structured Wikipedia knowledge, the constraints between learning objects are identified. Because a large set of reusable digital resources include text and web pages, Microsoft word and pdf file formats, the proposed approach is focused on the learning objects which more easily can be assigned a sort of keyword-based representation of their content. As part of an ongoing research, we are currently collecting evaluation test results to prove the validity of the approach.

2 Prerequisite Extraction

Given a pair of learning objects, lo_i and lo_j, the relationship $lo_i \rightarrow lo_j$ specifies the *ordering constraint* under which the topic containing lo_j is sequenced first. The set of those conceptual prerequisite constraints defines how two concepts are related to each other and can be used to derive instructional design rules that must be validated against the course, e.g.,"all topics covering broader concepts are sequenced before those more specialized".

Each learning object can include a variety of different topics. For this reason, two steps are required: (1) the identification of a knowledge base that contains a taxonomy of the topics and (2) a methodology for assigning to each object a subset of those topics.

Because manual ontology engineering requires great effort, especially if the ontology must be kept up to date with future topics, we try to overcome such problems by relying on Wikipedia, a wide coverage multilingual online encyclopedia developed by a large number of users. Each published article p can belong to one or more categories $C_p = \{c_1, c_2, \cdots, c_n\}$, subset of available ones on Wikipedia $C_p \subset C_w$. The C_p categories describe the domains related to the article. To organize Wikipedia for easy access to pages, contributors are given guidelines for categorizing articles and naming new categories.

Categories themselves may have subcategories, or reversely, supercategories. However, the categories form that weak conceptually-related thesaurus including a variety of semantic similarity relationships. On the other hand, prerequisites are mostly based on hierarchical relationships, such as IS-A, hypernym-hyponym, part-whole et cetera. Other taxonomies that explicitly include those kinds of relationships (e.g., Wordnet) are not frequently updated or more likely fail to include technical or specific concepts discussed in high education courses.

Given two learning objects lo_i and lo_j, we run the Wikipedia Miner toolkit[3] for detecting and disambiguating the Wikipedia topics when they are mentioned in the textual content extracted from lo_i and lo_j, obtaining two subsets of Wikipedia articles, respectively.

For studying the potential correlation between the prerequisite relationships of pairs of LOs and the two sets of Wikipedia articles describing the concepts covered by the LOs we formulate three hypotheses.

The first one is structural-based. Given two learning objects lo_i and lo_j, and the related subsets of Wikipedia articles, we can see that each article is assigned to one or more categories. We can obtain the two sets of categories associated with the two learning objects, C_{lo_i} and C_{lo_j}, respectively. Given two categories $c_i \in C_{lo_i}$ and $c_j \in C_{lo_j}$, we denote with $c_i \rightarrow_w c_j$ the shortest direct path through the Wikipedia taxonomy connecting c_i to c_j, where c_i is a more general category. The function $d : (C_w, C_w) \rightarrow \mathbb{Z}$ returns the shortest length of $c_i \rightarrow_w c_j$, ∞ if it does not exist.

The first hypothesis **H1** states that $lo_i \rightarrow lo_j$ exists if:

$$\exists c | d(c, c_{loi}) < d(c, c_{loj}) \wedge d(c, c_{loj}) < \infty \wedge \frac{max(d(c, c_{loi}), d(c, c_{loj}))}{d(c, c_{loi}) + d(c, c_{loj})} > \alpha \quad (1)$$

where $\alpha \in (0, 1]$ is a constant and $c_{lo_i} \in C_{lo_i} - (C_{lo_i} \cap C_{lo_j})$, $c_{lo_j} \in C_{lo_j} - (C_{lo_i} \cap C_{lo_j})$. In summary, given two distinct categories, each from one of two learning objects, if the distance that connects them, even through a common ancestor category, is less then a given threshold, the prerequisite relation exists. The order of the two learning objects is determined by analyzing how deep the c_j category is placed in the taxonomy in comparison with the category c_i.

The other two hypotheses are content-based. The hypothesis **H2** states that if lo_j has been associated with an article that contains a link to a page associated with lo_i at the beginning of the description, $lo_i \rightarrow lo_j$ exists. If the authors have found the necessity to define a concept by means of other concepts, probably the former one is more specific then the latter. The last hypothesis **H3** states that if the Wikipedia associated with lo_i is substantially longer than the one of lo_j, $lo_i \rightarrow lo_j$ exists. The rationale is that more general topics need longer discussions to be described than a very specific one.

3 Early Evaluation

We briefly give account to the criteria we are currently following to assess the appropriateness of the proposed approach. The research question of this study is to observe whether there is statistical relationship between the criteria for each hypothesis we introduced and the presence of a prerequisite relationship.

[3] http://wikipedia-miner.cms.waikato.ac.nz.

Table 1. Average precision, recall and F1 measures for the evaluated hypotheses.

	Precision	Recall	F1
H0	0.394	0.231	0.291
H1	0.501	0.363	0.421
H2	0.493	0.041	0.075
H3	0.540	0.300	0.386

The analyzed data is obtained from a large set real online courses that cover various different topics. The prerequisite relationships are identified by the help of a group of teachers. We analyzed four computer science courses.

For estimating the effect of each criterion, we are currently making use of traditional Information Retrieval measures, namely, Precision, Recall and F1-measure. Table 1 reports the average values for every hypothesis over the four courses. . H0 hypothesis represents the baseline that, for each pair $< lo_i, lo_j >$ randomly assigns the $lo_i \rightarrow lo_j$ relationship. In spite of the few input courses considered, the outcomes shows significantly deviations from a random approach that does not consider the content of the LOs.

The low recall of H2 hypothesis can be partially justified by the wrong annotations provided by the Wikipedia miner tool. By manual editing the annotations with the correct Wikipedia articles associated with the learning objects, the hypothesis reached similar recall values in comparison with the other ones.

4 Related Work

To the best of our knowledge, our work makes the first attempt to exploit weak-semantic taxonomies such as Wikipedia for the sequencing of learning objects.

Scheines *et al.* [10] use casual models search to identify prerequisites among knowledge components represented as latent variables. The approach does not analyze the content of learning objects but exploits test data collected measuring the student skills after attending the courses. Similarly, Voung *et al.* [11] propose to analyze large-scale assessment to determine the dependency relationships between knowledge units.

5 Conclusion and Future Work

Preliminary attempts to identify prerequisite relationships between learning objects have been done through the discussion of three hypotheses. We are currently concluding the experimental evaluation of the proposed approach. Early preliminary results on four courses are promising.

As for the future work, learning objects might cover particular skills that do not have compulsorily to be labeled to Wikipedia articles. For example, both "recognize task bars" and "dependency markers" depend on the "uses of Gantt charts". While all those learning objects will likely cover similar topics, prerequisites exists though. Content-based approaches might fail to find distinctive elements to find those relationships. One possible solution is the combination of multiple taxonomies and web corpora that can be analyzed in order to find valuable relationships, which can then be included in the prerequisite identification [2]. If two learning objects reference one another, a single representation of the covered topics can be defined by analyzing the learning path and the underneath motivations that the author of the didactic material has considered through those citations [5].

As for the Wikipedia taxonomy, different types of Wikipedia categories exists, each one based on the type of information they encode. Assuming that the IS-A and similar relationships are the only ones in Wikipedia is inaccurate and can negatively affect the precision of the inference. Further examinations are required.

Once the prerequisite identification has been correctly validated, the recommendation of learning objects can be extended by querying the learning repositories in search of new didactic material that has not been previously included by the instructor, e.g., learning objects covering similar topics. By profiling current users interests and their reactions to the retrieved objects (see for example recent advances on information sharing in social environments introduced in [1,6]), clusters of similar users can be identified in order to share among them objects that results in the maximization of the preference satisfaction and performance assessments.

References

1. Arru, G., Feltoni Gurini, D., Gasparetti, F., Micarelli, A., Sansonetti, G.: Signal-based user recommendation on twitter. In: Proceedings of the 22nd International Conference on World Wide Web Companion, pp. 941–944. WWW 2013 Companion, International World Wide Web Conferences Steering Committee, Republic and Canton of Geneva, Switzerland (2013). http://dl.acm.org/citation.cfm?id=2487788.2488088
2. Biancalana, C., Gasparetti, F., Micarelli, A., Sansonetti, G.: Social semantic query expansion. ACM Trans. Intell. Syst. Technol. **4**(4), 60:1–60:43 (2013). http://doi.acm.org/10.1145/2508037.2508041
3. Brusilovsky, P., Vassileva, J.: Course sequencing techniques for large-scale web-based education. Int. J. Contin. Eng. Edu. Lifelong Learn. **13**, 75–94 (2003)
4. De Marsico, M., Sterbini, A., Temperini, M.: A framework to support social-collaborative personalized e-learning. In: Kurosu, M. (ed.) HCII/HCI 2013, Part II. LNCS, vol. 8005, pp. 351–360. Springer, Heidelberg (2013)
5. Gasparetti, F., Micarelli, A., Sansonetti, G.: Mining navigation histories for user need recognition. In: Stephanidis, C. (ed.) HCI 2014, Part I. CCIS, vol. 434, pp. 169–173. Springer, Heidelberg (2014)
6. Gurini, D.F., Gasparetti, F., Micarelli, A., Sansonetti, G.: iSCUR: interest and sentiment-based community detection for user recommendation on Twitter. In: Dimitrova, V., Kuflik, T., Chin, D., Ricci, F., Dolog, P., Houben, G.-J. (eds.) UMAP 2014. LNCS, vol. 8538, pp. 314–319. Springer, Heidelberg (2014)

7. Limongelli, C., Lombardi, M., Marani, A., Sciarrone, F.: A teacher model to speed up the process of building courses. In: Kurosu, M. (ed.) HCII/HCI 2013, Part II. LNCS, vol. 8005, pp. 434–443. Springer, Heidelberg (2013)
8. Limongelli, C., Sciarrone, F., Vaste, G.: LS-PLAN: An effective combination of dynamic courseware generation and learning styles in web-based education. In: Nejdl, W., Kay, J., Pu, P., Herder, E. (eds.) AH 2008. LNCS, vol. 5149, pp. 133–142. Springer, Heidelberg (2008)
9. Micarelli, A., Gasparetti, F.: Adaptive focused crawling. In: Brusilovsky, P., Kobsa, A., Nejdl, W. (eds.) Adaptive Web 2007. LNCS, vol. 4321, pp. 231–262. Springer, Heidelberg (2007)
10. Scheines, R., Silver, E., Goldin, I.: Discovering prerequisite relationships among knowledge components. In: Stamper, J., Pardos, Z., Mavrikis, M., McLaren, B. (eds.) Proceedings of the 7th International Conference on Educational Data Mining. pp. 355–356. European Language Resources Association (ELRA), May 2014
11. Vuong, A., Nixon, T., Towle, B.: A method for finding prerequisites within a curriculum. In: Pechenizkiy, M., Calders, T., Conati, C., Ventura, S., Romero, C.J. Stamper, J. (eds.) The 4th International Conference on Educational Data Mining (EDM 2011), pp. 211–216 (2011)

Understanding of the Students' Behavioral Intention to Use Online Discussion Site (ODS) Using Rasch Analysis

Azizah Jaafar[1] and Prasanna Ramakrisnan[1,2(✉)]

[1] Institute of Visual Informatics, National University of Malaysia (UKM), 43600 Bangi, Selangor, Malaysia
azizah@ivi.ukm.my, prasanna@melaka.uitm.edu.my
[2] Faculty Computer and Mathematical Sciences (FSKM), University Technology MARA (Melaka), 77300 Merlimau, Melaka, Malaysia

Abstract. In this paper, we analyzed students' behavioral intention to use online discussion site (ODS) using existing measurement. As this online discussion site is widely used in education for student-student and student-lecturer interaction, we need to understand how this site is accepted by the students. This study proposes a statistical method for understanding student responses toward intention to use ODS. We analyze the intention to use ODS by using existing seven indicators: online course design, user interface design, previous learning experience, perceived usefulness, perceived ease of use perceived interaction and intention to use. All the 23 validated items from the seven indicators were combined into a single construct to measure intention to use by using Rasch analysis. The student's intention to use online discussion available in Universiti Teknologi MARA (UiTM) e-learning portal was investigated. The responses received was investigated using Rasch analysis. The analysis displayed visually all the 23 item through person-item distribution map (PIDM) with WINSTEP 3.68.2 software. This reveals the likelihood of student intention to use ODS. Using the PIDM we can easily identify most and least agreed items in a measurement model. Thus this analysis can be applied in any study to identify the items that need further improvement based on user's actual responses.

Keywords: Intention to use · Online discussion site (ODS) · Rasch analysis

1 Introduction

Online discussion site (ODS) is widely being used by many higher institution for teaching and learning purposes. It is used as a complementing tool for students to share their knowledge related to subject online. This tool is usually embedded in the e-learning portal. In Universiti Teknologi MARA (UiTM), students and lecturers are connected online using ODS. They are able to discuss subject related matter at any time and from anywhere using this tool. For successful utilization of the ODS, the discussion platform need to be used by the students. There are many factors that influence the students usage of the ODS. But this study interest is to look at the students response on

C. Stephanidis (Ed.): HCII 2015 Posters, Part II, CCIS 529, pp. 247–252, 2015.
DOI: 10.1007/978-3-319-21383-5_42

intention to use the ODS. Therefore the existing intention to use ODS [1] is re-validated [2] for studying the students responses on intention to use the ODS.

The probability of using the ODS for discussing on-line will decrease if the students do not show any intention using the ODS. So the success of providing a platform for on-line 6 discussions should be guided by the analysis of student's response towards the intention to use ODS. It was also identified that intention to use evaluation was commonly conducted on websites and information systems. There is a lack in intention to use ODS evaluation because most of the evaluation intention to use is associated with the overall design of e-learning systems. As the ODS is part of the e-learning system, the intention to use ODS only is not widely evaluated. However, a study has shown that there is a need to further investigate ODS designs (e.g. Harman and Koohang [3]). Therefore, an existing intention to use model is used to measure the ODS. Most of the study related on ODS are focused on model development and testing. But this study will explore further on the students pattern of response towards intention to use ODS. There by, this study also proposes a statistical method called Rasch analysis for understanding the response pattern.

2 Rasch Analysis

The Rasch analysis is applied to measure latent traits (e.g., ability or attitude) in various disciplines. Users' responses are used to understand their latent traits in a measurement scale. Location of items and users of the measurement scale is estimated by the Rasch analysis from the proportion of responses of each user to each item. The probability of success depends on the differences between the ability of the person and the difficulty of the item.

In the Rasch analysis, a user who is more developed has a greater likelihood of endorsing all the items; and easier tasks are more likely to be endorsed by all users [4]. The item difficulty and person ability are expressed in logits through transformation of the raw score (ordinal scale) percentage into success-to-failure ratio or odds. This odds value is then converted to its natural logs (interval scale). The scale resulting from the Rasch analysis of the ordinal response has the properties of an interval scale. This scale is linear, and the numbers tell how much more of the attribute of interest is present.

The basic assumption of the Rasch model is each user is categorized by his or her ability; and each item by a difficulty; user and item can be presented by numbers along one line and lastly the probability of observing any particular scored responses can be computed from the differences between the numbers [4]. Thus the model can be used to link the person to the items that have relative ordering of latent variables.

The purpose of this study is to show how to understand the user's response towards ODS design. It is done through the Rasch analysis by examining the item hierarchy of a measurement model. Data from previous work on intention to use was used for this study purpose [2]. Data analysis includes establishing the item hierarchy for ordering items from greater probabilities to endorse (bottom) to lesser probabilities to endorse (top). The findings from this study will provide evidence for understanding of meaningful activities in a measurement model towards ODS.

3 Intention to Use Measurement Model

Measurement model shows the relationship between the indicator variables (items) and the underlying latent variables or constructs [5]. The constructs are variables used in the measurement model. They are not directly measure but the indicators (items) are used to measure those constructs. For intention to use measurement model, the indicator variables and the underlying construct had been identified in previous study [6].

An individual's intention and usage of technology is commonly studied using the technology acceptance model (TAM). TAM was developed and validated by Davis based on the theory of reasoned action (TRA) [7, 8]. Based on this model an individual's attitude towards using a particular system is influenced by its perceived ease of use and perceived usefulness. Davis defined perceived ease of use (PEU) as "the degree to which an individual believes that using a particular system would be free of physical and mental effort" and perceived usefulness (PU) as "the degree of which a person believes that using a particular system would enhance his or her job performance". There are many previous studies which have applied the TAM model to investigate students' intention to use e-learning technologies [9–21]. Examples of technologies that support e-learning are the learning management system, blogs, the internet forum, social networking sites, wikis, instant messaging etc. However most of studies used the TAM to examine the concept of e-learning systems. But the extended TAM model [1] was re-validated [2] for exploring the students response pattern towards intention to use ODS.

4 Method

The data was collected from full time undergraduate student at Universiti Teknologi MARA (UiTM). The participants were all user of i-learn portal. Seventy seven responses were collected from the survey distributed manually and online. The instrument used for this study were adopted from [1]. The indicator variables and their underlying constructs were revalidation using Rasch analysis. The study were conducted to test the validity and reliability of the measurement items [2]. Based on the study conducted, item reliability after removal of item UID2 was increased to 0.71. It shows that there replicability in the instrument. The item reliability result is used to identify if there is any occurrence of replicability if the items in the instrument were tested with another sample of the same size. In conclusion there were 24 items in original instrument and after removal of one item (UID2) the final instrument consist of 23 items. Thus further study on understanding the students pattern of responses toward intention to use ODS will use only 23 item.

5 Finding and Discussion

The Rasch model can be used to establish a hierarchy of person and item together in a single person-item distribution map (PIDM). It displays the distribution of respondents on the left and the distribution of item agreement towards the measurement model on the right. Additionally, the PIDM also shows the most relevant items for measuring success of the measurement model and are at the bottom of the map.

The item is located by the number of persons getting a specific item correct or endorsing a specific item. While the person is located by number of items they are able to answer correctly or endorse. In applying the Rasch model, item locations are often scaled first. This part of the process of scaling is often referred to as item calibration. The mean for item is always zero because the Rasch model sets the mean of the item as a starting point (0 logits) for the calibration.

The location of an item on PIDM corresponds with the person's location at which there is a 0.5 probability of a correct response or endorsement of the item. Hence the probability of a person agreeing to the items below them will increase when moving down the PIDM.

The PIDM was explored for a better understanding of user responses towards the measurement model. The PIDM linking item difficulties to the person's endorsement ability of the sample across the four response scale (strongly agree, agree, disagree and strongly disagree) is presented in Fig. 1. More intention to use items are located at the bottom of PIDM while least intention to use items are displayed at the top of PIDM.

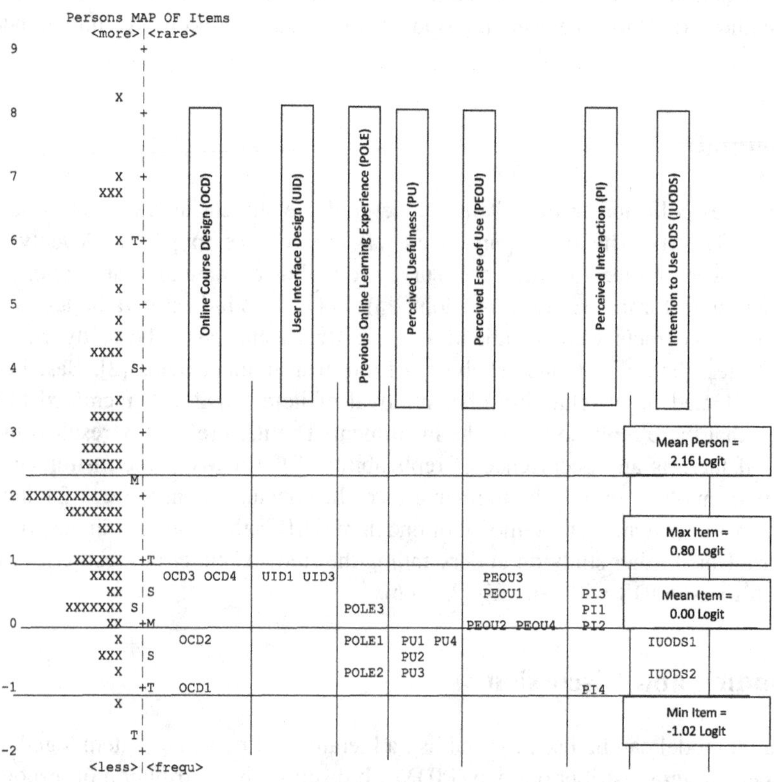

Fig. 1. The person-item distribution map (PIDM)

It was found that from the standpoint of the average group of students (mean person = 2.16 logit), all the items were plotted "much more easy to endorse". The most difficult item to endorse was "UID1" (0.80 logits) while the least difficult item was "OCD1" (−1.02 logits).

The both the items (UID1 and UID3) underlying the user interface design factor were at the highest location with UID1 = 0.80 logits and UID3 = 0.65. Thus user interface design factor items mostly disagree by the student because it is location at the highest location in the scale. The findings offer evidence to suggest that aspect related to user interface design are more difficult for students to endorse agree. There are some elements (e.g. layout design) in the user interface of the current ODS need to be investigated further. Therefore the designers need to further improve the user interface of the ODS to increase student intention to use ODS.

6 Conclusion

The Rasch analysis proposed as a statistical method for understanding students feedback toward ODS. It provides potential information on the evaluation of constructs in the activities involved by the students. The finding show how users actual responses were analyze. From the analysis, it was identified that the current ODS user interface design need to be further improved to increase the students intention to use ODS.

Developers and designers can use Rasch analysis for investigating user's actual responses on the system or website design. Any existing instrument can be adapted or newly development instrument can be used to understand items or constructs that need further improvement in the study. Therefore we propose Rasch analysis for exploration of user responses.

References

1. Liu, I.-F., Chen, M.C., Sun, Y.S., Wible, D., Kuo, C.-H.: Extending the TAM model to explore the factors that affect intention to use an online learning community. Comput. Educ. **54**(2), 600–610 (2010)
2. Ramakrisnan, P., Jaafar, A., Yatim, N.F.M., Mamat, M.N.: Validating instrument quality for measuring students' acceptance of an online discussion site (ODS). In: 2013 International Conference on Advanced Computer Science Applications and Technologies (ACSAT), pp. 475–478 (2013)
3. Harman, K., Koohang, A.: Discussion board: a learning object. Interdisc. J. Knowl. Learn. Objects **1**, 67–77 (2005)
4. Bond, T., Fox, C.: Applying the Rasch Model: Fundamental Measurement in the Human Sciences. Lawrence Erlbaum, Mahwah (2007)
5. Hair, J.F., Ringle, C.M., Sarstedt, M.: PLS-SEM: indeed a silver bullet. J. Mark. Theory Pract. **19**(2), 139–152 (2011)
6. Chiu, C.-M., Wang, E.T.G., Shih, F.-J., Fan, Y.-W.: Understanding knowledge sharing in virtual communities: an integration of expectancy disconfirmation and justice theories. Online Inf. Rev. **35**(1), 134–153 (2011)

7. Davis, F.D., Bagozzi, R.P., Warshaw, P.R.: User acceptance of computer technology: a comparison of two theoretical models. Manage. Sci. **35**(8), 982–1003 (1989)
8. Davis, F.D.: A Technology Acceptance Model for Empirically Testing New End-User Information Systems: Theory and Results. Massachusetts Institute of Technology, Cambridge (1985)
9. Liu, S.-H., Liao, H.-L., Peng, C.-J.: Applying the technology acceptance model and flow theory to online e-learning users' acceptance behavior. E-learning **4**(H6), H8 (2005)
10. Park, S.Y.: An analysis of the technology acceptance model in understanding university students' behavioral intention to use e-learning. Educ. Technol. Soc. **12**(3), 150–162 (2009)
11. Roca, J.C., Chiu, C.-M., Martínez, F.J.: Understanding e-learning continuance intention: an extension of the technology acceptance model. Int. J. Hum. Comput. Stud. **64**(8), 683–696 (2006)
12. Masrom, M.: Technology acceptance model and e-learning. Technology **21**, 24 (2007)
13. Ong, C.-S., Lai, J.-Y.: Gender differences in perceptions and relationships among dominants of e-learning acceptance. Comput. Hum. Behav. **22**(5), 816–829 (2006)
14. Saadé, R.G., Nebebe, F., Tan, W.: Viability of the 'technology acceptance model' in multimedia learning environments: a comparative study. Interdisc. J. Knowl. Learn. Objects **3**(2), 175–184 (2007)
15. Van Raaij, E.M., Schepers, J.J.L.: The acceptance and use of a virtual learning environment in China. Comput. Educ. **50**(3), 838–852 (2008)
16. Ngai, E.W.T., Poon, J.K.L., Chan, Y.H.C.: Empirical examination of the adoption of WebCT using TAM. Comput. Educ. **48**(2), 250–267 (2007)
17. Pituch, K.A., Lee, Y.: The influence of system characteristics on e-learning use. Comput. Educ. **47**(2), 222–244 (2006)
18. Lee, B.-C., Yoon, J.-O., Lee, I.: Learners' acceptance of e-learning in South Korea: theories and results. Comput. Educ. **53**(4), 1320–1329 (2009)
19. Sanchez-Franco, M.J.: WebCT–the quasimoderating effect of perceived affective quality on an extending technology acceptance model. Comput. Educ. **54**(1), 37–46 (2010)
20. Lee, Y.-C.: An empirical investigation into factors influencing the adoption of an e-learning system. Online Inf. Rev. **30**(5), 517–541 (2006)
21. Liaw, S.-S.: Investigating students' perceived satisfaction, behavioral intention, and effectiveness of e-learning: a case study of the blackboard system. Comput. Educ. **51**(2), 864–873 (2008)

Pump It up! – Conception of a Serious Game Applying in Computer Science

Daniela Janßen[1(✉)], Christian Tummel[1], Anja Richert[1], Daniel Schilberg[2], and Sabina Jeschke[1]

[1] IMA/ZLW & IfU, RWTH Aachen University, Aachen, Germany
{Daniela.Janssen, Christian.Tummel, Anja.Richert, Sabina.Jeschke}@ima-zlw-ifu.rwth-aachen.de
[2] Institute of Robotics and Mechatronics, University of Applied Sciences Bochum, Bochum, Germany
Daniel.Schilberg@hs-bochum.de

Abstract. Student attrition in mechanical engineering at German universities currently lies at about 40 %. A lacking sense of practical relevance for a future career are often named as reasons to quit studies. Over the past decade online games have become very popular for educational purposes. The approach of game-based learning, however, has proven to be suitable to motivate students. At RWTH Aachen University engineering students are imparted the relevance of computer science for their field through an e-learning environment including the online game *Pump it up!* The paper describes the conception and game design of the game including didactical and technical requirements related to it.

Keywords: Serious games · Game-based learning · Virtual worlds · Higher education · Computer sciences

1 Introduction

Digital media establish new possibilities of innovative ways of teaching and learning in higher education. With the arisen development of e-learning, the emerging tendency of serious games and the concept of game-based learning (the application of games with the aim of learning with digital media [1]) for educational purpose is an ongoing increasing trend. Mayer et al. talk about "a digital turn in the use of games and simulations for learning and training" [2]. At the same time, student attrition in mechanical engineering at German universities currently lies at a relatively high rate, approximately 40 %. A lacking sense of achievement and the lack of practical relevance for a future career are often named as reasons to quit studies. The missing of practical relevance is often embedded in the curriculum of engineering education because of a largely missing reference to the engineer profession. Evaluation results in the lecture "Computer Science in Mechanical Engineering" at RWTH Aachen University show that most students are unaware of the relevance of computer science in mechanical engineering as well as their importance and application in future career which has a negative effect on students' motivation. On the positive side, 60.5 % of engineering students prefer situations in which they have to find their own practical

C. Stephanidis (Ed.): HCII 2015 Posters, Part II, CCIS 529, pp. 253–258, 2015.
DOI: 10.1007/978-3-319-21383-5_43

solutions [3]. A promising approach combining self-controlled acting with enjoyment is the game-based learning approach. By now one third of the German population regularly plays computer games, two thirds of them play every day [4]. Games have the power of engaging, motivating and emotionally involving students. Therefore, it can be expected that educational games increase students' learning motivation as well as demonstrate the practical relevance of academic content.

2 Related Work

An increasing number of studies have shown that serious games provide an effective environment for the purpose of learning, for example [5, 6]. This research field is also a controversially debated field when it comes to the effectiveness of serious games. On the one hand, a lot of researchers, e.g. [1, 7] point out that the application of serious games improves learning, motivation as well as performance. Several studies, e.g. [8] show the positive effect of educational games in math, science and military education. Van Eck [9] supports the positive effects of game-based learning by a review of experimental research. Mayer et al. [2] give an overview of several authors which examine the effects of game-based learning. Pivec [10] sees in the "application of games and simulations for learning […] an opportunity for learners to apply acquired knowledge and to experiment, get feedback in form of consequences and thus gain experience in a 'safe virtual world'". Wilson et al. [7] examine the relationship between game attributes and learning outcomes. Furthermore, games encourage different learning approaches such as active learning, experimental learning and problem-based learning [5]. Consequently, it can be stated out that games have a positive impact as related to cognitive, skill-based and affective outcomes [7].

On the other hand there are several researchers [11, 12] who assess that the empirical effectiveness of game-based learning is quiet a mystery. Gunter et al. [13 cited in 14] report that "the effectiveness of an educational game is often based on enhancing learning motivation and social interactions rather than the effectiveness of knowledge acquisition" [14], an effect which is a quite unexplored [14]. Wilson et al. [7] claim a lack of research which combines game elements to learning outcomes.

To summarize, it can be stated that despite the huge number of research of the effectiveness of game-based learning there are a lot of open research question. But in light of the positive learning outcomes of serious games in higher education, it is worth to continue further research of the effectiveness of Serious Games on learning outcomes as well as the relationship between games and their impact on learning as a direct or indirect process and what the mediating variables are [7].

3 Conception of the Online Game *Pump It up!*

According to De Gloria et al. [15] the following aspects are important in order to develop serious games: the underlying theory respectively the didactical concept, the academic content as well as the game design which are described in detail below.

3.1 Didactical Concept: Game-Based Learning Approach

Playing games is related to having fun [16]. Brandstätter et al. [17] state that emotions such as enjoyment have an important function in motivation processes: motivated behavior is aimed to gain positive emotions and to avoid negative ones. A well-known model of motivation is the concept of flow by Csikszentmihalyi [18]. Flow describes the involvement in an activity. Weibel and Wissmath [19] also describe the feelings while playing games as "the sensation of being involved in the gaming action". This emotional state fosters students' motivation in the learning process. Because of its activating and participating approach the game-based learning model by Garris et al. [20] is used as the underlying didactically concept of *Pump it up!* (Fig. 1).

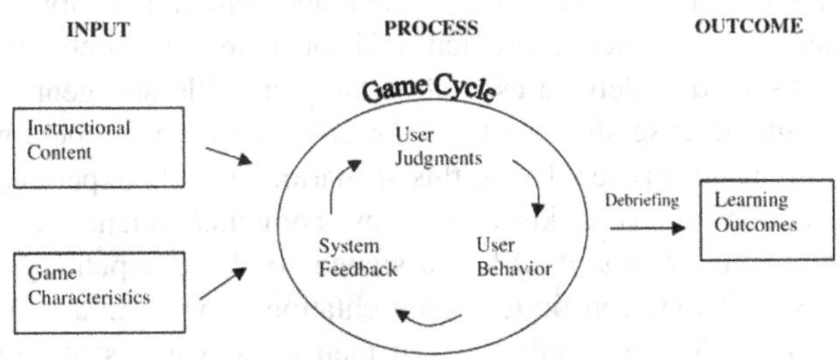

Fig. 1. Game-based model (Source: Simulation Gaming 33(4), p.445)

This model is based on constructivist learning theories after which students generate knowledge by making experience in a certain environment, in this context by playing the game [15]. Consequently students are seen as active participants of *Pump it up!,* who generate knowledge through the experience of playing. Giving frequent and transparent feedback regarding the level of completion provides the basis for long-term motivation. The key component of the model is the game cycle in which the students are in a "repeated judgment-behavior-feedback loop" [20]. This enables students to evaluate their actions and personal benefit. By playfully applying computer science skills through *Pump it up!,* students get feedback, gain practical experiences in terms of computer science and learn the importance of it for their future career.

3.2 Game Design and Content of *Pump It up!*

The game design includes the theoretical conception of the game world, rules and characters with regard to a certain target group. According to Pivec and Moretti [16] *Pump it up!* is developed along the following game design steps: learning outcomes of the game, define target group, define the game and shape the game idea, elaborate the details (storyline), evaluate the game idea, (technical) implementation of the game.

It is crucial for students to know and fully understand the final desirable outcome beforehand. This enables students to evaluate their actions and personal benefit. *Pump it up!* has the following **learning outcomes:** The overall aim is to maximize the motivation of those learners who perceive their task field to be too monotonous, theoretical or complex. Furthermore, students experience the importance and application of basic knowledge on computer science for their later career in the field of mechanical engineering. Students get a stronger practical relevance of computer science as well as deepen their knowledge from the lecture and of the practical course. A self-controlled, practical learning is fostered. Students learn how to integrate single commands into a complex program and realize further procedural steps typical for the industry as they are often found in the human-robot cooperation.

The **target group** of *Pump it up!* are engineering students which attend the lecture "Computer Science in Mechanical Engineering". *Pump it up!* will take up the already existing project-based task as part of this lecture. In the practical course, students apply lecture contents in teams by hands-on work. Engineering students focus especially on content of mechanical engineering and machine construction. Therefore, the relevance of computer science is an underrepresented field for them. After defining the learning outcomes the **game idea** is defined as well as the game title and genre. The game is entitled *Pump it up!* because students have the task to program robots which in turn manufacture pump adapter pipes. Using this scenario, students experience the importance and application of basic knowledge on computer science in the field of mechanical engineering. *Pump it up!* is assigned to the computer game genre of simulation [21]. Simulations constitute a representation of a real in a virtual world and are a practical context for the reality without their consequences like manufacturing errors and are therefore especially valuable in engineer's hands-on education [22]. In context of *Pump it up!* students have to program the two robots of each assembly cell to precisely execute the demanded task and to cooperate with other robots. Thereby students learn the realization of further procedural steps. The tasks are embedded in a **storyline** along a brewery scenario. In this scenario the start-up company *Pump it up*! gets the order to produce new pump adapter pipes for a brewery. In order to do so, different sub-steps are required. The students move from one level to another once they have successfully completed the lower level i.e. successfully manufactured the pump adopter pipes meeting the geometric and mechanical requirements (Fig. 2).

Afterwards, they have to implement this information in the form of a pseudo code, the syntax of this code is given to the students. The student who delivers the highest quality result in the shortest period of time will win. Thus, students will learn about the relation between the quality of the implemented program and the quality of the

Fig. 2. Screenshot of programming in *Pump it up*

manufactured good. Several possible game ends depending on the leaner's performance and various levels make it possible to customize the game to the respective level of students' knowledge, learning pace and rate of performance.

Before the game goes into action, the beta-version will be tested with students in order to receive didactical and technical feedback.

Up to **technical implementation** *Pump it up!* is set up as a browser game. The main technological objective is to play the game on different devices like notebook, tablet, pc or smart phones. For achieving platform independence the implementation of the game must be independent from the operating system e.g. Windows, IOS or Android as well as the game is constructed on HTML5, JQuery and CSS3 technologies.

4 Conclusion and Outlook

Driven by the lack of high student attrition in mechanical engineering at German Universities and the lack of practical relevance in computer science, the promising approach of game-based learning is applied in the engineering science at the RWTH Aachen University. Combining learning with engagement students get the possibility to experience practical relevance of computer science in a virtual learning environment in *Pump it up!* During the development of the game the students' requirements are collected and entered in the developing process in a didactical and technical way. The next steps include the programming and implementation of the game.

Besides the online game, further research steps are planned in context of applying Serious Games into higher education. In order to provide students more complex tasks and a higher immersion, the game-based learning approach is extended to 3D virtual learning environments, e.g. using a so called virtual theatre [22] or different versions of mixed learning environments as suggested by Hoffmann et al. [23]. Therefore, in further research activities we will focus on virtual environment using 3D glasses in order to enter more virtual reality and to increase the immersion in the game to facilitate students learning as the next education level.

References

1. Prensky, M.: Digital Game-Based Learning. Paragon House, Minneapolis (2007)
2. Mayer, I., Warmelink, H., Bekebrede, G.: Learning in a game-based virtual environment: a comparative evaluation in higher education. Eur. J. Eng. Educ. **38**(1), 85–106 (2013)
3. Derboven, W., Winker, G.: Ingenieurwissenschaftliche Studiengänge attraktiver gestalten. Vorschläge für Hochschulen. Springer, Heidelberg (2009)
4. Bundesverband Informationswirtschaft, Telekommunikation und neue Medien e.V. http://www.bitkom.org/de/themen/54906_68946.aspx
5. Oblinger, D.: The next generation of educational engagement. J. Interact. Media Educ. **8**, 1–18 (2004)
6. Kapp, K.M.: The Gamification of Learning and Instruction. Pfeiffer, San Francisco (2012)

7. Wilson, K.A., Bedwell, W.L., Lazzara, E.H., Salas, E., Burke, C.S., Estock, J.L., Orvis, K.L., Conkey, C.: Relationships between game attributes and learning outcomes: review and research proposals. Simul. Gaming Publ. **40**(2), 217–266 (2009)
8. McFarlane, A., Sparrowhawk, A., Heald, Y.: Report on the educational use of games: an exploration by TEEM of the contribution which games can make to the education process (2002). https://pantherfile.uwm.edu/tjoosten/LTC/Gaming/teem_gamesined_full.pdf
9. Van Eck, R.: Digital game-based learning. it's not just the digital natives who are restless. Educause Rev. **41**(2), 17–30 (2006)
10. Pivec, M.: Editorial: play and learn: potentials of game-based learning. Br. J. Educ. Technol. **38**(3), 387–393 (2007)
11. Papastergious, M.: Digital game-based learning in high school computer science education: impact on educational effectiveness and student motivation. Comput. Educ. **52**(1), 1–12 (2009)
12. Ke, F.: A case study of computer gaming for math: engaged learning for gameplay? Comput. Educ. **51**(4), 1609–1620 (2008)
13. Gunter, G.A., Kenny, R.F., Vick, E.H.: Taking educational games seriously: using the RETAIN model to design endogenous fantasy into standalone educational games. Educ. Tech. Res. Dev. **56**(5–6), 511–537 (2008)
14. Tsai, F.H., Yu, K.C., Hsiao, H.S.: Exploring the factors influencing learning effectiveness in digital-game-based learning. Educ. Technol. Soc. **15**(3), 240–250 (2012)
15. De Gloria, A., Belloti, F., Berta, R., Lavagnino, E.: Serious games for education and training. Int. J. Serious Games **1**(1) (2014). doi:http://dx.doi.org/10.17083/ijsg.v1i1.11
16. Pivec, M., Moretti, M. (eds.): Game-Based Learning: Discover the Pleasure of Learning. Pabst Science Publishers, Lengerich (2008)
17. Brandstätter, V., Schüler, J., Puca, R.M., Lozo, L.: Motivation und Emotion. Springer, Heidelberg (2013)
18. Csikszentmihalyi, M.: Finding Flow. The Psychology of Engagement with Everyday Life. Basic Books, New York (1997)
19. Weibel, D., Wissmath, B.: Immersion in computer games: the role of spatial presence and flow. Int. J. Comput. Games Technol. **2011**, 1–14 (2011)
20. Garris, R., Ahlers, R., Diskrell, J.E.: Games. Motiv. Learn. Res. Pract. Model Simul. Gaming **33**(4), 441–467 (2009)
21. Adler, F.: Computerspiele als Lernmedium und ihr Einsatz in den Ingenieurwissenschaften. Erarbeitung eines Analyse- und Entwicklungsmodells (2008). http://opus.bibliothek.uni-augsburg.de/opus4/frontdoor/deliver/index/docId/1288/file/Dissertation_Adler_Frederic_2008.pdf
22. Ewert, D., Schuster, K., Johansson, D., Schilberg, D., Jeschke, S.: Intensifying learner's experience by incorporating the virtual theatre into engineering education. In: Proceedings of the 2013 IEEE Global Engineering Education Conference, EDUCON (2013)
23. Hoffmann, M., Schuster, K., Schilberg, D., Jeschke, S.: Bridging the gap between students and laboratory experiments. In: Shumaker, R., Lackey, S. (eds.) VAMR 2014, Part II. LNCS, vol. 8526, pp. 39–50. Springer, Heidelberg (2014)

Badminton's Multimedia Courseware of Interactive Design Based on the MOOCs Mode

Mao Jie(✉)

College of Sports Engineering and Information Technology,
Wuhan Sports University, Wuhan 430079, China
Jiem027@163.com

Abstract. Interactive play an important role in the design of multimedia courseware. The multimedia courseware in this paper is based on the platform with PowerPoint 2010. It completed and implemented by PowerPoint. It is the most common software to make courseware; its interactive interface is friendly; it has simple operation. I use VBA technology to design the aspects of interactive and achieve the design about human-computer interaction of sports multimedia courseware and make a combination with computer multimedia technology and physical education teaching. What's more, it provided the means of applied computer technology for Physical Education. It has the promotion of high value and widely used.

1 Introduction

MOOCs originated in twentieth Century 60's Douglas Engelbart proposed a research project, begin to implement from 2008, the earliest practice at Harvard university and Standford university. However, the concept of MOOCs China introduced only in the past two years. This new online course development mode, change the past the traditional network that release resources, learning management systems and learning management system and more integrated open cyber source of the old curriculum development model. The MOOCs teaching mode impact mode reform of China's higher education, physical education in the institutions of higher education for the special education mode also will be faced with tremendous change. This paper study the interaction design of college sports technology curriculum MOOCs mode and college sports curriculum multimedia teaching technology type [1–4].

2 MOOCs Teaching Mode

2.1 MOOCs New Teaching Mode

The MOOCs teaching mode comes from the basic connectionist theory and network learning, which is different from the traditional teaching mode (teach + Learning) and the current open teaching form, is composed of M (Massive) +O (Open) +O (Online) +C (Course) four factors combined to Fig. 1, is a brand-new teaching mode. It brings in

C. Stephanidis (Ed.): HCII 2015 Posters, Part II, CCIS 529, pp. 259–264, 2015.
DOI: 10.1007/978-3-319-21383-5_44

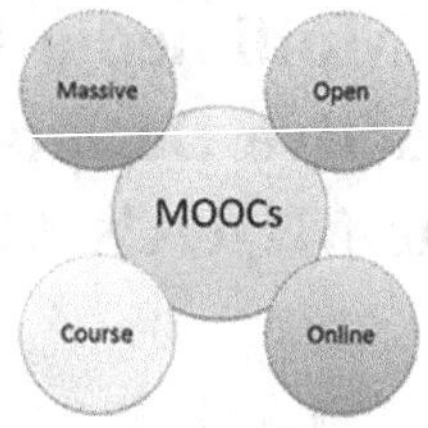

Fig. 1. The composition of the MOOCs teaching mode

the promotion of Global Institute is not only to the traditional teaching mode of impact, also is to reform the teaching system of China's vibration [5, 6].

2.2 Traditional Sports Curriculum Teaching Mode

Mao Zhenming has such a definition of sports teaching model in physical education teaching theory: Sports teaching mode of physical education is set up in a sports teaching thought and theory under the guidance of the program, which includes the structure of teaching process is relatively stable and the corresponding teaching method system, mainly reflected in the design and implementation of physical education teaching on hope and the conception of physical education teaching model consists of three basic elements: namely the guiding ideology of teaching, teaching process, the structure of corresponding law system. This relationship between the three is: the structure of teaching process is the support of the teaching model of "skeleton"; teaching method system is filled with the teaching process of "muscle"; and the guiding ideology of teaching is embedded in the "skeleton" and "muscle", and play the role of coordination and command of the role of the "nerve". The guiding ideology of teaching (neural) embodies the theory teaching mode; the structure of teaching process (skeletal) reflects the stability of the teaching mode; teaching method system (muscle) reflects the sports teaching mode of visual and operable sports.

Sports teaching mode while in constant innovation, but the traditional skill type sports teaching mode, physical education teaching system of teaching motor skills as the main objective [7, 8].

3 The Design of Multimedia Courseware Interactive Link

3.1 The Design of the System Structure

The multimedia courseware interactive design includes video, explanation and practice constitutes three parts, multimedia courseware interactive link design structure diagram in Fig. 2. The three part of the functions are as follows:

- Video insertion: video display, video dynamic on-demand, video capture and real-time display.
- Automatic explanation: TTS language reading.
- Exercises and Tests: Review module, Exercise module, Test module.

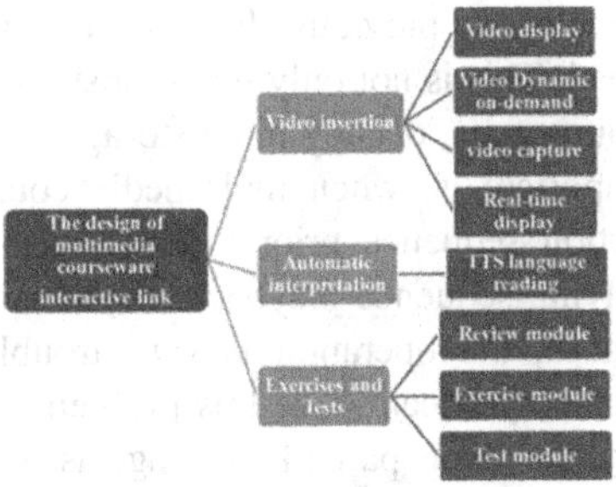

Fig. 2. Multimedia courseware interaction design structure diagram

3.2 Interactive Video Design

Interactivity is the most important difference between the multimedia courseware and other teaching media and teaching material. Multimedia courseware interactivity manifests in no hurry to use more rich media to show the form of content, but also can flexibly control the frequency and order of contents appear, show different content and the feedback information to different learners. In MOOCS mode, can be used to reflect the form of interactive means. Teaching in the course of interaction is very important, especially the sports teaching course. The point of this design is in the video interaction, according to the MOOCS mode of sports curriculum multimedia playback function is described in detail.

First of all, the general solution of video is a video display, especially for the sports teaching in Colleges and universities of media courseware, analysis of all kinds of video insertion methods and advantages into play, and interactive link and the design of the video. In PowerPoint software making video courseware in many ways, the use of controls also many, control method is a ideal method. Using this method, there are many options button, for example: Windows Media Player and Shockwave Flash Object. Windows Media Player controls can be used to any audio and video playback of the controls support, Shockwave Flash Object controls can be used to play the animation file. This design uses the control is a Windows Media Player, set up a video path and file name in Windows Media Player control properties, but also can set the playback control bar, the playback slider bar and video attribute bar, making courseware content and insert video better combination.

Secondly, we choose a personalized video playback control, to realize the use of VBA technology. Video control tools mainly with play, pause, fast forward, rewind and end control functions of playing control tools, which use Textbox, image, multi page control objects to display, the playback control tool of various control buttons.

3.3 Dynamic On-demand Video

The traditional video production is to insert a video page, sports training standardized action and scientific methods, so in the multimedia courseware of physical education curriculum, we need a large amount of video data as a reference. For example, badminton project, a set of training video less including more than a dozen video more than 100. If in accordance with the previous slide insert a video to make courseware, will bring the huge workload. This is not only time-consuming and laborious, but also increases the size of the courseware, occupy more storage space to load and run speed slows down, the more important is, when multimedia courseware playing, only in accordance with the insertion sequence prior video is also in accordance with the multimedia courseware playing sequence playback. If you want to skip a video, or go back to view a video before, the operation is very troublesome, so bring a poor interaction, and dynamic video just can solve this problem.

In the interface design, the main part of the page is a video playback window. Below the video window is a combination of drop-down box, so as to achieve the realization of multi video playback in the leaflet in PPT. The video options displayed in the combo box, and the establishment of broadcast links.

3.4 Video Capture and Real-Time Display

Video capture and real-time display of the idea is for students to grasp the correct technical movement of badminton. Through the camera to capture the student movement and real-time display, compared with the standard action courseware, to correct technical movement irregularities.

3.4.1 Interface Design

Real time display interface is mainly composed of "turn on" and "turn off" two space button switch camera control, interface design is shown below in Fig. 3. To open the camera, the window on the left of the screen will display the real-time camera captures images. At the same time, the right side of the window as an example video, there are two control buttons below the window, were "display" and "turn off", broadcast and control of the example video.

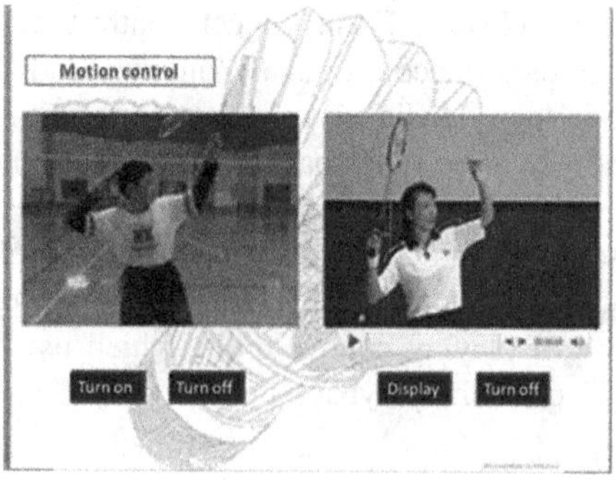

Fig. 3. Interface design

3.4.2 Realizing Method

At present, simple realization of real-time display function of VBAproject or insert Flash call camera method. Our design by means of selecting to insert Flash controls.

Create a SWF file, real-time video production to obtain the camera, you can use the Flash provided by the Camera class from the camera to capture video system. In the Flashplayer display, need to use the Video class of surveillance video, which added to the display list (Fig. 4). Detailed design steps are as follows.

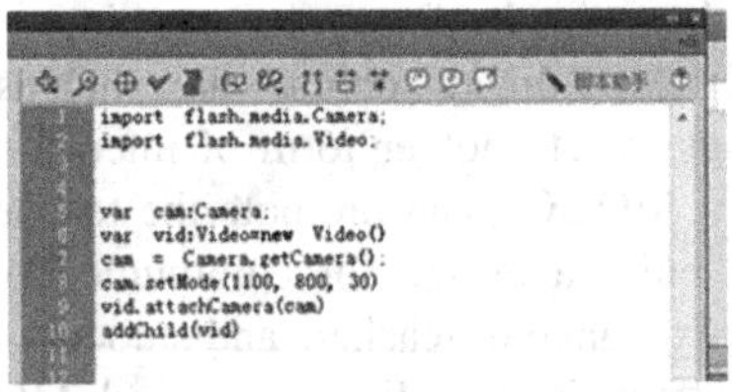

Fig. 4. Surveillance video class: Video()

First, create a named cam Camera class and a named vid Video class: var cam: Camera;var vid:Video = new Video();Use the Camera class getCamera () method, create a connection with the computer camera: cam = Camera.getCamera ();Setting in pixels to capture video width and height, the default value is only 160 and 120. So, video interface width and height is set to 1100 and 800, the request rate for data capture camera set to 30 frames per second: cam.setMode(1100, 800, 30). Then, use the Video class to the attachCamera () method to real-time video capture is added to the Video object: vid.attachCamera (cam), and Add an instance of the Video class to display the list of addChild (VID), you can view real-time video image.

4 Conclusion

4.1 Design Highlights

Design of the interactive courseware should use the convenient and compact software, in which all kinds of text, pictures, animation, sound, video should constitute reasonable, more need to be illustrated, dynamic and static combination. The design of the innovation lies in the development of PowerPoint software using VBA technology, and the use of various control tools in development tools, such as buttons, text boxes, option box etc. The design scheme of multimedia courseware creating custom, increase the operability and interactive features, so as to change the design of PowerPoint courseware interactivity disadvantages of poor. We innovate design of video capture and display in real time, for students to grasp the correct technical movement of badminton. Through the camera to capture the student movement and real-time display, compared with the standard action, thereby timely correcting technical action irregularities. Through the real-time interaction, is students deepen impression, improve teaching effect.

4.2 Enhance Interaction Between Teachers and Students

With a lot of technical action in sports teaching materials, it is difficult for students to observe clearly the moment, teachers cannot pause and playback in the demonstration process, which influence the teaching effect. By means of the camera to capture images of video contrast examples video, make students technical specification of action, to help students quickly grasp the learning content. Through interactive multimedia courseware, students can have a deeper understanding of action.The disadvantage is the lack of multimedia courseware can not realize the communication of teacher and student, the teacher will lose the leading role, teaching effect will be decreased. Through the interaction of the multimedia courseware, such as the use of video display real-time interactive settings, meet another form of interaction between teachers and students under the mode of MOOCs, can promote the teachers and students to teach and study enthusiasm, to build a bridge for communication between teachers and students, to strengthen the exchange of teachers and students, arouse the interest, so as to enhance the teaching effect. Today, E-learning and MOOCs the impact of the traditional education technology and education form, no matter what kind of education form is in order to better serve for the education.

Acknowledgment. We thank Zheng Yizhen, Lu Qi and Du Yunyun for helpful discussions and the referees for greatly improving the manuscript. The research was supported by Wuhan Sport University, the Teaching Study Foundation.

References

1. Liu, Q., Shi, D.: Multimedia Courseware Design Cases and Course. Tsinghua University Press, Beijing (2012)
2. Qiao, L., Zhang, J.: Theory and Practice of Multimedia Courseware. Tsinghua University Press, Beijing (2011)
3. Zheng, A., Cao, G.: Visual Basic Practical Course. Publishing House of Electronics Industry, Beijing (2010)
4. Wu, L., Tan, X.J.: Access Database Technology and Application. Beijing University of Posts and Telecommunications Press, Beijing (2011)
5. Wang, Y.: Cross-media reading: the new trend of ubiquitous reading integrated O2O and MOOCs. China Educ. Technol. **1**, 22–28 (2015)
6. Wang, Z., Chen, L., Zheng, Q.: The development track of MOOCs and three forms of practice. China Educ. Technol. **7**, 25–33 (2014)
7. Mao, Z.: Teaching Strategies of Physical Education. Higher Education Press, Beijing (2011)
8. Mao, Z., Yu, S.: Sports Teaching Method Skills and Case. Beijing Normal University Press, Beijing (2012)

Development of STEAM Educational Games Focused on Aesthetic and Bodily Expression in K-12 Science Class

Hyung Sook Kim[1,2], Hale Kim[1,3], and Yong Hyun Park[1](✉)

[1] Major in Human Art and Technology, Graduate Program in Robot Engineering, Inha University, Incheon, South Korea
{khsook12,hikim}@inha.ac.kr, yhpark81@gmail.com

[2] Major in Dance, Department of Kinesiology, Inha University, Incheon, South Korea

[3] Department of Information and Communication Engineering, Inha University, Incheon, South Korea

Abstract. The purpose of this study is to introduce gesture recognition-based STEAM educational games using Kinect. The game is instructional media for evoking a student's interest and helping students understand in a STEAM education class. We suggested a STEAM education program that consisted of visualization of the science knowledge through aesthetic and bodily expression for middle school science class. In the development process of this STEAM program, the main challenge was an instruction method of scientific knowledge of human body anatomy and physiology. Gesture recognition-based game including science learning material should be an excellent educational tool to make student comprehend and understand complex science knowledge. In addition, the game is an excellent tool to visualize the contents. The gesture recognition-based educational game and the STEAM program were offered to model demonstration middle schools, entitled as 'STEAM leaders' schools' in South Korea. The result of the trial lesson is this game motivated and increased students' activities and learning. 55.8 % of the students responded that this program was satisfied and gesture-recognition based game were interesting. We believe that this educational game is suitable for STEAM education in science, dance and physical education class. Gesture recognition-based game by Kinect would be an excellent answer for the next generation's instructional media.

Keywords: Gesture recognition-based game · NUI · Bodily expression · STEAM education · Science · Dance · Kinect

1 Introduction

Nowadays, many researches were conducted to investigate the effect of educational games on students' learning in a variety of subjects, not only software engineering, computer science but also mathematics, language, and science [1, 2]. The previous researches have reported that educational games enhance the interest of students and

C. Stephanidis (Ed.): HCII 2015 Posters, Part II, CCIS 529, pp. 265–270, 2015.
DOI: 10.1007/978-3-319-21383-5_45

increase their learning motivation [3]. Computer games also are powerful tools for visualization and interaction. In the classroom, the teacher uses several visualization tools in learning scientific topics from a blackboard to TV because it helps students understand scientific conceptual relationship [4].

The classical style lecture which using passive communication media composed of only text and images is difficult for a student to visualize the topic of science class. To overcome this shortcoming in curricular delivery, many teachers use much animation and motion picture learning materials. These animated learning contents is more capable to attract student's interest than the text so that this visualized contents can help students comprehend and understand scientific knowledge. However, this approach could induce only students' passive learning.

The importance and benefits of active learning were accepted by education profession and teachers [5]. A computer game is the typical active communication media. A game is the best tool ever for active and interactive learning. While students are playing a game, they are doing, acting, and interacting with contents. In this idea is the main motivation of this study. We develop the educational contents for students to interact and learn the science class materials using Kinect. Using this gesture-recognition based game with NUI, students can move their body actively and receive the rapid feedback from a teacher and co-learners.

In the science class, many students feel difficulty and are boring to study the knowledge of the science curriculum. So, many teachers use the teaching method that is to introduce the elementary content firstly and to teach more difficult one gradually. In this process, the primary challenge is to conduct rapid and precisely evaluate and to give adequate feedback to the student about how exactly students understand it. There is an effective way that check of the result of playing an educational game with the Kinect and big screen with a projector in the science class.

Gesture recognition-based interface is an excellent educational tool to make students more active. Learning through body movement could be a good way to learn not only kids but also the high school students [6]. Kinect is an NUI device that offer the unique way to control the computer through the body movement. So, gesture recognition-based game including science learning material should be an effective educational tool to make student comprehend and understand complex science knowledge. In addition, body movement is related to Dance and Physical Education. So, we suggested a steam education program that consist of visualization of the science knowledge and aesthetic and bodily expression.

The purpose of this study is to introduce application using Natural User Interface (NUI) for evoke a student's interest in STEAM science class. The classical style lecture which using learning material composed of text and images is boring to students. To overcome this shortcoming, gesture recognition-based educational game could be the best option. Gesture recognition-based game including science learning material should be a good educational tool to make student comprehend and understand complex science knowledge. In addition, the game is an excellent tool to visualize the contents.

1.1 Adopting the Concept of Dance Your Ph.D.

'Dance your PhD' is an online contest that challenges scientists to explain their PhD thesis topic quickly with the Dance video. In 2008 Science Magazine and the American Academy for the Advancement of Science (AAAS) hosted the first ever 'Dance Your PhD Contest' in Vienna, Austria. Moreover, till now the competition has continued.

The rules are simple;

1. *You must have a Ph.D., or be working on one as a Ph.D. student.*
2. *Your Ph.D. must be in a science-related field.*
3. *You must be part of the dance.*
4. *Solo dancers or teams are allowed, but the prize goes to the PhD author.*

This contest concept is a good trial to explain easily and to visualize complicated science knowledge. This concept is a representative example of STEAM education. In science class, students learn and organize scientific knowledge, and they compose dance about that scientific knowledge in dance class.

2 Development of STEAM Education Program

2.1 STEAM Program for Bodily Expression for Science Education

We suggested a STEAM education program that consisted of visualization of the science knowledge through aesthetic and bodily expression for middle school science class. The program's scientific contents were the human body anatomy and physiology in middle school curricular level. This STEAM program designed by development team organized by artists, scientists, engineers, curriculum specialists, teachers.

STEAM education is an acronym referring to the academic fields of Science, Technology, Engineering, Art, and Mathematics. Nowadays STEAM fields become the most essential because the arts-based education offers opportunities for students to develop his creativity and imagination. Aesthetic and bodily expression based on scientific knowledge could be a good approach for designing STEAM education program.

In the development process of this program, the main challenge was an instruction method of scientific knowledge of human body anatomy and physiology. This content is not easy for students to comprehend the contents of the class. Before aesthetic and bodily expression of something, the student must understand that. In this point of view, gesture recognition-based game including science learning material should be a good educational tool to make student comprehend and understand complex science knowledge. In addition, the game is an excellent tool to visualize the contents.

In the class plan, student played first gesture recognition-based game in order to learn human body anatomy, such as organs name, location, function and physiological process. When students were using this game, they moved their body to control the gesture recognition-based game. This activity is helpful in two ways. First, it is more effective way to learn scientific knowledge through body movement with visualized contents than watching a scientific animation. Learning through the body movement is helpful to organize scientific knowledge. Second, it is a good preparation and practice for aesthetic and bodily expression. Gesturing is a good warm-up to the bodily expression. Playing gesture recognition-based game pulled students out of their comfort zone by icebreaking activity.

So, we suggested a STEAM education program that consist of visualization of the science knowledge and aesthetic and bodily expression. In addition, body movement is related to dance and physical education. It could be an STEAM education including Science, physical education, and dance classes. Therefore, this gesture recognition-based education game is suitable for STEAM education.

2.2 Development of Educational Game

The game was developed using Windows Presentation Foundation (WPF) and Kinect for Windows Developer Toolkit ver. 1.8. In SDK, Control Basics of WPF – C# Sample was modified for creating main GUI of the educational game. The images of games are collected via the Google images searches.

The educational game is the human body anatomy and physiology in middle school curricular level. The game's playing is matching and arranging the images and test blocks. The contents include that body anatomy, such as organs name, location, function and physiological process. Table 1 shows the summary of specific contents.

There are two kind of game to play. One is a drag-and-drop matching game. Another is an arrangement game. Kinect, NUI interface device, was used for the controller of the game. If the player wants to drag up the image, he should straighten the arm forward, palm facing towards the sensor and make a fist with his hand. Then he should move the images into right position along background image. To drop-down is the opening of the closed fist. The stopwatch measures the time from when the game is started until it is finished. The gameplay time is recorded in order to induce competition (Fig. 1).

Table 1. STEAM educational game contents

Level	Program	Contents
• Middle school	• Digestive system organs	Matching digestive organ images diagram along the anatomical body image (stomach, pancreas, small intestine, large intestine)
	• Components of blood cells	Matching blood cell images (white blood cell, red blood cell, platelets along) along appropriate text descriptions
	• Cell division – mitosis and meiosis	Arrange cell division phase images (mitosis: prophase, prometaphase, metaphase, anaphase, telophase, cytokinesis, meiosis: interphase, prophase, metaphase, anaphase, white blood cell, red blood cell, platelets along)
	• Embryonic and fetal development	Arrange embryonic and fetal development period images (2 cells, 16 cells, morula, blastocyst, implantation)

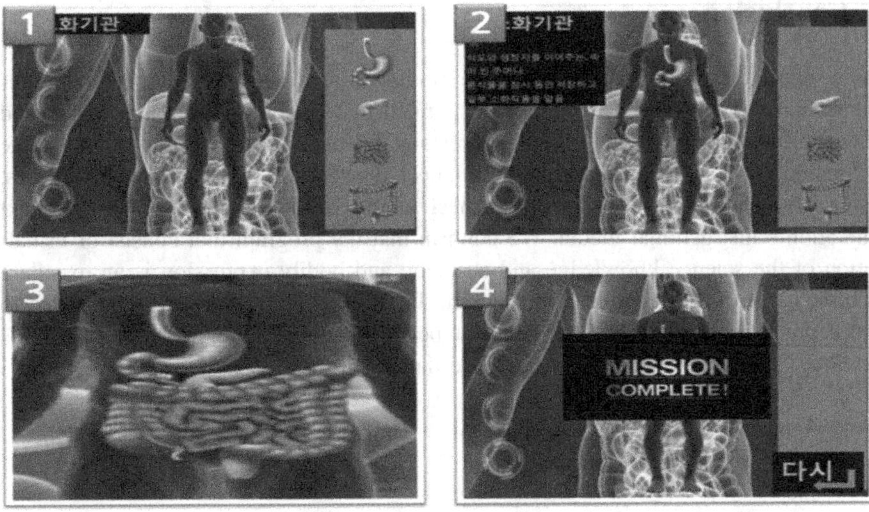

Fig. 1. The capture images of the educational game (digestive system organs)

3 Demonstration Lesson and Students' Feedback

The gesture recognition-based educational game and the STEAM program were offered to a demonstration middle school, entitled as 'STEAM leaders' school' in South Korea. Lessons took place in the science laboratory and classroom. The instructional devices to set the lessons included a computer, a Kinect, a projector and screen, and speakers. After the demonstration lesson, the questionnaire was surveyed for program satisfaction of the students. The result of the survey was that 55.8 % of the students responded that this program was satisfied and gesture-recognition based game were interesting (Fig. 2).

Fig. 2. Students playing the educational game using Kinect during science class

4 Conclusion

The result of the trial lesson is this game motivated and increased students' activities and learning. 55.8 % of the students responded that this program was satisfied and gesture-recognition based game were interesting. We believe that this educational game is suitable for STEAM education in science, dance and physical education class. Gesture recognition-based game by Kinect would be a great answer for the next generation's instructional media. We confirm that the program that consist of visualization of the science knowledge and aesthetic and bodily expression is an excellent example of the STEAM education program. In addition, body movement is related to Dance and Physical Education. It could be an extended STEAM education class including Science, physical education, and dance classes.

Acknowledgement. This work was supported by INHA UNIVERSITY Research Grant.

References

1. Foti, L.T., Hannafin, R.D.: Games and multimedia in foreign language learning-using back-story in multimedia and avatar-based games to engage foreign language learners: a pilot study. Int. J. Emerg. Technol. Learn. **3**, 40–44 (2008)
2. Sung, H.-Y., Hwang, G.-J.: A collaborative game-based learning approach to improving students' learning performance in science courses. Comput. Educ. **63**, 43–51 (2013)
3. Yang, Y.-T.C.: Building virtual cities, inspiring intelligent citizens: digital games for developing students' problem-solving and learning motivation. Comput. Educ. **59**, 365–377 (2012)
4. McClean, P., Johnson, C., Rogers, R., Daniels, L., Reber, J., Slator, B.M., Terpstra, J., White, A.: Molecular and cellular biology animations: development and impact on student learning. Cell Biol. Educ. **4**, 169–179 (2005)
5. Bonwell, C.C., Eison, J.A.: Active learning: creating excitement in the classroom. 1991 ASHE-ERIC higher education reports. ERIC (1991)
6. Yang, J.C., Chen, C.H., Jeng, M.C.: Integrating video-capture virtual reality technology into a physically interactive learning environment for English learning. Comput. Educ. **55**, 1346–1356 (2010)

Out-of-Class Online Language Learning Partnership Between Russian and American Students: Analysis of Tandem Project Results

Marina Kogan[1(✉)], Nina Popova[1], Konstantin Shestakov[2], and Lonny Harrison[3]

[1] Department of Linguistics and Cross-Cultural Communication, Peter the Great St. Petersburg Polytechnic University, Saint Petersburg, Russia
m_kogan@inbox.ru, ninavaspo@mail.ru

[2] Online Language School, WEBILANG, Omsk, Russia
konstantin73@yandex.ru

[3] University of Texas at Arlington, Arlington, TX, USA
lonnyharrison@uta.edu

Abstract. A telecollaborative project between Russian and American students is analyzed in terms of its organization, technology, and linguistic and intercultural aspects involved. Conditions for creating a collaborative environment are described, with the conversational topics, intended outcomes, and some pitfalls of the project being accentuated. The main conclusion of the project is the necessity of introducing intercultural aspects well in advance in order to teach students to distinguish the cultural dimension of their communication in the tandem sessions of the project.

Keywords: Communicative skills · Native speaker · Non-native speaker · Instructor · Telecollaborative project · Student groups · Language level · Videoconference · Drawbacks of the project · Mistake correction

1 Introduction

One of the reputable ways of developing learners' communicative skills is their participation in tandem projects with partners from target language countries. Out-of-class interaction with native speakers (NS) is crucial to practice conversation and interaction management in real-life contexts. Such projects allow the participants to preserve the balance of interests because each of the participants plays two parts by turns: both of a learner of the foreign language and expert of the mother tongue. This decreases the risk of "face loss," stimulates negotiation of meaning of unknown words and notions, and contributes to familiarization with little-known cultural realities [1, 2]. Eventually it increases learners' motivation to study and "learners' confidence and intercultural competence." To make it more efficient, a proper preliminary task design stage should be paid serious attention [3].

Some researchers believe that "all language interactions between native speakers and non-native speakers have a cultural dimension even though it may not be foregrounded" [4], thus becoming intended outcomes of collaborative projects. Online intercultural

C. Stephanidis (Ed.): HCII 2015 Posters, Part II, CCIS 529, pp. 271–276, 2015.
DOI: 10.1007/978-3-319-21383-5_46

activities have become popular and are more and more successfully integrated into the foreign language classroom [5] in the format of telecollaboration.

The technology by which long-distance exchanges are carried out and the degree of access to it have an undeniably strong impact on the course of the exchange. Most commonly used communication tools today are still more text oriented, while video- and audio-based tools are gaining in importance. This consideration seems encouraging as we describe our pilot research into an online language learning partnership between Russian and American students, which was a semester-long project in 2013–2014 intending to evaluate the following aspects of collaborative learning:

- whether it increases the participants' motivation in language learning;
- whether the learners negotiate meaning effectively and whether native speakers can be real experts in the explanation of linguistic issues;
- which conversational topics are the most suitable for this type of collaboration;
- which format and technical means are suitable for this type of collaboration.

2 Background

The project under consideration grew out of the following prerequisites:

1. the steady interest in innovative approaches (particularly based on using ICT) in SLA which has been manifested for years through different projects at the Linguistics and Cross-Cultural Communication Department of SPbPU (see for example, [6, 7]);
2. substantial experience of Webilang developers in running Russian-American tandem projects for second language learners for 5 years (mainly for students of Omsk Law Academy and their American counterparts). (For details, see [8, 9]).

To create conditions for a collaborative environment for Russian students and teachers of English, and American students and teachers of Russian, the site Webilang.com was designed in 2012. The site offers a venue for delivering courses led by **native speaker instructors** and projects where students are connected with **native speaker students**. Webilang has audio and text blogs, a virtual classroom for synchronous communication, and a learning management system (LMS) called *Webilang Intranet* (Fig. 1).

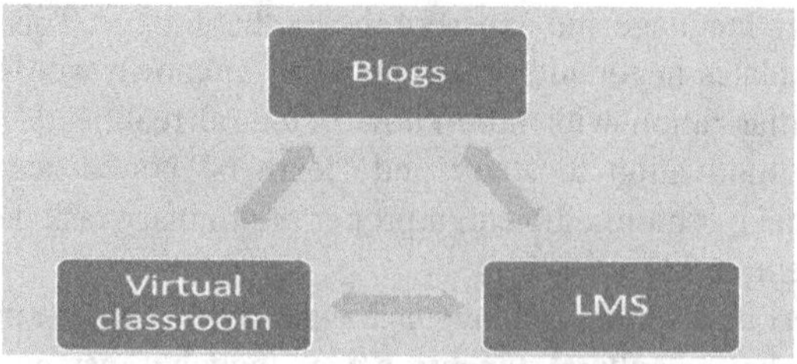

Fig. 1. The Webilang site architecture

3 Procedure

Instructors and learners met in the audio-video synchronous environment for eight sessions (1 h to 1 h 30 per session).

The project between a group of 8 SPbPU (St. Petersburg Polytechnic University, St. Petersburg, Russia) master's students majoring in civil engineering and a group of 5 UTA (University of Texas at Arlington, Arlington, TX, USA) university students studying Russian lasted for 14 weeks during the fall semester of 2013–2014. Five mini-groups of two to three students were formed. Students recorded each dyadic or triadic meeting with their partner/s and send recordings to their instructor. Instructors checked the submitted tasks, analyzed the discussions, and prepared individual recommendations for participants for the next meeting.

Students were required to do writing tasks related to the topic under discussion beforehand, so that their native speaker partners could correct it and provide feedback during the on-line session. It was agreed that the tasks should be alternatively conducted in English and in Russian during each on-line session. At the end of the course all the participants were asked to complete a final fourteen-item survey. Twelve of them were 7-point semantic differential scale questions aiming at measuring students' attitude toward learning English, their English teacher and English-speaking counterparts; their motivation to learn English; degree of anxiety while speaking the FL/TL in and outside the classroom; and preferences in suggested communication tasks.

The role of the instructors' collaboration in making decisions on task choice and sequencing [3] and preventing possible failures of telecollaborative projects [10] is of extreme importance. Most examples of task sequencing in the literature generally follow three different stages in their exchange: (1) an introduction/opening phase which gives learners the opportunity to get to know their remote partners and the latter's culture better through information exchange; (2) a comparative phase, in which students use different types of tasks to engage in comparisons of different aspects of their home and target cultures, and (3) a final stage, in which a result is produced in the form of a piece of work reflecting the students' collaboration [3]. According to the above schemata the instructors agreed upon the course design presented in Table 1.

4 Results and Discussion

The analysis of the questionnaire data from the Russian participants of the project showed that they have a high motivation to learn General English (M = 6.7) and English for practical purposes (career growth, participation in international conferences, exchange programs, etc.) (M = 6.6), and a very positive attitude towards learning English (M = 6.7), and toward their American partners (M = 7) and the English teacher (M = 6.7). Despite the last finding, students noticed that they felt more nervous while speaking at the lesson (M = 4) than during telecommunication sessions with their American partners (M = 1.9).

As for the course syllabus, the students approved of all the topics, except for the last one, which was the most professionally oriented. The reasons might be various: for example, it was not elaborated well enough by the instructors, which is crucial for

Table 1. Main topics and intended outcomes in Webilang course program

Task type	Description	Intended outcomes
(1) Information exchange on *cultural and geographical autobiographies*	1. Establishment of personal relationship with partners through answering a series of questions prepared by both parties beforehand 2. Presenting favorite locations to the partner and discussion through *Virtual Touring Around One's Native City*	Establishment of personal relationship with partners/increased awareness of cultural differences
Engaging in informal discussion based on *provoking newspaper articles*	Students are provided with general questions (topics 3&4 in our course) 3. *Science & the Future of the World* 4. *Global Warming: A Real Problem or a Bluff?*	Learner independence/development of fluency in the target language
Carrying out virtual *interviews on education,* producing a written report based on an interview process.	5. Group discussion on *Peculiarities of Russian and American systems of Higher Education* in an on-line conference mode	Familiarization with the differences in Russian and American systems of Higher Education
(2) comparison and analysis of job issues	6. Conducting *Job Interviews* based on the analysis of a target language CV prepared and sent to partner beforehand so that she/he can correct it and make up related questions in a partner's target language	Familiarization with the specificities of hunting for a job in the USA and Russia
(3) Collaboration on product creation	7. *Developing and promoting a new device* aimed at focusing on communication and productive activity for professional purposes	Mastering teamwork among students and developing reciprocity

success of such kind of task [11], requiring higher-order cognitive skills, according to the revised Bloom's taxonomy. Another matter of importance is that the last task was mainly oriented toward Russian students majoring in civil engineering, ignoring the fact that some of the American participants were from the Humanities domain and were not interested in device design.

According to the instructors' report and the students' diaries, the principal drawback of the project was related to technical glitches such as faulty connections or problems with sound and image (no sound, poor image, distortions, etc.). The participants noted that technical problems had decreased their "useful" communication time. The experts stress technical difficulties remain the most important disadvantage of synchronous voice-based CMC projects. Therefore, teachers should be prepared to face and solve these kinds of unavoidable problems when using this medium [12].

Participants also criticized the complexity of the procedure for recording sessions on the Webilang platform. They recommended using a simpler and more easily available platform such as Skype or social networks in future telecollaborative projects. The participants also wished that they had more freedom to choose materials for discussion (films, songs, poems, articles, TV programs).

Despite these drawbacks, some of the participants arranged additional meetings using Webilang. One of them was devoted to idiomatic expressions in American English and Russian. When asked during a follow-up interview 6 months after the project had finished if they continued to contact their partners, the Russian participants answered that they hadn't, stressing that if the project had continued they would have found ways to overcome such obstacles as the lack of free time and the above-mentioned difficulties. This proves that despite high internal motivation to communicate with native speakers of the target language, learners need external support, an organized framework, a teacher's feedback, and an opportunity to report about their findings in order make such contacts long-lasting.

The main positive feature of the project was a very friendly atmosphere created by the mutual attitudes of the participants toward one another. Most of them would smile and even laugh during the sessions when discussing certain funny words and expressions in both languages. Both parties, especially the Russians, tried to make sure they were properly understood and repeated the necessary words over again for better comprehension by their American counterparts.

The following weaknesses were also noted and should be taken into account in future telecollaborative projects:

- The assumed "balance of interests" during each session (regular taking of turns and target/native language use) was not often preserved. Course instructors pointed this out in their after-session recommendations, but it did not improve the situation to a great extent. This is probably difficult to avoid if the project mainly runs outside the classroom.
- The Russian participants were more active, aggressive, and direct in correcting their partners' mistakes, but at the same time demonstrated friendliness by facial expression and gestures. Thus, pre-teaching hedging structures and ways of politely interrupting partners (in both the native and target language) is desirable in such projects in the future. The Americans did not correct their partners unless the mistake resulted in communication failure. For example, no corrections were made in the question asked by a Russian participant, "*How much the house costs?*"
- Another shortcoming was a lack of instruction concerning the necessity of collecting more examples of appropriate language use by native speakers.
- The forth drawback of the project was lack of participation on the part of the American students, as the Russian participants were generally more active. Unfortunately, lack of participation on one side jeopardizes the quality of the whole project.

5 Conclusion

Reflecting on our experience with the Webilang tandem learning project, we would definitely advocate for the continuation of similar projects in the future. In spite of certain pitfalls, partially of a technical nature, we consider the positive learning atmosphere to be the main achievement of this project. Taking into account the fact that direct instructor intervention into the communication process is less effective, one recommendation for the future of tandem learning projects is to draw attention to the problem of intercultural aspects well in advance. Students should be encouraged to be more active in their communication and see the enormous opportunities for cultural interaction afforded by the project.

Acknowledgements. The authors would like to acknowledge and express their gratitude to Karina Victorova and Larisa Dostal', who were instructors of the Russian and American groups, respectively, in this project.

References

1. Tudini, V.: Form-focused social repertoires in an online language learning partnership. J. Pragmatics. **50**(1), 187–202 (2013)
2. Van der Zwaard, R., Bannink, A.: Video call or chat? Negotiation of meaning and issues of face in telecollaboration. System **44**, 137–148 (2014)
3. O'Dowd, R., Waire, P.: Critical issues in telecollaborative task design. Comput. Assist. Lang. Learn. **22**(2), 173–188 (2009)
4. Levy, M.: Culture, culture learning and new technologies: towards a pedagogical framework. Lang. Learn. & Technol. **11**(2), 104–127 (2007)
5. O'Dowd, R.: Foreign language education and the rise of on-line communication: a review of promises and realities. In: O'Dowd, R. (ed.) Online Intercultural Exchange: An Introduction for Foreign Language Teachers, pp. 17–40. Multilingual Matters, Clevedon (2007)
6. Almazova, N., Kogan, M.: Computer assisted individual approach to acquiring foreign vocabulary of students major. In: Zaphiris, P., Ioannou, A. (eds.) LCT. LNCS, vol. 8524, pp. 248–257. Springer, Heidelberg (2014)
7. Kogan, M., Popova, N.: Integration of open internet resources into an ESP course of English for complex safety students. In: Barr, D. (ed.) WorldCALL-2013: Global Perspectives on CALL, pp. 145–148. Glasgow (2013)
8. Shestakov, K., Harrison, L.: Intercontinental Russian-English workshop. In: Barr, D. (ed.) WorldCALL-2013: Global Perspectives on CALL, pp. 305–309. Glasgow (2013)
9. Shestakov, K.: International cooperation of language learners and language teachers in learning management system: methodology and results. In: Modern Technologies for Training in Companies and Educational Institutions. Moscow (2011)
10. O'Dowd, R., Ritter, M.: Understanding and working with 'failed communication' in telecollaborative exchanges. CALICO J. **23**(3), 623–642 (2006)
11. Vetter, A., Chanier, T.: Supporting oral production for professional purposes in synchronous communication with heterogeneous learners. ReCALL **18**(1), 5–23 (2006)
12. Bueno Alastuey, M.C.: Perceived benefits and drawbacks of synchronous voice-based computer-mediated communication in the foreign language classroom. Comput. Assist. Lang. Learn. **24**(5), 419–432 (2011)

Non-calibrated Peer Assessment: An Effective Assessment Method for Student Creative Works

Jinshuang Li(✉), Yu Zhang, and Kening Gao

Computing Center, Northeastern University, Shenyang, China
{ljs, zhangyu, gkn}@cc.neu.edu.cn

Abstract. In online education, peer and self assessment has got a lot of attention because it serves as a useful tool for scaling the grading of open-ended works. But peer and self assessment does not always produce accurate results because of some reasons. Firstly, experts and students may grade at different scale; Secondly, students are inclined to rate themselves higher than to rate others; Thirdly, some students may not take the assessment seriously; Fourthly, correcting for grader biases also need complex computation. In this paper, we present a non-calibrated peer grading method to solve the problems mentioned above. We make 4 experiments with 5-category rating scale showing that our method can get good performance, which convinces that it can be an effective assessment method for student creative works.

Keywords: Non-calibrated peer assessment · Wisdom of crowds · Online education · Peer assessment · Self assessment

1 Introduction

It is well known that online education has much better advantage than traditional education since everyone can participate and access the online course freely. But how to assess the students by homework or exam, especially the open-ended work, is a challenging problem.

The answer of open-ended work is not objected, so it is not possible for automated assessing. The only way we can try is human grading, but experts grading cannot be used in massive online education for tens of thousands students in a single course. Peer and self assessment provide a practical way for student assessment in massive online education, but it does not always give accurate and convinced grades. In this paper, we concerned this problem and try to solve it in a simple and reasonable way.

The remainder of the present paper is organized as follows. In Sect. 2, we discuss the present method for student assessment in massive online education. In Sect. 3, we introduce our solution to this problem. In Sect. 4, we present our experiment and practice. Conclusion is presented in the final section.

C. Stephanidis (Ed.): HCII 2015 Posters, Part II, CCIS 529, pp. 277–282, 2015.
DOI: 10.1007/978-3-319-21383-5_47

2 Peer Assessment and Self Assessment in Massive Online Education

Assessment of students' work means that students submit some works with requirements; the teachers can test how the student can solve a problem and also assess the students' ability of technique skill and creativity. But assessment of students' work also needs time and energy. Peer assessment and self assessment is an effective way to fix the problem, and it does have good performance used in massive online open courses.

Peer assessment and self assessment, is an calibrated assessment,which offer an opportunity to scale both assessment and learning to global classrooms, has been adopted in many classes, including 79 MOOCs on the Coursera platform alone [1]. Here we introduce the main steps of peer and self-assessment briefly.

1. Professors assign the homework to the students.
2. Students hand in the homework.
3. Assessment training. Students first grade some submissions with a grade given by professor as a standard. When the grade given by the student and the professor are close, or when the student has assessed several works (e.g. 5 submissions), then the student can move to the next phrase.
4. Peer assessment. Students assess a certain number of peer submissions.
5. Self-assessment. Students assess their own works after assessing other submissions.
6. Calibration of the results. The algorithm for the calibration is still an open problem.
7. Release and feedback of the final grade results.

It is a very effective way for assess the open-ended work of students. But it has some problems listed below:

- Professors and students may grade at different scale. Though after training phase in step 3, the difference could be reduced, it cannot be eliminated. For some open-ended works, every work has its own characteristic; it is very difficult to unify the view. Moreover, the view of professors is not always correct.
- Students are inclined to grade themselves higher than to grade others. Especially if the grading mark is very important for the student's final grade, it is hard for students to assess their own works objectively. A lot of research show that students are inclined to grade them higher, even knowing that professors involving in the assessment.
- Unlike professors, some students may not take the assessment seriously. Students may make the assessment emotionally, such as giving high marks for familiar students, depressing others' marks for heighten their own, or grading at different scale at different time.
- Calibration of grader biases also need complex computation, which is also an unsolved question. It is very difficult for the students understanding how the grade generated, and it is not helpful for students to improve work quality.

Above all, peer and self assessment is not so convincing compared with expert assessment. In some study show that the students often prefer to professor assessment, even though the grade given by professor is lower than the grade given by other students. We aim at fix the problems mentioned above and present a method which we introduce in the next section.

3 Non-calibrated Peer Assessment

3.1 Non-calibrated Peer Assessment Method

There are two kinds of the open-end works. One is simulated works, such as imitating, facsimile, and Layout using word processing software etc. The other is creative works, such as writing essay, programming, and drawing etc. In intuition, the first kind works have uniform Criteria, Assessment training can make the student's judgments as same as the teacher's judgments. But the second kind works, the creative works, have not uniform criteria. Such as program developing, every student has a different design, even use different software. The standard how assess the technical level of each creative work is difficult to unify. It would be very difficult to achieve effects for assessment training.

Focusing on the need for assessing the creative works, we provide a Non-calibrated Peer Assessment:

1. Professors assign the work to the students with rubric.
2. Students submit their work online.
3. Professors assign the assessment task to students, and students make the assessment. There are some avoiding rules for the assignment.
4. Professors calculate the assessment result and inspect the assessment quality.
   (a) Removing unreasonable assessment: If a student grade unreasonably for one item (e.g. he grade a mark for an unfinished work), his all assessment for this work will be obsolete.
   (b) Calculating the marks: removing the extreme values and average other values.
   (c) Punishment for the irresponsible students.
5. Professors announce the assessment results. Then students can question about it.
6. After revision of the assessment results, the professors announce the final results.

3.2 Theoretical Basis

The theoretical basis of the Non-calibrated Peer Assessment is the wisdom of crowds. It is the process of taking into account the collective opinion of a group of individuals rather than a single expert to answer a question [2, 3]. Non-calibrated Peer Assessment accord with the eight conjectures of the wisdom of crowds [4]:

- It is possible to describe how people in a group think as a whole (a). After training, students can assess works made by the same or similar technique under the same marking criterion.
- In some cases, groups are remarkably intelligent and are often smarter than the smartest people in them (b). There are plenty of students who involve in the assessment, and some students are more experienced than professors in some field,

such as social investigation, project research, students are more adaptable to do this kind of job.
- The three conditions for a group to be intelligent are diversity, independence, and decentralization (c). Obviously, the students from massive online course meet the conditions definitely.
- The best decisions are a product of disagreement and contest (d). There are a thousand Hamlets in a thousand people's eyes. Everyone has his or her own perspective when assessing open-ended work. The view of teachers is not always the best or the most reasonable.
- Too much communication can make the group as a whole less intelligent (e). There is no need of communication for the students to assess each other's work.
- Information aggregation functionality is needed (f). As we mentioned before, the submission and assessment of homework are both done online with fully developed function.
- The right information needs to be delivered to the right people in the right place, at the right time, and in the right way (g). The system of submission and assessment meet this demand.
- There is no need to chase the expert (h). Though students are not experts, they have studied the course systematically. Students can make the assessment independently without the experts.

As we can see, choosing students to do the subjective assessment meet every characteristics of the wisdom of crowds, so it can be used effectively.

4 Experiment and Practice

We make our practice and experiment based on Liaoning ShareCourse of China [5], which is a platform of massive online courses. Unlike some other online courses, we provide our materials once for all. We think it will help students study more freely. We take *"Fundamentals of Computer Applications*" as our course for experiment. We have above 2100 students in this course and we choose 336 students in 12 classes for this experiment. We use four assessment works for experiment with 4 assessment items for every works. Here we introduce our experiment with Work 1 as an example.

1. Requirement of works: It must be a creative work. The developed tools for works is recommended but not restricted. Work 1 is a video work with specific topic. Students should choose one from three topics. For the recommended tool, we provide necessary auxiliary materials for help, such as case video.
2. Evaluation dimension: We set 4 dimensions for the video work, each set 6 options for every index with value 0–5, which represents "not finished", "very poor", "poor", "just fine", "good", "very good" separately.
3. Assignment of assessment: We announce the assessment procedure. We emphasize that the students who make unreliable assessment would be punished. It means that if a student give a mark deviating the average mark too much, the mark will be put away and he will be punished by 10 % cut down for his own work.

4. Students have two weeks to hand in works on the website of platform under direction [6].
5. Assignment of students for assessment: For every student involving in the assessment, he cannot assess the works of his classmates. Every works will be assessed by at least 8 people with randomly assignment.
6. Assessment procedure: Under the supervising of professors, students are organized to do the assessment at the same time. The user interface to assessment is very simple and students can log in and do the assessment even without direction.
7. Calibration of the assessment results: In this phrase, we remove all the unreliable assessment. If a student grade unreasonably for an item, such as grading a high mark for an unfinished work or grading a zero mark for a finished work, his all assessment for this work will be obsolete.

Here we show the result of our all four experiments. Table 1 present the statistics of the evaluators. As shown in Fig. 1, precise assessment is 88.1 % and 1 bias percent is 11.0 %; bias above 1 is 0.9 %. For one particular work, the result is almost unchanged. AVE means average score and $\lfloor AVE \rfloor$ and $\lceil AVE \rceil$ means floor integer and ceiling integer separately.

Table 1. Statistics of the evaluators

	Work 1	Work 2	Work3	Work 4	Sum
Assessment items	8784	1644	4884	1924	17236
Number of evaluators	259	65	189	71	584
Number of evaluators above 10	84	0	39	0	123
Number of evaluators above 9	73	9	79	7	168
Number of evaluators above 8	36	1	41	15	93
Number of evaluators above 7	29	13	23	17	82
Number of evaluators above 6	23	21	3	19	66
Number of evaluators above 5	14	21	4	13	52

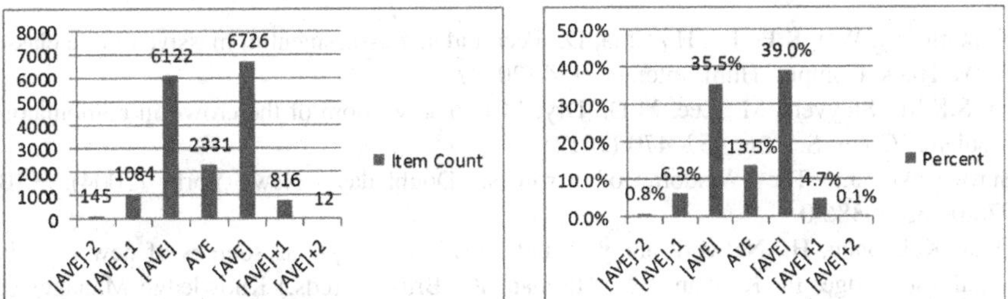

Fig. 1. The result of assessment for all four works

8. Announcement of the assessment results for one week. Students are able to inspect all the other students' works. If a student gets a higher mark, he will get more inspection by others. So it not only helps students get good experience, but also helps professors inspect cheating behavior.
9. Announcement of the final results.

After finished assessment, 20 works have been extracted from different level works. 12 teachers assess these works, each teacher assesses 10 works, and each work is assessed by 6 teachers. Teacher assessment results and student assessment results have good consistency: although the scores are different, the order remains consistent.

We studied using spiral assessment (student improve their works on the second round assessment.). Students must explain in what aspects improved. The result show that the quality of work has significantly improved.

5 Conclusion

We proposed an effective method for student assessment for the creative work. We found that the method can be used in massive online course for the assessment of open-ended works. It not only helps improving the working effectiveness of professors, but also makes students understand what they studied more clearly.

Compared to peer assessment, our method has three advantages: First, students do not need to be trained. Although students and teachers have different perspectives, the outcome of the assessment will be no difference. Second, we have no self assessment phrase. It will depress the down side effect for the assessment. Third, the criterion of grading is open to everyone, which is easy to understand and inspect. It will help to attract students to involve in the assessment work and make some progress.

Acknowledgment. Research was sponsored in part by the Liaoning Science and Technology Projects (2013217004-1) and Fundamental Research Funds for the Central Universities (N130316001).

References

1. Kulkarni, C., Wei, K.P., Le, H., Chia, D.: Peer and self assessment in massive online classes. ACM Trans. Comput. Hum. Interact. **9**, 4 (2013)
2. Yi, S.K.M., Steyvers, M., Lee, M.D., Dry, M.J.: The wisdom of the crowd in combinatorial problems. Cogn. Sci. **36**, 452–470 (2012)
3. Surowiecki, J.: The Wisdom of Crowds. Doubleday, New York (2004). ISBN 978-0-385-50386-0
4. Oinas-Kukkonen, H.: Network analysis and crowds of people as sources of new organisational knowledge. In: Koohang, A., Harman, K., Britz, J. (eds.) Knowledge Management: Theoretical Foundation, pp. 173–189. Science Press, California (2008)
5. Liaoning ShareCourse of China. http://sharecourse.upln.cn/
6. Peer assessment for O2O education. http://pa.neu.edu.cn

Cooperative Writing Peer Feedback in Online Moodle System

Hsin-Yi Lien(✉)

Graduate School of Education, Ming Chuan University, Taoyuan, Taiwan
Maggielien61@gmail.com

Abstract. This study investigated the effects of three cooperative peer feedback environments on the English writing performance of tertiary level nonnative English speakers and their perceptions of web-based cooperative writing. Using a counter-balance design, thirty tertiary level students were randomly assigned to use three different online writing tools: a wiki, a forum and a workshop using the Moodle system. All participants completed three cooperative writing tasks and two individual writing tasks as pre and posttests. The results revealed that participants provided different types of feedback, eliciting actual revision from their peers, which contributed to better cooperative writing. Peer feedback benefited overall writing performance as well as idea generation, organization, writing conventions, sentence fluency, word choice and voice. An analysis of questionnaires indicated that students harbor positive attitudes toward the three online cooperative writing tools.

Keywords: Cooperative writing · Peer feedback · Online moodle system

1 Introduction

This exploration of computer-assisted instruction (CAI) employed a computer-mediated communication (CMC) interface as a means of facilitating anonymous peer feedback for the writing of students of English as foreign language (EFL). According to [1], information and communication technologies offer revolutionary and thriving learning environments for students to collaboratively work with peers. These technologies may include blogs, social media, websites, wikis, forums, and workshops. The implementation of peer assessment in higher education has been promoted by researchers for years. Reference [2] indicated that reviews given by peers enhance the revision portion of the writing process. Studies on the use of social learning wikis claim that they contribute to foreign language learning [3, 4]. A wiki is an online collaborative space enabling users to create, edit and give comments, allowing for more pragmatic learning [5]. Reference [6] also revealed that wiki use allows the coexistence of both communication technology and pedagogical features, enabling deep and sustained learning for students. Reference [4] investigated the use of a forum, blog and wiki on the writing progress of EFL learners as well as their perceptions toward the instruments. The results from questionnaires, interviews and text analysis revealed a blended learning course involving in-class instruction and online writing activities indeed benefited writing performance and the learners held positive impressions of the online writing tools.

C. Stephanidis (Ed.): HCII 2015 Posters, Part II, CCIS 529, pp. 283–289, 2015.
DOI: 10.1007/978-3-319-21383-5_48

Reference [7] questioned the levels of usability and sociability associated with wikis and forums. Their results pointed to a lack of functionality in wikis, with students citing a lack of tools for editing, slow responses or problems copying and pasting. Students tended to prefer forums to the wiki. Still, the learners valued the collaborative learning process that was made available through the sharing of online documents. Reference [8] also made a comparison of wikis and forums in problem-based tasks and analyzed the differences that emerged in the discourse and actions of learners when they engaged with each platform. Their findings suggest that the use of a wiki instead of a threaded discussion board resulted in more collaborative learning. Previous empirical studies on virtual collaborative learning environments only investigated the use of either wikis or thread discussions [9, 10] or both [8]. No previous research has explored the simultaneous implementation of three online social interaction tools (a wiki, a workshop and a forum) in an EFL writing class. The present study therefore aims to probe the effects of online interaction tools on the writing performance of EFL learners, as well as their perceptions toward those instruments. Based on the aim of this research, we present the following two research questions regarding the use of wikis, forums and workshops:

1. Do these three online learning tools benefit the writing performance of EFL learners?
2. What perceptions do EFL learners have with regard to these three online learning tools?

2 Method

The study utilized a blended learning course design [4, 11], involving classroom instruction and out-of-class online writing activities. The participants were thirty freshmen taking *English Composition I* in a college in northern Taiwan. They received face-to-face instruction in class, and outside the classroom they were required to conduct online peer assessment, peer editing, or online discussion using the Moodle system, which provides open-source e-learning software known as the Course Management System (CMC), the Learning Management System (LMS), or the Virtual Learning Environment (VLE) [12]. A writing task was administered as a pretest for the counter-balance design, then participants were randomly assigned into three cooperative peer feedback environments: wikis, forums and workshops using the Moodle system. Each group of students completed three writing tasks and took turns using each of the three online social environments. Students were instructed to participate in peer editing for the wiki, peer assessment in the workshop and online discussions in the forum. All of the students were required to upload their first drafts to the Moodle system and then engage in social interaction according to assigned Moodle activities. The wiki offered space in Moodle for peer reviews and collaborative work on individual writing assignments. Moodle Workshop functioned as a platform for peer response sessions and the participants gave their comments and evaluations using rubrics and criteria provided by the system. The forum provided versatile opportunities for group members to have online discussions. Responses to a student's initial post were displayed on a single page in the forum.

The participating students were required to revise their drafts after receiving peer comments. They then uploaded their edited draft to an online grading system called WriteToLearn. This instant grading system evaluates the writing performance of students through examining six traits of writing including ideas, organization, conventions, sentence fluency, word choice and voice. After this process, students completed a questionnaire to explore their perceptions of the three collaborative online environments and examine their reflections on the online writing process. The questionnaire included items rated on a five-point Likert scale. It also included open-ended questions. Data regarding page views, discussions and history modules were also collected from the wiki, forum and workshop systems throughout the eighteen-week process.

3 Results

3.1 Three Online Writing Tools

The present study aimed to investigate differences in writing performance that may emerge after student use of three collaborative online learning tools: a wiki, a forum and a workshop. The students wrote five compositions in total, including one pretest, one posttest and three essays. These were assessed by an online instant grading system. Table 1 shows that the participants performed much better on the final four writing tasks (M = 3.80, 3.87, 3.53 and 3.77) that were submitted after engaging in collaborative online environments. The differences among the students appeared to be smaller in the posttest (SD = 0.77) for which their lowest score was 3. Significant differences were found for the scores on all four compositions ($p < .001$) as shown in Table 2.

Table 1. Descriptive statistics of composition scores

Writing task	N.	Min.	Max.	Mean	Std. D.
Pretest	30	1	5	2.20	1.00
Essay 1	30	3	5	3.80	0.85
Essay 2	30	2	6	3.87	0.90
Essay 3	30	2	5	3.53	0.78
Posttest	30	3	5	3.77	0.77

Using a counter-balance design, the present study analyzed the differences among the writing scores of participating students after their involvement with three collaborative online environments. The students engaging in the forum (M = 3.83) performed slightly better than those using the wiki (M = 3.60) and the workshop (M = 3.77). When examining performance over the six traits, the students scored moderately higher in convention than in the other five traits as shown in Table 3. However, no significant difference was found among the three online tools (F = 0.60, p = 0.55) when it came to overall score or the six traits, as shown in Table 4.

Table 2. Comparison of writing performance (N = 30)

	Paired differences					t	df	Sig.
	Mean	Std. D	Std. error mean	95 % confidence interval of the difference				
				Lower	Upper			
Pretest -essay 1	−1.57	1.01	0.18	−1.94	−1.19	−8.53	29	0.00
Pretest -essay 2	−1.60	0.97	0.18	−1.96	−1.24	−9.09	29	0.00
Pretest -essay 3	−1.67	1.09	0.18	−2.07	−1.26	−8.35	29	0.00
Pretest -posttest	−1.33	1.03	0.18	−1.72	−0.95	−7.10	29	0.00

$P < .001$

Table 3. Descriptive statistics of writing scores after participating in the collaborative online environments.

	Wiki		Forum		Workshop		Sum	
	Mean	SD	Mean	SD	Mean	SD	Mean	SD
Idea	3.40	1.0	3.63	0.96	3.54	1.10	3.54	1.02
Organization	3.33	0.80	3.53	0.94	3.49	0.89	3.49	0.88
Convention	3.73	0.91	3.80	0.85	3.81	0.88	3.81	0.87
Fluency	3.50	0.86	3.80	1.00	3.70	0.81	3.70	0.89
Choice	3.57	0.97	3.73	0.87	3.68	1.14	3.68	0.97
Voice	3.63	0.89	3.87	0.90	3.77	0.92	3.77	0.90
Overall	3.60	0.81	3.83	0.87	3.77	0.86	3.73	0.85

Table 4. Comparison of writing performance after participating in the three collaborative online environments.

		Sum of squares	df	Mean square	F	Sig.
Overall	Between groups	0.867	2	0.433	0.601	0.551
	Within groups	62.733	87	0.721		
Idea	Between groups	0.956	2	0.478	0..455	0.636
	Within groups	91.367	87	1.05		
Organization	Between groups	1.156	2	0.578	0.747	0.477
	Within groups	67.333	87	0.774		
Convention	Between groups	0.422	2	0.211	0.273	0.762
	Within groups	67.367	87	0.774		
Fluency	Between groups	1.8	2	0.9	1.133	0.327
	Within groups	69.1	87	0.794		
Choice	Between groups	0.556	2	0.278	0.291	0.748
	Within groups	83.1	87	0.955		
Voice	Between groups	0.867	2	0.433	0.529	0.591
	Within groups	71.233	87	0.819		

Table 5. Reflections on the benefits of using the three online tools (N = 30)

Statement	Percentage
I learned some practical writing skills from reviewing the writing of others	23.33 %
I was able to observe the different writing styles of others	23.33 %
My feedback contributed to the writing of others	16.67 %
It was a novel experience to give my classmates grades	16.67 %
I loved the three different online writing tools. They were very practical in various ways	13.33 %
The online writing tools were beneficial	10.00 %
We were able to exchange our ideas	10.00 %
I learned from the mistakes of others	6.67 %

3.2 Perceptions of Learners

86.7 % of the students agreed that online collaborative activities benefited their writing performance. 96.7 % of the students indicated that they revised their drafts based on the comments of their group members. In reflecting on the usage of the wiki, the forum and the workshop, some students discussed the advantages and difficulties encountered when using the online tools, also mentioning the comments they received and the interactions they had with their group members, as shown in Tables 5 and 6. The learners reported that they learned about different writing skills (23.33 %), various writing styles (23.33 %), that they learned from others' mistakes (6.67 %) and that they learned by exchanging ideas (10.00 %). However, the participants indicated that technical problems (16.67 %), unprofessional comments (13.33 %), inability to access the computer (10.00 %) and lack of feedback from others (13.33 %) distressed them.

Table 6. Reflections on the disadvantages of using three online tools (N = 30)

Statement	Percentage
I was not familiar with methods for using the tools, especially the workshop platform	16.67 %
Some of the comments or feedback were not professional	13.33 %
The workshop platform could only give grades but not comments which would have been more useful	13.33 %
Sometimes, I couldn't find a computer to access the systems	10.00 %
Some serious comments were useful but some feedback was useless	13.33 %
Some comments were too general, not very specific	10.00 %
I preferred to give comments in person in class	13.33 %
Sometimes I didn't receive feedback from others and I couldn't revise my draft	13.33 %
Sometimes I didn't know how to grade the paper	6.67 %
I was afraid to add sentences to my classmates' papers, so I only focused on grammar	6.67 %

4 Discussion and Conclusion

The present study investigated the writing performance of EFL learners and their perceptions of three asynchronous online writing tools – a forum, a workshop and a wiki. Adult language learners appear to benefit from online social interaction such as peer assessment, peer editing or online discussions. This study affirms the positive effects these collaborative online environments can have on the writing process and writing performance of students. Significant differences were found in their writing performance after participating in these online environments. The results correspond to those found in previous studies on the benefits of utilizing online collaborative learning environments [4, 6]. To further examine the differences in learners' writing performance after using wiki, forum and workshop, no significant difference among using three online tools is detected. However, the writing scores of learners who engaged in the forum slightly outperformed the scores students obtained after using the wiki or workshop. This result is in opposition to that of [8], who reported that the use of a wiki contributed more to collaborative learning than did threaded discussion boards. In sum, a blended learning course design indeed provides students opportunities to cooperate and interact with others outside of the classroom. Through the use of these tools, learning is no longer limited to class instruction only. The majority of participants held positive attitudes toward online assessments, editing or grading, and they expressed that those collaborative activities were practical and useful. Nonetheless, some of them pointed out minor problems that were distressing to them, such as the inability to access a computer, lack of familiarity with the system or unprofessional feedback from their peers. Therefore, it would seem that it is essential to equip students with the skills needed to deal with these systems, training them in grading, giving comments, and editing the writing of their peers while implementing web-based platforms.

References

1. Wheeler, S., Yeomans, P., Wheeler, D.: The good, the bad and the wiki: evaluating student-generated content for collaborative learning. Br. J. Educ. Technol. **39**(6), 987–995 (2008)
2. Trautmann, N.M.: Interactive learning through web-mediated peer review of student science reports. Educ. Tech. Res. Dev. **57**, 685–704 (2009)
3. Ducate, L., Anderson, L., Moreno, N.: Wading through the world of wiki: an analysis of three wiki projects. Foreign Lang. Annu. **44**(3), 495–524 (2011)
4. Miyazoe, T., Anderson, T.: Learning outcomes and students' perceptions of online writing: simultaneous implementation of a forum, blog, and wiki in an EFF blended learning setting. System **38**, 185–199 (2010)
5. Glassman, M., Kang, M.J.: The logic of wiki: the possibilities of the web 2.0 classroom. Comput. Support. Collab. Learn. **6**, 93–112 (2011)
6. Carroll, J.A., Diaz, A., Meiklejohn, J., Newcomb, M., Adkins, B.: Collaboration and competition on a wiki: the praxis of online social learning to improve academic writing and research in under-graduate students. Australas. J. Educ. Technol. **29**(4), 513–525 (2013)

7. Kear, K., Woodthorpe, J., Robertson, S., Hutchison, M.: From forums to wiki: perspectives on tools for collaboration. Internet High. Educ. **13**, 218–225 (2010)
8. Ioannou, A., Brown, S.W., Artino, A.R.: Wikis and forums for collaborative problem-based activity: a systematic comparison of learners' interactions. Internet High. Educ. **24**, 35–45 (2015)
9. Ioannou, A.: Online collaborative learning: the promise of wikis. Int. J. Instr. Media **38**(3), 213–223 (2011)
10. Vasquez, M., Potter, R.E.: A (closer) look at collaboration using wiki. J. Appl. Res. High. Educ. **5**(2), 145–155 (2013)
11. Graham, C.R.: Blended learning systems: definition, current trends, and future directions. In: Bonk, C.J., Graham, C.R. (eds.) The Handbook of Blended Learning: Global Perspectives, Local Designs, pp. 3–21. Pfeiffer, San Francisco (2006)
12. Suvorov, R.: Using Moodle in ESOL writing classes. TESL-EL **14**(2), 1–11 (2010)

Using Digital Document Network System for Group Learning Activities

Kenji Matsunaga(✉) and Kyoko Yoshida

School of Network and Information, Senshu University,
Kawasaki-shi, Kanagawa, Japan
{matunaga,k-yoshida}@isc.senshu-u.ac.jp

Abstract. With the increasing volume of privately-owned digital documents it is becoming more important to manage the documents for effective use. For document management, we propose a digital document network system. The system has been improved for use as a group-learning assistance system. In this paper the functions added to the system are explained. The validity of the system was evaluated by observing the behaviors of the students who used the learning assistance system for their learning and by interviewing them.

Keywords: Digital document · Group learning

1 Introduction

People acquire knowledge from the content of privately-owned paper documents and books and write notes or put sticky notes on them. For digital documents, the volume of which has been increasing dramatically in recent years, application software has been developed with a function for putting notes on the digital documents. With both paper documents and digital documents, it is important to understand the relation between documents in order to enrich one's knowledge of a target field. The digital network system [1–3] that we propose controls digital documents related to a certain field. The user puts marks on the documents and creates links between the marks. By doing so, the user can save the relation between the documents and establish a network of documents. By searching the documents in the network with a keyword or following the links, the user can easily recapture information that he/she previously accessed.

We recently improved the system to make it a group-learning assistance system. If multiple students develop a digital document network of a specific field, they can learn from each other and acquire rich knowledge that they could not obtain by themselves.

In this paper, the functions of the digital document network system are introduced in Sect. 2. In Sect. 3, functions added for group learning are explained. Students actually used the system for learning. The results of the observation of the students and the evaluation of the improved system are presented below.

2 Digital Document Network System

The proposed digital document network system creates a network of privately-collected digital documents by adding marks, notes, and links (Fig. 1).

C. Stephanidis (Ed.): HCII 2015 Posters, Part II, CCIS 529, pp. 290–294, 2015.
DOI: 10.1007/978-3-319-21383-5_49

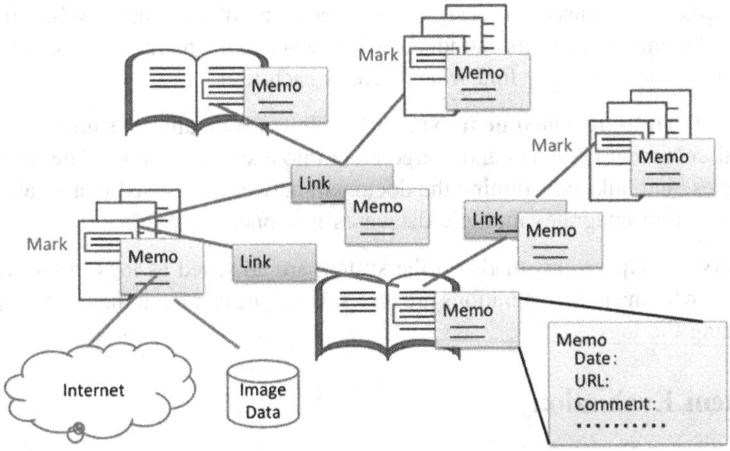

Fig. 1. Digital document network

A mark is a place that a user designates in a document. A link connects two marks. A note can be put on a mark or link. A network of documents can be formed by repeating these operations.

The notes in the document network can be searched with keywords. One can move on the links between the marks with the help of the notes and find related documents successively. By associating the accumulated documents with each other in this manner, we can use the collection of documents as a knowledge base.

This system was originally developed for researchers or specialists to organize and coordinate documents of specific areas of expertise. If this organizing and coordinating action is replaced with a learning action, the system can be used also by students. Students can register documents provided as learning materials and documents that they collect and put marks, notes, and links on the documents to deepen their knowledge.

3 Function Enhancement for Group Learning

The system was improved by adding the following four functions to make it a group-learning assistance system.

1. User registration and user designation
2. Mark display
3. Merging of multiple document networks
4. Log browsing

The four functions are explained below.

User Registration and user Designation. To find who is using the system, one can designate before starting the operation who is going to use the system. If the same user uses the system successively, the user who made the previous operation is automatically set to current user. Therefore designation of user is only necessary when the user is changed.

Mark Display. Each user can designate his/her own color of mark. When finding a mark on a document, the users can identify the owner of the mark from the color. With this function, one can easily find what interests each user.

Merging of Multiple Document Network. The system allows students to create individual document networks and merge them into a single network. The documents, marks, notes, and links constituting the document network are saved in a database. The merging function integrates multiple databases into one.

Log Browsing. Operations made on the system are all saved as logs in the database. The data of who made the operations are also saved. One can track the learning process by exploring the logs.

4 System Evaluation

Making a network of collected material is effective for learning a new field and deepening knowledge. If the network is made by multiple learners, the effect is enhanced. To find out whether the system is effective as assist system for multiple users to develop knowledge of a new field of study in their group work, two university students were employed as examinees to perform the experiment (Fig. 2). The process of the experiment was observed to evaluate the system.

The experiments were performed in the following steps:

1. The students collected materials related to a one-day lecture from the Internet and saved them in pdf document files. (About 60 min)
2. The students put notes on the original lecture materials and newly-collected materials and made links between the materials that were related to each other. (About 60 min)
3. The networks that two students made separately were merged into one.
4. Each student tried to find what documents the other student collected and what notes and links the other student had added. (About 30 min)
5. Teachers joined the group and made comments or instigated discussions. (About 30 min)

The title of the lecture used for the experiment was "Case example of mistaken arrest for posting a threat on a bulletin board." Examinees A and B collected 21 and 8 materials respectively from the Internet, added 27 and 16 notes respectively, and created 15 and 8 links respectively.

Student examinees' comments:

- Even when looking for the same thing, we reached different documents. This could deepen each other's understanding.
- The system allows me to find out about another person's learning process. In particular, when one finds the content of another's notes or the location of another's links, it motivates each other's learning.
- Even when we choose the same material, the location or the content of the notes could be different between us. It was interesting that we can find the location or content of each other's notes.

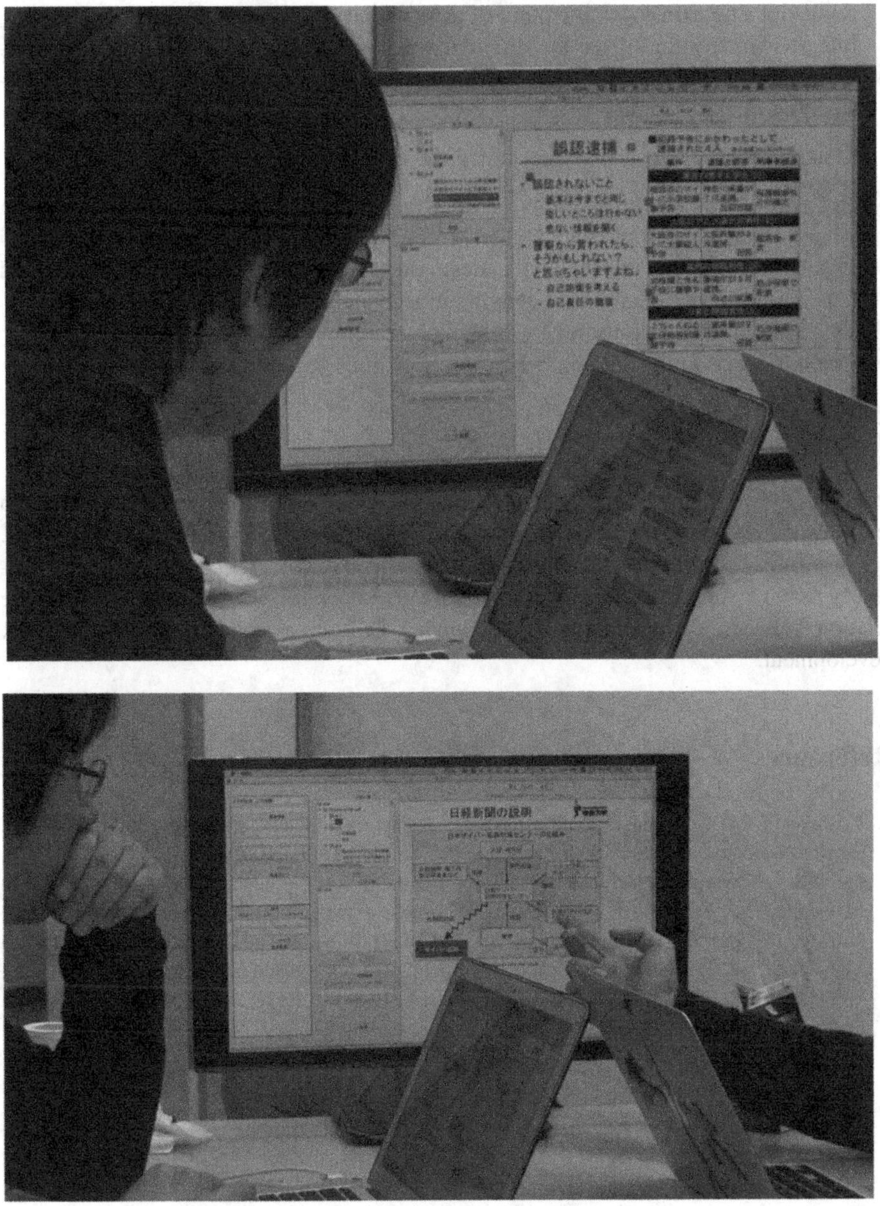

Fig. 2. Students discuss by using the system

- When I browse the Internet, I sometimes get lost. However in this case, there is a core document that is lecture material and we can browse the network based on it.
- The texts of that day's lecture are placed in parallel. This arrangement does not show a clear relation between them and could be improved.

- Some put a note on a specific point of a document and some put a note on a heading line. It is interesting to see the different ways in which people consult documents.
- In particular, finding how others add notes and links is useful for a deeper understanding of the lecture.

Comments of the teachers who joined the experiments:

- Not only seeing the final results of what the students found out but also knowing what reference materials they studied and how they studied is effective.
- I could find out what the students understood. Also, from the notes and links I could find out how widely and how deeply the students learned about the subject.
- This system would be useful for reference searching in our seminar.
- The difference in the set number of notes or links between students is interesting.

5 Conclusions

In this study we improved the system for making a digital document network for group learning and evaluated the improved system. This paper presents analysis of the results.

In future we will and add more functions effective for group work. As it is necessary to have support for developing an effective network, we will give shape to the relation between various kinds of knowledge and set a standard for the network development.

References

1. Yoshikoshi, M., Matsunaga, K., Yoshida, K.: A personal document network building system for digital document searches. In: Stephanidis, C. (ed.) HCII 2013, Part II. CCIS, vol. 374, pp. 458–461. Springer, Heidelberg (2013)
2. Matsunaga, K., Yoshida, K.: A personal document network building system for organizing knowledge. IPSJ SIG technical report, vol. 2013-IS-125, no. 10, pp. 1–5 (2013) (in Japanese)
3. Matsunaga, K., Yoshida, K.: Digital document network system for organizing individual knowledge. In: Yamamoto, S. (ed.) HCI 2014, Part I. LNCS, vol. 8521, pp. 396–403. Springer, Heidelberg (2014)

See the Flex: Investigating Various Display Settings for Different Study Conditions

Michael Saenz, Joshua Strunk(✉), Kelly Maset, Erica Malone, and Jinsil Hwaryoung Seo

Texas A&M University, College Station, TX, USA
{itsmemichaelsaenz, ermalone91}@gmail.com,
{joshau.p.strunk, kellymaset, hwaryoung}@tamu.com

Abstract. We present FlexAR, a kinetic tangible augmented reality (TAR) [5] application for anatomy education in varied learning situations. Learning anatomy is fundamental to every health profession as well as related domains such as performance, physical therapy, art, and animation. For example, dancers need to learn anatomy to care for their bodies and learn to move efficiently. Anatomy has traditionally been taught in two dimensions, particularly for those in non-medical fields such as artists and physical education practitioners. Medical students often gain hands-on experience through cadaver dissections [8]. However, with dissection becoming less practical, researchers have begun evaluating techniques for teaching anatomy through technology. Our goal is to develop TAR interfaces to enhance the effectiveness of learning gross anatomy in group and individual study settings. We believe that once expanded FlexAR could be effective as a standalone or supplementary tool for both group and individual learning.

Keywords: Augmented reality · Tangible user interface · Education · Human anatomy

1 Introduction

A significant drawback of learning anatomy through traditional reading material is the difficulty students have piecing together disparate 2D images into knowledge of 3D structures. In the past, this has been solved through the use of cadavers for dissection, which gives students hands-on experience anatomical structures. Recently, however, this has become less practical for a number of reasons. For one, this method of instruction does not afford students room to make mistakes or repeat procedures. Furthermore, as rising ethical concerns limit the availability of cadavers for dissection, the costs of acquiring them rise. In light of these issues, we present FlexAR, an AR application that combines a tangible interface and GUI to teach anatomy. FlexAR combines the written information available from traditional reading materials with the spatial learning one would acquire from anatomical dissection. Users have the ability to study anatomy at their preferred pace using their study method of choice, freely exploring gross anatomy or selecting specific structures for closer examination.

C. Stephanidis (Ed.): HCII 2015 Posters, Part II, CCIS 529, pp. 295–300, 2015.
DOI: 10.1007/978-3-319-21383-5_50

2 Related Work

In developing a tangible augmented reality (TAR) interface that enhances the efficiency of learning gross anatomy in group and individual study settings, we decided to look at prior work which focuses on augmented reality (AR) applications for anatomy education. Prior work relating to the use of AR for anatomy education is detailed in Juanes' paper [3]. This paper introduces a tool for augmenting 2D images from a book with static 3D models on mobile devices. This allows the user to view the structure of particular body parts in 3D space without the need for physical models. However, we believe that having a dynamic model will improve the user's ability to understand spatial relationships and the effect of movement on different systems. For our research we focus on demonstrating the flexion and extension of various muscle groups as the result of movement of the arm using an articulated tangible as a controller. Another related application which uses a TAR interface is ARnatomy. ARnatomy aims to create a tangible user interface (TUI) by using dog bones to control the display of information on a mobile device such as a smartphone or tablet [4]. Though this application does include dynamic text, there is little interaction between the user and the tangibles themselves; the tangible controls only the location of the text onscreen and there is no interaction between the user and mobile device. Thus, this application is useful primarily as a tool for memorizing written information. In FlexAR we fuse interaction with a graphical user interface (GUI) and TUI, allowing the user to manipulate a physical model to drive the animation of a 3D digital overlay and highlight and display the information of individual muscles.

3 System Description

FlexAR consists of a camera device as well as a tangible human arm skeleton which drives the animation of a 3D model projected over the skeleton on the device. The application uses a TAR interface in which the tangible controls interaction with the system, providing an ideal setting for the user to explore the model in 3D space. While traditional instruction employs materials such as books, diagrams, and standalone physical anatomical models, our current prototype combines written information witha tactile model to serve as a self-contained learning module. The GUI within the application supplements the TAR interface with written information, which is displayed over the 3D projection.

The prototype consists of the physical arm model accompanied by our application, which can be run on several different devices. The application uses multiple image targets affixed to a physical model of a human arm skeleton to control the animation of a 3D overlay of the arm displaying the bones and major muscles of the human arm. As users manipulate the physical model, the animation of the physical model is updated accordingly so that they can observe the extension and contraction of the muscles and articulation of the bones as well as major anatomical features. Another form of interaction with application is the ability to select muscles, highlighting them on the overlaid model and displaying their written information. In this way, users can explore anatomical structures from multiple angles and learn at their own pace.

4 Design Implementation

The augmented reality system was implemented using a number of programs and development tools. The 3D overlay was created in Autodesk Maya [1] before being imported into the multiplatform game engine Unity [7] for integration with our application, and all scripting was done in C# using Unity's integrated development environment (IDE) MonoDevelop. Three different implementations of the project were made for each supported device: desktops, tablets, and wearables.

The assets for the 3D overlay were developed in Maya using our physical arm model and Gray's Anatomy [2] as reference. To enhance immersion, the physical and digital models had to align as closely as possible in appearance and be anatomically correct. After the skeleton was modeled, each muscle was modeled and textured separately in order to allow them to be selected individually. The movement and deformations were created using a combination of a simple rig and blendshapes, which were set up in such a way as to match the range of motion possible with the physical model. Once the assets were completed, they were exported to Unity for integration with the application (Fig. 1).

To expedite the development process and allow the application to be built for multiple platforms, we built the augmented reality system using the software development kit (SDK) Vuforia, a mobile AR library implemented by QUALCOMM Incorporated [6], as an extension for Unity. Vuforia relies on camera feed to track image targets, projecting a 3D overlay relative to the position of detected targets onscreen. For *FlexAR*, we used 4 targets: 1 to determine the basic position of the arm and the others to control the rotation of the shoulder, elbow, and wrist joints of the 3D model (Fig. 2).

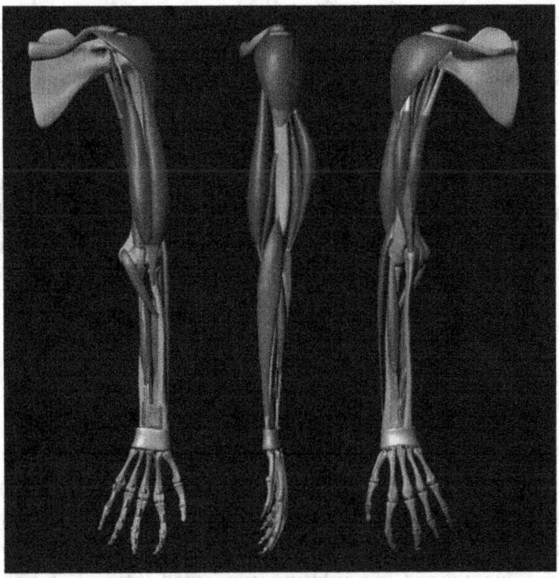

Fig. 1. Front, side, and back views of the final digital assets in their anatomically neutral starting position

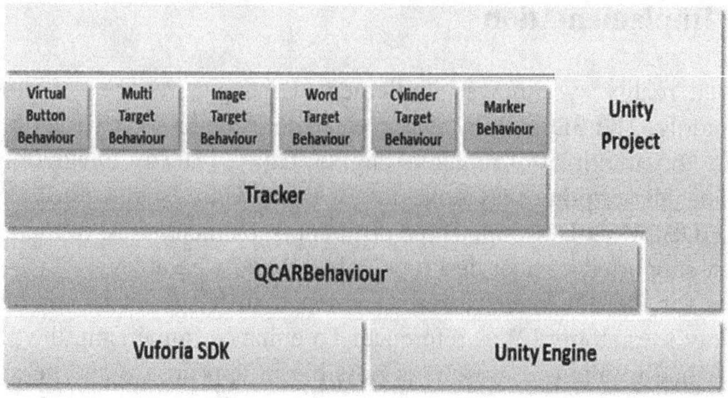

Fig. 2. High-level system overview of the vuforia SDK unity extension

In our initial primary observations, we found that users had difficulty selecting individual muscles in 3D space. A common suggestion was to introduce direct interaction with a GUI rather than with 3D overlay selection. Rather than having to select individual muscles, users could instead display information using tabs labeled with the names of the muscles. We found that this implementation provided a more intuitive experience for the user.

5 Preliminary Observations

5.1 Protocol

To test FlexAR, we observed participants interacting with our prototype in a lab environment. We observed nine university-level participants from a variety of backgrounds including art, dance, and computer engineering. The people we observed were divided into three groups of equal size. The project was built for three different devices – a desktop with a webcam, an Android tablet, and Epson Moverio BT-200 glasses – and each group interacted with one of these devices. For this iteration we focused on usability, interaction, and user experience. Participants arrived at the lab one at a time. After a brief instruction period, each was permitted to explore the application on their own. In the first phase, we observed the interactions with the system using the tangible. Next, participants were instructed to interact with the GUI. Participants were then given the opportunity to freely use the prototype.

5.2 Discussion

The feedback we received was generally positive. Participants listed a number of areas in which they believed FlexAR would be useful. Several students compared it favorably to using anatomy textbooks to train medical personnel. A few mentioned its potential as a reference in the process of creating joint systems for 3D animation, and one participant who specialized in sculpting expressed interest in being able to view static structures from multiple angles.

From the preliminary observations we noticed several things. First, the tablet was too large and difficult to handle at the same time as the tangible. Some participants who had a second person control the tangible did not experience these issues. We inferred that tablets are unsuitable for individual study using TAR-based applications but may be useful for group studying because of the difficulty of interacting with both the device and tangible simultaneously without a partner. What we found most interesting, however, were our observations regarding the desktop and the smart glasses. Many participants gave us feedback stating that the desktop would be ideal for learning as a group or class while the glasses would be most useful in individual learning settings or where mobility was the most important factor. Using the desktop, one person - such as an instructor or group leader - could interact with the application in front of the camera while the others observed the screen. This would be most useful for guided learning. In contrast, the glasses would work best for those wishing to study independently or during individual assignments. Consequently, we plan to focus on these two devices in our continuing research (Fig. 3).

Fig. 3. From left to right: users of a desktop with webcam, Android tablet, and Epson Moverio BT-200 glasses

6 Future Work

Motivated by the positive initial feedback we received, we are currently furthering our research and expanding our prototype to include not only the arm but also other key regions such as the torso. A larger tangible would likely enhance the user's sense of immersion into the application and bring us closer to our goal of being able to replace cadaver dissection as an effective method of teaching anatomy spatially.

7 Conclusion

FlexAR is a prototype tool for teaching anatomy through the use of augmented reality. We believe that it contributes to education by giving users both written and 3D visual information about anatomy without the need for dissection or traditional study materials. In its current state it is useful as a tool for studying the muscles of the arm, but when expanded shows promise as an application for teaching the anatomy of multiple complete body systems, both for individuals and large groups across a wide range of disciplines.

References

1. Autodesk Maya. http://www.autodesk.com/products/maya/overview/
2. Gray, H., Pick, T.P., Howden, R.: Myology. In: Gray's Anatomy, chapter 4, section 7, pp. 442–455. Running Press, Philadelphia (1974)
3. Juanes, J., Hernández, D., Ruisoto, P., García, E., Villarrubia, G., Prats, A.: Augmented reality techniques, using mobile devices, for learning human anatomy. In: Proceedings of the Second International Conference on Technological Ecosystems for Enhancing Multiculturality (TEEM 2014), pp. 7–11. ACM, New York (2014)
4. Seo, J., Storey, J., Chavez, J., Reyna, D., Suh, J., Pine, M.: ARnatomy: tangible AR app for learning gross anatomy. In: ACM SIGGRAPH 2014 Posters (SIGGRAPH 2014), Article 25, p. 1. ACM, New York (2014)
5. Billinghurst, M., Kato, H., Poupyrev, I.: Tangible augmented reality. In: Proceedings of SIGGRAPH Asia 2008 (Courses), pp. 1–10 (2008)
6. Qualcomm Vuforia. https://www.qualcomm.com/products/vuforia/
7. Unity. http://unity3d.com/
8. Winkelmann, A.: Anatomical dissection as a teaching method in medical school: a review of the evidence. Med Educ. **41**(1), 15–22 (2007)

Development of Intuitive Force Presentation Method Using Stopper Mechanism for Skill Training

Masamichi Sakaguchi(✉) and Mingoo Lee

Nagoya Institute of Technology, Nagoya, Aichi 466-8555, Japan
saka@nitech.ac.jp

Abstract. In skill training, there are many information and most of skill training depends on watching the skill. However the novice can not acquire the force information by watching the skill. So the trial and error process is required for the skill training. We describes some methods guiding the exerting force of novice to exert the target force at target position. The methods present spring from the target position for the novice exerting target force. Because watching the skill is also important in skill training, the presenting methods intend for presenting the force information without the visual information. The spring element makes the novice actively exerting force. And the stopper and latch element display how much pushing down the spring. The force guiding method use mechanical elements controlled by the brake linear actuator like the spring, stopper and latch. In this paper, the concept and purpose of the method and the validity of the method are described.

Keywords: Skill training · Skill transfer · Force guiding · Force presentation · Robot-mediated training

1 Introduction

There are various kinds of skills. In order to achieve a better performance, motor skills are playing a key role on various kinds of tasks. For instance, skills like piloting, ceramic art, forging, sports and surgical operation need motor skills.

Previous studies of robot-meditated training or teaching use path-following, target-hitting and peg-in-hole task [1]. These tasks are used for evaluating, and most of presented method are assist the purposed task. And these studies concern not exerting the same force and same movement of master of skill but task result. There are various paradigms for training and skill transfer [2,3], force training and learning studies [4,5]. As a study of observation of the sensation of touch, gibson [6] emphasized the difference of touching and being touched and says passive touch plus kinesthesis is insufficient.

In this study, we propose a method, that the trainee gets the guiding information and perceives whether exerting the target force or not. In this paper,

C. Stephanidis (Ed.): HCII 2015 Posters, Part II, CCIS 529, pp. 301–306, 2015.
DOI: 10.1007/978-3-319-21383-5_51

we introduce the concept of the operating force guiding method using mechanical elements. We made 1-DOF device and evaluated the validity of method. In Sect. 2, the concept and purpose of the proposed method is described. In Sect. 3, device is described. In Sect. 4 experiment procedure and result are described. Finally, discussion and conclusion are described in Sects. 5 and 6. And an example of application is indicated in Sect. 7.

2 Concept and Purpose

The main purpose of this paper is finding a good method for generating environment of matching target force and position. As illustrated in Fig. 1, skill training processes have direct teaching, watching and training. Direct contact teaching, like grabbing tennis racket with novice, has limitation that the body of novice disturbs master's skill. And watching and imitating process can't transfer invisible information like the force information of master. Our aiming application is measuring the master's invisible information without disturbance and presenting the information to the novice. Though the trajectory always depends on the force, there are skills like tennis, which is difficult to measuring the force of master. So the proposed method is used for the skills allowing measuring master's force.

Figure 2 shows the proposed methods for exerting target force at target position. It makes a training environment transferring the force information from the master to the novice. The proposed methods use some mechanical elements. In this methods, presenting a spring which returns the exactly same force of the novice with displacement. The spring make a environment to exert force. Though using a passive elements like spring can't maintain the presenting force by control, the merit of using spring is that we can make a environment for exerting target force actively and the position is stable. When the novice interacts with the training device. The stability of position is only satisfied by equilibrium of force, and spring satisfies equilibrium of force.

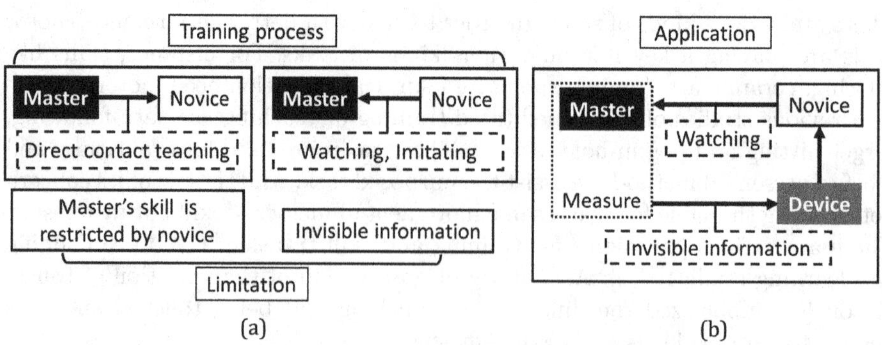

Fig. 1. (a) Training process and limitation of traditional training. (b) Aiming application of presenting method.

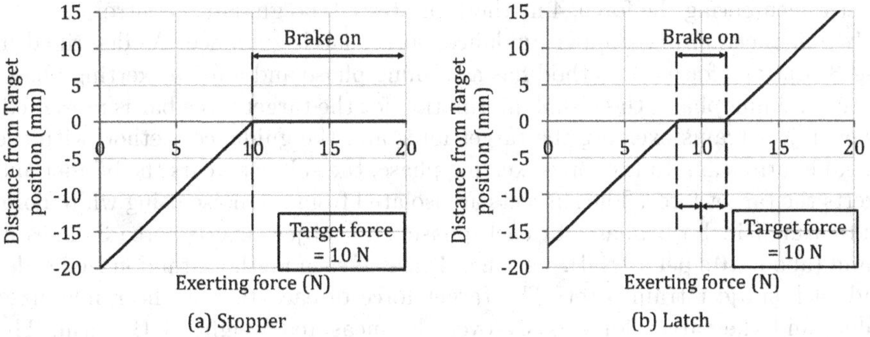

Fig. 2. Methods for exerting target force at target position. (a) Using spring with stopper. novice perceive the target position by the rigid body contact boundary. (b) Using spring with latch. novice perceive the target position by the rigid body contact section

There is two important point for using this method in skill transfer application. The one is non-visual information for force presenting. In the traditional apprentice system, watching the skill is important for learning and imitating the skill. There are many information like the posture, center of gravity and movement of foot. So the methods restricting the eye of the novice like a force status bar can restrict information in skill training. The other is separating the master from the novice. When master teach the novice directly, the skill environment of the master is changed because of the weight of the novice or restriction of movement. By using skill transferring device, the master transfers the skill information on the usual state.

3 Device

The experimental system is composed of a linear guide actuator and a force sensor. The force sensor is placed on the stage of the linear guide, and subjects push down on the top of the force sensor. The device is controlled to present spring by using the position control of a linear guide and the force information. The linear guide (LX26, lead 5 mm, MISUMI) are actuated by the AC servo brake motor (SGMJV-A5ADA2C, 50W, YASKAWA Electric). We use the force sensor with parallel plate structure (A5056). The device presents 1 degree of freedom force information.

4 Experiment

4.1 Experimental Procedure

In this experiment, we confirm that the validity of the mechanical elements guidance. In the process, the novice exerts the target force using the right hand, after remembering the force. 4 methods are tested: no guidance(control), spring-only guidance, spring-stopper guidance, spring-latch guidance. As described in Fig. 3 (a), task for each method has a training phase and a force exerting phase. In the training phase, the visual information for the target force bar is presented. The subject trains exerting the target force and the guidance method with the visual information. In the force exerting phase, the subject wears the blinder and exerts the target force. The subjects are isolated from the noise using white noise and earmuff in both phase. In each phase, the subject exerts force 3 times in 1 min (about 10 s per 1 trial). 1 set has 4 task of each method, randomized order and each subject train 3 set. The target force of each task is the randomized value, and the target force is set over the measured weight of the arm. The age of 8 subjects are twenties, and the are right handed. The subjects have no experience in the device in set 1. Set 1 is conducted a week before set 2, and set 3 is conducted after a week of set 2.

The error value of each trial is calculated from the section of exerted force 5 s in Fig. 3 (b). The exerted force is F_{exert}, the target force is F_{target} F_{error} is the mean of absolute value of $F_{exert} - F_{target}$ during 5 s of exerting force. Each task of a set has 24 data of F_{error}.

4.2 Result

Group 1 is no guidance and spring method, which depends on only human recalling ability, and group 2 is stopper and latch method, which presents information for displacement using break. We compare the two groups. Figure 4 shows the box plot data of the F_{error}. Results of all sets are compared using tukey kramer test. The stopper method is significantly better than the group 1, and the latch method is significantly better than the group 1, except no guidance method in set 3. The F_{error} of no guidance of set 3 is significantly smaller than that of set 1. The Fig. 4 (d) shows that Likert-type evaluation of perception. 1 is difficult to perceive the target force, and 5 is easy to perceive the force.

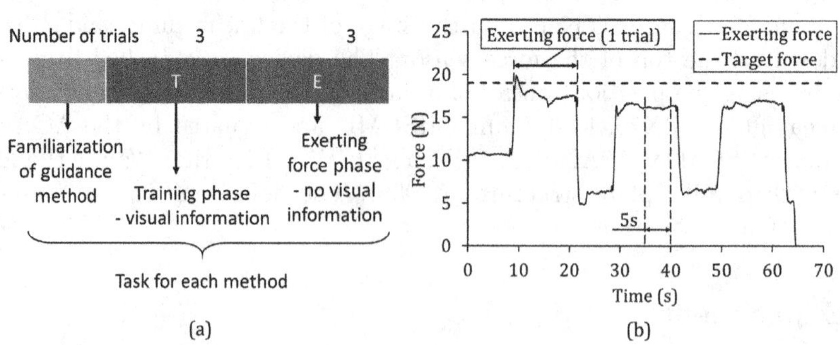

Fig. 3. (a) Structure of task for each method. Training the target force, and exerting force 3 times. (b) A sample of one phase. Force exerting time of a trial is about 10s, and use data of 5 s each trial.

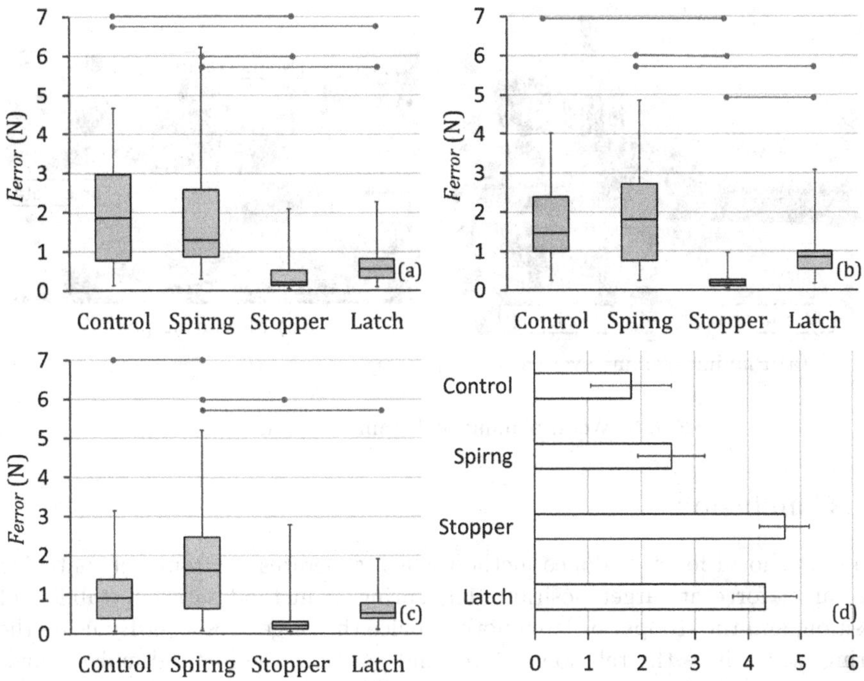

Fig. 4. Box plot of F_{error}. (a) Set 1. (b) Set 2. (c) Set 3. (d) Likert-type evaluation. Lines above the graph show significant diffenrence (tukey-kramer test)

5 Discussion

Using stopper and latch with spring in guidance shows significantly better performance in exerting 1 DOF constant force. Compared to other method, F_{error} of no guidance methods significantly smaller in set 3. This may shows that the no guidance and normal way of learning has faster adaptation speed. Though the novice exerts force more than the target force, the right target position is presented to novice passively. In the process of repeated training, we expect that the novice can get the feedback information of force, and achieve training the target force at the target position.

The presented method is using intuitive and purposive information which is the rigid body contact. Because of the simplicity, the information confuses the operator with the other axis information. So multiple degree of freedom increase complexity of perception and may require visual information. For example, 3-D vision can be used for presenting difference of target force by using the position gap of tool from the right position.

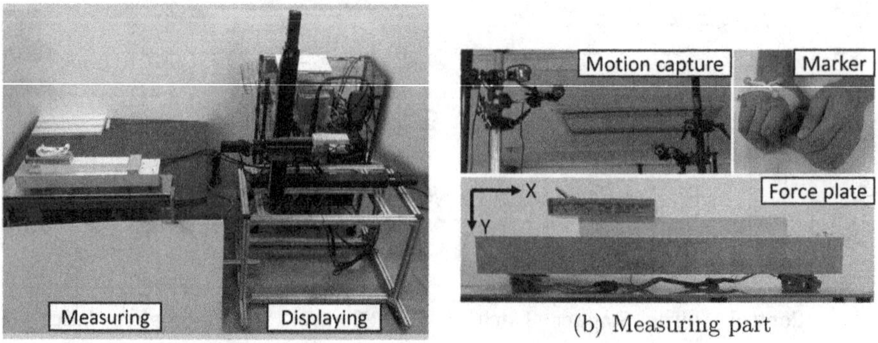

(a) Planing training system (b) Measuring part

Fig. 5. Wood planing skill training application

6 Conclusion

We have shown force guidance method which generates environment matching the target force at target position. The spring of method satisfies stability of position, and the stopper or latch notify novice the target position. By using the spring, which fixes the relation of force and position, the method make a environment of matching the position and force. The 1-DOF device of the methods guides the constant target force without visual information. 2-DOF force and guiding force with movement experiments are required for future application.

7 Application

From the result, spring-stopper is the most intuitive method in presented methods. By using the method, we develop wood plaining skill training system as shown in Fig. 5. The training system measuring 2DOF position and 2DOF force information. And display 2DOF position and 2DOF force information using spring-stopper method.

References

1. Powell, D., O'Malley, M.K.: The task-dependent efficacy of shared-control haptic guidance paradigms. IEEE Trans. Haptics **5**(3), 208–2019 (2008)
2. Gillespie, R.B., O'Modhrain, M.S., Tang, P., Zaretzky, D., Pham, C.: The virtual teacher. Proc. ASME IMECE-DSC **64**, 171–178 (1998)
3. Henmi, K., Yoshikawa, T.: Virtual lesson and its application to virtual calligraphy system. In: Proceedings of IEEE ICRA, pp. 1275–1280 (1998)
4. Morris, D., Tan, H., Barbagli, F., Chang, T., Salisbury, K.: Haptic feedback enhances force skill learning. In: Proceedings of IEEE WorldHaptics, pp. 21–26 (2007)
5. Kikuuwe, R., Yoshikawa, T.: Haptic display device with fingertip pressing function for motion&force teaching to human. In: Proceedings of IEEE ICRA, pp. 868–873 (2001)
6. Gibson, J.J.: Observations on active touch. Psychol. Rev. **69**(6), 477–491 (1962)

Towards a Visual and Tangible Learning of Calculus

Patricia Salinas(✉), Eliud Quintero, Xavier Sánchez, and Eduardo González Mendívil

Tecnológico de Monterrey, Campus Monterrey, Eugenio Garza Sada 2501 Sur, 64849 Monterrey, Mexico
{npsalinas,eliudquintero,sax,egm}@itesm.mx

Abstract. The Augmented Reality Application we present here is an educational resource meant to help transform the teaching of Mathematics. It takes advantage of the didactic potential of this emergent technology in order to create graphical representations for mathematical reasoning. We identified the spatial visualization skill as a cross-curriculum content that has been taken for granted, and we took on the task of designing an educational resource to improve the development of this skill. The application involves some topics that belong to conventional courses of Calculus I, II and III at College.

Keywords: Augmented reality · Calculus · Technology · Visualization

1 Introduction

The emergent technology of Augmented Reality (AR) brings the opportunity to transform the way we interact with Mathematics. Dealing with mathematical knowledge involves dealing with symbolic representations necessarily. Numerical, algebraic and graphical are the standard representations, and their exchange is an important issue for the learning of Mathematics.

We consider the graphical representation as the one that requires more cognitive effort in order to understand and explain a behavior. We believe that a well-conceived graphical representation can give students' mind a stable support in order to deal with other mathematical representations. With that in mind, our proposal is to elaborate visual approaches for the students in order to foster their interaction with mathematical knowledge.

We believe that problems related to the learning of Math are associated with how we conceive this science and how it is reflected in the teaching process. Aiming to change the perception of students about mathematical knowledge, we propose working on a new pedagogy to approach students with this revised knowledge [1, 2, 3].

We share the point of view about digital technology offering the opportunity to create new forms of symbol-focused experience. Particularly, the idea of co-action guides our design process in the AR application. We strongly look for an understanding about the way digital technology can be effectively integrated into mainstream education and become an active participant of the cognitive process [4, 5].

C. Stephanidis (Ed.): HCII 2015 Posters, Part II, CCIS 529, pp. 307–312, 2015.
DOI: 10.1007/978-3-319-21383-5_52

We work at Monterrey Institute of Technology and Higher Education, a private educational institution in Mexico. Our educational model cares for the integration of technology in the learning process. Our particular concern is Mathematics Education, and as part of an innovation program, we have been combining the use of emerging digital technologies and educational methods in order to nourish a positive attitude from students for the learning of Mathematics.

Today we identify ourselves as TEAM, *Tecnología Educativa para el Aprendizaje de las Matemáticas*. We took on the challenge of creating a multidiscipline team that could lead an innovation process for the learning of Calculus in our Campus.

Technology changes the way we learn, and students in this millennium are already prepared to live learning experiences through visual and gestural interaction. As TEAM we are confident of the advantages on this new constantly-developing paradigm. We seek to transform the learning of Mathematics through an enjoyable interaction with technology. Augmented Reality technology has been the first choice to begin our research about its advantages.

2 The AR Application: Towards a Visual and Tangible Mathematics

Thinking in traditional content of the three Mathematics courses for Engineering, we identified spatial visualization as the mathematical skill that deserves to be explored by AR.

The application considers three levels, named: *From 2D to 3D*, *Solids of Revolution* and *3D Surfaces*, which can be associated with Mathematics I, II, and III in College. Below we describe each level and its features.

2.1 First Level: From 2D to 3D

The first part of the application studies the transition from a 2D curve to a 3D surface; through 'accumulation in time-space' of different curves. It starts with a known curve-form where different graphical effects will take place as shown in Table 1.

The curves will be shaped by the graphical effect that corresponds to the presence of the parameter k in the algebraic expression.

Table 1. Different graphical simulations for level 1

Graphical effect	Parabola	Sine	Circle
Original	$y = x^2$	$y = \sin x$	$y = \sqrt{1 - x^2}$
Vertical scroll	$y = x^2 + k$	$y = \sin x + k$	$y = \sqrt{1 - x^2} + k$
Horizontal scroll	$y = (x + k)^2$	$y = \sin(x + k)$	$y = \sqrt{1 - (x + k)^2}$
Contraction expansion	$y = kx^2$	$y = k \sin x$	$y = k\sqrt{1 - x^2}$
other		$y = \sin kx$	$y = \sqrt{R^2 - x^2}$

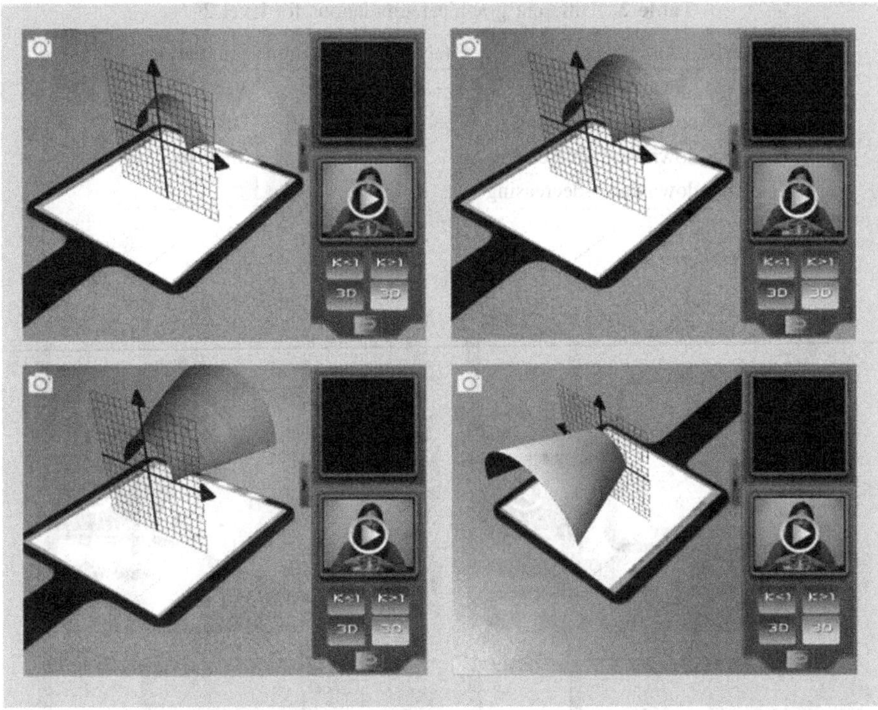

Fig. 1. Different frames of the simulation in level 1

The curve images are originally in 2D, but an animation occurs with the graphical effect simulating a 3D surface. Successive curves are placed in parallel planes situated so near in such a way that the surface begins to take its own shape. With the effect of the parameter (*k*) and simultaneously the "motion of time" through the successive copies in parallel planes, the 3D visualization takes place. Figure 1 illustrates this process.

2.2 Second Level: Solids of Revolution

The second level of the application considers four curves behavior, as shown in Table 2. UI contains buttons leading to a total of 24 simulations.

Each curve behavior includes both the case with rotation of the curve performed around the x-axis and also around the y-axis. In each case, the visualization of the solid and the method for volume calculation acknowledged as 'disk' and 'shell', are simulated with AR technology.

Taking advantage of the AR possibilities, we included the visualization of the solid of revolution before the introduction to the methods for calculating its volume. We decided to produce a simulation in order to mentally construct the solid, performing a natural cognitive process to visualize it. Figure 2 illustrates part of the visualization simulation.

Table 2. Different graphical simulations for level 2

Curve Behavior	Function	Rotation	Simulation
Concave upwards-increasing	$y = x^2$	x axis	Visualizing
Concave upwards-decreasing	$y = 2 - \sqrt{x}$	y axis	Disk method
Concave downwards-increasing	$y = \sqrt{x}$		Shell method
Concave downwards-decreasing	$y = 4 - x^2$		

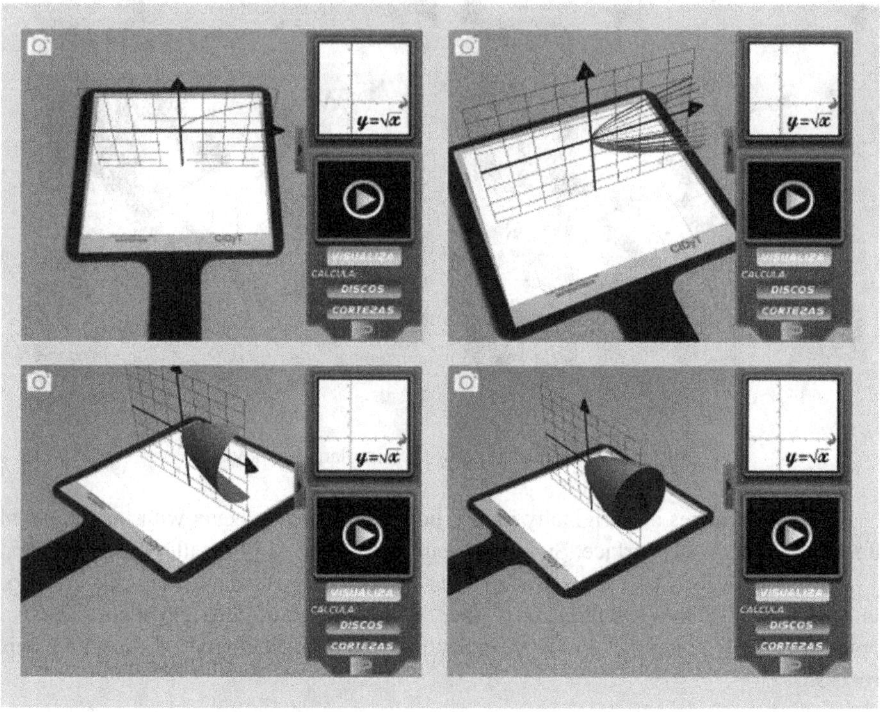

Fig. 2. Different frames of the simulation in level 2

2.3 Level 3: 3D Surfaces

The third and last level of the AR app consists of 3D surfaces, seen as the graph of a two-variable function. A variety of functions with different features is presented in order to illustrate the kind of behavior that is possible in a 3D space. Table 3 shows the functions considered, as well as intersections with the surface produced by planes which are parallel to the XY, XZ, YZ planes.

The innovation we introduced in this level is the simulation of a process now performed from 3D to 2D. It consists of a return to the 2nd dimension when the surface in 3D is affected by the intervention of parallel planes to the coordinate planes XY, YZ

Table 3. Different graphical simulations for level 3

Function	Intersections	Visualization
$z = x^2 + y^2$	xz plane	3D
$z = x^2 - y^2$	yz plane	2D $\leftrightarrow$ 3D
$z^2 = x^2 + \frac{y^2}{25}$	xy plane	
$z = \frac{1}{2}\lvert x^2 - y^2 \rvert$		
$z = y \sin x$		

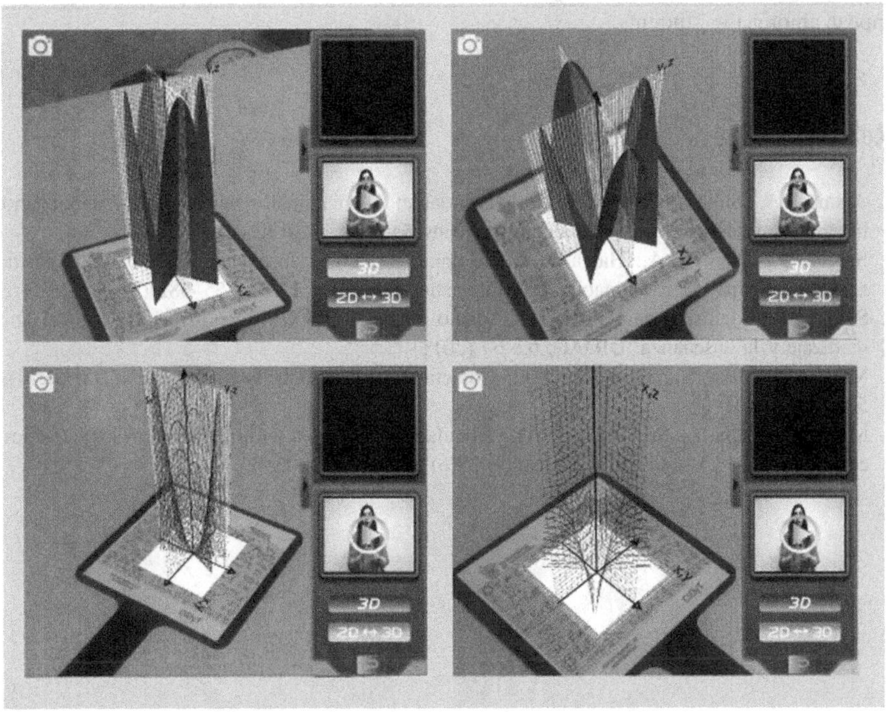

Fig. 3. Different frames of the simulation in level 3

and XZ. This visual process of cutting and rebuilding the surface promotes a cognitive evocation of a new way to visualize the surface. Figure 3 shows part of the simulation process.

3 Concluding Remarks

As TEAM we care for the actual changes that education is experiencing. It is not difficult to recognize that the university model of education, remaining for hundreds of years, nowadays is being challenged. Top Educational Institutions are looking for innovation. Reinvention about the usefulness of time and space for the teaching and learning event makes us aware of the great potential of emergent technologies.

We take part of this reinvention for the impact in the learning of Mathematics. Here we presented the possibility to offer students a visual and tangible Math. They can interact with it inside and outside the classroom. But mostly it has been our main concern to conceive an AR App that performs a simulation to be adopted cognitively. Spatial visualization is not a mathematical topic considered in the syllabus, and we are not stating it should be. Instead, we are identifying mathematical skills that make a great difference when learning Mathematics, and try to integrate digital technology in order to develop those skills. This way, mathematical knowledge should be better understood and because of this, a better attitude for its learning should eventually appear among the students.

References

1. Alanís, J.A., Salinas, P.: Cálculo de una variable: Acercamientos newtoniano y leibniziano integrados didácticamente. El Cálculo y su Enseñanza **2**, 1–14 (2010)
2. Salinas, P., Alanís, J.A.: Hacia un nuevo paradigma en la enseñanza del Cálculo. Revista Latinoamericana de Investigación en Matemática Educativa **12**(3), 355–382 (2009)
3. Salinas, P., Alanís, J.A., Pulido, R.: Cálculo de una variable: Reconstrucción para el aprendizaje y la enseñanza. DIDAC, 62–69 (2011)
4. Moreno-Armella, L., Hegedus, S.J.: Co-action with digital technologies. ZDM **41**(4), 505–519 (2009)
5. Moreno-Armella, L., Sriraman, B.: The articulation of symbol and mediation in mathematics education. ZDM Mathematics Education **37**(6), 476–486 (2005)

Effect of Interactive E-Learning on Pupils' Learning Motivation and Achievement in Mathematics

Yuan-Zheng Wang[1] and Chii-Zen Yu[2,3(✉)]

[1] Department of Network System, Toko University, Puzi, Chiayi, Taiwan
ycz@mail.toko.edu.tw
[2] Department of Industrial Design, National Cheng Kung University, Tainan, Taiwan
[3] Department of Animation and Game Design, Toko University, Puzi, Chiayi, Taiwan

Abstract. The main purpose of this study was to investigate the effect of interactive e-learning on pupils' learning motivation and achievement in mathematics. To compare the effect of e-learning and traditional instruction on children's learning motivation and achievement in mathematics, a quasi-experimental design was adopted in this study, with pretests and posttests being administered to different groups of students. Third grade students in a class at an elementary school in Chiayi County were selected as the study subjects. They were assigned to the experimental group and the control group. The experimental group received a assistant instruction which with the e-learning platform. The control group received a traditional assistant instruction. The conclusions of this study are listed below:First, the comparison of e-learning and traditional instruction on the learning effects has statistically difference and promote significantly. Second, the students' learning motivation has been significantly increased with using the e-learning for assistant teaching.

Keywords: E-learning · Mathematics instruction · Learning motivation · Learning achievement

1 Introduction

E-learning includes many kinds of electronically supported learning [1–8]. It is promoted in elementary school. This study adopted questionnaire survey to discuss pupils' learning motivation and achievement with interactive E-learning in mathematics. The data were analyzed by SPSS for descriptive statistics, independent sample t-test, and one-way ANOVA.

Hung presents that E-learning is a significant method to promote students' learning achievement for elementary school math course [9]. Chang presents that E-learning is a significant method to promote students' learning achievement for a new tech issue [10]. Hung presents that e-Learning System (web) for Music Redemptive Instruction can effectively improve the students' attitude towards music learning [11]. Tsai presents

C. Stephanidis (Ed.): HCII 2015 Posters, Part II, CCIS 529, pp. 313–317, 2015.
DOI: 10.1007/978-3-319-21383-5_53

that the students' learning achievement has significantly increased with the application of the Moodle Platform [12].

2 Method

The purpose of the study is the design of an interactive e-learning to assist in the teaching of Division and Fractions in an elementary school math course. To compare the effect of e-learning and traditional instruction on children's learning motivation and achievement in mathematics, a quasi-experimental design was adopted in this study, with pretests and posttests being administered to different groups of students. Third grade students in a class at an elementary school in Chiayi County were selected as the study subjects.

The data were analyzed by SPSS for descriptive statistics, independent sample t-test, and one-way ANOVA. The students' satisfaction degree of the above seven aspects were surveyed. The Likert five-point scale was adopted to calculate the points.

The procedure of the research survey is as follows:

a. Pre-test: Using Cronbach α coefficient to examine internal consistency of the questionnaire.
b. Analyzing the result of pre-test: After retrieving the questionnaire, we conduct reliability analysis and consult professionals' advice to revise the questionnaire. The ultimate questionnaire is formed.
c. Formal test: Proceed with the survey of the 180 questionnaire.
d. Analyzing the result: Proceed with statistical analysis.

3 Result

After retrieving the questionnaire, we go on to data analysis and presenting statistical data. They were grouped according to their mathematics scores on a preceding test. An S-shaped grouping method was used to divide the subjects into Group A (experimental group) and Group B (control group), with the groups subsequently learning two course chapters. Two independent-sample t tests were performed. The pretest results showed that the t-test values for the chapter on division and fractions were .212 ($p > .05$) and .358 ($p > .05$) for Groups A and B, respectively; neither of which was significant. The results suggested that no significant difference existed between Groups A and B regarding their ability to learn the chapter on division and fractions. To understand differences in the posttest scores between the two groups, two independent-sample t tests were performed. Tables 1 and 2 show the t-test results of the chapter on division and fractions. As shown in Table 1, the t-test value of the posttest scores for the chapter on division was 1.182 ($p > .05$) for the two groups, which was not significant; Group A achieved greater improvement than did Group B. As shown in Table 2, the t-test value of the posttest scores for the chapter on fractions was −1.511 ($p < .05$) for the two groups, which was significant.

Table 1. T-test results of the posttest scores for the various student groups after learning the chapter on division.

Group	N	Mean	SD	t-test	P
Experimental group (group A)	12	85.92	12.169	1.182	.250
Control group (group b)	12	78.58	17.717		

Table 2. T-test results of the posttest scores for the various student groups after learning the chapter on fractions.

Group	N	Mean	SD	t-test	P
Control group (group A)	12	78.25	14.473	−1.511	.049
Experimental group (group B)	12	85.75	9.285		

According to the students' mathematics scores on the preceding test, the students were divided into a high-score group (top 27 %), middle-score group (46 %), and low-score group (bottom 27 %) to understand whether these groups of students showed significant differences in academic performance before and after interactive e-learning instruction. A one-way analysis of variance was performed. As shown in Tables 3 and 4, the F values of the pretest and posttest for the chapter on division were 9.25 ($p < .05$) and 8.83 ($p < .05$), respectively; the F values of the pretest and posttest for the chapter on fractions were 29.46 ($p < .05$) and 19.54 ($p < .05$), respectively. The results for the three groups were significant, indicating that significant differences in learning achievement existed among the groups of students.

To examine the influence of interactive e-learning instruction on the students' learning motivation, the students were administered a pretest and posttest involving a scale of motivation to learn mathematics. The scale encompassed six dimensions: self-efficacy, active learning strategies, the value of mathematical learning, nonperformance goals, achievement goals, and learning incentives. Paired-sample t tests were performed on the pretest and posttest scores. As shown in Table 5, the average posttest score for each motivational dimension was greater than the average pretest score ($p < .05$). For the entire scale and for each dimension, the t-test results were significant,

Table 3. Analysis of variance for the chapter on division for students of all levels of academic achievement.

		SS	df	MS	F-test	P
Pretest	Between groups	2805.667	2	1402.833	9.25	.007
	Within groups	1365.333	9	151.704		
	Total	4171.000	11			
Posttest	Between groups	1078.917	2	539.458	8.83	.008
	Within groups	550.000	9	61.111		
	Total	1628.917	11			

Table 4. Analysis of variance for the chapter on fractions for students of all levels of academic achievement.

		SS	df	MS	F-test	P
Pretest	Between groups	2658.000	2	1329.000	29.46	.000
	Within groups	406.000	9	45.111		
	Total	3064.000	11			
Posttest	Between groups	770.750	2	385.375	19.54	.001
	Within groups	177.500	9	19.722		
	Total	948.250	11			

Table 5. Paired-sample t-test results of the pretest and posttest scores on the motivation to learn mathematics scale.

Aspects	pretest		posttest		T-test	P
	Mean	SD	Mean	SD		
Self-efficacy	3.11	.72	3.32	.64	−4.71	.000
Active learning strategies	2.98	.55	3.15	.49	−6.38	.000
The value of mathematical learning	3.20	.44	3.32	.40	−3.08	.005
Nonperformance goals	2.63	.29	2.78	.26	−4.10	.000
Achievement goals	3.58	.51	3.93	.46	−6.31	.000
Learning incentives	2.82	.28	3.58	.41	−17.4	.000
Total	3.04	.41	3.34	.39	−17.4	.000

indicating that the students' motivation to learn mathematics improved following the interactive e-learning instruction.

4 Conclusions

The main purpose of this study was to investigate the influence on pupils' learning motivation and achievement with interactive e-learning in mathematics.The results of this research are as follows:

1. A significance difference (improvement) in learning achievement existed between the students who received traditional instruction and those who received interactive e-learning instruction. The posttest mathematical scores of the students who received interactive e-learning instruction were significantly higher than those of the students who received traditional instruction.
2. After receiving interactive e-learning, students of all levels of learning achievement improved their learning achievement. Among these three groups of students, the low-score group demonstrated the greatest improvement.
3. As shown in the results, the average posttest score for each motivational dimension was greater than the average pretest score ($p < .05$). For the entire scale and for each

dimension, the t test results were significant, indicating that the students' motivation to learn mathematics was significantly enhanced after receiving interactive e-learning.

References

1. Rosenberg, M.J.: E-learning:Strategies for Delivering Knowledge in the Digital Age. The McGraw-Hill, New York (2001)
2. Masie, E.: The road to an e-learning strategy planning for future of learning. Learn. Decis. **9**, 17–30 (2002)
3. Cassarino, C.: Instructional design principles for an eLearning environment a call for definitions in the field. Q. Rev. Distance Educ. **4**(4), 455 (2003)
4. Cooper, A.: The challenge for e-learning. Open Prax. **1**, 8–11 (2004)
5. Horton, W.K.: E-learning by design. Pfeiffer, San Francisco (2006)
6. Doolittle, P., Mariano, G.: Working memory capacity and mobile multimedia learning environments: individual differences in learning while mobile. J. Educ. Multimedia Hypermedia **17**(4), 511–530 (2008)
7. Pan, A.Z.: A Study on applying didgital learning to the accounting recovery teaching. Master's thesis, National Changhua University of Education, Taiwan (2006) (in Chinese)
8. Hsu, C.H.: The effects of integrating power point multimedia on seventh graders' cognitive learning outcomes and motivation — circulation system. Master's thesis, National Taiwan Normal University, Taiwan (2009) (in Chinese)
9. Hung, C.H.: the effectiveness of an interactive website in teaching a commonmon factors and multiples course at the elementary level. Master's thesis, National Yunlin University of Science and Technology, Taiwan (2007) (in Chinese)
10. Chang, T.H.: Use moodle platform to implement nanotechnology curriculum: take grade fifth as an example. Master's thesis, National Taichung University of Education, Taiwan (2008) (in Chinese)
11. Hung, W.J.: The study of applying an e-Learning system for music redemptive instruction in The Elementary School. National Changhua University of Education, Taiwan (2007) (in Chinese)
12. Tsai, M.H.: An action research on using moodle platform to develop e-learning curriculum of mathematics teaching in Junior High School. Master's thesis, National Changhua University of Education, Taiwan (2008) (in Chinese)

HCI in Health

Learning-Training System for Medical Equipment Operation

Ren Kanehira[1(✉)], Kazinori Kawaguchi[1], and Hideo Fujimoto[2]

[1] FUJITA Health University, 1-98 Dengakugakubo, Kutsukake-Cho, Toyoake, Aichi 470-1192, Japan
kanehira@fujita-hu.ac.jp
[2] Nagoya Institute of Technology, Nagoya, Japan
fujimoto@vier.mech.nitech.ac.jp

Abstract. A clinical engineer has to do a lot of work including the management, the operation, and the maintenance of various medical equipments, requiring highly specialized techniques and up-to-date knowledge. However, it is very difficult for him to master such an enormous amount of knowledge within the limited time as university student, particularly the ability for trouble shooting to ensure safety. In order to solve these problems, this study presents an education system for clinical engineers with a representative education and training case for the operation of heart-lung machines. Although two contents, i.e., the basic operation and trouble shooting, respectively, should be included in such a training system, we pay more attention to the basic operation in this paper.

Keywords: Computer training_system · E-learning system · Skill science · Medical equipment · Clinic engineer

1 Introduction

A clinical engineer (CE) has to do a wide range of work including the management, operation, and maintenance of various medical equipments, requiring highly specialized techniques with advanced knowledge [1].

However, it is very difficult to train students or other learners to become qualified CEs who have to master so many techniques within a very limited period of time in university. As the results, the CEs quite often feel the lack of knowledge and skill when they start working in a hospital after graduation.

On the other hand, with the advanced technologies such as computer-support systems, multimedia, CG, and VR, together with a lot of new display equipments, not only visual data but also data for other human senses can be provided to the learner, ensuring a quick and effective training effect [2–6]. Following the advancing trends of medical engineering, we have studied several education/training systems [7–9]. And more recently, a computer-supported education system for clinical engineers focused on operations of medical machines was presented [10, 11].

The conventional E-learning method, though, focuses mostly on the learning of knowledge like that from textbook, paying less attention to how to operate medical

C. Stephanidis (Ed.): HCII 2015 Posters, Part II, CCIS 529, pp. 321–327, 2015.
DOI: 10.1007/978-3-319-21383-5_54

systems. Obviously, the knowledge learnt from textbook only cannot be compared with that from experience (empirical knowledge), body movements (embodies knowledge), and explicit knowledge in addition to the knowledge from textbook [12]. In this study, we present an education system for clinical engineers with a representative case for the operation. Although two contents, i.e., the basic operation and trouble shooting, respectively, should be included in such a training system, we are discussed by focusing on education and training for basic operation in this paper.

2 Education and Training for Clinical Students

One problem emerges to the students that all of them have to take national licenses for doctor or clinical engineer without much chance to do realistic and enough medical treatments on patients. Furthermore, there may be similarly less chance to operate medical machines even in their practice period in hospitals. Obviously, practice should be done as many as possible for reducing any medical accident. Therefore, effect methods of learning the methods of operation, confirming what is a safety operation, experiencing emergency cases, knowing the avoidance of dangers, and so on, have always been the research subjects of university.

Being the same in the Department of Medical Engineering in our university, the students have to master both medical knowledge and engineering one within their limited university time. Furthermore, they need to be trained with practical techniques to operate various clinical equipments at a high level of safety. The huge contents and limited time span bring to students a lot of pressure.

We did a questionnaire last year on the 4th grade students in our university by asking "did you forget the operation sequence of heart-lung machines after you have become the 4th grade student (right before the hospital practice). Surprisingly, all 31 students regardless of gender answered with "yes, I forgot"! The reasons may be multiple, but "less chance to touch and operate the medical system" becomes the dominant (Fig. 1).

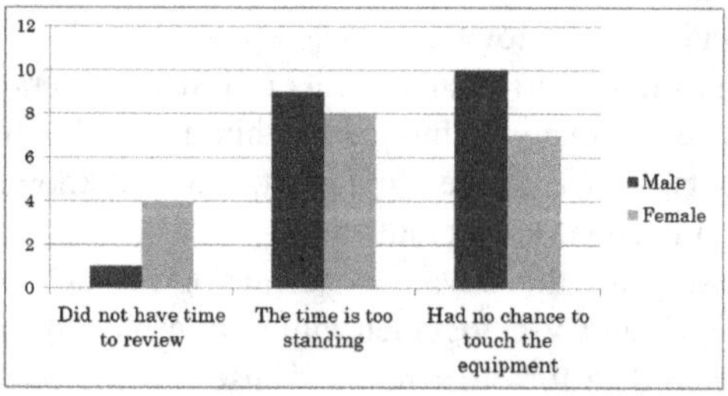

Fig. 1. Questionnaire results (1)

Therefore, it becomes much more important to build up a computer-added training system for CEs to match the increased medical need, and the importance should be increasing with time.

Another questionnaire was put upon the 4th grade students by asking "do you want to use a computer simulation system capable of providing simulated experience in the preparation and review of your text". The answers divided by different training items are shown in Fig. 2, in which 90 % of students answered "yes".

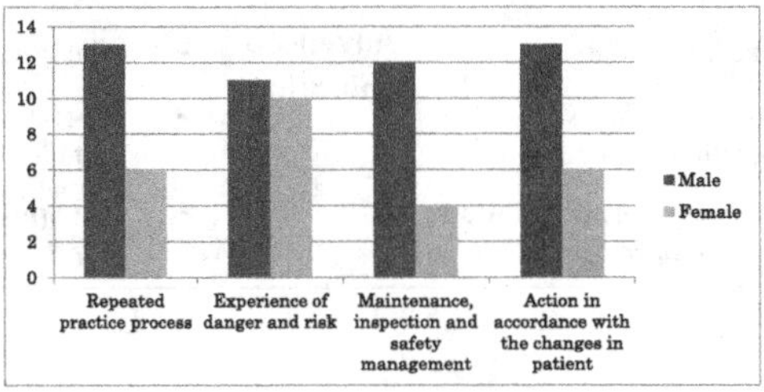

Fig. 2. Questionnaire result (2)

As stated above, it is very much expected by the students to have a training system using the advanced computer technology with multimedia presentation, particularly those with operational capability and towards different clinical equipment.

3 Teaching of Basic Operation Methods on Heart-Lung Machine

3.1 Instruction to the Construction of Extra-Corporeal Circuit

The teaching system is made for students in the 3rd grade for a better understanding on heart-lung machine operation and related knowledge.

A heart-lung machine is such an artificial system to replace temporarily the function of blood circulation and oxygen introduction of a patient. Such a medical treatment is also called "cardio-pulmonary bypass". The heart-lung machine has been taken as a typical example of clinical systems with complex circuits and numerous parts, requiring particular operations and most importantly, directly related to the life supporting of a patient.

We divided the contents of the training system into two parts, i.e., the basic training for the most fundamental operations and the trouble-shooting during practical treatments, as demonstrated in Table 1. This study focuses on the basic operation training.

In learning operation of heart-lung machines, it is considered difficult to master skills from textbook together with necessary operations within a short period of time because the medical machines differ from each other in makers and years of production.

Most importantly, operations must be taken without any mistake because they may relate directly to the patient's life. Therefore, such knowledge as the circuit construction, the machine parts and their functions, the determination of operation parameters, the safety devices and monitors, and the correct operation sequence, are required.

For this purpose, the instruction of basic operations of the extra-corporeal circuit was taken as an example. The figures and graphs from textbook are made comparable

Table 1. Contents of the system

Operation training system of the heart-lung machine			
	Basic procedures		**Troubleshooting**
Fundamentals	➢ Circuit configuration	**Advanced Operations**	➢ The trouble types
	➢ Basic knowledge		➢ The trouble types
	➢ Time series tables of operating procedures		➢ Operation process with detailed operation methods
	➢ The operation presentation by video presentation		➢ Confirmation of learning effect

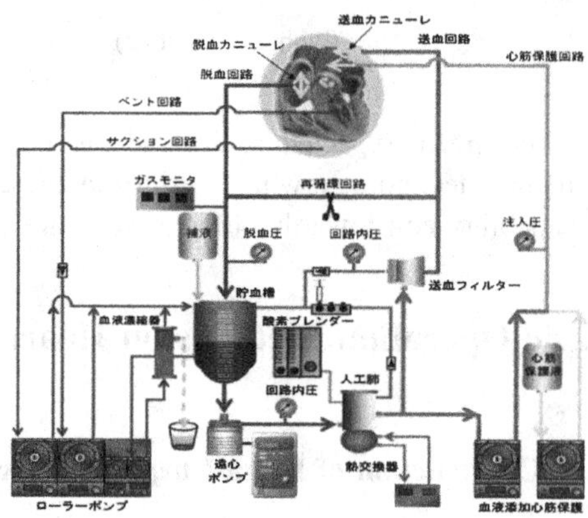

Fig. 3. Extra-corporeal circuit figure in a textbook

to the practical circuits displayed on a computer screen. Figure 3 is the flat figure of the circuits to help the students to get a rough understanding of the system at first.

Figure 4 shows the construction of circuits by photo images taken from a practical machine. It is understood that the shape of each parts, the connection of circuits are demonstrated very vividly. In addition, the names of parts, the detail of each image, and the related knowledge, function, and operation key points, are also demonstrated.

3.2 Operation Sequence by Time Series Presentation

A model operation sequence with video made under the advices of experienced clinical engineers was produced as the time series table. Related knowledge was made into a database, with which the operation contents and sequence, the easy-occur mistakes and the prevent methods were summarized to form digital text and connected with retrievals and networking.

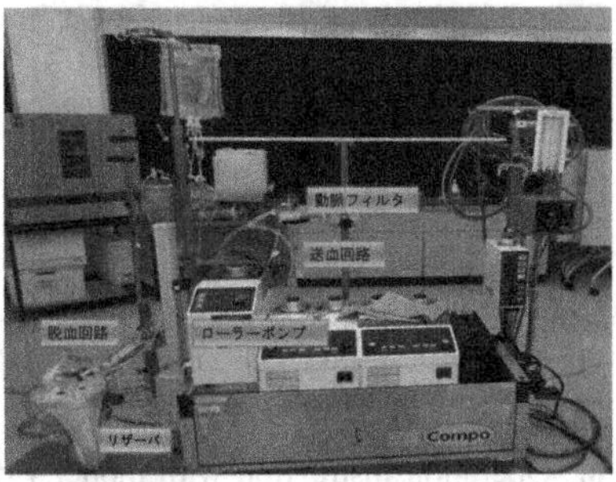

Fig. 4. Circuit construction with practical machine images

The study case using the above operation sequence table is as the following:

(1) To get the total flow of operations; (2) Study the related knowledge and operation points from explanations; (3) Get detailed by retrieval and networking; (4) Summarize the model video into the time series and make it visible when necessary.

Figure 5 shows the time series table of the operation. Knowledge/Images/Video in the right hand are linked with operation sequence in the left hand. For example, the star mark links to the related knowledge to the related page with knowledge represented by instructions with description sentence and tables. When click the Image, it is demonstrated as a detailed photo and suitable descriptions.

手順	ポンプ	心筋保護液	知識	写真	動画
<1> ポンプスタートの準備	・ポンプが停止していることを確認 ・脱血サイド(1本)、送血サイド(1本)、リサーキュレーション回路(1本)に鉗子で閉めてあるかしっかり確認する。		★	■	●
	・リザーバレベルを一番高いレベルにする。 ・手の届く位置に鉗子、手回し用クランクを用意する。		★	■	●
<2> ポンプスタート (部分体外循環開始)	・ヘパリン投与とACT値確認 ※ACT値400以上でないと開始してはいけない。		★	■	●
術野の指示で開始	・送血チューブの鉗子外す。 ・チューブを手で軽く押し拍動を確認 ・『ポンプスタートします。』 ・100～200ml送血 ・『脱血開始します。』 ・インデックス2.4にあわせる。→術野に知らせる。	※送血圧に注意する！ ※イニシャルドロップを避ける	★	■	●
<3> トータルバイパス (完全体外循環開始)	・冷却スタート		★	■	●

Fig. 5. Time series table of operation sequence

3.3 Instruction with Model Video

It is easier to memorize an operation with one's eyes tracking the traces of a moving body than keeping them staring at typed words in textbook. In fact, the model operation text was produced using the images and video taken from a real machine and real operation after consulting experienced clinical engineers. The parts in text can be emphasized by magnifying, added with new words or red colored to help the students for better understanding. Figure 6 demonstrates an example of operation instruction by video.

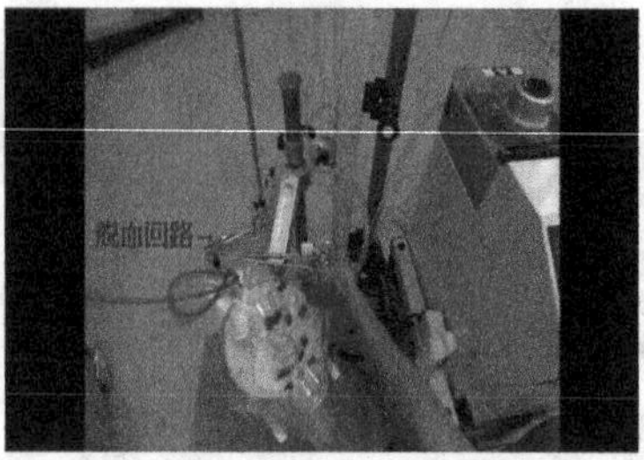

Fig. 6. Operation instruction with model video

4 Conclusions

A training system for operations on heart-lung machines was studied for the "Practice of Circulation Support Technologies" of the 3rd grade student in university.

As the content for the basic operation knowledge learning, the circuit construction and model operation methods were presented with digital text. Instruction on operation sequence was provided with time series table with necessary links to related knowledge, images and videos. A combination of audio-visual stimuli provided by multimedia led to a better understanding and higher efficiency in the training.

The effect of system was evaluated with the questionary on the trained students of the department. Over 80 % of them confirmed the usefulness of the system in helping them to master necessary skills and knowledge during study. It is expected that a much higher training efficiency can be obtained with further accomplishment of the present training system.

Acknowledgments. This study was supported by JSPE KAKENNHI Grant Number 25350304. I would like to thank clinical engineers and 4th grade students for cooperation of research studies.

References

1. Japan Association for Clinical Engineers (2014). http://www.ja-ces.or.jp/ce/
2. Watanabe, K., Kashihara, A.: A view of learning support research issues based on ICT genealogy. Jan. J. Educ. Technol. **34**(3), 143–152 (2010)
3. Japan e-learning, Education IT Solutions EXPO. http://www.edix-expo.jp/en/Home/
4. Journal of Japan Association for Simulation-based Education in Healthcare Professionals, vol. 1 (2013). http://square.umin.ac.jp/model/
5. Noh, Y., Segawa, M., Shimomura, A., Ishii, H., Solis, J., Hatake, K., Takanishi, A.: Development of the evaluation system for the airway management training system WKA- - 1R. In: Proceedings of the Second IEEE RAS/EMBS International Conference on Biomedical Robotics and Bio Mechatronics (2008)
6. Sueda, T.: Development of a Training Simulator for Extracorporeal Circulation with a Heart-Lung Machine, Hiroshima University (2010). http://hutdb.hiroshima-u.ac.jp/seeds/view/3/en

7. Kanehira, R., et al.: Development of an acupuncture training system using virtual reality technology. In: Proceedings of 5th FSKD, pp. 665–668. IEEE Press (2008)
8. Kanehira, R., Yang, W., Narita, H., Fujimoto, H.: Insertion force of acupuncture for a computer training system. In: Wang, F.L., Deng, H., Gao, Y., Lei, J. (eds.) AICI 2010, Part II. LNCS, vol. 6320, pp. 64–70. Springer, Heidelberg (2010)
9. Kanehira, R., Yang, W., Fujimoto, H.: Education and training environments for skill mastery. In: Wang, F.L., Lei, J., Lau, R.W.H., Zhang, J. (eds.) CMSP 2012. CCIS, vol. 346, pp. 451–458. Springer, Heidelberg (2012)
10. Kanehira, R., Narita, H., Kawaguchi, K., Hori, H., Fujimoto, H.: A training system for operating medical equipment. In: Li, S., Jin, Q., Xiaohong, J., Park, J.J. (eds.) Information Technology in Medicine and Education. LNEE, vol. 269, pp. 2259–2265. Springer, Heidelberg (2013)
11. Kanehira, R., Hori, H., Kawaguchi, K., Fujimoto, H.: Computer-supported training system for clinical engineer. In: Stephanidis, C. (ed.) HCI 2014, Part II. CCIS, vol. 435, pp. 89–94. Springer, Heidelberg (2014)
12. Furukawa, K.: Skills Science Introduction: Approach to the elucidation of embodies knowledge. Ohmsha (2009)

A New Assessment Model of Mental Health

Jingqiang Li(✉), Ning Zhao, and Bingxia Hao

Research Institute of Civil Aviation Safety,
Civil Aviation University of China, Tianjin, China
jqli@cauc.edu.cn, mcn1989@126.com,
haobingxia6219@163.com

Abstract. Traditionally, mental health has been considered as a mental state with absence of mental illness symptoms. According to the Dual-Factor Model of Mental Health, mental health is a complete state, which includes the presence of a positive state of human capacities and functions as well as the absence of disease or infirmity. However, these models haven't investigated the mechanism of action of the regulatory or intermediary factors behind individual's current state of mental health. From this point, this article constructs a new assessment model of mental health: Neuro-Trait-State-Balance model (NTSB). The NTSB model considers three aspects as follows: (1) assessing the dominant performance (adaptive state) and implicit mechanism (adaptive trait) to clarify the present situation of mental health; (2) assessing the neural mechanism of the adaptive trait and analyzing the relationship between the characteristics of higher nervous activities and mental health to clarify the implicit mechanism; (3) assessing the degree of needs balance to know the variation trend of mental health state. In addition, it can indirectly improve the intervention strategies of mental health.

Keywords: Mental health · Assessment · Adaptive trait · Adaptive state

1 Introduction

In recent years, various countries around the world increasingly focused on mental health, although the number of all sorts of psychological problems have not declined. According to the World Health Organization, about 450 million people worldwide are affected by mental, neurological or behavioral problems at any time [1]. At present, the most frequent tools are the Symptom Checklist 90 (SCL-90), Self-rating Depression Scale (SDS), Self-rating Anxiety Scale (SAS) etc. [2, 3]. They all assess psychological disorders instead of mental health. By questioning the classic view considering the mental health and psychological disorder as the two poles of a continuum, Keyes proposed the double construct hypothesis [4]. Subsequently, empirical research indicates that positive and negative mental health are mutually independent but interrelated structures. Mental health and psychological disorder are different constructs which have a causal and interacting covariant relationship [3, 4]. This also shows that using the scales of evaluating psychological disorder to assess mental health is not suitable. Therefore, it is necessary to reflect on the traditional mental health model and explore a more effective mental health model.

C. Stephanidis (Ed.): HCII 2015 Posters, Part II, CCIS 529, pp. 328–333, 2015.
DOI: 10.1007/978-3-319-21383-5_55

The essence of the mental health is a kind of state [4]. Keyes points out that the process of understanding mental health covers three stages: negative mental health, positive mental health, and complete mental health [5]. These traditional assessment models only evaluate the mental health status and cannot prevent, maintain, promote individual mental health or eradicate psychological disorder fundamentally. It is necessary to further investigate the modulatory or intermediary function mechanism behind individual's current state of mental health. Thus, this article constructs a new mental health assessment model to elaborate the mechanism.

2 The Evolution of Mental Health Assessment

Under the negative mental health stage, mental health was thought as no mental symptoms because the stage viewed health as the absence of disability or disease [4]. Here, mental health was a one-dimensional structure, and mainly regarded psychopathology as an indicator, which involved internal disorders (e.g. anxiety) and external disorders (e.g. behavior disorder). The studies are confined within the perspective of neuropathology. Later, Jahoda believed the absence of mental illness cannot be applied to effectively defining mental health. It was necessary but not sufficient [6]. With the rise of positive psychology, the researchers further treated subject well-being as the indicator of mental health. They deemed that mental health is a positive mind state. For instance, in the studies of Keyes et al., mental health is directly defined as well-being [7]. And then, in whole mental health stage, the Dual-Factor Model of Mental Health (DFM) [7–9] (Keyes, 2005; Suldo & Shaffer, 2008; Doll, 2008) emerged. DFM showed that mental health was a complete state, which included the presence of a positive state as well as the absence of disease or infirmity. The integration of negative indicators (e.g. neuropathology) and positive indicators (e.g. subjective well-being) goes beyond the unilateralism of one dimension in the negative and positive stage. This has made a more comprehensive understanding of mental health. According to this model, the people are divided into four or six groups [7–9]. While DFM proposed the operational concepts and verified the two-dimensional diagnosis standard and classification standard, its mechanism of the regulatory or intermediary factors behind mental health status has not yet been assessed.

3 The Assessment Model of Mental Health

Currently, the main assessment criteria for mental health are divided into six categories: the normal distribution in statistics, the standards compliance in sociology, the pathogeny and symptoms in medicine, subjective experience standard, life adaptation standard and psychological maturity and development standard. Also, the "social adaptation" is treated as a basic standard. However, the "social adaptation" standard was doubted to have one-way obedience from individual to society which leads to the emergence of the "development" standard [10]. Nevertheless, due to pressure from adaptation, "development" also presented compulsivity and thus Yu came up with the two-dimensional standard of "positive adaptation, active development" [11]. The two-dimensional standard of "adaptation" and "development" also refers to the nature of mental health as a good condition of internal and external coordination and active adaptation. Mental health includes adaptive state and adaptive trait. Adaptive state is one's condition as adaptive now, and may be altered with the changes of internal and external environment. While adaptive trait is the stable, durable tendency that is developed gradually with the features of personality, which will gradually adjust one's psychological condition to an adaptive state. The dominant performance of mental health is the adaptive state, and its recessive mechanism is the regulation and process of the adaptive trait. The relative stability of mental health determines the level of the mental health status, in which the adaptive trait plays a role in them. The stable behavior patterns embodied by the behaviors of the neural mechanism are the adaptive trait. As a state, the volatility of mental health status also determines the variability.

3.1 Mental Health State and Quality

Good psychological state and adaptive behavior are the outward expressions of mental health. The adaptive state reflects a good relation in the process of individual psychology interacting with the environment. According to the objects of adaptation, such as environment, society and oneself, adaptation can be divided into natural adaptation, social adaptation, self-adaptation or mental adaptation. The adaptation state is characterized by: (1) the existence and absence of individual psychosomatic symptoms, (2) the individual discretion of subjective well-being, (3) whether personal psychology and behavior conforming to or meeting the conditions, specifications and rules of environment. These three aspects provide a comprehensive assessment of the adaptive state of mental health respectively from the internal negative factors, internal positive factors and the matching degree of individual and external perspectives.

The relationship between adaptive trait and adaptive state is as to "nature" and "performance". Adaptive trait is the core layer of psychological structure and the sources of psychological activities. Adaptive state is the skin layer, which reflects the states of certain adaptive traits. From the functions of the adaptive trait, it is the endogenous factors of the adaptive state, which has important direct effects and adjusting effects to the level of mental health. While considering the functions of the adaptive state, good mental health state reflects the soundness and a higher level of the adaptive trait to some extent.

3.2 Neural Mechanism of Mental Health

According to Pavlov's theory of higher nervous activity, the basic process of higher nervous activity is excitatory and inhibitory [12]. Excitation and inhibition can connect, restrain and transform each other mutually. There are three basic characteristics [12]: strength (the ability to accept intense stimulation and persistent work), flexibility (the rapidity of these processes) and balance (the balance of the degree of excitation and inhibition). The excessive tension of higher nervous activity processes will weaken the nervous system [12] and the accumulation of tensions unimproved for a long time will reduce the body's resistance to the pathogenic factors and then speed up the production of neurosis. For example, the overstrain of inhibitory process (such as enduring psychological pain for a long time with the greatest patience), the excessive tension of excitatory process (such as pretending to be calm and hiding sadness), the overstrain of flexibility (such as living conditions suddenly worsening), the conflict between excitation and inhibition (such as the overlap of joy and sorrow in the short term). Neurosis, meanwhile, also causes deviation from the normal level to neural activities and cortical dysfunction, which will aggravate the state of illness or bring about new diseases. Under the influence of unfavorable factors, higher nervous activities will evolve in the pathological direction such as neuroticism developing into neurosis, and psychoticism developing into mental illness.

In addition, the neural activity can indirectly influence the mental health status by different behavior patterns. The individuals with a weak type of nervous system easily show the control and prevention of activities in the conditions without stimulation and their abilities of directing, controlling and executing activities are suppressed in threatening situations. Their mental health states are at an average level. While the individuals with a strong type of nervous system usually conduct good fallback behaviors in situations with high stresses, and their mental health is in good condition.

3.3 Variation Trend of Mental Health State

With a change of environment, an individual will initiate the psychological balance-oriented mechanism to coordinate his condition and make it recover or develop into a new harmonious state. Mental health varies between uncoordinated state and coordinated state, which reflects a process of dynamic change. Bandura thinks that the adaptive behavior depends on not only the strengthening of the appropriate stimulation outside, but also the subjective psychological expectation [13]. Proper expectation is a necessary condition to adaptive behavior. Rotter further argues the significance of adaptation is to achieve some degree of balance between the freedom of motion of behavior potential (the psychological expectations of the goals achieved) and the needed value (personal goal value) [14]. Therefore, appropriate expectations and corresponding personal goal value will produce adaptive behavior, but when the needed value for a goal is too high and the expectation to the goal achieved is too low, it will create an unhealthy adaptive state. Thus, the key to the change of psychological health state depends on the balance between individual needs and expectations.

3.4 The Assessment Model of Mental Health

Figure 1 indicates the above-mentioned logical relationship and illustrates the Neuro-Trait-State-Balance model (NTSB). It is summarized as following:

- T-S. The essence of mental health is a kind of positive state. Good psychological state and adaptive behavior are outward expressions of mental health, and the endogenous factor of mental health is the influence of the adaptive trait. Therefore, it is necessary to evaluate both the dominant performance and the recessive characteristics of mental health in order to make clear the present situation of mental health.

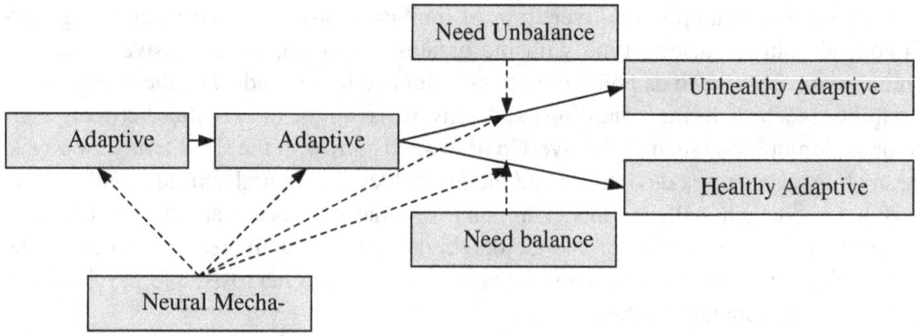

Fig. 1. The assessment model of mental health (Notes: Dashed line shows an influence relationship; solid line shows a causal relationship).

- N. The physiological basis of the adaptive trait is the neural mechanism. The adaptive-state is the external performance of the neural mechanism to some extent. The neural mechanisms also indirectly influence the changes of mental health state through certain action ways or types. As a result, assessing the neural mechanisms and analyzing the relationship between the characteristics of higher nervous activities and mental health clarifies the implicit mechanism of mental health.
- B. The balance of psychological needs and expectations is the driving force of the changes of mental health state. Thus, evaluating the degree of balance of psychological needs helps understanding the change tendency of mental health state.

3.5 Targeted Interventions of Mental Health

The NTSB model can also guide the intervention of mental health. The individual adaptive trait has a recessively mediate or moderating effect on the obtainment of positive mental health status and the elimination of negative mental health status. For this reason, the intervention of mental health not only eliminates the adverse psychological states or cultivates subjective well-being. The elimination of psychological symptoms does not mean the mental health is in a good condition. The scientific validity is also questionable because the stability of subjective well-being is poor. The goal of mental health intervention and treatment is to improve patients' subjective well-being and psychological resources (positive psychological quality) in order to achieve a complete mental health state. Only by taking into account both the state and the trait of mental health can be improved the pertinence and efficiency of intervention. In addition, for people with different adaptive traits, we also should adopt different guidance and intervention strategies. For instance, for neurotics, we should advise them to adopt positive emotional regulation strategies under pressure, which will make them more likely to experience the feeling of success and improve their efficacy of managing negative emotions and therefore reduce mental health problems.

4 Summary

The NTSB supports that the mental health is not merely the absence of mental illness or a high level of subjective well-being, but also a complete state of the combination of the two parts as DFM. The difference is that NTSB further suggests the mental health can be decided by certain psychological qualities. NTSB considers three aspects in assessment of mental health. The model evaluates the positive and negative factors of mental health to understand the state of mental health, assesses its neural basis to analyze the influence mechanism, and also assesses the needs balance to know the variation trend of mental health. In addition, the model can also direct the intervention of mental health. Through improving mental resources, the adverse psychological states can be eliminated and the subjective well-being can be cultivated. Moreover, different intervention strategies should be adopted according to different characteristics.

References

1. World Health Organization: Global Health Risks: Mortality and Burden of Disease Attributable to Selected Major Risks. WHO Press, Switzerland (2009)
2. Li, J.: An analysis of use frequency of psychological health measurement tools and suggestions. J. S. China Normal Univ. (Soc. Sci. Ed.) **3**, 119–123 (2007). (in Chinese)
3. Tong, H.J., Yang, Y.J., Li, L.H., et al.: Development of the mental health style questionnaire and the test of double constructs hypothesis. Chinese Ment. Health J. **6**, 473–477 (2010). (in Chinese)
4. Keyes, C.L.M.: Toward a science of mental health. In: Snyder, C.R., Lopez, S.J. (eds.) Oxford Handbook of Positive Psychology, pp. 89–95. Oxford University Press, New York (2009)
5. Antaramian, S.P., Huebner, E.S., Hills, K.J., et al.: A dual-factor model of mental health: toward a more comprehensive understanding of youth functioning. Am. J. Orthopsychiatry **4**, 462–472 (2010)
6. Jahoda, M.: Current Concepts of Positive Mental Health. Basic Books, New York (1958)
7. Keyes, C.L.M.: Mental illness and/or mental health? investigating axioms of the complete state model of health. J. Consult. Clin. Psychol. **3**, 539–548 (2005)
8. Suldo, S.M., Shaffer, E.J.: Looking beyond psychopathology: the dual-factor model of mental health in youth. Sch. Psychol. Rev. **1**, 52–68 (2008)
9. Doll, B.: The dual-factor model of mental health in youth. Sch. Psychol. Rev. **1**, 69–73 (2008)
10. Jin, D.C.: Living standard and development standard on mental health. Psychol. Sci. **4**, 253–255 (1993). (in Chinese)
11. Yu, G.L., Zeng, P.P.: Teacher's mental health and its improvement. J. Beijing Normal Univ. (Humanit. Soc. Sci.) **1**, 20–27 (2005). (in Chinese)
12. Chilingarian, L.I.: I.P. Pavlov's theory of higher nervous activity: landmarks and developmental trends. Neuro-Sci. Behav. Physiol. **1**, 39–47 (2001)
13. Bandura, A.: Social Learning Theory. Prentice-Hall, Englewood Cliffs (1971)
14. Mearns, J.: Social learning theory. In: Reis, H., Sprecher, S. (eds.) Encyclopedia of Human Relationships, pp. 1537–1540. SAGE Publications, Thousand Oaks (2009)

"Fit" Determining Nurses' Satisfaction of Nursing Information System Usage

Hsien-Cheng Lin[1(✉)] and Chen-Chia Chen[2]

[1] Fooyin University Hospital and Fooyin University, Kaohsiung, Taiwan
u0028909@nkfust.edu.tw

[2] China Medical University Hospital, Taichung, Taiwan

Abstract. In the digital age, nursing units must more than ever be able to utilize nursing information system (NIS) to enhance efficiencies, effectiveness, and decision-support, and get timely answers to questions, when they arise in daily clinical and administrative practice. Previous researchers have suggested that satisfaction status is established on the degree of fit, when achieve a good fit between the users' requirements and technological capabilities to attain optimal use satisfaction. Thus, this study attempts to understand how impact of fit of individual requirement-technological capability on user satisfaction through the holistic perspective of fit within the nursing context. The results indicate that the fit of users' perceptions-technological capabilities interaction is a more important factor than individuals' factor of users' perceptions or technological capabilities in users' satisfaction of information system usage.

Keywords: Fit · Satisfaction · Nursing information system

1 Introduction

The use of a Nursing Information System (NIS) is widespread in modern healthcare organizations. Approximately 95 % of healthcare organizations have adopted NIS to support nursing clinical practice and general administration in Taiwan [1]. An NIS is defined as the emerging applications of the information technology to help nurses deliver or acquire accurate and real time clinical information to or from patient, physician, or other healthcare providers to ensure quality healthcare [2]. Previous studies have verified that NIS can assist nurses in making clinical decisions, as well as increasing their efficiency and effectiveness in their daily routines [1, 3]. Goodhue & Thompson (1995) [4] and Parkes (2013) [5] suggest that the degree of users' satisfaction is established on fit, i.e. when a good fit is achieved between the users' requirements and technological capabilities to obtain optimal use satisfaction. However, the perspectives of previous studies are incomplete since they ignored the fit relationship between users' perceptions and technological capabilities impacting users' satisfaction [6–8]. This study argues that nurses perceived fit of individual requirement-technological capability influences nurses' satisfaction with NIS usage.

This study is approved by the Institutional Review Board of the Fooyin UniversityHospital (No: FYH-IRB-103-09-02-A).

C. Stephanidis (Ed.): HCII 2015 Posters, Part II, CCIS 529, pp. 334–339, 2015.
DOI: 10.1007/978-3-319-21383-5_56

Hence, we attempt to tests whether the fit of users' perceptions- technological capabilities interaction is a more important factor than individuals' factor of users' perceptions or technological capabilities in users' satisfaction of information system usage through the perspective of fit as covariation in the context of nursing work.

2 Theoretical Background, Research Model and Hypotheses

Figure 1 displays the research models of this study. Consequently, several hypotheses will be developed and tested.

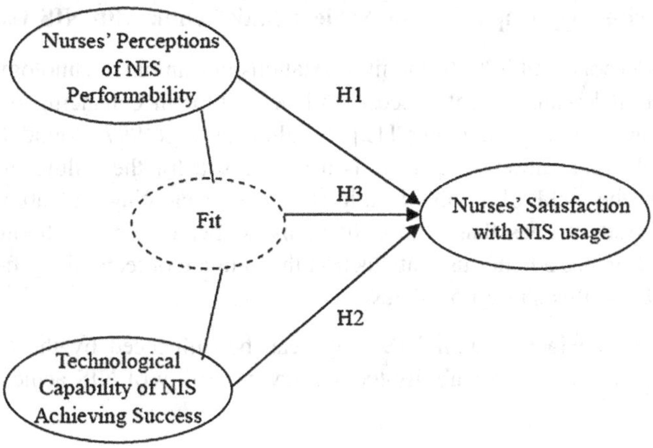

Fig. 1. Research model

2.1 Nurses' Perceptions of NIS Performability and Nurses' Satisfaction with NIS Usage

In the field of healthcare informatics, previous literatures have identified that the degree to which healthcare professionals perceive the performability of a healthcare information system has a significant influence on the users' satisfaction of healthcare information system applications [1, 6]. Moreover, according to Lee et al. (2008) nurses are more likely to have higher satisfaction than physicians by adopting an electronic healthcare system when they perceive that the device provides friendly-interface, compatibility, accurate and real-time information [9]. Thus, this study postulates:

H1: Nurses' perceptions of NIS performability are significantly related to nurses' satisfaction with NIS usage.

2.2 Technological Capability of NIS Achieving Success and Nurses' Satisfaction with NIS Usage

Technological capability is an important factor impacting user satisfaction with information system applications [8]. Sarker et al. (2005) declared that user perceived continuity in the availability of technology functional support from a device is a key antecedent of user satisfaction and continued use of the information system [10]. Otieno et al. (2007) [11] through an investigation of 1666 nurses found that technological quality of electronic medical records has a positive correlation with user satisfaction. Thus, this study postulates:

H2: Technological capability of NIS to achieve success is significantly related to nurses' satisfaction with NIS usage.

2.3 Fit Between Nurses' Perceptions of NIS Performability and Technology Capability to Achieve Satisfaction with NIS Usage

According to Yusofs et al. (2006) the fit of relationships among technology, staff skills and organizational management process will be helpful in enhancing organizational performance and strategy planning [12]. Southon et al. (1997) found that poor fit among several organizational elements is a key reason for the failure of technology acceptance in the field of public health [13]. By integrating the abovementioned insights, this study argues that a good fit of users' perceptions- technological capabilities interaction has a better use satisfaction than human or technology factors on use satisfaction. Thus, this study postulates:

H3: Nurses' satisfaction with NIS usage can be influenced by the fit of nurses' perceptions of NIS performability-technology capability of NIS achieving success

3 Methods

3.1 Instrument Development

The measures to be used in this study were obtained from previous literature. Items for measuring nurses' perceptions of NIS performability were adapted from Davis et al. (1989) [14], while scales used to measure technology capability of NIS achieving success was adapted from Chenet al. (2015) [15], and Petter & Fruhling (2011) [16]. Nurses' satisfaction with NIS usage measures was adapted from Chen et al. (2015) [15]. This study employed multi-item five-point Likert scales anchored by 5 = "strongly agree" and 1 = "strongly disagree." Pretests were examined by 30 registered nurses before they were used in the selected target population.

3.2 Data Collection

The questionnaire was distributed to 200 registered nurses at 4 healthcare institutions. All hospitals already had established and widely employed NIS offering support services for nurses' clinical and administrative affairs. 153 questionnaires were returned. Of these, 11 were incomplete. The valid sample size was 142, with an effective response rate of 71 %.

4 Results

4.1 Measurement Model Assessment

This study used a CFA to estimate the reliability and validity of the scales of measurement items. The scales' convergent and discriminant validity were examined as demonstrated in Table 1. The Cronbach's alpha of all constructs, which displayed an adequate reliability, was > 0.7, the threshold suggested by Hair et al. (1998) [17]. The items' factor loading, which recommends an acceptable outcome for discriminant validity according to Antony et al. (2002) [18], was > 0.7 in all instances. All values of average variance extracted (AVE) were greater 0.5 displaying an acceptable convergent validity. Additionally, the composite reliabilities (CR) for all constructs were above 0.7; all values well exceeded the required threshold of 0.6, showing good composite reliability. Table 1 displays the AVE square root values on the diagonal line, which surpass the values on the non-diagonal line that are correlation coefficients between inter-construct correlations. Therefore, the results showed powerful evidence of good discriminant validity.

Table 1. The results of construct correlations

Constructs	Mean	S.D	Nurses' perceptions of NIS performability	Technological capability of NIS achieving success	Nurses' satisfaction with NIS usage	
Nurses' perceptions of NIS performability	3.888	0.780	0.375***	**0.825**		
Technological capability of NIS achieving success	3.730	0.886	0.444***	0.301**	**0.816**	
Nurses' satisfaction with NIS usage	3.861	0.558	0.407***	0.317***	0.378***	**0.780**

Note: Square root of Ave extracted for each latent construct is displayed in diagonals.

$p^{**}<0.01$, $p^{***}<0.001$

4.2 Structural Model Assessment- the Perspective of Fit as Covariation

This study compared the coefficients of determination (R^2) of the two models to examine the goodness of fit of the research model. The direct effects model variance explained 13.1 % (R^2 = 26.7 % vs. 39.8 %) less variance in nurses' satisfaction with NIS usage. The values of R^2 were greater than 10 % in the model, which implied that latent variable regressions were significant in this study [19]. Thus, the results hint at the acceptance of the fit over the main effects model. Moreover, nurses' perceptions of NIS performability, technological capability of NIS achieving success, and fit have significant influence on nurses' satisfaction with NIS usage (β = 0.244; 0.207; 0.433, t-value = 3.303; 3.117; 5.110, respectively); hence hypotheses 1, 2 and 3 were supported.

5 Discussions

The findings show that the fit of nurses' perceptions of NIS performability and the technological capability of NIS achieving success was found to have a significant impact on nurses' satisfaction with NIS usage. The fit of nurses' perceptions -technology capability interaction is a more important factor than individuals' factors of users' perceptions or technological capability with respect to users' satisfaction with information system usage; it determines the success or failure with NIS implication. Therefore, this study suggests that nursing department supervisors can apply the concept of holistic fit and assist in developing and evaluating an appropriate type of NIS for achieving better performance.

References

1. Lu, C.H., Hsiao, J.L., Chen, R.F.: Factors determining nurse acceptance of hospital information systems. CIN- Comput. Inform. Nurs. **30**(5), 257–264 (2012)
2. Ammenwerth, E., Rauchegger, F., Ehlers, F., Hirsch, B., Schaubmayr, C.: Effect of a nursing information system on the quality of information processing in nursing: an evaluation study using the HIS-monitor instrument. Int. J. Med. Inform. **80**(1), 25–38 (2011)
3. Lee, T.T., Lee, T.Y., Lin, K.C., Chang, P.C.: Factors affecting the use of nursing information systems in Taiwan. J. Adv. Nurs. **50**(2), 170–178 (2005)
4. Goodhue, D.L., Thompson, R.L.: Task-technology fit and individual performance. MISQ **19** (2), 213–236 (1995)
5. Parkes, A.: The effect of task-individual-technology fit on user attitude and performance: an experimental investigation. Decis. Support Syst. **54**(2), 997–1009 (2013)
6. Shoham, S., Gonen, A.: Intentions of hospital nurses to work with computers. CIN- Comput. Inform. Nurs. **26**(2), 106–116 (2008)
7. Jen, W.Y., Chao, C.C.: Measuring mobile patient safety information system success: an empirical study. Int. J. Med. Inform. **77**(10), 689–697 (2008)
8. Chatterjee, S., Chakraborty, S., Sarker, S., Sarker, S., Lau, F.Y.: Examining the success factors for mobile work in healthcare: a deductive study. Decis. Support Syst. **46**(3), 620–633 (2009)
9. Lee, T.T., Mills, M.E., Bausell, B., Lu, M.H.: Two-stage evaluation of the impact of a nursing information system in Taiwan. Int. J. Med. Inform. **77**(10), 698–707 (2008)
10. Sarker, S., Valacich, J.S., Sarker, S.: Technology adoption by groups: a valence perspective. J. Assoc. Inf. Syst. **6**(2), 37–71 (2005). Article 3
11. Otieno, O.G., Toyama, H., Asonuma, M., Masako, K.P., Keiko, N.: Nurses' views on the use, quality and user satisfaction with electronic medical records: questionnaire development. J. Adv. Nurs. **60**(2), 209–219 (2007)
12. Yusof, M.M., Paul, R.J., Stergioulas, L.K.: Towards a framework for health information systems evaluation. In: Proceeding the 39th Hawaii International Conference on System Sciences 5: Article 95a (2006)
13. Southon, F.C.G., Sauer, C., Grant, C.G.: Information technology in complex health services: organizational impediments to successful technology transfer and diffusion. J. Am. Med. Inform. Assoc. **4**(2), 112–124 (1997)

14. Davis, F.D., Bagozzi, R.P., Warshaw, P.R.: User acceptance of computer technology: a comparison of two theoretical models. Manage. Sci. **35**(8), 982–1003 (1989)
15. Chen, V.J., Jubilado, R.J.M., Capistrano, E.P.S., Yen, D.C.: Factors affecting online tax filing: an application of the IS success model and trust theory. Comput. Hum. Behav. **43** (February), 215–262 (2015)
16. Petter, S., Fruhling, A.: Evaluating the success of an emergency response medical information system. Int. J. Med. Inform. **80**(7), 480–489 (2011)
17. Hair, J.F., Rolph Jr., E.A., Ronald, L.T., William, C.B.: Multivariate Data Analysis, 5th edn. Prentice Hill, Upper Saddle River (1998)
18. Antony, L., Leung, K., Knowles, G., Gosh, S.: Critical success factors of TQM implementation in Hong Kong industries. Int. J. Qual. Reliab. Manage. **19**(5), 551–566 (2002)
19. Falk, R., Miller, N.: A Primer for Soft Modeling. University of Akron Press, Akron (1992)

Research on Health Management System Based on Clouding Computing

Qi Luo([✉]) and Tianbiao Zhang

College of Sports Engineering and Information Technology, Wuhan Sports University, Wuhan 430079, China
ccnu_luo2008@126.com

Abstract. Cloud computing involves deploying groups of remote servers and software networks that allow centralized data storage and online access to computer services or resources. The health management system based on clouding computing was proposed in the paper. The system is composed of the following modules such as client module, expert module, healthy management organizations module, accumulated points and rank management module, task listing and evaluation module, cloud server network platform module. Though application in the system, the individual user data has no longer stored in the medical institution, but the individual user data has stored in the cloud server, which can be accessed anytime and anywhere. A large number of servers are composed of statistical and learning distributed platform. Behavior information and physical data can be extracted from the mass data automatically, which can be output factors and standardization of physical data. The same type of samples is extracted, which can achieve a group of experts and users by many-to-many model. Health standards databases are constructed though bidirectional user and expert evaluation. The system is an open and interactive system among user, health management organization and expert.

1 Introduction

The health management system (HMS) is an evolutionary medicine regulative process proposed by Nicholas Humphrey in which actuarial assessment of fitness and economic-type cost-benefit analysis determines the body's regulation of its physiology and health. This incorporation of cost-benefit calculations into body regulation provides a science grounded approach to mind-body phenomena such as placebos that are otherwise not explainable by low level, noneconomic, and purely feedback based homeostatic or allostatic theories [1, 2].

Many medical symptoms such as inflammation, fever, pain, sickness behavior, or morning sickness have an evolutionary medicine function of enabling the body to protect, heal or restore itself from injury, infection or other physiological disruption.

The deployment of self-treatments have costs as well as benefits with the result that evolution has selected management processes in the brain such that self-treatments are used only when they provide an overall cost benefit advantage. The brain controls such physiological process through top down regulation.

External treatment and the availability of support is factored into the health management system's cost benefit assessment as to whether to deploy or not an evolved self-treatment.

C. Stephanidis (Ed.): HCII 2015 Posters, Part II, CCIS 529, pp. 340–344, 2015.
DOI: 10.1007/978-3-319-21383-5_57

Placebos are explained as the result of false information about the availability of external treatment and support that mislead the health management system into not deploying evolved self-treatments. This results in the placebo suppression of medical symptoms.

Based on it, The health management system based on clouding computing was proposed in the paper. The system is composed of the following modules such as client module, expert module, healthy management organizations module, accumulated points and rank management module, task listing and evaluation module, cloud server network platform module. Client module includes users logging management module and user behavior information acquisition device. Expert module includes expert logging management module and Experts program assistant editing module. Healthy management organizations module includes healthy management organizations logging management module, healthy management organizations and healthy management organizations assistant editing module. Task listing and evaluation module includes task listing module, task pool, task evaluation module, standardization program output module, and emergency module. Cloud server network platform module includes behavior and information identity module, physical information identity module, standard program database and system basic task generating module.

2 Cloud Computing

Cloud computing is a computing term or metaphor that evolved in the late 2000 s, based on utility and consumption of computing resources. Cloud computing involves deploying groups of remote servers and software networks that allow centralized data storage and online access to computer services or resources. Clouds can be classified as public, private or hybrid.

Cloud computing relies on sharing of resources to achieve coherence and economies of scale, similar to a utility (like the electricity grid) over a network. At the foundation of cloud computing is the broader concept of converged infrastructure and shared services [3].

Cloud computing, or in simpler shorthand just "the cloud", also focuses on maximizing the effectiveness of the shared resources. Cloud resources are usually not only shared by multiple users but are also dynamically reallocated per demand. This can work for allocating resources to users. For example, a cloud computer facility that serves European users during European business hours with a specific application (e.g., email) may reallocate the same resources to serve North American users during North America's business hours with a different application (e.g., a web server). This approach should maximize the use of computing power thus reducing environmental damage as well since less power, air conditioning, rack space, etc. are required for a variety of functions. With cloud computing, multiple users can access a single server to retrieve and update their data without purchasing licenses for different applications.

The term "moving to cloud" also refers to an organization moving away from a traditional CAPEX model (buy the dedicated hardware and depreciate it over a period of time) to the OPEX model (use a shared cloud infrastructure and pay as one uses it).

Proponents claim that cloud computing allows companies to avoid upfront infrastructure costs, and focus on projects that differentiate their businesses instead of on infrastructure. Proponents also claim that cloud computing allows enterprises to get their applications up and running faster, with improved manageability and less maintenance, and enables IT to more rapidly adjust resources to meet fluctuating and unpredictable business demand. Cloud providers typically use a "pay as you go" model. This can lead to unexpectedly high charges if administrators do not adapt to the cloud pricing model [4, 5].

The present availability of high-capacity networks, low-cost computers and storage devices as well as the widespread adoption of hardware virtualization, service-oriented architecture, and autonomic and utility computing have led to a growth in cloud computing. Companies can scale up as computing needs increase and then scale down again as demands decrease.

Cloud vendors are experiencing growth rates of 50 % per annum. Figure 1 is the structure of cloud computing.

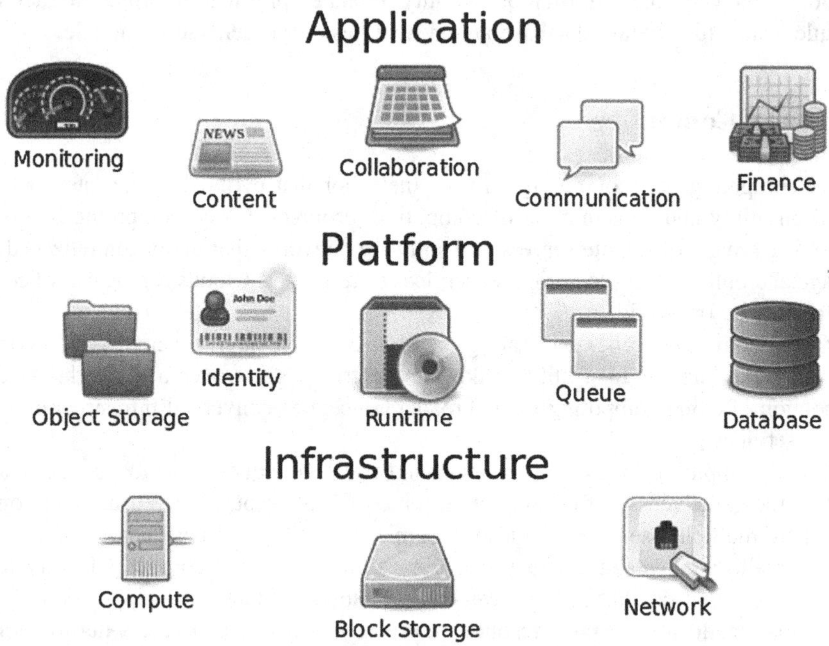

Fig. 1. The structure of cloud computing

3 Health Management System Based on Clouding Computing

The system is composed of the following modules such as client module, expert module, healthy management organizations module, accumulated points and rank management module, task listing and evaluation module, cloud server network platform module. Client module includes users logging management module and user behavior information acquisition device. Expert module includes expert logging management module and Experts program assistant editing module. Healthy management organizations module includes healthy management organizations logging management module, healthy management organizations and healthy management organizations assistant editing module. Task listing and evaluation module includes task listing module, task pool, task evaluation module, standardization program output module, and emergency module. Cloud server network platform module includes behavior and information identity module, physical information identity module, standard program database and system basic task generating module.

The structure of the system is Fig. 2.

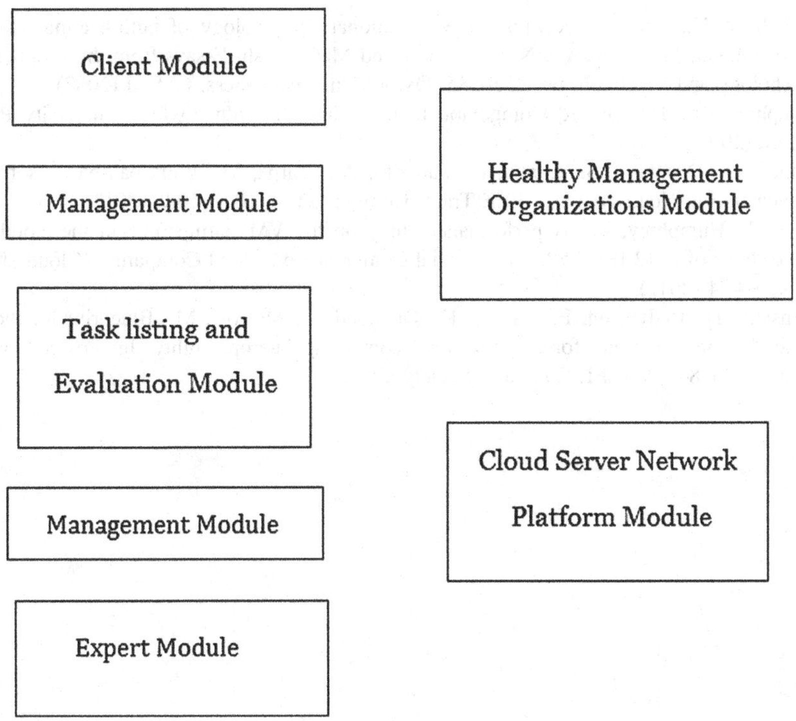

Fig. 2. The structure of the system

4 Conclusions

Though application in the system, the individual user data has no longer stored in the medical institution, but the individual user data has stored in the cloud server, which can be accessed anytime and anywhere. A large number of servers are composed of statistical and learning distributed platform. Behavior information and physical data can be extracted from the mass data automatically, which can be output factors and standardization of physical data. The same type of samples is extracted, which can achieve a group of experts and users by many-to-many model. Health standards databases are constructed though bidirectional user and expert evaluation. The system is an open and interactive system among user, health management organization and expert.

Acknowledgments. This paper work is supported by 2015 the youth foundation of Wuhan Sports University, China (Research on key technologies of health monitoring cloud platform for college students).

References

1. Humphrey, N.: Great expectations: the evolutionary psychology of faith-healing and the placebo effect. In: Humphrey, N. (ed.) The Mind Made Flesh: Essays from the Frontiers of Psychology and Evolution, pp. 255–285. Oxford University Press, Oxford (2002)
2. Humphrey, N.: The Oxford Companion to the Mind, 2nd edn. Oxford University Press, Oxford (2004)
3. Bruneo, D., Distefano, S., Longo, F., Puliafito, A., Scarpa, M.: Workload-based software rejuvenation in cloud systems. IEEE Trans. Comput. **62**(6), 1072–1085 (2013)
4. Mao, M., Humphrey, M.: A performance study on the VM startup time in the cloud. In: Proceedings of 2012 IEEE 5th International Conference on Cloud Computing (Cloud 2012), pp. 423–424 (2012)
5. Bernstein, D., Ludvigson, E., Sankar, K., Diamond, S., Morrow, M.: Blueprint for the intercloud – protocols and formats for cloud computing interoperability. In: Proceedings of ICIW, pp. 328–336. IEEE Computer Society (2009)

Designing A Mobile Application for Complementary and Alternative Medicine: A Usability Approach

Miloslava Plachkinova(✉), Guillaume Faddoul, and Samir Chatterjee

Claremont Graduate University, Claremont, CA, USA
{miloslava.plachkinova, guillaume.faddoul, samir.chatterjee}@cgu.edu

Abstract. The use of complementary and alternative medicine (CAM) is growing rapidly, and this trend has a significant impact on conventional healthcare. The lack of CAM disclosure between patients and physicians presents a serious challenge for successful treatment. The current study addresses this problem by proposing a CAM mobile application designed with a focus on usability. The goal of the study is to provide a platform where patients, physicians, and CAM practitioners can communicate, exchange ideas, and share their experiences. The mobile application is centered on the needs of the different user groups, and it provides an easy to navigate interface with responsive design, which is based on best practices in human-computer interaction. The study extends current knowledge by incorporating design science principles in the application development process and focuses on the usability of the proposed artifact to ensure successful communication on CAM between patients, physicians, and CAM practitioners.

Keywords: Complementary and alternative medicine · Mobile healthcare · Mhealth · Usability · Human computer interaction · HCI · Design science

1 Introduction and Background

The use of complementary and alternative medicine (CAM) in the United States has been constantly growing in the last couple of decades [1–3]. In 2007, almost 4 out of 10 adults had used CAM therapy in the last 12 months [4]. The trends indicate the increasing influence of CAM on healthcare and the demand to integrate both approaches to achieve better outcomes and improved quality of care.

In spite of the growing use of CAM and its documented benefits, still many patients do not disclose the use of such therapies to their physicians. This can be due to: physician disinterest, anticipation of negative physician response, belief the physician is unable or unwilling to contribute useful information, and perception that disclosure of CAM is not relevant [5]. Further, discussions of biomedical treatment are much more frequent with CAM practitioners and CAM practices are poorly integrated into the medical encounter with physicians. Such a misbalance represents a serious challenge in medical communication [6] and can potentially lead to harmful treatment and adverse effects of prescribed medications.

C. Stephanidis (Ed.): HCII 2015 Posters, Part II, CCIS 529, pp. 345–349, 2015.
DOI: 10.1007/978-3-319-21383-5_58

There are numerous calls for medical practitioners to acknowledge the concerns and beliefs that drive patients' healthcare decisions and work with patients so that the use of CAM is acknowledged and the patients' needs, beliefs and concerns are respected [7–9]. Yet, accomplishing such a major shift in physicians' perception and attitude is still difficult to achieve.

2 Proposed Solution

We propose a mobile application that can improve the communication process between patients, physicians, and CAM therapists. We approach the CAM disclosure problem from a design science perspective [10, 11], and we integrate principles of HCI and usability in the design, development, and evaluation of the CAM mobile application. Mobile applications for CAM have been overlooked by researchers in the past. Existing CAM mobile applications have been created mostly from a business perspective, and there is lack of a scientific approach to the development process. Thus, a more rigorous method involving HCI and usability principles is needed to improve the quality and effectiveness of CAM mobile applications. The research question that guides this study is the following: How can a mobile application be designed to improve communication between patients, physicians, and therapists and how it can address the lack of disclosure of CAM therapy based on: (1) demonstrated usability, utility and usefulness of the artifact, and (2) transfer of successful design science principles to mobile application development?

2.1 Theories Informing the Design

Due to the existing lack of trust among patients, physicians, and CAM practitioners, we integrate in the design process theory of social capital which involves social cohesion to build trust and to engage individuals [12]. To improve the usability of the mobile application, we also refer to theories on "deep" and "thick" trust [13, 14], and we explore in more detail the specific needs of individuals in the community [15]. To develop a high quality application and ensure its adoption by the community, we also apply patterns of persuasion suggested by [16]. In addition, we elicited requirements from best practices established in prior literature and observations on other applications for healthcare, well-being, and health promotion. We also consulted with two experts on CAM.

2.2 Design Science Approach

The research approach we utilize for this study is based on design science principles suggested by [10]. They discuss an iterative approach to designing, building, and testing artifacts, which consists of the following three cycles: relevance, rigor, and design.

Starting from the application context, the relevance cycle begins when the research requirements and the acceptance criteria for evaluation are identified. When the problem is defined, the rigor cycle starts. In this case, theories on CAM, mobile applications, and healthcare communication are used to inform the design. The requirements and theories identified earlier are used as inputs to the design cycle. A prototype of the mobile application is currently ongoing using experimental situations before field testing. The mobile application prototype will then be made available to the public and an evaluation will be performed. Based on the feedback obtained from users (patients, CAM practitioners, and physicians) a number of iterations will occur.

2.3 Description of Artifact

The main function of the CAM mobile application is to serve as a platform for communication between patients, physicians, and CAM practitioners. Upon registration users are asked to identify themselves with one of these three categories which promotes trust in the community and improves the communication process among the individuals. When interacting with the application, users are prompted to watch a series of CAM videos and are encouraged to participate in a discussion about them. The ultimate goal is to generate high quality content on CAM and engage all stakeholders in the communication process. Figure 1 presents some mock screens to illustrate some of the activities a user can perform using the mobile app:

Fig. 1. CAM mobile application mock screens

3 Evaluation

To evaluate the proposed mobile application, we apply a test plan suggested by [17]. In Stage 1, we are currently testing the technical effectiveness of the application. In Stage 2, we will test the relative usability of the application, with users being timed while they perform standardized tasks in order to examine the usability of the application and whether the user interface is easy to navigate. For these two stages we are collecting both quantitative and qualitative data. In Stage 3, we will examine whether the mobile application actually impacts CAM disclosure by conducting pre and post semi-structured interviews with patients, physicians, and CAM practitioners.

4 Conclusion

The current study extends knowledge on CAM mobile applications and provides a number of advances to science and practice. First, it identifies gaps related to CAM disclosure and provides a solution to improve the communication process. Second, by considering best practices in HCI and usability testing, we propose a more successful strategy for building and managing a CAM mobile application. Third, we add knowledge on CAM mobile applications which is still a relatively unexplored area. We transfer successful models from mHealth HCI to establish a solid foundation for future research and motivate developers to take a more rigorous approach when creating mobile applications for CAM purposes.

References

1. Su, D., Li, L.: Trends in the use of complementary and alternative medicine in the United States: 2002–2007. J. Health Care Poor Unders. **22**(1), 296–310 (2011)
2. Barnes, P.M., et al.: Complementary and alternative medicine use among adults: United States 2002. Semin. Integr. Med. **2**(2), 54–71 (2004)
3. DiGianni, L.M., Garber, J.E., Winer, E.P.: Complementary and alternative medicine use among women with breast cancer. J. Clin. Oncol. **20**(suppl 1), 34–38 (2002)
4. Barnes, P.M., et al.: Complementary and alternative medicine use among adults and children: United States, 2007. In: US Department of Health and Human Services, Centers for Disease Control and Prevention, National Center for Health Statistics Hyattsville, MD (2008)
5. Adler, S.R., Fosket, J.R.: Disclosing complementary and alternative medicine use in the medical encounter: a qualitative study in women with breast cancer. J. Fam. Pract. **48**(6), 453–458 (1999)
6. Chao, M.T., Wade, C., Kronenberg, F.: Disclosure of complementary and alternative medicine to conventional medical providers: variation by race/ethnicity and type of CAM. J. Natl Med. Assoc. **100**(11), 1341 (2008)
7. Robinson, A., McGrail, M.: Disclosure of CAM use to medical practitioners: a review of qualitative and quantitative studies. Complement. Ther. Med. **12**(2), 90–98 (2004)
8. Saxe, G.A., et al.: Disclosure to physicians of CAM use by breast cancer patients: findings from the women's healthy eating and living Study. Integr. Cancer Ther. **7**(3), 122–129 (2008)
9. Sibinga, E.M., et al.: Parent-pediatrician communication about complementary and alternative medicine use for children. Clin. Pediatr. **43**(4), 367–373 (2004)
10. Hevner, A., Chatterjee, S.: Design Research in Information Systems: Theory and Practice, vol. 22. Springer, New York (2010)
11. Hevner, A., et al.: Design science in information systems research. MIS Q. **28**(1), 75–105 (2004)
12. Sirianni, C., Friedland, L.: Social capital and civic innovation: learning and capacity building from the 1960s to the 1990s. In: Annual Meetings of the American Sociological Association (1995)
13. Lewis, J.D.: Trusted Partners: How Companies Build Mutual Trust and Win Together. Simon and Schuster, New York (1999)

14. Putnam, R.D.: Bowling Alone: The Collapse and Revival of American Community. Simon and Schuster, New York (2000)
15. Radin, P.: To me, it's my life: medical communication, trust, and activism in cyberspace. Soc. Sci. Med. **62**(3), 591–601 (2006)
16. Weiksner, G., Fogg, B.J., Liu, X.: Six patterns for persuasion in online social networks. In: Oinas-Kukkonen, H., Hasle, P., Harjumaa, M., Segerståhl, K., Øhrstrøm, P. (eds.) PERSUASIVE 2008. LNCS, vol. 5033, pp. 151–163. Springer, Heidelberg (2008)
17. Kushniruk, A.W., Patel, V.L., Cimino, J.J.: Usability testing in medical informatics: cognitive approaches to evaluation of information systems and user interfaces. In: Proceedings of the AMIA Annual Fall Symposium. American Medical Informatics Association (1997)

Innovations in OSH Trainings - Social Skills of Safety Instructor *Versus* On-line Training

Joanna Sadłowska-Wrzesińska[1(✉)] and Izabela Gabryelewicz[2]

[1] Poznan University of Technology, Poznan, Poland
joanna.sadlowska-wrzesinska@put.poznan.pl
[2] University of Zielona Góra, Zielona Góra, Poland
i.gabryelewicz@ibem.uz.zgora.pl

Abstract. A systemic approach to the issue of safety which participation of both workers and managerial staff is a part of is a trusted way of creating safety culture. The implementation of safe work in everyday practice is not easy, but possible. The OSH specialist plays a key role here, as changing workers' attitudes and values is an effective way to improve safety at the workplace. The OSH specialist must have high professional qualifications, including social competence. He most often acts as a safety educator or safety instructor. The article presents results of the research conducted on a group of 215 workers. The workers underwent the obligatory OSH training, after which the increase of their knowledge was analysed. What is more, their subjective preferences as to the form of OSH training were later determined.

Keywords: OSH training · OSH instructor · E-learning

1 Introduction

Computers are more and more often used in training people. Thanks to them a trainer may share his knowledge with the use of both text and graphics. He or she may also find specific information in the Internet. One of the most popular methods in this respect is e-learning. One of its biggest advantages is that the student may choose the best time and place to learn, as well as the pace of learning. What is more, the student may choose the appropriate scope of the material. Thanks to constant access to the material he may come back to difficult issues, analyse them again or comment on fora. It is a convenient solution for people who for some reasons cannot participate in traditional indoor training and therefore are unable to access the whole material.

However, contemporary OSH training didactics emphasizes teamwork skills. It is more and more often indicated that teamwork has an inspiring influence on the workers. It boosts their activity, co-operation, rational work management and responsibility for real effects. Interpersonal relationships within a group may help eliminate organizational difficulties and, as a result, tasks are easier to solve. In some cases the relationships and interpersonal communication may become more important than the task itself. Teamwork inspires building bonds among people, gaining new experiences and learning the ways to overcome difficulties. What is more, it is also much more fascinating and absorbing than individual work. It may also – in case of

C. Stephanidis (Ed.): HCII 2015 Posters, Part II, CCIS 529, pp. 350–355, 2015.
DOI: 10.1007/978-3-319-21383-5_59

OSH trainings build common responsibility for the safety of oneself and the rest of the team. This way safety culture in an organization is created [1].

2 Objectives and Methods

The aim of the research is to evaluate the OSH knowledge of office workers before and after the mandatory OSH training. It was also supposed to analyse the preferences of the trainees as to the form of training [2]. The methods chosen for the research were diagnostic poll method and achievement tests. To carry out the research a particular form (diagnostic poll) was prepared together with a number of examination questions (test) for the participants of period training. All of the participants held office workplaces. The researchers had to comply with the training dates and training places of particular companies. Before the training started, the employees were asked to fill in the form and answer test questions. The training, which started afterwards, lasted 8 classes, 45 min each. After the training, the employees were asked to answer the same test questions. The result of both tests were used to analyse the level of OSH knowledge of the participants before and after the training. The diagnostic poll answers help collect research material as far as work experience, the number of OSH trainings, the form of previous trainings and training form preferences were concerned. The research included five groups of workers from Poznań. The trainings were held in appropriately prepared conference rooms in respective workplaces on following days: the 16th of April, 2014; 22nd of April, 2014, 26th of April 2014, 29th of April, 2014, 6 of May, 2014 within the working hours.

3 Research Results

3.1 The Increase of Knowledge

Test questions help establish the level of OSH knowledge of the trainees before the period training. The test contained 20 multiple questions. In each of them the trainee was supposed to mark one out of three questions. To pass, one had to answer 12 questions correctly. Only 30 % of the participants passed the test before the training (28 % women and 32 % men). The remaining 70 % of office workers did not have sufficient OSH knowledge. Among those who passed, the most numerous group were women aged 36 to 45 (31 % of all the passed tests). As to men, those aged 36 to 45 and 46 to 55 had the best scores.

Comparison of the input and the output with regard to age groups and work experience is shown in Figs. 1 and 2. The period training was the most successful with office workers aged 26 to 35 and 56 to 65, because the test was passed by 77 % of the members of the first age group and 64 % of the members of the fourth age group. As far as work experience is concerned, the training was the most beneficial for those who were employed shorter than 5 years, as 94 % of them improved their score. Those with 5 to 10 years of work experience, as 66 % of them also improved their score. The score was later used in further analysis.

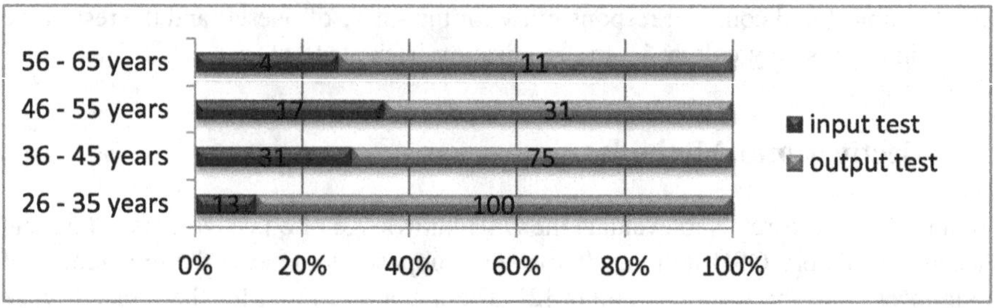

Fig. 1. Compilation of positive scores obtained after the input test and the output test according to age.

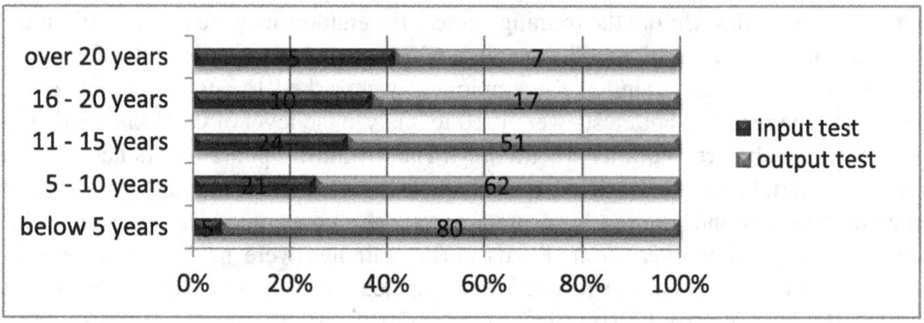

Fig. 2. Compilation of positive scores obtained after the input test and the output test according to work experience.

3.2 Preferred Form of Training

The information obtained from the form help visualise the number of training taken by the participants as well as where they happened and which methods were applied. They also made it possible to show preferences of employees as to the methods of period training. The number of period training as well as the work experience of office workers is shown in Table 1.

Table 1. The number of completed the period trainings of office workers

	office workers									
The number of trainings / Work experience	females					males				
	1	2	3	4	5	1	2	3	4	5
below 5 years	42					38				
5-10 years	18	17				16	11			
11-15 years		19	13				12	7		
16-20 years			9	2				5	1	
above 20 years				2	2				2	1

Period OSH trainings, in which the respondents have previously taken part in, varied as to the method applied (Fig. 3). All of them underwent the initial, 8 h training in their workplace. The forms which require the presence of an OSH instructor are seminar (a lecture or a lecture with multimedia presentation - 67 %) and seminar with exercises (59 %). A considerable part of the respondents were also trained in ways which make it possible to choose the place and time, such as: e-learning (76 %) or controlled self-study without a computer (31 %).

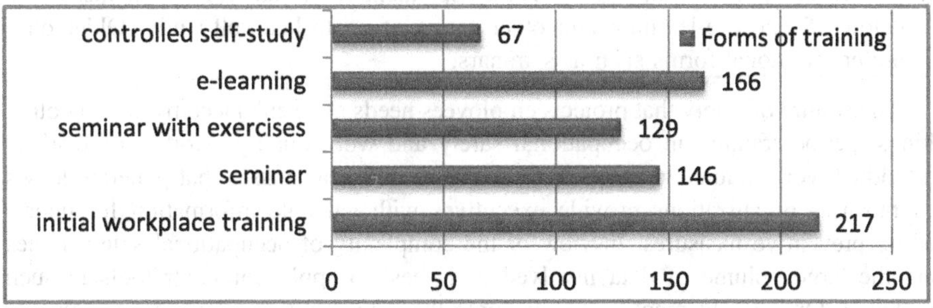

Fig. 3. Forms of accomplished OSH trainings

As to the preferred forms of period training, most people have chosen e-learning (66 %) and controlled self-study (25 %). The most prominent in those were younger respondents, aged 26–35 and 36–45. Older respondents have preferred traditional methods such as seminars (23 %) and seminars with exercises (17 %) (Fig. 4).

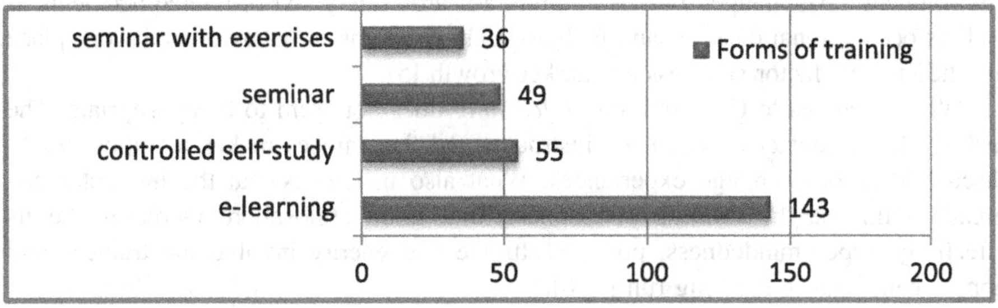

Fig. 4. Preferred forms of OSH period trainings

4 Conclusions of Research

The analysis of research material, collected thanks to well-chosen methods, techniques and tools, led to certain conclusions:

1. Before the period OSH training the respondents exhibited a low level of knowledge. Only 30 % obtained a positive result of achievement test.

2. The worst results were obtained by young employees aged 26–35 who had maximum 5 years of work experience. Low level of OSH knowledge may result from a small number of accomplished trainings.
3. Respondents with work experience over 16 years obtained much higher results which may prove that their period trainings had been effective, as work experience corresponds with the number of accomplished period trainings.
4. In the second test (output test) all the respondents got a positive result. Period trainings make it possible to raise the level of OSH knowledge by even 90 %.
5. Preferences of OSH trainings forms are dependent on the age of respondents. Those below 45 chose e-learning and other forms of controlled self-study. Older ones prefer traditional forms such as seminars.

The culture of safety that protects employees needs to be enhanced by, among other things, period training in occupational safety and work quality. Models of work at individual workstations and models of accidents and near misses that generate losses for business organizations provide executives with valuable information for undertaking preventive measures. In view of the complexity of occupational safety issues and the large volume of data involved, it is best to apply computer tools in such modeling. One should mention for example the solutions that allow to use valuable management support tools such as Visual Interactive Modeling (VIM) and Multimedia Information Management Systems [3, 4].

The working environment is changing very dynamically - there are new threats: physical and psychological. The psychological ones include time pressure, excessive workload, violence or the risk of violence, harassment or mobbing, intimidation, and fear of losing the job. The results indicate that this new type of threat causes serious health problems for workers, which is a serious financial burden both in the country and across Europe. Over the years not only the types of risk occurring in the human environment have changed but also attitude towards safety. Work-related accidents as well as occupational diseases and pathological symptoms of behavior in a work place are the greatest factor suppressing market growth [5].

When it comes to OSH training, *e-learning* does not seem to be appropriate. The lack of direct contact between the instructor and the trainees makes it impossible to discuss ideas or exchange experiences. What also matters is that the instructor can greatly influence the training atmosphere, and good atmosphere increases the its effectivity. Open-mindedness, positive attitude and energy involve the trainees and appear beneficial in the long run [1, 6].

Younger employees prefer e-learning as a comfortable and easy method, but one may assume that such beliefs are ungrounded as young employees lack experience.

5 Summary

Systematic staff trainings is crucial from both legal and economic point of view. Such trainings are regulated by the Polish law.

Lack of trainings, which deal with occupational risks, hazard identification and prevention of accidents at work and occupational diseases, may have detrimental consequences. The employees have to be systematically trained how to minimalise risk at work and how to work with machines and devices [7].

Depending on the type of industry, the human factor is recognized as the cause of up to 80 % of failures. This means that the human more or less directly contributes to a significant part of the failures. In order to reduce this problem there are many different methods and approaches that are used for obtaining the fallibility of the human [8, 9] – it is believed that training in 48 % leads to reduce human error [9, 10]. In Poland e-learning trainings are an innovation and OSH e-learning trainings are considered easy and comfortable. It is necessary for the conclusions to become a basis for further work on the development and implementation of effective OSH training methods.

References

1. Sadłowska-Wrzesińska, J.: Rozwój kompetencji społecznych specjalisty bhp – wyzwanie dla systemu kształcenia. In: Przedsiębiorczość i Zarządzanie, pp. 41–55, ISSN: 1733-2486, Łódź (2014)
2. Mroczkowski, P.: Mandatory OSH training contrasted with the feeling of safety among managerial staff, unpublished master's thesis. Supervisor: Sadłowska-Wrzesińska, J., WSHiU, Poznan (2014)
3. Dahlke, G., Jasiak, A.: Ergonomic modeling of work environment in the mechanical engineering enterprise with using of the hypermedia techniques. In: 11th International Conference on Human - Computer Interaction, 22th-27th July, Caesars Palace - Las Vegas, NV USA (2005)
4. Jasiulewicz-Kaczmarek, M., Drożyner, P.: Social dimension of sustainable development – safety and ergonomics in maintenance activities. In: Stephanidis, C., Antona, M. (eds.) UAHCI 2013, Part I. LNCS, vol. 8009, pp. 175–184. Springer, Heidelberg (2013)
5. Sadłowska-Wrzesińska, J.: Analysis of psychosocial risk in the context of the objectives of macroergonomics. In: Peter, V. (ed.) Advances in Social and Organizational Factors, pp. 277–285. AHFE Conference, Krakow (2014). ISBN 978-1-4951-2102-9
6. Kowal, E., Gabryelewicz, I., Kowal, A.: Jakość i efektywność szkoleń BHP. In: Knosala, R. (ed.) Innowacje w zarządzaniu i inżynierii produkcji, T. 2, Oficyna Wydaw. Polskiego Towarzystwa Zarządzania Produkcją, pp. 537–547, ISBN:978-83-930399-6-8, Opole (2014)
7. Górny, A.: The knowledge and the skills of the OHS staff in process of occupational risk assessment. In: Proceedings of 17th World Congress on Ergonomics (CD-ROM, 9–14 August 2009, Beijing, China, 2009). IEA (2009)
8. Misztal, A., Butlewski, M., Jasiak, A., Janik, S.: The human role in a progressive trend of foundry automation. Metalurgija **54**(2), 429–432 (2015). ISSN 1334-2576
9. Butlewski, M., Jasiulewicz-Kaczmarek, M., Misztal, A., Sławińska, M.: Design methods of reducing human error in practice, safety and reliability: methodology and applications. In: Proceedings of the European Safety and Reliability Conference, ESREL 2014, pp. 1101–1106 (2015)
10. Kariuki, S.G., Lowe, K.: Integrating human factors into process hazard analysis. Reliab. Eng. Syst. Saf. **92**(16), 1764–1773 (2007)

On the Sharing of Nursing Care Information with Employees in Japanese Companies

Yumiko Taguchi[1(✉)] and Yoko Ogushi[2]

[1] Shohoku College, 428, Nurumizu, Atsugi, Kanagawa 243-8501, Japan
taguchi@shohoku.ac.jp
[2] Niigata University, 8050, Ikarashi 2-no-cho, Nishi-ku, Niigata 950-2181, Japan
ogushi@econ.niigata-u.ac.jp

Abstract. In this study we consider ways of sharing nursing information that enable companies to understand the nursing care burdens of their employees. To explore our topic we review the measures companies take for their caretaking employees, the employees' roles as caretakers, the views of employees who have experienced nursing care, and various case studies.

Keywords: Caretaker with fulltime employment · Sharing of nursing care information with employees

1 Introduction

Japan is a super-aged society, a quarter of whose population is aged at least 65 years old. According to an employment status survey in the Japanese public by the Ministry of Internal Affairs and Communications, about 2.9 million (4.5 %) of the 64 million workers in the country work as caretakers for other members of their families. These caretakers engage in daily care chores to support their relatives in everyday activities such as changing clothes, having meals, using the bathroom, moving, etc. Sixty percent of these family caretakers are aged in their 40 s and 50 s. Over the past five years, caretaking and nursing care responsibilities have forced 49 million workers out of jobs or into new careers. In other words, labor turnover due to caretaking and nursing care responsibilities totals more than 10 million persons every year [1]. According to a recent report, the number of people requiring nursing care rises rapidly after the age of 75 [2]. In ten years, all of Japan's "baby boomers" (born from 1947 to 1949) will be aged over 75 years old. When this happens, the number of baby boomers requiring nursing care will surely increase [3]. This, in turn, will increase the number of caretaking chores to be done and further aggravate the trend of job displacement.

Many workers in their 40 s and 50 s are core members of their companies with strong experience in their fields. When they are suddenly forced to quit, their companies may be unprepared to find qualified replacements and suffer economic loss as

C. Stephanidis (Ed.): HCII 2015 Posters, Part II, CCIS 529, pp. 356–360, 2015.
DOI: 10.1007/978-3-319-21383-5_60

a result. The health of these companies can only be safeguarded if preemptive steps are taken to prevent their employees from suddenly leaving. Managers, human resource staff, and bosses in offices should understand the nursing care burdens of their employees and prepare practical systems to retain them. They should also cultivate their human resources in advance to ensure that other employees can take over the roles of colleagues forced to take temporary leaves of absence. First, managers should try to understand the nursing care burdens of their employees and consider ways to share information on nursing care in advance. The purpose of this study is to consider ways of sharing of nursing care information that enable companies to understand the nursing care burdens of their employees. To explore our topic we review the measures companies take for their caretaking employees, the roles of employees as caretakers, the views of employees who have experienced nursing care, and various case studies.

2 Measures Companies Take for Employees Who Are also Caretakers and the Views of Employees Who Have Experienced Nursing Care

According to a basic statistical survey on gender equality in employment management in Japanese by the Ministry of Health, Labour and Welfare [4], about half of the companies surveyed know whether their employees have nursing care burdens. There are two ways to elucidate the actual nursing care burdens a workforce bears: voluntary self-declaration by employees and direct questioning on the topic by bosses and colleagues in interviews. Employees generally volunteer information on their nursing care burdens more often than employers set up interviews to clarify those burdens. As measures to help employees balance work with caretaking, about 80 % of the companies surveyed indicated that they "Prepare a family-care leave system such as granny leave or the like." The other 20 % selected either of the following responses: "Monitor how employees balance work with caretaking" or "Make a workplace where employees can easily take leave such as family-care leave or granny leave." According to interviews with workers who have experienced caretaking, they manage to handle their nursing care burdens by taking paid holidays, taking absences, and leaving work early without relying on any special leave systems. These employees explained that their workplace cultures made it difficult to use the systems or that they had failed to get their bosses and colleagues to understand the heavy burdens they bore [5]. Companies clearly need to create workplace cultures that encourage their employees to use of these systems without hesitation.

3 Case Studies on Measures Companies Take to Balance Work and Caretaking

The three case studies below describe the measures companies take to help their employees balance their work and caretaking burdens. The type of business and measures taken are indicated for each.

3.1 Company A (A Small or Medium-Sized Company)

- Business type: Welfare industry.
- Measures taken: Company A offers a granny leave system and provides a home-visit nursing care service and welfare equipment. The company also tries to create an atmosphere where employees with caretaking burdens will easily share their distress. When caretaking employees talk at the workplace, the company grasps the caretaking and nursing care burdens their employees bear and shares information about them within the workplace.

3.2 Company B (A Small or Medium-Sized Company)

- Business type: Accounting agency service.
- Measures taken: Company B allows employees to work three-day weeks and five-hour days. When employees consult with their bosses, the bosses grasp the caretaking and nursing care burdens their employees bear.

3.3 Company C (A Large Company)

- Business type: Trading company.
- Measures taken: Company C offers systems corresponding to the phases of caretaking, that is, before caretaking, during preparations for caretaking, during caretaking (including caretaking leave), and after the return from caretaking leave. A family-care leave system, granny leave system, short-hour working system, and staggered work shift system are all offered. Several tools to support caretaking are also provided, including manuals, seminars, individual consultations, and interviews at different phases of caretaking. In addition, the company allies with an external agency to provide more detailed forms of support such as remote caretaking, care for the elderly, and interviews with caretaking employees for mental care.

3.4 Considerations on the Case Studies

The factor that allowed Company A and Company B to successfully balance work and caretaking was a workplace atmosphere where caretaking employees could easily consult with bosses and colleagues, that is, an atmosphere where employees could use the system without hesitation. Detailed support corresponding to the phase of caretaking, such as that provided by Company C, encourages employees and prompts them to use caretaking support systems.

4 An Approach for Sharing Nursing Care Information with Employees

Companies nowadays have an almost complete grasp of whether their employees have children or not. When employees inform them of an impending birth in their families, some companies efficiently share information about birth, childrearing, and return to work by using groupware. In the case of caretaking, some companies share nursing care information with employees by communicating face to face at the workplace, as described earlier in Sect. 3. As more employees become caretakers in the future, managers, human resource staff, and bosses in offices will ideally have a system for sharing and reviewing nursing care information with employees.

4.1 Applying Several Personnel-Management Systems

Some Japanese companies formerly used personnel-management systems such as "JINJIBUGYO" by OBC or "JINZAIBAKO" by Watakei Intelligence System Corporation. These systems can set data on their employees' birthdates, ages, and cohabitating family members. Yet none of these systems was set up to accommodate data representing nursing care conditions in employee families. A new system capable of managing nursing care conditions in families and the nursing care burdens of employees clearly needs to be created.

4.2 Basic Policy for Sharing Nursing Care Information with Employees

This section describes the purposes of sharing nursing care information and an approach to actualize sharing.

4.2.1 Purposes

The purposes of sharing nursing care information diverge between the field-level and manager-level. The purpose at the field-level is to enable nursing care support suited to the nursing care burdens of employees and the balanced continuation of their work at the workplace. The purpose at the manager-level is to gain an overview of the nursing care burdens of employees, the support system for caretaking, and the support needs both for the whole company and individual departments.

4.2.2 Approach to Actualize Sharing Information

The following three conditions must be arranged in order to actualize the purpose at the field level. The first condition is a workplace environment where employees can share information about their nursing care burdens without inhibition or restraint. To achieve such an environment, confidential relationships among staff members in the field should be built up in advance. Managers, meanwhile, should be aware that anyone can bear nursing care burdens and should encourage staff members in the field to help each other. The second condition is IT communications infrastructure in the workplace, such SNS messaging links with the boss when circumstances make face-to-face communication difficult. The third condition is a repository of caretaking data gained through communication, with thorough information on the roles of employees in caretaking, the health of employees, and support needs, all readily viewable by the boss. This purpose at the manager-level can be attained by providing data on the numbers of caretaking employees by age, by department, and by their specific caretaking burdens, as well as the numbers who take advantage of the company's support system.

5 Conclusion

This study considered how nursing care information should be shared as a means of helping companies understand the nursing care burdens of their employees. In the near future we plan to create a concrete framework for promoting the sharing of nursing care information with employees based on the result of this study.

References

1. Employment Status Survey (in Japanese). http://www.stat.go.jp/data/shugyou/2012/pdf/kgaiyou.pdf
2. White Paper on Aging Society. http://www8.cao.go.jp/kourei/whitepaper/w-2012/zenbun/pdf/1s2s_3_2.pdf (in Japanese)
3. The National Census. http://www.e-stat.go.jp/SG1/estat/Csvdl.do?sinfid=0000124606 (in Japanese)
4. Basic Survey of Gender Equality in Employment Management. http://www.mhlw.go.jp/toukei/list/dl/71-25r-07.pdf
5. Saito, M., et al.: Seeking a solution to reconciling work and care: preliminary considerations about balance among work, life, and care. Ritsumeikan Rev. Ind. Soc. **49**(4), 119–137 (2014). (in Japanese)

Preliminary Guidelines to Build a Wearable Health Monitoring System for Patients: Focusing on a Wearable Device with a Wig

Junwoo Yoo[1(✉)], Nockhwan Kim[1], Jeongho Keum[1], Ji Hwan Ryu[1], Minjae Park[1], Jihoon Lee[1], Byung-Chull Bae[2], and Jundong Cho[1]

[1] Department of Human ICT Convergence, Sungkyunkwan University, Suwon, Korea
grochi@gmail.com
[2] School of Games, Hongik University, Sejong, Korea
byungchull@gmail.com

Abstract. We have previously developed a wearable health monitoring system embedded in a wig. In this paper we introduce our system and derive preliminary guidelines to build such wearable devices for healthcare purposes. The major goal of the system is to monitor and detect falling in addition to measuring heart rate, body temperature, and current location of a patient who is wearing the device, and send text messages to pre-configured recipients in emergency. Preliminary guidelines were developed using a focused group interview with healthcare experts, which include form factor, wearing area, motivation, target, and additional functions. We are currently in the process of developing an improved device based on the derived insights.

Keywords: Wearable systems · Connected healthcare · Fall detection

1 Introduction

Wearable health monitoring systems have been under the spotlight recently, especially among the research community and the health industry. The market size of wearable healthcare is estimated to be approximately 2 billion dollars and is expected to reach 41 billion dollars by 2020. [3, 5] However, many existing products and services have not been successful in the market.

In this paper we summarize our previously developed wearable device, embedded in a wig, which is focused on healthcare for patients. The wig form has at least two advantages. First, the wig has a larger surface area that can be attached to the skin, compared to other wearable devices such as smart watches. As a result, the wig form factor can incorporate more sensors than traditional devices can. Second, a wig is considered as a personal accessory that enhances the wearer's appearance. It is also perceived as a fashion accessory, which fits well with the needs of the wearable devices market that sets a high value on fashion. Further, the wig is naturally a good form factor that makes the device completely transparent, both to wearers and observers. That is the major motivation that we develop a health monitoring system using the wig form

C. Stephanidis (Ed.): HCII 2015 Posters, Part II, CCIS 529, pp. 361–365, 2015.
DOI: 10.1007/978-3-319-21383-5_61

factor. We also built preliminary guidelines for developing such a system by interviewing healthcare experts.

2 Related Work

This section compares the differences between another wig-formed wearable device and our system, and then addresses diverse efforts to develop fall detection systems.

2.1 Smart Wig

Tobita and Kuzi conducted a research on a wearable device using a wig [7]. They suggested certain advantages of using a smart wig and some potential examples in their paper. Tobita and Kuzi introduced two key functions, navigation and presentation, as applications of the wig-formed wearable device. While their analysis identified two important functions and advantages of the smart wig, it did not focus on healthcare.

2.2 Fall Detection System

A fall is unintentional and happens against one's own intentions. Technically a fall refers to one's sudden change of position to the ground/floor or a lower position compared to a primary position [6]. Existing fall detection solutions mainly employ two major mechanisms for the fall detection. The first mechanism analyzes acceleration to detect falls. Lindemann et al. [4] integrated two bi-axial accelerometers into a hearing aid housing. They used three trigger thresholds for acceleration and velocity to detect falls. The other mechanism utilizes both acceleration and body orientation information to detect falls. Bourke and Lyons [1] developed a threshold-based fall-detection algorithm using a bi-axial gyroscope located in the sternum. They measured angular velocity, angular acceleration, and change in trunk angle to detect falls. Fall-detection algorithms have been implemented using various forms. However, wig-formed devices have rarely been employed to implement fall detection systems.

3 Design and Approach

3.1 System Architecture

The goal of our system is to monitor patients' specific physical states (specifically falling), as well as physiological data (e.g., heart rate and body temperature), and situational information (e.g., current location). Our system has also capability of sending text messages to pre-configured recipients such as the patients' family members, nurses, and doctors in emergency. As shown in Fig. 1(a), the system consists of three parts: input module (which collects data from patients), Micro-Controller Unit (MCU, which processes and communicates with a smartphone application), and output module (which rings an alarm with a buzzer and LED). As shown in Fig. 1(b),

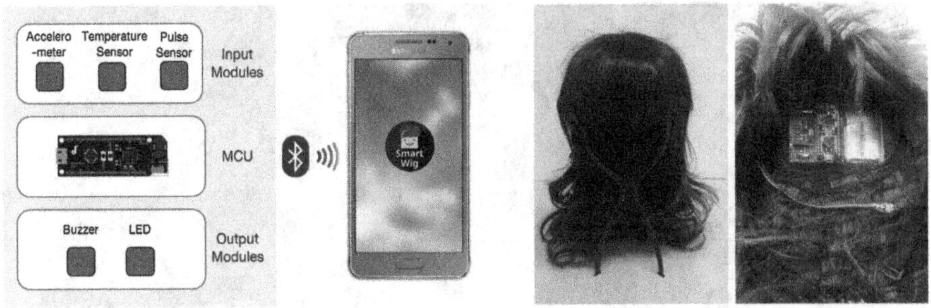

(a) (b)

Fig. 1. (a) Our system consists of three parts (Input module, MCU, and Output module, which communicates with a smartphone application via Bluetooth). (b) Prototype using a wig.

we developed a prototype using a wig, in which an integrated circuit board having various sensors, modules, and battery is attached to the inside of a wig.

The validity of the fall-detection algorithm in our system has been shown in our previous paper [2]. The primary targets of our system are patients who suffer from physical deterioration and hair loss induced by chemotherapy. We measured the acceleration and the change in trunk angle using a tri-axis accelerometer to detect falls. Our fall detection solution could distinguish four different stages related to falls: normal, dynamic transition, analogous falling, and falling.

3.2 Application

We developed an Android application (See Fig. 2), which is wirelessly connected to the hardware systems and has two functionalities: monitoring the patient's state and emergency alarm. The application displays the patient's physiological data as shown in Fig. 2(a), highlighting abnormal data in red when undesirable situations occur (Fig. 2(b). When the undesirable situations continue for more than 5 s, a pop-up alarm appears as shown in Fig. 2(c). A text message including the patient's current location is send to pre-configured recipients automatically unless the patient chooses "Immediate Alarm" or "Cancel Alarm" within 5 s.

4 Interview with Healthcare Experts

After developing the prototype, we conducted a focused group interview with three healthcare experts at the cancer department in Samsung Medical Center in order to validate the practicality of our prototype. The healthcare experts include the head of cancer education division, a medical researcher, and a senior registered nurse. Through the interview with them, we could identify several primary considerations for developing wearable healthcare devices such as form factor, wearing area, motivation, target, and additional functions. The results of the interview are as follows.

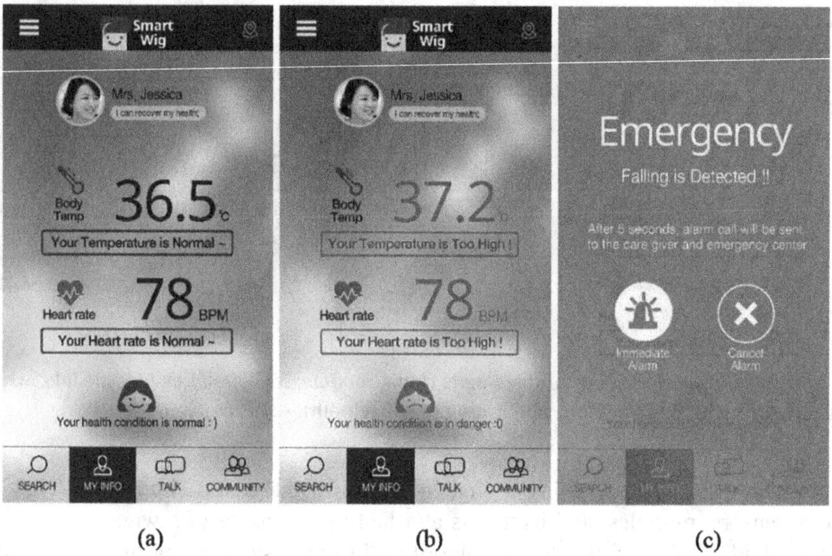

Fig. 2. Android application working with the proposed wearable device

Form Factor All the experts agreed that patients may be uncomfortable with the wig. It is primarily because patients may use the wig only occasionally, especially in social settings. According to them, patients would prefer using scarves or hats rather than wigs. Therefore, the use of wigs may not be practical.

Wearing Area When we asked about the appropriate area for wearing such a device, the healthcare experts stated that head is hardly suitable for patients because they don't frequently wear even a hat. They instead suggested that arms (e.g., a watch or a wrist band) or waist (e.g., abdominal binder) would be more suitable as wearing areas for such devices since patients are used to wearing devices in those areas.

Motivation As wearable devices for healthcare require the user's constant wearing to collect data, it is important to keep users motivated to wear the device constantly. People generally do not have a strong motivation for healthcare. Appropriate and timely feedback (e.g., visualized statistics) can be of help to give motivation to the user.

Target The healthcare experts suggested that the major target users of such systems should be medical staffs since their opinions are more influential than patients. They unanimously agreed that such a device that is specially devised to prevent falling is greatly useful because "falling" is a critical issue for patients in (and out of) the hospital.

Additional Functions The experts also suggested several specialized functions for the system such as fall prevention by prediction. For example, the system can prevent a fall by providing an alarm when the common patterns of typical falls are detected or monitored from the analysis of the data relating to the patient's body balance.

In sum, the interview helped us create the following preliminary guidelines to build a healthcare wearable system for monitoring the states of patients. First, the wig-formed device is not recommended because of the rarity of patients with hair loss and its use of discomfort. Second, arm or waist, which is more conventional areas for health monitoring, is recommended as the area for wearing such devices. Third, at the prototype development stage, medical requirements should outweigh usability improvement since the target users would be mostly medical staffs. Fourth, additional features such as "prevention of falls by prediction" would be necessary.

5 Conclusions and Future Work

In this paper we recapitulated a healthcare wearable device in the form of a wig [2], and suggested preliminary guidelines to develop a wearable health monitoring system based on the results of a focused group interview with healthcare experts. These methods helped us derive the primary considerations for such systems: form factor, wearing area, motivation, target, and additional functions.

We are currently developing and testing a small pouch-shaped device that can be attached to either arm or waist. Its primary target users are medical staffs and patients as presented in the preliminary guidelines. In future we plan to conduct a study to evaluate our system in two cases: falls and normal daily activities.

Acknowledgment. This research was supported by the Ministry of Trade, Industry and Energy (MOTIE), Korea, through the Education Support program for Creative and Industrial Convergence (Grant Number N0000717).

References

1. Bourke, A.K., Lyons, G.M.: A threshold-based fall-detection algorithm using a bi-axial gyroscope sensor. Med. Eng. Phys. **30**(1), 84–90 (2008)
2. Kim, N., Ryu, J.H., Park, M., Keum, J., Yoo, J., Lee, J., Cho, J.D.: Smart wig for patient with chemotherapy induced alopecia: emphasis on fall detection and emergency alert. In: Proceedings of HCI Korea, 2014, pp. 246–252. Hanbit Media Inc. (2014)
3. Koenig, P., Elsler, L., Binder, S.: The wearable health revolution. Soreon Research report, vol. 1. Soreon Research (2014)
4. Lindemann, U., Hock, A., Stuber, M., Keck, W., Becker, C.: Evaluation of a fall detector based on accelerometers: a pilot study. Med. Biol. Eng. Comput. **43**(5), 548–551 (2005)
5. Pantelopoulos, A., Bourbakis, N.G.: A survey on wearable sensor-based systems for health monitoring and prognosis. IEEE Trans. Syst. Man Cyber. Part C Appl. Rev. **40**(1), 1–12 (2010)
6. Tinetti, M.E., Speechley, M., Ginter, S.F.: Risk factors for falls among elderly persons living in the community. N. Engl. J. Med. **319**(26), 1701–1707 (1988)
7. Tobita, H., Kuzi, T.: SmartWig: wig-based wearable computing device for communication and entertainment. In: Proceedings of the International Working Conference on Advanced Visual Interfaces, 2012, pp. 299–302. ACM (2012)

Assistive Technologies and Environments

An Evaluation of AccessBraille: A Tablet-Based Braille Keyboard for Individuals with Visual Impairments

Hanan Alhussaini[1(✉)], Stephanie Ludi[2], and Jim Leone[1]

[1] Information Science and Technology Department, Rochester Institute of Technology (RIT), Rochester, NY 14623, USA
{haal125, jalvks}@rit.edu

[2] Software Engineering Department, Rochester Institute of Technology (RIT), Rochester, NY 14623, USA
salvse@rit.edu

Abstract. Braille is a different symbolic alphabet that is used by people with visual impairments to communicate. Since the use of smartphones has become an essential part of peoples' lives, we should benefit from this connection and use smartphones as a training tool. AccessBraille is an iPad application that helps users practice Braille in different interactive ways. The goal of AccessBraille is to provide training for novice Braille individuals who want to practice Braille. A usability test was conducted to evaluate the usability of the app, validate the app's capability of facilitating the practicing of Braille characters and discover ways to enhance the app design and use. Data was collected and later analyzed to assess the difficulty involved with task completion.

1 Introduction

The Braille system, designed by Louis Braille in 1825, is a well-established method used in reading and writing [1]. Each character in Braille consists of six binary dots each numbered from one through six. The number of these dots and their combinations distinguish one character from another. Braille has proven its capability as a fast form of text entry [2].

AccessBraille is an iPad accessibility application to help users practice Braille in different interactive forms [3]. This system is designed as an educational tool for pre-college students who have had problems learning the essential US Braille characters. The goal of AccessBraille is to provide a practicing app for students who want to practice Braille beside their vocabulary and writing skills that will ease Braille literacy. The app has a menu on the left side of the screen with options where users can navigate through. The typing screen on the app consists of the 6 Braille columns, delete, and space options as shown in Fig. 1. The AccessBraille app consists of three elements: practice Braille (a standalone free typing keyboard to encourage users to type words using Braille), flashcards (listening game where the system speaks a letter/number and the users enter the equivalent Braille), and time trip (a text adventure that is an audio text test to practice spelling skills after hearing words).

C. Stephanidis (Ed.): HCII 2015 Posters, Part II, CCIS 529, pp. 369–374, 2015.
DOI: 10.1007/978-3-319-21383-5_62

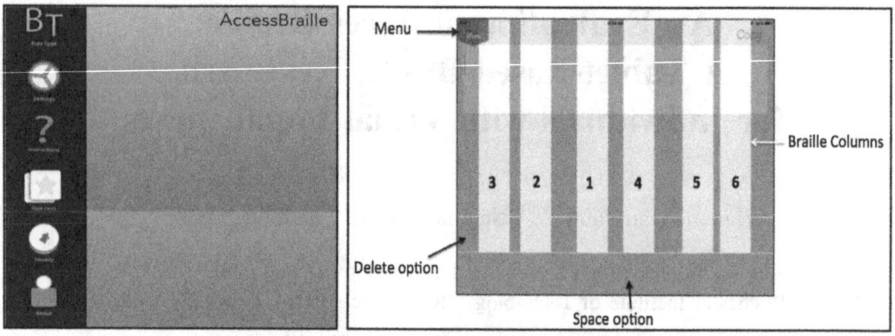

Fig. 1. The AccessBraille app with the menu system (left) and the typing screen (right)

A usability test was conducted to evaluate the AccessBraille system. The usability test consists of a number of techniques used to experiment with a system [4]. The usability test requires different scenarios where participants are observed by the test conductor while using the system to help define the problem areas and participants' preferences. There are different techniques used to gather data from participants during the test such as think aloud protocol, taking notes, and pre- and post-questionnaire [4]. The usability test answered these questions: How many errors do users make when using the system on average? What are the types of errors users make when using the AccessBraille system? And what is the proper writing speed that visually impaired users can maintain while using the system?

2 Related Work

BrailleTouch system is a touchscreen application used by people with visual impairment to text using the Braille language [5]. It contains a keyboard that works as an iPod/iPad application. There are six buttons on the system; each indicates one of the six cells in the original Braille language. Users use both hands to hold the screen facing away from them and use their fingers to type as if they were typing on a physical keyboard. There is no need to change the fingers' position to type after placing them, but users can reset the position of the buttons.

VBGhost is an educational smartphone game for low vision or blind people [6]. Players using this game can play against the computer or another player to add letters to the word without completing the growing word fragment. Players type the letters using the Braille language on a touchscreen, and get an audio feedback from the phone.

3 Test Methodology

This test used a within-subjects test design where each participant performs all tasks together [4], and in the same order. There were 8 participants noted as p1 to p8, where 3 were from Rochester Institute of Technology and 5 were attendees from The 16th

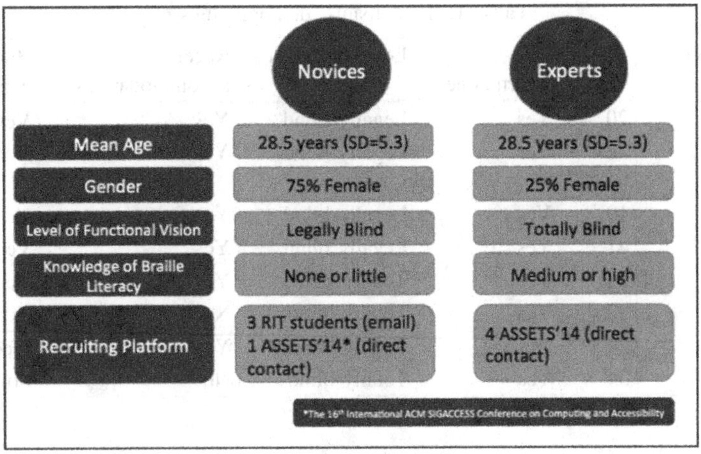

Fig. 2. User profile

International ACM SIGACCESS Conference on Computers and Accessibility (ASSETS'14). The participants fell under the following categories: Braille novices with little to no experience with Braille, and Braille experts with medium to high experience with Braille. Figure 2 gives a summation profile of the participants.

Participants sat in a table with the moderator, and the iPad mini was placed in front of them. A video camera was set up on the table as well and focused on the iPad mini. Participants started the task scenarios from the main screen of the iPad mini. All participants were instructed to focus upon navigating through the menu and initiate the 6 columns by swiping on screen. There are 4 task scenarios participants performed: task 1 was to write and then re-write the word 'Milk' using practice Braille, task 2 was to write the sentence 'Ice Coke' using practice Braille, task 3 was to listen and type the first five words using flash cards, and task 4 to solve the puzzle using time trip.

4 Results and Discussion

Table 1 highlights participants' demographics including their level of functional vision and Braille experience. 50 % of the participants are female, and the largest group of participants is in the 18–25 age group. The youngest participant is 19 years old, and the oldest is 41 years old. Half of the participants are totally blind either since birth (p5, p7), or since a specific age (p8 at age 6 years old), and the other half are legally blind. 75 % of the participants are able to read and write Braille grade 1 or grade 2. However, with this high percentage of Braille knowledge, only one participant (p5) reported her Braille knowledge as very high. 75 % of the participants have used other Braille learning keyboards before.

The test results showed differences between novice Braille participants' performances compared to experts. This includes task completion time, error counts, and hint counts. Braille novices spent most of their time trying to remember the letters'

Table 1. Participants' demographics

ID	Gender	Age	Use smartphone	Level of vision	Received accommodations	Braille experience
P1	F	20	Yes	Legally blind	Yes	Very low
P2	F	22	Yes	Legally blind right eye	Yes	Very low
P3	M	19	Yes	Legally blind	Yes	Very low
P4	F	41	Yes	Legally blind	Yes	Very low
P5	F	24	Yes	Totally blind	Yes	Very high
P6	M	32	Yes	Totally blind	No	High
P7	M	24	Yes	Totally blind	Yes	Medium
P8	M	34	Yes	Totally blind	No	Low

combinations, typing other letters incorrectly, asking for hints, and then typing the letters. Thus, Braille experts took less time when doing all tasks.

Braille experts made fewer errors in all the tasks compared to novice participants as shown in Fig. 3. The mean number of errors made by all tasks expert participants is 34.25, and novice participants is 60.75. There were three types of errors users made in the test: typing one letter instead of another, trying to remember the letter combinations, and tracking the columns' locations.

The first type of error occurred to all participants when trying to type one letter and by mistake type another one by not touching the whole letter combination. The second type, which is the most common error, happens only to novice participants when they play with Braille combinations to explore the letters and remember their location for the future. The third type happens to totally blind participants only when they are trying to remember the columns' positions when they move their hands away. Mostly, it ends up happening when they recreate the columns again. Braille novices requested letter combination hints in all tasks, while experts did not, except for one participant (p8) who asked for 4 hints in task 1 and task 4.

The test results showed that totally blind participants faced more obstacles than legally blind participants, which includes: navigating through the menu, remembering

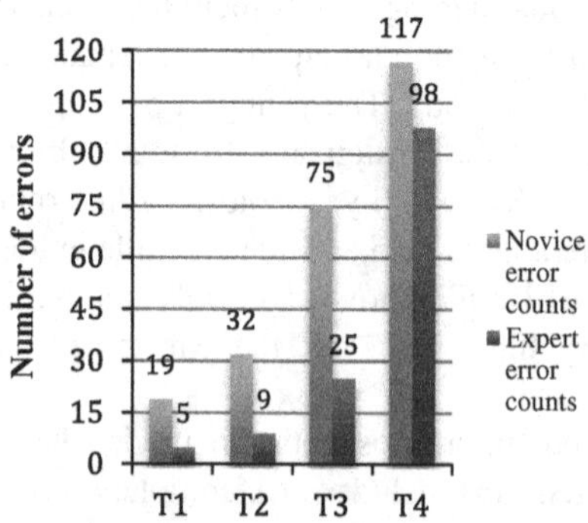

Fig. 3. Participants' error count

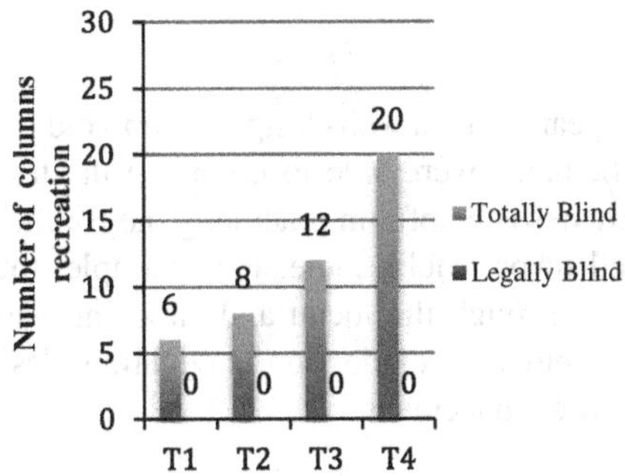

Fig. 4. Number of times participants tried to remember the columns' locations.

the Braille columns' locations, and trying to delete the last Braille entry. Totally blind participants move their fingers up and down to explore the menu, but when they swipe up more than 2 times, they get lost and frustrated, and then ask where the menu is.

Totally blind participants cannot remember the Braille columns' locations after initiating them. Participants in general move their fingers after creating the columns, but totally blind participants spend more time trying to match their fingers with the columns and sometimes reinitiate the columns. Figure 4 shows the number of times participants tried to remember the locations of the columns they just created.

Moreover, Totally blind participants sometimes typed a combination that results in more than one letter; when they delete it, only one letter is deleted and not the whole entry. Since the voice command doesn't say the deleted letter, they don't know what was deleted and ask for clarification.

5 Usability Problems and Recommendations

A number of problems were identified in the AccessBraille app. First, navigating through the menu where totally blind participants have difficulties navigating through the menu and choosing the right option. Second, the Braille columns move up and down while users are typing and that makes them frustrated and ask how to type space, return, or delete. Third, the voice command speaks too fast when reading a word, an instruction, and a sentence. Fourth, deleting the last letter since participants, especially totally blind ones; always have the problem of deleting the last entry. They expect the delete action to delete the last entry not the last letter.

A number of recommendations were suggested that could help enhancing the app and making it more usable. First, change the menu layout, so each icon will be in a separate page. Second, make the Braille columns activate automatically, and add a sound feedback, so whenever users touch one of the columns, it would say the number of that column. Also, make the size of each of the columns wider than the regular finger width. Third and last, make the delete action delete the last entry participants typed not the last letter.

6 Conclusion

The AccessBraille app appears to be a well-designed app void of major usability issues. The majority of the participants were able to complete the tasks given to them. The functionality this app provides is helpful in practicing the Braille language. Some of the interface elements proved to be troublesome. For example, totally blind participants face difficulties navigating through the menu and choosing various options. Our recommendations for improvement include app navigation design modification, oral feedback and app function enhancement.

References

1. Oliveira, J., Guerreiro, T., Nicolau, H., Jorge, J., Gonçalves, D.: BrailleType: unleashing braille over touch screen mobile phones. In: Campos, P., Graham, N., Jorge, J., Nunes, N., Palanque, P., Winckler, M. (eds.) INTERACT 2011, Part I. LNCS, vol. 6946, pp. 100–107. Springer, Heidelberg (2011)
2. Frey, B., Rosier, K., Southern, C., Romero, M.: From texting app to braille literacy. In: Extended Abstracts on Human Factors in Computing Systems, CHI 2012, pp. 2495–2500 (2012)
3. Ludi, S., Timbrook, M., Chester, P.: A tablet-based approach to facilitate the viewing of classroom lecture by low vision students. In: Miesenberger, K., Fels, D., Archambault, D., Peňáz, P., Zagler, W. (eds.) ICCHP 2014, Part II. LNCS, vol. 8548, pp. 591–596. Springer, Heidelberg (2014)
4. Rubin, J., Chisnell, D.: Handbook of Usability Testing: How to Plan, Design, and Conduct Effective Tests, 2nd edn. Wiley, Indianapolis (2008)
5. Romero, M., Frey, B., Southern, C., Abowd, G.D.: BrailleTouch: designing a mobile eyes-free soft keyboard. In: Proceedings of the 13th International Conference on Human Computer Interaction with Mobile Devices and Services, MobileHCI 2011, pp. 707–709 (2011)
6. Milne, L.R., Bennett, C.L., Ladner, R.E.: VBGhost: a braille-based educational smartphone game for children. In: Proceedings of the 15th International ACM SIGACCESS Conference on Computers and Accessibility, ASSETS 2013, article no. 75 (2013)

An Assisted Living Home for Alzheimer's Patient in Saudi Arabia, A Prototype

Sulaf Almagooshi(✉), Mona Hakami, Maha Alsayyari, Wafa Alrajhi, and Sarah Alkoblan

King Saud University, Riyadh, Saudi Arabia
almagooshis@acm.org

Abstract. Number of patients with Alzheimer's disease (AD) is increasing every day. As it target and destroy brain cells. And in order to avoid the high cost of care institutions of Alzheimer's patients, we should provide a safe environment for them. Ambient Assisted Living (AAL) technologies can provide such environments. AAL is used to supervise and assist people with disabilities who cannot rely on themselves as patients of Alzheimer's. In this paper we present a prototype of a house that has been equipped with Arduino micro-controller to suit the Alzheimer's patients. By monitoring the behaviour of the patients, the system will interact by sending a message for the caregiver if a risk action was detected. The evaluation of the early prototype system involved evaluating the monitoring system as well as the devices.

Keywords: AAL · Alzheimer · Arduino · Physical computing

1 Introduction

In Saudi Arabia, experts have estimated that the chances of being diagnosed with Alzheimer's doubled every 5 years [1]. Though the Ministry of Health (MOH) at Saudi Arabia has no official statistics as it stated in its website, they have declared that there are at least more than 50 thousands Alzheimer's patients in Saudi Arabia, most of them are women [1]. Though this number might be insignificant, In a study that explored the Co-morbidities of patients with dementia in Saudi Arabia, The study have found that 18.2 % of sample consisted of 77 patients with dementia have presented with cardiovascular risk factors [3], This results have expanded the problem scope as World Health Organization (WHO) have reported that cardiovascular diseases are accountable for 45 % deaths in Saudi Arabia [4].

Fortunately, Ambient Assisted Living (AAL) technologies have evolved in the past two decades. These technologies aim to offer an easier lifestyle for patients having cognitive or/and physical disabilities through enhancing the quality of life as well as reducing the need for social and medical care [5]. Under this scenario, patient's treatment will take place at home by using the AAL technologies, which can be done by monitoring their daily life activities and evaluation of critical data, sending alarms and making recommendations in case of need [6].

C. Stephanidis (Ed.): HCII 2015 Posters, Part II, CCIS 529, pp. 375–380, 2015.
DOI: 10.1007/978-3-319-21383-5_63

It is evident that deploying AAL technology will enhance the quality of life for Alzheimer's patient and it would ease the burden of responsibility of continuous monitoring felt by the caregiver. However, as stated by specialists at the Saudi Alzheimer's Association, a lot of families dealing with Alzheimer's have not deployed any technology that would help them on daily basis.

This paper deploys those technologies into customizing a house that suit Alzheimer's patient needs. Using Arduino, a physical computing sketch kit [7], a prototype of a house was built taking into consideration different aspects that may affect the design of the house; such as culture and architecture layout. Subject Matter Experts included doctors, specialists and caregivers, validated the prototype.

2 Inspiration

An assisted living home is a home that had been customized to enhance the quality of life for disabled person who live in it [8]. These homes had been equipped with technologies that contribute into discovering insights of patient behaviours. These insights have a great value for caregivers and doctors into diagnosing the patient stage of Alzheimer's and therefore adopt to more related course of treatments.

In this section, we explore the literature for implemented AAL project to introduce it in the prototype.

The In-Home Monitoring System (IMS) [9] is a sensor-based monitoring system, sensors deployed within this system varied between: pressure switch pads, temperature sensors for the stove and motion detectors. In [10] researchers have conducted a need perception study that targeted elderly who lived in a home with IMS embedded, the study have concluded a positive attitude toward smart home technologies in general.

The Aware Home Project [11] is a program within Georgia Tech Broadband Institute's Residential Laboratory. The project goal is to explore the ubiquitous computing related to elderly healthcare problems. One of the functionalities of The Aware Home it offer is to analyse the extended behaviour. As defined by researchers, an extended behaviour is 'either in time or in time and space'. Such as moving objects around the home, a stochastic context-free grammar (SCFG) technology was used in conjunction with detectors.

3 Building a Prototype

In Software Engineering field, building a prototype have been recognized to be the base of a software development model. It is since 1987 where Bullet and Brooks have highlighted that software development process will not be simplified unless it becomes visual. [15] The prototype was used by software engineers as a tool to better understand the requirements [16]. As it offers the user "functionality" of the design [15], the interactions with prototype can enable the user to grasp the dynamics of the desired system [16].

4 Methodology

This section describes the four prototyping development stages from establishing the prototype objectives to the final stage of evaluating the prototype.

4.1 Establish Prototype Objectives

Taking care of Alzheimer's patient requires high physical ability, emotional capabilities, and financial aid. The demands of day-to-day care, the change of family roles, and difficult decisions about getting external help could be difficult to handle. The main objective of this project is to raise the awareness of AAL technologies and its uses for Alzheimer's society by building a throwaway prototype that suit Alzheimer's patient needs. The aim of developing a prototype is to create an easy to evaluate model in short-time with low-cost.

4.2 Define Prototype Functionality

This project depends on monitoring and detecting patient activities. The system will assist the patient immediately once an error activity has been accrued. Interactively, this system would send text messages to the caregiver or/and taking an immediate action. Figure 1 shows the context diagram of Alzheimer's patient home prototype. In this prototype, sensors have been built in the oven, sink, refrigerator, bedroom and on the main door intended to detect and prevent dangerous situations. The functionality of the prototype has been determined by Alzheimer's patient caregivers as well as knowledge shared by Saudi Alzheimer Disease Association.

The key stakeholders of this house are Alzheimer's patient, the caregivers, and the health care provider. Using AAL technology will allow caregivers to monitor the patient actions from remote location. Caregiver's concentration and physical pressure will be reduced by reducing the number of working hours. Furthermore, the caregiver and the health care provider will take the advantages of the system through receiving different kinds of reports about patient's behaviour (Table 1).

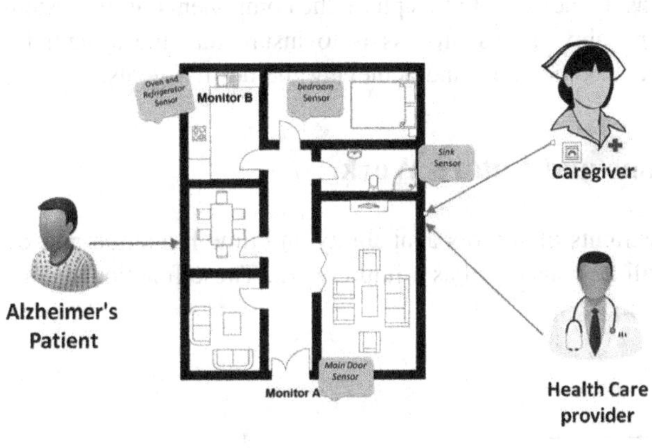

Fig. 1. Context diagram of Alzheimer's patient home

Table 1. Prototype functionality

Sensors	Patient action	System response	Notification
Sink	Left the water tap open for a specific period	Close the water tap	Sending SMS message to the caregiver
Oven	Forgot the stove on without usage for a specific period	Switch off the stove	
Refrigerator	Left the refrigerator door open without usage for a certain time	Close the refrigerator door	
Bedroom	Fell out of bed	No action	
Main door	Open the main door	No action	

4.3 Develop Prototype

Our prototype simulate the functionality of two parts namely, the main door and the oven sensors. In the early stage having fewer parts in a prototype is almost better as stated by Yang, "Prototypes with fewer parts correlate with better design outcome, as do prototypes that have fewer parts added to them over the course of development. Also committing more time to a project is not necessarily associated with a successful design outcome." [12]. To build this prototype we use Arduino Uno microcontroller since it has huge market and open source [7], in addition we use various sensors to monitor the house. Global System for Mobile communications (GSM)[1] shield has been bulged in the Arduino board with a Subscriber Identity Module (SIM) card in order to send notification messages. Figures 2 and 3 show the main door and the oven that have been developed in the prototype including the Arduino, sensors and other components.

4.4 Evaluation Prototype

The evaluation of the early prototype system involved evaluating the monitoring system as well as the devices. In this phase the components of the system will be tested individually. The aim of this process is to insure that the system is well working according to the specifications and achieving the desired goals.

5 Limitations and Future Work

Due to the constraints of sensors availability and time limitation part of the prototype functionality will be considered as a future work. These functions include refrigerator, sink and bedroom.

[1] http://arduino.cc/en/Reference/GSM.

Fig. 2. Oven prototype

Fig. 3. Main door prototype

6 Conclusion

Ambient Assisted Living AAL experiencing significant development in the last decade. Using AAL technologies, we can control and reduce the risks that may surround a patient of Alzheimer's because these technologies provide the ability to monitor the health and safety of the patients. Using AAL, we developed a prototype of a house for an Alzheimer's patients. We identified and monitored several locations at the house to assist the patient. Using Arduino, we monitored these locations, send a message for the caregiver if a risk action was detected, and also sometimes an action is performed to reduce the danger that might result from forgetting some of the devices such as the oven. Consequently, we tried to minimize the risk that might surrounds the patient.

Acknowledgment. The authors extend their appreciation to the Deanship of Scientific Research at King Saud University for funding the work through the research group project number RGP-VPP-157. The authors would like to thank Dr.Areej Al-Wabil for her comments and support and to those who assisted in the development of the prototype: Arwa Alabdulkarim, Sarah Alyemni, Wea'am Alrashed and Noura Alhakbani.

References

1. Ministry of Health: Annual Report – 2013. Ministry of Health, Saudi Arabia (2013)
2. Duthey, B.: Background paper 6.11: Alzheimer disease and other dementias. In: A Public Health Approach to Innovation, pp. 1–74 (2013)

3. Karam, G., Lynn, I.: Dementia: a review from the Arab region. Arab J. Psychiatry **24**(1), 77–84 (2013). (Papers are submitted in electronic form)
4. WHO report. http://www.who.int/nmh/countries/sau_en.pdf
5. Rialle, V., Ollivet, C., Guigui, C., Hervé, C.: What do family caregivers of Alzheimer's disease patients desire in smart home technologies? **1**, 1–17 (2009). doi:10.3414/ME9102
6. Costa, R., et al.: Ambient assisted living. In: 3rd Symposium of Ubiquitous Computing and Ambient Intelligence 2008. Springer, Heidelberg (2009)
7. Arduino. http://arduino.cc/en/Reference/HomePage
8. Rashidi, P., Mihailidis, A.: A survey on ambient-assisted living tools for older adults. IEEE J. Biomed. Health Inform. **17**(3), 579–590 (2013)
9. Alwan, M., et al.: In-home monitoring system and objective ADL assessment: validation study. In: International Conference on Independence, Aging and Disability (2003)
10. Demiris, G., et al.: Senior residents' perceived need of and preferences for "smart home" sensor technologies. Int. J. Technol. Assess. Health Care **24**(01), 120–124 (2008)
11. Abowd, G.D., et al.: The aware home: a living laboratory for technologies for successful aging. In: Proceedings of the AAAI-02 Workshop "Automation as Caregiver" (2002)
12. Yang, M.C.: A study of prototypes, design activity, and design outcome. Des. Stud. **26**(6), 649–669 (2005)
13. Sedha, R.S.: T.B. of Applied Electronics (M.E.). S. Chand, New Delhi (2008)
14. Helander, M.G., Landauer, T.K., Prabhu, P.V.: Handbook of Human-Computer Interaction. Elsevier, Amsterdam (1997)
15. Brooks, F.P.: No silver bullet. Essence and accidents of software engineering. IEEE Comput. **20**(4), 10–19 (1987)
16. Sommerville, I., Sawyer, P.: Requirements Engineering: A Good Practice Guide. Wiley, New York (2005)

Requirements Engineering of Ambient Assisted Living Technologies for People with Alzheimer's

Afnan AlRomi, Ghadah AlOfisan, Norah AlRomi, Sulaf AlMagooshi, and Areej Al-Wabil(✉)

Prince Sultan University, Riyadh, Saudi Arabia
aalromi@kacst.edu.sa, ghada.othman-al-ofisan@hp.com, n.alromi@tamkeen.it, almagooshis@acm.org, awabil@pscw.psu.edu.sa

Abstract. A rapid growth in the ambient assisted living technologies (AALTs) is being witnessed due to the aging society. Evidence suggests that AALTs empower the elderly's involvement with their surroundings, and hence; improves the quality of their living. Therefore, public service organizations (e.g. The Saudi Alzheimer's Disease Association (ALZ)) have been established with the aim to raise awareness about AD, in order to reach a comfortable lifestyle for all elders with AD. Moreover, this fact is the motivation behind addressing our problem in the paper. Each AALT has its own special requirements in usage, care, extensibility, reusability, scalability and adaptability. More importantly, there are many other factors that have great influence on those requirements. In this paper we will investigate some of these factors, such as: the environment, the caregiver's experience, and the elder's age, culture, and social structure. Furthermore, adaptability and cultural factors are the pivots of our study, to show their influence on designing AALT and specifying their requirements.

Keywords: AAL · Alzheimer · Requirement engineering · Design consideration

1 Introduction

Due to the aging society, a population of 35 billion people worldwide are developing Alzheimer's Disease (AD) [1], and the number has exceeded 50 thousands of elders in Saudi Arabia [2]. Alzheimer's Disease is known as a degenerative brain disease [3]. AD is a progressive deterioration in memory and cognitive skills (i.e. thinking and reasoning). Furthermore, AD can be identified and diagnosed at an early stage in order to help individual's administering treatment. Alzheimer's Association has formed a list of warning signs for Alzheimer's. As an example of such signs that disrupt daily life: memory loss (i.e. Dementia), challenges in solving problems and planning, confusion with time or place, difficulty in conversations and completing tasks [4]. To help assess those elderly's, monitor and diagnose AD early and support aging in place, assistive and intelligence technologies have been introduced. Those technologies are referred to as "ambient assistive living technologies" (AALTs). AALTs are aware of the elderly's presence, sensitive to their movements and gestures, and responds to them

C. Stephanidis (Ed.): HCII 2015 Posters, Part II, CCIS 529, pp. 381–387, 2015.
DOI: 10.1007/978-3-319-21383-5_64

adaptively [8, 9]. AALTs improve the quality of the elderly's living [5]. Subsequently, there is an emergence towards the use of AALTs in healthcare and homecare domains [6, 7].

More importantly, there are many other factors that have influence on those requirements. In this paper we investigate some of these factors, such as: the environment, the caregiver's experience, and the elder's age culture, and social structure. Furthermore, adaptability and cultural factors are the pivots of our study, to show their influence on designing AALT and specifying their requirements.

2 Background

The evolution of AALTs has started by addressing heterogeneous users to facilitate many services and monitor the user interactions with the environment for various reasons, such as data prediction of future activities. EasyLiving [10] and Carelab [11] are one of the initial AAL projects that began under the category of smart environments that provides a cohesive user experience by detecting activities and behaviour patterns [10, 11]. AwareHome [12], I-Living [13] and BelAmI [14] are as well other smart environment but with the focus on the assistive living perspective such as addressing security and safety concerns [14].

Many of existing AALTs have the capability to address more than what they were designed and built for, as slight adjustments and modifications broaden their target users. Some of them have even high potential in serving more specific users with their current highly suitable technology, such as MavLab [15]. One of the most AALTs that wasn't designed for elders with AD specifically, but for elderly and disabled in general is MavLab (i.e. MavHome lab) [15]. MavHome is a smart environment utilized to monitor the health of elders and people with disabilities, and assist them in carrying out daily activities at home by themselves. It provides a novel data mining and prediction algorithm that learns how to detect patterns from the collected data. Moreover, it detects anomalies in their regular activities, which thereby might be of great help in the case of AD, where the detected outliers is useful to monitor the progress and level of AD the elderly is reaching. The SmartHouse system [16] as well carries out the same mechanism as the MavHome, and can be adapted for AD patients too. Moreover, below are three AALTs developed for elders with AD and their state of art.

ALZ-MAS is a multi-agent system aimed to enhance the assistance and healthcare for Alzheimer's patients [17]. The system integrates different technologies for context awareness agents to collaborate with, such as radio frequency identification, wireless networks and automation devices. All information gathered by these tools are processed by agents as the writers have justified the employment of agent in their system because "as they possess the capability of adapting themselves to the users and environmental characteristics".

3 Problem

Recent research in healthcare and informatics had shed light on the inadequate support available for people with AD, and the increasing need for a sustainable model of assistive technology provision for people with AD and their caregivers.

It can be argued that AALTs -which were developed in other countries- might not necessarily be embraced by target user populations in Saudi Arabia due to variations in socio-cultural context. And as each AALT developed for Alzheimer's patients is based on one certain culture, and this is for the variations that are in the daily life activities between cultures. This is affecting the adaptation of those technologies to different environments due to the socio-cultural factors and how they translate to functional and non-functional requirements. Consequently, these design considerations affect the usability of these technologies when integrated with the targeted environment. Adapting existing AALTs to our culture requirements is what we will be investigating.

4 Methodology

As reported in the literature [33], it is recommended to use semi-structured interviews to investigate requirements in the context of AD patients' needs. It is also suggested in [34] to involve experts from various fields to form a multidisciplinary perspective. Participants in our research are categorized into three categories:

Category (1): Specialists from the Saudi Alzheimer Disease Association in which they represent the caregivers' perspective.
Category (2): Industrial engineer, Dr. Eng. Shady Aly.
Category (3): Geriatric psychiatrist, Dr. Fahad Al-Wahhabi.

The adopted research design strategy is an exploratory design conducted in two phases as follows:

Phase 1 - Data Collection: Literature Review: Reviewed the state of art and studied related literature on Alzheimer's disease, AAL tools in general and AAL tools for Alzheimer's patients related studies are studied and analyzed in depth to derive a set of requirements in which these tools perform.

Semi Structured Interviews: Interviews are conducted in person. We interviewed specialists from the Saudi Alzheimer Disease Association. The objective of these interviews is to investigate and discuss the cultural factors and their effects on Alzheimer's patients in Saudi Arabia. We have also interviewed a geriatric psychiatrist. Our goal is to explore the psychological perspective of elderly with Alzheimer's diseases. All interviews are analyzed qualitatively.

Surveys: All questions in the questionnaires are educed after reviewing the literature. The targets of the survey are engineers, as we wanted to reflect on the deployment of AAL tools from engineering respective.

Phase 2 – Data Analysis: Tools review is shared with Category (1), the goal is to observe how they will reflect on existing technology, and they shared their concerns and reflection in terms of pros and cons. After receiving the output from Category (1) on tools review, we have summarized their reflection along with interviews and survey analysis to form design considerations as seen in Table 1.

Table 1. General requirements

Type	Tool name	Design consideration
Memory aid	Memory glasses [18]	1. DC4. Experts from all categories show concerns regarding wearable technologies, as they experienced that AD patients are not necessary cooperative when instructed to carry them, as they tend to remove them
	Memoclip [19–21]	2. DC1. Experts in categories one and three had touched on the social aspect of wearable technologies. As they add a distinguishable element that pins them out as AD patients, whereas caregivers prefers them to blend with the community
	Interactive symptom assessment and collection (ISAAC) [22]	3. DC7.1.2 Category one experts one have questioned AD patients' perception of using such technologies. As deriving a positive acknowledgement of the audio alert requires a level of familiarity of interaction with technology (i.e. to touch the screen in order to stop the audio) 4. DC7.2.3 The system shall add Arabic in the available languages
Navigation aid	Opportunity knocks [23]	5. DC1 Local AD patients don't use public transportation. Private transportation is available for Male patients if they are capable of driving, whereas Female patients require a male driver as local regulations prohibits female driving
	Activity compass [24]	Refer to point 3. DC7.1.2
Motion detection tool	Talking motion detective [25]	6. DC4 The audio customization feature offers adaptability
	Motion detector with remote alarm [26]	Interaction is only with caregivers; therefore, no design consideration for AD patients
Environmental aid	Possum primo [27]	Refers to point 4. DC7.2.3
	Alert-IT door activity monitor [28]	7. DC8 Category three experts have highlighted the usage of labels in requesting the caregiver (i.e. pressing the "HELP" button).

(*Continued*)

Table 1. (*Continued*)

Type	Tool name	Design consideration
		As 5 % of local population is illiterate; therefore adding an image that illustrates the meaning of HELP is recommended
Wandering and tracking aid	MindMe [29]	8. DC1.4 Carried devices might be disposed or forgotten by AD patients. Therefore, experts in all three categories have recommended the separation of the device's functionality from the patient's control, where they shall function without the patient's cooperation (i.e. carrying the device)
	GPS shoe [30]	9. DC1 Category one experts have suggested the shoes to be customized to local designs
Physiological/functional aid	Fall detector [31]	10. DC1 Experts in all categories have emphasized on the privacy aspect, where users tend to find having cameras in their living environment uncomfortable
	Bedwetting alarm [31, 32]	This technology addresses a matter which falls out of the cultural requirements scope, where it is concerned with physiological functions

4.1 General Requirements and Design Considerations

Table 1 illustrates the general requirements elicited and educed from the previously listed AAL tools, and design considerations that evolved from the experience and knowledge of subject matter experts (SMEs) in all three categories.

5 Conclusion

In this paper we have proposed a set of design constrains that needs to be taken into consideration while deploying those technologies in our culture for ambient assisted living technologies for AD patients. Three categories of different disciplines experts were involved in reviewing a pool of AAL tools. The resulted set of design constraints suggest that the variation in socio-cultural context presented in Saudi Arabia might demand an adoption mechanism in order to raise those tools effectiveness.

We believe and aim that the investigation of those design constraints could assist AD patients indirectly by designing tools that suit their culture best and therefore ease their lives. Those design constrains could be seen as a primality requirements for manufactures as they could use them as guidelines to design AAL tools.

References

1. Alzheimer's Disease International, Dementia: a public health priority. http://whqlibdoc.who.int/publications/2012/9789241564458_eng.pdf
2. Ministry of Health, World Alzheimer's Day. http://www.moh.gov.sa/en/HealthAwareness/healthDay/2013/Pages/HealthDay-019.aspx
3. Chan, H.L., Hsu, W.C., Meng, L.F., Sun, M.H.: Event-related evoked potentials in Alzheimer's disease by a tool-using gesture paradigm. In: 2013 35th Annual International Conference of the IEEE Engineering in Medicine and Biology Society (EMBC), pp. 4299–4301. IEEE, July 2013
4. Alzheimer's Association, Basics of Alzheimer's Disease. Accessed 10 April 2014, from Alzheimer's Association. https://www.alz.org/national/documents/brochure_basicsofalz_low.pdf
5. Aghajan, H., Augusto, J.: Thematic issue: evaluating ambient assisted living components and systems. J. Ambient Intell. Smart Environ. (JAISE) **7**(3)
6. McNaull, J., Augusto, J.C., Mulvenna, M., McCullagh, P.: Data and information quality issues in ambient assisted living systems. J. Data Inf. Qual. (JDIQ) **4**(1), 4 (2012)
7. Acampora, G., Cook, D.J., Rashidi, P., Vasilakos, A.V.: A survey on ambient intelligence in healthcare. Proc. IEEE **101**, 2470–2494 (2013)
8. Costa, R., et al.: Ambient assisted living. In: 3rd Symposium of Ubiquitous Computing and Ambient Intelligence 2008. Springer, Berlin (2009)
9. Riva, G.: Ambient intelligence in health care. Cyber Psych. Behav. **6**(3), 295–300 (2003)
10. Brumitt, B., Meyers, B., Krumm, J., Kern, A., Shafer, S.: EasyLiving: technologies for intelligent environments. In: Thomas, P., Gellersen, H.-W. (eds.) HUC 2000. LNCS, vol. 1927, p. 12. Springer, Heidelberg (2000)
11. Ruyter, B., Pelgrim, E.: Ambient assisted-living research in carelab. Interactions **14**(4), 30–33 (2007)
12. Kientz, J.A., et al.: The Georgia tech aware home. In: CHI 2008 Extended Abstracts. ACM (2008)
13. Wang, Q., et al.: I-Living: an open system architecture for assisted living. In: SMC (2006)
14. Anastasopoulos, M., et al.: Towards a reference middleware architecture for ambient intelligence systems. In: ACM Conference on Object-Oriented Programming, Systems, Languages, and Applications (2005)
15. Das, S.K., Cook, D.J.: Health monitoring in an agent-based smart home by activity prediction. In: Proceedings of the International Conference on Smart Homes and Health Telematics, vol. 14 (2004)
16. Barger, T.S., Brown, D.E., Alwan, M.: Health-status monitoring through analysis of behavioural patterns. IEEE Trans. Syst. Man Cybern. Part A Syst. Hum. **35**(1), 22–27 (2005)
17. Corchado, J.M., Bajo, J., Tapia, D.I.: ALZ-MAS: Alzheimer's special care multi-agent system. In: Proceedings of the Workshop on Health Care. ECAI, vol. 6 (2006)
18. DeVaul, R.W.: The memory glasses: wearable computing for just-in-time memory support. Doctoral dissertation, Massachusetts Institute of Technology (2004)
19. Beigl, M.: MemoClip I. http://www.teco.edu/research/ubicomp/memoclipI/. Accessed 9 Dec 2007

20. Beigl, M.: MemoClip: a location-based remembrance appliance. Pers. Ubiquit. Comput. **4**(4), 230–233 (2000)
21. Patterson, D.J., Liao, L., Gajos, K., Collier, M., Livic, N., Olson, K., Wang, S., Fox, D., Kautz, H.: Opportunity knocks: a system to provide cognitive assistance with transportation services. In: Mynatt, E.D., Siio, I. (eds.) UbiComp 2004. LNCS, vol. 3205, pp. 433–450. Springer, Heidelberg (2004)
22. Gorman, P., Dayle, R., Hood, C.A., Rumrell, L.: Effectiveness of the ISAAC cognitive prosthetic system for improving rehabilitation outcomes with neurofunctional impairment. NeuroRehabilitation **18**(1), 57–67 (2003)
23. Patterson, D.J., Liao, L., Gajos, K., Collier, M., Livic, N., Olson, K., Wang, S., Fox, D., Kautz, H.: Opportunity knocks: a system to provide cognitive assistance with transportation services. In: Mynatt, Elizabeth D., Siio, Itiro (eds.) UbiComp 2004. LNCS, vol. 3205, pp. 433–450. Springer, Heidelberg (2004)
24. Patterson, D., Etzioni, O., Kautz, H.: The activity compass. In: Papers presented at the Proceedings of the 1st International Workshop on Ubiquitous Computing for Cognitive Aids. Goteborg, 9 Dec 2007
25. Robinson, L., et al.: Keeping in touch everyday (KITE) project: developing assistive technologies with people with dementia and their carers to promote independence. Int. Psychogeriatr. **21**(03), 494–502 (2009)
26. The Alzheimer's Store. Motion Detector. The Alzheimer's Store. http://www.alzstore.com/alzheimers-motion-detector-p/0093.htm. Accessed 12 Sept 2014
27. Technical Solutions Australia. Primo! Environment Control. Innovative Assistive Technology. http://tecsol.com.au/cms123/index.php?page=shop.product_details&cid=18&part=subcat&flypage=flypage.tpl&product_id=330&category_id=34&option=com_virtuemart&Itemid=53&vmcchk=1&Itemid=53. Accessed 12 July 2014
28. Alert-it Care Systems, Door Activity Monitor. Alert-it Care Systems. http://www.alertit.co.uk/Documents/Pdf/Handbooks/UH1115_P161B_Door_Activity_Handbook.pdf. Accessed 12 July 2014
29. MindMe. Alarm and Locate. MindMe. http://www.mindme.co.uk. Accessed 12 Sept 2014
30. GPS Shoe: Accessed 12 Sept 2014 from GPS Shoe, May 2012. http://www.gpsshoe.com
31. Bharucha, A.J., Anand, V., Forlizzi, J., et al.: Intelligent assistive technology applications to dementia care: current capabilities, limitations, and future challenges. Am. J. Geriatr. Psychiatry **17**(2), 88–104 (2009)
32. Pollack, M.E.: Intelligent technology for an aging population: the use of AI to assist elders with cognitive impairment. AI Mag. **26**(2), 9 (2005)
33. Hawkey, K., et al.: Requirements gathering with Alzheimer's patients and caregivers. In: Proceedings of the 7th International ACM SIGACCESS Conference on Computers and Accessibility, pp. 142–149 (9 Oct 2005)
34. Bono-Nuez, A., et al.: Ambient intelligence for quality of life assessment. J. Ambient Intell. Smart Environ. **6**(1), 57–70 (2014)

"See Medication": An Arabic Assistive Mobile Application for Asthmatic Visually Impaired Patients

Afnan F. Alsadhan[1], Sarah M. Bin Mahfodh[1], Nada M. Alsuhebany[2](✉), Hind A. Bin Ajlan[1], Hana A. Al-Alashaykh[2], Asma A. Alzahrani[2], and Rafeef M. Aqel[2]

[1] College of Computer and Information Sciences, King Saud University, Riyadh, Saudi Arabia
aalsadhan@ksu.edu.sa,
{sarah.binmahfodh, hind.binajlan}@gmail.com
[2] College of Pharmacy, King Saud University, Riyadh, Saudi Arabia
{nalsuhebany, hana.alashaykh, rafeef.aqel}@gmail.com,
aaz.alzahrani@yahoo.com

Abstract. This paper introduces the development of See Medication system that helps visually impaired patients or low-vision patients who are suffering from asthma to know about their medications by VoiceOver. "See Medication" is an interactive healthcare system that works as a channel between mainly asthmatic visually impaired patients and pharmacists. This system consists of two components: mobile application and website. It is available in two languages: Arabic and English, in order to serve a broader population. The aim of the application is to improve the quality of utilizing asthma medications and raising the independence of visually impaired patients.

Keywords: Asthma · Visually impaired · iOS app · Pharmacy

1 Introduction

Asthma is a chronic disease of the airway of the lungs. Around 235 million people suffer from asthma. It occurs in all countries regardless of the level of development [1].

Nowadays, mobile technology is starting to transform into healthcare [2]. Since June 2014, a shift in the digital market has occurred, as the average daily use of health and fitness apps grew by 62 %, exceeding the use of apps overall, at only 33 % growth [3]. There are various medication tools that could help patients to identify their drugs and understand the instructions found in the market as a solution for this problem; such as pillboxes and medication reminders with sounds and alert. Some mobile applications on different platforms such as iOS and Android were developed to help asthmatic patients. The "Asthma Buddy" [4] application enables the patients to record their medications, email their action plan to their doctors and have access to education materials. The "AsthmaMD" [5] application helps to track the asthma condition and how medications are helping the patient. Also, it connects doctors to it so they could

C. Stephanidis (Ed.): HCII 2015 Posters, Part II, CCIS 529, pp. 388–391, 2015.
DOI: 10.1007/978-3-319-21383-5_65

conduct research. The "Use Inhaler App" [6] helps the patient to mange the inhaler technique by a video assistance and has a dose reminder too.

Despite the usefulness and benefits of the available applications that target asthmatic patients, visually disabled patients are still finding it not easy to identify their medications, and the need for assistive aid to help them safely recognizing their drugs and managing their medication use is also not fulfilled. Many pharmacists are facing challenges with visually impaired patients, either blind or very low vision patients, in tailoring the best care plan that fits their needs. The World Health Organization (WHO) estimated that 285 million people are visually impaired worldwide: 39 million are blind and 246 million have low-vision [7].

See Medication project targets all asthma patients, especially visually impaired patients by providing barcodes to all their medications and the ability of the mobile application to scan it and read it for the patient.

2 Method

This extended abstract presents "See Medication", an interactive healthcare system that works as a channel between asthmatic blind patients and pharmacists. The system serves different types of users, so it involves an iOS mobile application for patients and a website for management, and both connected to one comprehensive database, which contains medication information, patient record and pharmacist log. "See medication" aims to help asthmatic patients to identify and utilize their medications effectively and to improve the independence of visually impaired patients.

2.1 Mobile Application

The application was developed for iOS devices. According to the consumer preferences presented in an article conducted by J. Morris and J. Mueller, that assessed blind and deaf preferences for Android and iOS smartphones. The percentage of blind smartphone users who prefer iPhone is 86 %, while only 18 % of the blind users preferred Android. In terms of ease of use, 85 % of blind iPhone users described their devices as 'Easy' or 'Very easy' to use. On the other hand, 42 % of blind Android smartphone owners described their devices as 'Easy' or 'Very easy' to use [8].

Visually impaired patients can easily use the application after enabling the VoiceOver on the device. And the application provides different features, which are as follows:

1. **Medication Scan** – it reads and displays medication's information after scanning the medication's QR-code on the container.
2. **Puff counter** – it counts and displays the number of remaining puffs in the inhaler.
3. **Medication List** – it shows all patients' medications with details.
4. **Reminder** – it reminds the patient about his/her doses, time to refill, and expiry date of the medications.
5. **Weather Alert** – it notifies the patient when there is any dust in the air, so that he/she can take precautions.

6. **Peak Flow Meter** – it allows the patient to enter the last measured peak flow reading, to determine in which zone the patient is (Classified into three zones: green, yellow, and red according to the disease control status).
7. **How to use inhalers** – video and audio educational materials.

2.2 Website

The website works as management tool, where the administrator is authorized to register, delete and modify pharmacist. In addition, the pharmacists are allowed to register the patients, update patients' profile, and update medications information, also to manage the patient's action plan.

3 Results

The proposed "See Medication" project has two main components: the website and the iOS application. Figure 1 shows the scenario of the project in general. Pharmacist uses the website to add a new patient, whom is assigned to, with complete information that includes; demographics, new medication list and the action plan. Then, the website synchronizes all patient's information on his/her installed iOS application on iPhone device. Patient is able to review the current medication list, including the each medication's information, weather status, and receive medication notifications. Also patient can follow up his/her plan with puff counter function and peak flow functions.

Fig. 1. General scenario of see medication

3.1 Preliminary Evaluation

An evaluation was performed to verify the correctness as well as the accuracy of the application. A group of seven visually impaired people with a good experience in using mobile phones in daily life was invited to try the application using iOS7 smart phones.

The participants ranged in age between (18–30) years old. At the beginning, an introduction about the App and its functions was given with brief explanation about how to use it. Then, they were asked to utilize each function of the mobile application.

At the end of the test, the participants were surveyed about their experience. The answers ranged from strongly agree to strongly disagree. Table 1 shows the responses to the survey questions according to Likert scale (1 = strongly disagree, 5 = strongly agree).

Table 1. Mean response for seven visually impaired people. 1 is strongly disagree, 5 is strongly agree.

Usefulness as an assistive application	4.66
Ease of use	4.71
Reliability of the application	3.85
Satisfaction	3.28

The survey mean response results show a positive feedback of the application. However, the satisfaction had the lowest score, with emphasize on barcode method improvement to make it easier to handle.

4 Conclusion

In this extended abstract we presented the development of "See Medication" system. This system is designed to help asthmatic visually impaired patients to improve their independency, medication utilization, keeping the disease condition well controlled and to reduce the confusion between medications or medication overdose by facilitating their medication identification before administration, medications' reminders to improve adherence, providing comprehensive and easy to understand information and instructions, sending alerts when medication is near to expire or when the weather is dusty. To insure the safety for the patient, "See Medication" enables pharmacists track the patients, and control their action plans.

For future development, See Medication will be developed for Android devices, to reach and help more patients.

Acknowledgement. The authors extend their appreciation to the Deanship of Scientific Research at King Saud University for funding the work through the research group project number RGP-VPP-157.

References

1. Asthma. World Health Organization, Nov 2013. www.who.int/mediacentre/factsheets/fs307/en/
2. Collins, F.S.: Mobile technology and health care. NIH Winter **5**(4), 2–3 (2011)
3. Viswanath, K., Nagler, R.H., Bigman-Galimore, C.A., McCauley, M.P., Jung, M., Ramanadhan, S.: The communications revolution and health inequalities in the 21st century: implications for cancer control. Cancer Epidemiol. Biomark. Prev. **21**(10), 1071–1078 (2012)
4. Asthma Buddy (2012). https://appsto.re/us/kq1VG.i
5. AsthmaMD (2014). https://appsto.re/us/R1O0u.i
6. Use Inhalers App (2012). https://appsto.re/us/rZJbP.i
7. Visual impairment and blindness. World Health Organization, Aug 2014. http://www.who.int/mediacentre/factsheets/fs282/en/
8. Morris, J., Mueller, J.: Blind and deaf consumer preferences for android and iOS smartphones. In: Langdon, P.M., Lazar, J., Heylighen, A., Dong, H. (eds.) Inclusive Designing: Joining Usability, Accessibility, and Inclusion, pp. 69–79. Springer, London (2014)

Development of Serious Game for the Upper Arms Rehabilitation: "Balance Ball Rhythm Game" Case Study

Sung-Taek Chung[1], Sung-Wook Shin[1], and C.J. Lim[2(✉)]

[1] Department of Computer Engineering, Korea Polytechnic University, Seoul, Korea
{unitaek, napalza}@kpu.ac.kr

[2] Department of Game and Multimedia Engineering, Korea Polytechnic University, Seoul, Korea
scjlim@gmail.com

Abstract. Accuracy, repeatability and activity are very critical factors for rehabilitation of hemiplegic patients. Rehabilitation exercise should be done regardless of space, time and cost. Recently, interesting functional games, which induce active participation, have gained increasing attention. In the current study, a balance ball has been developed that can contract the user muscle and help in natural joint rotation by stimulating the upper arm muscle of hemiplegic patients. Additionally, a functional game was also developed that can engage the patients with rhythm game and training contents. The balance ball can detect the upper arm motion by an acceleration sensor and offered sense of reality and immersion with buttons and haptic sensors. The game applied Fitt's law to test accurate motion and two tutorial contents that induced their motion based on MFT. The level of difficulty can also be chosen to help intensive training for the motion with low scores from the tutorials and the patients can even do the upper arm rehabilitation exercise while listening to music.

Keywords: Motion detect · Accelerometer · MFT (Manual function Test) · Serious game · User interface

1 Introduction

'Stroke' refers to cerebrovascular disease or accident in general. It is the most common neurological disease whose incidence rate increases with people's age and is known as the second cause of death after cancer [1]. Although development of modern medicine increased the survival rate of the stroke patients, 90 % or more of them suffer from certain types of disabilities, such as movement disorder, sensory disorder or cognitive disorder followed by chronic health problem called as hemiplegia [2]. Hemiplegia causes weakness in the muscles of upper and lower arm or face, muscle modulation disorder, weakened muscle tone and subsequent paralysis from unilateral brain damage as well as synergy where several groups of muscles move at the same time, instead of a single muscle [3, 4]. Hemiplegic patients need early rehabilitation exercise within three to seven days of its occurrence before spasticity develops, which is the biggest obstacle

C. Stephanidis (Ed.): HCII 2015 Posters, Part II, CCIS 529, pp. 392–398, 2015.
DOI: 10.1007/978-3-319-21383-5_66

to normal movement. Functional reorganization of cerebral activation area by brain plasticity has been acknowledged as the most influential hypothesis on movement function recovery [5]. To facilitate the functional reorganization of the brain during rehabilitation, factors, such as activity, accuracy and repeatability of patients are important to consider. Among these, accuracy and repeatability can be achieved through rehabilitation exercise performed with the subjective viewpoint of the therapist; however, such exercise is not enough to generate a patient's interest and invoke his/her active participation [6]. This implies that it is difficult to execute continuous and steady rehabilitation exercise. As a solution to this problem, serious game is gaining attention which can improve motion detect ability of the brain and perform rehabilitation exercise among others [7]. The serious game uses body senses more than the general games and increases a patient's will to participate by maximizing user satisfaction [8]. However, the existing content of the serious game was designed for those without hemiplegia and is thus very difficult for the hemiplegic patients to use. Therefore, a customized content is necessary which would have a reasonable difficulty level and an easy interface.

In the current work, a spherical device was developed with the aid of which the hemiplegic patients who cannot move their upper arms can undergo easy upper arm rehabilitation exercise. This device would enable only light muscle contraction and natural joint rotation with minimal pain through stimulation of upper arm muscles along with free movement of hand, wrist and arm. It would also try to engage the patients in the rehabilitation exercise that may be boring and repeating by combining intriguing contents with a rhythm game.

2 Development of Balance Ball Device

Figure 1 shows the balance ball designed in this study. The patients can do upper arm rehabilitation exercise by placing their hand on the top of the ball (Fig. 1a) and tilting it in the direction they want, with the movement of their wrist, elbow and shoulder as if it is rolling. The device can help the patients to tilt their weakened upper arm and again return it to the center. The device has a fixed pendulum in the middle so that the patient's hand and wrist can rest on it comfortably. It also has five buttons that can increase the variety of the content and test finger movement or gripping power depending on certain events. Besides, the switch would allow changing the set up depending on the hand used, which means that both right and left hand can be used. It applies a haptic sensor that can provide force feedback for the users to transmit information realistically and heighten sense of immersion. Through extension, abduction, radial deviation and ulnar deviation movement of wrist with the device, the patients can reduce pain through light muscle contraction and natural joint rotation and prevent spasticity. Figure 1b shows the hardware inside the balance ball. The gradient of the balance ball can be calculated with acceleration sensor (ADXL335 3 axis acceleration sensor module) and acceleration data of X, Y and Z axis that have ±3.6 dps(deg/s). Acceleration and gradient were estimated using Eqs. (1) and (2).

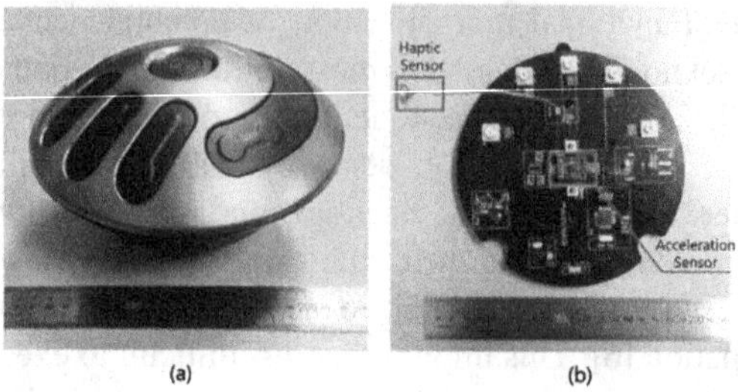

Fig. 1. (a) External, and (b) internal appearance of fabricated balance ball

$$a_i = \frac{V_{out} - V_{offset}}{S} \quad (1)$$

$$\theta_i = \operatorname{asin}(a_i) * \frac{180}{\pi} \quad (2)$$

Where a_i is the i acceleration value of each axis, V_{out} is the current output value of the sensor that changes by gravitational acceleration, V_{offset} is the sensor value when gradient is '0', S is the sensor sensitivity, θ_i is the angle that was obtained from the acceleration value of each axis. The angle value was obtained from acceleration sensor output value by gradients and the movement of the balance ball was mapped on a two-dimensional plane.

3 Rehabilitation Contents Development

With increasing aged population, the number of incidence of stroke is also rising. About 56 % or more of the patients suffer from hemiplegia, having everyday life quite challenging [9] and most of them face great difficulties in finding suitable treatment facilities.

The current work developed rehabilitation contents that can induce upper arm movement using the balance ball wirelessly connected to PC, a proper platform for treatment and rehabilitation exercise of hemiplegic patients regardless of space, time and cost. The balance ball gives feedback using vision, hearing and touch. The patients can also enjoy the treatment process themselves while performing tasks with enhanced motives under a safe environment. With the purpose for rehabilitation of hemiplegic patients, the current approach used minimum resources with 2D, comprising balance ball device test, two staged tutorial and rhythm game. The flow chart is shown in Fig. 2.

In order to test whether the balance ball operates satisfactorily or not, the balance ball device examine the contents, created for the hemiplegic patients, using the Fitt's law (see Fig. 3). Fitt's law is a certified tool that can evaluate cursor movement and clicks on the computer screen. The test used distance (D), width (W) and angle (A) between the cursor and the target to set up the level of difficulty. The values used

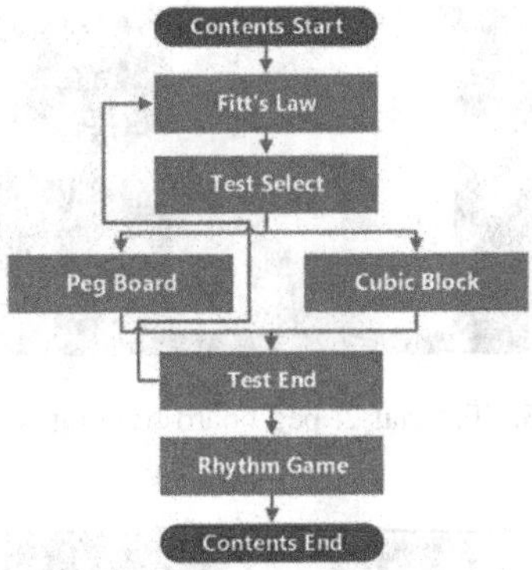

Fig. 2. Game flow chart

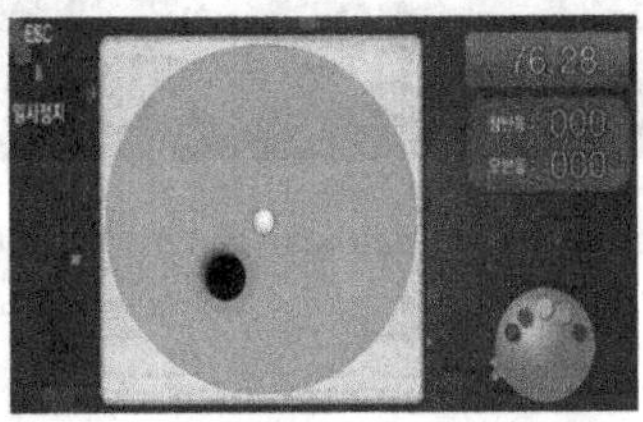

Fig. 3. Fitt's law testing screen

were as follows: D = 125, 250 and 375 pixels, W = 50 and 100 pixels, A = 0°, 45°, 90°, 135°, 180°, 225°, 270° and 315°. Depending on the randomly decided location of holes by stages, forward reaction and backward reaction were measured and at the end of the balance ball device test was a tutorial.

Tutorial 1 of Fig. 4 calculated the number of goals made into the basket in 30 s. The score was saved at the end of the game before Tutorial 2 appeared in Fig. 5. Tutorial 2 calculated the number of hitting the balls, which came out randomly within the circle in 30 s, by pressing the button of the matching color. For scoring, MFT (Manual Function Test) was applied. Different scores recorded during the training can verify the effect of

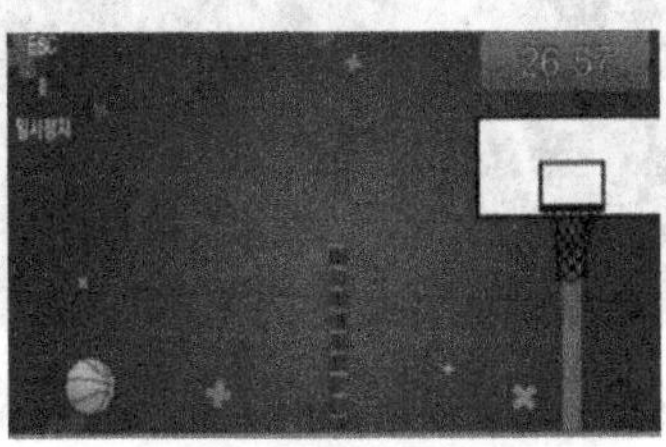

Fig. 4. Tutorial 1: cubic block training screen

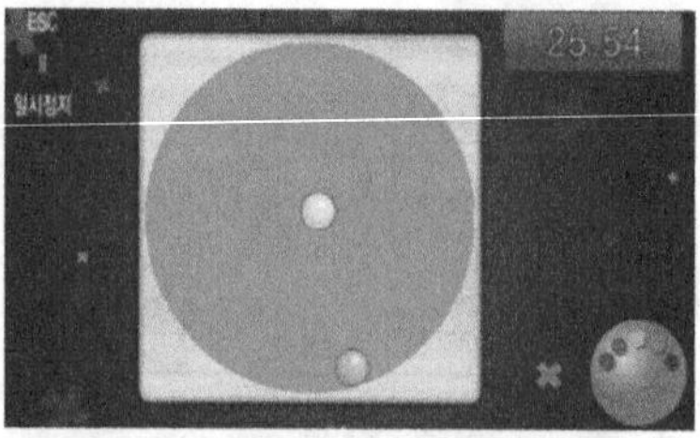

Fig. 5. Tutorial 2: peg board training screen

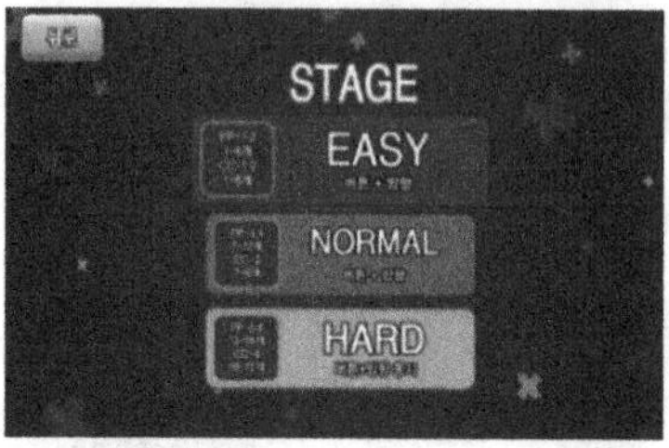

Fig. 6. Difficulty level choice screen for rhythm game

the rehabilitation as the user's measuring reference. Added scores of Tutorial 1 and 2 decide the level of difficulty for the rhythm game, as shown in Fig. 6. The level can be chosen as easy, normal or hard. Furthermore, this game was designed to focus on the training of those who obtained a relatively low total score from the sum of tutorial 1 and 2 (Fig. 7).

The rhythm game has two songs from which the user can choose. When the nodes come down in the song, the user has to move toward the node direction through the movement of the balance ball and presses the button for the corresponding node. The score consists of Perfect, Good, Miss and Max Combo in order and is leveled after the game is over.

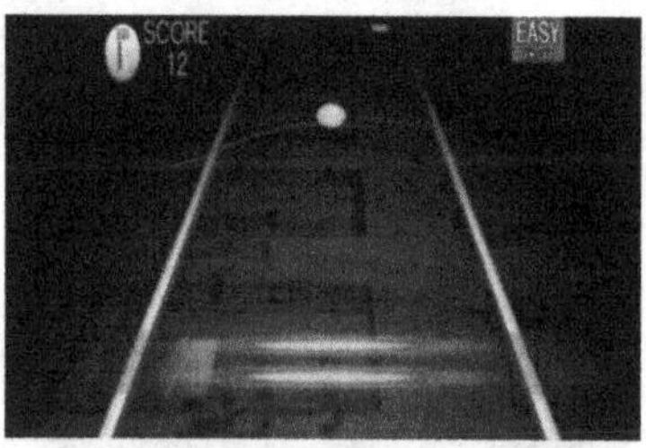

Fig. 7. Playing screen of rhythm game

4 Conclusions

The paper presented a rehabilitation device that used acceleration sensor for upper arm rehabilitation of hemiplegic patients. The spherical balance ball helped the user pay attention to the activity by providing force feedback with a vibration motor. It also measured accurate angle of device tilting through motion using the acceleration sensor. Since both hands can be used and the device can induce upper arm joint rotation and muscle contraction, it is expected to be a proper model for upper arm rehabilitation that reduces pain and helps to overcome spasticity.

Future studies should be performed in the direction that allows various motions that use gyro sensor as well as acceleration sensor and a wide range of rehabilitation exercise.

This study also developed rehabilitation contents using the balance ball for rehabilitation of the hemiplegic patients. The game, based on the upper arm rehabilitation, uses vision, hearing and touch to provide feedback, thus lets the patients enjoy and engage in the treatment process. It also promotes motives under a safe environment. The system is expected to help the patients' rehabilitation exercise.

Additionally, analysis on the effect of rehabilitation contents on treatment should be performed. For wide applicability of the rehabilitation contents, development of tailored training contents, which emphasize gaming aspect for rehabilitation patients that cannot perform difficult motions, should also be targeted through basic analysis.

Acknowledgement. This research was supported by the MSIP (Ministry of Science, ICT and Future Planning), Korea, under the C-ITRC (Convergence Information Technology Research Center) support program (NIPA-2014-H0401-14-1003) supervised by the NIPA (National IT Industry Promotion Agency).

References

1. Anderson, G., Vestergarrd, K., Ingermann-Nielsen, M., Lauritzen, L.: Risk factors for post-stroke depression. Acta Psychiatr. Scand. **92**, 193–198 (1994)
2. Feigenson, J.S.: Stroke rehabilitation. Outcome studies and guidelines for alternative levels of care. Stroke **12**, 372–375 (1981)
3. Sharp, S.A., Brouwer, B.J.: Isokinetic strength training of the hemiparetic knee: effects on function and spasticity. Arch. Phys. Med. Rehabil. **78**, 1231–1236 (1997)
4. Bobath, B.: Adult Hemiplegia: Evaluation and Treatment. Butterworth-Heinemann, Oxford (1990)
5. Kwon, Y.H., Lee, M.Y., Park, J.W., Kang, J.H., Yang, D.S., Kim, Y.H., Ahn, S.H., Jang, S. H.: Differences of cortical activation pattern between cortical and corona radiata infarct. Neurosci. Lett. **417**, 138–142 (2007)
6. Teasell, R., Bayona, N., Salter, K., Hellings, C., Bitensky, J.: Progress in clinical neurosciences: stroke recovery and rehabilitation. Can. J. Neurol. Sci. **33**, 357–364 (2006)
7. Christian, S., Thomas, P., Hannes, K.: Full body interaction for serious games in motor rehabilitation. In: Proceedings of the 2nd Augmented Human International Conference. ACM (2011)

8. Lim, C.J., Chung, S.T., Lim, D.W., Jeong, Y.G.: Development of motion based serious game: "falling" case study. Korean Society for Computer Game **25**, 117–125 (2012). (in Korean)
9. Luke, C., Dodd, K.J., Brock, K.: Outcomes of the Bobath concept on upper limb recovery following stroke. Clin. Rehabil. **18**, 888–898 (2004)

Towards a Google Glass Based Head Control Communication System for People with Disabilities

James Gips[1(✉)], Muhan Zhang[2], and Deirdre Anderson[2]

[1] Information Systems Department, Boston College, Chestnut Hill, MA, USA
james.gips@bc.edu
[2] Computer Science Department, Boston College, Chestnut Hill, MA, USA
{muhan.zhang, deirdre.anderson}@bc.edu

Abstract. We have developed Noggin and Glass Gab, two Google Glass based systems to allow people with disabilities to choose Yes or No and spell out messages just by moving their head. Our goal is to allow people who cannot speak and do not have reliable control of their hands to communicate just with head movements. The advantage of using Google Glass is that the user, perhaps in a wheelchair, does not need a notebook computer or tablet computer. The system displays a pointer on the Google Glass screen and Yes and No buttons (Noggin) or an onscreen keyboard (Glass Gab). The user moves the pointer by head movement. Selection is made using dwell time, by having the pointer dwell over the buttons or letters for a second. The user can have Google Glass speak the message. Head motion is detected using the three axis gyroscope built into Glass.

Keywords: Assistive technology · Access to mobile interaction · Adaptive and augmented interaction · Alternative I/O techniques · Architectures and tools for universal access · Interaction techniques · Wearable technology

1 Introduction

Computer technology plays an increasing role in allowing people with severe disabilities to live fuller lives. For over 20 years our lab at Boston College has been developing assistive technologies to allow people with no voluntary control of their hands or legs and no ability to speak to communicate through eye movements or head movements. These technologies initially required a desktop computer. Assistive technologies based on desktop computers were a major boon for people with disabilities, but they required a person to use the technology at the place where the computer was located. With the development of powerful notebook computers and then tablet computers the technologies became mobile. Technologies that run on notebook computers and tablets can accompany a person with disabilities, for example on a wheelchair. Now with the advent of Google Glass and other wearables, the assistive technologies could be with the person always. The person could literally wear the assistive technology. Google Glass may or may not continue as a viable product. Some

C. Stephanidis (Ed.): HCII 2015 Posters, Part II, CCIS 529, pp. 399–404, 2015.
DOI: 10.1007/978-3-319-21383-5_67

head mounted wearable products will succeed. We hope that the systems described here will be forerunners of assistive technologies for head mounted wearables in the future.

2 Past Work

At Boston College we developed two assistive technologies, EagleEyes and Camera Mouse, before the work on Google Glass.

2.1 EagleEyes

EagleEyes [1–3] allows people with the most severe physical disabilities, people who cannot mover their arms, legs, or heads and cannot speak, to control the computer just through eye movements. Almost all of the people using EagleEyes are children or young adults. Most were completely locked in, with no way to communicate before using EagleEyes. Many were thought to have no mental life, no intelligence [4, 5].

Some of the people using EagleEyes have genetic disorders such as Reyes Syndrome, Trisomy 18, or Spinal Muscular Atrophy Type 1. Some have disabilities resulting from birth, such as Cerebral Palsy. Some suffered drowning accidents or strokes. For most, EagleEyes provides the first means for people to communicate, to show their intelligence.

EagleEyes works through five electrodes placed on the head, around the eyes. EagleEyes measures the vertical and horizontal electrooculogram (EOG), an electrical signal that is proportional to the angle of the eyes in the head. The EOG signals are amplified, filtered, digitized, and used to control the mouse pointer on the screen. Selection is done using dwell time; holding the mouse pointer above a spot on the screen for half a second causes EagleEyes to issue a mouse click. EagleEyes is a general mouse replacement system that allows a person to control the mouse pointer on the screen just with eye movements.

Since the EOG indicates the angle of the eye in the head, people with voluntary head movement can control the mouse pointer just with head movements alone or with a coordinated combination of head movements and eye movements.

EagleEyes is manufactured and distributed by the Opportunity Foundation of America (OFOA) under license from Boston College. Currently they are distributing about two EagleEyes systems per week to families and schools.

2.2 Camera Mouse

Camera Mouse [6, 7] allows people with disabilities to control the computer just with head movements. Camera Mouse uses the built-in camera in a Windows computer or any standard USB webcam to track a location on the head, for example the corner of an eyebrow, specified by the user or selected by the program. As the person moves the head, the mouse pointer moves accordingly. Move your head to the right, the mouse pointer moves to the right, and so on. As with EagleEyes, selection is done using dwell time. Camera Mouse is a general mouse replacement systems, so it works with any standard Windows software.

Camera Mouse is used by many adults with disabilities as well as children. Camera Mouse is available for free download at cameramouse.org. Currently there are over 1,000 downloads per day. Since the program first was made available at the website in 2007 there have been over 2,700,000 downloads.

3 Google Glass

Glass is a lightweight, head-mounted system first made available to the public in the Explorer edition in April 2013. See Fig. 1. Glass is a complete wearable computer system that features a 640 × 360 display, voice control, a touchpad, a 5 megapixel camera, a speaker, Wi-Fi, Bluetooth, a 3 axis gyroscope, and a 3 axis accelerometer. In our software we make use of the display, the gyroscope, and the speaker. The display is the equivalent of a 25 in. high definition screen from eight feet away.

On January 15, 2015 Google halted sale of Glass to the general public, though promising there would be improved versions available in the future. Several companies have head mounted display systems available or in development. There are two types of head mounted display systems. Some are closed systems where the user can see just computer generated images. Some, like Glass, allow the user to see the computer generated image in front of the real world image. The techniques developed in our software are applicable to both types of head mounted systems.

4 Noggin

Noggin is a program for Glass developed by Muhan Zhang in the summer of 2014. Noggin allows the user to move a yellow circle "mouse pointer" on the screen with head movements. Noggin displays a Yes, No, and Enter button on the screen. Noggin allows a user to answer Yes or No questions by selecting the answer on the screen.

Fig. 1. Google glass, explorer edition

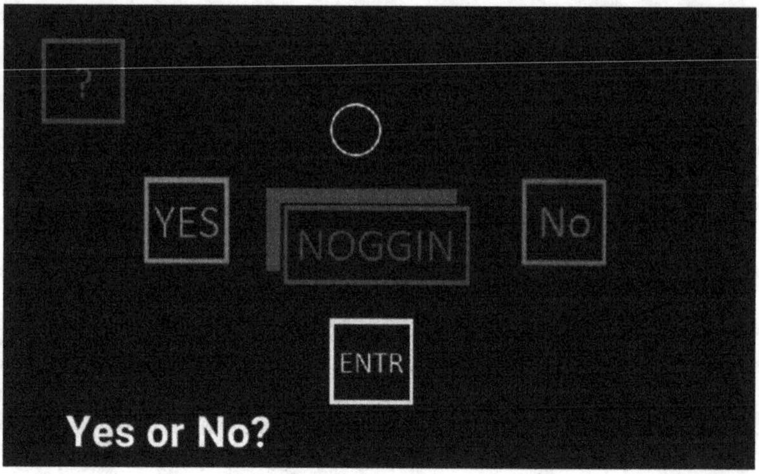

Fig. 2. Noggin screen. The yellow circle is the "mouse pointer" (color figure online)

Noggin then speaks Yes or No. See Fig. 2. Noggin provided a proof of concept of the ability to use the gyroscope to sense head movements to move a mouse pointer with reasonable accuracy.

Noggin for Google Glass is developed in Java using the Glass Development Kit, an additional layer of abstraction on top of the Android Development Kit. Graphics for the app heavily utilizes the AndEngine game engine library. Advantages to this engine are that it is powerful, light, and actively developed by an employee of Zynga with a wide proliferation in the Android mobile gaming world. The major disadvantage is the lack of documentation.

5 Glass Gab

Glass Gab is a program for Glass developed by Deirdre Anderson in the fall of 2014 and winter of 2015. Glass Gab allows the user to spell out a message using an onscreen keyboard. See Fig. 3. Glass Gab makes use of the code base developed for Noggin.

As the user rotates his or her head the program senses the rotation through the changes in the gyroscope settings and moves the yellow circle "mouse pointer" accordingly. If the circle is kept above a letter for one second the letter is selected and added to the end of the message. In addition to the letter keys, a space key, delete key, clear key, and speak key are included.

Initially we were concerned that the user might not have the accuracy to select from 30 targets, but it seems to work after some practice. It took Deirdre 38 s to spell out the 14 character message BOSTON COLLEGE. Of course 14 of the 38 s were required for the dwell times to select the letters. There is more experimentation we could do to improve the mapping between gyroscope changes and pointer movement.

Fig. 3. Glass gab screen. The user has spelled out Boston College

6 Discussion

Three generations of devices allow for a person to control the mouse pointer on the screen by head movements. EagleEyes senses head movements, actually changes in the angle of the eye in the head, through electrodes. Camera Mouse senses head movements with a visual tracking algorithm using a webcam. Noggin and Glass Gab sense head movements though changes of readings of a gyroscope. Camera Mouse is using translational movements while Noggin and Glass Gab are using rotational movements of the head.

Noggin and Glass Gab point the way for assistive technologies using future versions of Google Glass and other head mounted displays.

References

1. Gips, J., Olivieri, P.: EagleEyes: an eye control system for persons with disabilities. In: Eleventh International Conference on Technology and Persons with Disabilities, Los Angeles (1996)
2. Tecce, J.J., Gips, J., Olivieri, P., Pok, L., Consiglio, M.: Eye movement control of computer functions. Int. J. Psychophysiol. **29**, 319–325 (1998)
3. DiMattia, P., Curran, F.X., Gips, J.: An Eye Control Teaching Device for Students Without Language Expressive Capacity: EagleEyes. Edwin Mellen Press, Lewiston (2001)
4. At a Glance, A Computer Comes Alive. New York Times, New York, 4 Aug 1996. http://www.nytimes.com/1996/08/04/education/at-a-glance-a-computer-comes-alive.html

5. Using Her Eyes to Talk. KTUU TV, Anchorage, 12 Aug 2014. http://m.ktuu.com/news/using-her-eyes-to-talk/27426080
6. Gips, J., Betke, M., Fleming, P.: The camera mouse: preliminary investigation of automated visual tracking for computer access. In: Proceedings of RESNA 2000, pp. 98–100. RESNA Press, Arlington (2000)
7. Betke, M., Gips, J., Fleming, P.: The camera mouse: visual tracking of body features to provide computer access for people with severe disabilities. IEEE Trans. Neural Syst. Rehabil. Eng. **10**, 1–10 (2002)

A Comparative Study: Use of a Brain-Computer Interface (BCI) Device by People with Cerebral Palsy in Interaction with Computers

Regina Heidrich[1(✉)], Francisco Rebelo[2], Marsal Branco[1], João Batista Mossmann[1], Anderson Schuh[1], Emely Jensen[1], and Tiago Oliveira[2]

[1] Universidade Feevale, Novo Hamburgo, Brazil
{RHeidrich, marsal}@feevale.br,
{mossmann, anderschuh, emelyjensen}@gmail.com
[2] Universidade Técnica de Lisboa, Cruz Quebrada, Lisbon, Portugal
Frebelo@fmh.ulisboa.pt, t.oliveira2010@gmail.com

Abstract. This article presents a comparative study among people with cerebral palsy and healthy controls, of various ages, using a brain-computer interface (BCI) device. The research is qualitative in its approach. Researchers worked with observational case studies. People with cerebral palsy and healthy controls were evaluated in Portugal and in Brazil. The study aimed to develop a study for product evaluation in order to perceive whether people with cerebral palsy can interact with the computer and to gauge whether their performance is similar to that of healthy controls when using the brain-computer interface. Ultimately, it was found that there are no significant differences between people with cerebral palsy in the two countries, as well as between populations without cerebral palsy (healthy controls).

Keywords: Brain computer interface · Interaction · Cerebral palsy

1 Introduction

This article presents a comparative study among people with cerebral palsy and healthy controls, of various ages, using a brain-computer interface (BCI) device. The study was conducted with people with cerebral palsy and healthy controls from Portugal and Brazil. A brain-computer interface (BCI) allows a person to transfer commands directly to a computer. Instead of using a keyboard, mouse or other input device, the user of this interface simply sends commands via brain waves and the computer responds to them.

People with cerebral palsy, who have their cognitive function preserved, but are unable to communicate or move, or both, require technological learning aids. The use of learning objects may involve concepts and knowledge through experimentation practices, which would not otherwise be possible. In this manner, it is possible to simulate educational situations, thus facilitating the process of school inclusion for these people. Therefore, it is clear that new techniques should be designed within

C. Stephanidis (Ed.): HCII 2015 Posters, Part II, CCIS 529, pp. 405–410, 2015.
DOI: 10.1007/978-3-319-21383-5_68

accessibility guidelines, so as to ensure more inclusive digital environments. The term learning object generally applies to educational materials designed and built in small sets in order to maximize learning situations in which the resource can be used. The basic idea behind them is that the objects are like the blocks with which the learning context is to be built. The IEEE Learning Technology Standards Committee [1] goes further: according to this institution, "any entity, digital or nondigital, that can be used or re-used or referenced during technology-supported learning". An environment, in learning objects, is a software that has a goal, and in which the student makes decisions that interact with the actions of the interaction environment itself, resulting in a new condition. Thus, new learning proposals seek to provide learning scenarios that encourage the development of intellectual autonomy and this is achieved through learning processes that promote reasoning and collective problem-solving [2]. Learning objects in the form of games present themselves as an assistive technology that provides prosperous contributions to develop applications geared at teaching.

Cerebral palsy (CP) is a disorder of posture and movement resulting from an injury to the immature brain during the pre-, peri or postnatal periods [3–6]. In 2006, the Executive Committee for the Definition of Cerebral Palsy [7] formulated a definition that describes cerebral palsy as a group of permanent disorders in the development of posture and movement, attributed to non-progressive disorders that take place during fetal or infant development.

2 Brain Computer Interface - BCI

Specific papers on BCI were collected from the literature. Many were found in the medical field, some in education, and none that mentioned people with disabilities and cerebral palsy using BCI. Scientists in various parts of the world have conducted many studies. A survey between Coventry University and the Universidad Veracruzana [8] presented a usability evaluation of the device MindSet (MS) by NeuroSky. An interesting aspect was to investigate whether the MS readings could be combined with the data generated by the user.

2.1 Operation

- The process begins with the user's intention
- The intention to communicate or control something triggers a complex process in certain areas of the brain.
- The activation of certain brain areas causes a difference with adjacent areas.

The hardware used in this project is called MindWave [9]. It is developed by NeuroSky and works as a BCI (brain-computer interface). Its objective is to use the brain as a communication interface with the machine. It converts electrical brainwaves and analog processes into digital signals to make measurements available to feed the user interface of games, computers, and medical research applications.

- Easy to use
- Non-invasive
- Single dry sensor
- Allows for mobility
- Access to both the raw data or data filtered through optimized algorithms
- Platform open for any industry

3 Objectives

- Develop a study for product evaluation in order to determine whether people with cerebral palsy are able to interact with the computer;
- Compare the performance of people with cerebral palsy to the performance of healthy controls using the brain-computer interface MindWave by NeuroSky.

3.1 Specific Objectives

- Learn whether people with cerebral palsy can use the NeuroSky MindWave to perform a control task for a graphic element;
- Understand the emotional experience resulting from using MindWave;
- Learn whether there are differences between the use of MindWave by people with cerebral palsy, and by healthy controls;
- Understand the main limitations of MindWave when used by people with cerebral palsy.

4 Materials and Methods

- The research is qualitative in its approach. This research was developed with a case study design. This choice is justified by the fact that the case study is a design that allows for a multifaceted, in depth research of a single social phenomenon. Researchers worked with observational case studies. Stake [10] suggests that the object of participant observation can be the work conducted in classroom and new teaching methods. The author has suggested that the case study is the study of the particularity and complexity of a case, in order to understand its activities within special circumstances.
- People with cerebral palsy and healthy controls were evaluated in Portugal and in Brazil.
- The purpose of the study was explained to all participants;
- Before each game, the objective and mode of interaction was explained (attention/meditation).

- Participants with CP performed the test individually, in the presence of two researchers and an Occupational Therapist from AFID, in Portugal. Healthy participants performed the test individually, in the presence of an investigator.
- In Brazil, the participants with cerebral palsy patients were receiving care at the physiotherapy outpatient clinic at Feevale University and the healthy controls were undergraduate students from the same University.
- Participants experienced four games, in the following order:

  - "Burn" game
  - "Float" game
  - "MindtyAnt" game
  - "Jack Adventure" game

In the Burn game, the subject must concentrate in order to blow up a barrel. When the required level of attention is achieved, the barrel explodes, recording the time. After the explosion, the barrel goes back to burning again, and so time can always be improved. Three attempts were made, and the time data for all three were recorded.

Float is a game that measures levels of relaxation. Unlike Burn, here, the subject needs to be relaxed in order to achieve the goal, causing a ball to levitate the highest and for the longest time possible. After three attempts, the time and the height (in meters) of the attempts were recorded.

MindtyAnt is a game in which the user focuses his or her attention levels to help an ant push a piece of food towards the nest. There are 16 stages that challenge the user's ability to concentrate and sense of timing, combining mind control with the use of a keyboard. For the testing, three attempts were made at the 1st level of the game (which only uses mind control, without the keyboard), and the time was recorded).

Jack's Adventure is a game in which the goal is to reforest other planets. Jack is the protagonist, who travels to other planets in his spaceship to help his alien friends tackle environmental problems, such as air pollution and sandstorms. At each new stage of the game, the levels of concentration required to make Jack plant the trees increase. In this game, the user played until they were not able to pass a level at the first attempt. The time for each level the user passed without losing was recorded.

During the games, data on three successful attempts was collected.

Objective variables were recorded for all games:

- Time of game control (given by the game itself);
- Total time for all three successful attempts (collected with a stopwatch).
- Subjective variables were recorded for all games:
- Discomfort;
- Pain.

At the end, each participant was asked about the following subjective variables:

- Which game did you like the most?
- Which game did you like the least?
- Which was the easiest game?
- Which was the hardest game?

5 Discussion

There were no significant differences found among people with cerebral palsy in the two countries and also none found between populations without cerebral palsy, based on the games Float, MindtyAnt and Jack Adventure.

In terms of physical design, the MindWave headset fits about 87.9 % of the population, however improvements can be implemented to make it more effectively adjustable for different percentiles. The experience with the use of this product was observed to be very positive in the samples studied.

The MindWave product showed that it is able to fulfill the promise it sets out to deliver, even in special populational niches, as in the case of people with cerebral palsy.

BCI devices can be great allies to adapt interfaces so they can be used by most people without the need of motion to control elements or tools.

6 Conclusions

After a comprehensive analysis of the MindWave product as a communication interface for games, it was observed that the product is able to fulfill the promise it sets out to deliver, even in special population niches, as in the case of people with cerebral palsy.

BCI technology provides a way to interact with machines, products, and systems, and, as such, is of great importance to their study, since BCI already makes it possible to adapt machines, products and systems to populations with mobility difficulties in order to improve their performance, turning disabilities into mere differences in execution, but with mean performance similar to those of healthy people. Thus, we can use brain functions to design safer systems, and more efficient operations, while advancing knowledge on brain functions in relation to procedural and cognitive performance in tasks that are required by the outside world.

During the first stage of the research, at UTL in Lisbon, pre-tests were applied and it was found that people with cerebral palsy, regardless of their age, have results similar or equal to those of healthy adults. After applying the tests in Brazil, very similar results were observed. Thus, we can envision a field of study with great chances of success in the school field, as well as in the workplace. It was also found that, among the various groups of researchers from prestigious universities, there was no published research exploring the use of BCI by people with cerebral palsy.

References

1. IEEE Learning Technology Standards Committee. Draft Standard for Learning Object Metadata. http://ltsc.ieee.org/wg12/files/LOM_1484_12_1_v1_Final_Draft.pdf
2. Barros, L.A.: Suporte a Ambientes Distribuídos para Aprendizagem Cooperativa. Universidade Federal do Rio de Janeiro, Rio de Janeiro (1994)

3. Finnie, N.R.: O Manuseio em Casa da Criança com Paralisia Cerebral, 3rd edn. Manole, São Paulo (2000)
4. Schwartzman, J.S.: Paralisia Cerebral. Arquivos Brasileiros de Paralisia Cerebral. **1**, 4–17 (2004)
5. Sankar, C., Mundkur, N.: Cerebral palsy - definition, classification, etiology and early diagnosis. Indian J. Pediatr. **72**, 865–868 (2005)
6. Geralis, E.: Crianças com Paralisia Cerebral: Guia para Pais e Educadores, 2nd edn. Artmed, Porto Alegre (2007)
7. Executive Committee for the Definition of Cerebral Palsy: A report: the definition and classification of cerebral palsy April 2006. Dev. Med. Child Neurol. **49**, 8–14 (2007)
8. Rebolledo-Mendez, G., Dunwell, I.: Assessing NeuroSky's usability to detect attention levels in an assessment exercise. In: Jacko, J.A. (ed.) Human-Computer Interaction New Trends, pp. 149–158. Springer, Berlin (2009)
9. Neurosky MindWave. http://www.neurosky.com/biosensors/eeg-sensor
10. Stake, R.E.: The Art of Case Study Research. Sage, London (1995)

Indoor Wheelchair Navigation for the Visually Impaired

Manar Hosny(✉), Rawan Alsarrani, and Abir Najjar

College of Computer and Information Sciences,
King Saud University, Riyadh, Saudi Arabia
mifawzi@ksu.edu.sa, rawan.alsarrani@gmail.com,
abbenabid@KSU.EDU.SA

Abstract. Visually impaired (VI) people face many daily life challenges. It is often difficult for them to recognize where they are, and they may feel disoriented or completely isolated. Moreover, people who have other motor disabilities besides visual impairment face even more difficulty. For example, when using a wheelchair, they usually need a personal assistance to help them navigate to their destination, since they cannot use a cane or other manual assistive devices. To help these people, we aim to develop an indoor wheelchair navigation system. The system is divided into three components: a positioning system, a navigation system and a VI system interface. In the current research, we focus on the design of the navigation system, which will build the optimal path for a VI user on an electric wheelchair. To navigate, the user chooses a destination and their route preferences. A specially designed algorithm will construct an optimized path to the destination, by processing a map of the environment and the route preferences. The algorithm will take into account particular route features customized to the needs of the VI, such as: being free of obstacles, having few turns, being close to walls, and accommodating clues and landmarks. Our navigation system uses the A* shortest path algorithm for path construction, after adapting the objective function to take into account multiple criteria that fit the requirements of a visually impaired. The output of the algorithm is the moving directions, which will be fed back to the wheelchair as commands to direct its movement to the desired destination.

Keywords: Indoor navigation · Visual impairment · Path planning · Human computer interaction · Wheelchair navigation · Optimization · User centered design

1 Introduction

Visually impaired (VI) people often have difficulty knowing their location and navigating to a desired destination without human assistance or travel aids. Among the visually impaired, there are also those who suffer other disabilities like mobility impairment. These people even face more challenges while moving, and may feel disoriented or completely isolated. For example, when using a wheelchair, VI people often need a personal assistance to help them navigate to their required destination, since they cannot use a cane or other manual assistive devices to know their way.

C. Stephanidis (Ed.): HCII 2015 Posters, Part II, CCIS 529, pp. 411–417, 2015.
DOI: 10.1007/978-3-319-21383-5_69

Today, technology has helped people with different types of disabilities to improve their lives. For the visually impaired, supplemental navigational guidance is necessary for their independence and wellbeing. Navigation involves finding a collision-free path that connects the location of the user to a desired destination.

A holistic indoor navigation system for the VI can be divided into three components (Fig. 1): a *Positioning System (Positioner)*, a *VI User Interface System,* and a *Navigation System (Navigator).* The Positioner focuses on gathering information about the navigation environment and the current position of the user, and tracks their location during navigation. The VI User Interface gets the preferences of the user regarding the navigation path and the desired destination. The Navigator receives information from the Positioner and the VI Interface. It processes the map of the environment by identifying obstacles and other surrounding features that are important for consideration in the navigation process. It then computes the optimal path between the current position and the destination, with respect to the VI conveniences and preferences. The path is finally translated into moving directions that are fed back to the wheelchair to guide its move.

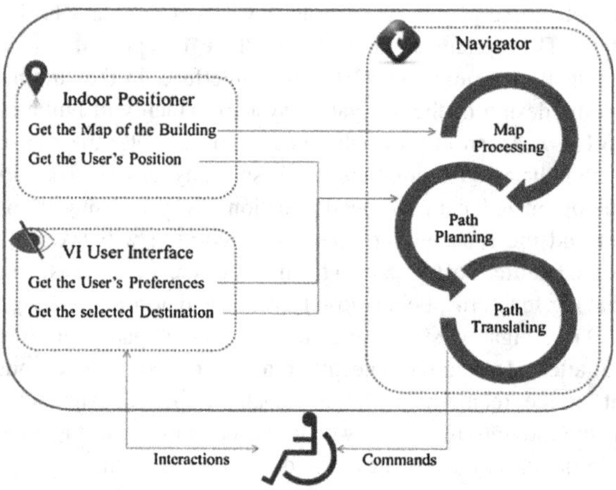

Fig. 1. Indoor navigation system architecture

In the current research we assume that the Positioner and the VI Interface systems are already implemented, and we focus on the Navigator. Specifically, we develop a path finding algorithm for navigating wheelchair-dependent VI people. Besides being obstacles free, the path should account for the needs of the VI in terms of having few turns and being close to walls. Also, it should take into consideration clues and landmarks that can help the visually impaired recognize their surroundings and navigate easily to the destination.

We adopt here a user centered design (UCD) approach to gather the requirements of the VI user in the local context. To plan the best path, we will adopt the famous A* search algorithm. We present in this paper the main components of the system, the design methodology, and an overview of the path planning algorithm.

The rest of this paper is organized as follows: Sect. 2 is a short review of related work. Section 3 provides the details of the proposed approach, and finally Sect. 4 is the conclusion and future work.

2 Related Work

The main component of the navigation system is path planning, which computes an appropriate path between two locations. A feasible path is a path that does not collide with static or dynamic obstacles in the environment, where the environment could be *indoors* or *outdoors*. We review next some literature on indoor navigation.

The authors in Ref. [1] develop an indoor routing algorithm for the sighted and compare it with a blind routing algorithm. They aim to calculate optimal indoor route for blind people who are traveling with a white cane. The algorithm differentiates between clues, landmarks, obstacles, and hazards over the feasible paths, and selects the optimal route by comparing the distance and the number of landmarks along the path.

In Ref. [2] a path planning algorithm is developed for VI people in an indoor environment. The problem is concerned with finding a path that connects different points of interest (POI), while taking into account some safety consideration, such as avoiding hazards and minimizing the distance traveled. Dijkstra/A* algorithms are used for path planning by finding a sequence of nodes that act as a "virtual hand-rail" path.

The report in Ref. [3] describes the navigation layer in an indoor navigation system for a visually impaired pedestrian. A path to the destination is computed by taking into account the length of the route and some user preferences, such as the number of turns and the convenience of the cells through which the user moves. To build the optimal path, Dijkstra's algorithm is used after adapting it to fit the user preferences.

The work in Ref. [4] presents a path finding algorithm for the visually impaired in an indoor environment, specifically a shopping market. The A* algorithm is used to find the shortest path as part of a navigation system that combines RFID technology, a central processing system, and a voice assisted guiding system.

Increased use of wheelchairs is expected along with the increase in life expectancy of elderly people. A system that automatically guides the movement of the wheelchair would be a great help for users with severe mobility. Despite this, path planning research for wheelchair movement is scarce. An example of a navigation system for wheelchair users is in Ref. [5]. The user chooses a destination from a map of using BCI (brain computer interaction). Then the system processes the brain signals, determines the destination, and constructs an obstacles-free path. Directions are then input to the wheelchair, leading the user automatically to the destination.

3 Proposed Approach

We adopt in this system a user centered design (UCD) approach, by taking the needs and preferences of the user into account throughout the design process. UCD is adopted because the user population has special needs and their requirements may not be immediately available or can be derived from a similar system. In addition, we specifically target users in the local context, which has language, cultural, and technological requirements that may differ from systems developed elsewhere. Finally, to our knowledge, existing navigation assistance systems have been designed for either visually impaired or wheelchair users, but not both. Figure 2 shows a schematic diagram of the UCD approach as followed in our research.

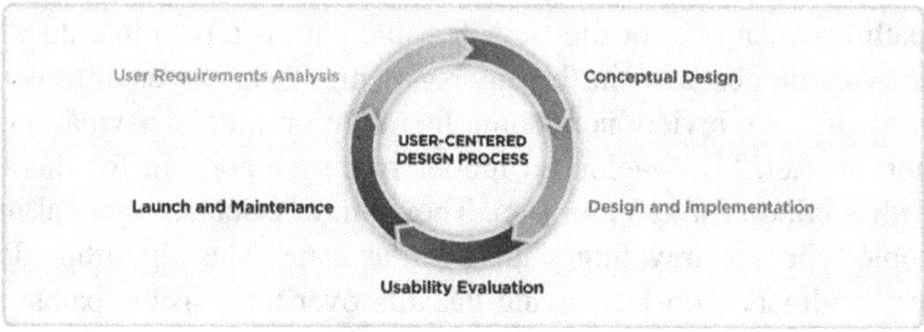

Fig. 2. UCD approach

3.1 User Requirements Analysis

First, an exploratory survey was conducted to understand the behavior of VI users in the local context. The questions targeted the following areas: (1) user demographic information, (2) characteristics of the preferred navigation path, and (3) environmental (surroundings) features that may assist or hinder the navigation process.

The survey was posted online with the help of VI online Twitter society, and was distributed in a VI rehabilitation center. The survey yielded overall 25 responses.

We can summarize the findings of the surveys as follows: the most important features in the movement path for the VI (in priority order) are: straight-line, minimum number of turns, and shortest distance. Also, the majority prefers moving near walls, although quite a few indicated that it is not preferred. On the other hand, stairs and escalators are mostly not preferred. Obviously, obstacles in the path should also be avoided and moving near them should be restricted.

In addition to the above design implications, we could also utilize findings in the literature (e.g. [1, 2]), where special environmental features are divided into three classes: (1) Point of Interest (POI), a place or an object that is a potential destination (e.g. a specific room or shop); (2) Landmark (LM), a location that can help the user verify their position (e.g. a water fountain, or a voice enabled map), and (3) Walking Area (WA), which includes a path where the user can move comfortably.

3.2 Conceptual Design

The conceptual design task can be divided into three phases with respect to the Navigator: Map Processing, Path Planning, and Path Translating.

Map Processing. To plan the path, the environment map should be available. The map will be divided into a grid of equal sized cells, and will identify obstacles' locations and any features that can help in the planning process, such as POIs, LMs, etc. Figure 3 shows an example of a simple map processed as above, where for a VI, moving near blue cells is preferred, while moving near read cells is unsafe.

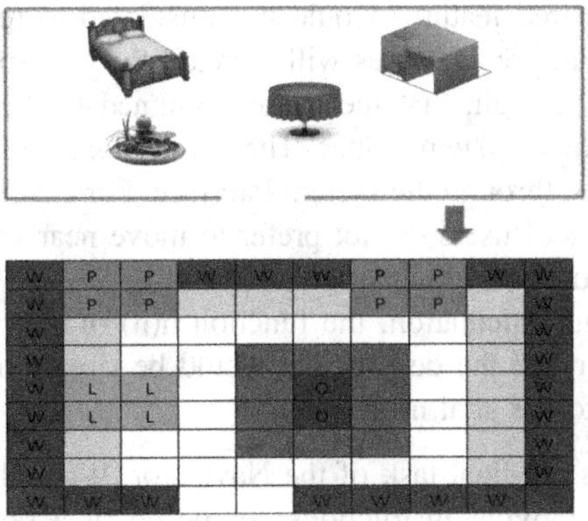

Fig. 3. Environment map: W (Wall), P (Point of interest), L (Landmark), and O (Obstacle)

Path Planning. The A* (A star) algorithm is a widely used search algorithm for finding the shortest path between two points. It uses a heuristic to guide itself to find the optimal path, by estimating the remaining distance from the current state to the destination. Assuming a grid based environment, like the one described in the map processing above, the A* algorithm starts from a specific starting node/cell S. Then it uses an evaluation function f(n) to guide the selection of a neighboring node to be visited next.

$$f(n) = g(n) + h(n) \tag{1}$$

where g(n) represents the cost of the path from the starting node S to any node n, and h (n) represents a heuristic estimated cost from any node n to the destination D.

In our system we use the Manhattan distance to compute the length of the path, where only four possible moves are allowed (horizontal and vertical). Diagonal movements are prohibited, since they are not applicable for wheelchair movement.

To calculate the cost function g(n) in (1), we are concerned with the path distance and the desirable and un-desirable path features encountered in the path. The path will add one of its adjacent cells at each movement. Thus, the number of nodes that the path passes through represents the total distance. In addition, for every undesirable path feature encountered in the path (e.g. obstacle, near obstacle, stairs/escalators, and near stairs/escalators) a penalty value will be imposed. Moreover, to avoid jerky movements of the wheelchair, the number of turns in the path will also be penalized, such that any change from horizontal to vertical or vise versa will be considered as a turn. So, the cost function can be expressed as follows:

$$g(n) = w1 \times L + w2 \times T + w3 \times C(n) \tag{2}$$

where w1, w2, and w3 are weights in the range [0,1] that determine the importance of each term in the function, and w1 + w2 + w3 = 1. L is the total distance of the path up to the node n. T is total number of turns up to the node n, and C(n) is the cost of node n.

To calculate the cost of each node, neutral cells will be initialized to some positive default value. Then, desired features would be considered as reducing the cost (negative penalty), while undesired features will increase the cost (positive penalty).

It should be noted, though, that the values assigned to the cost of each cell, as described above are default system values. These values can be customized according to individual preferences, through the system interface. For example, our survey results indicated that over 36 % of users do not prefer to move near walls. In such case, the user may put a low priority on this particular feature.

To complete the path calculation, the function h(n) of (1), which is the heuristic estimate of the cost to reach the destination, would be simply the Euclidean distance from the current node to the goal node.

Path Translation. It is the final task of the Navigator. It simply involves translating the obtained path into moving instructions composed of a series of directions and distances that can be fed back to the wheelchair to direct its movement to the desired destination.

4 Conclusions and Future Work

In this research we have considered the design of a navigation system for a visually impaired user on a wheelchair. The system relies on a user centered design (UCD) approach to identify the needs and requirements of users in the local context. After determining the main requirements, we have designed a path planning optimization algorithm to generate an optimized path that will fit the user needs, taking into account a number of desired and undesired path features. The system is currently under implementation using JAVA programming language. The testing phase will follow, where different maps of the environment will be tried and the generated paths will be evaluated first from a theoretical standpoint, with respect to achieving the best objective function. Then, usability evaluation will follow where the system will be evaluated by visually impaired users, to examine whether or not it is fit for their needs and preferences. After the testing phase, the navigation component discussed here will be integrated with the positioning and the VI interface components to form a complete indoor navigation system for the visually impaired.

References

1. Swobodzinski, M., Raubal, M.: An indoor routing algorithm for the blind: development and comparison to a routing algorithm for the sighted. Int. J. Geogr. Inf. Sci. **23**(10), 155–1343 (2009)

2. Wu, H., Marshall, A., Yu, W.: Path planning and following algorithms in an indoor navigation model for visually impaired. In: Second International Conference on Internet Monitoring and Protection, 2007 (ICIMP 2007), pp. 38–38. IEEE (2007)
3. Tissot, N.: Indoor navigation for visually impaired people-the navigation layer. ETH Zürich Technical report (2003). http://www.mics.ch/SumIntU03/NTissot.Pdf
4. Kilinçarslan, M.: Implementation of a path finding algorithm for the navigation of visually impaired people. MS thesis in Computer Engineering, Atilim University, Ankara (2007)
5. Alrajhi, W., Hosny, M., Al-Wabil, A., Alabdulkarim, A.: Human factors in the design of BCI-controlled wheelchairs. In: Kurosu, M. (ed.) HCI 2014, Part II. LNCS, vol. 8511, pp. 513–522. Springer, Heidelberg (2014)

Assessment of Electronic Write-in Voting Interfaces for Persons with Visual Impairments

Ashley Ongsarte[1], Youxuan Jiang[2], and Kyla McMullen[3(✉)]

[1] Department of Computer Science, Mills College, 5000 MacArthur Blvd, Oakland, CA 94613, USA
aongsarte@mills.edu

[2] College of Engineering and Computing, Miami University, 501 E High St, Oxford, OH 45056, USA
jiangy9@miamioh.edu

[3] Department of Computer and Information Science and Engineering, Gainesville, FL 32611, USA
kyla@cise.ufl.edu

Abstract. In 2002, the Help America Vote Act (HAVA) mandated that all Americans should have an equal opportunity to vote with privacy and security. However, current electric voting technologies have unsuccessfully provided barrier-free access for people with visual impairments to write in a desired candidate's name without assistance. The present work describes a new e-voting technology where voters independently use a mouse to interact with a virtual audio keyboard that provides the ability to type, check, and modify a write-in candidate choice. The goal of this work is to create an accessible, accurate, and independent keyboard based interaction mechanism for visually impaired voters. The interface was assessed using 16 participants. Performance was measured in terms of voting speed, accuracy, and preference. The system was compared to a voting technology that uses a linear method to select letters. Results indicated that performance using the linear write-in interface was significantly better than the virtual keyboard. The results also revealed an interesting distinction between human muscle memory and spatial memory.

Keywords: Visual impairments · Write-in voting · Accessibility · Spatial memory

1 Introduction

The United States (US) Constitution guarantees that every citizen has the right to vote for the candidate(s) of his or her choice, not excluding persons with disabilities. In October of 2002, as a response to the controversial aftermath of the 2000 presidential election, the US Congress passed the Help America Vote Act (HAVA), which is the first legal requirement that mandated equal voting access for blind and visually impaired citizens [5]. HAVA requires all states to replace punch card and lever based voting systems with advanced technology to provide independent, accurate, and secure voting access for visually impaired voters. HAVA also funds programs to improve the accessibility and quality of voting. This includes establishing at least one accessible

C. Stephanidis (Ed.): HCII 2015 Posters, Part II, CCIS 529, pp. 418–423, 2015.
DOI: 10.1007/978-3-319-21383-5_70

voting system for individuals with disabilities at each polling location and educating voters and poll workers on voting procedures and ballot casting.

An ever-present challenge for visually impaired voters is overcoming the difficulty of writing in a candidate's name within a short period of time. For example, in a telephone survey conducted in 2008 by the National Federation of the Blind (NFB) Jernigan Institution, visually impaired voters expressed challenges writing in the names of candidates because the process of choosing the letters was tedious and there was no feedback to confirm that the correct selection occurred [4].

2 Related Work

Many electronic voting systems have been created that include write-in features for voters with visual impairments. For example, Vote-Trakker was developed to afford a portable touch screen display with a QWERTY computer keyboard for blind and visually impaired voters to type in their desired candidates' names. However, the noncomputer users who are unfamiliar with the QWERTY keyboard and the synthetic computer voice could develop a fear of the keyboard interface and not be able to use the write-in feature of Vote-Trakker [2].

To provide independent voting for people with visual impairments, regardless of their computer familiarity, AutoMARK voter assist terminal (VAT) is designed as an optical scan ballot marker, which contains a touch screen on a base that has a keypad that is marked by Braille on the right side of the screen. The keypad has a square select button surrounded by four arrow buttons that point to different directions that represent up, down, back, and forward for easy identification [3], which allows visually impaired voters to scroll through the letters shown in alphabetical order on the screen as they are read through the headphones, and press the select button to type it. Although users can check if the name is entered correctly at any time while writing, several potential problems for write-in voting are still posed. First, AutoMARK does not have a modifying feature for users to correct their typing mistakes. Consequently, users have to restart the entire typing process if they make a mistake. Second, AutoMARK does not provide feedback to indicate successful typing, so users have no way to verify if the letter they are typing is what they want as they press the select button. Third, AutoMARK does not allow direct access to each letter. Users have to linearly search through the letters alphabetically before selecting their desired letter, which is extremely time consuming. Lastly, the AutoMark keypad is on the right side of the screen, which forces left-handed voters to use their right hand in an unnatural way or use their left hand in an unnatural position.

To assess those challenges faced by visually impaired voters while writing in candidates, the present work investigates the impacts of using different write-in interfaces on time, accuracy, and preference. The system designed for this study resembles a standard QWERTY keyboard, which allows the listener to directly access each letter by operating the interface using either left or right hand rather than manually scrolling through each letter in the alphabet. The present work also assesses performance when using a familiar, alphabetically ordered keyboard. User performance with both virtual keyboard interfaces was compared to performance using a system in which the user input names linearly by holding down a key as the letters of the alphabet are read, and releasing the key to select the letter.

3 Methods

3.1 Participants

Sixteen participants (8 women and 8 men) with normal hearing who were undergraduate and graduate students participated in the study. All listeners were between the ages of eighteen and thirty. All of the participants self-reported average to excellent typing skills. The experiment required about 1.5 h of participation and was completed in one session. Participants were paid $10 per hour. Before participating, each person gave consent by reading and signing a consent form.

3.2 Apparatus

Experiments were conducted in an IAC soundproof booth in the university's Psychology Department. Each participant was seated at a table in front of the iMac system/Apogee Duet audio interface with the Beyerdynamic headphones in place. The keyboard had raised regions on the left and right arrow keys, shift key, and the play button so the participants could easily locate buttons needed to complete the tasks. The system rendered the auditory stimuli using OpenAL. Standard mouse to screen cursor mapping was used.

The two virtual keyboard systems designed for the study were designed to resemble a standard and an alphabetically ordered keyboard (Fig. 1 - top left and right panels). Users were given a mouse, which was used to hover over the virtual keys as its specific letter was read audibly. To end the write-in task, the user pressed the "Enter" key and heard the word "enter" spoken. To ensure that users stayed within the bounds of the keyboard, each participant heard a bell sound if the mouse cursor moved beyond the keyboard.

User performance with both virtual keyboard interfaces was compared to performance using a linear system. In the linear interface (Fig. 1 - bottom panel), the

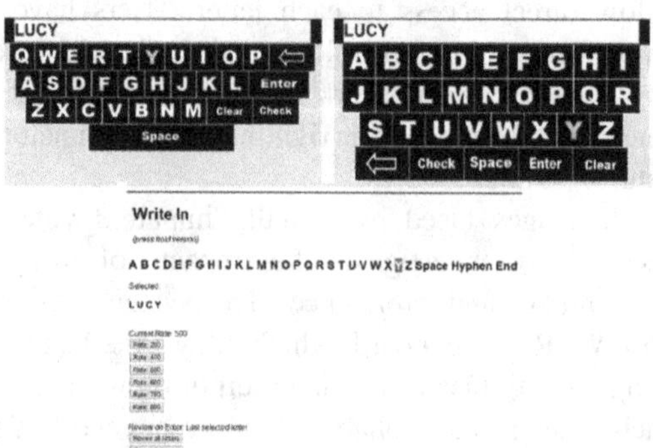

Fig. 1. Typing interfaces used in the study. QWERTY virtual keyboard interface (top left), alphabetical virtual keyboard interface (top-right), linear interface (bottom).

participant held down the left and right arrow keys on the keyboard to traverse the alphabet and used shift keys to select a letter. The left and right arrow keys on the physical keyboard were marked with raised buttons to inform the user of their location.

3.3 Procedure

A within-subjects experiment was performed using 16 blindfolded participants, which is a common practice in many studies for visually impaired interfaces. Figure 2 displays the experimental procedure, which consisted of three distinct phases. First, each participant took an audiogram to ensure that they had normal hearing. Next, each participant completed five sets of write-in voting tasks using a keyboard interface (QWERTY or alphabetical) and the linear interface, in a randomly determined order. Half of the participants began with the linear interface while the other half began using one of the virtual keyboard interfaces (QWERTY or alphabetical). Finally, the participant took a qualitative survey to assess their experience using both systems.

4 Results

The results indicate that performance using the linear interface was significantly faster than using either of the two keyboard interfaces. This trend was seen in all 5 typing tasks. Figure 3 depicts the results for the task of typing a voting candidate's first and last name. No significant difference was observed between the virtual keyboard

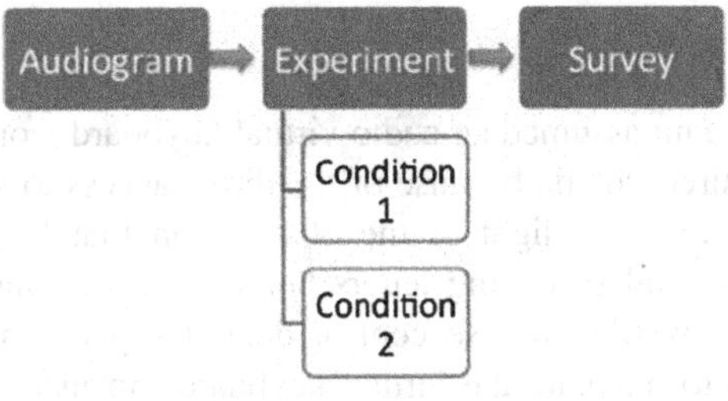

Fig. 2. Flowchart of the experimental design

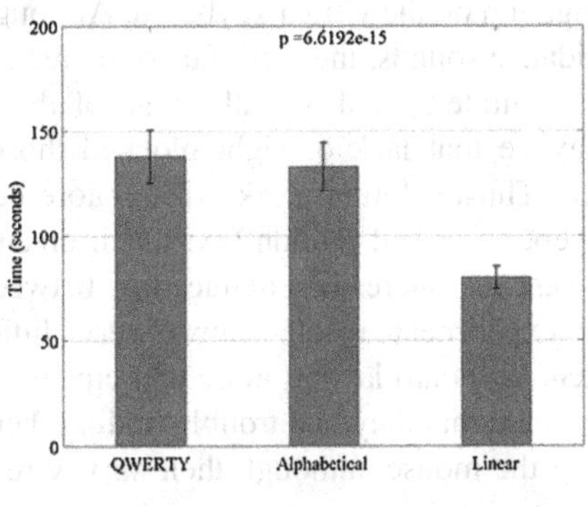

Fig. 3. Completion time for typing a first and last name

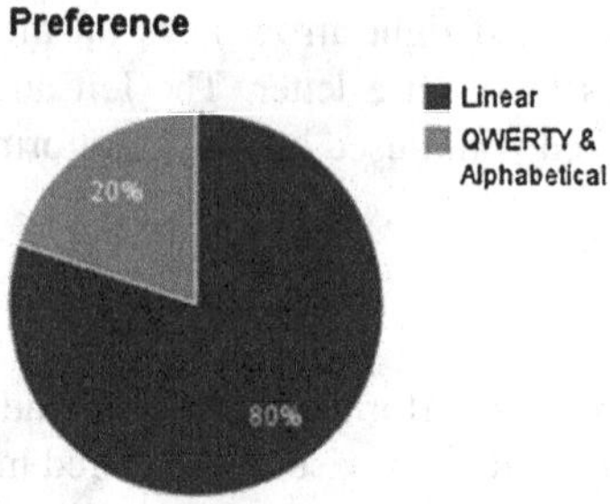

Fig. 4. Overall participant preference for virtual interface as compared to the linear interface

interfaces. This finding may suggest that no matter the chosen layout, individuals with visual impairments may prefer using an egocentric navigation method rather than environment-centered navigation while finishing short distance navigation tasks, such as mouse navigation on the virtual keyboard.

Figure 4 indicates that most participants preferred using the linear write-in system as compared to the keyboard write-in systems. Many participants found it difficult to navigate the virtual keyboard and locate the desired letters using mouse control alone, which suggests a delineation between spatial and muscle memory, as many self-reported to be proficient typers. Associating this finding with the fact that procedural memory is the least likely memory to be forgotten, future studies can investigate how muscle memory helps people learn performance in low-level attention contexts.

5 Discussion

Initially, the research team assumed an audio virtual keyboard would decrease write-in time for visually impaired voters, because of the direct access to select desired letters. This assumption was made in light of the observation that linear write-in systems require users to traverse all preceding letters before selecting their desired letter. In contrast, the results show that mouse control degrades performance for users who cannot see the screen to navigate the virtual keyboard, no matter the chosen layout. Individuals with visual impairments may prefer using an egocentric navigation method rather than environment-centered navigation to complete short distance navigation tasks, such as mouse navigation on the virtual keyboard. Although the virtual interfaces contained speech and guidance sounds, they still failed to create the necessary cues for participants to create an accurate spatial mental image of the virtual keyboard. One cause of this finding may be that lack of sight blocked those users' perception of self-motion on the screen. Thusly, future work will explore ego-centered navigation that incorporates the perception of self-motion (ex: touchscreen).

The results also suggest an interesting delineation between spatial and muscle memory. Although the experiment result shows very little difference between QWERTY and alphabetical keyboard layout, more participants disliked the QWERTY keyboard. Participants reported that they had trouble finding their desired letters on the QWERTY keyboard using the mouse, although their survey results indicated average or above typing skills. It is not clear why the participants did not establish a mental image of the QWERTY keyboard that they use each day to type.

Acknowledgements. The authors would like to thank the Distributed Research Experience for Undergraduates (DREU) for affording the opportunity for the authors to perform this research.

References

1. Burton, D., Uslan, M.: The ballot ballet: the usability of accessible voting machines. In: American Foundation for the Blind AccessWorld Magazine (2004)
2. Conrad, F.G., Bederson, B.B., Lewis, B., Peytcheva, E., Traugott, M.W., Hanmer, M.J., Herrnson, P.S., Niemi, R.G.: Electronic voting eliminates hanging chads but introduces new usability challenges. Int. J. Hum. Comput. Stud. **67**(1), 111–124 (2009)
3. McClendon, J.: A new approach to voting: an accessible voter verifiable paper ballot. Master's thesis, Auburn University (2009)
4. Piner, G.E., Byrne, M.D.: The experience of accessible voting results of a survey among legally-blind users. In: Proceedings of the Human Factors and Ergonomics Society Annual Meeting, vol. 55, pp. 1686–1690. SAGE Publications (2011)
5. Shambon, L.M.: Implementing the help America vote act. Election Law J. **3**(3), 424–443 (2004)

Tool for Alternative and Augmented Communication: A Study Implemented in Hospitals Environment to Support Pedagogical Therapies

Ednilson G. Rossi[1(✉)], Janaina C. Abib[1], and Luciana A. Rodrigues[2]

[1] Federal Institute of São Paulo, Araraquara, SP, Brazil
{ednilsonrossi, janaina.abib}@gmail.com
[2] Centro Universitário Barão de Mauá, Ribeirão Preto, SP, Brazil
lu_arodrigues@yahoo.com.br

Abstract. Communication is a basic need of human beings. It is required in professional, social and personal relationships, establishing a fundamental aspect for survival. Communication can be considered a set of signs that refers to behaviors that occur among two or more persons and which provide a way to create meanings between them. When individuals have no forms of communication or have some form of communication, but this is not enough to maintain communication links, establishing social relationships, it is necessary to use some resources to promote communication, integrating this individual in social life. Adapt and create alternative ways of communication is essential for people with disabilities or lack of oral communication to interact with their peers into the work, social and personal environments. For these adaptations it is common to use alternative and augmented communication tools (AACT), for example, uses of alternative communication boards and applications to support the communication process, using images, videos and technological resources to support the communication. The objective of this research is propose the development of prototypes with medium fidelity to facilitate patients with disabilities to learn and communicate, and understanding their distinctions in learning and interacting during communication process.

Keywords: Communication process · Alternative and augmented communication · Communications technologies

1 Introduction

The communication can be considered a set of signs that refers to behaviors that occur among of two or more persons and which provide a way to create meanings between them. The term alternative and augmented communication (AAC) is defined as other forms of communication beyond the oral communication, such as the use of gestures, sign, facial expressions, use of alphabet boards, graphic symbols, use of sophisticated computer systems with synthesized speech and others [6]. Thus, communication is considered as alternative when the individual has no other form for communication,

C. Stephanidis (Ed.): HCII 2015 Posters, Part II, CCIS 529, pp. 424–429, 2015.
DOI: 10.1007/978-3-319-21383-5_71

excepted oral communication, and it is considered augmented when the individual has some form of communication, but this is not enough to maintain communication links or establishing social exchanges. The purpose of this project is the development of an alternative tool using interactive media and expanded interaction with touchable and voice communication devices in Portuguese. This tool can provide a significantly difference to a person's life that has any kind of restriction or is unable to communicate, especially those with boundaries regarding communication, such as difficulties and speech limitations.

This paper is organized as follow: concepts and contextualization are presented in Sect. 2. Section 3 presents our prototypes and the development process of the prototypes. Finally, the Sect. 4 presents the conclusions and future works.

2 Concepts Involved and Contextualization

Cards and boards with graphics symbols are used as features to alternative and augmented communication. This collection of images used in cards and graphical boards shares common characteristics and is designed to address different requirements or needs of all kind of users with disabilities in communication. One of the most used symbolic systems in the world is the PCS (picture communication symbols), created in 1980 by an American speech therapist named Mayer Johnson [1]. The PCS system has the following characteristics: clear and simple designs, easy recognition, suitable for users of any age. The system is easily combined with other figures and photographs for creating individualized communication resources.

There is software based on PCS system that allows communication of individuals with pre-recorded or synthesized voices. A voicer is an electronic recording/playback resource that helps people to communicate. Using these devices, the users can express their thoughts, feelings and desires by choosing and pressing an appropriate message that is pre-recorded on the device. Messages are accessed by keys which are associated with images (pictures, symbols, pictures) or words that correspond to the recorded sound. However, the interface of voicers is not suitable for many people, especially people with physical disabilities or other conditions that act directly on the human brain. Furthermore, the use of overlapping images on keyboards creates some limitations based on usage of images, symbols and words.

Thus, the aim of this project is to develop an application of alternative and augmented communication to be used to any user with an appropriate interface, allowing the user to have the ability to communicate and become part of society. During the study we defined a set of users and what type of application they need, because we know that different users need different interfaces: a user with autism needs a different communication tool if we compare with one user with cerebral palsy, for example [4, 7]. After our first prototype implementation, intended for a specific type of user - with cerebral palsy, other interfaces were implemented, allowing the use of application by a greater number of users, also with cerebral palsy but with different limitations, fitting the special needs of each user. Probably, in the near future, more interfaces will be required.

3 Experiments and Prototypes to Supporting Alternative and Augmented Communication

Prototypes are graphical representations, not necessarily functional, of a system (or part of a system) in the design phase. They can be models, drawings and screens designed to simulate user interaction with a system [5]. According to [3], build prototypes is a very good way to explore ideas for a project before investing time and resources in its implementation. It is sort of test and consolidates ideas using cheaper resources and its used have a fast development process. Prototyping is an effective technique to test hypotheses and check the user's needs in early development phase, when it's quite cheap making changes in the design [2].

In this project the prototyping allowed us to design and evaluate the IVA tool and realize during the requirements gathering the needs of design another interfaces, with new forms of interaction, since users have different characteristics and needs for interaction.

3.1 IVA Prototype – an Alternative and Augmented Tool

The prototype of IVA tool was designed to enable the communication of patients with cerebral palsy that live in a hospital in Brazil and educational psychology professionals, as a tool to support therapy sessions, allowing patients to express themselves. We also included some functionality that support some activities performed during the therapy sessions.

Figure 1 shows the layout of the main interface of the developed tool. The logo is available at the top left of the screen; the navigation buttons are located at the top right: they allow access to basic functions of the tool: eat (a), drink (b), play music (c), play games (d), how I feel (e) and speak (f).

The user can choose the button/option EAT (as showed in Fig. 2) and select the possible food menu - all options were suggested by professionals involved and the

Fig. 1. Home screen of IVA prototype

Fig. 2. Option EAT detailed

images were chosen to fulfill what patients know and used in their daily activities. Clicking on the image, the prototype emits a sound corresponding to the text of the selected button and the sound is repeated every time an option is selected. The same procedure occurs for other areas: Drink, Play Music, Play Games and How I Feel.

The Speak button is under development, and it will propose a simplified alphabetic keyboard, so the patient can type complete sentences, to express what they think, feel or want. The numeric keypad, displayed on the homepage, was a request of the educational psychologists to allow patients with skills and mathematical knowledge, use the numeric keypad to make small calculations - this functionality was already used during some therapies with numeric cards of paper and was incorporated into the IVA prototype. It's important emphasize that in the main interface as well as other tool's screens were designed by the professionals already involved with the patients and the functionalities can be inserted, removed and changed according to the needs of patients and professionals.

During requirements collecting and initial tests with patients, we noticed that some patients were more affected by hands and arm movements. Thus, a new functional prototype was created for patients with cerebral palsy with reduced control of hands and arms and they are no able to use touch, or use conventional mouse, or pointers.

3.2 Adaptations and New Forms of Interaction

The new prototype has interaction mechanism with bigger objects and reduced amount of options, but enables communication of the patients with reduced control of arms and hands, and combines concepts of multimedia and communication boards, allowing a visual and voice interaction between the patient and professionals involved in the pedagogical therapies.

This new interface consists in a set of images and sounds to be exposed to the user and the interaction is through a click on an adapted mouse (two separate boxes simulating a conventional mouse, with one left and one right sensors), which was called " boxes clicks" – Fig. 3.

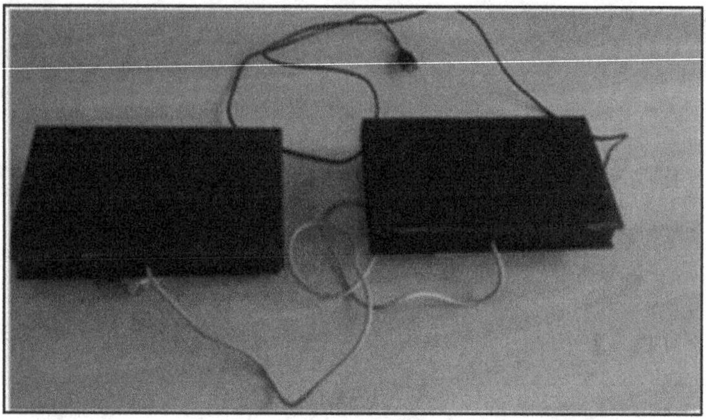

Fig. 3. Boxes clicks

The new part of the prototype has a fully visual interface; the screen can display three images, as shown in Fig. 4, with the middle image is highlighted (see Fig. 4) and is the image selection. The left image is the option that was previously presented and the right image is the next option being displayed. For each image or interaction performed, the corresponding sound is presented referred to the image/interaction selected, in order to stimulate the hearing and oral communication of the patient.

The user, by hitting the left side of the "boxes clicks" is choosing that s/he wants to select and/or execute the highlighted option, and the prototype provides the contents of the selected option and triggers the corresponding sound. By hitting the right side of the "boxes clicks" another option appears highlighted: the next option. The options are arranged on a carousel, which is repeated at the end of each set of options. The choice of an option of the carousel allows patients to participate in therapies with technological resources. In the initial tests with users, some chose to use the "boxes clicks" with feet and a new adaptation is being prepared to make it more resistant.

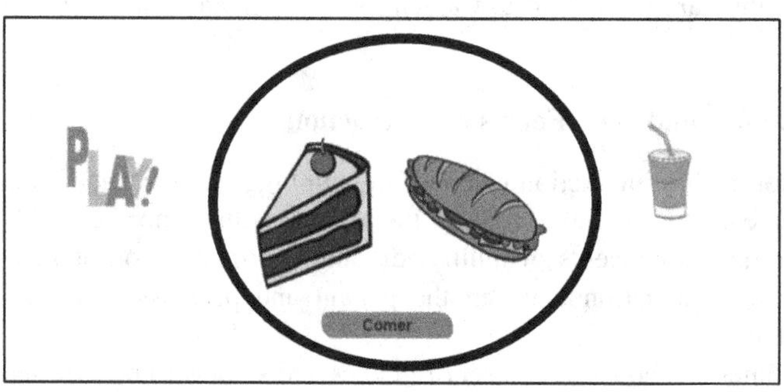

Fig. 4. Main new interface

4 Conclusion and Future Work

We present prototypes developed to support the process of communication between therapists and patients with little or no oral communication during the therapy sessions in a hospital.

Other existing tools were tested but they did not meet the needs of these users - most have multiple disabilities and the tested tools do not provide specific support for cognitive difficulties and motor difficulties at the same time. Even our prototypes have been adapted for each user and many of the users appropriated the offered resources on their own way.

We understand that people with multiple disabilities need specific technology to support communication and that these resources have be tailored to each user. Our prototypes are constantly evolving and adapting to serve patients in their therapy.

Acknowledgements. We thank Caioby Aleixo Ripoli Fiochi and Fabiana Oliveira by the implemented prototypes. Also we thank Federal Institute of São Paulo by the financial support.

References

1. Mayer-Johnson, R.: The Picture Communication Symbols: Combination Book, Sprial edn, p. 378. Pittsburgh, Mayer-Johnson (1989)
2. Snyder, C.: Paper Prototyping: The Fast and Easy Way to Define User Interfaces. Morgan Kaufmann Publishers, San Francisco (2003)
3. Berkun, S.: The Art of UI Prototyping. In: Microsoft Corporation. ESSAYS. Nov/Dec 2000. https://msdn.microsoft.com/en-us/library/ms993294.aspx
4. Abib, Janaina Cintra, Rodrigues, Luciana, Gotardo, Reginaldo: Tool to help the communication for autists. In: Kurosu, Masaaki (ed.) HCI 2014, Part III. LNCS, vol. 8512, pp. 211–220. Springer, Heidelberg (2014)
5. Abib, J.C., Theodoro, L.A.: Protótipo de Ferramenta para Apoio na Divulgação de Conhecimento. In: Proceedings of XII International Conference on Engineering and Technology Education, Dili, vol. 12, pp. 103–108 (2012). (In Portuguese)
6. Beukelman, D., Mirenda, P.: Augmentative and Alternative Communication, 2nd edn. Brookes, Baltimore (2005). http://www.pbrookes.com/aac/. ISBN 1-55766-333-5
7. ASSOCIAÇÃO AMERICANA DE PSIQUIATRIA. *DSM-IV-TR*: Manual diagnóstico e estatístico de transtornos mentais. 4.ed. Rev. Artmed (2002). (In Portuguese)

Access All Areas: Designing a Hands-on Robotics Course for Visually Impaired High School Students

Valerie Stehling(✉), Katharina Schuster, Anja Richert, and Sabina Jeschke

IMA/ZLW & IfU, RWTH Aachen University, Aachen, Germany
{Valerie.Stehling,Katharina.Schuster,Anja.Richert, SabinaJeschke}@ima-zlw-ifu.rwth-aachen.de

Abstract. In recent years, student laboratories have been established as effective extracurricular learning areas for the promotion of educational processes in STEM fields. They provide various stimuli and potentials for enhancements and supplements in secondary school education [8]. Most courses, however, do not offer full accessibility to all students. Those who e.g. suffer from visual impairment or even sightlessness find themselves not being able to participate in all tasks of the courses. On this account, the Center for Learning and Knowledge Management and Institute of Information Management in Mechanical Engineering at RWTH Aachen University have redesigned one of their robotics laboratory courses as a first step towards accessibility. This paper presents the work in progress of developing a barrier-free course design for visually impaired students. First feedback discussions with the training staff shows that even little changes can sometimes have a huge impact.

Keywords: School laboratories · Barrier free · LEGO mindstorms · Visual impairment · Highschool students

1 Introduction

Extracurricular school laboratories have proven to be an effective way to let students playfully experience the fundamentals of robotics, computer science or other technology-related topics. In combination with a hands-on approach, e.g. by working with LEGO MindStorms, they get a chance to learn on a cognitive, emotional and haptic level. While this is a widespread approach these days, not every pupil, however, is able to participate in courses like these due to a lack of accessibility. Ludi e.g. states that "awareness of potential career paths and access to adequate preparation remain barriers to students who are visually impaired" [5]. Due to their impairment or lack of sight it is rather impossible for them to fully participate in a programming process or when building a robot using e.g. LEGO MindStorms sets.

To overcome this sort of discrimination, the Center for Learning and Knowledge Management and Institute of Information Management in Mechanical Engineering of RWTH Aachen University have teamed up with a group of experts in order to develop

C. Stephanidis (Ed.): HCII 2015 Posters, Part II, CCIS 529, pp. 430–435, 2015.
DOI: 10.1007/978-3-319-21383-5_72

a special barrier-free course design. This group of interdisciplinary researchers and practitioners – psychologists, school and university teachers, experts in the field of accessibility as well as robotics etc. – took the original course design from an existing robotics course for high school students and transformed it into an accessible course design by applying specific changes. Applying solely technical adjustments to the course, however, cannot be fully sufficient in the development of a new and adequate course design. Therefore, all changes applied to the course went hand in hand with an adjustment of teaching and learning strategies.

When designing a programming course for pupils with handicaps in a first step these strategies as well as required tools have to be thoroughly identified. The resulting new course design allows students with a handicap such as impairment of sight to access the same courses and benefit from the same experiences as their fellow pupils. This paper will present the original course design followed by results from the expert design workshops in terms of technical and didactical adjustments to the course. Finally it will present first indications through feedback discussions on the achievements made in first courses.

2 Original Course Design: "Roborescue" and "Rattlesnake"

In the original robotics course design high school students are given the chance to get an insight in building and programming robots using LEGO Mindstorms sets in a school laboratory. The main focus of the course lies on the construction and programming of various robot models with LEGO Mindstorms construction kits. By using the graphical programming interface NXT-G, which is also suitable for non-professionals, students find an easy access into the world of programming [1].

In order to prepare and motivate students for a future career in robotics, they can try their hands at building, programming and testing robots in a highly interactive and playful environment. The course allows them to experience the fascination of robotics by letting the students create either a "rescue robot" [2] that can search for virtual victims in a simulated rescue mission or a "rattlesnake" that snaps shut when someone crosses its field of vision. The choice of the scenario is subject to the age of the students – lower grades build a rattlesnake which is easier to build and to program while junior and senior classes go on a more complex rescue mission. Within this storyline, the four main tasks of the course are embedded: an introduction giving basic theoretical information, the construction phase, the programming process as well as the reflection or evaluation phase. The underlying didactical course concept focuses on own experiences made as a basis for all implicit learning processes. These processes primarily run playfully, practically and experimentally [1].

The school laboratory where the courses take place, however, is not located at school – it has been set up at RWTH Aachen University. This allows high school students to take a peek into the daily routine at University and is meant to facilitate the decision making process when it comes to choosing further steps after graduating from high school [3].

3 Enabling Higher Accessibility for Visually Impaired Students

3.1 Expert Design Workshops

In order to facilitate the process of redesigning the robotics course and reach a higher accessibility, researchers from RWTH Aachen University invited a team of interdisciplinary experts. In a series of expert design workshops, the roadmap of the redesign was created. The main goal of these workshops was to identify the key aspects of required adjustments in order to reach a distinctively higher level of accessibility.

In the course of the workshops, the participants gradually developed a grid of these requirements. In a first step they divided the course into its individual phases based on the established approach by Vieritz et al. [10]. They used the different phases of the course and analyzed the requirements and necessary adjustments for each individual part compared to those of the original course design. These phases are the introductory part, the construction phase, the programming phase as well as the phase for reflection. Combining their different experiences and testing single elements by simulating specifying eye disfunctions, the experts came to results in terms of requirements for each phase. These results are being presented and discussed in the chapters below divided into technical as well as didactical adjustments. At the end of chapter three, the developed grid gives a summarized overview of the results from the workshops.

3.2 Technical Requirements

Due to continuous research and rapid technical advancement, today, being visually impaired does not automatically exclude one from working on and with e.g. smaller objects or computers. It does, however, bring about specific technical requirements which have to be considered when designing a robotics course. According to the results of the design workshops, the identified requirements especially include auxiliary means which can be summed up as objects, software and computer settings. There are a lot of different eye dysfunctions which call for support by different objects. In order to increase accessibility these objects are e.g. magnifiers and common magnifying glasses. Other important objects for the different phases of the course are cameras and reading devices, printed handouts for every phase, additional lighting for the building process and sorting boxes for robot components.

In terms of software, screen readers such as JAWS or Dolphin, graphic programming using e.g. NXT-G [1] as well as textual programming using e.g. JBrick [6, 7] should be provided in the programming phase. Finally, the computers provided should allow for adjustments of graphic contrast on computer screens. These adjustments should also be possible on the provided work tables. Nevertheless, there is no "universal remedy" for increasing accessibility. In preparation of the course the teaching staff should therefore always acquaint themselves with the participants in order to be prepared for any special requirements the students might have.

3.3 Didactical Adjustments

Not every measure taken is helpful for every sort of handicap and not all changes can be made at once. In the presented case a fundamental distinction between different degrees of visual impairment up to sightlessness has been essential groundwork for further research and course development. Most advancements and adjustments have to be made gradually in order to reach full accessibility. This has proven to be a very helpful approach in the process of designing the new course. Some degrees of visual impairment, for example, are even contrary to one another [5], so there is a need for different technical as well as didactical approaches in one course to reduce or extinguish existing barriers for all participating students.

As a first result and requirement, printed manuals should be provided for the first three phases, the introductory part, the construction as well as the programming phase. This allows students to reread instructions at their individual pace.

Time has also proven to be one of the main but often underestimated factor [4]. Visually impaired students need to be given more time to work on their tasks in terms of reading instructions, following presentations as well as building and programming. The more severe the impairment is, the more time will be needed to finish a task. In addition to that, additional time needs to be invested in giving detailed information regarding the content of e.g. manuals or presentations, repeating this content, reflecting processes, practicing as well as post-processing. Practitioners from the workshop have come to the subjective conclusion that the time necessary for a traditional course design should be at least multiplied by four after monitoring their own ability to work through the tasks of the class by wearing glasses that simulate an eye dysfunction. On an average it took them four times as long to finish the assigned tasks. Further research and evaluations of the course will have to prove whether that factor needs to be adjusted.

Another important adjustment relates to the teacher-student ratio. It has to be increased compared to traditional course designs which of course takes up additional time and resources on the teaching end. The required ratio can differ vastly as students have very diverse needs in terms of support. As we also know from Silva et al., even students without handicap perceive and process experiences in different preferred ways [9]. This has been confirmed also by the practitioners. Therefore, the supervisors need to provide a high level of flexibility regarding supervision and support throughout the course. Lastly the practitioners identified presorting the sorting boxes used in the construction phase as a helpful measure in the building process which does no longer exclude visually impaired students from the haptic and tangible experience of building a robot themselves.

Every course is highly influenced by diversity aspects and a thorough preparation and awareness of all possibilities and influences as well as a pre-analysis of the expected target group of each course proves to be the key to a successful course design. Table 1 sums up the results from the workshop in a grid.

Table 1. Results from the workshop: requirements for the new course design

Phase	Content	Original Course Design and equipment	Technical Requirements for a barrier free course	Didactical Requirements for a barrier free course
Introduction	Theoretical Input	Power Point Presentation	- Laptops with screen readers - Magnifying glasses	- Detailed explanations and descriptions of what the slide shows - Repetition of content - Simple slide design with high contrast - Printed Manuals
Construction	Building of the robot	Unsorted boxes	- Sorting boxes - Magnifying glasses - Reading Device - Graphic contrast on work tables	- Pre-sorting of components - Room for extra time and practice - Continuous supervision and support - Printed construction manuals
Programming	Programming of the robot	Laptops	- Contrast settings - Screenreader (JAWS/Dolphin) - Extra lighting - Printed Manual instead of beamer - On-screen magnifier - Graphic programming	- Continuous supervision and support - Room for extra time and practice - Printed programming manuals
Reflexion	Reflecting the Processes and Outcomes			Room for extra time

4 Conclusion and Outlook

The paper has described the process of redesigning of a robotics course from an educational robotics laboratory. The redesign was performed in order to increase accessibility of the course for visually impaired students. The evaluation of an expert workshop has brought about a concept for the redesign which has been implemented and is currently being tested in a second run with various groups of visually impaired students. The developed grid of the workshop suggests that smaller as well as bigger adjustments to the designated phases of the lecture can lead to a higher level of accessibility. First anecdotal but enthusiastic feedback from the students leads to the gentle assumption that the applied changes suggested by the experts were successful.

Nevertheless, a huge part of the adjustments needs to be individually taken considering the needs and requirements that the specific dysfunctions of the target group bring about. At this point of research, there is no "one-fits-all"-solution to the challenge. As a consecutive step, evaluations of the designed courses will allow for a thorough analysis and serve the pursuit of continuous improvement. Additionally, it will be the key to future research. In order to broaden the range of accessibility, further research will have to focus on full accessibility also for blind students as well as other impairments such as hearing and e.g. physical disabilities.

References

1. Hansen, A., Hees, F., Jeschke, S.: Hands on robotics. Concept of a student laboratory on the basis of an experience-oriented learning model. In: Proceedings of the International Conference on Education and New Learning Technologies, EDULEARN 2010, 5–7 July 2010, IATED, pp. 6047–6057. Barcelona (2010)
2. Jeschke, S., et al.: A rescue robotics PBL course. In: Proceedings of the ISCA 25th International Conference on Computers and their Applications (CATA), 24–26 Mar 2010, pp. 63–68. USA (2010)
3. Jeschke, S., et al.: What's it like to be an Engineer? Robotics in Academic Engineering Education. In: Proceedings of the Canadian Conference on Electrical and Computer Engineering (CCECE), 4–7 May 2008, pp. 941–946. Niagara Falls (2008)
4. Kabátová, M., et al.: Robotic activities for visually impaired secondary school children. In: Proceedings of 3rd International Workshop Teaching Robotics, Teaching with Robotics Integrating Robotics in School Curriculum, pp. 22–31 (2012)
5. Ludi, S., Reichlmayr, T.: Developing inclusive outreach activities for students with visual impairments. In: Proceedings of the 39th SIGCSE Technical Symposium on Computer Science Education 2008, pp. 439–443. USA (2008)
6. Ludi, S., Reichlmayr, T.: The use of robotics to promote computing to pre-college students with visual impairments. ACM Trans. Comput. Educ. **11**, 20 (2011)
7. Ludi, S., et al.: JBrick: accessible lego mindstorm programming tool for users who are visually impaired
8. Reuter Sebastian, et al.: Robotic Education in the DLR_SCHOOL_LAB RWTH AACHEN. In: Proceedings of the International Technology, Education and Development Conference INTED 2015, in Process (2015)
9. Silva, D., et al.: Transforming diverse learners through a brain-based 4MAT cycle of learning. In: Proceedings of the World Congress on Engineering and Computer Science 2011, vol 1, WCECS 2011, October 19–21. San Francisco (2011)
10. Vieritz, H., Schilberg, D., Jeschke, S.: Early accessibility evaluation in web application development. In: Stephanidis, C., Antona, M. (eds.) UAHCI 2013, Part II. LNCS, vol. 8010, pp. 726–733. Springer, Heidelberg (2013)

Visual Approach of a Mobile Application for Autistic Children: Little Routine

Wan Fatimah Wan Ahmad(✉) and Iman Nur Nabila Azahari

Computer and Information Sciences Department,
Universiti Teknologi PETRONAS, 31750
Tronoh, Perak Darul Ridzuan, Malaysia
fatimhd@petronas.com.my, nabilaazahari@gmail.com

Abstract. With the rise of mobile technology, visual approach can be implemented in mobile applications in order to help Autistic children. Nonetheless, those mobile applications that does not entirely uses actual pictures in their visual approach method that helps these children with their core drawback, which is the lack of independence. Therefore, this paper aims to present a visual approach of a mobile application, Little Routine, to assist autistic children. Requirement gathering is conducted through literature review of research papers, interviews and observations. At the same time, the methodology is based on rapid application development (RAD). Little Routine has been developed based on the requirements from the experts and literature. The tool used to develop the prototype is App Inventor and Android Software Development Kit. Later, usability test was conducted with a specialist, teachers and children to examine the effectiveness of the mobile application. The results showed that the respondents were satisfied with the mobile application. It is hoped that the application will assist autistic children in their daily routine.

Keywords: Mobile application · Autistic · User testing · Visual approach

1 Introduction

Mobile application is rising as a common trend in world's development. People's productivity can be increased with the aid of smart phones and tablets, as it is easy to use. Therefore, using mobile application, many developers create apps that give benefits and assist people every day. This can also be a platform to aid disabled group such as autistic children. Autism is a developmental disability that happens in the first three years when a child is born. It is known as a neurological disorder that influences the growth of the brain, resulting in struggles with learning, communication, and social interaction [1]. Nonetheless, visual are their area of strength.

Hence, this project aims to present a prototype through visual approach for educating autistic children. The prototype is an interactive application that teaches the children based on their daily surroundings. This mobile app will act as a tool for autistic children to enhance their independence skills. This will improve other major drawbacks as well like communication and social skills.

C. Stephanidis (Ed.): HCII 2015 Posters, Part II, CCIS 529, pp. 436–442, 2015.
DOI: 10.1007/978-3-319-21383-5_73

2 Literature Review

2.1 Technology and Education

Understanding towards technology has been growing for the past decades. People are more driven to use technology everyday which enable to increase their efficiency. Thus, technology has now come up to assist other sectors, including education sector.

Additionally, mobile technology has penetrate the education market, as well as making disabled student's lives simpler. For an autistic child, it is essential to keep them interested in learning, as they are easily distracted. Therefore, with the aid of mobile technology devices like iPad or tablets, they can be more focused and motivated to learn. Most autistic kids respond well to the visual display that tablet offers and even though sometimes technology is inconvenient, with tablet, it is definitely easier for kids with autism than without it [2].

2.2 Understanding Autism and Autism Spectrum Disorders

Autism Spectrum Disorders (ASD) are a group of disorders with complex neurological growth and major characters, which include social and communication limitation, sensory impairments and repetitive stereotype behaviour [1]. ASD is not an uncommon sickness; it affects approximately 1 in every 165 persons [3]. It is also known as a life-long disorder with no exact cure. However, with fast intervention and excellent educational practices, the disorder may see a rapid improvements.

Autistic children face countless obstacles daily; however, their complications in socializing are most challenging [4, 5]. Social interaction difficulties include trouble in peer interaction, drawback in using and understanding non-verbal communication, and restricted imitation of other's actions and sounds [6]. Effective social skills are crucial to build successful interactions in home and society [9]. Nonetheless, this particular project aims to develop the independent skill of autistic children.

Developing the skills of autistic children is quite a challenge as each of them has different symptoms and unique in their own ways. Thus, the major areas of education that must be concentrated are communication, social, and independence. Communication is highly important to sustain one's life. However, most autistic children are having difficulties in languages skill, whereby it is hard for them to digest what others are saying [7]. By enhancing language, it can aid in developing socialization and interactions of autistic children with other people [8].

2.3 Learning Theories and Approach

There are various approaches and treatments, which include Applied Behaviour Analysis (ABA), Social Communication, Emotional Regulation and Transactional Support (SCERTS) and Visual Approach [10]. ABA is the strategy, application, and assessment of environmental adaptations to produce socially meaningful enhancement in human behaviour [11]. ABA approach comprises the practice of direct observation and evaluation. However, SCERTS encourages a broad educational approach that provides an opportunity and sequence of progressive goals by concentrating on significant, realistic progress within daily routines at school, home, and in the society [12]. Visual Approach uses pictures or other visual items to communicate with autistic children as they are visually oriented [13]. Autistic children go through their daily routine by visual supports. It eases them to recall what happens afterward. Most applicable visual items used are by using actual pictures. Actual pictures helps the children to understand better and able to relate with their surroundings. Visual approach has been implemented in many mobile applications however, those apps do not entirely uses actual pictures in their method.

2.4 Previous Related Works

There are several development of mobile application for autism that have been done over the past few years. However, these works have minor setbacks in assisting autistic children.

The Choiceworks app is a learning tool for assisting children to accomplish their daily routines (morning, day and night). This app is aimed for caregivers to offer clear and reliable support to child's independence, and emotional directive either at home or in public [14]. Still, some setbacks the interface include too crowded with many elements and symbols, which can be confused.

Proloquo2go is another communication application designed for autistic children. The idea is an alternative communication solution for children, to help them by constructing sentences using symbols, which will enhance their communication skills [15]. However, this particular app only focuses on communication and lack routine assessments that can improve their independent skills.

3 Little Routine

The developed mobile application is called "Little Routine". The main idea of Little Routine is to teach and assist children with autism to recognize and learn daily activities, as well as routine in various places at home, such as in bathroom, living room, kitchen and bedroom by adopting visual approach. It uses pictures and video to communicate with autistic children as they are visually oriented as supported by [13]. The tool used to develop the prototype is App Inventor and Android Software Development Kit. Figure 1 shows the flow of the prototype app that comprises routine activities. Figure 2 displays the main page of the app, which shows a picture of a house. The app interface has minimal elements with sound effects and the app applies colourful actual pictures. Figure 3 shows the routine selection page, whereby children can choose which routine location they want to perform. There are four options, which are bathroom, kitchen, living room and bedroom.

Figure 4 displays one of the routine examples, which is the bathroom routine. The interface is simple and easy to understand for the children. They have to click on the picture of which routine they want to learn whether it is the bathtub, toilet, sink, and toothbrush. Each of the picture will then be directed to a video. Figure 5 displays the

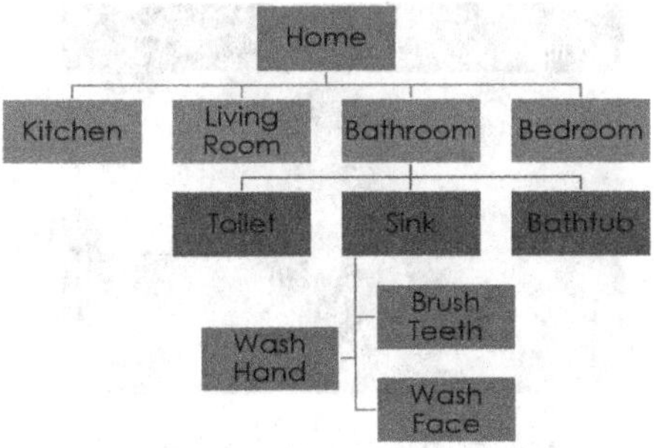

Fig. 1. Flow of prototype

Fig. 2. Main page home

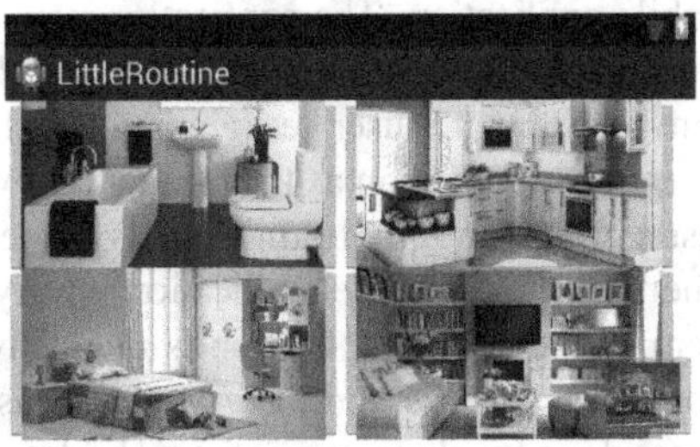

Fig. 3. Routine selection page

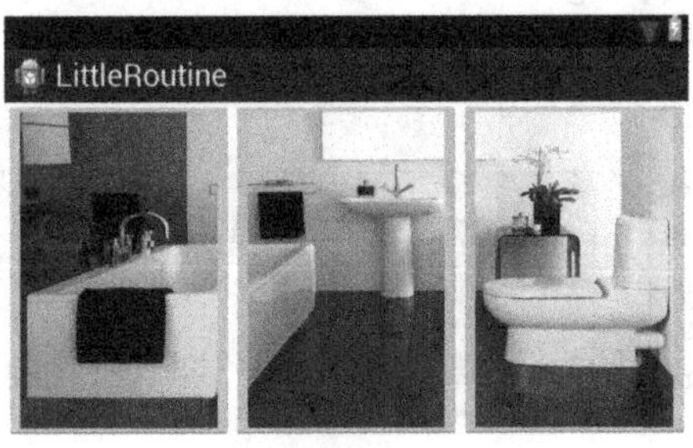

Fig. 4. Bathroom routine recognition

Fig. 5. Routine training video

next phase of the routine, which is the routine training page. This page shows an easy way to perform child's everyday routine through an interactive video display.

4 User Testing

User testing has been conducted with a total of 10 participants. It has been divided into 3 categories that is one specialist, 4 teachers and 5 students. The details of the testing and results are discussed below.

User testing done with the specialist was the first cutover phase. The specialist had observed the design of the prototype. The comments include: The application should focus to overcome one specific setback of the child; use few animated pictures and symbols; simple interface design. As a result, this project managed to come up with a second version of the mobile application. The application now focuses on developing the child's independent skills and only uses actual pictures with a simpler interface.

Four teachers were involved in the user testing process. It is believed that it is important for teachers to test the application as they know best what the children need. Figure 6 displays the result from the user testing involving teachers. From the user testing, 80 % of the teachers claimed that the application is very helpful to be used by the students. 60 % of them said that the application is interactive. Furthermore, 80 % agreed that the application is easy to use and they would all use it again.

Another user testing was done by observing autistic children to further comprehend the effectiveness of the application prototype. Since the target group of this application is limited, only 5 students were involved in the user testing process. Figure 7 displays the result from the user testing. Since the children are unable to respond verbally, the testing was done by observing their facial expressions. It was found that 4 of the

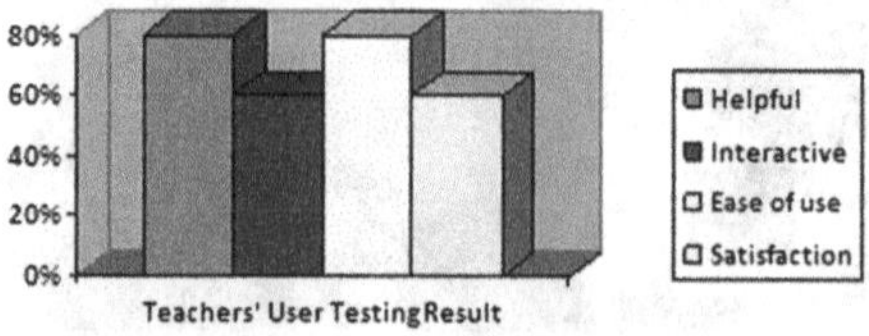

Fig. 6. Teachers' user testing result

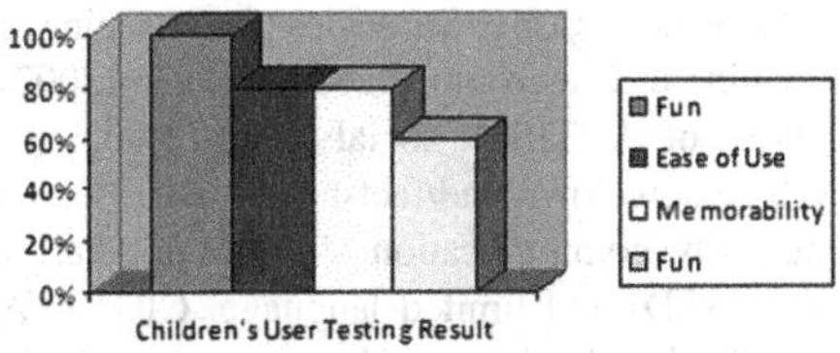

Fig. 7. Children's user testing result

students played with the application continuously. However, 2 of them did not understand the video shown in the application. Unfortunately, 1 of them did not follow or imitate the routine shown. Overall, the results are supported by the claim by [8] that using toys, objects, and routines will attract the child to communicate.

5 Conclusion

The paper discussed a mobile application prototype based on visual approach to educate autistic children. Thus, a prototype named 'Little Routine' has been developed. Little Routine is a mobile application targeted to attract and motivate autistic children to learn daily routine skills, as well as to enhance their independent skills. Based on the user testing, it is found that most of the teachers are very interested with the application. They also believed that the application is definitely helpful to aid autistic children as the 80 % responded well during the user testing. This mobile application strives to support and assist autistic children in enhancing their daily activities, especially in their independent skills, which subsequently gives an impact on their communication and social abilities.

The next recommendation is to add more routines in the application which allow them to learn and explore more knowledge by themselves. The next phase of Little Routine will include routines at school, playground and other places.

Acknowledgment. The authors would like to thank Universiti Teknologi PETRONAS and others who have been involved directly or indirectly in this research.

References

1. Virginia Department of Education. Foundational Competencies. Guidelines for Educating Students with Autism Spectrum Disorders, pp. 6–12 (2010)
2. Agency for Healthcare Research and Quality "AHRQ". Therapies for children with autism spectrum disorders. A Review of the Research for Parents and Caregivers (2010)
3. Notbohm, E.: Ten things every child with autism wishes you knew (2013). www.autismspeaks.org/sites/default/files/images/10_things.pdf. Accessed 10 Feb 2014
4. Alberta Learning. Chapter 2: characteristics associated with autism spectrum disorders. Teaching students with autism spectrum disorders, pp. 9–19 (2003)

5. Millar, M., Scott, D., McSorley, O.H.: Strategies for teaching communication. Autism Spectrum Disorders: A Guide to Classroom Practice, 21–26 (2002)
6. Brereton, A.: Core features of AUTISM: social skills (2011). www.med.monash.edu.au/spppm/research/devpsych/actnow/download/factsheet05.pdf. Accessed 14 Feb 2014
7. Lewis, M.:. Developing early communication skills in toddlers & young children with autism spectrum disorder (ASD) and limited language. CIGNA Autism Education Series (2011). http://www.yai.org/getinvolved/events/downloads/developing-early.pdf
8. Poliakova, N., Palkhivala, A.: Social impairment in children with autism spectrum disorder (2008). www.ccl-cca.ca/pdfs/ECLKC/other/AutismAbilitiesSpring2008.pdf
9. NIDCD Communication Problem in Children with Autism (2010). www.nidcd.nih.gov/staticresources/health/voice/NIDCD-Communication-Problems-in-Children-with-Autism-FS.pdf. Accessed 22 Feb 2014
10. Stone, W., Ruble, L., Coonrad, E., Hepburn, S., Pennington, M., Burnette, C., Brigham, N.B.: TRIAD social skills assessment. Assessing Children with Autism Spectrum Disorder, pp. 2–11 (2010)
11. Najdowski, A.C.: Using ABA for the treatment of Autism: the CARD program (2010). http://www.autismoaruba.org/wp-content/uploads/Dr.-Adel-Nadjowski-%E2%80%93-CARD-PROGRAM.pdf
12. British Columbia. Characteristics Associated with Autism. Teaching Students with Autism: A Resource Guide for Schools, pp. 9–27 (2000)
13. Loring, W., Hamilton, M.: Visual supports & autism spectrum disorders (2011). http://kc.vanderbilt.edu/kennedy_files/VisualSupports-March2011.pdf. Accessed 15 Feb 2014
14. About Choiceworks App (2007). http://www.beevisual.com. Accessed 20 Feb 2014
15. Who is Proloquo2Go for? A voice for those who cannot speak: Proloquo2Go (2013). http://www.assistiveware.com/product/proloquo2go. Accessed 1 April 2014

Development of a Game that Visually-Impaired People Can Actively Enjoy

Sadahide Yoshida and Kyoko Yoshida(✉)

School of Network and Information, Senshu University, Tokyo, Japan
{ne230116, k-yoshida}@isc.senshu-u.ac.jp

Abstract. Recreational activities have an effect of improving the quality of life, but the recreational activities that visually-impaired people can enjoy are quite limited. "Passive" recreational activities that one can enjoy by reading, watching, or hearing (in particular those that visually-impaired people can enjoy) have increased through the development of synthesized voices. However, there are still only a few recreational activities such as sports and games that they can proactively participate in and enjoy. Videogames are one of such "active" recreational activities popular among visually-impaired people, however, interviews revealed that it requires a huge amount of effort for them to enjoy videogames. In the present study we developed a game that visually-impaired people could also actively enjoy.

Keywords: Dance game · Visually-impaired people · Kinect

1 Introduction

Recreational activities can reduce various stresses caused in our daily life, serving as an enhancer of QOL (Quality of Life). However, most types of recreational activities such as watching TV, movies, or plays, enjoying sports, reading books, and playing games require eyesight. Therefore, visually-impaired people can only enjoy limited types of recreational activities. The number of passive types of recreational activities that visually-impaired people can enjoy with content encompassing reading, watching, or listening has been increasing. However, there are still few active types of recreational activities such as sports, computer games, and board games that they can voluntarily participate in, analyze, and enjoy.

In this study, we developed a game that visually-impaired people could enjoy with the following aims: "The game shall not rely on the player's vision," "the game shall be enjoyable to both sighted and visually-impaired people," "the game shall not require complicated explanations on how to play," and "the game shall motivate players to continue to play it".

C. Stephanidis (Ed.): HCII 2015 Posters, Part II, CCIS 529, pp. 443–447, 2015.
DOI: 10.1007/978-3-319-21383-5_74

2 Background

In Japan, playing videogames is a form of recreation familiar to visually-impaired people. The Pokémon game and "Taiko no Tatsujin" game are particularly popular [1, 2]. Also, fighting games are popular among serious visually-impaired "gamers" [3, 4]. Interviews with visually-impaired people indicated that they needed to memorize many things and devise their own ways of playing the games in order for them to enjoy them. In contrast, a survey result showed that most visually-impaired people were eager to play sports [5].

These games are popular because players can understand the situation by sound. In Pokémon, for example, the voices made by the characters, the sound effects of actions, and the sound effects of striking an obstacle change depending on the power gauge of the characters. Visually-impaired people enjoy the game by making an effort to memorize these sounds and creating a map in their brain by virtually walking all over the game world. They can also enjoy other games since the games contain a lot of sound information that can compensate for visual information. Of course, a great deal of work is necessary for them to enjoy the games just like sighted people.

In foreign countries, there are game-specific forums for visually-impaired people [6]. The games for visually-impaired people in these forums are mostly adventure games, arcade games, and board games, with only a few action games, sports games, and racing games (Fig. 1). Namely there are many games that allow players to enjoy the game stories and/or require them to take time analyzing, along with a few games that require the players' quick response. However, the fact that sports and fighting games are popular indicates that visually-impaired people would want to play action games and sports games. In this study we developed a dance game that people can play by actually moving their bodies.

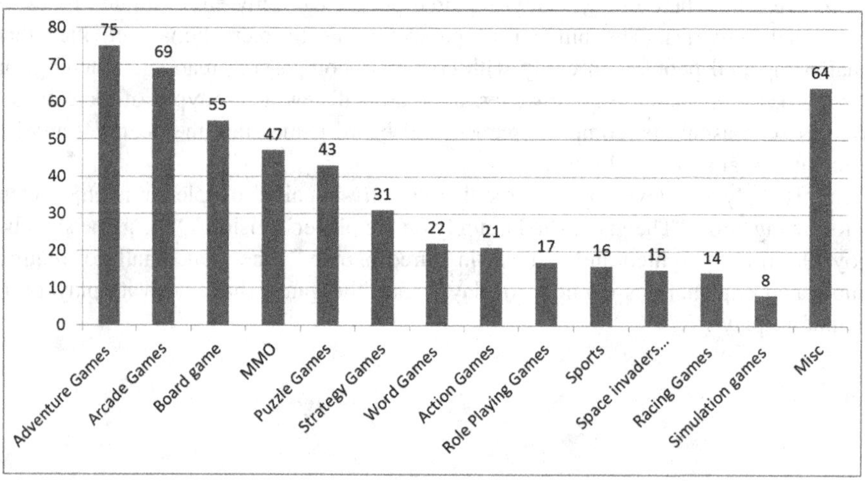

Fig. 1. The number of audiogames

3 Overview

In this study we developed a dance game that people can actively enjoy. The game is used in the following manner.

1. Music for dancing is registered.
2. A tutor dances as a model to record model data.
3. A player learns the dance according to the model data.
4. After learning the dance, the player actually dances and is rated on how accurately he/she dances.

If the player is not satisfied with the score, he/she can return to Step 3, learn the dance again, and try the game in Step 4 again. By doing this repeatedly, the player can pursue the improvement of his/her dancing.

Our developed dance game consists of two systems: Acquiring model data system, and dance scoring system. The present game incorporated the system of acquiring model data and the dance scoring system. Kinect was used to capture the player's body motion. The player plays the game by dancing to music in front of Kinect. A space of 1.8 m × 1.8 m would be necessary for Kinect to capture the entire body of the player (Fig. 2).

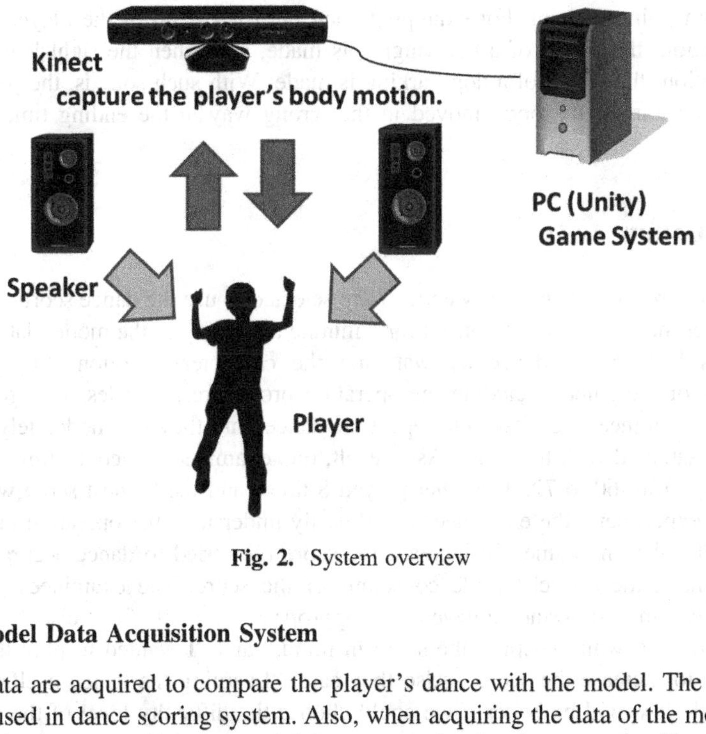

Fig. 2. System overview

3.1 Model Data Acquisition System

Model data are acquired to compare the player's dance with the model. The acquired data are used in dance scoring system. Also, when acquiring the data of the model, one can specify breaks at which the model dance stops for the choreography. For example, when a player makes a downward swinging motion of his/her arm, the start time of the motion when the player raises their arm up and the ending time when the player finishes swinging it down are recorded and the system recognizes the motion from the start time to the ending time as a single motion. The start and ending times of the motion are saved in a text file in the form of flags and time stamps.

3.2 Dance Scoring System

This system scores the dance that the player learned. It compares the player's dance with the model and informs the player if the difference is large. The score is based on how accurately the player could follow the dance model.

For rating, the three dimensional coordinates of five points of the player's body are compared with those of the model data. If the player's body coordinates deviate from the model by an amount larger than, for example, one third of the length from the player's elbow to the wrist, the system determines the deviation of the motion.

The motion measurement is performed three times a second. For example, for 3-min. music, the dance is compared with a model 540 times (180 [sec] × 3 [times] = 540) and the number of deviating motions from the model is counted to reduce the score. If 54 motions are judged as deviating, 90 % of the motions of the player were correct and thus the score is 90.

A sound is created to indicate which of the five points deviated most. The sound differs from point to point. For example, when the right hand of the player makes a wrong motion, the sound of a bell ringing is made, and when the right leg makes a wrong motion, the sound of a dog barking is made. With such sounds, the player can know which part of the body moved in the wrong way at the ending time of each motion.

4 Evaluation

Two sighted examinees in their twenties were selected to use the dance scoring system. In the experiment, a character danced for a minute according to the model data and the examinees learned the dance by watching the character's motion (Fig. 3). The instruction of the game, including the operation procedure and rules, was given verbally. The examinees were asked to repeat the dance until they felt moderately tired or they were satisfied with the score. As a result, one examinee played 11 times and the scores were from 60 to 72. The other played 8 times and the highest score was 92.

In the experiment, the examinees could easily understand the operation procedure and rules to play the game. To increase the score they tried to dance accurately and repeated the game actively while conscious of the score. The examinees gave the following comments: "Dancing gave me an appropriate amount of exercise," "I tried to dance accurately while keeping the score in mind," and "I wanted to play the game repeatedly to increase the score". Also they said, "Learning the dance itself was difficult". and "It would be better if we could choose the difficulty level of the dance".

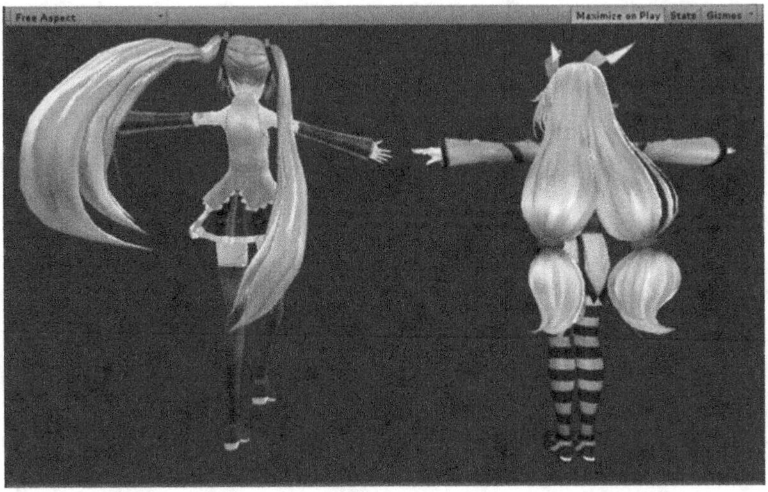

Fig. 3 Screenshot of the character's dancing motion

5 Conclusions

A future work will be to incorporate the tutorial system so that a player who does not know a dance motion can learn it by himself/herself. The future work will also include making all the systems verbally-controllable without eyesight. Also, not only the motion of hands and feet but also other body parts need to be measured for more accurate dance evaluation by adding more coordinate measurement points, such as fingertips and head, to the five points for which the coordinates are measured

References

1. Pokemon. http://www.pokemon.com/us/
2. Taiko no Tatsujin. http://taiko.namco-ch.net/taiko/
3. Street Fighter V. http://www.streetfighter.com/us/sfv
4. SOULCALIBUR V. http://soulcalibur.com/
5. The investigation report regarding exercise and sports for the National visually impaired rehabilitation assistance facility graduates
6. http://www.rehab.go.jp/achievements/japanese/19th/paper20.html
7. AudioGames.net. http://www.audiogames.net/

Fitness and Well-Being Applications

Investigating the Role of Haptic Stimulation in Mobile Meditation Tools

Antoinette Leanna Bumatay(✉) and Jinsil Hwaryoung Seo

College Station, Texas A and M University, College Station, TX, USA
{aleannab, hwaryoung}@tamu.edu

Abstract. Previous studies have shown that mindfulness meditation and paced breathing are effective tools for stress management. There are a number of mobile applications currently available that are designed to guide the breath to support mindfulness meditation and paced breathing practices. However, these focus mainly on audio/visual cues and are mostly non-interactive. Our goal is to develop a mobile meditation tool focusing on haptic cues. To investigate the effectiveness of the system, we conducted user studies. This study explores the following questions: How effective is haptic guidance on its own? And how may the addition of haptic feedback enhance audio based guidance? Preliminary analysis support the value of haptic guidance in mobile meditation tools.

Keywords: Meditation · Technology · Haptic device

1 Introduction

Stress is physical response that affects us all in varying degrees throughout our lifetime. Throughout history, people have developed various practices to cope with stress. Many of these focus on bringing awareness to the body and breath. Previous studies have supported that mindfulness meditation and paced breathing are effective tools for stress management [1]. Within the past year there have been huge strides in development and commercial interest regarding health and fitness portable tools [2]. There are a number of commercial mobile apps currently available designed to guide the breath to support mindfulness meditation and paced breathing practices; however, these focus mainly on audio and visual cues and are non-interactive. Overall, there has been limited research done towards integrating meditation with technology, especially in the realm of haptic use and interactivity in portable meditation tools. This study will focus on how effective haptic rhythm guidance is in comparison with different modalities (audio and audio-haptic).

2 Related Work

2.1 Traditional Methods of Relaxation

As stress is undeniably universal, there have been many techniques and practices previously developed to assist in stress management and the promotion of relaxation.

C. Stephanidis (Ed.): HCII 2015 Posters, Part II, CCIS 529, pp. 451–456, 2015.
DOI: 10.1007/978-3-319-21383-5_75

The breath is one of our primary contacts with our parasympathetic nervous system. Often during bouts of stress or panic attacks, our sympathetic nervous system activates "fight or flight" mode. Breathing is the only component of the autonomic nervous system that can be controlled consciously. Control of the breath stimulates the parasympathetic nervous system, triggering a relaxation response [3]. Paced breathing has been shown to be a valid tool in managing stress and anxiety [1].

The relationship of the body to its environment can be obtained through bringing awareness to the senses. Although, tactile exploration is underexplored in this particular area, there is evidence of the sense of touch being incorporated in traditional relaxation practices. Touch is an extremely personal and intimate sense. It is used to create a personal space, only experienced to those directly exposed to the action. The use of therapeutic touch is often used to help people relax [4]. Similarly, the tactile sense has also been incorporated in meditation through the physical manipulation of objects with the hands, such as the creation of a zen garden or the handling of baoding balls and prayer beads [5].

2.2 Technology Driven Methods of Relaxation

Recently, there has been a shift in focus in technology to fitness and health related devices. In this age of technology and innovation, there exists a lot of opportunity to supplement existing practices. Breathe with the Ocean, explored various systems featuring an environment with audio (ocean wave sounds), haptic (touch blanket), and visual (light) stimuli. It was noted that most users found the synchronization between the wave-like patterns from the haptic blanket and the audio waves pleasing [6]. Another project, the Heartbeat Sphere featured a spherical object designed to assess and reflect a person's heart rate through soft pulsing vibrations and colorful lights. This is intended to invite the user to be mindful of her heartbeat [7]. There are also numerous commercial mobile phone applications available on the market that offer meditation or paced breathing guidance. Audio utilized ranges from guided meditation voice narrative to natural sounds (e.g. water, birds) to percussive sounds (e.g. bell chimes, gongs, meditation bowls). Visual guidance often appears in the form of meters filling and emptying, objects expanding and contracting, or animated graphs. Few offer haptic components, and those that do have abrupt pulses that feel jarring. You Can't Force Calm [8] was an exploratory study that designed and evaluated techniques to support respiratory regulation to reduce stress and increase parasympathetic tone. It incorporated breath sensor input and visual and audio feedback. Evidence from this study supported that auditory guidance was more effective than visual at creating self-reported calm. It would be interesting to further this exploration of mobile tools into the physical and subjective effects of haptic stimulation.

3 Case Study

We investigated how haptic modality in a mobile meditation system affects a user's relaxation experience. We conducted user studies comparing different modalities implemented in a mobile device.

3.1 System Design

We developed a mobile phone application in Android Studio. The application has the ability to produce haptic, audio, or audio-haptic outputs to act as a breathing guide for the user. The application has manual and biofeedback interaction mode. Biofeedback mode utilizes an external sensor, the Zephyr BioHarness 3, in order to determine the user's current breathing rate. The breathing guide is initially set to match the user's rate, slowly increasing the interval to decrease the user's breathing rate. The program continuously monitors the user's ability to match the guide and adjusts the breathing interval accordingly. Manual mode allows the user to manipulate the breathing interval in real time with a slider. Figure 1 contains a diagram of the overall system and a visual description of the various breathing guide modalities. A pillow was used to encase the mobile phone, helping to soften and amplify vibrations. This also allowed the user to relax with their hands wrapped around the pillow (Fig. 2).

3.2 User Study

We obtained 21 undergraduate and graduate university students for our user study. The study lasted three days for each participant. Users were separated into three different modality groups (haptic only, audio only, and combination audio-haptic) based on a pre-filter questionnaire. Groups contained 6 to 7 participants each. Each participant was able to control the system manually and interactively through a biofeedback sensor. In this paper, we analyzed only manual sessions. Both quantitative and qualitative data are used for analysis. Quantitative data included the following: breathing rate, heart rate variance, user preference (choice on Day 3), and the short stress surveys (before and after each sit). Qualitative data was gathered by a general feedback on-site interview at the end of each session. The recorded interview data was coded and analyzed focusing on "key theme" arising from the participants' experiences.

4 Results

The stress survey contained an analog scale that read very tense to very relaxed. Participants marked their current relaxation state on the scale before and after each meditation sit. The participant's mark was converted to a real number on a scale of 0 (very tense) to 10 (very relaxed). We calculated the user's subjective change in relaxation by the difference of the converted values. Overall, each group experienced an increase in relaxation state (Fig. 2b). The haptic group obtained the greatest average

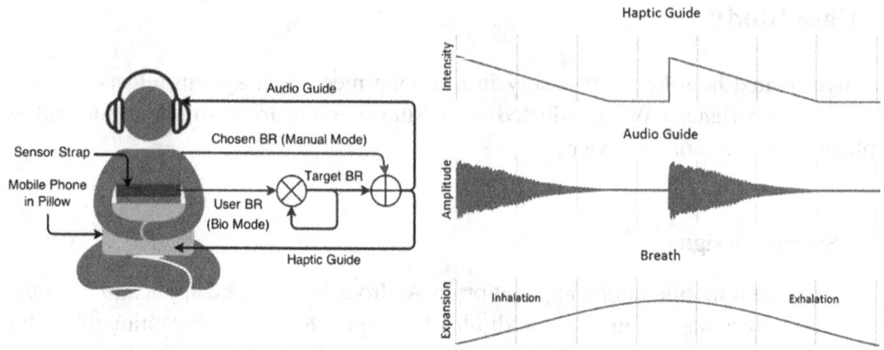

Fig. 1. (a) System diagram with interaction modes: manual and biofeedback. BR: Breathing Rate. (b) The haptic guide describes the intensity of the phone's vibration. The audio guide describes the amplitude of the gong chimes. The vibration pulse and/or gong chime marks the beginning of the inhalation/exhalation.

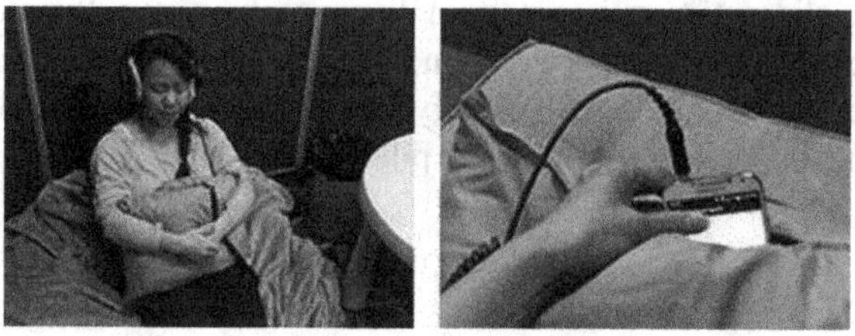

Fig. 2. (a) Participant using device. (b) Participant inserting phone into pillow pocket.

change in relaxation at a value of 4.4. The audio and audio-haptic group had average changes in relaxation with values of 4.1 and 3.4 respectively.

The stress survey also contained 5-point Likert scale items of various adjectives adopted from the Stress Arousal Checklist [9]. Stress adjectives were given a positive or negative ranking, and summed together, to quantify the user's current stress level. We calculated the user's change in stress by finding the difference before and after each meditation sit and mapped to a scale from 0 (no change) to 10 (greatest possible change). Overall, participants did experience an increase in objective relaxation, as inferred from a decrease in quantitative stress (Fig. 2a). Again, the haptic group felt the greatest decrease in quantitative stress after using the application with an average value of 2.9. The audio group followed behind with a value of 2.0. The audio-haptic group experienced the least amount of quantitative stress relief with a value of 1.6.

Difficulty of the session (Fig. 3c) indicates the observed level of difficulty the user had in following the breathing guide. Each session was described using the following adjectives: gradual, flat, and bumpy (Fig. 4). A gradual section is characterized by a steady decrease in average BR. A flat section is characterized by a stable value of average BR. A bumpy section is characterized by an unstable BR. This value was calculated by determining the fraction of time the user's breathing pattern was bumpy

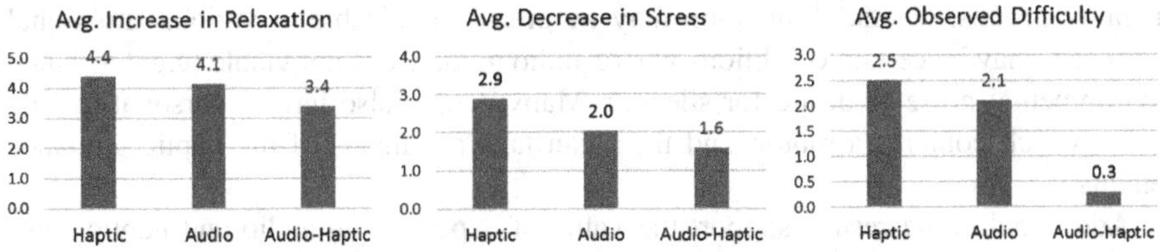

Fig. 3. Average change in (a) subjective relaxation and (b) objective stress, and (c) observed difficulty for each of the modality groups.

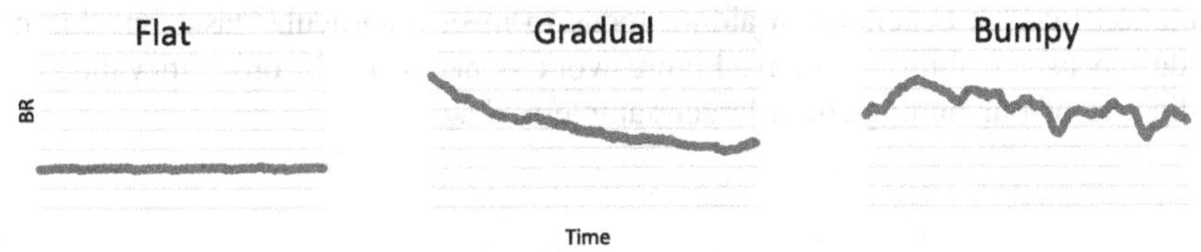

Fig. 4. Graph descriptions of breathing rate (BR) over the session duration: (a) flat, (b) gradual, and (c) bumpy.

during the session. It was then converted on a scale from 0 (completely smooth) to 10 (completely bumpy). Out of the three guidance feedback systems, the audio-haptic guide was significantly the easiest to follow. The average difficulty participants had following the audio-haptic guidance was 0.3 session versus 2.5 and 2.1 for the haptic group and audio group respectively.

To iterate, each user only experienced one type of modality for the duration of the study. However, a few users made comments directly addressing the haptic feedback they experienced. Three users commented that the vibration pulses from the pillow reminded them of a heartbeat or a cat purring. Participant A liked the subtleness of the effect, commenting, "*Normally when I try to meditate on my own I get severely distracted... But I liked how the vibrations made you aware that you were doing something. But you weren't really aware of it*". One user initially found the vibration pulses unpleasant as they were reminiscent of a phone ringing. However, by the end of the session, he was able to remove that negative association. Two people commented how they liked how the sounds and the vibrations worked together. Participant H reflected, "*I actually found the gong noise a lot more relaxing... for some reason I realized this is actually a good noise. I like this... And I felt that... had the vibrations not been there I don't know if it would have the same effect*". Overall, users tended to enjoy the addition of the haptic stimulation.

5 Discussion

Our preliminary analysis suggests the effectiveness of haptic stimulation on its own in mobile meditation tools. On average, participants in the haptic group experienced the greatest increase in subjective relaxation and decrease in objective stress of all three modality groups. Haptic stimulation may be greatly applicable to various situational use. There may be certain conditions where audio guidance is not viable (e.g. too much environmental noise or desire for silence). Many people also have a personal mobile device which contains a motor, and thus, can take advantage of the haptic guidance benefits.

Additionally, the results support the value of experiencing audio and haptic stimulation simultaneously. The participants in the audio-haptic group followed the breathing guide with more ease on average compared to participants experiencing only one type of feedback. However, our results suggest that the ease of following the guide did not necessarily lead to a greater feeling of relaxation. Multimodal audio-haptic stimulation may be beneficial in aiding focus to meet a particular task, but this may impede the user's ability to relax. Future work is necessary in order to validate the significance of our findings on a larger sample scale.

References

1. Brown, R.P.: Sudarshan kriya yogic breathing in the treatment of stress, anxiety, and depression: part ii-clinical applications and guidelines. J. Altern. Complement. Med. **11**(4), 711–717 (2005)
2. Pitstick, B.: RESEARCH PAPER: CES 2014 Wearable & Fitness Tech Trends- Going Mainstream | Moor Insights & Strategy. Moor Insights and Strategy (2015).http://www.moorinsightsstrategy.com/research-paper-ces-2014-wearablefitness-tech-trends-going-mainstream/. Accessed 30 January 2015
3. Seaward, B.: Managing Stress: Principles and Strategies for Health and Well-Being - BOOK ALONE. Jones & Bartlett Publishers, Sudbury (2008)
4. Gagne, D., Toye, R.C.: The effects of therapeutic touch and relaxation therapy in reducing anxiety. Arch. Psychiatr. Nurs. **8**(3), 184–189 (1994)
5. Wernik, U.: The use of prayer beads in psychotherapy. Mental Health Relig. Culture **12**(4), 359–368 (2009)
6. Dijk, E.O., Weffers-Albu, A.: Breathe with the ocean: a system for relaxation using audio. In: Haptic and Visual Stimuli, Special Symposium at EuroHaptics 2010, Haptic and Audio-Visual Stimuli: Enhancing Experiences and Interaction, pp. 47–60 (2010)
7. Thieme, A., Wallace, J., Johnson, P., Lindley, S., McCarthy, J., Olivier, P., Meyer, T.D.: Can we introduce mindfulness practice through digital design. In: Proceedings of BCS HCI (2012)
8. Wongsuphasawat, K., Gamburg, A., Moraveji, N: You can't force calm: designing and evaluating respiratory regulating interfaces for calming technology. In: Adjunct proceedings of the 25th annual ACM symposium on User interface software and technology, pp. 69–70. ACM, October 2012
9. King, M.G., Burrows, G.D., Stanley, G.V.: Measurement of stress and arousal: validation of the stress/arousal adjective checklist. Br. J. Psychol. **74**(4), 473–479 (1983)

A Usability Evaluation of Fitness-Tracking Apps for Initial Users

Ana Carolina Tomé Klock and Isabela Gasparini(✉)

Graduate Program in Applied Computing (PPGCA),
Department of Computer Science, Santa Catarina State University (UDESC),
Joinville, Santa Catarina, Brazil
actklock@gmail.com, isabela.gasparini@udesc.br

Abstract. Nowadays, there are many different mobile apps designed to help people start and continue practicing physical activities. This paper aims to analyze the usability of the most used apps for walk through inspection methods, focusing especially on the core tasks available. This paper presents the problems found and the comparison between the five analyzed apps. Through the results, the goal of this study is identifying the usability problems to help improving user interaction with physical activity monitoring apps.

Keywords: Usability evaluation · Inspection method · Heuristic evaluation · Ergonomic criteria · Fitness-tracking apps

1 Introduction

The International Telecommunications Union estimates that there are about 7 million mobile phones in the world today [1]. At the same time, according to the World Health Organization [2], in 2008 there were already more than 1.4 billion adults (twenty years or more) overweight.

These two statistics together make clear that technology can and must help people to be healthier and have a better quality of life. Nowadays, there are many apps developed to engage people to make physical activities and diet control. Nevertheless, sometimes what should help may become a barrier: if people do not know how to use these apps, then they will be inefficient and people give up using them.

Based on the global problem of overweight and the easy access to technology, this paper aims to find the apps designed for walking or running that has better usability in the most trivial activities by performing a heuristic evaluation by ergonomic criteria.

This paper is structured as follows. Section 2 presents the usability concept, the inspection method and explains the ergonomic criteria evaluation technique. Section 3 discusses the five fitness-tracking apps evaluated. In Sect. 4 we introduce the methodology of the usability evaluation and in Sect. 5 we detail the results. Section 6 presents our conclusion of this paper.

C. Stephanidis (Ed.): HCII 2015 Posters, Part II, CCIS 529, pp. 457–462, 2015.
DOI: 10.1007/978-3-319-21383-5_76

2 Usability Evaluation by Ergonomic Criteria

Usability is one of the most important quality factors in human computer interaction which ensures that interactive products are easy to learn, effective to use and enjoyable from the users' perspective [3]. The challenge to develop more usable applications has led to the emergence of a variety of methods, techniques and tools for treating usability issues [4]. One of these methods is the inspection method, where researchers or experts critic, predict and model aspects of the interface in order to identify the main usability problems [3]. To perform the inspection, evaluators are put in the place of potential users and they try to identify problems that users would face when interacting with the system [5]. There are several methods of evaluation by inspection, such as heuristic evaluation, cognitive walkthrough, the use of recommendations, guidelines, etc. [6]. In this paper, we focus on heuristic evaluation by the Ergonomic Criteria [7]. The ergonomic criteria act as a guide to design and evaluate the user interface, and each criterion consists of a definition, a rationale, examples and some comments to avoid ambiguity [8].

Bastien and Scapin [8] created a set of eighteen ergonomic criteria and the eight major ergonomic criteria are: (1) Guidance, (2) Workload, (3) Explicit Control, (4) Adaptability, (5) Error Management, (6) Consistency, (7) Significance of Codes and (8) Compatibility. Each criterion is explained below, along with their sub-criteria.

Guidance is how the system guides users to reach their goal, ensuring the "learning capacity" and it is divided into *Prompting* (providing labels and masks, letting users know what should be done), *Grouping* (giving visual organization to the system, and this can be: *by Format* – according to shapes and colors – or *by Location* – according to logical organization of system's data), *Immediate Feedback* (letting users know what is happening) and *Legibility* (formatting fonts, colors and alignments to give more visibility) [8].

Workload is how the system reduces the cognitive load, showing only what is needed and letting users decide what they want to read and to do [8]. This criterion is also subdivided into *Brevity* (focusing on short reading and fast data input – called *Concision* – and reducing the number of steps to reach users goals – called *Minimal Actions*) and *Information Density* (also tries to reduce the read, but focuses on what is necessary and what is superfluous to the user, not the size of the information) [8].

Explicit Control involves the *Explicit User Action* (the system processes exactly what users request – nothing more and nothing less – and when they request – neither before nor after) and *User Control* (provides appropriate actions – like cancel, pause, resume, and exit – so users can select them if they want to) [8].

Adaptability is how the system becomes more anatomical according to the user profile and is divided into *Flexibility* (letting users customize the system according to their needs) and *User Experience* (letting users reach their goals in different ways: with a step-by-step instructions for novice users and shortcuts for experienced users) [8].

Error Management is how the system prevents, reduces and helps users to get recovery from errors and it is divided into *Error Protection* (error prevention in the input data and dangerous actions, like deleting data), *Quality of Error Messages* (assuming that the error messages are only effective when they show what is wrong) and *Error Correction* (letting users know how to fix what went wrong) [8].

Consistency means keeping the same interface design pattern for similar contexts and using different styles for different things [8]. **Significance of Codes** refers to the relationship between the codes and its references (such as the use of "F" for female) [8]. **Compatibility** is how the system imitates the real world, using the similar provision of fields like in paper form, for example [8].

3 Fitness Apps

To conduct the heuristic evaluation, the five free fitness-tracking apps most downloaded in Play Store until the second half of 2014 were selected, which were (in this order): RunKeeper, Nike + Running, Runtastic, Runtastic Pedometer and Endomondo Sports Tracker. The search focused on apps designed for walking or jogging tracking. Because of available resources, we analyzed Android's version of each app.

RunKeeper is a GPS based app designed to track walking, jogging, cycling and other indoor and outdoor fitness activities. Beyond its tracking functionality, RunKeeper has other main functionalities, e.g. tracking user's weight loss, syncing with user's heart rate monitors and sharing user's activities on social networks [9].

Nike + Running is a GPS based app, but it focus on jogging and coaching users to be ready to marathon races [10]. It shares users' runs on social networks. Nike + Running warns its users when their shoes are worn-out (if users specify which shoes are used in each activity).

Runtastic is a GPS based app and it tracks walking, jogging and cycling (among other activities, like RunKeeper). Runtastic shares users' activities on social networks and syncs with heart rate monitors. Runtastic provides tips about health on a YouTube channel and it has a partnership with Universal Music Group to create a fitness-focused music compilation [11].

Runtastic Pedometer is a gyroscope based app focused on walking. Based on the theory that everyone should walk 10,000 steps per day, Pedometer Runtastic helps users to control this daily achievement [12]. As well as the apps mentioned above, Runtastic Pedometer allows the user to monitor their activities (speed and distance) and share their steps amount in social networks.

Endomondo Sports Tracker is a GPS based app to track walking, jogging, cycling (and other activities). Endomondo was designed to motivate people to keep doing exercises, based on the theory that social interaction stimulates people to continue practicing exercises [13]. Endomondo syncs with user's heart rate monitor and shares data on social networks.

4 Inspection Evaluation Process

As a first step of this evaluation, the five applications have been downloaded and installed on a smartphone Motorola Moto X, model XT1058, with Android operating system in the version 4.4.3 (popularly known as "Kit Kat") and screen resolution of

1280 × 720 pixels. At that time (July 2014), the latest versions available for download were installed: RunKeeper in the version 4.6.4, Nike + Running in the version 1.4, Runtastic in the version 5.1.2, Runtastic Pedometer in the version 1.5 and Endomondo Sports Tracker in the version 10.2.7.

In the second stage, an exploratory research was conducted in each app to check the coverage of their tasks. Unfortunately, the scope of the apps were different: in some apps were found more than ninety different tasks (RunKeeper and Endomondo), while others did not exceed fifty tasks (like Nike + Running and Runtastic Pedometer).

Thereby, a list of main activities was created to define what would be evaluated. This list has fifteen activities: (1) Sign up; (2) Sign in; (3) Start walking; (4) Pause walking; (5) Stop walking; (6) Distance (i.e. check distance walked); (7) Duration (i.e. check the duration of the walk); (8) Calories (i.e. check burned calories); (9) View performed route on map; (10) Share data on social networks; (11) View data of previous walks; (12) Inform weight; (13) Inform height; (14) Change unit of measurement and; (15) Delete data of a previous walk.

While the list has only basic activities, some apps do not have all activities and such cases will not be considered, namely: Runtastic Pedometer does not monitor the burned calories in the free version; Runtastic Pedometer cannot show the map because it does not use GPS and; RunKeeper does not get users' height. Then, we conducted the evaluation of each app and each task in the same order as described above.

When evaluating the tasks, the apps were rated for each criterion and sub-criterion. If the criterion were fully satisfied, it was rated "OK" (i.e. the criterion is in accordance). If the criterion was not satisfied by the task, it was rated as "Not OK". If it was not possible to evaluate the criterion (if the task was not available or criterion was not applicable for that task), it was rated as "N/A", meaning "Not Applicable".

5 Results

After doing the heuristic evaluation based on ergonomic criteria, the results were gathered for each task and for each app.

In the first task, *Sign up*, RunKeeper was the best rated app, satisfying 14 of 18 ergonomic criteria. One criterion not satisfied by RunKeeper (and by Endomondo) is *Immediate Feedback*, because both apps allow users to input their data before testing the Internet connection and, if users are unable to connect before closing the app, the inputted data would be lost. Nike + Running, Runtastic and Runtastic Pedometer did not satisfy *Information Density* criterion, because users must input their postal code – for Nike + Running – or their birthday – for Runtastic and Runtastic Pedometer – to sign up, and these information should not need to be mandatory.

In the second task, *Sign in*, RunKeeper was also the best app, since it satisfied 17 of 18 ergonomic criteria. The only problem was related to its *Flexibility*, because users cannot remove unnecessary items of the interface. This problem occurred in all other apps.

The third task, *Start walking*, was best represented by Endomondo, which ensured that 14 of 18 criteria are fulfilled. One criterion not satisfied was *Flexibility*, since the app allows users to see exactly three indicators (such as distance, calories and duration), not allowing users to add or remove a different amount of indicators. This criterion has not been satisfied in all other apps.

The fourth task, *Pause walking*, was OK by Endomondo Sports Tracker, Nike + Running and RunKeeper. All these apps satisfied 14 criteria, also failing in the *Flexibility* criterion, not allowing users to remove unwanted data of the interface.

The fifth task, *Stop walking*, had almost the same results of the fourth task, where RunKeeper and Endomondo Sports Tracker had 14 satisfied criteria. Nike + Running did not satisfy the criterion *Distinction by Location*, since the stop button is not close to the pause button.

For the sixth task, *Distance*, RunKeeper, Nike + Running and Endomondo Sports Tracker were the best apps. These apps satisfied 13 criteria, failing in the *Adaptability* criterion (including *User Experience* and *Flexibility* sub-criteria). None of the apps had shortcuts to facilitate the adaptation and use for more expert users.

The seventh task, *Duration*, had the same result for all apps: 13 criteria satisfied and 2 criteria not satisfied (*Flexibility* and *User Experience*).

In the eighth task, *Calories*, RunKeeper, Nike + Running and Endomondo Sports Tracker satisfied 13 ergonomic criteria and they had problems to satisfy the *Adaptability* criterion. In addition, Runtastic Pedometer could not be evaluated, since this task is not included in the free version.

The ninth task, *View performed route on map*, had similar results to the eighth task. RunKeeper, Nike + Running and Endomondo Sports Tracker satisfied 12 criteria and there were still problems to satisfy *Adaptability* criterion. Runtastic Pedometer did not support this activity.

In the tenth task, *Share data on social networks*, and in the eleventh task, *View data of previous walks*, Nike + Running and Endomondo Sports Tracker satisfied more criteria (14 in the tenth task and 15 in the eleventh task). In the twelfth task, *Inform weight*, RunKeeper and Endomondo Sports Tracker satisfied 16 of 18 criteria. In the thirteenth task, *Inform height*, Endomondo Sports Tracker was the only app to satisfy 16 criteria and RunKeeper did not support this task. In the fourteenth task, *Change unit of measure*, and in the fifteenth task, *Delete a previous walk*, all the apps satisfied 13 criteria.

Summarizing, the following results can be found: RunKeeper satisfied 70.37 % of the criteria, Nike + Running satisfied 74.07 %, Runtastic satisfied 70.74 %, Runtastic Pedometer satisfied 61.85 % and Endomondo Sports Tracker satisfied 77.04 %, being the app with most satisfied criteria. Also, RunKeeper and Endomondo Sports Tracker had 9.26 % of their tasks not satisfied, while Nike + Running had 12.22 %, Runtastic had 15.56 % and Runtastic Pedometer had 13.70 %. This means that RunKeeper and Endomondo Sports Tracker could be considered easier to use for initial users. Also, RunKeeper had 20.37 % of its tasks not available or not applicable to evaluate, Nike + Running, Runtastic and Endomondo Sports Tracker had 13.7 % and Runtastic Pedometer had 24.44 %. Nike + Running, Runtastic and Endomondo could be considered more complete for trivial tasks than the others because of this. These results can be visualized in Fig. 1.

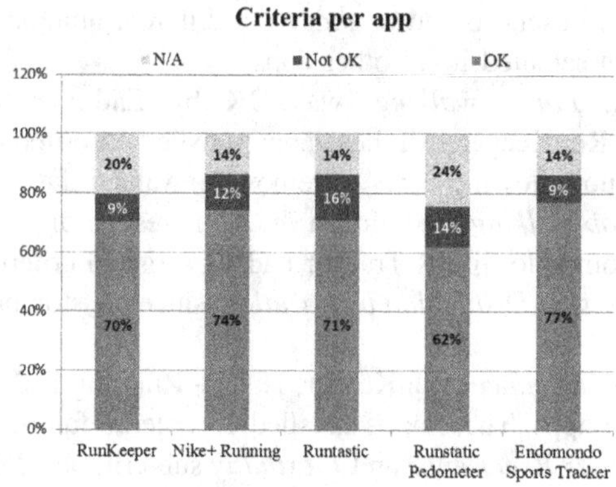

Fig. 1. Results achieved through inspection evaluation by ergonomic criteria of each app

6 Conclusion

The results revealed the importance of conducting a usability evaluation. The inspection was able to identify several usability problems in all apps. This paper identified many problems that can be faced by potential users of fitness-tracking applications, especially in relation to the main and most used tasks. As future work, we will conduct further usability evaluations, involving users through controlled experiments, to understand the usability problems related to the different types of users and the consequences of these problems.

References

1. International Telecommunication Union facts and figures. http://www.itu.int/en/ITU-D/Statistics/Documents/facts/ICTFactsFigures2014-e.pdf
2. World Health Organization. http://www.who.int/mediacentre/factsheets/fs311/en
3. Fernandez, A., Insfran, E., Abrahão, S.: Usability evaluation methods for the web: a systematic mapping study. J. Inf. Softw. Technol. **53**(8), 789–817 (2011)
4. Rogers, Y., Preece, J., Sharp, H.: Interaction Design: Beyond Human-Computer Interaction, 3rd edn. John Wiley, Hoboken (2011)
5. Barbosa, S.D.J., da Silva, B.S.: Interação humano-computador. Elsevier (2010)
6. Nielsen, J., Mack, R.L.: Usability Inspection Methods. Wiley, New York (1994)
7. Bastien, J.C., Scapin, D.L.: Evaluating a user interface with ergonomic criteria. Technical report n. 2326, INRIA, Rocquencourt, France (1994)
8. Bastien, J.C., Scapin, D.L.: Ergonomic criteria for the evaluation of human-computer interfaces. Technical report n. 156, INRIA, Rocquencourt, France (1993)
9. RunKeeper Official Website. http://runkeeper.com/
10. Nike + Running Official Website. https://secure-nikeplus.nike.com/plus/products/gps_app/
11. Runtastic Official Website. https://www.runtastic.com/
12. Runtastic Pedometer Official Website. https://www.runtastic.com/en/apps/pedometer/
13. Endomondo Sports Tracker Official Website. https://www.endomondo.com/

Research on Intelligent Exercise Prescription System for Civil Servant

Qi Luo(✉) and Wei Deng

College of Sports Engineering and Information Technology,
Wuhan Sports University, Wuhan 430079, China
ccnu_luo2008@126.com

Abstract. Public servant refers to the people who work in the government institutions of various levels and execute the mission of state administrative functions and powers. Civil servant is in sub-health status and is high dangerous group of some chronics. Civil servant has a highly recognition about the value of sport for health and has desire to participate in it. But because some objective and subjective reasons, Civil servant cannot participate in exercise and is lack of targeted and scientific. The intelligent exercise prescription system for civil servant has been proposed by the following method such as literature, expert interviews, experimental test, software engineering method, data mining, system dynamics modeling. The intelligent exercise prescription system based theory on artificial intelligence and assessment of fitness-health include these achievements. The intelligent exercise prescription system is the life-style and rest/work system and chronics of civil servant taken into account deeply so as to ensure the feasibility and targeted and scientific of exercise prescription.

1 Introduction

Public servant refers to the people who work in the government institutions of various levels and execute the mission of state administrative functions and powers. Practice has shown that civil servants need to own health-related fitness such as physical and psychological to guarantee them competent in the posts. However, the properties and characteristics of civil servants' work easily lead to their fitness problems. Firstly, Due to the heavy working strength, long working hours, lacking of physical activities, the public servant's rates of metabolism and basic metabolism is lower, blood circulation is worse, the functions of human organs and main joints is decline, which easily make them got chronic occupational diseases, such as obesity, angiocardiopathy, arthritis. Secondly, the public servant' ability which resists disease and adapts to environment become decline because of many social intercourses, stimulation of tobacco and wine, the excessive intake of all kinds of high-calorie or high cholesterol foods. Finally, the fast pace of life, mental nervous have led to various psychological problems associated with job stress increased..

Based on it, The intelligent exercise prescription system for civil servant has been proposed by the following method such as literature, expert interviews, experimental test, software engineering method, data mining, system dynamics modeling. The intelligent exercise prescription system based theory on artificial intelligence and

C. Stephanidis (Ed.): HCII 2015 Posters, Part II, CCIS 529, pp. 463–466, 2015.
DOI: 10.1007/978-3-319-21383-5_77

assessment of fitness-health include these achievements. The intelligent exercise prescription system is the life-style and rest/work system and chronics of civil servant taken into account deeply so as to ensure the feasibility and targeted and scientific of exercise prescription.

2 Decision Support System

A Decision Support System (DSS) is a computer-based information system that supports business or organizational decision-making activities. DSSs serve the management, operations, and planning levels of an organization (usually mid and higher management) and help to make decisions, which may be rapidly changing and not easily specified in advance (Unstructured and Semi-Structured decision problems). Decision support systems can be either fully computerized, human or a combination of both.

While academics have perceived DSS as a tool to support decision making process, DSS users see DSS as a tool to facilitate organizational processes [1]. Some authors have extended the definition of DSS to include any system that might support decision making. Sprague (1980) defines DSS by its characteristics [2].

DSS tends to be aimed at the less well structured, underspecified problem that upper level managers typically face; DSS attempts to combine the use of models or

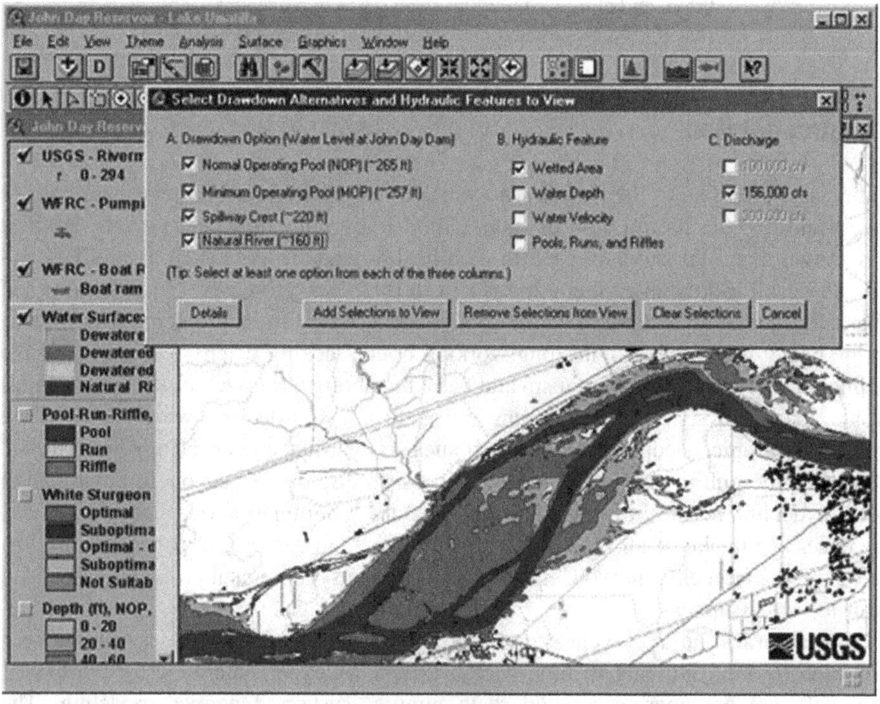

Fig. 1. Example of a decision support system

analytic techniques with traditional data access and retrieval functions; DSS specifically focuses on features which make them easy to use by non-computer people in an interactive mode; and DSS emphasizes flexibility and adaptability to accommodate changes in the environment and the decision making approach of the user. DSSs include knowledge-based systems. A properly designed DSS is an interactive software-based system intended to help decision makers compile useful information from a combination of raw data, documents, and personal knowledge, or business models to identify and solve problems and make decisions.

Typical information that a decision support application might gather and present includes: inventories of information assets (including legacy and relational data sources, cubes, data warehouses, and data marts),comparative sales figures between one period and the next, projected revenue figures based on product sales assumptions [3, 4].

Example of a Decision Support System is Fig. 1.

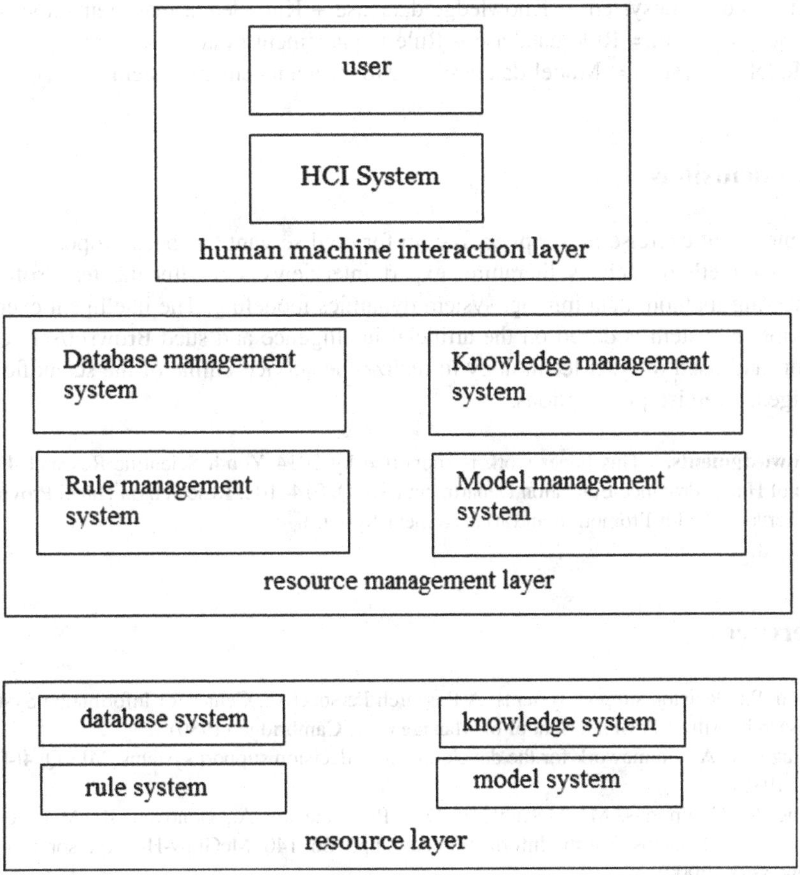

Fig. 2. The structure of intelligent exercise prescription system for civil servant

3 Intelligent Exercise Prescription System for Civil Servant

Basing on Decision Support System theory, The structure of Intelligent Exercise Prescription System for Civil Servant is Fig. 2.

Setting up the system is based on three levels, including the resource layer, information processing layer, human machine interaction layer. From the structure, resource database is mainly composed of database, knowledge database, rule database and model database. Resource management layer is composed of four database management systems. Among the various management systems, which is related to each other. So, the resources can be called accurately, reasonably and conveniently. Human-computer interaction layer can realize direct dialogue between user and system, which can provide a convenient entrance of decision support for users.

From the elements of the system, the system consists of four major subsystems.

- Database subsystem = Database + Database management system
- Knowledge subsystem = Knowledge database + Knowledge management system
- Rule subsystem = Rule database + Rule management system
- Model subsystem = Model database + Model management system

4 Conclusions

The intelligent exercise prescription system for civil servant has been proposed by the following method such as literature, expert interviews, experimental test, software engineering method, data mining, system dynamics modeling. The intelligent exercise prescription system is dazed on the artificial intelligence and sued Browser/service as support and used internet technology to realize the service online of the scientific and intelligent exercise prescriptions.

Acknowledgments. This paper work is supported by 2014 Youth Scientific Research Foundation of Hubei Province Education Department (No. Q20144102, Research on Hubei Provincial Civil Servant Health Promotion and Management System).

References

1. Keen, P.: Decision support systems: A Research Perspective. Center for Information Systems Research, Alfred P. Sloan School of Management, Cambridge (1980)
2. Sprague, R.A.: Framework for the development of decision support systems. MIS Q. **4**(4), 1–25 (1980)
3. Haag, S., Cummings, M., McCubbrey, D.J., Pinsonneault, A., Donovan, R.: Management Information Systems: For the Information Age, pp. 136–140. McGraw-Hill Ryerson Limited, New York (2000)
4. Wright, A., Sittig, D.: A framework and model for evaluating clinical decision support architectures q. J. Biomed. Inform. **41**, 982–990 (2008)

Prototype of a Shoulder and Elbow Occupational Health Care Exergame

Wilson Nava, Cesar Andres Ramos Mejia(✉), and Alvaro Uribe-Quevedo

Military Nueva Granada University, Bogota, Colombia
{u1201153,u1201161}@unimilitar.edu.co,
alvaro.j.uribe@ieee.org

Abstract. The use of gaming in non-entertainment scenarios have impacted learning, therapy, exercising and training scenarios, among many others. In terms of occupational health care, it can provide motivation and monitoring, while complementing surveys and medical examinations. The success of the exercise depends on several factors, from understanding the guides, the demonstrations and its causes and consequences. Related works in this area have approached this problem with different type of games and motion tracking to boost engagement and the acquisition of data. This work presents the development of a shoulder and elbow exergame using motion capture as a complimentary tool to traditional means of occupational health care exercising. The presented solution in this project tracks the user upper limb to provide feedback that may help improve the exercising experience through charts that can be sent to a health care specialist.

Keywords: Data · Game · Tracking

1 Introduction

Upper-limb musculoskeletal disorders are rising among the global population caused by occupational work habits, such as stress, repetitive movements, excessive forces, sedentary and sports practices [1, 2], as a result the quality of life of nearly 15.3 % of the world's population is being affected [3].

A solution to this problem is exercising; however, this activity requires motivation which varies from person to person, affecting the rate of success. In occupational health, this activity may help reducing the risk of suffering from a musculoskeletal disorder and even though this should provide enough motivation to engage into active pauses and self-health care, they are not practice due to the repetitive movements, lack of feedback and motivation, poor or nonexistent interactive scenarios, and unclear guides and explanations [4] Virtual Reality (VR) can provide tools for overcoming these challenges by offering immersion and interaction features in computer generated worlds that allow the user to perform activities within a controlled environment where rewards, feedback and clear goals are presented and provide engagement to the player [5]. Through the interaction with a VR environment the user can be distracted from the main activity (exercising) which results in the performance of a desired action within a

C. Stephanidis (Ed.): HCII 2015 Posters, Part II, CCIS 529, pp. 467–472, 2015.
DOI: 10.1007/978-3-319-21383-5_78

treatment with an entertaining experience, an example of such application can be found in cases where the pain feeling is reduced as a consequence of the engagement in a game [6].

Given the ample development and evolution of affordable tracking devices ranging from electromechanical solutions with inertial sensors [7], image processing [8], myography [9], electro encephalographic signals [10], along with the trend of having more natural and accurate interactions [11], several developments can be found on the literature taking advantage of these technologies. Several exercising scenarios have benefited from exergaming in scenarios such as in stroke rehabilitation, autism children physiotherapy [12], and elderly care [13]. At a commercial level fitness exergames have been developed with the goal of providing interactive and engaging scenarios that allow enhancing the user's experience [14], without providing feedback on the accuracy of the movements, mainly focusing on the experience of having a good time.

In this paper, the authors present the development of an upper limb exergame focused on the shoulder and the elbow active pauses, joints required to perform several daily tasks. The process involved analyzing the upper limb and the active pauses so the movements could be programmed as game mechanics to provide engagement while monitoring their correct execution with non-invasive motion tracking.

2 Exergame Development

The game development required the characterization of the upper-limb, ranges of motion, common musculoskeletal disorders and their exercises. This process provides sufficient information for designing the game's formal, dynamic and dramatic elements within the chosen scenarios.

2.1 Upper Limb Analysis and Exergame Design

The upper-limb is composed of the shoulder (3 Degrees of Freedom (DOF)), the elbow (1 DOF) and the wrist (2 DOF), supported by the humerus, ulna and radius, these allow to perform flexion/extension and adduction/abduction rotations as presented in Fig. 1.

Daily activities involving choosing and grabbing objects require arm movements using the shoulder and the elbow, however, when affected the disorders involving the rotator cuff require abduction and internal/external rotations exercises while standing straight with the elbows horizontally aligned. During this activity the elbows must remain at a 90° angle without moving the shoulder from its position (Fig. 1). In the case of the elbow the exercise requires to hold both of them tight and close to the torso using an elastic band to provide resistance for the flexion/extension movements [15] (Fig. 1). These exercises are recommended to be performed o regular basis from a minute to five during working hours to help reduce the risk of musculoskeletal disorders.

With the information from the exercises and their required movements within the time constraints of occupational health the game is designed to provide a suitable active pause environment based on motion capture at a 1.3 m from the sensor. The interaction is setup to use gestures to encouraging the use of the upper limb and create familiarity

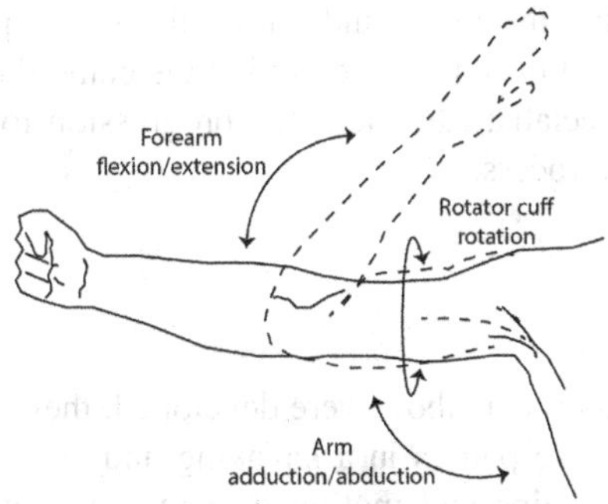

Fig. 1. Upper limb DOF and shoulder and elbow exercises

with the user interface. The game elements are defined as follows: the goal of the game is to provide entertaining active pauses for shoulder and elbow that feedback the player and a healthcare specialist with recorded motion data; the rules of the game are to reach the goal on each level, to accomplish them, the player is required to properly execute the movements and overcome the presented obstacles while gathering each level collectibles; the feedback is provided in terms of scores, motion graphs and on-screen tips about the importance of exercising.

On a general basis, the GUI allows choosing the menus, to pause, to continue and to exit of the application. During the game the user's movements are tracked using a Kinect to trigger the virtual characters actions and this data is saved to a chart that allows quantifying the experience and validate if the user is doing the exercises correctly or incorrectly so a healthcare specialist could do a closer follow up.

Two scenarios were implemented, a kayaking minigame for the shoulder and a snow skiing for the elbow, these were selected after a survey on which virtual environment would the user prefer; most of the participants expressed interest on scenarios not available to them which were also validated with healthcare specialists. The implementation followed the architecture presented in Fig. 2.

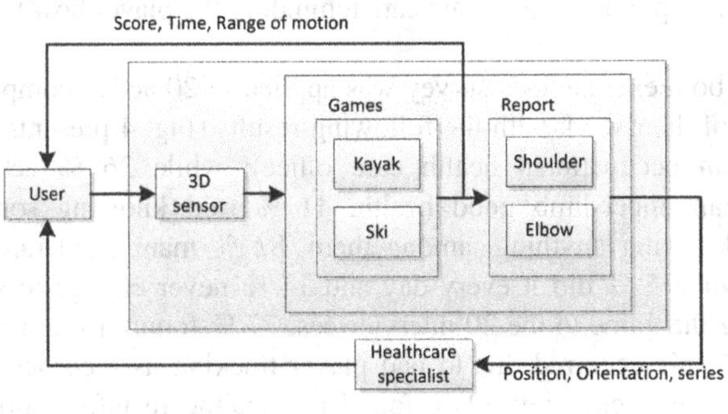

Fig. 2. System Architecture

For the development Unity and Microsoft's Kinect SDK were used. The scenarios modeled, textured, rigged and animated with 3D authoring software and then imported to Unity. Scripts were programmed to allow interactions and reactions accordingly to the user inputs when using the menu and within the game, providing the feedback, scores, tips and penalties. At the end of the session the game show the collected data so the user or health care specialist can check the progression for performing corrective measures to improve the process.

3 Results

Two exergames for shoulder and elbow were developed, they provide scenarios where the player can practice active pauses in a kayaking and snow skiing virtual environment. Both games provide tips and motion data in graphics for assessing the progression. Figure 3 presents the developed games along with the user executing the movements.

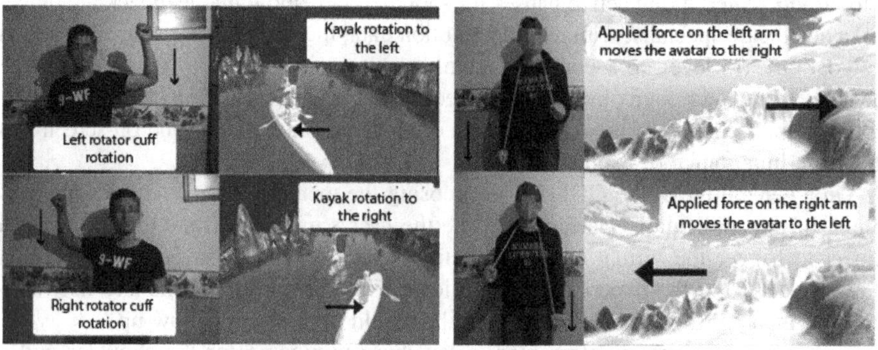

Fig. 3. Shoulder kayaking and elbow skiing exergames

To provide feedback both games indicate with red and green on-screen buttons if the motion was poorly or well executed respectively and if the mistakes occur three consecutive times a popup message appears reminding the player how the movement is performed.

To validate both exergames a survey was applied to 20 active computer users who use it for most of their work with the following results (Fig. 4 presents a player using the games at an occupational health care office): while 36 % acknowledge the importance of an upper-limb good health, 41 % said knowing some and 23 % expressed not knowing anything, among them, 82 % manifested rarely performing active pauses while 5 % did it every day and 14 % never engage in such activities. After presenting the game to the 20 interviewees, 77 % found it intuitive to use while 23 % disagreed, this occurred due to bad player tracking as a consequence of room lightning and player's clothing; 32 % found the healthcare information very useful, while 64 % found it normal due to previous knowledge and 5 % founded of little use; the popup messages when making mistakes during the game were found very appropriate by 94 % and 1 % found inadequate, for most of the users this was a result from tracking challenges which help them to improve the experience, however, it was also found that the popup message caused distraction during the game. Finally, when asked if the game was motivational enough to using it continuously as an active pause complimentary too, 95 % declared that they would and 5 % stated that a game was not required as it was already a routine practice. The motion capture information was validated with healthcare specialists who after observing the data could identify if the motion ranges were within the expected, it is worth noting that there weren't any abnormalities detected on the collected data, however, the when the tracker failed, the information couldn't be assessed.

Fig. 4. Test at an occupational health care office

4 Conclusions

The development of exergames not only impact users with specific needs due to their conditions, but also impact people in other scenarios such as the practice of active pauses that may help preventing health risks. Due to its broad commercialization the Kinect is tool that participants manifest having or being interested into acquiring one due to its affordability. The quantification of the motion by providing feedback on how well the movements were performed interested all participants due to the possibility of quantifying the exercising activity. Health care specialists that participated were very interested as it could provide more information about the user so they could better assess the player's progression. Finally, the system was well accepted and thus, future works will be on improving data acquisition with possibly a Kinect 2 or wearable sensors, as it was a factor that affected the player's experience; improved visuals and more exercising scenarios.

Acknowledgements. The authors wish to thank the Mil. University Nueva Granada for their support on project ING-1545. Also thanks to the Virtual Reality Center along with Dr. Bibiana Moncayo and Dr. Claudia Robayo.

References

1. Shiri, R., Viikari-Juntura, E.: Lateral and medial epicondylitis: role of occupational factors. Best Pract. Res. Clin. Rheumatol. **25**(1), 43–57 (2011)

2. Cruz, F., Almazánn, A., Pérez, F., Sierra, L., Villalobos, E., Ugalde, H.G., Ibarra, C.: Lesiones en el hombro ocurridas durante la práctica de deportes. In: Ortho-tips, vol. 5, pp. 65–78, Medigraphic Artemisa (2009)
3. World report on disability (2011). www.who.int/disabilities/world_report/2011/report/en/
4. Burdea, G.: Keynote address: virtual rehabilitation-benefits and challenges. In: 1st International Workshop on Virtual Reality Rehabilitation (Mental Health, Neurological, Physical, Vocational) VRMHR, pp. 1–11 (2002)
5. Rizzo, A., Kim, G.: A SWOT analysis of the field of virtual reality rehabilitation and therapy. Presence **14**(2), 119–146 (2005). MIT PRESS
6. Hoffman, H.G., Patterson, D.R., Carrougher, G.J., Sharar, S.R.: Effectiveness of virtual reality-based pain control with multiple treatments. Clin. J. Pain **17**(3), 229–235 (2001). LWW
7. Wingrave, C.A., Williamson, B., Varcholik, P.D., Rose, J., Miller, A., Charbonneau, E., Bott, J., LaViola, J.: The wiimote and beyond: spatially convenient devices for 3D user interfaces. IEEE Comput. Graphics Appl. **30**(2), 71–85 (2010)
8. Chang, Y.-J., Chen, S.-F., Huang, J.-D.: A kinect-based system for physical rehabilitation: a pilot study for young adults with motor disabilities. Res. Dev. Disabil. **32**(6), 2566–2570 (2011). Elsevier
9. Nuwer, R.: Armband adds a twitch to gesture control. New Sci. **217**(2906), 21 (2013). Elsevier
10. Lievesley, R., Wozencroft, M., Ewins, D.: The Emotiv EPOC neuroheadset: an inexpensive method of controlling assistive technologies using facial expressions and thoughts? J. Assistive Technol. **5**(2), 67–82 (2011). Emerald Group Publishing Limited
11. Furntratt, H., Neuschmied, H.: evaluating pointing accuracy on kinect V2 sensor. In: International Conference on Multimedia and Human-Computer Interaction MHCI (2014)
12. Pogrzeba, L., Wacker, M., Jung, B.: Potentials of a low-cost motion analysis system for exergames in rehabilitation and sports medicine. In: Göbel, S., Müller, W., Urban, B., Wiemeyer, J. (eds.) GameDays 2012 and Edutainment 2012. LNCS, vol. 7516, pp. 125–133. Springer, Heidelberg (2012)
13. Gerling, K.M., Schild, J., Masuch, M.: Exergame design for elderly users: the case study of SilverBalance. In: Proceedings of the 7th International Conference on Advances in Computer Entertainment Technology. ACM (2010)
14. Jin, S.A.A.: Avatars mirroring the actual self versus projecting the ideal self: the effects of self-priming on interactivity and immersion in an exergame, Wii Fit. CyberPsychol. Behav. **12**(6), 761–765 (2009)
15. Green, A.: Lesiones crónicas masivas del manguito rotador: evaluación y tratamiento. J. Am. Acad. Orthop. Surg. (Ed Esp) **2**, 365–375 (2003)

An Investigation of the Usability and Desirability of Health and Fitness-Tracking Devices

Ashton Pfannenstiel and Barbara S. Chaparro(✉)

Wichita State University, Wichita, KS, USA
ashtonpfannenstiel@gmail.com,
barbara.chaparro@wichita.edu

Abstract. This study investigated the usability and functionality of 6 different fitness tracking wristbands that have been suggested to improve and encourage healthy behaviors. While many previous studies assess the accuracy and behavioral effects of fitness tracking devices, limited research has been done to analyze the usability and desirability of these products. Participants were asked to rate their impressions of six fitness tracking devices - the Garmin Vivofit, Jawbone Up24, Fitbit One, Basis B1 Band, Misfit Shine, and the Tom Tom Multisport – before and after usage. Participants were also asked to describe the main factors contributing to their overall preference and likelihood to purchase and/or use each device. Results indicate that participants are initially more likely to favor, small, lightweight devices that have a display. After wearing the devices, the most valued features were attractiveness, long battery life, waterproof, and a heart rate monitor. The study suggest that a "one size fits all approach" to the design of fitness tracking devices may not be the most effective method to promote the actual use of the technology.

Keywords: Wearables · Beauty technology · Usability methods and tools Mobile products · ISO · Usability

1 Introduction

According to Comstock [1], 19 million wearable fitness tracking devices are owned this year, a figure that is expected to triple in the next 3 years. Despite this success, it is suggested that the early appeal and fascination with the devices does not last. This leaves companies eager to discover what factors appeal the most to individuals in the market for fitness tracking devices. However, Quinlan [3] suggests that this "one-size-fits all approach" is what limits the desirability of these products. In order to appeal to a greater number of potential users, Quinlan [3] states that fitness devices need to be versatile and considerate of people with different, or limited, abilities.

Versatility is very important in terms of fitness devices as one third of the population is considered obese. As a result, flexible material that can be size adjusted is crucial if the market is to expand farther than people who are already considered fit.

Kelly [2] reports 6 trends that are becoming more popular and may even be necessary for a device's popularity. The first trend is that "devices are getting smarter,"

C. Stephanidis (Ed.): HCII 2015 Posters, Part II, CCIS 529, pp. 473–477, 2015.
DOI: 10.1007/978-3-319-21383-5_79

meaning that fitness trackers do not just report activity, but they now instruct users on how active they should be. Second, smartphone extension is an important function in order for users to have quicker access to their data and additional features. Users also expect beauty from their fitness devices as many companies aim to make their products look more like jewelry, or offer products in a variety of colors. The integration of social networks increases the desirability of products as well, as individuals hope for products that will fit into other components of their lives. In addition, innovation, or new and unique features, encourage consumers to purchase or upgrade fitness tracking devices. The sixth and final trend, heart rate monitoring, is now an expected functionality. However, unlike previous devices, which required an extra chest strap to monitor heart rate, consumers now desire devices that utilize wrist sensors [2].

The current studies will explore available fitness tracking devices and their appeal towards consumers. The goal of the study is to discover how to make wearable fitness tracking technology more desirable to a greater number of individuals outside of the more athletic, fitness-focused community.

2 Method

2.1 Participants

Nineteen participants (10 male, 9 female) were recruited from a Midwestern university between June and July 2014. Participants ranged in age from 18 to 45 (m = 27.63). 17 of the 19 participants were unfamiliar with any fitness tracking device and two had experimented with a step counting device not used in this study.

2.2 Materials

Six fitness tracking devices, and their packaging were evaluated. The devices and packaging were labeled A through F. Participants rated their first impressions and final impressions using a paper 50 point scale. Other materials used during the study included: a tube sock and quarter, a Samsung Chromebook, and a "Feature Ratings" survey. Prior to the study, each participant was asked to complete a background questionnaire.

2.3 Procedure

Packaging. Before seeing any of the devices, each participant rated the packaging of the devices using the 50 point scale. For the first 2 questions, the participant was not allowed to touch the device. Instead, he/she was asked to instruct the researcher where to place each package on the scale. The participant was then allowed to touch and read the packaging. They were asked to explain what influenced their overall opinion of each package.

First Impressions. The packaging was removed and replaced with the 6 devices. Each participant was asked to rate the devices based on his/her first impressions. Again, He/she was not actually allowed to touch the devices and were asked to instruct the researcher where to place each device on the 50 point scale. They were asked to explain what factors influenced their overall first impressions of the devices.

Tasks. Each participant was asked to put on each device in a randomized order and complete the following representative tasks with each one: 1. Put on the device, 2. Walk around/Get a feel for the device, 3. Reach into a sock to pull out a coin (to simulate pocket), 4. Type on a laptop keyboard, and 5. Remove the device.

Final Impressions. After completing the tasks with all 6 devices, participants were asked to rate their final impressions of the devices using the 50 point scale. After rating each attribute, participants were asked to explain their ratings for the devices, specifically the highest and lowest rated device. To conclude the study, the participant was given a "Feature Ratings" survey. The survey consisted of a list of features that can be found on different fitness tracking devices. The participant indicated how important he/she think each feature is. The study took approximately 60–75 min to complete.

3 Results

Packaging. A one-way repeated measures ANOVA indicated significant differences for expense, $F(5, 85) = 6.82$, $p < .01$, eta2 = 0.28, quality, $F(3.38, 57.54) = 6.30$, $p < .05$, eta2 = 0.27, amount of features, $F(5, 85) = 16.42$, $p < .01$, eta2 = 0.49, and the likelihood to buy each device, $F(5, 85) = 14.74$, $p < .01$, eta2 = 0.46, when participants were asked their opinions about device packaging. Based on packaging, participants perceived Jawbone as being significantly cheaper than the Garmin, Fitbit, and Tom Tom. Overall, the Jawbone was believed to be lower quality than the other 5 devices. The Jawbone was also thought to have less features. The Jawbone was rated significantly lower than the Garmin, Fitbit, Basis, and Misfit, when asked which device the participant would buy.

First Impressions. A one-way repeated measures ANOVA indicated significant differences for weight, $F(5, 85) = 58.91$, $p < .01$, $eta^2 = 0.77$, and comfort, $F(2.82, 48.82) = 7.91$, $p < .01$, $eta^2 = 0.31$, when participants were asked about their first impressions of the devices. Overall the Basis and Tom Tom were perceived to be significantly heavier than all the other devices. The Basis was perceived as less comfortable than the Garmin and Misfit, while the Tom Tom was believed to be less comfortable than Garmin, Fitbit, and Misfit.

Final Impressions. A one-way repeated measures ANOVA indicated significant differences for comfort, $F(5, 85) = 11.92$, $p < .01$, eta2 = 0.41, masculinity/femininity of the device, $F(2.55, 43.36) = 18.17$, $p < .01$, eta2 = 0.51, and the likelihood to buy each device, $F(5, 85) = 3.32$, $p < .05$, eta2 = 0.16, when the participants were asked about their final impressions. After trying on and performing tasks with each device, the Basis and Tom Tom were considered less comfortable than the Garmin, Fitbit, and Misfit.

Overall, the Basis and Tom Tom were viewed as more masculine than the other 4 devices. Similarly the Misfit was rated more feminine than all the devices except the Jawbone. When asked which device they would buy, the Fitbit was rated significantly higher than the Basis (Fig. 1).

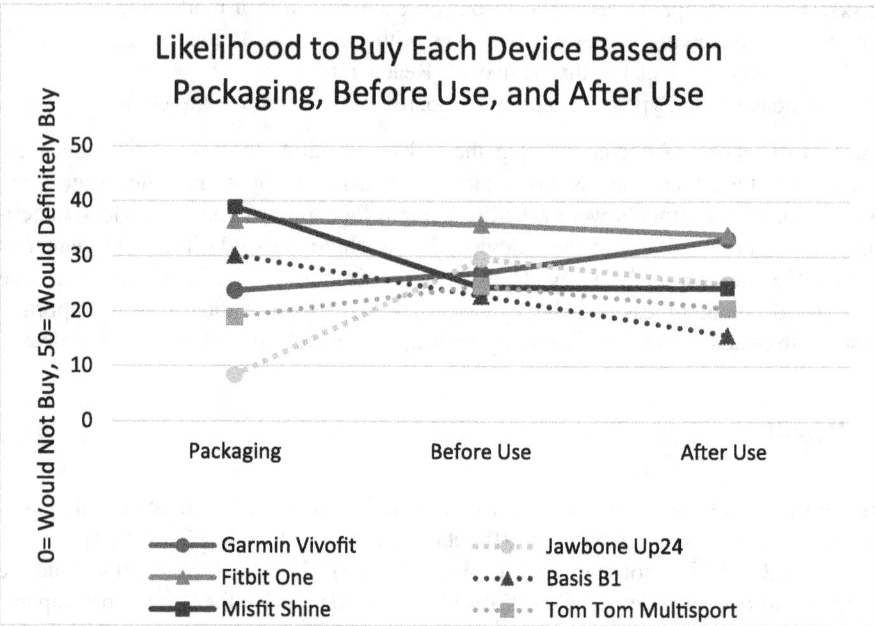

Fig. 1. Likelihood to buy each device based on packaging, before use, and after use

A one-way repeated measures ANOVA indicated significant differences for the likelihood to wear each device while exercising, $F(5, 85) = 4.35$, $p < .01$, eta2 = 0.20, during one's daily routine, $F(3.55, 60.40) = 7.02$, $p < .01$, eta2 = 0.29, and while sleeping, $F(3.22, 54.84) = 5.66$, $p < .01$, eta2 = 0.25. Participants indicated they were more likely to wear the Fitbit than the Basis while exercising. During their daily routine, they were more likely to wear the Garmin and Fitbit than the Basis. They also indicated that they would rather wear the Garmin than the Basis or Tom Tom while sleeping.

At the end of the study, participants were asked to rate the importance of the fitness tracking features. The features rated "important" or "very important" most often included the aesthetic/attractiveness of the device, the amount of battery life, being waterproof, containing a heart rate monitor, and having separate modes for different activities such as running, swimming, biking, etc. The features most often considered "not important" or "not important at all" included sleep tracking, smartwatch capabilities (i.e. smart alarms, social media notifications, etc.), having an accompanying phone app, GPS, food logging, and the ability to wear the device in different ways (versatility).

4 Discussion

The results indicate that participants are less willing to purchase a device if the packaging looks cheap. Although there were significant differences in the perceived weight and comfort of the devices, initially this did not create a significant difference in the likelihood to buy each device. After trying on the devices, participants believed they would be more likely to buy the more gender neutral, inconspicuous device (Fitbit or Garmin) over the more uncomfortable, "masculine," device that presented the most difficulty while completing the tasks (Basis or Tom Tom). Not only would they be more likely to buy this type of device, they would also be more likely to wear the device while exercising, during their daily routine, and while sleeping. The results imply that these particular individuals would be more drawn to devices that would not interrupt their daily lives or attract any outside attention. This is consistent with the participants' comments, as they were most likely to make remarks regarding the size and weight of the devices. Although the participants frequently commented that the small, lightweight devices, particularly the Fitbit, would be easy to lose, this did not seem to affect the overall preference. In addition, the most frequent positive comment made about the heavier, bulky devices was the fact that they had a display. As a result, the most favored devices were small, light devices that also had a digital display (Fitbit and Garmin). Typically, individuals indicated they would prefer a device that they could forget they were even wearing. Participants also indicated a desire for simplicity and rated the more complex features such as food logging, sleep tracking, smartwatch capabilities, etc. as "not important" or "not important at all".

The study was limited as the participants recruited were all college students. This may not accurately reflect the overall target population. In addition, participants may have been influenced by the brands of the devices. Multiple participants commented on the fact that they had seen or used other Garmin and Tom Tom products in the past (i.e., GPS). As a result, their past experiences with the brand may have influenced their opinion of the specific device.

Future studies should examine preferences among different populations. For example, understanding the preferences of serious athletes versus the preference of less active individuals would have very important marketing implications, especially if the goal is to appeal to the average consumer. Gender differences and age differences should also be explored. Longitudinal studies examining device preferences over a prolonged usage would also be useful in improving the likelihood of continued use of fitness tracking technology and overall consumer satisfaction.

References

1. Comstock, J.: Study: 19 M fitness wearables in use today, to triple by 2018, 25 November 2014. http://mobihealthnews.com
2. Kelly, C.: Biggest fitness tracker trends from CES 2014, 14 January 2014. https://everymove.org
3. Quinlan, J.: Why fitness wearables can't be one-size-fits-all, 16 April 2014. http://venturebeat.com

Development of an Open Electronics User Inerface for Lower Member Occupational Health Care Exergaming

Estefania Ramos-Montilla(✉) and Alvaro Uribe-Quevedo

Mil. Nueva Granada University, Bogota, Colombia
estefa.ramos0102@gmail.com, alvaro.j.uribe@ieee.org

Abstract. According to the World Health Organization 15 % of the global population suffers some form of musculoskeletal disorder. To prevent such affection, workers are encouraged to engage into active pauses during work hours to lower the risk of suffering any type of disorder. Although aware of the consequences, workers tend to avoid active pauses due to lack of time or motivation, unclear guides or ignorance regarding the effects of bad occupational health habits. An approach to overcome such challenges can be found in exergames, as they provide means to increase user motivation and clear instructions by taking advantage of motion tracking to better execute the active pauses. Wearable sensor are currently providing affordable solutions that track data more accurately in contrast to gaming devices, in this work, an open electronics interface is implemented within an exergame to motitave the execution of lower member active pauses within an office environment.

Keywords: Health · Sensor · Tracking

1 Introduction

Musculoskeletal disorders is a major concerned recognized by the World Health Organization that affects the quality of life, these can result from occupational health risks caused by excessive work, bad postures, sedentary and repetitive tasks, among many others [1, 2]. A strategy to minimize the risks and improve the worker's health is achieved through the practice of active pauses, however, it success is challenging because it depends on motivation and understanding on what needs to be correctly done. Current assessments in occupational health use visual observation and surveys, making it subjective and difficult to follow as the worker may not perform the pauses or report them when examined [3].

The engagement and assessment challenges can be approached with exergames, research in this area has resulted in the development of applications in fitness, rehabilitation and entertainment involving different scenarios and body parts [4]. These developments have been evolving along computer graphics and user interfaces (UIs), resulting in more realistic and natural interactions with motion controllers that can provide experiences which can be assessed by a health care specialist to improve the benefits and impact of the physical activity [5].

C. Stephanidis (Ed.): HCII 2015 Posters, Part II, CCIS 529, pp. 478–483, 2015.
DOI: 10.1007/978-3-319-21383-5_80

Interactive motion capture developments have provided approaches using expensive equipment, such as high performance motion capture systems using suits and multiple infrared cameras [6], however these technologies face a major challenge due to costs and space requirements [7]. This problem has been recently tackled using affordable devices such as gaming controllers like the Kinect and the Wii remote control [8], and smartphones and custom devices [9]. The Kinect for example, requires adequate space to properly capture the player and depending on lighting conditions its accuracy may be affect, however it has been in used in full body and segmented body parts exergames with success [10]. The Wii remote control also poses challenges in terms of its attachment to body due to its size and weight (initially only had an accelerometer, but current version includes a gyroscope as well), it has also been used in several exercising scenarios, proving adequate for exergaming [11]. Smartphones have also been studied as tools for encouraging healthier activities because they are commonly used and most have several sensors that allow detecting user motion to use it as game mechanics [12, 13]. Finally, the use of wearable sensors is providing more accurate solutions to track motion capture; these can be tailored to specific needs and don't depend on a manufacturer's choice (common scenario in smartphones where every device has different types and quality of sensors), current developments are focusing on wireless and realistic motion tracking to provide sufficient data to better assess the exercising activities [14, 15].

In this paper the authors focused on a computer work scenario, in this case, the most common health risks are due to repetitive tasks, bad postures and sedentary caused by being seated most of the day. A lower member exergame was chosen as the leg is the most important body part used for locomotion, hence its care is of great importance to avoid circulatory and muscle disorders. The goal is to provide motivation and data with an affordable solution based on Arduino + Processing to accurate capture flexion and extension movements that can be perform within a computer working environment without requiring guides or attending to exercising sessions. The tracked information allows the worker and the health care specialist to learn about how well the exercises are being performed.

2 System Development

The system development is comprised of a lower member kinematics and active pause analysis to design the game and the system architecture, with this information the motion capture device is implemented using open electronics equipment and commercial inertial sensors with wireless communications to allow motion freedom to the player without constraining the exercise.

2.1 Lower Member Analysis and Exergame Design

The lower member is composed of a support (bones) and actuator (muscles) system with six degrees of freedom (DOF) from the hip (3) to the knee (1) and finally, to the ankle (2). An active pause requires the worker to take at least five minutes from

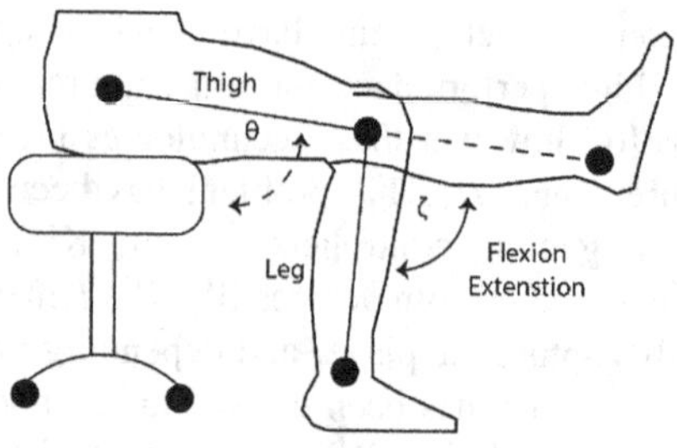

Fig. 1. Lower limb links, DOF and active pause movement

working activities to perform a series of exercises focused on different body parts. A common practiced exercise is the seated hamstring curl that requires repetitive leg rotations from 0° to 90° as presented in Fig. 1 This movement requires only one DOF, allowing to analyze the leg as a serial kinematic chain with three joints, the length of each link depends on the player's leg and thigh measures, and the flexion/extension rotations vary accordingly to the active pause exercise.

To represent the movement of the leg a forward kinematics analysis is performed as the angles are known from the exercises executed by the player; this model allows mapping the user's motion capture data with the virtual avatar in the exergame.

2.2 System Architecture

To develop the exergame the system architecture is defined as presented in Fig. 2, the main input is received from the player who can configure the thigh and leg lengths for the game to properly display the avatar and motion capture movements; another input is provided by the health care specialist, who indicates the amount of repetitions and acceptable ranges of motions, which may vary from player to player. The main mean of interactions is a the wearable sensor that the player places at the leg, the device is composed of an open electronics Arduino Uno board with a 9 DOF sensor that sends the information to the computer program through Bluetooth. When the game application receives the data, the virtual avatar's leg accordingly to what the player did, assigning scores and recording the movements for later assessment.

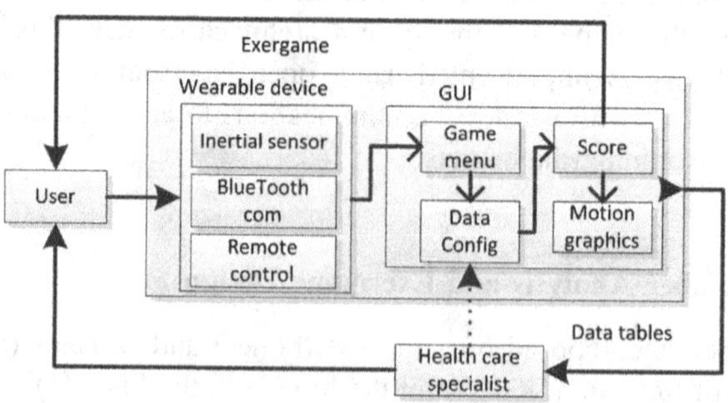

Fig. 2. System architecture

2.3 Game Design

The first elements to define for the exergame are the goal, the rules and the feedback. The system presented in this project has two main goals quantify the lower limb– leg active pause with motion captured data and encourage the workers into executing them within a more compelling setup. The rules of the exergame require the player to correctly execute the movements as these allow reaching the goal through flexion and extension rotations. The feedback is provided in several forms, one is the displayed score in the GUI, the avatar performing the movements, the motion graphics and the data tables, all of these allow improving the active pause execution by the player and the health care specialist.

With these elements in mind and considering the chosen the active pause exercise, the designed gaming scenario consisted in a ball kicking game where depending on the angle and angular velocity the player needs to reach certain objects at different distances.

2.4 Programming and Motion Capture

The exergame programming required reading the accelerometer and gyroscope data and write the values into the homogenous transformation matrix presented in (1). In this case as the model requires only one DOF the matrix is simplified with the following Denavit-Hartenberg values: $\boldsymbol{\theta_i}$ (Thigh: $\boldsymbol{\theta_1}$, Leg: $\boldsymbol{\theta_2}$), $\boldsymbol{d_i}$, $\boldsymbol{\alpha_i}$: 0 (no abduction or adduction considered), $\boldsymbol{a_i}$: (Thigh and leg lengths depending on each user) [16].

$$^{i-1}T_i = \begin{bmatrix} Cos\theta_i & 0_i & 0 & a_iCos\theta_i \\ Sin\theta_i & Cos\theta_i & 0 & a_iSin\theta_i \\ 0 & Cos\alpha_i & Cos\alpha_i & 0 \\ 0 & 0 & 0 & 1 \end{bmatrix} \quad (1)$$

With the rotation information the kinematics model allows transforming the virtual avatar leg with the player's movement. The game was programmed using angular movement, collisions and parabolic motion to kick the ball and send it to the objectives.

3 Results

To use the exergame, the user attaches the wireless device to his leg as presented in Fig. 2. To start the game the user uses a wireless controller to access menu and settings where it configures the lengths of the avatar's leg and exercise duration and repetitions. The game provides information regarding how to perform the exercises, its benefits and how to use the wearable sensor, once the setup is finished the player can start the game and engage into the active pause, while standing or seating.

The exergame was tested with ten users (five practiced sports and the other five didn't) kicking the ball with occupational health care specialists also participating. Motion capture data was obtained from the thigh and leg by placing the sensor around

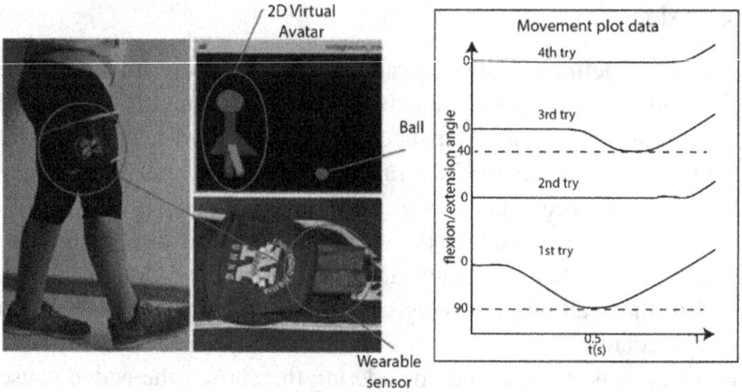

Fig. 3. Exergame components, test and motion graphics

them as presented in Fig. 3. A survey to acquire information about the experience and potential future works was applied to the participants.

From the survey it was possible to observe the users attention being caught, both groups found the development interesting, however, those who practice sports only manifested interest in the data as it could help them improve the performance while the other group concluded that gaming elements could motivate them into engaging and continuously practice the active pauses. Some challenges that arose from the test that affected the motion capture where the placement of the sensors and the comfort associated if it was tight or loose, where they asked if it was possible to have a smaller device, however, when placed correctly the users engaged into the game to get the score while perfecting the motion through the game's visuals and graphics. Regarding the graphics, players where focused on getting the game right that the geometry primitive avatar didn't caused any negative feedback, however, they manifested that a 3D scenario would also be interesting due to depth perception.

4 Conclusions

The developed exergame provided an entertaining scenario to practice leg hamstring curl active pauses; the game can be configured to work with gaming and monitoring elements modules to address the needs of occupational health care and fitness. A size restriction was met with the chosen materials as a consequence of using elements easily found in the market, however, the size can be reduced and this is part of future works, along with further developments in full body models and motion capture.

Acknowledgements. The authors wish to thank the Mil. University Nueva Granada for their support on project ING-1545 and also acknowledge the support of the Virtual Reality Center.

References

1. Jäger, M., Arbeitsschutz, B., Steinberg, U., Pekki, T.: Prevención de trastornos musculoesqueléticos en el lugar de trabajo, W. H. Organization, Ed., World Health Organization (2004)
2. World report on disability (2011). www.who.int/disabilities/world_report/2011/report/en/
3. Burdea, G.: Keynote address: virtual rehabilitation-benefits and challenges. In: 1st International Workshop on Virtual Reality Rehabilitation (Mental Health, Neurological, Physical, Vocational) VRMHR (2002)
4. Göbel S., Hardy S., Wendel V., Mehm F., Steinmetz R.: Serious games for health: personalized exergames. In: International Conference on Multimedia (2010)
5. Väätänen, A., Leikas, J.: Human-centred design and exercise games. In: Design and Use of Serious Games (2009)
6. Moeslund, T., Hilton, A., Krüger, V.: A survey of advances in vision-based human motion capture and analysis. Comput. Vis. Image Underst. **104**(2), 90–126 (2006)
7. Debevec, P.: The light stages and their applications to photoreal digital actors. In: SIGGRAPH Asia (2012)
8. Francese, R., Passero, I., Tortora, G.: Wiimote and Kinect: gestural user interfaces add a natural third dimension to HCI. In: International Working Conference on Advanced Visual Interfaces (2012)
9. Pogrzeba, Loreen, Wacker, Markus, Jung, Bernhard: Potentials of a Low-Cost Motion Analysis System for Exergames in Rehabilitation and Sports Medicine. In: Göbel, Stefan, Müller, Wolfgang, Urban, Bodo, Wiemeyer, Josef (eds.) GameDays 2012 and Edutainment 2012. LNCS, vol. 7516, pp. 125–133. Springer, Heidelberg (2012)
10. Bird, M.L., Cannell, J., Callisaya, M., Moles, E., Smith, S.: A single case study using Jintronix software for stroke rehabilitation and Kinect motion tracking for physical rehabilitation using a putt to stand aid and standby table. In: Smart Strokes 2014 Conference (2014)
11. Wingrave, C.A., Williamson, B., Varcholik, P.D., Rose, J., Miller, A., Charbonneau, E., Bott, J., LaViola, J.J.: The wiimote and beyond: spatially convenient devices for 3D user interfaces. Comput. Graphics Appl. **30**(2), 71–85 (2010)
12. Wylie, C.G., Coulton, P.: Mobile exergaming. In: International Conference on Advances in Computer Entertainment Technology (2008)
13. Chittaro, L., Sioni, R.: Turning the classic snake mobile game into a location–based exergame that encourages walking. In: Bang, M., Ragnemalm, E. (eds.) PERSUASIVE 2012. LNCS, vol. 7284, pp. 43–54. Springer, Heidelberg (2012)
14. Alshurafa, N., Xu, W., Liu, J.J., Huang, M.C., Mortazavi, B., Roberts, C.K., Sarrafzadeh, M.: Designing a robust activity recognition framework for health and exergaming using wearable sensors. Biomed. Health Inform. **18**(5), 1636–1646 (2014)
15. Mortazavi, B., Nyamathi, S., Lee, S.I., Wilkerson, T., Ghasemzadeh, H., Sarrafzadeh, M.: Near-realistic mobile exergames with wireless wearable sensors. Biomed. Health Inform. **18** (2), 449–456 (2014)
16. Hartenberg, R.S., Denavit, J.: Kinematic synthesis of linkages. McGraw-Hill, New York (1964)

Impact of Intermittent Stretching Exercise Animation on Prolonged-Sitting Computer Users' Attention and Work Performance

Sy-Chyi Wang[1(✉)] and Jin-Yuan Chern[2]

[1] Department of E-Learning Design and Management, National Chiayi University, Chiayi, Taiwan
kiky@mail.ncyu.edu.tw

[2] Department of Health Care Administration, Chang Jung Christian University, Tainan, Taiwan
chern@mail.cjcu.edu.tw

Abstract. The prevailing use of computers and the Internet has contributed to popular symptoms of visual impairment, musculoskeletal injuries, and even emotional disorders nowadays. While certain ergonomics software packages have thus been designed to avoid or relieve the symptoms, some studies raised concern about possible decline in attention and work performance. This study aimed to explore the effects of the computer stretch/massage software on extended computer users' attention and work performance. The Neuroscience brainwave monitor was used to evaluate the participants' attention. Thirty college students who work more than 4 h a day in front of computer were recruited and evenly distributed to two groups. The participants in the experimental group were asked to perform the task on computer for 30 min with a stretch program on, which was set to pop-up every 10 min for about 30 s each. The control group took no breaks or interventions. The results show that the computer break software did not decrease the participants' attention scores. Meanwhile the experimental group demonstrated higher work performance scores. It is suggested that during prolonged sitting computer work, breaks and body movements are necessary for better attention and work performance.

Keywords: Stretching exercise animation · Brainwave · Attention score · Work performance

1 Introduction

Computer and Internet use is becoming increasingly commonplace at home, in school, and at work nowadays. The benefits of increased convenience, connectivity, and flexibility that the computer and Internet has brought to us are tremendous. However, these new technologies also add more stress and new demands to our lives. A population-based prevalence study showed that on average children and adults in the US spent 54.9 % of their waking time, or 7 h 42 min per day, in sedentary behaviors, or leading a sedentary lifestyle (Matthews et al., 2008). It has been shown that extended computer use may contribute to symptoms of visual impairment (commonly dry eyes),

C. Stephanidis (Ed.): HCII 2015 Posters, Part II, CCIS 529, pp. 484–488, 2015.
DOI: 10.1007/978-3-319-21383-5_81

musculoskeletal injuries (e.g., neck, shoulder, and low back pain), skin problems, and even emotional disorders (Hayes et al., 2007). Among the many possible causes of injuries, not taking regular breaks from computer work has been acknowledged as an important factor (Broughton, 2008).

In dealing with these computer-related health issues, more and more ergonomics software packages have been designed to prompt computer users to take a break and guide them toward regular exercise. Although the relevant programs showed positive effects on health behaviors and conditions (Marangoni, 2010; Van den Heuvel et al., 2003), Wang and Chern (2013) found that worries about decline in attention or work performance caused by the program's constant interruptions were also expressed by some of the research participants. Therefore, although most of the participants were aware of the benefits of the program toward their health and agreed on the necessity of the programs alike, they still hesitated to adopt the interventions.

For a long time, most researchers believe that attention is a limited resource and it will be used up overtime. Nevertheless, a recent study showed that brief interruptions could boost performance (Ariga and Lleras, 2011). Similar to building muscles, it is critical to rest and recover for the second round after sustained use. The problem is that most workers do not take enough breaks, especially breaks involving body movement (Trougakos, 2009). Research showed that 5-minute exercises improved children's performance on attention and reaction time (Hsieh, 2009). Massage therapy and yoga also showed positive effects on attention and mood improvement for students with Attention-deficit/hyperactivity disorder (ADHD) (Archer and Kostrzewa, 2012; Jensen and Kenny, 2004; Field, Quintino, Hernandez-Reif and Koslovsky, 1998).

In sum, research claimed that breaks with body movement would decrease visual and musculoskeletal discomfort for extended computer users, and the computer break/stretch programs also have similar effects on the computer symptoms. Research also found that brief distractions or breaks/exercises help improve attention and boosted work performance. However, the effect of the break/stretch programs alike on attention and work performance stays unknown. This study aimed to develop a user friendly computer program to deliver a series of 3D in-chair stretch and massage animation clips for prolonged sitting computer users, and to examine the program effect on people's attention and work performance.

2 Methods

This study recruited 30 college students aged 18–24 as research participants, who normally work more than 4 h a day in front of computer. The participants were asked to perform the task on computer for about 30 min with the designed stretch program on, which was set to pop-up every 10 min for 30–40 s each. The 30 participants were divided into two groups. The control group took no breaks or interventions throughout the task. The experimental group was told to follow the stretch animation movements. A pretest and post-test questionnaire was administered to elicit demographic information, symptom perception and mood state. The Neuroscience's brainwave monitor was used for the evaluation of the participants' attention. Figure 1 shows the experimentation process and a screenshot of work performance results.

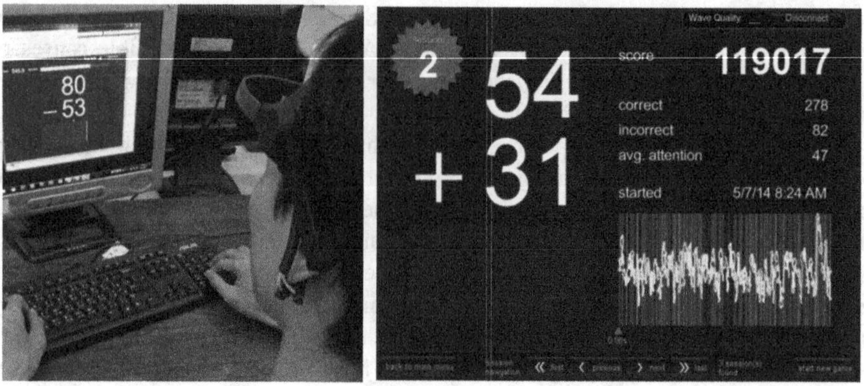

Fig. 1. Experimentation process (L) and a screenshot of work performance (R)

3 Results

The data were collected in three consecutive sessions. Overall, the difference in the attention scores (Fig. 2) between the control group (42.69 ± 2.70) and the experimental group (47.22 ± 4.03) reached statistical significance ($p < 0.005$). The result indicates that the computer break system for delivering the stretch program exerted a significant impact on the participants' attention.

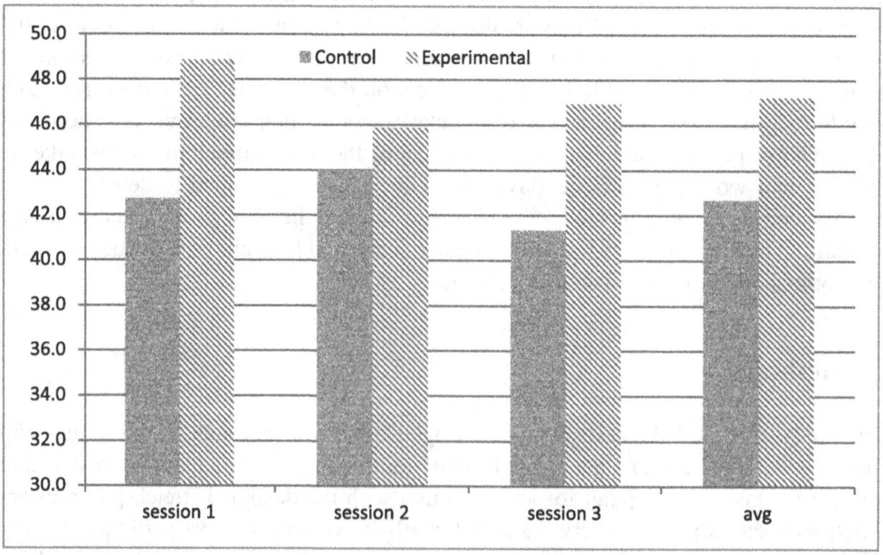

Fig. 2. Attention scores for three sessions and the means

Figure 3 shows the work performance scores for the control group and the experimental group respectively. The difference in means between the control group (76902 ± 23869.5) and the experimental group (99037 ± 36254.5) reached statistical significance (p = 0.029), indicating that the implementation of the computer break system for delivering the stretch program exerted a meaningful impact on the participants' working performance.

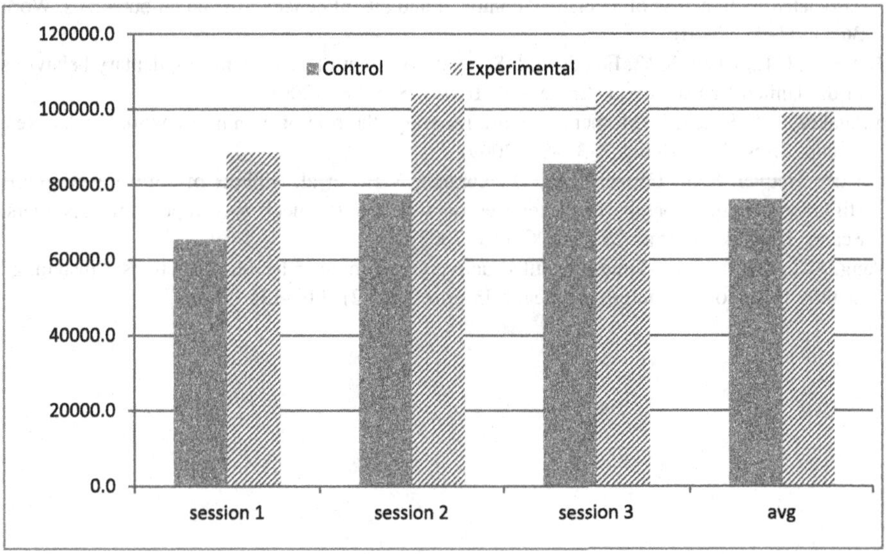

Fig. 3. Work performance scores for three sessions and the means

4 Conclusions and Suggestions

This study first called for attention on the negative effects of extended computer use and examined the potential benefits of computer break/stretch program. It is suggested that break and body movement are necessary during prolonged-sitting computer work. In brief, along with the increasingly severe problems associated with extended computer use, we need to figure out a way to balance the harm the computer has brought to us, particularly for this tech-savvy generation.

References

Archer, T., Kostrzewa, R.M.: Physical exercise alleviates ADHD symptoms: regional deficits and development trajectory. Neurotox. Res. **21**(2), 195–209 (2012)

Ariga, A., Lleras, A.: Brief and rare mental "breaks" keep you focused: deactivation and reactivation of task goals preempt vigilance decrements. Cognition **118**(3), 439–443 (2011). doi:10.1016/j.cognition.2010.12.007

Broughton, A.: Eurofound: Place of work and working conditions (2008). Retrieved January 14, 2012. http://www.eurofound.europa.eu/ewco/studies/tn0701029s/tn0701029s_4.htm

Field, T., Quintino, O., Hernandez-Reif, M., Koslovsky, G.: Adolescents with attention deficit hyperactivity disorder benefit from massage therapy. Adolescence **33**(129), 103–108 (1998)

Jensen, P.S., Kenny, D.T.: The effects of yoga on the attention and behavior of boys with attention-deficit/hyperactivity disorder (ADHD). J. Attention Dis. **7**(4), 205–216 (2004)

Hayes, J.R., Sheedy, J.E., Stelmack, J.A., et al.: Computer use, symptoms, and quality of life. Optom. Vis. Sci. **84**(8), E738–E755 (2007). doi:10.1097/OPX.0b013e31812f7546

Marangoni, A.H.: Effects of intermittent stretching exercises at work on musculoskeletal pain associated with the use of a personal computer and the influence of media on outcomes. Work **36**(1), 27–37 (2010)

Matthews, C.E., Chen, K.Y., Freedson, P.S., et al.: Amount of time spent in sedentary behaviors in the United States. Am. J. Epidemiol. **167**(7), 875–881 (2008)

Trougakos, J.P., Hideg, I.: Momentary work recovery: the role of within-day work breaks. Res. Occup. Stress Well-Being **7**, 37–84 (2009)

Van den Heuvel, S.G., Looze, M.P., Hildebrandt, V.H., et al.: Effects of software programs stimulating regular breaks and exercises on work-related neck and upper limb disorders. Scand. J. Work Environ. **29**(2), 106–116 (2003)

Wang, S.C., Chern, J.Y.: Time-scheduled delivery of computer health animations: "Installing" healthy habits of computer use. Health Inform. J. **19**(2), 116–126 (2013)

Location and Context Awareness

Dynamic Adaptation of Personalised Recommendations Based on Tourists' Affective State

Petr Aksenov[1(✉)], Andres Navarro[2], David Oyarzun[2], Theo Arentze[1], and Astrid Kemperman[1]

[1] Eindhoven University of Technology, Eindhoven, The Netherlands
{p.aksenov, t.a.arentze, a.d.a.m.kemperman}@tue.nl

[2] Vicomtech-IK4, Donostia/San Sebastian, Spain
{anavarro, doyarzun}@vicomtech.org

Abstract. The presented work in progress is on the inclusion of information about tourists' emotions in personalising their cultural program recommendations. Emotions are estimated unobtrusively and in real time from facial expressions during tourists' interaction with a dedicated 3D- and AR-based application for cultural tourism. The affective data so collected is used for creating an affective map of an area, where each attraction (point of interest) is assigned an affective score in accordance with the involved affective model. The main goal of our work is to use these affective scores in determining and recommending attractions and activities which suit, among other criteria, the tourist's current or desired affective state.

Keywords: Affective computing · Emotions · Recommendation · Tourism · Utility

1 Introduction

Within the context of this work, the suitability of a cultural attraction as a potential recommendation to a tourist relies on the concept of process utility that the attraction and its associated activities can generate with respect to satisfying the tourist's particular needs for leisure [1]. These needs are dynamic and they are connected to individual preferences, which has an impact on the activity choices tourists make [2].

Recommending attractions by determining their needs-based utility scores does not require knowing about one's emotions explicitly. However, previous research has demonstrated that tourists' emotions during a visit have a considerable impact on the perceived experience and satisfaction [3]. In turn, this may lead to changes in the utility score that a particular attraction is able to generate for a particular tourist.

From the perspective of awareness of the individual preferences, a tourist's affective state represents an additional dimension of these preferences. And the ability to know the expected or the desired (target) affective state allows us to introduce a correction to the utility score that would take into account how well a prospective

C. Stephanidis (Ed.): HCII 2015 Posters, Part II, CCIS 529, pp. 491–496, 2015.
DOI: 10.1007/978-3-319-21383-5_82

"affective" change to be acquired from experiencing a particular attraction meets this tourist's emotional preferences.

The approach we propose in this work is guided by two important trends in personalisation, which we combine together. On the one hand, we learn about one's affects from facial expression in a uniform automatic way and in real-time, a tendency that has been recently receiving more attention and interest in the area of location-based services [3, 4]. Besides, we also address the complex nature of the emotional experience of a cultural visit by aggregating prototypical and continuous emotional components, as further explained in Sect. 2.1. And on the other hand, by connecting our affective data with locations and places (cfr. [5–7]), we further address a particular area of personalised recommendations of cultural attractions and activities to tourists.

2 Overview of the Approach

As Fig. 1 illustrates, our approach rests on three building blocks. This section introduces and discusses each of them in detail.

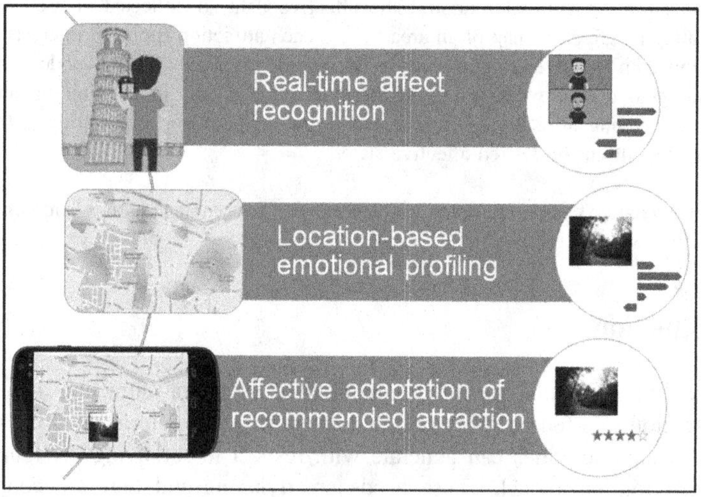

Fig. 1. Three building blocks of the approach to personalising recommendations using place-based affective data collected in real time.

2.1 Real-time Affect Recognition

As opposed to self-reported or expert observer assessment of the user's affective state, which can be biased by the user's capability to remember or explain [3], we estimate tourists' emotions systematically and unobtrusively from their facial expressions.

Being able to record the users' face during their interaction with a dedicated 3D- and AR-based application for cultural tourism, we learn about their emotions in a uniform way and in real-time, allowing us to make interpersonal relationships.

Using a two-step, deterministic detection of facial features and adjustment of deformable 3D face model [8], a lightweight and robust method for facial action tracking, a user's facial expression can be estimated on a mid-range mobile device.

In affect recognition, two main approaches are used to describe the emotions: a discrete set of emotional categories (i.e. six basic categories by Ekman [9]) or a multidimensional space where each dimension represents a quality of the emotion (i.e. valence/pleasure, arousal/activation, dominance [10]). Despite the limitations of both perspectives, there is extensive evidence of their value to describe emotions and we use both approaches to better capture the emotional experience of the tourist, as described in Sect. 2.2.

As a result, a continuous Valence-Arousal dimensional and a discrete categorical (anger, disgust, fear, happiness, sadness and surprise) estimation of the user's affective state is obtained in real-time that we can use for recommending certain attractions.

2.2 Location-Based Emotional Profiling

Similar to advertising or multimedia analysis using consumers' emotional response, we propose to aggregate the different estimated affective states of the tourists collected during their experience with a certain attraction into an emotional profile of that attraction. Examples of the aggregation of users' emotional response based on their location can be found from the analysis of social networks content, self-report applications or implicit sensor approaches [11].

However, tourist's experience during the visit of an attraction might be composed of continuous events that have a different impact on the overall emotional perception of that attraction. In fact, it has been proposed that while tourists remember a visit as a collection of highlighted discrete events, the often ignored continuous emotional experience influences the perception of the attraction [3].

For that reason, we argue that the emotional response of the tourists should be analysed in a multi-componential manner where the complex nature of their emotion can be better addressed. Following Russell's framework [12], we propose to incorporate in the emotional response analysis the following concepts: (i) "core affect", a neurophysiological continuous state that is consciously accessible as a simple representation, (ii) "mood", a longer in time but less intense emotional state, (iii) "prototypical emotional episodes", an event that matches the cognitive structure of causal connections and temporal order for a person concept of each emotion.

Including both core affect and prototypical emotional episodes components into the emotional profile of the attraction, which as explained previously are both recognised from the facial expression, we address the often forgotten but influencing continuous affective state during the visit and the more highlighted discrete emotional bursts. An aggregated profile will be reduced to an emotional dimensional vector, allowing the use of a distance function to compare profiles and to search for a target emotion. The inclusion of mood as an attraction transversal emotional bias will be explored in the future.

2.3 Affective Adaptation of Recommended Attractions

Following the discussion in Sect. 2.2, in order to compare two affective states we need to find the difference between them. For the adaptation purposes, our primary interest is not this difference itself but the utility it corresponds to, and the main assumption here is that small differences correspond to positive utilities. This is in line with a particular expectation that the situations when the attraction's affective state matches the tourist's desired state (no difference) should correspond to the maximum added value. Likewise, big differences are expected to produce negative utilities.

As an illustration of the collaborative contribution of both the needs and the affects to the cumulative utility score, we can think of two different attractions, A and B, that a tourist can visit. Attraction A has a higher needs-based utility score than B, with both scores emerging from the satisfaction of the tourist's respective needs and preferences. The affective profile set by the tourist as a target indicates the preference for activities with some higher values on the specified affects. From A's affective profile, which is a product of accumulating the affective responses left for A by previous tourists, the system is able to learn that this attraction corresponds to only marginal levels on the requested affects. This makes the difference between A and the target affective state big, which in turn decreases A's affects-based utility score. Attraction B, while having a lower needs-based utility score than A, matches a lot closer to the target affective state, which increases the affects-based contribution to its utility score. As a result, the needs-based (main) score and the affects-driven (complementary) score together produce a higher cumulative utility for B, making it the next most suitable recommendation.

Currently we are investigating which metrics and norms should be used for establishing the "affect-difference – affects-based utility" mapping. As we already mentioned earlier, one aspect of reasoning here is that the affects-based utility decreases as the difference increases, with the zero difference corresponding to the maximum utility value. In particular, big differences produce negative affects-based utilities, decreasing the cumulative utility and thus lowering the attraction's suitability. Another reasoning aspect that must be taken into account is that in general, each involved affective dimension is of different importance to the overall affective change and therefore needs to be assigned its own weight that would determine its contribution. This, in turn, means that solutions that spread unevenly in different affective dimensions can be equally suitable as they would produce the same cumulative utilities.

3 Evaluation Directions and Perspectives

An attraction's affective profile is a product of the analysis of emotional traces that previous tourists left for this attraction. It means that in order to involve these affective grounds into the recommendation process, we need to collect a sufficient amount of this affective history for each participating attraction. This preparatory activity can be performed using crowdsourcing, which has proved effective for similar tasks [11]. Following our approach to affect recognition, respondents' facial expressions will be analysed in real-time, forming in each case an instance of input for the corresponding attraction's affective profile. It must be noted here that affective profiles are adjusted accordingly as new affective responses arrive.

The main goal of our adaptation is to reflect on the tourist's affective preferences and the respective changes. And on the one hand, the arrangements for the evaluation depend on the success and the results of the crowdsourcing initiative. On the other hand, the performance depends also on the criteria used in comparing affective profiles as was covered in Sect. 2.3.

With the above considerations in mind, we outline our current perspective on the evaluation scenario, which aims to understand the usefulness of the corrections to the attractions' utilities introduced by taking tourists' affects into account in the proposed way. In the entry task the current and target affective states of the participants will be collected. The purpose of the target state is straightforward, and knowing about the current state is required for setting up the conditions for the affects-based utility's zero contribution. If a participant is satisfied with the current state, the two states are set to match. The utility-based recommendation engine receives these states and determines which attraction(s) have the highest utility value(s) in each of the two cases – with and without taking the affects into account. In the main task the participants' affective responses to both recommended attractions will be collected. Afterwards, the participants will be asked to rank to what extent (e.g., using a standard 7-point Likert scale) each attraction would suit for acquiring the target affective state.

4 Discussion and Future Steps

We have presented our work in progress on the dynamic adaptation of personalised recommendations of cultural programs based on tourists' affective state.

The application potential of the approach is two-fold: (i) certain attractions and associated activities can be recommended as the most suitable ones to the tourist who has set a desired affective state; (ii) a tourist's affective state on a certain activity/attraction can be the basis for recommending such an activity/attraction to future tourists whose affective profiles would match with the ones obtained from the affective data collected during tourists' previous experiences.

Our next steps in the short term will be devoted to elaborating on the already mentioned certain analytical and practical aspects of the approach. In particular, the details of the dimensional affective space to be used and the subsequent elaboration of the appropriate distance measures need to be addressed. This goes in line with the arrangements necessary for the crowdsourcing affective data collection step, the results of which will be used in planning and elaborating on the actual evaluation scenario. In the long-run, we plan to extend our emotional profiling to long-term affective states, considering the bidirectional relationship between an attraction experience and the tourist's mood, and to explore the influence of personality and culture in the emotional response of the tourist.

Acknowledgments. The research leading to these results has received funding from the European Community's Seventh Framework Program (FP7/2007-2013) under the Grant Agreement number 611040. The authors are solely responsible for the information reported in this paper. It does not represent the opinion of the Community. The Community is not responsible for any use that might be made of the information contained in this paper.

References

1. Arentze, T.A.: LATUS: a dynamic model for leisure activity-travel utility simulation. In: Proceedings of the 94th Transportation Research Board Annual Meeting (2014)
2. Arentze, T.A., Kemperman, A.D.A.M., Aksenov, P.: The role of dynamic needs in tourists' activity choice: design and results of a stated choice experiment. In: Proceedings of the International Choice Modeling Conference, Austin, TX (2015) (To appear)
3. Kim, J.J., Fesenmaier, D.R.: Measuring emotions in real time: implications for tourism experience design. J. Travel Res. **54**(4), 419–429 (2014)
4. Al-Husain, L., Kanjo, E., Chamberlain, A.: Sense of space: mapping physiological emotion response in urban space. In: Proceedings of the 2013 ACM Conference on Pervasive and Ubiquitous Computing, pp. 1321–1324. Adjunct Publication (2013)
5. Mody, R.N., Willis, K.S., Kerstein, R.: WiMo: location-based emotion tagging. In: Proceedings of the 8th International Conference on Mobile and Ubiquitous Multimedia, pp. 1–4 (2009)
6. Truelove, M., Winter, S.: Emotional cartography for crowd-sourcing elusive spatial concepts. In: Arrowsmith, C., et al. (eds.) Progress in Geospatial Science Research, pp. 512–532. RMIT University, Melbourne (2013)
7. Quercia, D., Schifanella, R., Aiello, L.M.: The shortest path to happiness: recommending beautiful, quiet, and happy routes in the city. In: Proceedings of the 25th ACM Conference on Hypertext and Social Media, pp. 116–125 (2014)
8. Unzueta, L., Pimenta, W., Goenetxea, J., Santos, L.P., Dornaika, F.: Efficient generic face model fitting to images and video. Image Vis. Comput. **32**(5), 321–334 (2014)
9. Ekman, P.: Basic emotions. In: Handbook of Cognition and Emotion, pp. 45–60 (1999)
10. Marsella, S., Gratch, J., Petta, P.: Computational models of emotion. In: Scherer, K.R., Bänziger, T., Roesch, E. (eds.) A Blueprint for Affective Computing: A Sourcebook and Manual. Oxford University Press, Oxford (2010)
11. Klettner, S., Huang, H., Schmidt, M., Gartner, G.: Crowdsourcing affective responses to space. Kartographische Nachrichten **2**(3), 66–72 (2013)
12. Russell, J.A.: Core affect and the psychological construction of emotion. Psychol. Rev. **110**, 145–172 (2003)

Dynamic Operations Wayfinding System (DOWS) for Nuclear Power Plants

Ronald L. Boring(✉), Thomas A. Ulrich, and Roger T. Lew

Idaho National Laboratory, Idaho Falls, ID, USA
{ronald.boring, thomas.ulrich, roger.lew}@inl.gov

Abstract. A novel software tool is proposed to aid reactor operators in responding to upset plant conditions. The purpose of the Dynamic Operations Wayfinding System (DOWS) is to diagnose faults, prioritize those faults, identify paths to resolve those faults, and deconflict the optimal path for the operator to follow. The objective of DOWS is to take the guesswork out of the best way to combine procedures to resolve compound faults, mitigate low threshold events, or respond to severe accidents. DOWS represents a uniquely flexible and dynamic computer-based procedure system for operators.

Keywords: Nuclear power plant · Computer-based procedures · Wayfinding · Severe accident

1 Introduction

1.1 Background

We propose a novel software tool to aid reactor operators in responding to upset plant conditions. The proposed Dynamic Operations Wayfinding System (DOWS) effectively serves as a global positioning system (GPS) navigator for the reactor operator to maintain safe plant operations despite emerging or unanticipated plant conditions. Current paper-based procedures are static, and they offer minimal flexibility in responding to plant upsets that occur: (1) below a certain setpoint (e.g., slow leaks), (2) beyond the design basis of the plant (e.g., severe accidents), or (3) in an unanticipated or unexampled manner (e.g., compound events). The operating procedures for all three are underspecified—in the first case, abnormal or emergency operating procedures are not warranted, but the condition falls outside normal operations; in the second case, the severe accident management guidelines are typically very broad and do not offer the operator useful step-by-step guidance in the face of failed systems; in the final case, compound events may force the operator down a procedure path that fails to resolve the most risk significant fault.

1.2 Existing Procedures in Nuclear Power Plants

A crew of nuclear power plant operators follow detailed procedures to cover a variety of plant contexts. These context-dependent procedures include: standard (or normal)

C. Stephanidis (Ed.): HCII 2015 Posters, Part II, CCIS 529, pp. 497–502, 2015.
DOI: 10.1007/978-3-319-21383-5_83

operating procedures (SOPs), abnormal operating procedures (AOPs), emergency operating procedures (EOPs), and severe accident management guidelines (SAMGs). The use of these procedures ranks from frequent for SOPs to extremely rare for SAMGs. The current regulatory framework in the United States means that existing plants exclusively maintain the use of paper-based procedures, while new builds are adopting various forms of computer-based procedures. These computer-based procedures follow a continuum specified in IEEE-Std-1786 [1]:

- *Type 1* procedures simply feature digitized, static versions of the paper-based procedures.
- *Type 2* procedures feature embedded indicators that are displayed as part of the procedures on a screen. Without the embedded procedures, reactor operators have to find indicators across the control boards [2].
- *Type 3* procedures combine the features of Type I and Type II procedures with soft controls. Rather than carry out actions on the plant using physical knobs, switches, and dials on the control boards, the operators can perform those activities with the press of an on-screen button in the procedures.

These three types of computer-based procedures offer significant advances over existing plant operations (while introducing some new types of failure opportunities [3]). However, they tend to follow the same format as the paper-based procedures they replace. In other words, with few exceptions [4], they do not respond or change the procedural path depending on the plant state or emerging circumstances. Perhaps it is appropriate to add a *Type 4* procedure to the existing taxonomy. We posit that a Type 4 procedure is one that adapts in response to changing conditions at the plant. Adaptation without optimization is fruitless. This is the main advantage of DOWS—it optimizes the procedure to allow the operator to respond in the safest and most efficient manner to emerging plant upsets.

2 DOWS Conceptual Overview

2.1 Purpose

The purpose of DOWS is to diagnose faults, prioritize those faults, identify paths to resolve those faults, and deconflict the optimal path for the operator to follow. The objective of DOWS is to take the guesswork out of the best way to combine procedures to resolve the compound faults. Further, the proposed DOWS is dynamic in that it adapts to changing conditions, thus becoming a uniquely flexible yet useful resource for operators. It is hypothesized that DOWS will reduce variability in operational outcomes when responding to changing or inadequately proceduralized events. Such variability has been a cause for considerable concern in prior operator studies (e.g., [5]). Minimizing operator performance variability while maintaining a dynamic response to complex and changing conditions are keys to ensuring DOWS is part of a fault-tolerant and resilient system.

2.2 Navigating a Physical World Map vs. a Procedure

DOWS builds on wayfinding algorithms to calculate dynamically the optimal route for the operator to complete a task. Just as a GPS navigator can accommodate wrong turns and road obstructions to lead the driver to the desired destination, DOWS treats plant conditions and states as constraints, plant risk as the criterion for preferred route selection, and operational goals as destinations. The objective is to craft a route for the operator to complete specific tasks, even if the plant conditions create unique scenarios not anticipated by procedure writers.

The task space for operators following procedures can easily be mapped to the types of environmental primitives used in contemporary wayfinding algorithms in computerized navigation aids. The primitives used in map-based navigation can be cross-walked to procedures as follows:

- *Starting Point → Current Operational Context:* In the physical world, the starting point represents the geographic coordinates where the person is currently. When following procedures, the context is usually an initiating event that triggers a particular procedure. For example, an alarm would trigger a particular AOP. This AOP determines the destination.
- *Destination → Desired End State:* The destination is, of course, the location to which the individual wishes to go. Likewise, any procedural action is designed to build toward a desired end state, typically a restoration of the steady state condition characteristic of the plant's normal operating mode.
- *Path → Procedure:* In the cartographic world, the path marks a route between two points. In nuclear operations, such a path is marked by a procedure that the operators follow in order to change the current state of the plant. A literal path moves through a fixed terrain; a procedure changes the terrain to map the process to the physical characteristics of the plant. Both path and procedure include several attributes.
- *Path Difficulty → Task Complexity:* A navigational algorithm may take attributes of the path into account (e.g., paved vs. unpaved roadway). In an operational context, this can be equated with task complexity—how easy or difficult it is to complete the task specified in the procedure. It is generally desirable to take the easiest procedural path, but other factors may dictate different priorities.
- *Path Length → Procedure Steps:* A short road may take longer than a long road simply due to speed limits. In operational terms, the number of steps of a procedure equates to the path length. Note that the number of steps is not always a good measure of duration, because steps are rarely of equal duration.
- *Path Duration → Time Required:* An important metric for navigational aids is how long it will take to reach the destination. For operations, where critical time windows may factor into the safety of the plant, one of the key measures is the time required to complete the procedure steps.
- *Intersection → Branching Point:* An intersection represents a waypoint along the path, after which an additional navigation route must be considered. For each alternate route, the factors under consideration such as path duration must be calculated to determine the optimal path among alternate routes. For procedure

following, a branching point represents the point at which the operator jumps to a different point in the current procedure or to a different procedure entirely. Rarely are such branching points optional—they are invariably followed if the conditions are met. For the purposes of procedure wayfinding, branching points may represent alternate priorities when confronting compoud faults and can help operators to prioritize optimal routes to follow through multiple, concurrent procedures.

- *Obstruction → System Fault:* An obstruction is an emerging condition (e.g., a traffic jam or detour) that prevents travel along the desired route. An equivalent situation during procedure following would be a sudden system fault that prevents the operator from activating required plant functions or even diagnosing current plant states. Obstructions and system faults require dynamic recalculation to find a new route.

This list is not exhaustive, but it provides a sample of how mapping can occur for both physical environments and procedural paths in reactor operations. It is not necessary to invent new algorithms (although it may be desirable to adopt different wayfinding strategies like simplest rather than shortest path [6]). Rather, it is necessary to translate these characteristics from the plant and the procedures into primitives that can be used to build maps through tasks. A particular facet of mapping these primitives becomes parsing procedural blocks of activities. Rather than take an entire 23-step EOP, for example, as a single path, that EOP should be divided into logical subpaths that can be combined to form an entire procedure. The parsing allows flexibility in the implementation of DOWS.

2.3 DOWS Implementation

The DOWS algorithm queries a variety of data (e.g., existing alarms, state of systems, plant mode, etc.) when predetermined parameters are met and analyzes this information. The output of the system includes the conclusion(s) of the analysis on a display that may include a system overview given at the appropriate level of detail. A context-based procedure with visual aids if needed will be displayed to assist the operator in taking the right action based on the system diagnosed faults. A level of confidence could be provided to the operator based on the algorithm's output. This could be based on data quality and quantity as well as risk significance of the faults. The operator is given the option to take other actions if merited.

DOWS builds on best practices for computer-based procedures (e.g., [1]), including the display of plant states and the use of soft controls. Required data are available to the operator within DOWS to aid in decision-making. Additionally, best features of GPS navigator displays will be incorporated, including the quick selection of goals (destinations), the overview of different paths, the display of information relevant to immediate task and situation awareness, warnings about impending obstacles toward goal completion, and the zoomable view to different levels of information.

3 The Need for DOWS

There is considerable cost in terms of resources to amend existing paper-based procedures to become computer-based procedures. The benefits may not be apparent, especially with the additional complexity of adding primitives to allow the system to navigate optimal paths. We conclude this paper with three distinct examples where the overhead to adapt procedures is quickly outweighed by the advantages afforded by DOWS:

- Idaho National Laboratory has developed a computerized operator support system (COSS) prototype [7] that is capable of early fault diagnosis. The challenge with such diagnosis is that the fault detection is often sufficiently sensitive to anticipate the issue before it has reached the threshold for an alarm. Early diagnosis can mitigate faults before they have an actual consequence on plant operations; yet, currently, the procedures are not written at this level. DOWS enables the system to provide relevant procedural guidance to operators to allow them to respond to the COSS and realize its potential.
- The SAMGs developed for severe accidents are not at the same level of detail as AOPs and EOPs, forcing operators to make many on-the-fly decisions without clear procedural guidance [8]. While severe accidents are extremely rare, operators responding to such an event must overcome severe psychological and physical stress, which do not make ideal companions to complex decision making. DOWS, when properly configured, can serve as an aid to allow operators to navigate the difficulties of severe accidents, prioritize responses, and work step-by-step toward achieving desired end states.
- In compound faults, there is often symptom masking, which makes it difficult for operators to diagnose the root cause of particular faults. For example, a steam line break may mask the symptoms of a co-occurring steam generator tube rupture [5]. Moreover, there may be conflicting indications that result in ambiguity when the operator needs to select the most appropriate procedure. Because procedures must be followed linearly, the operator potentially loses considerable time and minimizes the safety margin when he or she steps through an incorrect procedure. As such, resolving conflicting procedural paths becomes difficult and time-consuming in the prescribed linear process. DOWS can prevent false paths by shortening the number of potentially irrelevant prescripted steps in a procedure and by dynamically recalculating new procedure paths when warranted.

4 Conclusions

This paper has presented initial concepts related to DOWS. DOWS will initially be prototyped on a select number of scenarios and procedures (e.g., steam generator tube rupture masked by a steam line break) in order to establish a proof of concept for the design approach and to optimize the algorithm. A series of operator tests will be conducted to determine the efficacy of the wayfinding algorithm and the quality of the information presentation. An iterative design approach will be employed, refining the interface and algorithm over successive scenarios of increased complexity. The final design should as a result be scalable to other plant systems and will represent a significant, original technological advance to operator performance and overall plant resilience.

5 Disclaimer

This work of authorship was prepared as an account of work sponsored by an agency of the United States Government. Neither the United States Government, nor any agency thereof, nor any of their employees makes any warranty, express or implied, or assumes any legal liability or responsibility for the accuracy, completeness, or usefulness of any information, apparatus, product, or process disclosed, or represents that its use would not infringe privately-owned rights. Idaho National Laboratory is a multi-program laboratory operated by Battelle Energy Alliance LLC, for the United States Department of Energy under Contract DE-AC07-05ID14517.

References

1. Institute of Electrical and Electronics Engineers: IEEE Guide for Human Factors Applications of Computerized Operating Procedure Systems (COPS) at Nuclear Power Generating Stations and Other Nuclear Facilities. IEEE Std 1786-2011, New York (2011)
2. Boring, R.L.: Information foraging in nuclear power plant control rooms. In: Proceedings of 2011 European Safety and Reliability (ESREL) Conference: Advances in Safety, Reliability, and Risk Management, pp. 654–660 (2011)
3. Boring, R.L., Gertman, D.I.: Current human reliability analysis methods applied to computerized procedures. In: Joint Probabilistic Safety Assessment and Management and European Safety and Reliability Conference, 16B-Th4-3 (2012)
4. Doutre, J.L., Pirus, D., Ratti, L., Audet, G.: N4 NPP's operation: preliminary tendencies. In: Enlarged Halden Programme Group Meeting, Lillehammer (1998)
5. Forester, J., Dang, V.N., Bye, A., Lois, E., Massaiu, S., Broberg, H., Braarud, P.Ø., Boring, R., Männistö, Liao, H., Julius, J., Parry, G., Nelson, P.: The International HRA Empirical Study: Lessons Learned from Comparing HRA Methods Predictions to HAMMLAB Simulator Data, NUREG-2127, U.S. Nuclear Regulatory Commission (2014)
6. Duckham, M., Kulik, L.: "Simplest" paths: automated route selection for navigation. In: Kuhn, W., Worboys, M.F., Timpf, S. (eds.) COSIT 2003. LNCS, vol. 2825, pp. 169–185. Springer, Heidelberg (2003)
7. Thomas, K., Boring, R., Lew, R., Ulrich, T., Vilim, R.: A computerized operator support system prototype. INL/EXT-13–29651, Idaho National Laboratory (2013)
8. Vayssier, G.: Present day EOPS and SAMG—Where do we go from here? Nuclear Eng. Technol. **44**, 225–236 (2012)

Context-Aware Systems for Complex Data Analysis

Adam Fouse(✉), Stacy Pfautz, and Gabriel Ganberg

Aptima, Inc., Woburn, MA, USA
{afouse, spfautz, ganberg}@aptima.com

Abstract. Increasingly there is a need to analyze a large quantity of diverse, multidimensional data in a timely, efficient manner. A computational awareness of context can improve the speed and accuracy of complex data analysis, and promote more effective human-machine collaboration. We describe ongoing work to develop a framework that monitors human-machine interactions, analyzes context, and augments the system (such as prioritizing information, providing recommendations, adapting an interface, adjusting the level of automation, proactively fetching data, managing notifications, sharing context with others, personalizing the system, etc.). We believe that we can facilitate complex data analysis by adapting systems to meet analysts needs based upon the varying demands of the tasks, priorities, resources, time, user state, and environment.

Keywords: Context-aware systems · Recommender systems · Complex data analysis · Interactive visualization

1 Introduction

The rapid increase in ubiquitous computing devices and the Internet of Things has created interest in computational awareness of context [1, 2]. In these settings, context is often primarily concerned with the social and environment setting in which actions are taking place. We apply similar concepts to support people performing data analysis in complex environments, such as geospatial awareness for disaster response, intelligence analysis, and healthcare. In these settings, useful information about context includes not only the social and environmental setting, but also the collection and characterization of relevant data, the history of interaction, and explicit or implicit tasking given to analysts. To support users working in such environments, we have developed a framework to monitor and analyze context in real-time, and applied this framework to improve interaction with analysis support systems.

Traditional data analysis and decision-support tools lack an understanding of context, such as the semantics of the information, how it relates to tasks, goals, and objectives, and even the workflow or cognitive strengths and limitations of the human analyst. The goal of incorporating these types of contextual information to guide interaction is to intelligently adapt or augment a system or application to best suit a user's current situation and needs.

C. Stephanidis (Ed.): HCII 2015 Posters, Part II, CCIS 529, pp. 503–507, 2015.
DOI: 10.1007/978-3-319-21383-5_84

2 Defining and Analyzing Context

Our work with developing context-aware systems for data analysis has been informed by several years of work across a variety of fields, including geospatial analysis, medical data analysis, and open-source intelligence analysis. Based on interviews with expert analysts in each of these fields, we have developed a working definition of context as it can be applied to the design of systems.

We define context as explicit and implicit situational information about entities, the environment, and their interactions which may impact interpretation or decisions [4]. In our experience, an effective context-aware application has three major functions, as illustrated in Fig. 1: First, monitor the context explicitly present within the system's environment and infer implicit context such as user state; Second, analyze and reason about goals and intent (including latent knowledge) within the contextual situation as a whole; Third, augment the environment or situation based on its understanding of the situation.

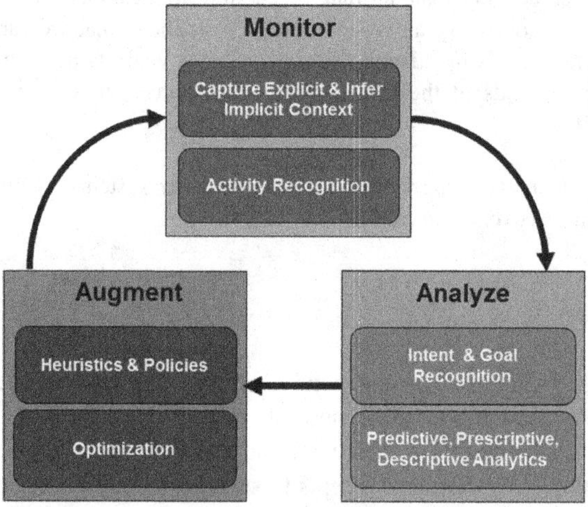

Fig. 1. Model for contextual awareness in data analysis systems [4]

Context data comes from a variety of sources, including system data, mobile devices, traditional computer activity tracking (such as keystroke or mouse clicks), instrumented user interfaces, neurophysiological sensors, or from optical and depth cameras. Analysis of context data is domain-dependent, but typically combines low-level activity recognition with higher level predictive analytics to hypothesize goals and intent. Details of this contextual analysis have been previously discussed [4]. Here, we focus on discussion of ways that we can augment the system by making use of the results of context analysis– for example, by proactively taking actions, adapting a user interface, managing notifications and recommendations, or personalizing the tool.

3 Applying Context to Interaction with Adaptive Systems

The primary benefit of recording and analyzing contextual information is to augment, adapt, or configure analysis systems to better support users. These online changes to system characteristics have the potential to make analysis faster and better by more directly supporting an analyst's current needs. However, applying these changes also has the potential to frustrate and confuse analysts, so care needs to be taken to design such changes in ways that align with work patterns and expectations.

Our efforts have focused on three ways that context can be applied to improve interaction with complex data: recommendations, adjustable automation, and personalization. In the following sections, we discuss these techniques as used in the general case of knowledge workers performing analysis of text-based documents, a description that can apply to a range of specific roles, from scientific researchers to intelligence analysts. While these roles may differ in their details, they share some common characteristics. Analysts across these domains are faced with collecting documents from a variety of sources, organizing these documents, extracting relevant information from those documents, and forming conclusions based on that information. We use document to refer generally to a range of text-based information, including blog posts, news articles, and scholarly publications.

3.1 Recommendation

Contextual information can be highly valuable for identifying information that could potentially be useful for an analyst's task at hand. Traditional keyword-based search techniques are limited by the analyst's skill in choosing the correct set of search terms, and potentially iterating through multiple sets of search results by using variations of the terms. When presented with long lists of search results, users may miss information that shows up beyond the first several results. Developing a model of the context of an analyst's work can help to find relevant information more quickly, and discover information that may be missed.

A key enabling technology for forming recommendations is modeling of information at a semantic level. We make use of third-party semantic entity extraction tools to process documents, and build a *semantic knowledge graph* that represents the documents and information in the system. This knowledge graph creates links between documents based on common reference to entities. We then make use of a range of algorithms, such graph analytics techniques used for collaborative filtering, to extrapolate from a current context to identify data accessible to the system that may be relevant to the analyst's current activity. For example, this may include documents that are related to those an analyst has already read, rated, or annotated.

While identifying related documents can help with finding more relevant information, pro-active recommendations require additional context information. In combination with identification of related documents, we also make use of models of analysis process to identify where additional reading and analysis would offer the most benefit. For example, if an analyst has created a collection of documents about a topic that are all from a single type of source, the system may suggest documents that are related, but from sources with different characteristics. Other recommendations could be to include information that will lead the analysts down new paths and broaden their perspectives, or information that is similar to information that has been rated highly or marked as relevant.

3.2 Adjustable Automation

Several analysis tasks are too difficult for either a human or automation to complete successfully alone with current techniques. Even when tasks can be independently completed, cooperation is likely to improve performance when the strengths of current automation are complementary to those of human analysts. A common goal of adjustable automation is to minimize training time and reliance on the adaptability of humans, and to design systems that are manageable by a wide variety of users in varying conditions. Automation can also assist human teammates to facilitate coordination and collaboration activities. There are several existing scales [3] that describe levels of automation, and in general they range from fully automated, to fully manual, to systems that require users to confirm or reject decisions the automation makes.

Context can be used here to automatically adjust automation levels depending on state, user preferences, and other constraints in the environment. Context can also be used along with resource allocation and constraint optimization algorithms when formulating and solving the problem of optimizing what information or tasks should be assigned at any given time, creating an adjustable automation policy. For example, documents can have a variety of tags and ratings, such as topic themes, source credibility, and topic relevance. Contextual information can be used to infer these values based on the knowledge gap, but whether the system should infer values or let an analyst manually determine the values is determined by the context of the analysts' activities. These applications of context also intersect with recommendations, allowing the system to better understand *when* and *how* recommendations should be presented.

3.3 Personalization

A critical challenge for designers of analysis support systems is designing tools that are flexible enough to support a wide variety of analysis tasks but don't overwhelm analysts with interface complexity. One area where this challenge is particularly relevant is the creation and configuration of visualizations. For complex data analysis, powerful visualizations are needed to navigate the data and form initial hypotheses. A variety of views may be needed to understand the development of information, including temporal visualizations for understanding events, geospatial visualizations for understanding spatial relationships, and node-link visualizations for understanding semantic relationships.

In the absence of context, creating and manipulating these visualizations can be a complex task in itself. By leveraging context, interaction with complex visualizations can be customized to the current context so that they can be simplified but remain powerful enough to improve the analyst's ability to do his or her job. For example, given the amount of information that is available, visualizations can quickly go from showing too little information to be useful to showing too much information and causing cognitive overload. Context information can be used to pre-select relevant data or automatically adjust filters so that a manageable amount of information is shown.

4 Discussion and Future Work

We have presented our ongoing work to incorporate context into systems supporting analysis of complex data. We believe this approach has great potential to create analysis systems that are tightly coupled to the needs of analysts and enable faster and better quality analyses.

Our primary goal for future work in this area is validation of the described approach. The goal is to improve the speed and/or quality of analysis, and application of context-aware system design has potential to achieve that goal, but as of yet we have no empirical evidence that this approach provides the expected benefits. Several evaluation efforts in multiple domains are at various stages of planning and execution.

In addition, while we have described our current framework for creating context-aware applications for analysis of complex data, we have also identified several paths for future work in this area. Many of these are related to the question of how to best adapt an interface based on an analysis of context. For example, we discussed possible ways for the system to suggest changes to context, some of which were implicit and some of which were explicit. An area for further research is to determine when different approaches should be used.

References

1. Abowd, G.D., Dey, A.K.: Towards a better understanding of context and context-awareness. In: Gellersen, H.-W. (ed.) HUC 1999. LNCS, vol. 1707, pp. 304–307. Springer, Heidelberg (1999)
2. Dourish, P.: What we talk about when we talk about context. Pers. Ubiquit. Comput. **8**(1), 19–30 (2004)
3. Parasuraman, R., Sheridan, T.B., Wickens, C.D.: A model for types and levels of human interaction with automation. IEEE Trans. Syst. Man Cybern. Part A: Syst. Hum. **30**(3), 286–297 (2000)
4. Pfautz, S.L., Ganberg G., Fouse, A., Shurr, N.: Leveraging context to improve human-system performance. AI Magazine (to appear)

User Situation-Aware Mobile Communication Method

Jungkih Hong, Scott Song(✉), Dongseok Kim, and Minseok Kim

Software R&D Center, Samsung Electronics Co., Ltd., Suwon, Korea
{jungkih.hong, sangkon.song, ds9.kim, msvic.kim}@samsung.com

Abstract. Communicating information through electrical mobile devices solely relies on static functions provided by the mobile devices. For example, when a caller uses the call function on a mobile device, the other caller at the receiving side has only two static functions to execute namely reject or answer. Under most of communication environment, the caller does not recognize the receiver's current context. In this paper, we propose SCS (Situation-aware based on Communication Service) platform to provide an appropriate method to express useful information based on user context like speak-able, read-able, gesture-able situations through mobile devices. In addition, the proposed method enables automatic configuration of personal preference and device attributes and living environment conditions reflecting current situation awareness [1].

Keywords: Situation-aware · Communication service · Mobile device · User context

1 Introduction

SCS is originally envisioned as a unique and seamless way to upgrade the traditional communication experience into something more collaborative and contextual for users (Fig. 1).

With speech or activity recognition capabilities, it has since grown into something far more flexible, enabling rich terminal to terminal communications for traditional usage scenarios like a user is talking to a friend, sending message, or sharing multimedia files. In any of these scenarios, SCS provides users better communication experience with friends, family or business. Since SCS provides peer-to-peer standpoint, it can expand into various service scenarios [2] that share context during a phone call.

In Sect. 2, various sources of situational awareness are defined and applications are explained in detail. In Sect. 3, system structure and features of server and client will be described in order to implement these functions. Sect. 4 discusses the conclusions of this paper and what the future development directions of SCS are.

2 Definitions and Applications

Various contexts are essential factors in order to establish appropriate communication services. Thus, SCS (Situation-aware based Communication Service) platform is to effectively integrate new services to get the goal with developed skills through the

C. Stephanidis (Ed.): HCII 2015 Posters, Part II, CCIS 529, pp. 508–513, 2015.
DOI: 10.1007/978-3-319-21383-5_85

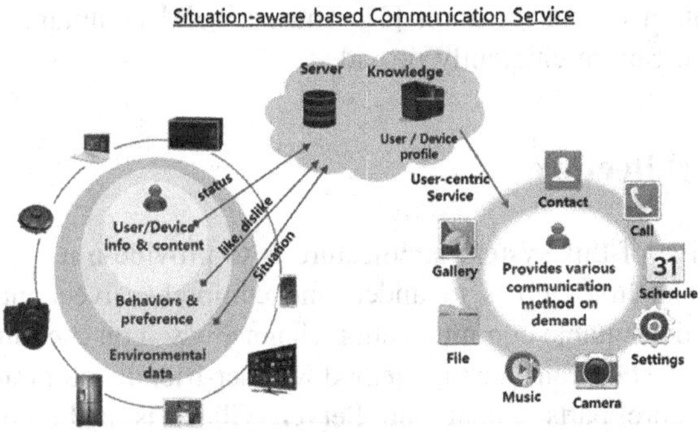

Fig. 1. Conceptual view of SCS

study of existing technologies based on the concept of Fig. 1. Furthermore, it was designed from the beginning with the market-oriented and practical service objectives.

2.1 Environmental Information

A mobile device can extract environment information through various sensors [3]. It can gather not only location-based information, but also user activities [4]. Thus, user environment information is a key factor to construct effective communication path. Upon activating a communication, different situations require particular ways of proceeding the communication. For example, a library requires quiet user activities and intended communication still must work well even though in a concert hall with full of noises. Financial or private information must not be leaked to others during a communication in public. In addition, communication should not disturb users too much while driving or jogging.

2.2 Pattern and History of User

Some context can be extracted through pattern and history of a user. Even though people are under the same environment, because user pattern and history are different for each person, situations can be differently interpreted. To infer a particular user situation for the context-aware communication, it is very important to extract and understand user pattern and history. For this, intelligent modeling must be needed to collaborate with a variety of user information like pattern and history.

2.3 Semantic Based

If there is insufficient information about user environment, the information directly extracted from user speech and conversation can also be a significant factor to provide situations based communication. If the solutions that recognize voice and text in a mobile device are collaborated with voice call and messaging, it can understand the subject and intention of conversation [5]. Thus, a valid communication path or an appropriate service can be efficiently provided.

3 System Architecture

The prime objective of this system architecture is to provide a user-situation friendly communication. The first step is to understand comprehensive context information. Second, it is to find a suitable communication channel based on user and device profile. Final step is to suggest or translate the method for user-friendly communication. SCS is designed with 2 core parts Client and Server. Client is gathering environmental information and providing services to a user and Server is a suitable communication channels. Figure 2 describes the modules within the two parts. The roles of these modules are as followings.

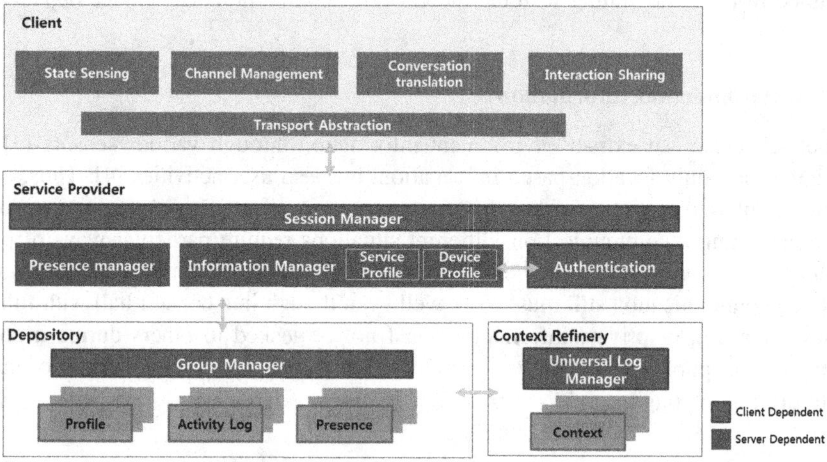

Fig. 2. SCS architecture diagram

Server composes Session Manager, Presence Manager, Information Manager, Group Manager and Universal Log Manager. Session Manager is a broker function which relays transmission between client and server. Information Manager manages profiles of service and device based on a user. Presence Manager provides real-time communication channel information and action status of a user based on profiles. Group Manager has some functions which collaborate with activity logs, profiles and presence. In addition, it infers the relation and actions for a valid communication in advance. Universal Log Manager stores and manages history and context based on user actions. After communication is terminated, all data which occur in all modules are moved to Universal Log Manager.

Client composes State Sensing, Channel Manager, Conversation translation, Interaction Sharing and transport abstraction. State Sensing detects all events occurring out of a device. Channel Manager provides communication channels based on contexts of a user. Conversation Translation has some functions. For instance, there are converting of dialog mode and inter-working with external modules such as voice recognition and language translation. Interaction Sharing processes real-time sharing of user actions and information happening in a mo-bile. Transport abstraction is an independent abstraction layer from physical connectivity and supports APIs to access to Session Manager in Server.

Figure 3 shows the flow of information updated. When user communication status is idle, devices send updated information to the server periodically for better service reliability. Updated information is stored to the depository by Group Manager and extracted context from the information is managed by Universal Log Manager. The gathered information creates contexts as below Fig. 4.

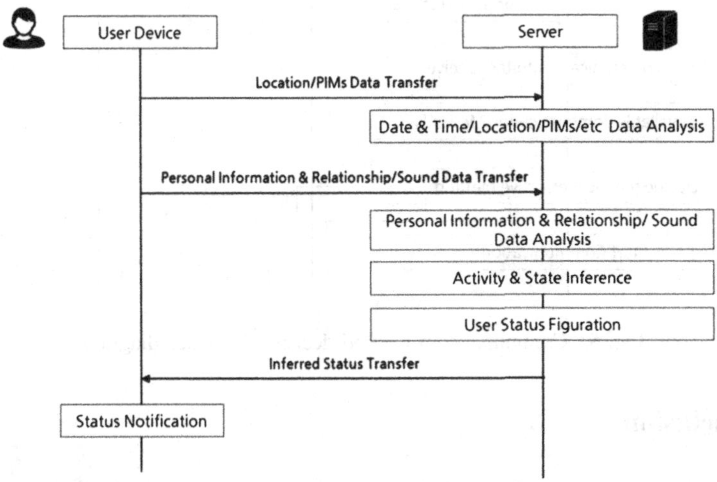

Fig. 3. Sensed data update sequence diagram

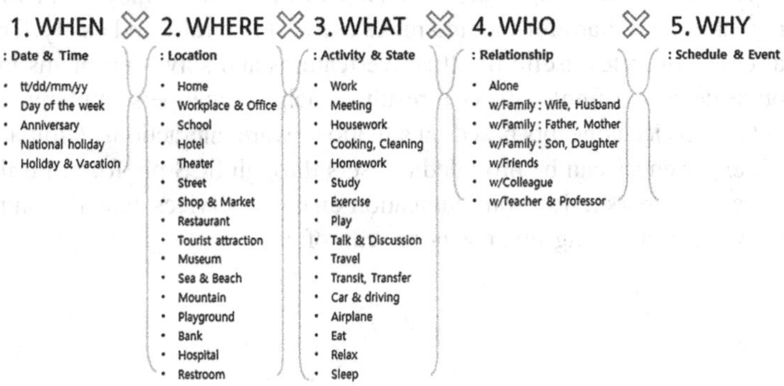

Fig. 4. Categorized 5 W form context

The Fig. 5 below shows the communication service sequence of SCS. In communication process, the server collects communication method candidates and provides the clients with the most proper one of them. Since this platform which reflects user preferences and purposes recommends or presets communication methods based on user action status or environments, users don't get disrupted even during communication.

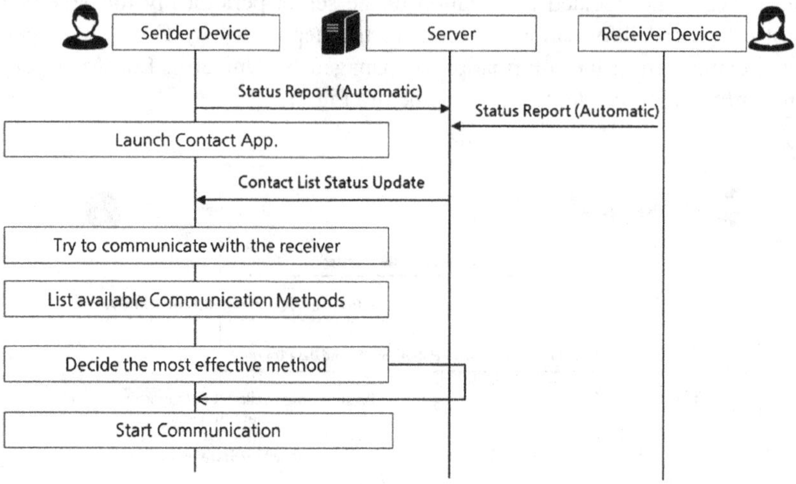

Fig. 5. Communication method decision sequence diagram

4 Conclusion

In the past, when a user uses communication functions, contextual information could not be used. As sensing technology is being improved and useful context information can be collected, experience level of user communication can be enhanced by using these features. Our design methodology is focused on delivering value to UX designers and developers. Users and application developers know what they want to do, but technology makes it too hard for them to make use of it naturally and easily. Thus, SCS platform already concretes useful or attractive features and solves problems in today's use of mobile device technology. As a result, it helps developers implement various communication service concepts based on situation-aware interactions. Ultimately, new and creative experiences can be provided to users through SCS platform. Furthermore, it can open a new market for communication-enabled services that is compellingly more attractive than anything other vendors can offer.

References

1. Endsley, M.R.: Toward a theory of situation awareness in dynamic systems. Hum. Factors **37**, 32–64 (1995)

2. Schilit, B., Adams, N., Want, R.: Context aware computing applications. In: Proceedings of 1st International Workshop Mobile Computer System Application, pp. 85–90. December 1994
3. Riva, G., Vatalaro, F., Davide, F., Alcaniz, M.: Ambient Intelligence. IOS Press, Amsterdam (2001)
4. Oh, J., Haas, Z.: Personal environment service based on the integration of mobile communications and wireless personal area network. IEEE Commun. Mag. **48**(6), 66–72 (2010)
5. Choi, Y.H.: Context-aware service using smart device in intelligent vehicle environment. J. Comput. Sci. Eng. **29**(268), 35–41 (2011)

Design Guideline on Location Based User Emotion Sharing Map Service

GeeYoung Noh(✉), DongNyeok Jeong, Sangsun Park, and Jundong Cho

Department of Human ICT Convergence, SungkyunKwan University, Suwon, Korea
{janle,nyeok,sangsun,jdcho}@skku.edu

Abstract. In this paper, we present our preliminary initial investigation about a Heart-map system that detect user`s emotion and visualize to cartography map on mobile service. For this project, we developed a wearable prototype to recognize emotions. Based on the prototype, we propose mobile application guideline for this concept functions. Then, We present the results of a in-depth interviews, scenario story board study with ten local people that we conducted with local people, and indicate guidelines for the Function of a Emotion-map systems. Through this project, individuals' emotion and evaluation could look at possibility that social network service(SNS) based on user's specific location. Furthermore, this research can suggest that effective emotion SNS based on system design guideline.

Keywords: Emotion map · Location sharing · Socialization · Mobile application

1 Introduction

Most studies were put in effort from times past in detecting and transferring human emotions. Recently, there has been significant development towards measuring human emotion and the possibility of transferring them to computers [1]. This change of paradigm has focused on utilizing information regarding internal and external human biological signals, a natural reaction that the user can provide appropriately when it is desired [1, 3]. For this, human emotion can be visualized by utilizing the bio-signal data with the external world we live in. The visualization of the emotions of people by displaying in a form of a map can be a good example of a service that can connect people within a society [2]. The current technology with smart phones can be seen as an initial a step as it is using location based map information service [4].

Considering the fact that the existing studies that 94.59 % of human emotion can be accurately measured through ECG and be classified into two contrasting feelings of joy and sorrow [9], a new service can be designed based on regions of human emotion. For an example, a service can be designed for sharing reviews on landmarks, emotions recognized from travel experiences, and reviews on restaurants solely based on human emotions. The data extracted from such reviews and recognized emotions can be categorized and be visualized by designing [2] an emotion map. A wearable device is

C. Stephanidis (Ed.): HCII 2015 Posters, Part II, CCIS 529, pp. 514–518, 2015.
DOI: 10.1007/978-3-319-21383-5_86

work in progress to appropriately measure emotions and effectively visualize such emotions related to designated locations. We have developed a prototype based on location based information for measuring human emotion designed to be measurable anywhere at any time by using biometric data of heart rate variability (HRV) [6].

Currently, there are two largely used human emotion recognition inference models. First, a two dimensional recognition model where it is categorized as: preference to neglect and activity to inactivity. Along with the valence-arousal model, human emotion can be distinguished into happiness, surprise, fear, anger, sadness and more [7]. The two models were used together to utilize the processing software Pulse sensor Amped Visulizer v1.1 which is based on recognizing five human emotions was used to extract the code and the data [6].

Following the previous work [6], this study will focus on providing a system design guideline from the data measured from the wearable device based on human emotion and the user's needs through user study and scenario. We present design space of an emotion map (The Heart-Map application, web site) that helps travelers, families and others to review decide restaurants, landmarks to visit and to leave feedbacks and emotions. We expect a more manageable design guideline for an interacting wearable device with a mobile phone as well as a web site and to see a more complete service.

2 User Study

We designed a user study as in [8], using a speed- dating storyboard study technique in which participants were Separately requested to debate and elaborate their opinions about three different scenarios about when searching for a specific location. We tried to find the user's thoughts and their wants and the possible dangers.

Method and materials. Recruited participants included both male and female in their 20 s and 30 s, mostly those comfortable and used to using smart phones based on a internet community site from a certain location called Mapo-Gu. The participants included: 2 single males in their 20 s, 1 married male in their 20 s, 4 single females in their 20 s, 3 married females in 30 s.

The experiment took a total of 90 min and it was divided into three different parts. First, the participants were given an introduction of the experiment and an initial demographic questionnaire was taken (15 min) following an in depth interview (20 min). Participant's needs and their daily lives as well as their motive. Second, by using the scenario board, the participants were shown the pictures of three different scenarios and after reading the descriptions and carefully understanding the situations they were encouraged to express their opinions and thoughts concerning the situations provided (30 min). Finally, the participants were given the opportunity to share thoughts, two in particular, on how to improve from the scenarios (25 min).

Demographics questionnaire. The initial demographics questionnaire was composed of 40 questions divided into three parts to appropriately categorize users: Part 1. Personal tendencies on using smart phones Part 2. Location selection methods Part 3. Personal standards on leaving reviews.

In Depth interview. The in depth interview was formed as a one to one interview to specifically find out how participants selected locations when traveling and why. They also were interviewed on their usual behaviors regarding searching for reviews on restaurants, leaving memos on pictures with family when traveling, and were interviewed regarding with all else concerning searching for locations.

3 Scenarios Storyboard Study

We conducted a Scenario user study using a paper storyboard to stimulate the users' discussion about finding a certain location. The scenarios provided show a set of different functionalities and situations of an imaginary concept.

Scenario 1. This scenario shows how a reservation can be made at a restaurant using the application. The wearable device will measure the user's emotions and leave reviews on that particular restaurant on the mobile phone. This scenario describes how linkage between wearable device and mobile phone is important how reviews from the application can be used to restaurants easily.

Scenario 2. This scenario shows how a family can transfer a emotion from a certain location to their mobile phones and leave a photos and memos. They can store their memories with each other and not just leave as it is. The scenario shows that using the push alarm and having the users write memos allowed to check the application's functions once again.

Scenario 3. This scenario shows a couple using the application to find a travel location with a certain concept or with certain atmosphere. The couple can search for locations with using emotion based keywords. The application shows feedbacks and other users emotion based reviews. Through this scenario, we show how user can control proper trip for their family and how to prepare for find famous landmark in foreign country.

4 Results

The affinity diagram was developed from the study considering user's main needs and their feedbacks. The affinity diagram was categorized into 3 different issues and was again subcategorized. We drew a list of needed and un-needed functions for the users. Most users felt comfortable using the application as they were already using a similar application on their mobile phone. 10 out of 8 users did not feel uncomfortable using the wearable device outside. Users felt the interlinked data from wearable device to the mobile phone was useful. 2 of the users questioned the reliability of measuring their emotions simply from the wearable devices. We describe some of the design issues from the study.

Emotion based map. Most participants preferred and felt eased mapping the emotion by colors rather than with words. A color's intrinsic effect had a strong impact towards the users' ability to view the map with ease. An opinion was raised if a simple keyword would be added to supplement and provide explanation for each color.

Interaction between wearable device and mobile application. Two of the users questioned the need for the wearable device for measuring their emotion. Other users seemed positive towards the device and felt that it was easy to use on their mobile phones. They also suggested having a pc-based emotion map for better visualization and for a wider look.

Review service and SNS. Most participants were already involved in travel and food communities. They were already sharing their data with others. They wanted real reviews from real users not from the owners themselves. They seemed positive tagging themselves to locations and leaving reviews on SNS but were concerned if their involvement will cause negative impact towards housing market or an overall negative insight towards a certain location.

5 Concept Prototype

Most of users' feedback was used to complete the prototype. The Information Architecture was formed using the study regarding the affinity diagram. Gathered data was able to be better sorted using the diagram. Mobile users feel most sensitive when facing complicated interfaces. The important fact is to structure the interface for them to be able to follow and use the interface without any troubles. The application shows the prototype (Fig. 1) where the colors show user's emotions regarding locations. The user can also type in a certain keyword to search for a location by using the wearable device and transfer his or her emotions towards that location into their mobile phone.

The user can apply the emotion data from measured by wearable devices using mobile application and leave reviews regarding each location. They can select three different mode for the following emotion map (1.) Emotion Map (main), (2.) Emotion graph, (3.) General Map. User also use the application when taking photos and using SNS leaving emotion factors inside. They can review using personal emotion data when they visit the various shops in the map and share to people through the SNS.

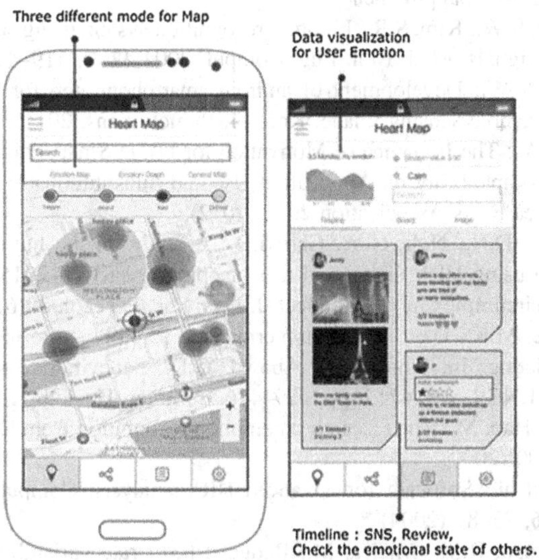

Fig. 1. Overview of the Heart-Map Mobile application prototype feature

Finally, Finally, the Mobile application allows users to see recommendations for happy place and allow user to share review information conveniently with other user, using categories for easier access.

6 Conclusions and Future Work

This study is based on examining user's emotions related to a particular location as well as his or her reviews by using a wearable device. The extracted data from the experiment will be used to develop emotion based map. The concept of the product and the importance of its functions were concerned from the interviews regarding users' needs as well as its expected scenario storyboard. The prototype was completed using the extracted data above and using the possible guidelines and beginning points of the project. In future work we plan to include considering and deciding whether the users' emotion will be measured automatically or manually based on usability tests. Most work will be focused on developing an algorithm towards testing and supplementing the limitations of the project and will be considering generalization as well as visualization of each location.

Acknowledgements. This research was supported by the Ministry of Trade, Industry and Energy(MOTIE), KOREA, through the Education Support program for Creative and Industrial Convergence.(Grant Number N0000717).

References

1. Jung, H.S.: Trends and prospects in healthcare wearable devices. In: KHIDI 2014 (2014)
2. Biomapping. http://biomapping.net/
3. Kim, K.H., Bang, S.W., Kim, S.R.: Emotion recognition system using short-term monitoring of physiological signals. Med. Biol. Eng. Comput. 2004 **42**(3), 419–427 (2004)
4. Kan, S.G., Lee, K.W.: Development of android smartphone app for corner point feature extraction using remote sensing image. Korea J. Remote Sens. 2011 **27**(1), 33–41 (2011)
5. Lee, J.A., Na, E.Y.: The Influence of Motivation for Using Smart Phone Applications And Innovativeness/Compatibility on Application Use and Substitution for Other Media/Living Equipments. Korea Press Assocication 2012 (2012)
6. Park, S.S., Jeung, D.N., Noh, G.Y., Cho, J.D.: A study on the human emotion infer in meaningful place using HRV signal and text mapping. In: KCHI 2015 (2015)
7. Russell, J.A.: A circumplex model of affect. J. Pers. Soc. Psychol. **39**(6), 1161–1179 (1980)
8. Davidoff, S., Lee, M.K., Dey, A.K., Zimmerman, J.: Rapidly exploring application design through speed dating. In: Krumm, J., Abowd, G.D., Seneviratne, A., Strang, T. (eds.) UbiComp 2007. LNCS, vol. 4717, pp. 429–446. Springer, Heidelberg (2007)
9. Jing, C., Liu, G., Hao, M.: The research on emotion recognition from ECG signal. In: ITCS 2009, pp. 497–500 (2009)
10. Niskanen, J.P., et al.: Software for advanced HRV analysis. Comput. Method Programs Biomed. 2004 **76**, 73–81 (2004)
11. Miu, A.C., Heilman, R.M., Miclea, M.: Reduced heart rate variability and vagal tone in anxiety. Auton Nerosci 2009 **145**, 99–103 (2009)

AR-Technology-Based Locationing System for Interactive Content

Satoshi Saga(✉), Ryota Oki, Shusuke Kawagoe, Wanjia Zheng, and Jiacheng Sun

University of Tsukuba, Tsukuba, Tennodai 1-1-1, Japan
saga@saga-lab.org

Abstract. In this research, we propose an interactive display system that has a simple implementation. The system is composed of a smartphone, PC, display, and cloud service; it realizes a CAVE-like immersive system by employing simple devices. Relative location information is acquired by the user's smartphone and a marker (or markers). Based on this information, the system renders the appropriate image in real time. In this paper, we describe the implementation and operation of the proposed system.

1 Introduction

In recent years, personal head-mounted displays (HMD) such as Oculus Rift have been distributed, and immersive virtual-world display systems, such as gaming environments, have drawn public attention. Not only HMDs but also immersive projection technology (IPT)-based displays such as the Cave Automatic Virtual Environment (CAVE) system have been developed as immersive displays. (The CAVE system is an immersive virtual reality environment where projectors are directed to several walls of a room-sized cube.) IPT display methods require displays or screens located around a user, whereas an HMD covers the user's eyes. Both systems interactively change the displayed image based on the user's movement and produce an immersive sensory experience.

However, both systems have several problems. IPT displaying methods require location sensors, multiple projectors, and multiple screens. These are expensive, lack portability and require a large space. Thus, the IPT display method is unsuited to personal use; its use is limited to research or large events. On the other hand, HMD realizes a personal immersive environment, and is now becoming more widespread. However, the system covers the user's eyes; thus, it cannot be used in everyday life. In addition, the display might induce virtual sickness owing to differences between the user's movement and the displayed image [1].

Here we propose novel but simple immersive display framework that employ smartphone, normal PC, LCD displays, and cloud service. In this study, we propose a simple, novel immersive display framework that employs a smartphone, a basic PC, an LCD display, and a cloud service. Using this framework, we create

C. Stephanidis (Ed.): HCII 2015 Posters, Part II, CCIS 529, pp. 519–524, 2015.
DOI: 10.1007/978-3-319-21383-5_87

simple interactive content and evaluate the functionality of the location information system. As shown in Fig. 1, a smartphone captures the displayed marker and sends the calculated relative location data to a location server in real time. An image server acquires the data and controls the displayed computer graphics. By controlling the displayed image based on location information regarding the user, the framework realizes a motion-parallax-based 3D display. By evaluating the latency of the system, we verify the functionality of the proposed framework and the capability of the framework to display interactive contents.

2 Related Research

In recent years, Oculus Rift has drawn attention as a personalized immersive display. The display has gyro, acceleration, and magnetic sensors, and estimates the orientation of the user. The information is used for generating interactive content for the user. Although the device can estimate the orientation of the user, location information cannot be estimated.

The CAVE system, the basis of IPT, was developed by Cruz, et al. [2]. The system has four screens surrounding the user; it displays immersive content to the screens using projectors. The user wears active-shuttered 3D glasses with a magnetic location sensor. The system estimates the location and orientation of the user from the sensor data and generates location-based binocular vision for the user. The system requires a magnetic location sensor and multiple projectors and screens. This setup is expensive, lacks portability, and requires a large space. Thus, the IPT display method is unsuited to personal use, and its use is limited to research or large events.

Another immersive system, called RoomAlive [3], displays wide immersive vision for a whole room, including the furniture. The system measures all of the shapes in the room and the location of the user and generates an appropriate displayed image. However, the system requires the setup of a camera and a projector system in the room, and measurement of the room beforehand.

Our proposed system estimates user location information and uses simple equipment (only a smartphone, a basic PC, an LCD display, and a cloud service). In the next section, we describe the proposed system.

3 Proposed System

In this paper, we propose a novel framework for obtaining more precise information in a simple manner in an urban environment where you can see many displays such as digital signage or large electronic billboards. Conventional augmented reality (AR) technology employs a homography matrix to calculate relative location information between a marker and a camera. This locating technology offers not only translation information but also rotation information. In addition, even if the marker is far away, once the camera captures it, the technology will derive the location information. Thus, we expand the technology to precisely measure the client's location.

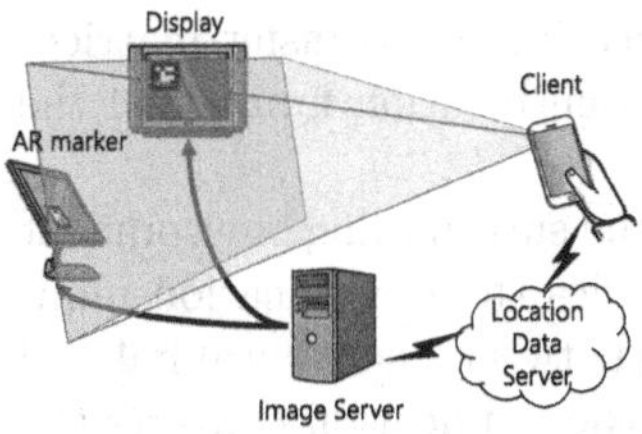

Fig. 1. Dataflow of the proposed system

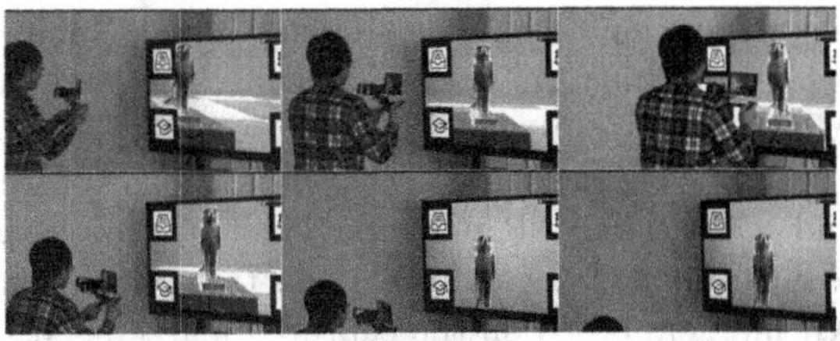

Fig. 2. A use case of the proposed system; He looks around a virtual work of art.

In this section, we explain the proposed system. A PC will display a marker on an LCD display, and a user will capture the displayed marker with a smartphone. The phone calculates relative location information and sends the data to a cloud-migrated location data server. With this system, we can create the basis of an indoor locating system. In addition, by employing the location information as feedback for displaying the content, we can easily construct interactive content.

3.1 System Flow

The system consists of a client terminal (a smartphone), a cloud-migrated location data server, a content server, and a display (Fig. 1). The client terminal acts as the viewpoint for the user; thus, the user holds the terminal in front of their face. AR markers are displayed on the displays. If the camera on the terminal captures a marker, the terminal calculates location information between the marker and the terminal. As the client device, we employ an android smartphone, and as the location server, we use the Heroku service. The location information is sent to the cloud server. To produce computer graphics, the image server acquires relative location information from the Heroku server. In this way, to construct interactive content, we can employ any client device and any image server that has a network connection. The AR marker does not have to be a dot pattern; it can be any natural image that does not interfere with the content itself. The interactive content works as follows: the users can see changes in the appearance of content according to their own movement. If the user moves left, the appearance changes to the image from the left point of view. If the user moves right, it changes to the image from the right point of view. Based on the viewpoint control of the user's location, a motion-parallax-based image is generated. Figure 2 shows a use case of the system.

4 Implementation

In this section, we describe the design of the implementation. This system requires fast data transfer to realize real-time responses to the user's movement. Thus, we chose WebSockets and designed a transfer protocol that is fast and compact. WebSockets provides bi-directional communication while keeping the connection open. The contents of the communication are transfer matrices between client terminal and AR markers, and the identification number of the AR marker.

On the client terminal, the application captures the surrounding environment and searches for AR markers. The application specifies the identification numbers of the markers and calculates transfer matrices between client terminal and AR markers based on the captured markers. Next, the application converts the transfer matrices into binary data using MessagePack [4] and sends the message to the location server, which uses Heroku [5]. For the terminal client, we use a Nexus 7 and an application built with an AR library, Metaio [6].

Next, we prepare a location server. The purpose of the location server is to process and relay the message to the application server. If the server knows the absolute position of the markers, it can also calculate the absolute position of the terminal. By returning the absolute position information to the content server, the content server can provide different positioning services to the user. For the location server, we employ a cloud server, Heroku.

Next, the content server receives the location data for the terminal from the location server. The server parses the relayed message and acquires the transfer matrices. Based on these matrices, the PC renders virtual images. For the prototype system, we employ the gaming engine Unity [7].

5 Experiment

To evaluate the functionality of interactive content with the proposed framework, we performed several experiments. First, we evaluated communication and processing delay in terms of a frame rate. Second, we performed experiments to validate the preciseness of the estimated location.

5.1 Interactivity

To evaluate the interactivity of the proposed system, we measured communication and processing delay in terms of a frame rate. During 3-second recordings of the transferred messages from the terminal to the content server, we acquired the frame rate of the system. Table 1 shows the measured results. Table 1 shows the measured results.

Table 1. Frame rate of the system

	Send	Receive
Average [ms]	56.6	57.6
Frame rate [fps]	17.7	17.4

Fig. 3. Experimental setup

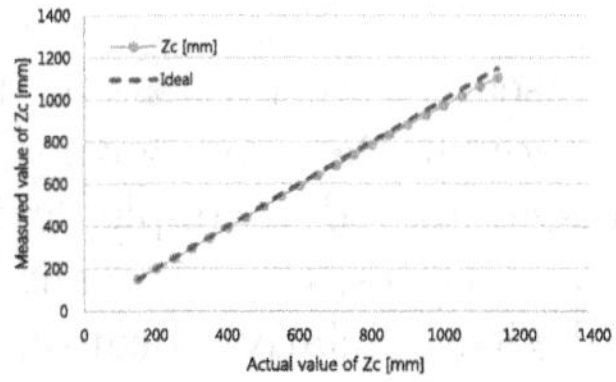

Fig. 4. Measurement result of translation (Z-axis)

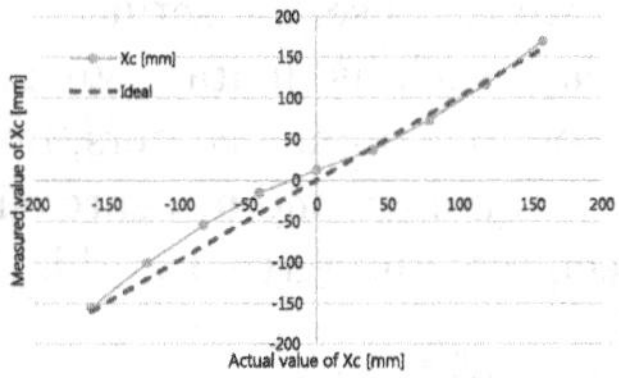

Fig. 5. Measurement result of translation (X-axis)

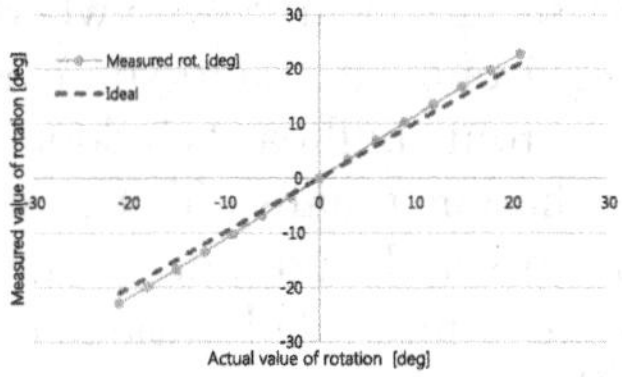

Fig. 6. Measurement result of rotation

5.2 Preciseness

To evaluate the preciseness of the location measurement, we measured translation and rotation data and compared them to the actual values. Figure 3 shows the experimental setup.

The center of the AR marker is the origin of the system; the normal direction of the marker is the z axis. The client terminal is placed in front of the AR marker. We set the client position X_c to be 0 mm and moved the client position Z_c, from 150 mm to 1150 mm at intervals of 50 mm and measured the transfer matrices. Figure 4 shows the results. Next, we set the client position Z_c to be 500 mm and moved X_c from -160 mm to 160 mm at intervals of 20 mm and measured the transfer matrices. Figure 5 shows the results. Third, we set the client at $Z_c = 500$ mm and rotated it around the origin by $\pm 16°$. Figure 6 shows the results.

5.3 Results

From the interactivity experiment results, the frame rate of the proposed system is around 17 frames per second. This is not high enough for a fully interactive system; however, some interactivity can be achieved. From the preciseness experiment result, the translation results show linear behavior that is very close to the actual values. In the Z-axis results, the maximum error rate is 17 %. On the other hand, the X-axis results show a maximum error rate of approximately 10 %. In the results for rotation, the error remains below approximately 3°.

6 Conclusion

In this research, we propose an interactive display system that makes a user feel as though they are gazing at a virtual space outside a window. The system is composed of simple devices, including a smartphone, a PC, a display, and cloud services; thus, it realizes an immersive CAVE-like system using only simple devices. Relative location information is acquired by the user's smartphone and a marker (or markers). Based on this information, the system renders the appropriate image in real time. From the experimental results, the system can display roughly 17 frames per second. In addition, the error rate of measurements is kept small. By making the server a cloud service, we can use this location service nearly everywhere. For example, we can use the service in an urban environment where you can see many displays such as digital signage or large electronic billboards indoors (e.g., in underground shopping centers, buildings, or shopping malls). Thus, we can expand the technology and measure client locations precisely, not only for interactions between real and virtual worlds, but also between multiple locations in the real world.

Furthermore, several precise vision-based local positioning technologies such as PTAM [8] or Smart AR [9] have been developed. These technologies do not employ recorded markers, but instead, use general objects to locate the client. With these technologies, our proposed system can be made more precise and immersive. In future work, we plan to incorporate these technologies with our system and propose more powerful applications.

References

1. Davis, S., Nesbitt, K., Nalivaiko, E.: A systematic review of cybersickness. In: Proceedings of the 2014 Conference on Interactive Entertainment, pp. 1–9. ACM (2014)
2. Cruz-Neira, C., Sandin, D.J., DeFanti, T.A.: Surround-screen projection-based virtual reality: the design and implementation of the cave. In: Proceedings of the 20th Annual Conference on Computer Graphics and Interactive Techniques, pp. 135–142. ACM (1993)
3. Jones, B., Sodhi, R., Murdock, M., Mehra, R., Benko, H., Wilson, A., Ofek, E., MacIntyre, B., Raghuvanshi, N., Shapira, L.: Roomalive: magical experiences enabled by scalable, adaptive projector-camera units. In: Proceedings of the 27th Annual ACM Symposium on User Interface Software and Technology, pp. 637–644. ACM (2014)
4. Furuhashi, S.: Messagepack. msgpack. org, 1, 2013
5. Middleton, N., Schneeman, R. et al.: Heroku: Up and Running. O'Reilly Media, Inc., California (2013)
6. Metaio GmbH. Metaio. http://www.metaio.com/. Accessced 20 March 2015
7. Unity Technologies. Unity. http://unity3d.com. Accessced 20 March 2015
8. Klein, G., Murray, D.: Parallel tracking and mapping for small ar workspaces. In: 2007 6th IEEE and ACM International Symposium on Mixed and Augmented Reality. ISMAR 2007, pp. 225–234. IEEE (2007)
9. Sony Inc. Smart AR. http://www.sony.co.jp/SonyInfo/News/Press/201105/11-058/. Accessced 20 March 2015

A Computational Location Model Based on Relative Information

Ruowei Xiao[1(✉)], Kazunori Sugiura[1,2], and Zhanwei Wu[1,2]

[1] Keio University, Minato, Japan
{ruoweixiao,uhyo}@kmd.keio.ac.jp,
zhanwei_wu@sjtu.edu.cn
[2] Shanghai Jiaotong University, Shanghai, China
zhanwei_wu@sjtu.edu.cn

Abstract. In this paper, we proposed the concept "relative location" as a complementary presentation to the traditional "absolute location", which were considered the traditional expression of locations and have pervaded the current locations based services (LBS). Two methods were introduced to make relative location computable and more useful. Prototypes with Data visualization interface were designed and evaluated to test usability of the proposed methods. User experiments shown that integrating relative location information into computing system may help to improve usability of location based applications.

1 Concept and Model

Recent researches on spatial applications suggest that today's absolute location based applications should be more human-centered and integrating more context information [1, 2, 3]. We argued that, relative location information, as widely used in human daily life, could meet this requirement by providing better social context. The existing concept of relative location in geography refers to locations in wide relations to other locations; while absolute location, on the other hand, uses coordinates. In contrary to absolute location's popularity, the usage of relative location in computing system is very limited.

Take one familiar daily usage of Google map as an example, the navigation from place A to B, which in its nature, reflects a relation between A and B based on "transportation methods". Furthermore, people also use the nearby function to find close restaurants or hotels around a specific location from time to time. Thus, both "spatial adjacency" and "functionality" are used as the clues to organize the outcome. All of these different kinds of relations mentioned above, belongs to but not cover the full range of "relative location". Still the social aspects of the concept, such as affiliation, community, and all the other relations defined by human activities, remained to be further utilized.

However, it's difficult to define and implement the concept. The challenges mainly lies in two aspects: On one hand, most relative location are described by human concepts, which are uncomputable; On the other hand, given that even the same location, different users may use different relative locations.

C. Stephanidis (Ed.): HCII 2015 Posters, Part II, CCIS 529, pp. 525–530, 2015.
DOI: 10.1007/978-3-319-21383-5_88

In order to introduce relative locations in a computable way, in this paper, we defined relative locations as follows:

- First, relative locations present a location with relations to other locations.
- Second, the relation from location B to A is defined as, how possible the user will use information of location B while he/she is handling spatial task regarding A. This relation could be denoted as RB → A.
- Third, the relations between location B and A are bidirectional, and not necessarily equals to one another, that is: RB → A ≠ RA → B.

To briefly illustrate the definition, if among every 100 times descriptions, there are 65 times that A is described as "A berthed opposite B" and the other 35 times A is described as "A is close to C", then RB → A = 0.65 and RC → A = 0.35.

As shown in the example, RB → A can be derived from either the statistical features of crowd behaviors or a specific user's data. While in the former occasion, the crowd statistics may be weighted and averaged, hence known as the AH(averaged human) model based. Similarly, we call the latter one SH(specific human) model based.

The main purpose of this paper is to study:

- First, whether the usability of current LBS interfaces can be further improved by leveraging complementary relative location information.
- Second, since differences may exist between methods using AH methods and methods using SH model, what are the advantages or disadvantages in various circumstance.

Our idea has been partially proved by the study of cognitive fit theory in the field of spatial cognition[4, 5]. It has been widely supported by facts and experiments that in problem-solving or decision-making process, performance on a task will be enhanced when there is a cognitive fit, or match between task information presentation and user's mental presentation. As the relative location presentation is much more common in our daily life than absolute locations, according to cognitive fit theory and our common sense, it's an intuitive premise that providing complementary relative location information shall increase the usability of current location based services and applications.

2 Design and Experiment

To further evaluate our idea, we have selected three most common spatial tasks among today's LBS to verify the concept usability of relative locations, respectively:

First, locate a certain place. In some occasions, people are pretty sure about their destination, in which situation web map is used as a navigation tool. While in the other, the word "destination" is a rather vague term, because it might refer to a certain type of locations rather than a fixed place. Or people may just simply find themselves lacking of detailed information to find a certain place using map applications. In the Google map, an accurate keyword, such as name or address, is often required to locate a place; while in the Google field trip, a web recommendation app that people use to find some hangouts, allow users to discover interesting places with or without simple place description. In this paper, our first task focused more on the latter aspect, since it was more common in daily life which has not been well supported by current computing system yet. Moreover, the relative location shows more advantages in handling this kind of spatial tasks as for its more human related nature. To further classify, the task specifically refers to:

Suppose you are an international exchange student in keio university hiyoshi campus. After you arrive on campus, you need to locate the most popular lamen restaurant and the biggest pharmacy as soon as possible.

Fig. 1. User interface used in task 1

To support this task, social activity data of keio students are collected, computed into relative location data, and visualized on an interactive map interface, with absolute location data from google map. White dots are used to display absolute location, while heat map with different colors are used to show relative location data indicating various activities across space. For example, blue means having a meal, red means studying, yellow means shopping, purple means transportation, etc. To better simulate the situation, 10 foreign students were selected as participates and divided into two groups. The control group use mere absolute location data (only white dot), and the experimental group use map interface shown in Fig. 1. Participates were allowed to use other websites to obtain more detailed information about certain locations. Time consumption and user satisfaction measured by 7 point likert scale were collected to compare performance between two groups.

Results shown, the experimental group achieved 17 % less time consumption and 0.6 more satisfaction score. In the discussion after experiment, participates' feedback show that the visualization of relative location data could help them to focus on a relative smaller region and jump quickly between different regions, thus make them more comfortable and effective.

Second, plan a route. In logistics, route planning refers to a classic optimization task that: given a certain group of points with more or less constraints, to find the shortest path or least duration to visit every point. However, the route planning in our life does not always stick strictly to this definition. Take travelling as an example, travelers may decide to go to the most attractive places first, and skip other less attractive places in consideration of time and cost. In this situation, computing system is hard to organize an optimistic route since the objective and constraints are both uncertain. Relative location, which derived from historical visiting data of travelers, could play a big role to solve this kind of problem. In this task, we discussed how relative location theory could better meet daily needs on route scheduling under varying uncertain conditions. To further classify, the task specifically refers to: Given 30 most famous attractions in Tokyo, select attractions in list and plan a one day journey.

To support this task, itineraries posted by travelers on a trip advice website were collected, relative location data were computed by travel records between every two location, data visualization were provided on a map interface. Users could click one location to open its information window and show relation data with other locations, or take an overview of all locations by closing the information window. The value of relation data from low to high were mapped into different colors from blue to red.

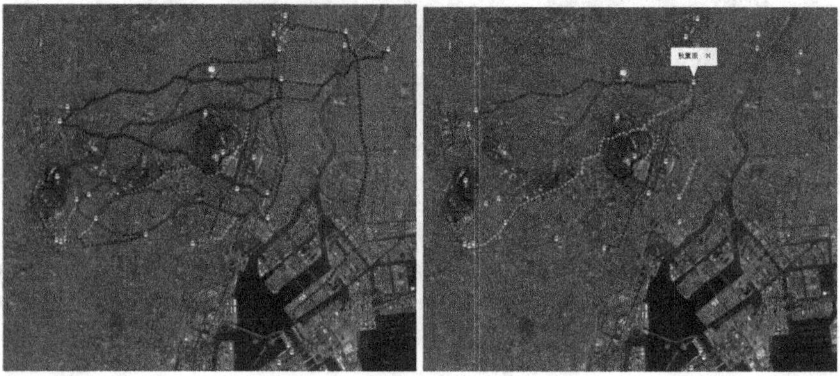

Fig. 2. User interface used in task 2

Participates were divided into 3 groups. Like the previous task, the control group use interface with mere absolute location, and the experimental group use the interface shown in Fig. 2. After the control group and experimental group finished their task, the third group will give each route plan a score. Score and time consumption were recorded to compare performance of two groups. Results shown, the experimental group achieved 62 % less time consumption and 9 % better score. Participates feedback confirmed that: (1) showing location relations derived from other traveler's experiences will help users to simplify their task and reduce cognitive burden; (2) the relative location contains more social information that reflects human activity across space, which could not be provided by absolute location.

Third, manage data in relation to locations. Nowadays, lots of extra information is attached to map interface, including: points of interests, news, photos, even sensors. Researches have shown that organizing data in spatial format is more consistent with human cognition than in tabular format, and thus result in a better performance in spatial tasks [6]. However, most map interfaces used by current apps only nail objects down on the map according to their absolute locations, e.g. coordinates. In this paper, we argued that by leveraging relative locations, the usability of location based applications could be further increased because it gives deeper social context than absolute location. For example, imagine you have taken some photos on the way to a tourist attraction and posted in Instagram. Now Instagram will display exactly where the photos were taken on the photo map, which may be some unknown roads. However, if the relation between these unknown roads with the tourist attraction on your trip is clearly visualized, the photo gallery will better describe your situation. Furthermore, using relative location could also help to group locations in a more meaningful way. To further classify, the task specifically refers to: After browsing 100 photos on the map, given 5 photos in sequence, find the corresponding photos on the map.

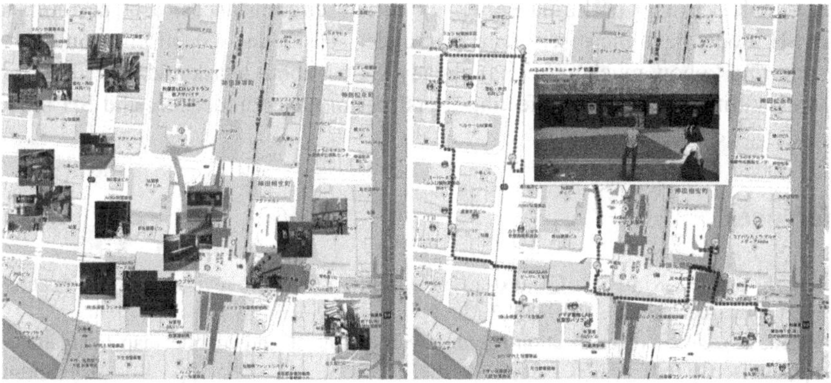

Fig. 3. User interface used in task 3

To support this task, two interfaces were provided, as shown in Fig. 3. The left one is similar to Instagram map interface, showing photos according to its absolute location. The right one attaches photos to nearby landmarks. Landmarks and relations between them are extracted and visualized by using the same technique in task 2. However, in this task, two models were used to generate relative location data, include: AH model, which means data are computed from travel routes of a crowd of people; and SH model, which mean data are computed from historical route of the participates themselves. To avoid bias, pictures from virtual reality environment are used instead of real photos.

Participates were divided into 3 groups, the first group is control group which use interface absolute location based interface (left one in Fig. 3), the second group is experimental group which use relative location based interface with AH model, the third group is another experimental group which use relative location based interface with SH model. Time consumptions were recorded to compare performance of three groups. Results shown, the third group achieved the best score, which is 5 % less than the second group and 18 % less than the first group. Screen capture show that participates in the control group have much more clicks and many of them are far away from the desired objects. One reason may be spatial cues that provided by relative location could help to limit down the search scope. Also, the fact that the third group achieved the best performance indicates that the SH model may give the best cognitive fit if users already have some experiences about objective space.

3 Conclusion and Discussion

All three tasks have shown, providing complementary relative location information with well-designed visualization method will give users more spatial cues about relations between locations. These relations are generated by human activities, and may be used to quickly recognize and manage spatial environments and objects, which result in: (1) In most circumstances, providing complementary relative location information helps to enhance user performance; (2) In certain circumstances, user performances under SH model have increased more than under AH model; (3) Information entropy, here referring to how much a user has already known about a task and related locations etc., was a critical factor that affecting users' performance under AH and SH models.

References

1. Hong, J., Suh, E., Kim, S.J.: Context-aware systems: a literature review and classification[J]. Expert Syst. Appl. **36**(4), 8509–8522 (2009)
2. Jokinen, K.: Usability in location-based services: context and mobile map navigation. In: Stephanidis, C. (ed.) UAHCI 2007 (Part II). LNCS, vol. 4555, pp. 401–410. Springer, Heidelberg (2007)
3. Nivala, A.M., Brewster, S., Sarjakoski, L.T.: Usability evaluation of Web mapping sites. Cartogr. J. **45**, 129–138 (2008)
4. Vessey, I.: Cognitive fit: a theory-based analysis of the graphs versus tables literature. Decis. Sci. **22**(2), 219–240 (1991). doi:10.1111/j.1540-5915.1991.tb00344
5. Vessey, I., Galletta, D.: Cognitive fit: an empirical study of information acquisition. Inf. Syst. Res. **2**(1), 63–84 (1991)
6. Dennis, A.R., Carte, T.A.: Using geographical information systems for decision making: extending cognitive fit theory to map-based presentations[J]. Inf. Syst. Res. **9**(2), 194–203 (1998)

Urban Interaction

Acceptance of Integrated Active Safety Systems in China

Junliang Chen[1(✉)], Zhengjie Liu[1], Paul A. Mendoza[2], and Fang Chen[2]

[1] Sino-European Usability Center, Dalian Maritime University, Dalian, China
cjl8989@gmail.com

[2] Interaction Design Collegium, Department of Computer Science and Engineering, Chalmers University of Technology, Gothenburg, Sweden

Abstract. Yearly almost 60,000 people are killed in traffic accidents in China due to the rapid growth of the number of vehicles and bad driving habits. There is a need to increase safety and cars are being equipped with new active safety technology known as Advanced Driver Assistant Systems (ADAS), which can help driver by warning before accidents occur. A simulator study with 16 participants was carried out at a driving simulator, which equipped with an integrated visual interface prototype developed by Chalmers University of Technology in Sweden. The interface presents information visually to the driver before any critical situation with help from three Advanced Driver Assistance Systems, Forward Collision Warning (FCW), Curve Speed Warning (CSW) and Lane Departure Warning (LDW). Questionnaires and open-ended interviews were held to subjectively measure the participants' attitude toward the sound warnings and visual interface. Questionnaire results showed that most participants thought the sound warning could facilitate their driving while most users' attitude towards the visual display warning were comparatively neutral. In order to better understand how ADAS technology can be designed to suite Chinese drivers, their behaviors and preferences. There is more work need to do.

Keywords: Advanced driver assistant system · Infotainment equipment · Active safety system · User acceptance

1 Introduction

In recent years, there are almost 60,000 persons killed by traffic accidents every year in China. This number is the largest of the world. According to the statistical date in China in 2004, the traffic accident caused by driver behavior counted 89.8 % of all. To alarm drivers before the accidents take place by identifying the dangerous driving actions should be good. Thus, it is of great help to equip vehicles with Advanced Driver Assistant System (ADAS), which can alarm drivers when danger is coming.

But the visual burden for drivers is becoming heavier due to more and more adoptions of controlling components, alerting system and infotainment equipment, while other channels (e.g., auditory and haptic channels) of drivers are still not made full use of. Hence, some researchers considered to convey information through other

C. Stephanidis (Ed.): HCII 2015 Posters, Part II, CCIS 529, pp. 533–538, 2015.
DOI: 10.1007/978-3-319-21383-5_89

channels, e.g., to adopt speech, earcon, audio and three-dimension sounds [1], to prompt drivers from crossing the line with steer vibration, or to emit the smell of coffee for a sleepy driver, etc. Today there are more than 30 ADAS being developed [2].

The design prototype consisted of sound warnings and visual information presentation. The visual information would give drivers advisory warnings that are showed continuously to the drivers throughout the scenario. The sound warnings would only ware if the encountered a critical situation [3]. The warnings that were issued (Fig. 1) were forward collision warning (FCW) when distance reaches a critical distance, curve speed warning (CSW) if the driver enters the curve with a too high speed and lane departure warning (LDW) if the driver unintentionally passes the line and does not use the turn-lights.

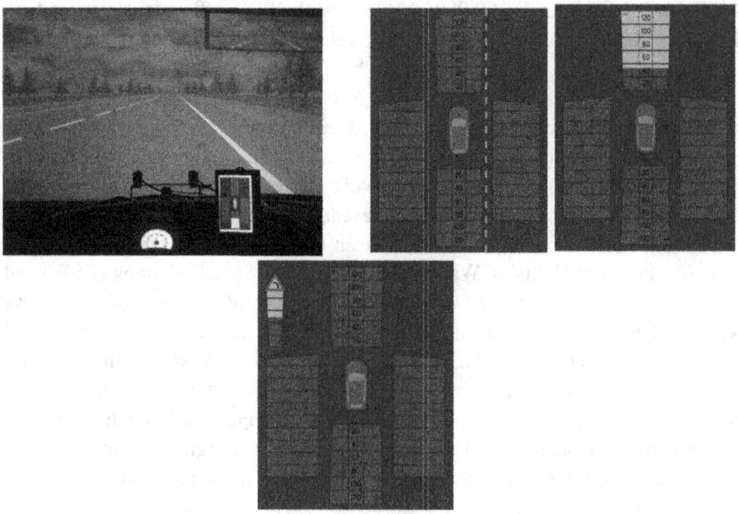

Fig. 1. Simulator setup and integrated ADAS interface

2 Method

The simulator setup consisted of a dashboard, steering wheel, adjustable seat, a projector projecting from behind, speedometer and the STISIM simulation software (Fig. 1). The whole system was mounted in the user experience lab of Sino-European Usability Center in Dalian Maritime University.

16 (8 males and 8 female) Chinese drivers were recruited. Driving years and yearly driving distances of the 16 drivers we finally chose are shown in Table 1.

The purpose of the simulator study was to evaluate the effectiveness and driver acceptance of the integrated ADAS interface and compare with only critical sound warnings. The driver drove 4 scenarios (1) baseline scenario (no ADAS information presented), (2) sound warning scenario, (3) visual display and sound warning scenario,

Table 1. Distribution of ages, driving years and yearly driving distance

Driving years	1~2	3~6	7~8	9~14
Number of drivers	4	3	6	3

Distance (km)	<5k	5k~15k	15k~50k
Number of drivers	5	6	5

and (4) baseline scenario. Questionnaires were answered after scenario (2), (3) and (4). Scenarios (2) and (3) were randomized to avoid learning effects.

Before the driving scenarios, each driver was asked to fill in a demographic questionnaire.

The first scenario was the baseline scenario which drivers drove for 15 min without warnings. The second scenario was either the sound warnings or display and sound warnings condition which were 30 min long. After each warning condition the drivers were asked to fill in a questionnaire to measure their subjective thoughts of the warning types. The third scenario was the left display warnings or sound warnings. The final scenario was another 15 min baseline scenario. The driver were asked to fill in a concluding questionnaire after this scenario.

A Likert scale with 7 levels was used in the questionnaires to measure subjective satisfaction. The concluding questionnaire was designed as a semi-open questionnaire, in which drivers could give explanations and comments to their choices.

Beside the above subjective date was collected, we also recorded some objective data from driver simulator, which is collisions, off road crashes, etc.

3 Results

The following is the analysis to questionnaires and recoded data.

3.1 Demographics Results

We found that 5 of them (31 %) thought their driving skills were above average, 9 (56 %) thought theirs were about average level, and 2 (13 %) thought theirs were below average. We also found that 12 of them had driven over speed limit, 4 had driven after drinking and 9 had the experience of fatigue driving.

3.2 Sound Warning Questionnaire Results

After analyzing the sound warning questionnaires, we found most of the drivers thought sound warnings were helpful for them. For example, the average score for the question "I believe that the sound warnings generally improved my driving…" was

5.06. For those thinking their driving skills were about average level or above average, altogether 11 drivers out of 16, the average score for this question was 5.4. We had correlation analysis to the acceptance levels of drivers to the sound warning system and the driving skills of them. The results showed that the Pearson correlation coefficient was −0.359 and $P = 0.172$. That revealed that driving skill and the acceptance level to the sound warning system were negatively correlative. Drivers with lower driving skill had higher acceptance level.

Table 2. Average scores for typical questions in sound warning questionnaire

Questions	Average score
Generally I found the sound warnings irritating (1-not at all, 4-neutral, very much)	3.38
The sound warnings generally improved my driving (1-not at all, 4-neutral, 7-very much)	5.06
I could imagine having these types of sound warning systems in my own car… (1-never, 4-neutral, 7-very much)	4.63

3.3 Visual Warning Questionnaire Results

After analyzing the data of visual warning questionnaires, we found most drivers held neutral opinions towards visual warning information, e.g. the average score to the question "I believe that the display information generally improved my driving…" was 4.44. Some drivers, especially those with lower driving skill, thought the warning display distracted their attention when driving. They said, "I didn't have time to see the display", "My car will deviate if I see the screen", etc. That revealed that processing the extra visual warning information might overload the driver's cognitive system. The drivers with low driving skill are afraid of moving their sights from the road, or they will miss important information of traffic situation.

Table 3. Average scores for typical questions in display warning questionnaire

Questions	Average score
Generally I found the display information irritating (1-not at all, 4-neutral, 7-very much)	4.00
The display information generally improved my driving (1-not at all, 4-neutral, 7-very much)	4.44
I could imagine having this type of display in my own car (1-never, 4-neutral, 7-very much)	4.94

3.4 Concluding Questionnaire Results

After analyzing the data of the conclusion questionnaires, we found that most of the drivers held positive opinions towards the sound warning system. They thought it could help them be aware of the potential danger when driving, especially on highway or when their attention was easy to be distracted. They were willing to have this kind of system. In Table 4, we can see that drivers held opinions to sound warning system after a baseline scenario. The average score increases from 5.06 (Table 2) to 5.25. The average score of acceptance to the visual warning system decreases from 4.44 (Table 3) to 3.63. The data of the conclusion questionnaire are more accurate on reflecting drivers' real feelings or opinions to ADAS after a second baseline scenario.

Table 4. Average scores for typical questions in conclusion questionnaire

Questions	Average score
I find the sound warnings irritating in real traffic (1-not at all, 4-neutral, 7-very much)	3.44
Generally I think the sound warnings irritating in real traffic (1-not at all, 4-neutral, 7-very much)	3.06
The sound warnings will warn too often in real traffic (1-not at all, 4-neutral, 7-very much)	4.06
The sound warnings can generally improve my real driving (1-not at all, 4-neutral, 7-very much)	5.25
The display information can generally improve my real driving (1-not at all, 4-neutral, 7-very much)	3.63

- About occasion and frequency of warnings

"I prefer to turn the system on when needed, e.g. driving at night, at high speed or with little traffic around." This reveals that ADAS is suitable for those types of driving situations and of little help to driving in busy city traffic.

"There is no need to alarm for crossing the line, or only alarm for too many times of crossing. Otherwise it is too often." We can lower the warning frequency. ……

4 Conclusions

The study showed that the use of integrated ADAS, either with the display or with sound warnings showed significant difference in collisions to the baseline driving.

The subjective results showed that the sound warnings were more accepted than the visual display warnings, and most users' attitude towards the visual display warning were comparatively neutral. Drivers acceptance should be considered when designing integrated ADAS for Chinese.

5 Discussion

Why is the less experience drivers think the sound is more acceptable? The reason may be they are more likely to take the three dangerous driving actions mentioned above in driving. And they are more likely to be nervous and panic when they encounter those kinds of danger. So they are easy to accept the sound warning system.

By analyzing the data from the questionnaires of 16 test sessions, we found that the drivers held positive opinions to the sound warning part of our ADAS. They thought it would improve their driving in real life. Scores for two related questions were 5.13 and 5.25. The drivers held neutral opinions to the visual warning part of our ADAS. Scores for two related questions were 4.44 and 3.63.

Bly revealed that reactions to auditory stimuli are faster than reactions to visual stimuli in certain cases [4]. So using sound warnings in ADAS is more helpful than visual warnings for drivers' quick reaction. Thus we think more sound stimuli should be taken in the design of ADAS.

Some drivers preferred speech as warnings in the test. They thought that would help them understand the meaning of the sounds. That is due to no special training for drivers on the sounds. Brewster mentioned that non-speech sounds are good for giving rapid feedback on actions [5]. Barker and Manji claimed that an important limitation of text is its lack of expressive capability [6]: It may take many words to describe something fairly simple. But in China, maybe the conciseness of Chinese pronunciation can find a new way for speech as warning sounds.

We will conduct further studies on sound types and warning occasions and frequency. We will start a new round of redesign and user research for our ADAS according to the results of this study. Due to the difference between the simulator and a real vehicle, like sense of position and speed, we should test our ADAS in a more real driving environment after passing laboratory tests, this should be very expensive.

Acknowledgement. The study described in this paper is supported by the project OPTIVe, which is funded by the Swedish government and Volvo.

References

1. Francesco, B., Riccardo, B., Alessandro, D.G., Massimiliano, M.: Using 3D sound to improve the effectiveness of the advanced driver assistance systems. Pers. Ubiquit. Comput. **6**, 155–163 (2002)
2. Lindgren, A.: Driving Safe in the Future? Driver Needs and Requirements for Advanced Driver Assistance Systems. Department of Computer Science and Engineering, Chalmers University of Technology, Gothenburg (2007)
3. Mendoza, P.A., Angelelli, A., Lindgren, A.: An Ecologically Designed Human Machine Interface for Advanced Driver Assistance Systems. Manuscript submitted for publication (2009)
4. Bly, S.: Sound and computer information presentation. Unpublished Ph.D. Thesis No. UCRL53282, Lawrence Livermore National Laboratory, Livermore, CA (1982)
5. Stephen, B.: Nonspeech auditory output. In: HCI Handbook 2008, pp. 247–264 (2008)
6. Barker, P.G., Manji, K.A.: Pictorial dialogue methods. Int. J. Man Mach. Stud. **31**, 323–347 (1989)

Interactive Navigation System for the Visually Impaired with Auditory and Haptic Cues in Crosswalks, Indoors and Urban Areas

Tianqi "Tenchi" Gao Smith(✉), Christopher Rose, Jeffrey "Wayne" Nolen, Daniel Pierce, and Alexander Sherman

3323 Shelby Center, Auburn University, Auburn, AL, USA
tzg0014@auburn.edu

Abstract. This Federal Highway sponsored study is aimed at creating an integrated human-computer system that the visually impaired could use to navigate through chaotic urban areas, indoors environment, as well as complex crosswalks. The system incorporates several redundant positioning systems in order to provide a robust solution to way finding. The main system components include global positioning system (GPS), visual odometry, pedometry, iPhone, Dedicated Short Range Communication (DSRC) radios, and tactile belt. The user will wear a laptop that contains a data processing program that collects data real-time from the devices and provides navigational feedback to the user's iPhone app and tactile belt.

Keywords: Visually impaired · Navigation · Global positioning system (GPS) · Visual odometry · Pedometry · Iphone application · Dedicated Short Range Communication (DSRC) radio · Tactile belt · Inertial Motion Unit (IMU)

1 Introduction

Vision plays a critical role in many people's lives. People use vision to navigate from place to place. However, many other people who cannot see or who have impaired vision navigate their way through the same places independently on a daily basis as well. There are some existing tools to aid blind navigation such as canes, Global Positioning System (GPS) that provides auditory signals [1], Radio Frequency Identification (RFID) [2], OEM ultrasound positioning system [3] and others. However, there are many technical difficulties in guiding the visually impaired through chaotic urban areas, indoors and complex crosswalks, where GPS signal is affected or blocked by the Urban Canyon Effect and walls. A conventional single navigational system becomes inaccurate and would drift farther and farther from the correct route if not corrected [4]. The dangerous traffic and loud ambient noise can also be a distraction and barrier for the blind users to receive the navigational instructions. There is a need for a more accurate and interactive navigation system for the blind and visually impaired community that is relatively easy to operate, light to carry, and provides users with concise and easy-to-interpret directional guidance.

C. Stephanidis (Ed.): HCII 2015 Posters, Part II, CCIS 529, pp. 539–545, 2015.
DOI: 10.1007/978-3-319-21383-5_90

2 System Components

This system incorporates three redundant positioning systems: visual odometry, pedometry, and GPS (Fig. 1) to increase the accuracy of navigation in different environments. The global positioning system (GPS) used in this study was augmented with and enhanced by visual odometry and pedometry. The visual odometry system was mounted to the chest, consisting of a stereo camera and an inertial measurement unit (IMU). The pedometry system was mounted to the foot using an IMU to detect footsteps to provide heading information and distance traveled. These components were combined with a Kalman filter for more accurate positioning than any single component can provide.

To find alternative delivery methods of the navigational systems than visual cues, the created system uses auditory and haptic cues instead to overcome the complicated ambient environment for the blind. An iPhone application (app) was created that is capable of reading its contents out loud as users hover over text. The iPhone was chosen because more than 60 % of the blind population in the US use iPhone and its Voice Over function, according to National Federation of the Blind (NFB) [5]. The app allows users to input origin and destination, provide estimated travel time and landmarks around the user in real time, as well as guidance to find access to destinations (ex. restaurants or shops). The user would also wear a tactile belt, which is wirelessly controlled by the iPhone app, to receive directional haptic cues. The app also allows volume adjustment and provided options to turn on or off the abovementioned features. In addition, Dedicated Short Range Communication (DSRC) radios are used to provide information on the location of crosswalks, crosswalk signals, and traffic light signals to users.

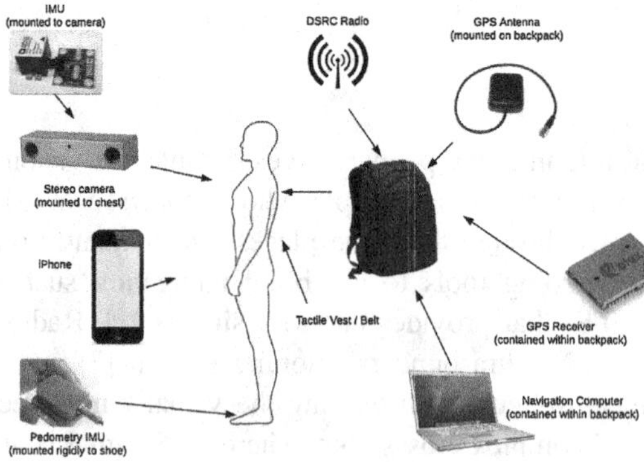

Fig. 1. System hardware components

Redundant Positioning Systems. For assisting the visually impaired as they commute unfamiliar environments, a confident global navigation solution must be attained. Such a system should provide ubiquitous positioning with the ability to handle various environmental conditions. For tracking the user's global position and orientation, an array of navigation devices are fused into one overall solution. The sensor suite consists of inertial measurement units (IMU), a stereo camera, and GPS. An IMU is capable of measuring accelerations and rotation rates in all directions. Provided perfect measurements from the device, a 3D position and orientation can be attained. The IMU is very common for navigation purposes because of its high sample rate and ability to operate in virtually all environmental conditions. For a MEMS grade IMU, like the one used in this project, the size, weight, power consumption, and cost are relatively low making it ideal for consumer products. In general, a MEMS grade IMU cannot be used for stand-alone navigation due to noisy, biased measurements. Coupling an IMU with other navigation systems can counteract such errors while maintaining the attributes of the inertial device. A stereo camera is used to perceive motion of the user. By comparing consecutive images from the camera, a "visual odometry" algorithm is capable of producing measurements of rotation and translation time period between frames. Such measurements are redundant to those produced from an IMU. By fusing redundant measurements, the accuracy and reliability of the navigation solution can be improved. Visual odometry does, however, rely on a certain number of stationary, visible objects in the camera frame. Such system suffers in highly dynamic environments (such as crowded streets, malls, subway station etc.) and low lighting scenarios. For this reason, complementary fusion with an IMU proves beneficial. For relating the navigation solution to points of interest throughout the user's commute, GPS provides positioning in a global reference frame. GPS is extremely common in navigation systems although it suffers in many scenarios. When the GPS receiver is surrounded by tall buildings or foliage, the signal's path from the satellite can be obstructed, causing erroneous position calculations. A GPS solution is also unavailable in virtually all indoor environments. Because of this, the IMU and camera systems are used to propagate the global navigation solution through sections of GPS unavailability.

Mapping. The bridge between the tactile belt and the navigation solution from the visual odometry, pedometry, and GPS systems is the mapping system for guiding the blind user from one location to another. The map consists of a network of nodes and linear links known as a graph. Each link has an associated weight determined by the length of that link between the two nodes at the ends of that link. Each node is a potential destination or point where the user must turn, while each link is a possible path for the blind user. For example, a city intersection could consist of four nodes with connecting links to show the possible paths around the block, as shown in Fig. 2. In this figure, the right intersection has four crosswalks for the corresponding four nodes and links. In the left intersection, a crosswalk does not exist, and as such, no link is present for that crosswalk. When the blind user enters a destination through the iPhone, a route is calculated using Dijkstra's algorithm, which is a path planning algorithm for finding the shortest path between two nodes in a graph [6]. Figure 2 shows two calculated paths for two desired goals. One goal is to reach a business meeting directly, and the other goal is to go to breakfast followed by the meeting. The calculated path from the hotel to the meeting (orange) takes the shortest route by crossing the road through the right intersection, traveling along the city block, and finally to the business meeting. The calculated path to breakfast and then to the meeting (purple) crosses the intersection, through a park, and then to breakfast. From the breakfast destination, the blind user travels to the intersection but is safely directed all around the intersection due to the lack of a crosswalk at that crossing. The tactile belt can guide the user to the next desired node with the knowledge of the user's current position from the redundant positioning systems explaining in earlier sections. The next section describes how the tactile belt guides the user to the next desired node along the linear link through notifications of either slight corrections to heading or a hard turn.

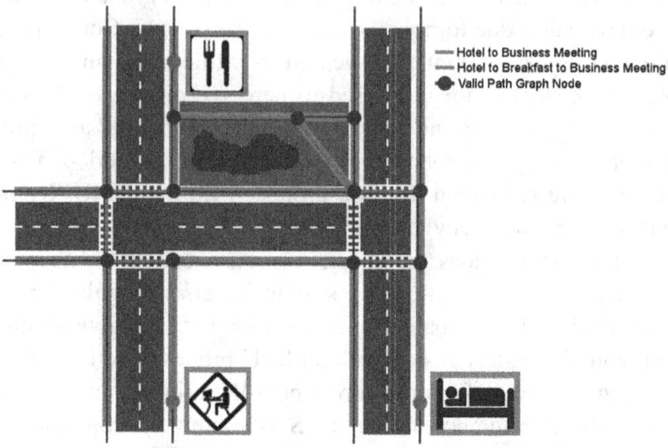

Fig. 2. Example of two calculated routes for two desired goals

Vibro-tactile Belt. The tactile belt's computer hardware is based from an Arduino Uno microcontroller. An Arduino was selected over alternatives due to its very low power consumption, Pulse-Width Modulation (PWM) output capabilities, and relative ease of use. The Uno's main chipset is an ATmega328 with a 16 MHz crystal and communicates over serial connection at 9600 baud rate. For the tactile belt unit, only four of the six PWM outputs are used, as the tactile belt has four vibrating motors. To power the DC motors, a separate circuit is needed outside the Arduino base. By using a transistor circuit, the high current loads needed to power the DC motors are isolated from the sensitive microcontroller. The Arduino is simply used to send a small pulse signal to a TIP120 NPN transistor. This specific transistor was chosen for its high current handling capabilities and overall robustness. Transistors typically have three pins – a base, emitter, and collector. The base of the transistor is connected to the Arduino's output, which is protected against surge currents by the use of a 1 k-Ohm resistor. Since the DC motors used for the belt have internal brushes, a standard 1N4004 diode is integrated into the circuit to only allow current to flow to the motor. DC brush motors have a propensity to send extremely high reverse voltage spikes when the motor comes to a stop, which is what the integration of diodes prevents. By oscillating the motor's ground and not the positive source, the transistor stays much cooler.

The vibrating motors were chosen based on overall vibrational intensity. Since the Arduino has a 5 V DC output, all the motors tested were 5 V motors of different size, weight, and rotational speed. The motors currently in use are low-torque, 3200- RMP motors that weigh 20 grams each. A larger motor was chosen for the user to sense feedback through a thicker jacket, if necessary. By using PWM, the motor's rotational speed can be adjusted to four distinct rotational speeds, each of which allows for a progressively more intense vibration. Four vibrating motors are integrated into the belt to guide the user. In order to be as unobtrusive and not overwhelming as possible, the belt is made with only four tactile user inputs. These four motors will be positioned 45 degrees off center from the standard cardinal directions, shown in Fig. 3.

Fig. 3. Tactile belt motor layout

The tactile belt is hard coded to accept different heading angles and use this information to delegate the direction of travel to the user. The four variables being passed from the laptop to the belt are heading angle, range, volume, and an emergency stop command. There are four different vibrating patterns for the UX (Fig. 4).

1. When heading is between −15 and 15 degrees from perpendicular, the belt will not send a vibrating response. This is a design aspect to make the UX less cumbersome and of an annoyance. For now the 15-degree variations have been arbitrarily chosen, but further testing will prove a more definitive cutoff.
2. Between −60 and −30 degrees, and 30 to 60 degrees from perpendicular, the area denoted by (2), is a path correction vibration. When the user's heading angle is between these cutoffs, a single vibratory pulse of 500 ms on each side will alert user to correct their path. If the user deviates to the right side of the defined path, a left side vibratory pulse will be issued. If the user deviates to the left side of the defined path, a right side vibratory pulse will be issued.
3. The region between −60 and −90 degrees, and 60 and 90 degrees is defined as the 'hard turn' region. When heading angle to the next node is in this region, the belt will pulse on the side of the body that turn occurs. (i.e. a left turn results in a tactile pulse of the left side front and back motors). The pulse will be of the pattern pulse-delay-pulse, where the pulses last for 500 ms apiece. This hard turn is differentiated from a path correction by the range to the next waypoint.

There is an emergency stop function that can override any command with a simple Boolean switch from the laptop. This e-stop pattern is pulse-delay-pulse-delay-pulse. The pulses are one second in length, and regardless of the volume setting, and pulsed at the maximum vibration volume. All four motors will also pulse during an e-stop command.

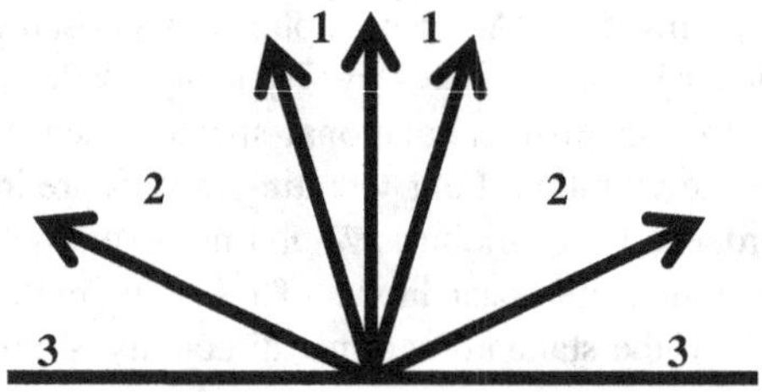

Fig. 4. Heading decision map

iPhone Application. The iPhone, recommended by NFB for its accessibility and wide use among the blind community, relays information with the navigational computer through Low Energy Bluetooth, interface with a designed graphical user interface and blind user through the iPhone's built-in accessibility capabilities, and communicate with the other components in the navigational system. Several communication protocols were explored for passing messages between the iPhone and the rest of the system. Wifi was not feasible due to a lack of support in many areas. While researching the applicability and usability of Bluetooth for this project, a fairly new technology called Bluetooth low-energy was also investigated. Upon further research, it was found that Bluetooth low-energy was the best choice. Software from another team on the project could only be implemented in Linux. In order to handle both the iPhone development and passing messages from the iPhone to the navigation system, a MacBook Pro runs Linux and Parallels, which is a platform that allows a user to run more than one operating system on a single computer. The OSX application Pro running Linux in Parallels (Parallels is a platform to run more than one operating system on one computer.) was built to send and receive messages to and from the iPhone opens a Transmission Control Protocol (TCP) port to send messages to a listening Robot Operating System (ROS) node, which then publishes the messages for the rest of the system to access. The OSX application also listens for messages and passes them to the iPhone when received. The iPhone's accessibility functions include voice over, zoom (for visually impaired), color inversion, larger or bolded text, as well as phone noise cancellation and LED flashing for the hearing impaired. Of particular interest to our project and the blind community is voice over. With voice over enabled on the iPhone, a voice will read the title of each page aloud, along with any selected text and the title of any labels or buttons highlighted. In addition to selected text and titles, various hints and suggestions, which the programmer can add or alter as needed, will be read aloud. Also, while voice over is enabled, navigating the iPhone becomes just as easy for the visually impaired as it is for the sighted. Simply swiping one finger to the right will progress forward across options and swiping left will progress back. When the desired option is found a double tap will select it.

3 Conclusion and Discussion

The three redundant positioning systems used in this study better assures positioning accuracy. The combination of auditory and haptic cues with volume adjust abilities provide users with multiple options of receiving directional guidance. And the iPhone application serves as the main user interface where visually impaired users take advantage of its Voice Over function to send command to the rest of the system and receive feedbacks accordingly.

This study is currently in the process of acquiring Institutional Review Board (IRB) approval for human subject testing. Upon approval, 12 visually impaired subjects that meet physical and other requirements will be recruited to test the system performance. Subjects will be asked to have the designed system mounted on them and walk on designated routes. Data will be recorded in real-time and will also be used post-experiment to simulate the subjects' gaits and routes in order to analyze the system performance.

Acknowledgement. The authors would like to thank the Federal Highway Administration for their generous support. This study is made possible by Federal Highway Grant # DTFH61-13-C-00006. The authors would also like to thank the GPS and Vehicle Dynamics Laboratory (GAVLAB) and Wireless Engineering Research and Education Center (CSSE) at Auburn University's technical support, Draper Laboratory's contribution on vision navigation system, and National Federation of the Blind (NFB)'s insight on the needs and feedbacks of the visually impaired community.

References

1. Loomis, J., Golledge, R., Klatzky, R.: GPS-Based Navigation Systems for the Visually Impaired. Lawrence Erlbaum Associates Publishers, New York (2001)
2. Chumkamon, S., Tuvaphanthaphiphat, P., Keeratiwintakorn, P.: A blind navigation system using RFID for indoor environments. In: 2008 5th International Conference on Electrical Engineering/Electronics, Computer, Telecommunications and Information Technology (2008)
3. Ran, L., Helal, S., Moore, S.: Drishti: an integrated indoor/outdoor blind navigation system and service. In: Second IEEE Annual Conference on Pervasive Computing and Communications (2004)
4. Fallah, N., Apostolopoulos, I., Bekris, K., Folmer, E.: Indoor human navigation systems: a survey, interacting with computers. Oxf. J. **25**(1), 21–33 (2013)
5. Chong, C.: Knowing what is good about the iphone and what is not (2014). Nfb.org
6. Dijkstra, E.: A note on two problems in connexion with graphs. Numer. Math. **1**(1), 269–271 (1959)

Domestic Electricity Consumption Visualized as Flowing Tap Water to Raise the Feeling of Waste

Yukio Ishihara[1(✉)], Makio Ishihara[2], Fumi Hirayama[1], and Keiji Yasukawa[1]

[1] Innovation Center for Medical Redox Navigation, Kyushu University, 3-1-1, Maidashi, Higashi-ku, Fukuoka 812-8582, Japan
{iyukio,hfumi,ykeiji}@redoxnavi.med.kyushu-u.ac.jp

[2] Faculty of Information Engineering, Fukuoka Institute of Technology, 3-30-1, Wajiro-Higashi, Higashi-ku, Fukuoka 811-0295, Japan
m-ishihara@fit.ac.jp

Abstract. In this study we visualize electricity consumption as flowing tap water in order to encourage people to save electricity by raising the feeling of waste. To save electricity, the mainstream is to present its consumption and quick feedback. Additionally we try to evoke the feeling of waste using flowing tap water. We build a prototype system to convert the amount of electricity being consumed into that of flowing tap water. Finally it is shown that the flow rate of tap water changes according to the amount of electricity consumption.

Keywords: Flowing tap water · Electricity consumption · Peripheral information · Ambient display

1 Introduction

After the Kyoto Protocol was negotiated in 1997 and coming into force in 2005, eco-friendly products and energy-saving household appliances started to be manufactured and gradually replaced the old ones in our homes to reduce greenhouse gas emissions. In 2011 there was the catastrophic event of East Japan earthquake, so we were all urgently required for further reduction of electricity consumption due to suspension of nuclear power plants across Japan for security check. This period turned to be a good opportunity to look deep into the way of daily use of electricity.

The mainstream to save electricity is believed to present its consumption in graph, which will be available as a part of Home Energy Management System (HEMS). This makes it easier to specifically find out what time and which room much electricity is consumed. To save electricity, it is also emphasized that quick feedback of the consumption is very important because it helps the residents to connect between the current consumption and the appliances being used. Although HEMS provides electricity consumption in graph, it is displayed on a screen, so it seems to be more effective to direct the consumption to the residents

C. Stephanidis (Ed.): HCII 2015 Posters, Part II, CCIS 529, pp. 546–550, 2015.
DOI: 10.1007/978-3-319-21383-5_91

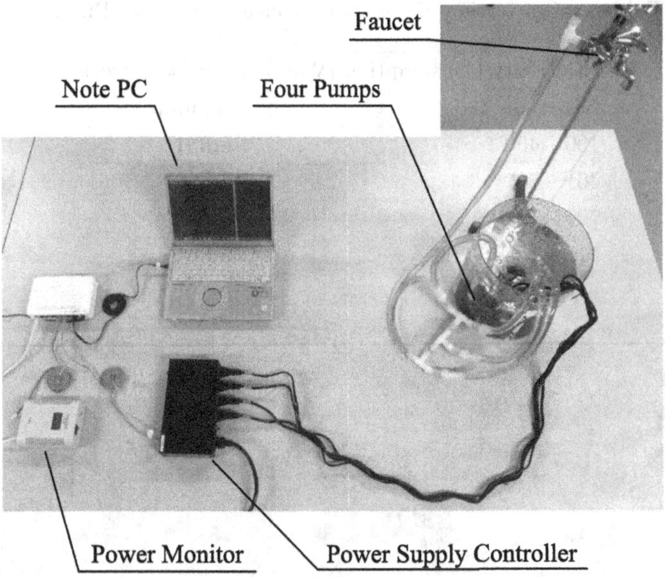

Fig. 1. Our prototype system.

in some other form. In this study, we take an approach of presenting electricity consumption as peripheral information.

Peripheral information is usually out of the focus of users' attention and does not interrupt their current work. When people are working on computers, for example, they will realize that it starts raining without their work interrupted when they hear the sound of raindrops hitting the ground, roof or the window. They may also realize that a near coffee shop opens because the beautiful smell of coffee comes up in the room. The peripheral information of the sound of raindrops and the smell of coffee does not interrupt their current work but it conveys much of what is going on around them.

In a HCI area, ambient displays were invented to provide peripheral information [1]. There are several studies to encourage people to improve their behaviors by introducing ambient displays in their life space. Rodríguez et al. [2] proposed a system for safe driving. Driving behavior of a driver is monitored and shown through a small mirror-hanging accessory, so the driver can realize his/her behavior but the driving is not interrupted. Hong et al. [3] built a flower-shaped physical avatar to provide feedback of how good/bad a user's posture is. When the user is slouching over a computer, for example, the avatar changes its posture and color to warn about his/her bad posture. Gustafsson et al. [4] made cords specially designed to illuminate depending on the amount of electricity being consumed.

The last study of Gustafsson et al. [4] is very relevant to ours. While cords illuminate to show electricity consumption in their study, we use flowing tap water. When people see flowing tap water with no intention of use, they cer-

Table 1. Conversion of electricity consumption into Pump#.

Electricity Consumption (Watt)	Pump# to work
Less than 100	No pumps
100 - 400	Pump1
401 - 700	Pump2
701 - 1000	Pump3
More than 1000	Pump4

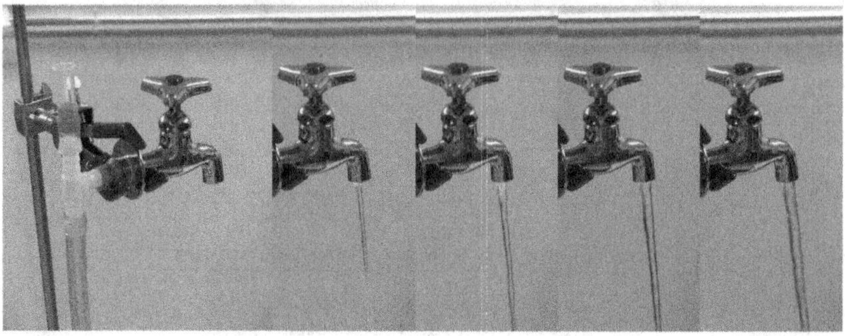

(a) (b) (c) (d) (e)

Fig. 2. Flowing tap water at four levels of flow rate. No pumps are working in (a). Pump1 to 4 are working in (b) to (e), respectively. Pump1 sucks the least water while Pump4 does the most.

tainly feel wasteful. As for electricity, they hardly feel it even though they know that standby electricity is being consumed all the time. We visualize domestic electricity being consumed as flowing tap water in order to let them feel wasteful as well as visualize the flowing electricity.

The rest of this manuscript is organized as follows. In Sect. 2, it is explained the way how electricity consumption is visualized as flowing tap water. Then our prototype system is demonstrated in Sect. 3. Finally we give concluding remarks in Sect. 4.

2 Electricity Consumption as Flowing Tap Water

Figure 1 shows our prototype system that comprises a power monitor (EGM801 manufactured by Miyakawa Electric Works Ltd.), a power supply controller (IP Power 9258 T manufactured by Aviosys International Inc.), four pumps and a note PC. The power monitor is connected to a fuse box and measures electricity being consumed by the household. After that the measured data is sent to a program running on the note PC then the program determines which pump to work as shown in Table 1. Each of the four pumps or Pump1 to 4 is previously adjusted to suck up water at one of four levels of flow rate. Pump1 sucks the

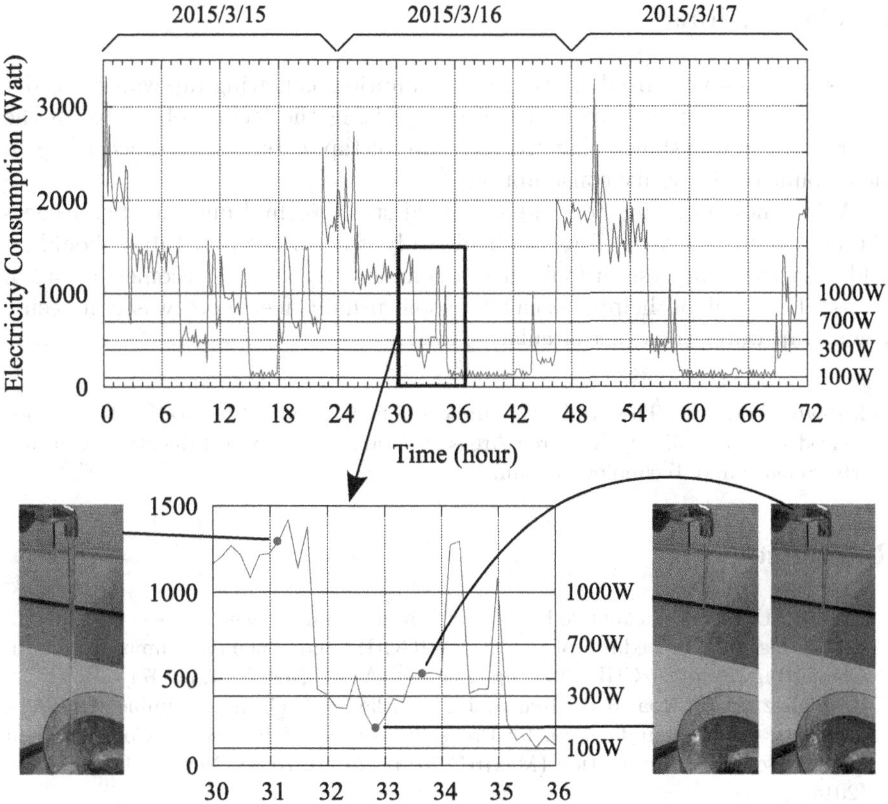

Fig. 3. Electricity consumption by a family for three days.

least water while Pump4 does the most (Fig. 2). These pumps are connected to the outlets of the power supply controller, and each of the outlets can be turned on/off separately by the program. Finally the program sends a signal to the power supply controller to turn on/off the pumps based on Table 1.

3 Experiment

We conducted an experiment in a research laboratory to make sure our prototype system works. First a family was asked to connect the power monitor to the fuse box of their home and measure the electricity consumption for three days. After the data was obtained, it was brought in the laboratory and reproduced on the note PC in order to simulate the electricity consumption of the home.

Figure 3 shows the measured electricity consumption. A part of the graph indicated by a rectangle is enlarged and shown below. Our prototype system was run based on the electricity consumption of Fig. 3. Three photos beside the enlarged graph show the flowing tap water at the three points of time. As a result, it was confirmed that the flow rate of the tap water changed according to the amount of electricity being consumed.

4 Conclusions

In this study we visualized electricity consumption as flowing tap water in order to encourage people to save electricity by raising the feeling of waste. In the experiment, it was shown that the flow rate of tap water changed according to the amount of electricity consumption.

We are now planning to conduct a field study to find out the effectiveness in practical situations. Before the field study, the pumps and tubes should be hidden so that our system looks like a common faucet and becomes a part of homes. This will be helpful because people usually feel more wasteful seeing flowing tap water than just circulating one.

Acknowledgement. This study was supported by Creation of Innovation Centers for Advanced Interdisciplinary Research Areas Program, Ministry of Education, Culture, Sports, Science and Technology-Japan.

References

1. Ishii, H., Ullmer, B.: Tangible bits: towards seamless interfaces between people, bits and atoms. In: Proceedings of the ACM SIGCHI Conference on Human Factors in Computing Systems (CHI 1997), pp. 234–241. ACM, New York (1997)
2. Rodríguez, M.D., Roa, R.R., Ibarra, J.E., Curlango, C.C.: In-car ambient displays for safety driving gamification. In: Proceedings of the 5th Mexican Conference on Human-Computer Interaction (MexIHC 2014), 26 pp. ACM, New York, NY, USA (2014)
3. Hong, J., Song, S., Cho, J., Bianchi, A.: Better posture awareness through flower-shaped ambient Avatar. In: Proceedings of the Ninth International Conference on Tangible, Embedded, and Embodied Interaction (TEI 2015), pp. 337–340. ACM, New York (2015)
4. Gustafsson, A., Gyllenswärd, M.: The power-aware cord: energy awareness through ambient information display. In: CHI 2005 Extended Abstracts on Human Factors in Computing Systems (CHI EA 2005), pp. 1423–1426. ACM, New York (2005)

Novel Route Depiction Method Based on Light Information for Map Applications

Namgyu Kang(✉) and Kana Takahashi

Department of Information Architecture, Future University Hakodate, Hakodate, Japan
{kang, b1011017}@fun.ac.jp

Abstract. In recent times, the number of users who use map apps on their smartphones has rapidly increased. When a pedestrian travels to a destination, he/she uses a nearby landmark for finding the route. However, in almost all map apps, routes are depicted considering daytime conditions. This implies that when a pedestrian uses such map apps at nighttime, he/she would need more information to determine whether a route is safe, such as the route's luminance level. Therefore, to address this need, we propose a new route depiction method based on light information. Furthermore, we verify the effectiveness of the proposed method through evaluation experiments involving 25 women participants. Experimental results show that the proposed method affects a user's choice of route; moreover, the proposed method is not only easy to understand and use but is also highly rated in *Kansei* aspects such as fun, interesting, and safety assistance.

Keywords: Map application · Light information · Depiction · *Kansei* value

1 Introduction

In recent times, map applications (apps) have become some of the most used apps in smart phones. A map app helps a user conveniently search and find his/her way to a destination [1]. When a user searches for a location using a map app, along with the route, visual information about landmarks, such as point of interaction, buildings, and signboards, is provided, which is immensely helpful in navigation. However, the availability of such visual information can change depending on weather conditions or the time of day. For example, visual information about landmarks in some map apps is typically described considering daytime conditions; therefore, when a user uses such a map app at nighttime, the availability of the visual information may be different as compared to that during daytime. Further, many users prefer a safe route at nighttime rather than the shortest path recommendation of typical map apps. For instance, Nakazawa reported that a user selects a route based on the availability of streetlights and number of open stores along the path [2]. According to Boyce's research team, how safe a person feels on a particular road varies depending on the illuminance level of the road [3]. Some recent studies have focused on the relationship between the luminance level of roads at night and the occurrence frequency of crime [4, 5]. In other words, a person's perception of safety, which typically depends on the luminance level of the route, is an important factor when selecting a route at night. However, there are

C. Stephanidis (Ed.): HCII 2015 Posters, Part II, CCIS 529, pp. 551–557, 2015.
DOI: 10.1007/978-3-319-21383-5_92

not many map apps that account for this need for safety when suggesting a route. Thus, to address this need, in this study, a new route depiction method that considers road luminance information is proposed. Further, we verify the effectiveness of the proposed method through evaluation experiments.

2 Proposed Method

In this section, first, we review some related works. Next, we survey the current situation of streetlights in Hakodate city. Then, based on the current situation of Hakodate streetlights and insights from previous work, we develop the underlying concept for the proposed method. Then, the proposed route depiction method, developed based on the concept and insights from previous work, is described.

2.1 Related Works

Google Maps is the most used map app in the world. Google Maps shows not only the shortest route to a destination but also information about real time traffic as well information about nearby destinations such as restaurants and shops (Left of Fig. 1). Yahoo! Maps shows not only the shortest route to a destination but also information about railroads and underground shopping arcades (Middle of Fig. 1).

However, the information in these two apps is provided considering daytime conditions. In contrast, the information of the NGY Night Street Advisor app is based on light information (luminance intensity). In this app, the illuminance level of a road is expressed by different colors. Red in this app indicates a bright road, and green indicates a dark road (Right of Fig. 1).

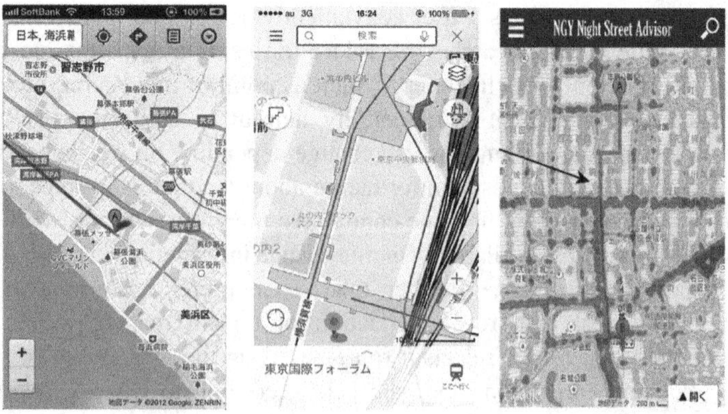

Fig. 1. Google maps, Yahoo! maps, and NGY night street advisor

2.2 Current Situation of Street Lamps in Hakodate City

Hakodate city was selected as the target city for the proposed method because of Hakodate's famous night view. Hakodate's night view is one of the most beautiful night views in the world similar to that of Hong Kong and Napoli.

According to the streetlight layout drawing of Hakodate (Fig. 2), there are two types of lamps, lamps intended to illuminate a road and lamps intended to prevent crime. Further, the operation hours of these lamps are different depending on seasons. Therefore, many tourists who visit Hakodate determine the operation hours of the lamps in order to enjoy the beautiful night view.

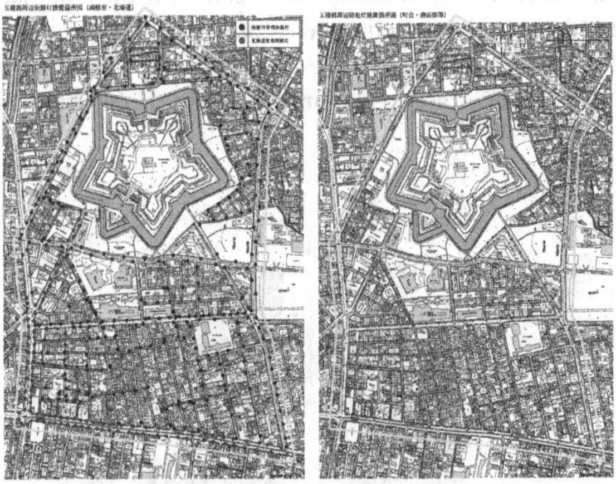

Fig. 2. Example of street lamp information in Hakodate

2.3 Concept for the Proposed Method

From previous studies, the concept "Grasping route and feeling safe, though it is night!" was extracted. In particular, women are the main target users for the proposed method. There are various light sources in our daily life such as natural sunlight, street lamp light, light from signboards, light from a store, and light from a car. In this study, we focus on changing sunlight intensity and light from street lamps.

The concept of the proposed method is to enable users to view the available light information for a route as well as indicate the presence or absence of landmarks.

2.4 Proposed Route Depiction Method

The proposed method for map apps of iPhone and other smart phone was developed based on the aforementioned concept (Fig. 3). The street lamp information was depicted on the map based on the streetlight layout of Hakodate. The proposed method has the following four functions:

1. Turn on and off the streetlight: A user is able to light and douse the streetlights on the map using the top left button on the screen. This function helps a user imagine the luminance conditions of a street at night. Figure 3 shows an example of the different background luminance levels of the map app. When user turns on and off the light, the lamps on the screen will fade-in and fade-out.
2. Adjusting the brightness level of sunlight: A user is able to change the background color to reflect the changing sunlight intensity using the white lever on the bottom of the screen.
3. Turn on and off landmark information: A user can view and hide landmarks on the map. If the background is too dark, it may become difficult for a user to read the information on the map, and therefore, hard to find the route to a destination owing to the blur on the screen. In such cases, a user can view the landmarks clearly on the map using the function. This function helps user to perceive night conditions while also being able to select the exact route to a destination on the map.
4. Zoom in and out: A user is able to zoom in and out of the map using this function (Fig. 4).

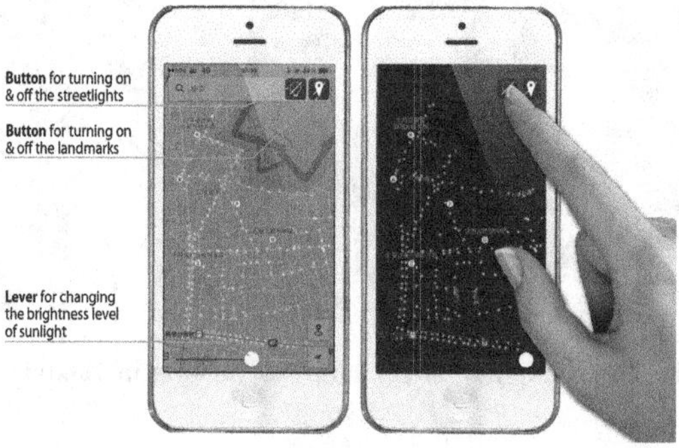

Fig. 3. Proposed route depiction method based on light information

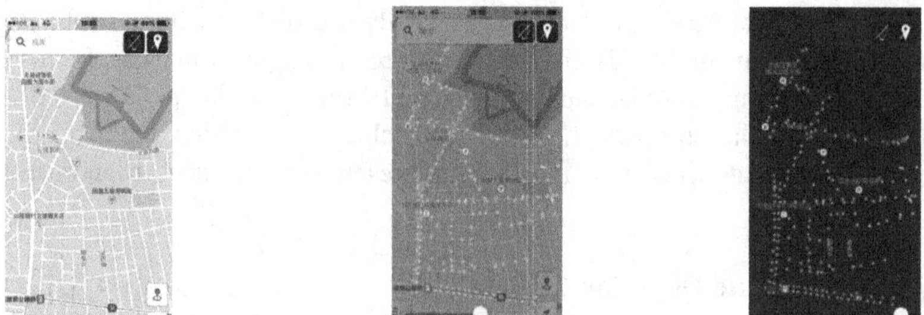

Fig. 4. Examples of streetlight information for changing sunlight intensities

3 Evaluation Experiment

3.1 Experimental Method

The *Kansei* evaluation experiment to verify the effectiveness of the proposed method was conducted with 25 participants at Future University Hakodate of Japan. All of the participants were young female students. First, the participants used both versions: the standard Google Maps version that only considers daytime conditions (existing version), and the Google Maps version implementing the proposed method (the light information version) for 10 min. Next, the following three features were evaluated: (1) fade-in and fade-out streetlights, (2) changing brightness level of sunlight, and (3) viewing and hiding landmarks on the map. Each feature was evaluated on a scale of 1 to 6 from the following eight *Kansei* aspects: (1) interesting, (2) fun, (3) easy to understand, (4) safety assistance, (5) user-friendly, (6) likability, (7) novelty, and (8) easy to perceive night conditions. Lastly, they selected a route from the specified start-point to a destination using the existing version and the light information version.

3.2 Results of the Experiment

Fade-in and Fade-Out Streetlights Feature. This feature was highly rated in the "novelty," "easy to understand," "fun," "safety assistance," "likability," and "easy to perceive night conditions" aspects. Figure 5 illustrates the evaluation result. These results imply that many users can easily understand the feature, fading in and out streetlights, and it helps them perceive night conditions. This feature helps assist a person to perceive the level of safety while also being fun and novel.

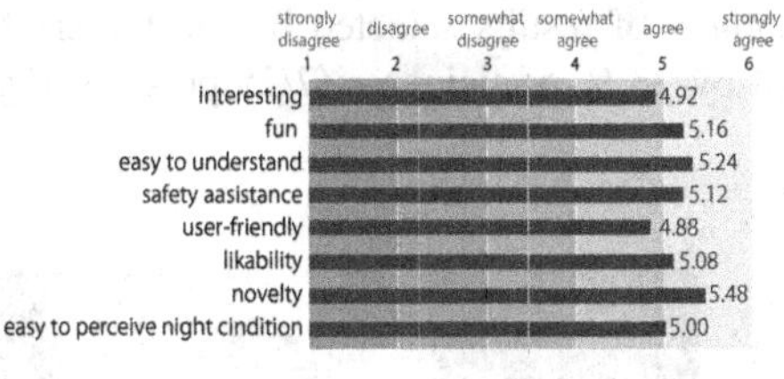

Fig. 5. Evaluation result of 'fade in and out streetlights' feature

Changing Brightness Level of Sunlight Feature. This feature was rated highly from the "novelty" aspect. Furthermore, other aspects such as "easy to understand," "likability," "interesting," and "fun" were also highly rated. Figure 6 illustrates the evaluation results. These results imply that the changing brightness level of sunlight feature is novel while also being fun, interesting, and likable.

Viewing and Hiding Landmarks Feature. This feature was rated highly in the "safety assistance" and "easy to understand" aspects. These results show that landmarks help users understand a street so that they can select an exact route. This process helps user to feel safer. However, this feature is not very helpful in "perceiving night

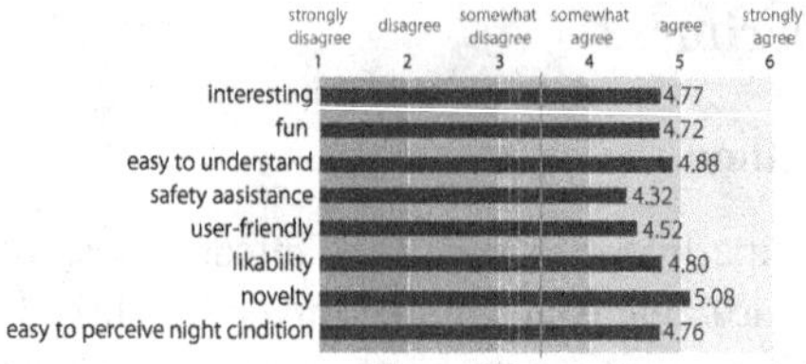

Fig. 6. Evaluation result of 'changing brightness level of sunlight' feature

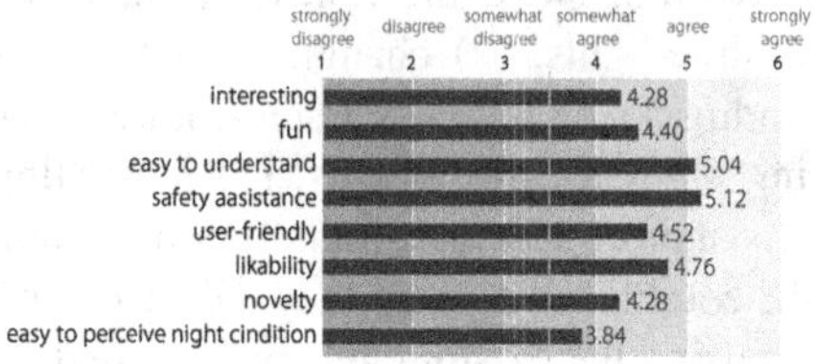

Fig. 7. Evaluation result of 'viewing and hiding landmarks' feature

conditions". In addition, almost all existing map apps have implemented this landmark function.

Selecting a Route Using Either Map Version. In the existing version, many participants selected the shortest and most convenient route. In the proposed method version, they selected a route depending on the concentration of streetlights; all participants selected a route different from the first route in the existing version. The result implies that preferred route to destination differs depending on daytime or night. Figure 7 shows the example of results selected by most users for each map version. Each route was selected by 28 % participants (7/25 person) (Fig. 8).

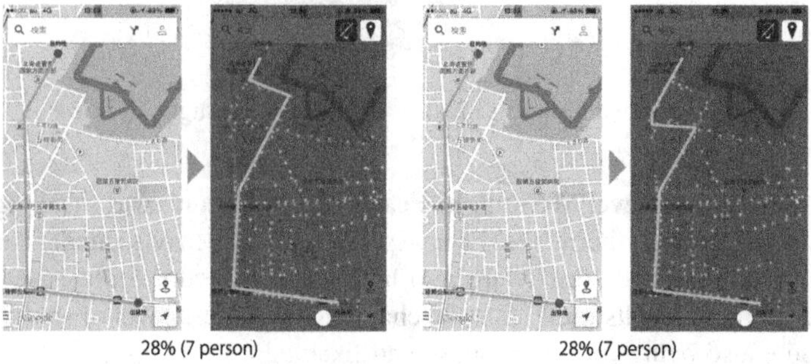

Fig. 8. Example of the results of selecting a route

4 Conclusion

The proposed method was highly rated in the aspects of "fun," "interesting," and "safety assistance." Moreover, almost all of the participants stated that the proposed method was easy to understand and use. The results of the experiment implied that users can search for a route to a destination without any stress for operating with *Kansei* value such as "fun" and "interesting." In addition, users can perceive the night conditions for a street, which helps users feel safer. From the evaluations experiment for route selection, it was confirmed that most users selected routes differently depending on whether it was daytime or nighttime. This result indicated that light information affects a user's route choice. From the experiment, it is evident that the proposed method is not only easy to understand but also is highly rated in terms of *Kansei* aspects such as fun, interesting, and safety assistance.

References

1. Google Maps, 29 May 2014. https://www.google.co.jp/intl/ja/maps/about/explore/mobile/
2. Nakazawa, K., Kita, N., Takagi, K., Inoue, T., Shigeno, H., Okada, K.: A dynamic map based on landmark's visibility. Inf. Process. Soc. Jpn **49**(1), 233–241 (2008)
3. Boyce, P.R., Eklund, N.H., Hamilton, B.J., Bruno, L.D.: Perceptions of safety at night in different lighting conditions. Light. Res. Technol. **32**, 72–91 (2000)
4. Mitsui, T., Mori, K., Namikawa, K.: Effects of retroreflective materials on recognition of pedestrian accidents at night. Int. Assoc. Traffic Saf. Sci. **33**(1), 88–97 (2008)
5. Kobayashi, S., Abe, T., Yoshizaki, K.: The Pedestrians avoidance behaviors toward a stranger on the nighttime streets. Archit. Inst. Jpn **556**, 69–75 (2002)

Exploration of Building-Occupant Communication Methods for Reducing Energy Consumption in Buildings

Saba Khashe(✉), Arsalan Heydarian, Joao Carneiro, and Burcin Becerik-Gerber

Sonny Astani Department of Civil and Environmental Engineering, University of Southern California, Los Angeles, CA 90089, USA
{skhashe, ydaria, jcarneir, becerik}@usc.edu

Abstract. Buildings consume enormous amounts of our nation's total energy use (38 %). Previous work showed that occupant actions and behaviors have significant impacts (more than 40 %) on building energy demand. Our main goal is to transform buildings into interactive living spaces that communicate with their occupants via agents and influence the way the occupants interact with their building to enable energy efficiency. As a first step towards this goal, we investigated effective communication methods aimed at influencing building occupants' energy-related behaviors. We hypothesized that human-building communication would be more persuasive if the interaction is seen as more social. To investigate the influence of social influence methods (e.g., foot in the door, rule of reciprocity, and direct request) on occupants' energy consumption behavior, experiments were conducted in which immersive virtual environments (IVEs) were used to model real-life office settings.

Keywords: Social influence methods · Immersive virtual environment · Compliance · Social features

1 Introduction

Rapidly growing energy use is exhausting energy sources and resulting in energy cost increases and has heavy environmental impacts, including ozone layer depletion, global warming, and the climate change. In developed countries, the building sector accounts for more energy consumption (38 % of nation's total energy use [1]) than the transportation sector and the industry sector which includes manufacturing, agriculture, and mining. Within the building sector, office buildings present opportunities in energy reduction due to their large share in energy consumption (18 %) [2] as well as the fact that occupants in commercial buildings are not in charge of energy bills and therefore, they are not motivated to take actions in reducing energy costs. Considering the increasing trends in buildings' energy consumption, efficient energy usage in buildings plays a vital role in reducing global energy demand and associated emissions. Therefore, energy efficiency in buildings is a prime objective for energy policy at the regional, national, and international levels [2]. Existing approaches to increase energy

C. Stephanidis (Ed.): HCII 2015 Posters, Part II, CCIS 529, pp. 558–563, 2015.
DOI: 10.1007/978-3-319-21383-5_93

efficiency in buildings fall into two broad categories: technological improvements and advancements in building systems (e.g., HVAC systems, lighting systems, sensors and sensing systems) and behavioral techniques (e.g. modifying behavior of an occupant by providing feedback (e.g., personal energy use)). Energy efficient occupant behavior provides higher savings with much lower costs than the investments in building equipment and it can be used in both new and existing buildings [3]. Previous work showed that occupant actions and behaviors have a significant impact (more than 40 %) on building energy demand [4]. In order to reduce office buildings energy consumption, this research focuses on novel human-building communication methods to influence occupants' behavior positively towards more energy efficient choices.

Our review of relevant research in the energy domain revealed some missing elements, which result in the failure of existing behavior change interventions to fully induce the possible changes in human behavior. In addition, follow-up studies conducted in energy domain to monitor the effects of the interventions over longer periods of time showed that the positive effects of the intervention were not maintained after the interventions were stopped for a while [5]. We argue that human-building communication needs continuous interaction. In fact, our main goal is to transform buildings into interactive living spaces that communicate with their occupants via agents and influence the way the occupants interact with their building to enable energy efficiency. As a first step towards this goal, we investigated effective communication methods aimed at influencing building occupants' energy-related behaviors.

2 Hypothesis

Social influence strategies in other domains (health, marketing, psychology) introduced approaches that have been successful in enhancing the effectiveness of intervention strategies that influence behavior. Existing influence strategies in energy domain failed to fully utilize social features. Social features are related to how humans interact with each other, requiring another person or an agent (in our study). Our objective is to investigate the effects of incorporating social influence methods (behavior-change tactics more commonly seen in face-to-face communication such as foot in the door, rule of reciprocity, and direct request) into the occupant-building communication. We hypothesized that social influence methods adopted in the design of our persuasive messages will influence the users' compliance with the energy saving messages.

3 Methodology

As the first step toward enhancing the human-building communication, we examined the use of social influence methods, such as direct requests and compliance-gaining techniques. Compliance gaining refers to the interactions, in which one individual (the agent) attempts to induce another person (the target) to perform a desired behavior that the target person otherwise might not have performed [6]. We tested the compliance-gaining strategies that have the greatest influence on behavior in the marketing literature, which are the (a) foot-in-the-door, and (b) role of reciprocity techniques [7–9]. In addition, we tested the effects of directly asking the participants to engage in the desired behavior, which is called (c) direct request.

To test the influence of these social influence methods in the context of office buildings – occupant communication, Immersive Virtual Environments (IVEs) are used to simulate a real-life office setting. Although performing such experiments is possible in existing buildings, there are several factors that could affect the results (e.g., cloudy/sunny weather in different days). IVEs give us the ability to manipulate complex, abstract objects and concepts while maintaining high experimental control. They also allow us to control for potentially confounding variables that exist in built environments and isolate the variables of interest. We designed an office environment in 3ds Max© and imported it to Unity 3D© to be used in an IVE.

The participants first were assigned randomly to one of the three groups of social influence strategies: a) foot-in-the-door, (b) role of reciprocity techniques, and (c) direct request (Table 1).

Table 1. Messages delivered to participants in different groups

Social influence method	Message
Foot-in-the-door	"Could you please do me a favor and open at least one of the blinds?" (Considering that blinds are near to the participant) and then "Could you please do me a favor and open the other blinds and turn off the artificial lights?" (Considering that the light switches are farther)
Rule of reciprocity	"Could you please do me a favor and turn off the artificial lights if I open the blinds for you?"
Direct request	"Could you please do me a favor and open the blinds and turn off the artificial lights?"

The messages were delivered through text and the participants were given an opportunity to comply with the message in the IVE. First, the participants were instructed to adjust the lighting levels (intensity levels) of the room to their most preferred settings by opening the blinds or turning the artificial lights on/off. Through real-time rendering, the virtual model dynamically adjusted the lighting levels as the participants turn the light switch on/off or opened/closed the blinds. Once the participants acknowledged their most preferred setting and were trained how to interact with the environment, they were immersed in the main scene where all the blinds were closed and the artificial lights were on. Then participants were exposed to different persuasive messages according to the condition to which they were assigned while performing a given task and then were given an opportunity to comply with different requests. The participants were asked to comply with the request by adjusting the lighting setting in an office and perform a set of activities, such as watching a video in the modeled environment using a head-mounted-display.

We observed the participants' compliance and, in a post survey, we ask the participants to explain the reasons behind their actions and to rate their intentions to use a similar suggestion system, if it were employed in their office in the future. Our intention was to understand how similar systems could be employed in the design of future buildings and operation of existing buildings. Additionally, the participants were asked to fill out a pre survey (personality test) and post surveys (group ideology survey and Technology Readiness Index) to conduct exploratory analyses on the effect of the participant attitudes and personalities with the way that they might interact with the suggestion system (Fig. 1).

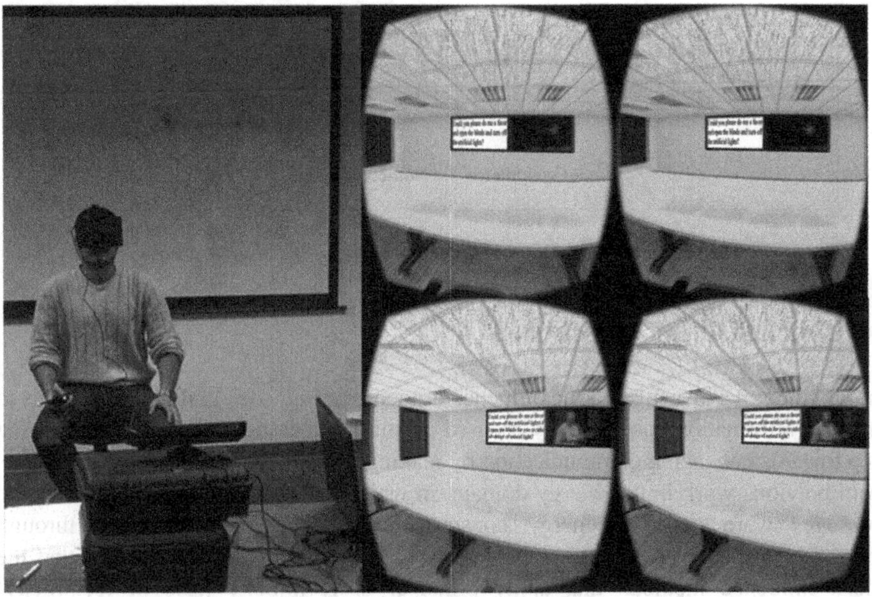

Fig. 1. Messages delivered in the IVE

4 Results

The results are presented based on the three social influenced methods commonly used in social science. Data were collected during an ongoing experiment that included 32 participants (59 % male and 41 % female). The participants were recruited from the graduate students in the University of Southern California. In general, 70 % of the participants complied with the message and the results indicated that among the social influence methods that were tested, role of reciprocity received the highest rate of compliance (Fig. 2).

When participants were asked how likely they were to use a similar suggestion system, if it were employed in their office, the results showed that 69 % of the participants rated the possibility as vey likely and somewhat likely, 10 % as undecided, and 21 % as unlikely or somewhat unlikely.

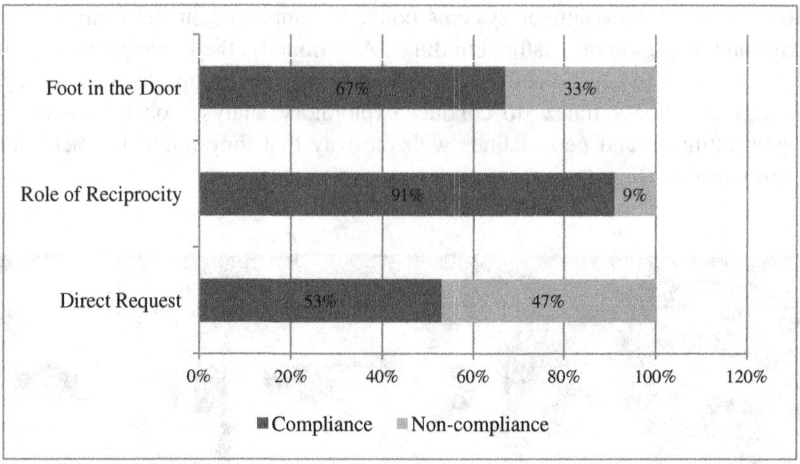

Fig. 2. Participants' compliance percentages in different groups

5 Conclusion and Discussion

In this study, we investigated the influence of incorporating social influence methods to improve information-based energy focused persuasive messages. It is an essential first step towards enhancing communication by making it more social. Our approach differs from previous work in the energy domain, in which the information-based persuasive messages were used or energy consumption feedback was provided through charts/tables (usually without another agent). The results of the test showed that the social influence methods that apply principal of reciprocity (rule of reciprocity) received more compliance followed by the methods that adapt repetitive requests (foot in the door) in comparison with the direct requests which neither use the principle of reciprocity nor repeated requests.

Acknowledgements. This material is based upon work supported by the National Science Foundation under Grant No. 1351701. Any opinions, findings, and conclusions or recommendations expressed in this material are those of the authors and do not necessarily reflect the views of the National Science Foundation.

References

1. Energy Information Administration's Annual Energy Outlook (2012). http://www.eia.gov/forecasts/aeo/er/excel/aeotab_2.xlsx
2. Pérez-Lombard, L., Ortiz, J., Pout, C.: A review on buildings energy consumption information. J. Energy Buildings **40**, 394–398 (2008)
3. Nisiforou, O., Poullis, S., Charalambides, A.: Behaviour, attitudes and opinion of large enterprise employees with regard to their energy usage habits and adoption of energy saving measures. J. Energy Buildings **55**, 299–311 (2012)

4. Azar, E., Menassa, C.C.: Agent-based modeling of occupants and their impact on energy use in commercial buildings. J. Comput. Civ. Eng. **26**, 506–518 (2011)
5. Abrahamse, W., Steg, L., Vlek, C., Rothengatter, T.: A review of intervention studies aimed at household energy conservation. J. Environ. Psychol. **2**(5), 273–291 (2005)
6. Wheeless, L.R., Barraclough, R., Stewart, R., Bostrom, R.: Compliance-gaining and power in persuasion. Commun. Yearb. **7**, 105–145 (1983)
7. Mowen, J.C., Cialdini, R.B.: On implementing the door-in-the-face compliance technique in a business context. J. Mark. Res. **17**, 253–258 (1980)
8. Rhoads, K.V., Cialdini, R.B.: The business of influence: principles that lead to success in commercial settings. In: Dillard, J.P., Pfau, M. (eds.) The Persuasion Handbook: Developments in Theory and Practice, pp. 513–542. Sage, Thousand Oaks (2002)
9. Malhotra, D., Bazerman, M.H.: Psychological influence in negotiation: an introduction long overdue. J. Manage. **34**, 509–531 (2008)

Survey Report of Wayfinding Experience Within Cities in China

Fung Ha Sandy Lai(✉)

Department of Information Art and Design Academy of Arts and Design, Tsinghua University, Haidian District, Beijing 100084, People's Republic Of China
jjsandylai@gmail.com

Abstract. Wayfinding is a kind of systematic communication system which helps people find their way by using elements of words, signage, maps, graphics, digital media, etc. This survey report focuses on how users use existing wayfinding design systems and wayfinding means in transportation services within cities in China. The method of paper surveys and online surveys were adopted to examine the effectiveness of existing wayfinding systems. Some elements of wayfinding systems such as the usability of the character design of 'Pinyin' (using Latin letters to help pronounce Chinese words), graphical information and digital means were also addressed. There were 196 valid interviews obtained in the paper survey at Beijing South Railway Station, and 35 valid responses from online survey which were given by foreigners with travel experience in China. Preliminary results indicated that the mobile internet is the most preferred wayfinding tool. Consistency, legibility and safety are important wayfinding principles.

Keywords: Wayfinding design · Mobile internet · Interactive information kiosk

1 Introduction

Wayfinding systems can be applied broadly in urban informatics, infrastructure service, transport service and so on. A definition of wayfinding was described by an experienced architect, Kelly C. Brandon: "*Wayfinding design is the process of organizing spatial and environmental information to help users find their way. It should not be considered different activity from traditional signage design, but rather a broader, more inclusive way of accessing all the environmental issues.*" [1].

Recently, the integration of new digital technologies with wayfinding design has become a hot topic in transportation services of smart city [2, 3] projects in China. These new digital technologies include mobile technology, interactive information kiosks, QR code [4], GPS systems, etc. However, some fundamental problematic wayfinding issues, such as misleading signs, irrational roadway wayfinding design, inconsistent 'Pinyin' character systems, etc., have to be attended and resolved before building a smart city project in order to avoid any inappropriate wayfinding design which may lead to an unnecessary waste of resources.

C. Stephanidis (Ed.): HCII 2015 Posters, Part II, CCIS 529, pp. 564–569, 2015.
DOI: 10.1007/978-3-319-21383-5_94

Being a part of the research project namely "Functionality and Usability of Interactive Wayfinding Design within Cities in China", this survey report aims to present the findings and the analysis from both the online survey and the field survey on wayfinding experience in China. Over two hundred local people and foreigners had participated in the two surveys. The objective was to identify the problems and shortfalls of the designs and the systems in order to find ways on improving the existing wayfinding experience. Through the findings and the analysis, it is shown that no matter what kind of new technologies are employed in the wayfinding design/system of the transportation facilities, majority of the people prefer to have a more direct, more accurate, faster and safer wayfinding path to find their way or information. The result also indicated that majority of the people rely on using the mobile internet to search destinations and information as it is more handy and effective to use.

2 Methods

In terms of the major wayfinding design elements (i.e. signage, color, text, graphical information with digital devices), field survey and online survey are used to assess the effectiveness of existing wayfinding design system in transportation service in cities within China. In both of the surveys, the target groups were invited to answer the questions given under two separate carefully designed questionnaires both with multiple-choice questions and open-ended questions.

2.1 Field Survey by Questionnaire

- Location: Beijing South Railway Station (Beijing, China)
- Target Group: Local Chinese
- Survey Period: 1st to 10th September 2014
- Sample Size: 200
- Age range: (1) 55 or above; (2) 36 to 54; (3) 15 to 35.
- Total Number of Valid Interviews: 196
- Survey Team: four (4) students from Tsinghua University

The reasons for choosing the above-mentioned survey period and location were that schools in Beijing usually start in Fall and many students and their parents from different cities are used to traveling to schools in Beijing via railway. Therefore, it was a better opportunity to meet up with the target group and to conduct the field survey during this period and location.

2.2 Online Survey

- Location: China
- Target Group: Foreigners

- Survey Period: 22th September 2014 to 5th October 2014
- Sample Size: 100
- Age Range: (1) 55 or above; (2) 36 to 54; (3) 15 to 35.
- Total Number of Valid Response: 35

The target group were foreigners who have either traveling or working experience in China. This online survey aimed to assess the usability and effectiveness of the 'Pinyin' character system in wayfinding, and preferences of using wayfinding tools and signage in transportation service within cities in China.

3 Findings and Analysis

From the survey results, the following findings were observed.

3.1 Preferences of Using 'Mobile Internet', 'Interactive Information Kiosk', and 'Information Center with Attendant'

- 74 % of local Chinese interviewees preferred to use 'mobile internet' to search for information, destinations and booking travel tickets. Majority of interviewees of the 55 or above age group tended to choose 'information center with attendant' as second choice. Only a few of the other age groups preferred to use 'interactive information kiosk'. (see Fig. 1)
- The younger age groups (i.e.15 to 35 age range and 36 to 54 age range) tended to choose 'mobile internet' rather than other means to search for destinations and information.
- In general, the reasons for not choosing 'interactive information kiosk' were that (1) interactive information kiosks are not easy to find (i.e. not enough); (2) not as interactive as compared to the attendant at the information counter; (3) interactive information kiosks have different interfaces and are difficult and slow to operate; (4) some people are not familiar with using digital technology.
- Many felt that the mobile internet was the most useful, efficient and accessible way of searching for information, e.g. via Google Maps or Baidu Maps.

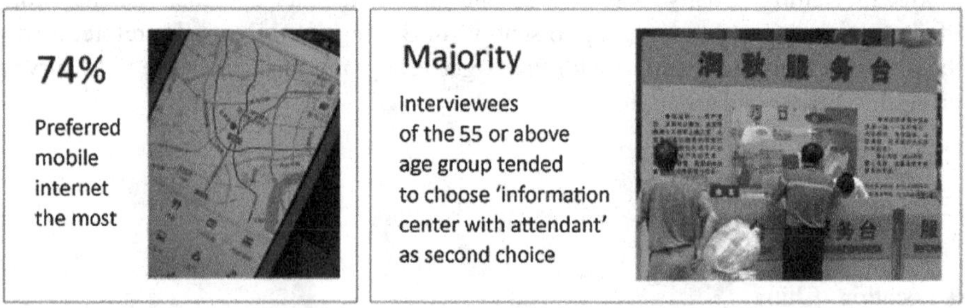
74%
Preferred mobile internet the most
Majority
Interviewees of the 55 or above age group tended to choose 'information center with attendant' as second choice

Fig. 1. Preferences of using wayfinding means for local Chinese interviewees

- The majority of people prefer to use a more direct, fast, accurate and convenient wayfinding mean to find their way, not necessarily via digital means

3.2 Graphical Information

Over 50 % of interviewees felt that most of the signage and graphical information are readable and clear. However, around 33 % expressed that some graphical information were not effective for wayfinding, e.g. the graphical arrow signs with text marking on the floor (see Fig. 2) may not be apparent as people normally glance at eye level and their views may be obstructed by the crowd walking around the railway station, especially during peak seasons like the public holiday of the *Lunar New Year* [5] or Autumn Festival.

Fig. 2. Graphical arrow signs with text marking on the floor

3.3 Effectiveness of the 'Pinyin' System in Roadway Signage for Foreigners

- 62 % respondents thought that the signage with 'Pinyin' was helpful in finding their destination. One of the common comments from the respondents is that having 'Pinyin' was especially helpful when he/she asked local people for directions. 'Pinyin' helped him/her pronounce the word accurately.
- However, it would be better if the 'Pinyin' letters were spaced out appropriately instead of all bunched together, e.g. 'Shanghailu' as one word is hard to read (see Fig. 3), whereas if it was spaced out, 'Shanghai Lu' it would be easier for foreigners to read.
- 'Pinyin' delivers little to no meaning to people who do not understand Chinese.
- The result indicates that legibility is important. Although the majority of foreign respondents felt that 'Pinyin' is useful, it seems that having no spacing in long 'Pinyin' characters may reduce the effectiveness and readability in wayfinding.

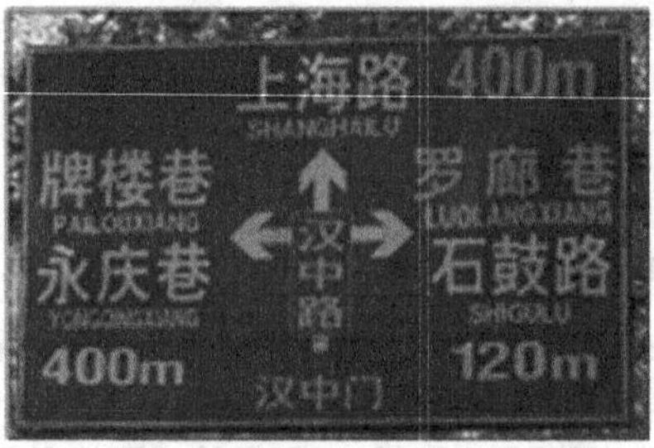

Fig. 3. Road sign with 'Pinyin'

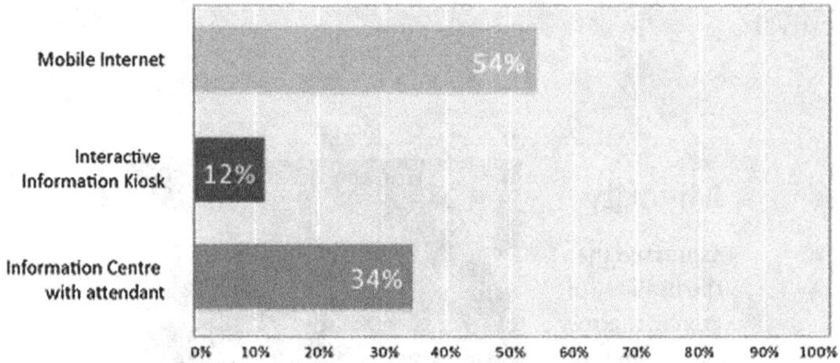

Fig. 4. Preference of using wayfinding means for foreign respondents

3.4 Preferences of Using Wayfinding Means for Foreigners

- 54 % of respondents preferred to use 'mobile internet', whilst 34 % of respondents chose 'information center with attendant', and only 12 % chose 'interactive information kiosk'. (see Fig. 4)
- In case there was no 'mobile internet', the result showed that almost all respondents preferred to choose 'information center with attendant' or ask someone directly near them for finding their destination rather than choosing 'interactive information kiosk'. This is especially true for younger age groups, as all of them chose the information center in this case.

4 Conclusion

The online survey results reflect that the mobile internet is the key platform for releasing and receiving information for wayfinding within cities in China. The majority of local and foreign people consider the mobile internet as a more handy, direct and effective means for wayfinding. According to the data analysis, it is indicated that the usability of interactive information kiosks is low. However, interactive information kiosks may still be necessary for a minority of users.

In the both surveys, if no mobile internet is available, most of the respondents preferred face to face communication with an attendant at the information center as the second choice for getting information rather than choosing to use the interactive information kiosk'. The reasons for that may be due to (1) foreign languages are not available on the interactive information kiosks (2) insufficient platform design and poor interface support in most of the interactive information kiosks, e.g. too many interface layers; loading time is too long for each interface.

Although the mobile internet may become the dominant tool for wayfinding, elements and principles of legibility, consistency and safety still need to be explored in the research for looking at the effectiveness in wayfinding within cities in China.

References

1. Brandon, K.C.: Wayfinding: kellybrandondesign.com (2014). http://www.kellybrandondesign.com/IGDWayfinding.html
2. Hu, Y.: Smart City: opportunity and challenge for enterprises: chinadaily.com, 15 December 2012. http://www.chinadaily.com.cn/bizchina/2012-11/15/content_15935688.htm
3. China announces 9 pilot 'smart cities: chinadaily.com, 13 August 2013. http://china.org.cn/china/2013-08/13/content_29707492.htm
4. Definition of QR Code: pcmag.com. http://www.pcmag.com/encyclopedia/term/61424/qr-code, http://china.org.cn/china/2013-08/13/content_29707492.htm
5. New Year travel rush starts with 3.62b trips: (Xinhua) chinadaily.com, 1 January 2014. http://www.chinadaily.com.cn/china/2014-01/17/content_17240283.htm

Algorithm to Estimate a Living Area Based on Connectivity of Places with Home

Yuji Matsuo, Sunao Hara, and Masanobu Abe(✉)

Graduate School of Natural Science and Technology,
Okayama University, Okayama, Japan
matsuo@a.cs.okayama-u.ac.jp,
{hara, abe}@cs.okayama-u.ac.jp

Abstract. We propose an algorithm to estimate a person's living area using his/her collected Global Positioning System (GPS) data. The most important feature of the algorithm is the connectivity of places with a home, i.e., a living area must consist of a home, important places, and routes that connect them. This definition is logical because people usually go to a place from home, and there can be several routes to that place. Experimental results show that the proposed algorithm can estimate living area with a precision of 0.82 and recall of 0.86 compared with the grand truth established by users. It is also confirmed that the connectivity of places with a home is necessary to estimate a reasonable living area.

Keywords: Living area · Dementia · Watch-out · GPS

1 Introduction

Thanks to the rapid spread of mobile phones, smartphones, and devices with Global Positioning System (GPS), location data is easily obtained. This is attracting increasing attention of new services and applications. In fact, numerous location-aware applications have been developed. In this study, we are attempting to develop a watch-over system for elderly people and children for two reasons. First, wandering is one of the most problematic behaviors of elderly people with dementia [1]. Surprisingly, it is reported that more than 10,000 people with dementia went missing in 2013 in Japan [2]. Family members or nurses bear a large burden of having to watch the people with dementia to prevent them from going missing. Second, parents also have a large responsibility of preventing their children from being kidnapped, having accidents, or being victims of crimes. For example, many parents have to take their children to and from school. To address this problem, some commercial products are available [3, 4]. Unfortunately, these products are not user friendly and effective; they have complicated procedures for setting the watch-out area, a poor precision of the watch-out area, and so on.

To solve this problem, we propose an algorithm that automatically determines a person's living area using his/her collected location data. Here, we consider a living area to be one of the most important areas to provide care for children and people with dementia. The living area is defined as a set that includes a person's home, important places that he/she frequently visits, and routes that connect them. The criteria for

C. Stephanidis (Ed.): HCII 2015 Posters, Part II, CCIS 529, pp. 570–576, 2015.
DOI: 10.1007/978-3-319-21383-5_95

determining the living area are as follows: (1) home and important places are connected by routes, (2) several routes between them should be available, and (3) the importance of a route is evaluated by its frequency of use. We believe the definition and its criteria are quite reasonable because home plays a central role in everyday life, and users have several routes to a particular place depending on contexts such as shopping lists, time constraints, accompanying people, and so on. Although some research has been performed on finding routes [5–7], the proposed algorithm is unique because it uses GeoHex [8] code and considers a route as a set of GeoHex codes; this results in implicitly expressing a route. Another advantage is that the precision of routes can be manipulated with this code.

This paper is organized as follows. In Sect. 2, we describe details of the proposed algorithm. In Sect. 3, we conduct evaluation experiments for three users. Finally, we conclude the paper and suggest future work.

2 Algorithm to Estimate Living Area

Figure 1 shows an outline of the proposed algorithm consisting of two steps. The first is the preprocessing of the collected location data and the second is the estimation of a living area.

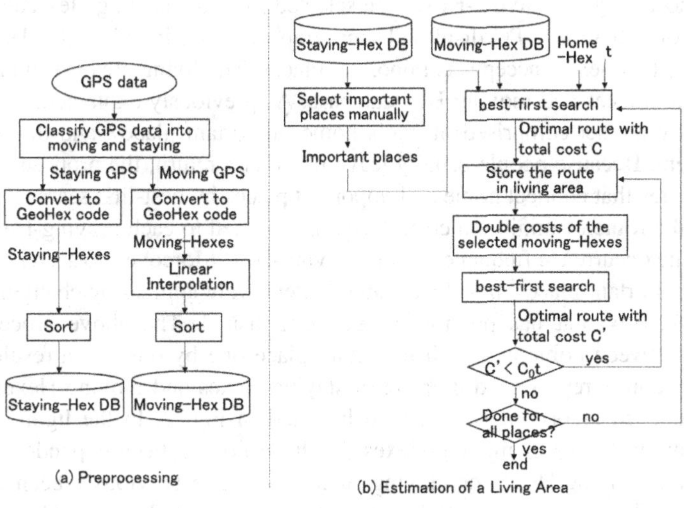

Fig. 1. An outline of proposed algorithm

2.1 Preprocessing for Collected Location Data

Location data of longitude and latitude is collected by GPS every 30 s. The preprocessing step has five procedures as follows. (1) On a daily basis, location data is classified into two states: staying and moving. The classification is performed using velocity and distance from the previous location. In the rest of this paper, based on these classifications, we refer to the GeoHex code of the staying state as staying-Hex and that of the moving state as moving-Hex. (2) Location data is converted into the GeoHex code that corresponds to a small area, a circle with a diameter of approximately 12 m. An aim of the procedure is to ignore small differences among location data because it is rare to obtain the exact same sequence of the data (longitude and latitude) even when people go to the same place taking the same route. This is necessary to accumulate location data over different days. (3) When consecutively sampled moving-Hexes are not adjacent, they are added to fill a gap by linear interpolation. Because location data is sampled every 30 s, a gap can occur between consecutively sampled moving-Hexes when a user moves fast. This procedure makes it possible to easily determine a route between places X and Y by checking if the adjacent moving-Hexes exist from place X to Y. (4) An occurrence frequency of each staying-Hex is counted, and after sorting all staying-Hexes by the frequencies, a staying-Hex database is generated. In this procedure, staying-Hexes located within a circle of 30 m diameter are merged because large buildings occupy several staying-Hexes. (5) An occurrence frequency of each moving-Hex is counted, and after sorting all moving-Hexes by their frequencies, a moving-Hex database is generated.

2.2 Estimating a Living Area

In the current implementation, important places are manually determined by each user. The n-th most frequent staying-Hexes are selected from the staying-Hex database, and are shown on a map in a PC display. Using graphical user interface (GUI), each user selects those that he/she accepts as important places. The living area is estimated using the important places and moving-Hex database. As previously explained, a living area is defined by the set comprised of one's home, important places, and the routes that connect them. Because people usually leave home and return, the proposed algorithm searches routes that connect home and important places by best-first search. The search aims to find a route of minimum cost. A cost is assigned to each moving-Hex; it is the inverse of the occurrence frequency of the moving-Hex. Moreover, to search alternative routes for important places, best-first search is iteratively applied by changing the cost of a moving-Hex that has previously been established. The above procedures are performed between home and each important place one by one. As a result, a living area of a person is represented by a set of staying-Hexes and moving-Hexes.

The proposed algorithm is explained in detail in Fig. 2. In the figure, OpenList contains staying-Hexes or moving-Hexes that have not yet been expanded and CloseList contains staying-Hexes or moving-Hexes that have previously been expanded. The example shown in Fig. 2 attempts to determine a route between Home-Hex and PlaceA-Hex. Here, a letter and a number shown in a Hex are a node ID and a cost, respectively. Hexes painted black indicate that they do not exist in either the staying-Hex or moving-Hex database. Further, an alphabet sequence in OpenList indicates a part of a route. For example, AE means that a user moves from Hex-A to Hex-E. The search is performed as follows. First, moving-Hexes that are adjacent to Home-Hex are expanded. Then, the expanded Hexes are sorted according to cost in increasing order, and the Hex with the lowest cost is expanded. As shown in Fig. 2, Hex A is expanded and added to CloseList because it has the lowest cost. In the same manner, Hex E is expanded and added to CloseList because the Hex sequence of AE has the lowest cost. In this manner, the Hex expansion and the updating of the open and close lists are repeated. Finally, in this example, an optimal route is obtained as a Hex sequence AEIJ. To find alternative routes, the search is continued after doubling the costs of the moving-Hexes used in the previously established route. The search for alternative routes is terminated when $C' > C_0 t$ is satisfied. Here, C_0 is the total cost of the first route, and C' is the total cost obtained by the repeated search, where t is a control parameter. Figure 3 shows an example of the alternative route search. The costs of moving-Hexes A, E, I, and J have doubled, and a new route CFLK is found.

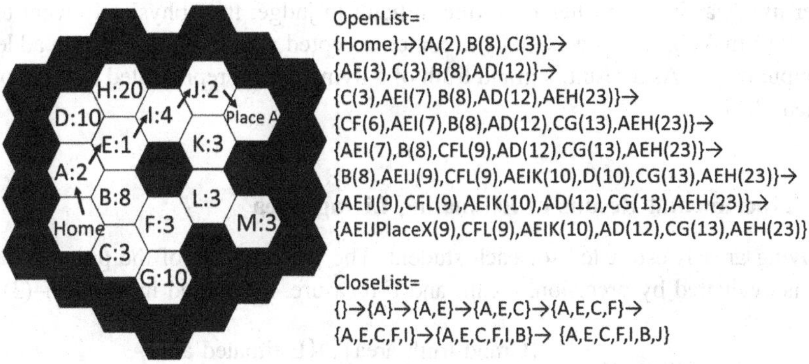

Fig. 2. An example of the best-first-search

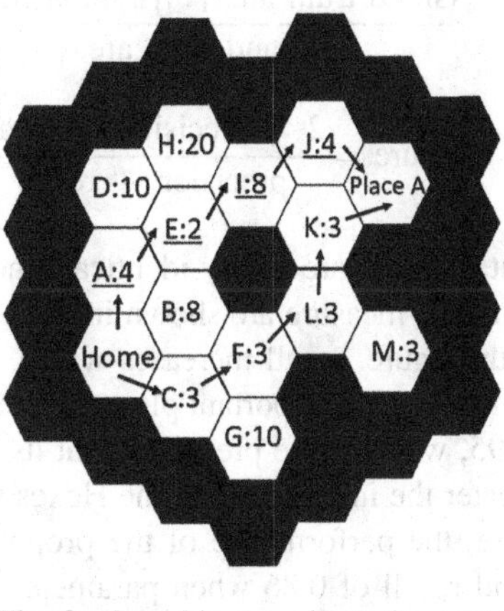

Fig. 3. Searching an alternative route

3 Evaluation of the Proposed Algorithm

The proposed algorithm is evaluated using location data collected from three users. Moreover, to observe the advantages of the proposed algorithm, we compared its performance with that of a conventional method that simply selects all GeoHexes counted more than 3 times as a living area.

3.1 Data for Evaluations

GPS data was collected every 30 s for 12 months for three graduate students of Okayama University. They live alone in Okayama city and travel to the university by walking or bicycling. Using the data, grand truth of a living area is created as follows. (1) The important places selected by each user were shown on a map in a PC display. Each user was asked to freely draw routes on the map using a GUI between home and the important places based on memory. The drawn routes were converted into GeoHex code and stored as the living area. (2) The routes generated by the proposed algorithm were shown on a map in a PC display over the GeoHexes selected in (1). Each user was asked to subjectively judge whether the generated routes were sufficient in defining his/her living area. For routes that were difficult to judge, they physically went to the site before making their decision. The routes accepted as the living area are added to the output of (1). As a result, a grand truth of a living area is represented by a set of the selected Hexes.

3.2 Experimental Results of Estimating Living Area

The living area is estimated for each student. The performance of the proposed algorithm is evaluated by precision, recall, and F-measure, as defined in Eqs. (1)–(3).

$$\text{precision} = \frac{\{\text{Grand truth area}\} \cap \{\text{Estimated area}\}}{\{\text{Estimated area}\}} \tag{1}$$

$$\text{recall} = \frac{\{\text{Grand truth area}\} \cap \{\text{Estimated area}\}}{\{\text{Grand truth area}\}} \tag{2}$$

$$\text{F - measure} = \frac{2 \times \text{precision} \times \text{recall}}{\text{precision} + \text{recall}} \tag{3}$$

Because the experimental results are nearly identical among the users, the average values of precision, recall, and F-measure are shown in Fig. 4. The x axis indicates the parameter t. As shown in the figure, recall increases with t. This means that there are several routes between home and each important place. When t is equal to 15, the recall is at its highest value of 0.95, whereas the precision is at its lowest value of 0.77. The lower the precision, the greater the inadequacy of the Hexes selected as the living area. According to the F-measure, the performance of the proposed algorithm is saturated with a precision of 0.82 and recall of 0.86 when parameter t is equal to 10.

Table 1 shows the precision, recall, and F-measure of the conventional method and proposed algorithm. We can see that the proposed algorithm outperforms the conventional method. Figure 5 shows examples of the estimated living area. As shown in Fig. 5(a), the conventional method generates numerous "Hex-islands" that have no connection to other Hexes. This is not acceptable for estimating a living area.

Judging from the results, the occurrence frequency of the GeoHexes is not sufficient to estimate a living area, and it is necessary to explicitly use the constraint that a

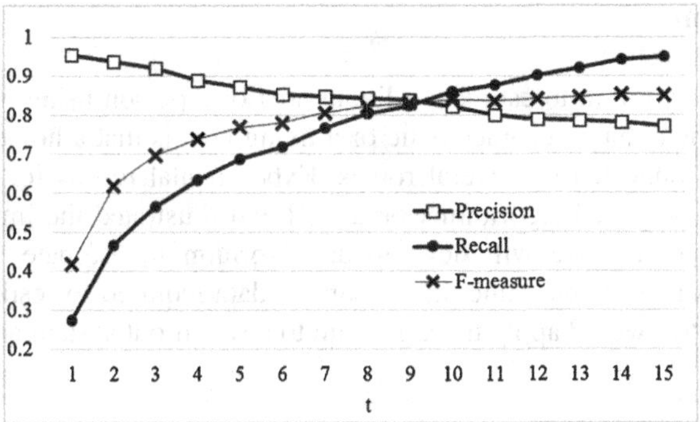

Fig. 4. Average performance for the three users

Table 1. Precision and recall of three users

	Precision		Recall		F-measure	
	Con-ventional	Pro-posed (t=10)	Con-ventional	Pro-posed (t=10)	Con-ventional	Pro-posed (t=10)
User A	0.30	0.84	0.26	0.82	0.28	0.84
User B	0.30	0.82	0.73	0.91	0.43	0.86
User C	0.60	0.81	0.67	0.85	0.63	0.83

Routes are missing in the dotted elliptical areas. This is inadequate for estimating the living area.

(a) Conventional method

All places are connected with routes. Several paths are clearly observed between staying places.

(b) Proposed algorithm

Fig. 5. An example of estimated living area for the three users

GeoHex must be a connection between a home and an important place. The performance of the proposed algorithm depends less on a user than the conventional method. This may be a direct effect of the constraint.

4 Conclusion

We propose an algorithm to estimate a living area of a person using his/her collected location data. The defining characteristic of a living area is that a home and important places must be connected by several routes. Experimental results for the three users showed that the proposed algorithm works well and illustrated the importance of the requirement. In future, we will develop an algorithm to estimate the location of important places and to determine the amount of data required for estimating a living area. Thereafter, we would apply the algorithm to a watch-out system and evaluate it in the field.

References

1. Lin, Q., Zhang, D., Chen, L., Ni, H., Zhou, X.: Managing elders' wandering behavior using sensors-based solutions: a survey. Int. J. Gerontol. **8**(2), 49–55 (2014)
2. https://www.npa.go.jp/safetylife/seianki/H24yukuehumeisha.pdf (in Japanese)
3. http://www.secom.co.jp/english/cocosecom/index.html
4. http://www.dokoiruka.jp/ (in Japanese)
5. Zhou, C., Shekar, S., Treveen, L.: Discovering personal paths from sparse GPS traces. In: Proceedings of the JCIS 2005 Workshop on Data Mining (2005)
6. Liao, L., Fox, D., Kautz, H.: Extracting places and activities from GPS traces using hierarchical conditional random fields. Int. J. Rob. Res. **26**(1), 119–134 (2007)
7. Yamada, N., Isoda, Y., Minami, M., Morikawa, H.: Incremental route refinement for GPS-enabled cellular phones. In: Proceedings of the Fifth International Conference on Mobile Computing and Ubiquitous Networking (ICMU 2010), pp. 87–93 (2010)
8. GeoHex. http://geogames.net/geohex/v3

Design of Interactive Instruction Systems for Travelers and Short-Term Visitors

Nuttaporn Noithong(✉) and Makio Ishihara

Fukuoka Institute of Technology,
3-30-1 Wajiro-higashi, Higashi-ku, Fukuoka 811-0295, Japan
mfml3011@bene.fit.ac.jp, m-ishihara@fit.ac.jp
http://www.fit.ac.jp/~m-ishihara/Lab/

Abstract. The purpose of this manuscript is to study about Interface design to develop an instruction system for tourists and short-term visitors. An instruction consists of 3 structures: sequence, selection and loop structures, and it is represented in 4 visual representations. Through the experiment in usability, this manuscript finds the best representation of instructions. The result shows that for sequence structure, representation P1(number) is the best, but representation P4 (slide) is the best for selection structure.

Keywords: Instruction system · Visualization · Interface design

1 Introduction

Nowadays, foreign tourists or short-time visitors often use technology such as smartphones to help them, for example, to translate words or to locate tourist attractions. In each country, there are many automatic machines which are very useful but there are some unclear icons and functions. In addition, the instructions on how to do something such as "How to buy a ticket" and "How to order food" are not sufficiently provided.

This paper is about the user interface design (UID) of applications that provide these instructions and discusses what visual representations of those instructions are preferred.

2 Description of Instruction

An instruction consists of three structures: sequence, selection and loop structures [1].

2.1 Sequence Structure

Sequence is a procedural structure that the next step is already determined. Figure 1 shows that the current step(yellow) is in the 2nd state and you can go into the 3rd state only. An example of the sequence structure is a beverage vending machine. Users have to insert some money before choosing the goods.

C. Stephanidis (Ed.): HCII 2015 Posters, Part II, CCIS 529, pp. 577–581, 2015.
DOI: 10.1007/978-3-319-21383-5_96

Fig. 1. Sequence structure

2.2 Selection Structure

Selection is a procedural structure that has a selection to choose before moving on to the next step. Figure 2 shows that from the current step, you can choose the next state from two. An example of the selection structure is a ticket vending machine. Users can choose to start from selecting a target or inserting money, or inserting card.

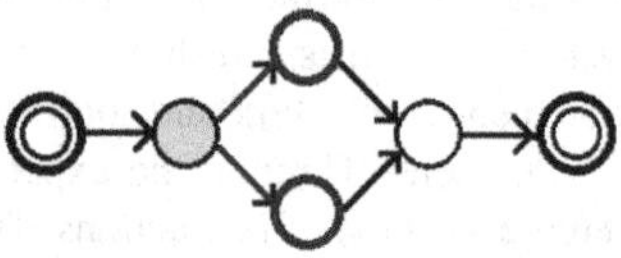

Fig. 2. Selection structure

2.3 Loop Structure

Loop structure is a procedure structure that iterates the same steps until not required. Figure 3 shows that at the current step, you can repeat to the first state, or go to the end. An example of the loop structure is a food-order machine of kaiten-sushi. Users can order sushi as much as they want until end and paying money.

Fig. 3. Loop structure

3 Visual Representations of an Instruction

Four visual representations P1 to P4 of an instruction are discussed in this manuscript. They are summarized below.

3.1 Visual Representation P1

All steps can be selected anytime. All buttons are available so users do not have to start from the first button. This representation uses numbers to show the order. Figure 4 shows an example of representation P1 with a vending machine. The 1st state is inserting coins and selecting a product is in the 2nd state.

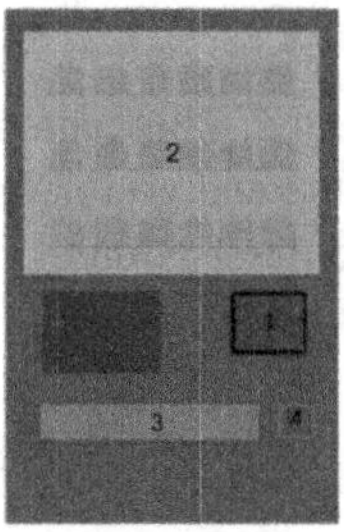

Fig. 4. Visual representation P1

3.2 Visual Representation P2

All steps can be selected anytime like P1, but using arrows instead of numbers to show the order. Figure 5 is an example of representation P2 with a vending machine. Arrows are drawn between the states such as from the state of inserting coins to the state of selecting a product.

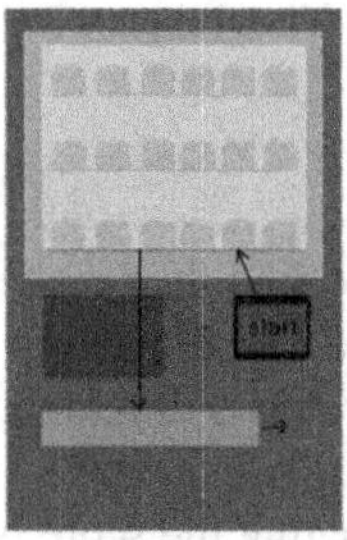

Fig. 5. Visual representation P2

3.3 Visual Representation P3

Only one step can be selected in order. The available button is only the next one. Users have to start the first button then the second will become visible. Figure 6 shows an example of representation P3 with a vending machine. The green-border button on the top is only one available button.

Fig. 6. Visual representation P3

3.4 Visual Representation P4

Previous and next steps can be selected. This pattern is similar to a slide-presentation. Users can go back to the previous step and go forward to the next step. Figure 7 shows an overall image at top-left side, and description of current state is shows in the middle. You can go back or go forward by buttons.

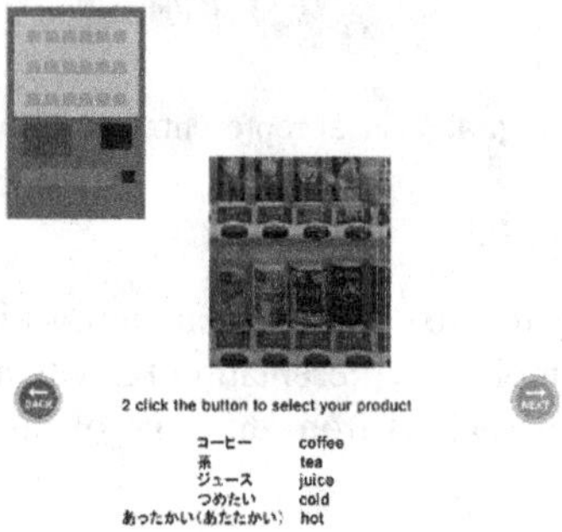

Fig. 7. Visual representation P4

4 Experiment and Result

The purpose of this experiment is to find the best representation of instructions. There were 5 subjects. Each subject was asked to use our instruction system in each of four representations of instructions for a vending machine and a ticket machine. The instruction for a vending machine has a sequence structures, and a ticket machine has a selection structure. After that, evaluating the score by questionnaires with a scale from 5(excellent) to 1(bad).

Figure 8 shows the average score of P1 to P4 representations. The red one is the score of the vending machine and the green one is the score of the ticket machine.

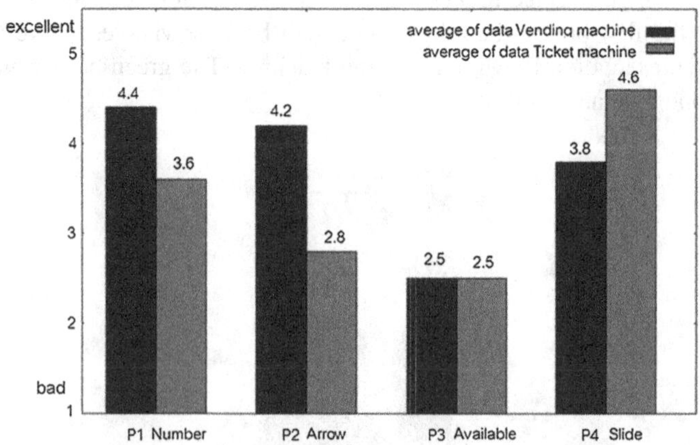

Fig. 8. Result

5 Conclusion

This manuscript discussed four representations of an instruction. The result revealed that limiting the available steps is better for increase in steps. Moreover, the explanation after clicking button is also important, such as text size and real-thing images which is easy to understand.

Reference

1. Dijkstra, E.W.: Note on structured programming. In: Dahl, O.J., Dijkstra, E.W., Hoare, C.A.R. (eds.) Structured Programming. Academic Press Ltd., London (1972)

Lessons Learned from the Development of a Rural Real Time Passenger Information System

Konstantinos Papangelis[1(✉)], Somayajulu Sripada[2], John D. Nelson[2], and Mark Beecroft[2]

[1] Cardiff School of Computer Science and Informatics, Cardiff University, Cardiff, UK
papangelisk@cardiff.ac.uk
[2] dot.rural Digital Economy Research Hub, University of Aberdeen, Aberdeen, UK

Abstract. In recent years, the advances in real-time transport telematics systems that use computer, communication, navigation and information systems, make the dissemination of the passenger information more effective and efficient. This led to real time passenger information systems to become more and more common. This paper explores the aforementioned in a rural context and presents lessons learned during the development of a rural real time passenger information system.

Keywords: Real time passenger information systems · Co-design · Rural areas

1 Introduction

Rural communities face a range of challenges associated with accessibility and connectivity. Limitations in transport infrastructure and services can diminish travel possibilities and hinder access to opportunities relating to employment, education, and business (Chamberlain and Crabtree 2013).

Technology has long been heralded as offering the potential to mitigate some of these barriers by providing alternative means of access and connectivity (Chamberlain et al. 2013). Though such transport technologies have been widely deployed in urban and suburban areas in the developed world, their application in rural and remote rural areas has been very limited.

In this paper, based on findings we discuss briefly the design of a technology that provides real-time travel information to rural passengers, and discuss the lessons learned.

2 Co-designing a Rural Mobile Real Time Passenger Information System

To facilitate the design of the technology a series co-design sessions, expert panels, focus groups, and walkthroughs were conducted. The initial design process involved two co-design sessions in the Scottish Borders (SB) with rural public transport

C. Stephanidis (Ed.): HCII 2015 Posters, Part II, CCIS 529, pp. 582–586, 2015.
DOI: 10.1007/978-3-319-21383-5_97

passengers that had previous experience with similar technologies and two sessions with participants in West Yorkshire (WY) that had no previous experience with similar technologies. The SB sessions involved six participants aged 19–21, and lasted approximately 150 min. The WY sessions involved 5 participants with an average age of 21 years old, and lasted approximately 180 min. In both the WY and SB sessions, we separated the participants into groups of two and showed them two videos. The first video illustrated the functions of the technology probe, while the second video showed the technology probe in action through various usage scenarios, as emerged from our previous studies[1]. The main purpose of the videos was to illustrate to both the WY and SB participants the technology we would like them to improve. After the videos, we gave the participants four scenarios illustrating real-world situations where RTPI would be needed for successful completion of the journey on time. The scenarios emerged from our ethnographic style study in the Scottish Borders, and the island of Tiree. The purpose of the scenarios was to blend a set of real, relatable, on-going activities in order to enable the participants in the co-design sessions to imagine a native futuristic look at how technologies could better support those activities.

After we gave some time for the participants to digest the scenarios, we gave them a set of functions and asked them to come up with their own functions, assign them to scenarios, and grade them as "must have" and "could be good to have". These were grouped as general functions, boarding-point functions, and on-trip functions. It should be noted that the functions we gave to the participants emerged during previous studies we conducted in various rural areas (see subsection X on page Y for more information).

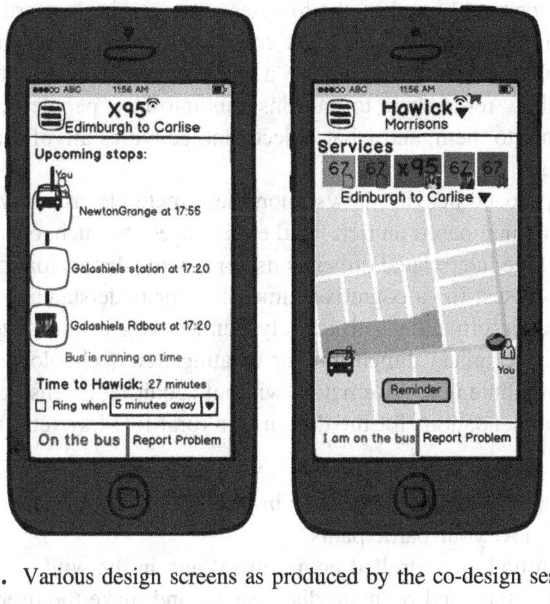

Fig. 1. Various design screens as produced by the co-design sessions

[1] Video 1 can be found at https://www.youtube.com/watch?v=3bY2X_FObCI, while video 2 can be found at https://www.youtube.com/watch?v=1Wgn-pMJAHA

After the end of this exercise we asked the participants to utilise the functions and the scenarios to design a smartphone application to improve the rural passenger experience and support the user during disruptions by primarily utilising the "must have" functions and secondarily the "could be good to have" functions. Each group produced a design that had variable levels of depth in different aspects. For example, the design of one group of participants from the WY session focused mainly on the social interaction between the users during disruption.

Based on the outcomes of the sessions in WY and SB, we created a design with inputs from two human-computer interaction experts and two transport studies experts that merged the design aspects, elements, and addressed several of the issues that emerged from the co-design sessions. The final design mainly concentrated on providing information regarding pre-trip, on-trip, and on boarding point, journey planning, supporting the rural passenger experience through social media, and disruption. Figure 1 illustrates various elements of the design.

3 Lessons Learned and Recommendations for Co-desining Rural Real Time Passenger Information System

There are many continuing arguments in the human-computer interaction and transport studies over which methods are appropriate when developing RTPI systems. These can depend on (i) who the user groups are (age, gender, sensory or physical impairments, novice versus experts), (ii) the task or tasks to be performed, (iii) the physical environment, and (iv) the social context.

A variety of approaches and methodologies are emerging as particularly useful in the design or RTPI systems. These involve engaging users in co-design and interactive experiences in order to elicit and capture a rich texture of individuals' experiences. These methods allow researchers to gain insights into how people travel, what information is important to them, and what objects and activities are of direct relevance to the design exercise.

Our design approach heavily draws upon these methods, as we were interested in capturing and designing based on rich lived experiences. As such, our overall design is characterised by three interrelated dimensions: (i) a social dimension for designing new practices and processes, (ii) a cognitive dimension for understanding the interference between providing information and actively contributing to the development of the system, and (iii) a technical dimension for creating new technologies that allow the participants to contribute new information without acquiring extensive technical skills.

Our key recommendations for the design of a rural RTPI system, based on lessons learned, include:

- Establish a panel of expert users early in project.
- Get to really know your participants.
- Study usage in both a controlled environment and in the wild.
- User props to initiate and promote discussions, and make the user the expert
- Use co-design activities to increase empowerment and buy-in.

- Use low-fidelity prototypes to encourage creative thinking before creating high-fidelity prototypes.
- Use high-fidelity prototypes to increase engagement.
- Encourage coding and validation of results during design sessions with users present.
- Use ethnographic studies, observations, and ride-alongs to provide physical and social context insights.

There are a number of challenges in these steps, such as recruiting the correct participants, identifying the objectives and metrics to determine if the design is achieving those objectives, and designing an initial relatively complex technology (or set of technologies). Our work indicates that these can be partially mitigated by employing a cyclical approach that is based on a small core user base that actively contributes to the improvement of the solution throughout its lifecycle. Such a proposed approach can be actualised with the SER model, which aims to transition the users from consumers of information to providers and, ultimately, meta-designers of the medium that conveys the information (Fischer 2011). Figure 2 illustrates this model.

In addition, we have identified a number of issues that should be taken into account when evaluating such systems. These include:

- Correct selection of evaluation metrics that reflect the objectives.
- Testing of the design to ensure that the presentation will not distract the users.
- Ensuring that, if scenarios are used, they are realistic for the user population and make use of significant portions of the design.
- Making sure that the data collection is feasible for the users and reasonable for later analysis. This is particularly true if the users are asked to mark up something or write something out.
- Making sure data from all users can be accumulated and compared against each other for analysis of the evaluation.

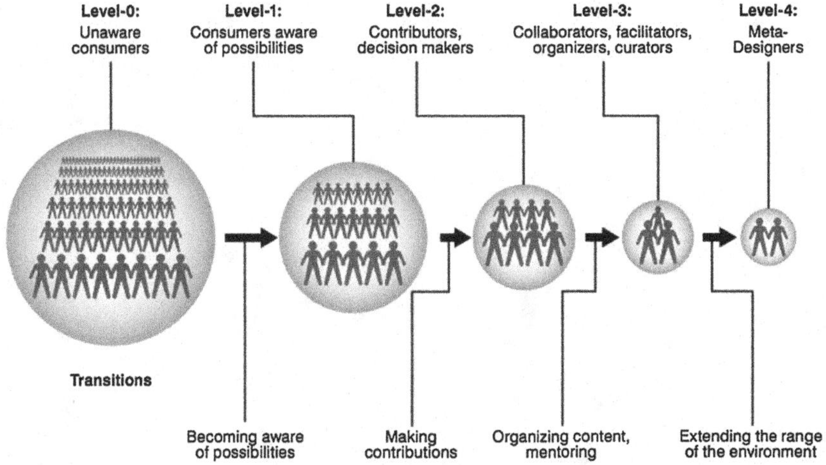

Fig. 2. The SER model (Fischer 2011)

Overall our lessons learned and subsequent recommendations fall under the concept of the "loose fit," and aim to balance the asymmetry of ignorance with the asymmetry of knowledge of the users when designing a rural RTPI system.

4 Discussion and Conclusion

In this brief paper we illustrated our co-design process and discussed lessons learned. The mobile RTPIS we co-designed focuses on capturing and sharing of both an individual's and a group's tacit knowledge, enabling the informed participation of people from all walks of life, and allowing the contributors to modify it according to their needs, leading to "living" information spaces. Our work indicates that, for the aforementioned reasons, a modular design approach that supports the users during various stages of their journey is needed, and that the design approach must include an initial key community of users that can provide an initial collection of domain knowledge in a setting that promotes continuous evolution of that knowledge.

References

Chamberlain, A., Crabtree, A.: Innovation in the wild: ethnography, rurality and participation. In: The 3rd Participatory Innovation Conference, PIN-C 2013. LUT Scientific and Expertise Publications, Lahti (2013)

Chamberlain, A., Crabtree, A., Davies, M.: Community engagement for research: contextual design in rural CSCW system development. In: Proceedings of the 6th International Conference on Communities and Technology 2013, C&T 2013. ACM, Munich (2013)

Fischer, G.: Understanding, fostering and supporting cultures of participation. Interact. Mag. **18** (3), 42–53 (2011)

A Market Analysis of Urban Interaction Design

Gianluca Zaffiro[1(✉)], Melissa Bracuto[1], Martin Brynskov[2], and Michael Smyth[3]

[1] Telecom Italia S.p.A., Future Centre, Turin, Italy
{gianluca.zaffiro, melissajose.bracutohernandez}@telecomitalia.it

[2] Department of Aesthetics and Communication, Aarhus University, Aarhus, Denmark
brynskov@cavi.au.dk

[3] Institute for Informatics and Digital Innovation, Edinburgh Napier University, Edinburgh, UK
m.smyth@napier.ac.uk

Abstract. Urban Interaction Design draws upon knowledge and approaches from a range of disciplines involved in the design of urban spaces, connecting them and establishing their interactions as a principle. It is also rooted in the wider field of interaction design, from which it takes much of its emphasis on behaviors at the human scale, putting the citizen at the center of the process of creating solutions in networked urban spaces. The paper presents the results of a preliminary survey that seeks to articulate, through best case examples, the challenges and opportunities for the field of Urban Interaction Design in the context of Smart Cities.

Keywords: Smart cities · User-centric approach · Interaction design

1 Introduction to Urban Interaction Design

Cities are increasingly characterized by urban environments permeated with data and augmented by technology. In fact ICT can be considered as a new layer of complexity to the city, where everything is digitally interconnected and interdependent. Interactions between city users and these environments are the central question in this context.

What is needed from the user point of view, which technologies can be used, how to "humanize" their impact, and finally how to design an answer to a need, are all questions at the core of Urban Interaction Design.

Urban Interaction Design can be seen as being grounded in the traditions of the Society, Technology and Arts [1], as depicted in Fig. 1.

The 'Urban' in urban interaction design signifies the emphasis on spatial aspects that affect human relationships, drawing on approaches from the social sciences.

'Interaction' refers to technology, particularly communication and networked technologies that convert the raw material of data into meaning that informs our decisions, at scales that range from citywide solutions to grassroots hacking and tinkering.

C. Stephanidis (Ed.): HCII 2015 Posters, Part II, CCIS 529, pp. 587–591, 2015.
DOI: 10.1007/978-3-319-21383-5_98

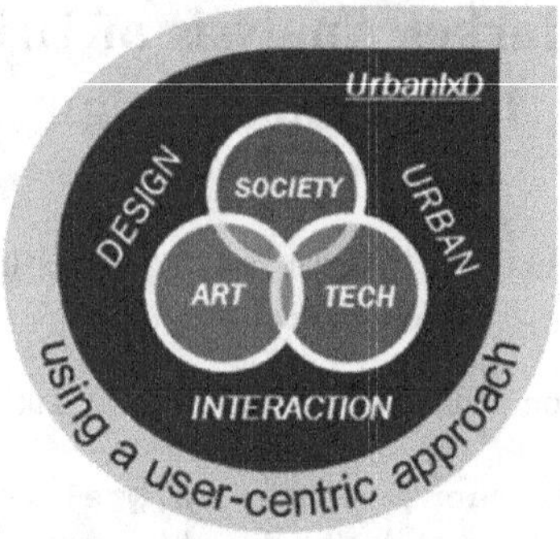

Fig. 1. Urban interaction design approach

'Design', the last part of the trilogy, draws on an interdisciplinary arts tradition, bringing critique and creativity into the mix, with an emphasis on both theory and practice [2].

2 Market Analysis

Urban Interaction Design innovates the way we can build Smart Cities, strongly adding the point of view of those for which the Cities are created, the Citizens. In the present study we analyze, by involving a panel of experts via an online survey, what are perceived to be the main challenges to innovate a Smart City, where the opportunities are foreseen, and what cases are already drawing upon this field.

2.1 Online Survey

An online survey which explores the perceived impact of Urban Interaction Design was deployed in two phases and run in 1H2014, reaching 122 experts worldwide. Most respondents are based in Europe (70 %) and almost evenly split between Industry (57 %) and University/Research (43 %) affiliations.

The first phase aimed at assessing the general opinions via 9 open-questions in the subjects of interest, such as the emerging issues in the Smart Cities and future opportunities and best practices for Urban Interaction Design.

The second phase was aimed at extending the sample size and converging the main categories of responses identified before. The survey was simplified to 5 multiple-choice questions and 2 open-questions.

2.2 Opportunities and Best Cases

Our preliminary analysis [3] shows that opportunities to introduce more solutions for the Smart Citizens lay particularly in areas such as smart governance, smart environment and smart living. This result is shown in the percentage mapping of the survey output (Fig. 2), where the percentage gap in total declared issues for the Smart Cities (dark grey in the figure) versus total suggested solutions (light grey) is 12 %, 6 % and 4 % respectively for the said areas. The assumption made here is that those areas where few solutions were suggested require more attention and effort in terms of future developments.

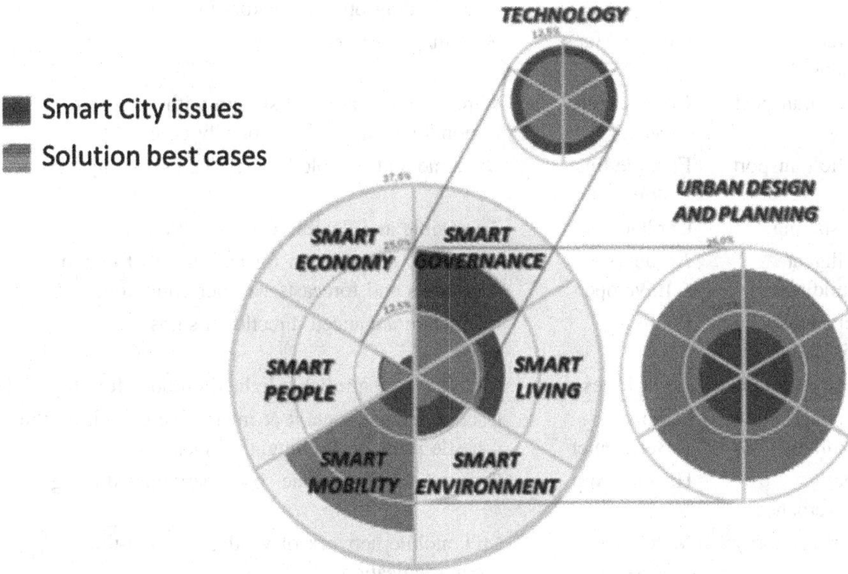

Fig. 2. Urban interaction design survey results

The respondents provided 104 examples of Smart City products or services that in their opinion were related to Urban Interaction Design. Among these we identified a 30 % as best cases according to the characteristics described in Sect. 1 of this paper, which are listed in Table 1.

The most representative of these is the Smart Citizens project [3], a platform to generate participatory processes of people in the cities. The objective of the platform is to serve as a node for building productive and open indicators by connecting data, people and knowledge. The idea is leveraging on several elements: involvement of the citizens in both the development and product deployment, integration of the solution in the smart city tissue, use of the most innovative open hardware and open software approaches.

Table 1. Urban interaction design best cases in the smart city context

Area	Best case	Description
Civic enlightenment	Bottle Bank Arcade Machine	Gamification for promoting plastic recycling (*)
Road security	Speed Camera Lottery	To get more people to obey the speed limit by entering a lottery for those who kept the limits (*)
Participated IoT	Smart Citizen Project	Citizen participation platform with low-cost sensors for creating open indicators in the cities
Interactive maps	Google Maps	Web mapping service
Green transport	Copenhagen Wheel	Wireless pedal assisted system with an App to monitor your ride and socially connect
Public transport	Flexible bus stop	Dynamic and flexible bus-service system by Philips
Car sharing	Car2Go	Accessible and flexible car rental system
Intelligent building	Xeromax Envelope	Interactive second-skin for building that records, presents and forecasts weather conditions (**)
Interactive display	Pointssign	Interactive advanced directional signs
Urban furniture	Light Lines	Modular & controllable lighted outdoor furniture (**)
Interactive exhibits	Danmarks Borgcenter	User-generated content & interactive exhibit on the castle ruins of Vordingborg, Denmark
Smart governance	Hackity App	Citizens App for public space participated design
Smart economy	Matching Markets	MIT mobile network of vendors w. real-time communication

(*) TheFunTheory; (**) Future Cities Lab

3 Conclusions

In this work we presented Urban Interaction Design as a new field with a user-centric approach based on the creative contamination of the Art, Society and Technology domains. We believe it can powerfully innovate the way we develop services in a networked urban environment, offering an effective tool to understand and tackle all challenges holistically.

In order to better understand this field and assess its potential and maturity level we conducted an online survey that prompted smart governance, smart environment and smart living as areas yet under-addressed in terms of available solutions at least with reference to the described approach.

Acknowledgment. The present work was conducted within the UrbanIxD Coordination Action, EU FP7-ICT Project Number 323687.

References

1. Brynskov, M. et al.: Urban Interaction Design. Towards City Making. Book Sprints, Europe (2014)
2. Mitrovic, I., Smyth, M., Helgason, I.: City|Data|Future: Interactions in Hybrid Urban Space (2014). www.urbanixd.eu
3. Bracuto, M., Zaffiro, G.: Urban Industry Report (2014). http://www.urbanixd.eu

Innovation Research on Service Design Collaboration Paths Oriented to Smart Cities - A Case Study in Living Lab

Yangshuo Zheng[1(✉)], Zhiyong Fu[1], and Taiping Zhu[2]

[1] Academy of Arts and Design, Tsinghua University, Beijing, China
zhengyangshuo@163.com, fudesign@263.net
[2] Institute of Art and Design, Wuhan University of Technology, Wuhan, China
44524437@qq.com

Abstract. This paper takes "Living Lab" as research example, analysis the social role of urban residents from "passive acceptance" to "active participation", and product design trends are changing from "traditional closed" to cross-border "open collaboration", and discuss the constitutes value system for Living Lab. With particular emphasis in article, Service design takes an irreplaceable internal driving force for the sustainable development of smart city and systematic social innovation. Smart city design should adhere to the user-centered service design, and continuously explore collaborative public participatory innovation paradigm.

Keywords: Smart city · Service design · Prosumer · Living lab

1 Introduction

Smart City has become the trend of future urban development. Currently, in the smart cities' construction process exists three main crux: firstly, pure IT driven mainly features takes more obvious and failed to achieve deep integration of IT technology and urban functions. Secondly, overall planning relatively subjective, did not take deep research based on the actual situation of different cities of the geographical environment, industry structure, people and culture, etc. Thirdly, due to the construction of smart city often involves multiple collaborate city administration, likely to cause poor implementation and bad effect. Top design concept and significance has been recognized, but top design also has some limitations. Need to reflect on is whether top design can solve all the problems of smart city construction?

The arrival of the big data era for the development of Smart City provides a new opportunity. With the new information media, urban residents to participate more actively in social innovation. From the digital to the smart of the city development process, the importance of service design has become increasingly prominent. Service design seeks to integrate and collaborate social elements, try to build an open and transparent, collaborative and innovative application platform, is a User-centered design philosophy and approach. In the smart city construction, should base on the human needs of urban residents, establish "design human city" as the core. To achieve

C. Stephanidis (Ed.): HCII 2015 Posters, Part II, CCIS 529, pp. 592–597, 2015.
DOI: 10.1007/978-3-319-21383-5_99

sustainable development of smart city, not only from a strategic top design, but also need new ideas through service design to explore new ways to collaborate and innovation.

2 Smart City Design Requires Public Collaborative Innovation

"Co-working" is not entirely a new concept, but a human population instinct in human society. The productivity of the information society is Rapidly improving, making the social division of labor more specialization, people are more willing to share information through collaboration with ways to seek their own value. In order to complete some complex research tasks, many large companies in the industry used to setting global experts to work together around the branch. For example, Boeing-787 is researched by Shenyang, Montreal, Seattle and other areas of the branch network engineers through the exchange of video conferencing and data processing programs, work together to complete the Boeing-787 core components development.

Along with ICT tools become more representative of IT popularity, "crowd-sourcing" model is increasingly on the rise. Through the Internet as a basis for social work, and every Internet user can play individual talent, and ultimately to promote the progress of the project through a collaborative approach. In public collaborative process, user's role arises from "passive acceptance" to "active participation", the individual is given greater force. Taking Wikipedia (Fig. 1) as an example, Wikipedia now has 31,240,000 entries, is an online encyclopedia has 16 million volunteers edited worldwide. Wikipedia via the Internet as a platform for brainstorming, brought thousands of collective intelligence together. Wikipedia flourished even a direct threat to the traditional classic "Encyclopedia Britannica". Till now, no longer issue Britannica print paper version.

Fig. 1. Wikipedia information service

Currently, the Internet has expanded to vast amounts of information aggregation platform for human society interaction. Public will take more participation in all levels of politics, economy and culture, make their voices heard and contribute their efforts. Society is bound to the "Nowhere is the center" model. Although the city's future development prospects still not very clear, but the role and status of urban residents has been greatly improved is unquestionable fact.

Smart City is a harmonious development of the city as the goal. Construction of smart city should take urban residents as core elements, the full application of big data, cloud computing, mobile Internet and other information technology tools, Build collaborative community participatory platform, and thus the formation of human progress and development of the city's as a virtuous cycle. Service design-driven social innovation will profoundly affect every aspect of the city, Ultimately create a good experience for every urban city dwellers.

3 Living Lab: Service Design Collaborative Innovation Paths

Small as a product, to a large city, future-oriented design requires a new design thinking, the core of which should be to enhance the interaction between users. Service design from the perspective of system theory, combine many factors together, such as design objectives, design principles, business strategy, process management, technological innovation. Setting interaction processes between users, products, environment; thus providing a good service and experience for users. Service Design most emphasizes the importance of user needs. Design and build an "User-centric" open collaborative innovation platform, will be more apt to popular demands, and explore the possibilities of business rules, cultural patterns, academic research.

Living Lab (LL) is a service design typical paradigm of collaborative innovation. The concept of LL was introduced in 1995 by Prof William Mitchell from MIT Media Lab and School of Architecture and city planning (Eriksson et al., 2005).Olavi Luotonen (ENOLL chairman) thought that, LL is a system for future economic and social forms. In this system, based on real life, user-driven research and innovation will be jointly create new services, new products and new social structure. LL can provide service enables users to actively participate in the research and innovation process. The most important feature of LL is to emphasis on people-oriented, user-centered and co-innovation.

With the user-centered innovation environment is increasingly complex, now LL has developed to 3.0 version. Experimental environment from a closed area expands to an open city, and become a main user-driven, future-oriented technological innovation

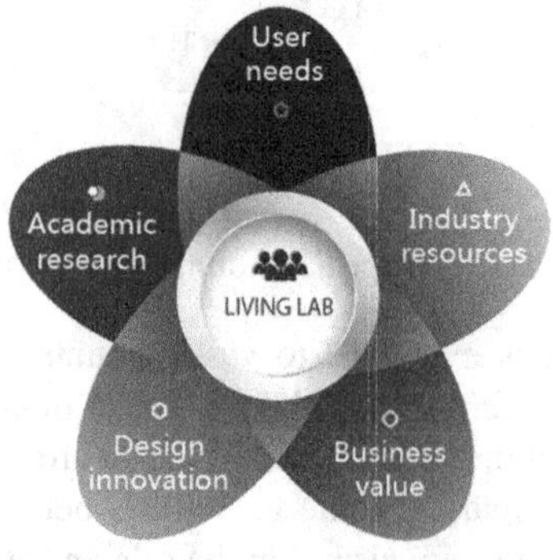

Fig. 2. LL consist elements

system, and innovative R & D new models. Living Lab brings design community, industry, business, academia, and other social groups and product users organically linked. By collaboration between users, designers and developers, Driving creativity, science and technology, culture in the form of better integration of product design (Fig. 2). LL can not only bridge the needs of society, user needs and product design activities, it is the epitome of an open society and a symbol of innovation.

4 Living Lab Value System Analysis

Relying on the city's residents as the main structure, as an open space in urban areas experiments, LL provides prototyping and testing platform for creation design and innovative applications. LL has distinctive SOLOMO attributes, to simulate a real environment for urban residents feel the design achievements in real-time.

LL integrates various types of users having chance to collaborate, combine the urban social needs and product innovation, technology research and development, advanced manufacturing and commercial operations, explore new design value, user value, business value and social value (Fig. 3).

4.1 Design Value

LL needs to capture the urban communities needs, predict usage scenarios, change user's participation process from the past test end, to the core research role into the design process. Today's product design philosophy has changed from the past to create a function to meet users, to based on the user to set the product features and other details. We can say that the rise of Living lab is brought to the traditional product design process of revolution.

4.2 User Value

LL capture real user groups attributes and build a participatory platform, build an information interaction space for different stakeholders, and takes as networking, distributed model. With the deepening applications of big data, mobile Internet tools, Diverse information media aggregation will help public more intelligent connection, product information interaction has great exploration space.

4.3 Business Value

LL is based on the localization of innovation. Every city has a unique charm of the city's character, there is a considerable mutual differences, which determines the static method should not be used to design for different cities. LL encourages users to share original ideas, research and creativity, which will inevitably lead to more regional style of products.

4.4 Social Value

Through the mass users participation innovation, LL help the city residents connected to each other. In the process of collaborative innovation, LL not only disseminate information technology concepts, improve information technology in the public's influence, While also help people further understand social innovation, and ultimately actively involved.

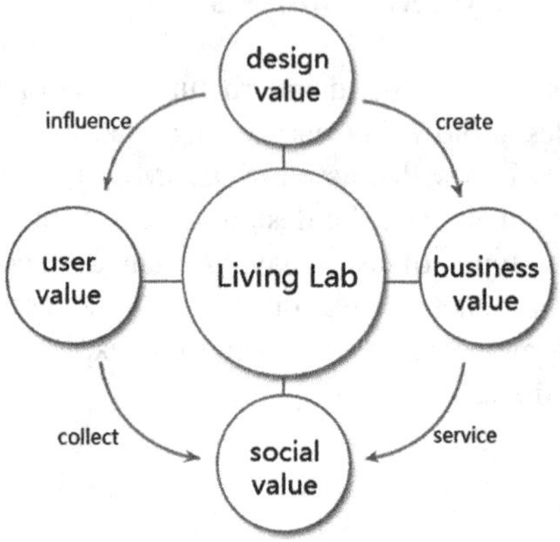

Fig. 3. Living lab value system analysis

5 Living Lab Case: Smart Living Lab Design

"Smart Living Lab" is founded in Tsinghua University (China), is an innovative environment for Living lab prototype of the smart city. Designers, engineers, brand experts, industry representatives, business professionals and design students and teachers participate in this professional collaboration platform, mainly for the future of urban life to create, experiment with different work tools and methods, and promote a specific type of product research, design and prototyping. "Smart Living Lab" seeks from the perspective of social humanities, focus on product design model can be implemented and potential business chances.

Via the internet help, "Smart Living Lab" across language, geography, culture intervals, convergence design global lab resources(including the United States, Australia, the Netherlands, etc.) for collaborative innovation, trying to create high-quality designs from the social, business, academic, and other perspectives. "Smart Living Lab" not only proved the feasibility of collaborative innovation from worldwide, but also reflects the young people trying to be creative, daring and innovative time spirits.

In the 2014 Beijing International Design Exhibition, "Smart Living Lab" constructed a communication participation platform for Beijing city residents, fully demonstrated the unique "Living lab" design concept :Not only smart city design works included ecology, transportation, living, education and entertainments, furthermore, take use of participatory co-design methodology, Expand knowledge sharing, research needs to explore a range of design activities. Held several workshops and collected user groups needs and behavioral data, more accurately grasp the public group behavior patterns and mental attributes, ultimately for applying to future smart city design (Fig. 4).

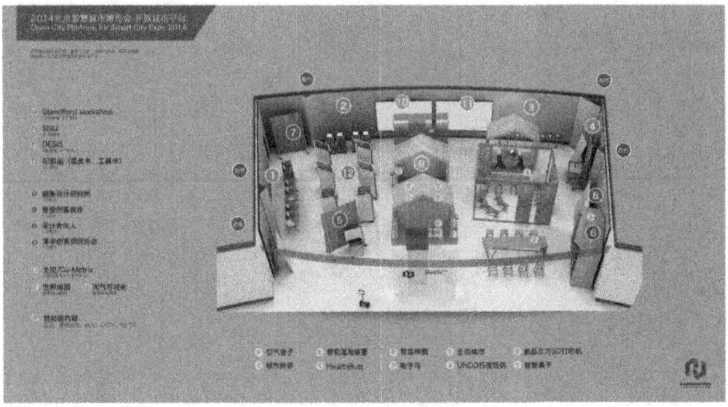

Fig. 4. Smart living lab design platform

6 Conclusion

Development of the city experienced a digital, networked era, gradually towards smart and service-oriented. Smart City is not limited to traditional spatial planning, it is innovation and inspiration regional area. Explore the development of smart city, requires a combination of advanced information technology tools, more needs to adhere to the concept of service design thinking to guide and encourage public participatory collaborative innovation, In an environment such as Living lab, to create smart lifestyle continuously together.

Automotive and Aviation

Multiple Scales Pilot Action Pattern Recognition During Flight Task Using Video Surveillance

Lu Ding[1(✉)], Jia Bo[1], Qi Wu[1], HaiYan Liu[2], and Shan Fu[1]

[1] Shanghai Jiao Tong University, Shanghai, China
dinglu@sjtu.edu.cn
[2] Commercial Aircraft Corporation of China Ltd, Shanghai, China

Abstract. Pilot action analysis is one of the most important aspects in objective measurement of flight crew workload. Pilot action patterns include distribution of action area, action duration, time and space interval between each of the actions, body posture, cross actions, action path and operation procedures. There are two main problems of pilot action pattern recognition. One is the issue of multiple scales in both time and space. The other is to locate action accurately. This paper presents a method of analyzing pilot action patterns during flight tasks by using video surveillance. Video data is obtained by setting up a single camera in real flight mission. We consider the cockpit as an intelligent environment and develop a new method to analyze pilot action patterns. The concept of intelligent environment is included. First, vision based pattern recognition method is used to locate moving targets in video. Then we use logical based method to recognition actions. The experiment results show that our approach is effective in workload assessment.

Keywords: Multiple scale · Activity recognition · Ontology · Pilot action patterns

1 Introduction

Minimum flight crew workload [1–3] is identified as one of the difficulties of civil transport category aircraft airworthiness certification issues which containing multi-disciplinary including human factors. Pilot action analysis is one of the most important aspects in studying minimum flight crew workload [4]. Workload is divided into 10 factors, among them 9 factors are pilot actions related: (1) Accessibility, ease and simplicity of operation; (2) Accessibility and conspicuity of necessary instruments; (3) Number, urgency and complexity of operating procedures; (4) Degree and duration of mental and physical effort; (5) Actions requiring a crewmember to be unavailable at his duty station; (6) Degree of automation provided in the aircraft systems to manage failures; (7) Communications and navigation workload; (8) Increased workload associated with any emergency; (9) Incapacitation of a flight crewmember. In each factor, we have some information that we need to figure out, such as task, distribution of action area, action duration, path of action, operation procedures and so on. In this

C. Stephanidis (Ed.): HCII 2015 Posters, Part II, CCIS 529, pp. 601–604, 2015.
DOI: 10.1007/978-3-319-21383-5_100

paper, we extract pilot action features from video data, and we use these features to analyze pilot action patterns, and then the results will be used in workload assessment.

Action is complicated, and it involves the problem of multiple scale. Multiple scale mainly manifest in time and space [5]. Different scales indicate different action patterns. We regard the cockpit as an intelligent environment, and we analyze the action pattern with the help of this environment. At a general level we can decompose the construct of an intelligent environment into three main components [6]. In the first instance we have the core sensing technology which has the ability to record the interactions with the environment. These may be in the form of for example video, contact sensors or motion sensors. A data processing module has the task to infer decisions based on the information gleaned from the sensing technology and with the third and final component providing the feedback to those within the environment via a suite of multi-modal interfaces. It has been the aim of this text to focus specifically on the data processing module, specifically focusing on the notion of activity recognition. Within the domain of intelligent environments some may have the view that the process of activity recognition forms the critical path in providing a truly automated environment. It is tasked with extracting and establishing meaningful activities from a myriad of sensor activations. Although work in this area is still deemed to be emerging, the initial results achieved have been more than impressive.

2 Activity Recognition

Activity recognition is the process whereby an actor's behavior and his/her situated environment are monitored and analyzed to infer the undergoing activities [7]. It comprises many different tasks, namely activity modeling, behavior and environment monitoring, data processing and pattern recognition. To perform activity recognition, it is therefore necessary to

1. Create computational activity models in a way that allows software systems/agents to conduct reasoning and manipulation.
2. Monitor and capture a user's behavior along with the state change of the environment.
3. Process perceived information through aggregation and fusion to generate a high-level abstraction of context or situation.
4. Decide which activity recognition algorithm to use, and finally
5. Carry out pattern recognition to determine the performed activity.

Monitoring an actor's behavior along with changes in the environment is a critical task in activity recognition. This monitoring process is responsible for capturing relevant contextual information for activity recognition systems to infer an actor's activity [8]. In terms of the way and data type of these monitoring facilities, there are currently two main activity recognition approaches; vision-based activity recognition and sensor-based activity recognition.

Traditional tracking is applied in 2d video space, it can provide moving information in 2D plane, but we can't get depth information. We use a new stereo vision-based model for multi-object detection and tracking in surveillance systems. Unlike most existing monocular camera-based systems, a stereo vision system is constructed in our model to overcome the problems of illumination variation, shadow interference, and object occlusion. In each frame, a sparse set of feature points are identified in the camera coordinate system, and then projected to the 2D ground plane [9]. A kernel-based clustering algorithm is proposed to group the projected points according to their height values and locations on the plane. By producing clusters, the number, position, and orientation of objects in the surveillance scene can be determined for online multi-object detection and tracking.

To enable long-term tracking, the key problem is the detection of the object when it appears in the camera's field of view. This problem is aggravated by the fact that the object may change its appearance thus making the appearance from the initial frame irrelevant. Next, a successful long-term tracker should handle scale and illumination changes, background clutter, and partial occlusions and operate in real-time. TLD [10] Method is proved to be an efficient method to track target in the video. TLD is a framework designed for long-term tracking of an unknown object in a video stream. The components of the framework are characterized as follows: Tracker estimates the object's motion between consecutive frames under the assumption that the frame-to-frame motion is limited and the object is visible. The tracker is likely to fail and never recover if the object moves out of the camera view. Detector treats every frame as independent and performs full scanning of the image to localize all appearances that have been observed and learned in the past. As any other detector, the detector makes two types of errors: false positives and false negative. Learning observes performance of both, tracker and detector, estimates detector's errors and generates training examples to avoid these errors in the future. The learning component assumes that both the tracker and the detector can fail. By the virtue of the learning, the detector generalizes to more object appearances and discriminates against background.

3 Experiment and Conclusion

In this paper, we aim at study multiple scale from the angle of space scale. We set up three scales: hand, arm, and body. We believe that a certain connections lies between each scales. Our main work content in this paper is to track the movement of pilot during flight task. The result will be further used to analyze pilot action.

First, vision based pattern recognition method is used to locate moving targets in video. Then we use logical based method to recognition actions. We also set up a series of experiments in dynamic flight simulators simulating real flight missions. Two camera are used to monitor the flight scene. We use stereo calibrate to get intrinsic and exterior parameter. TLD method is used to track pilot movement in the flight scene. Then we can get 3D coordinate of moving target. The multiple scale analysis can applied based on the position of moving target in 3D space.

The experiment results show that our approach is effective in pilot action recognition. We can track the movement of pilot in real-time and accurate positions in 3D space.

References

1. Hart, S.G., Staveland, L.E.: Development of NASA-TLX (Task Load Index): results of empirical and theoretical research. Adv. Psychol. **52**, 139–183 (1988)
2. Chen, L., Khalil, I.: Activity recognition: approaches, practices and trends. In: Activity Recognition in Pervasive Intelligent Environments, pp. 1−31, Atlantis Press, (2011)
3. Roscoe, A.H.: Assessing pilot workload. why measure heart rate, HRV and respiration? Biol. Psychol. **34**(2), 259–287 (1992)
4. Bakker, N.H., Tanase, D., Reekers, J.A., et al.: Evaluation of vascular and interventional procedures with time–action analysis: a pilot study. J. Vasc. Interv. Radiol. **13**(5), 483–488 (2002)
5. Chen, L., Nugent, C.: Ontology-based activity recognition in intelligent pervasive environments. Int. J. Web Inf. Syst. **5**(4), 410–430 (2009)
6. Chen, L., Nugent, C.D., Biswas, J., Hoey, J.: Activity Recognition in Pervasive Intelligent Environments. Springer, Heidelberg (2011)
7. Singla, G., Cook, D.J., Schmitter-Edgecombe, M.: Recognizing independent and joint activities among multiple residents in smart environments. J. Ambient Intell. Humaniz. Comput. **1**(1), 57–63 (2010)
8. Gu, T., Wang, X.H., Pung, H.K., et al.: An ontology-based context model in intelligent environments. In: Proceedings of Communication Networks and Distributed Systems Modeling and Simulation Conference, vol. 2004, pp. 270–275 (2004)
9. Cai, L., He, L., Xu, Y., et al.: Multi-object detection and tracking by stereo vision. Pattern Recogn. **43**(12), 4028–4041 (2010)
10. Kalal, Z., Mikolajczyk, K., Matas, J.: Tracking-learning-detection. IEEE Trans. Pattern Anal. Mach. Intell. **34**(7), 1409–1422 (2012)

Attentional Switch Characteristics are Correlated with the Performance of Simulated Aviation Task

Feng Du(✉), Jie Zhang, and Mengnuo Dai

Institute of Psychology, Chinese Academy of Sciences, Beijing 100101, China
duf@psych.ac.cn

Abstract. The present study explored what attentional switch characteristics are correlated with simulated aviation task performance. We measure the attentional switch characteristics based on three AB indices. When two targets are presented in a RSVP stream, the impairment in identification of the second target (T2) after correct report of the first target (T1) is attentional blink (AB). First, the overall switch cost is the AB magnitude which is the difference between the highest and lowest accuracy of T2 given correct report of T1 (T2/T1) across five T1-T2 intervals. Second, the general cost of processing T1 is measured by the average accuracy of T2/T1 across intervals. Finally, the AB dwell time is measured by the temporal interval when the accuracy of T2/T1 reach the lowest level across five T1-T2 intervals. The Multi-Attribute Task Battery (MATB) is used to simulate aviation tasks. The results show (1) AB dwell time is significantly correlated with the RT of monitoring dashboard;(2) average accuracy of T2/T1 is correlated with the performance of multiple tasks in the MATB including monitoring dashboard, resource management and tracking tasks. These results indicated that several AB indices might be useful for predicting the simulated aviation performance.

Keywords: Attentional switch characteristics · Attentional blink · Multi-attribute task battery · Simulated aviation performance

1 Introduction

When pilots are facing rapidly changing environment and dealing with multiple concurrent tasks in aviation, their cognitive systems are constantly overloaded with information flows. Attentions act as a goalkeeper of cognitive system to select more relevant information to aviation and filter out irrelevant information. Therefore, attentional characteristics of pilots are critical for predicting their aviation performance [1–4].

Since pilots are always facing multiple concurrent tasks in flight, they need to switch between tasks. These task switch usually requires switch in attentional set [5]. Thus the attentional switch characteristics might be a very important predictor for aviation performance. However, few studies examine whether attentional switch characteristics is correlated with aviation performance. Recent studies on Attentional blink shed light on this topic. The attentional blink (AB) refers to people's inability to

C. Stephanidis (Ed.): HCII 2015 Posters, Part II, CCIS 529, pp. 605–609, 2015.
DOI: 10.1007/978-3-319-21383-5_101

detect or identify a second target (designated T2) that follows within about five hundred milliseconds of an earlier target (T1) in the same location [6–8]. Visser and colleagues conducted a meta-analysis of previous AB work and found that the impairment caused by the attentional blink may be greatest away from the previously attended location [9]. This was further confirmed by several recent findings [10, 11]. Furthermore, Du and Abrams found that the benefit of the exogenous cue was reduced if the cue was presented within 100–200 ms after T1, when the attentional blink would be strongest, but it recovered as the interval between T1 and the cue increased [12–14]. Thus, the attentional blink provide a perfect measure of attentional switch characteristics.

2 Method

2.1 Participants

42 participants took part in experiments (25 males). All participants had normal or corrected-to-normal vision (including color vision). The experiment is approved by the internal review board of institute.

2.2 Attentional Blink

We adopt Attentional Blink to assess the attentional switch characteristics. Participants were required to report the two targets embedded in a RSVP stream [6]. After reporting the first target (T1) correctly, participants usually have difficulty in identifying the second target (T2). The impairment for reporting T2 is attentional blink (AB). The attentional switch characteristic were measure based on three AB indices. First, the overall switch cost is the AB magnitude which is the difference between the highest and lowest accuracy of T2 given correct report of T1 (T2/T1) across five T1-T2 intervals. Second, the general cost of processing T1 is measured by the average accuracy of T2/T1 across five T1-T2 intervals. Finally, the AB dwell time is measured by the temporal interval when the accuracy of T2/T1 reach the lowest level among those at five T1-T2 intervals.

The stimuli were displayed on a 17-in. CRT monitor with a resolution of 1024 × 768 pixels at a refresh rate of 85 Hz. The viewing distance is 60 cm. The background is black. Each trial began with the presentation of a fixation cross for 600 ms. The fixation cross was followed by 20 upper-case white letters (1.3° in height) sequentially presented at fixation. Letters were randomly chosen from all letters in the alphabet except the letter I. Each of the letters was presented for 40 ms and was followed by a 40 ms black screen. Thus SOA is 80 ms. The first target, T1, was a white digit randomly chosen between 2 and 9. It could appear in the tenth, eleventh, or twelfth frame in the stream.

The letters continued to change at the same rate after T1 was presented. T2 appeared in the 1st, 2nd, 3rd, 4th or 5th frames after T1. The T2 was a white letter chosen from letter A, B, X or Y. Participants were required to report both T1 and T2 as accurately as possible.

2.3 Multi-Attribute Task Battery (MATB)

We used Multi-Attribute Task Battery (MATB) to simulate aviation tasks [15]. As illustrated in Fig. 1, the MATB have four concurrent tasks including monitoring dashboard, manually tracking a target, verbal communication and resource management.

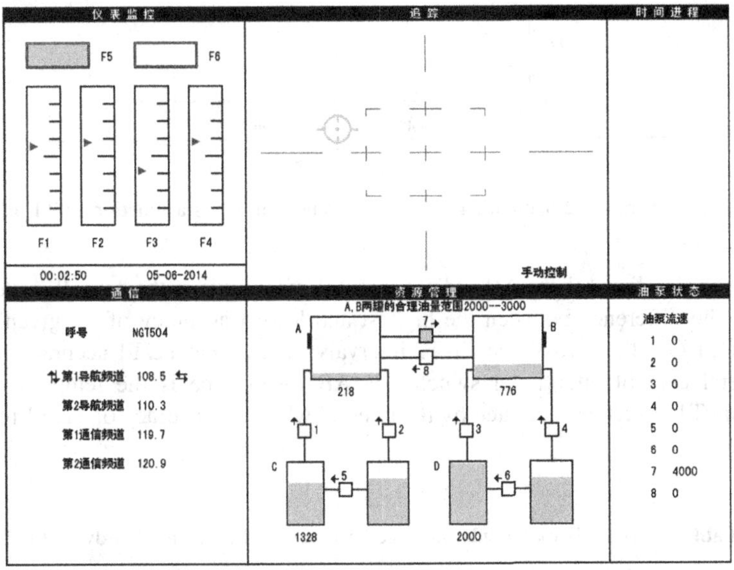

Fig. 1. Illustration of the interface in the Multi-Attribute Task Battery (MATB)

Monitoring Dashboard. Participants are required to monitor any abnormal signals on dashboard and press a key as soon as possible.

Manually Tracking a Target. Participants are required to constantly maintain the overlap between the center of green circle and the center of gray cross by using a joystick.

Verbal Communication. Participants are asked to monitor the verbal communication and adjust the frequency the communication channel as they are verbally instructed.

Resource Management. Participants were required to maintain the oil level within certain range for Tank A and B.

3 Results

One participant's AB performance is excluded from analysis based on 3 standard deviation criterion. The average T2 accuracy given correct report of T1 is listed in the Fig. 2. Attentional blink was observed in present experiment. The lowest T2/T1 accuracy is present at lag 3 (240 ms).

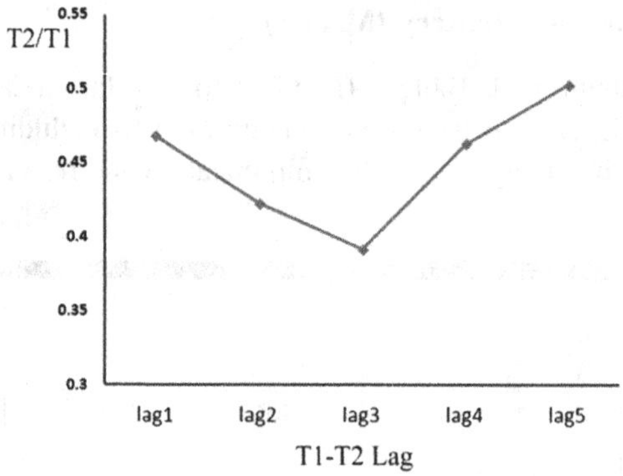

Fig. 2. The average T2 accuracy given correct report of T1 as a function of T1-T2 lags

Table 1 also listed there AB indices. (1) AB magnitude is the overall switch cost, which is the difference between the highest and lowest accuracy of T2 given correct report of T1 (T2/T1) across five T1-T2 intervals. (2) average T2/T1 accuracy measure the general cost of attentional switch. (3) AB dwell time is the temporal cost of processing T1, which is estimated by the interval when the accuracy of T2/T1 reach the lowest level.

Table 1. The AB magnitude, average accuracy of T2/T1 and AB dwell time

AB magnitude	Average accuracy	AB dwell time (ms)
0.31 ± 0.02	0.45 ± 0.02	236.1 ± 15.8

As Table 2 showed, (1) AB dwell time is significantly correlated with RT of monitoring dashboard; (2) average accuracy of T2 is positively correlated with the performance of three tasks' performance in the MATB including monitoring dashboard, resource management and tracking tasks. It is worth noting that performance get worse as RT of monitoring dashboard and tracking error increase. These results indicated that several AB indices might be useful for predicting the simulated aviation performance.

Table 2. The correlation between AB indices and MATB performance

	AB dwell time	AB magnitude	Average T2 accuracy
Monitoring dashboard (RT)	0.37*	0.14	−0.31*
Resource management	−0.24	0.23	0.36*
Tracking error	0.25	0.01	−0.30*

*indicate that two indices are significantly corrected.

4 Discussion

In flight, pilots are always facing multi-tasking situation. Attentional switch is naturally required by the multi-tasking situation in flight. As we expected, present study confirmed that indices of attentional switch can predict the performance of several tasks of simulated flight. For example, average T2/T1 accuracy, which measure the general cost of attentional switch, is positively correlated performance of three tasks of MATB. Therefore, we might be able to use attentional blink tasks to predict aviation performance.

Acknowledgement. This study was supported by grants from the National Natural Science Foundation of China (31470982 & 31200766), the key project of the Chinese Academy of Sciences (KJZD-EW-L04), and the scientific foundation of the Institute of Psychology, Chinese Academy of Sciences (Y4CX033008).

References

1. North, R.A., Gopher, D.: Measures of attention as predictors of flight performance. Human Factors: The Journal of the Human Factors and Ergonomics Society **18**, 1–14 (1976)
2. Hardy, D.J., Parasuraman, R.: Cognition and flight performance in older pilots. J. Exp. Psychol. Appl. **3**, 313–348 (1997)
3. Du, F., Ge, Y., Qu, W., Sun., X., Wu, J., Zhang, K., Zhang, L.: Attention, peri-personal perception, and visual displays in space. In: Human Performance in Space: Advancing Astronautics Research in China, pp. 4–5. Science/AAAS, Washington, DC (2014)
4. Wang, C., Tian, Y., Chen, S., Tian, Z., Jiang, T., Du, F.: Predicting performance in manually controlled rendezvous and docking through spatial abilities. Adv. Space Res. **53**(2), 362–369 (2014)
5. Du, F., Zhang, K., Abrams, R.A.: Hold the future, Let the past go: Attention prefers the features of future targets. Cognition **131**, 205–215 (2014)
6. Chun, M.M., Potter, M.C.: A two-stage model for multiple target detection in rapid serial visual presentation. J. Exp. Psychol. Hum. Percept. Perform. **21**, 109 (1995)
7. Raymond, J.E., Shapiro, K.L., Arnell, K.M.: Similarity determines the attentional blink. J. Exp. Psychol. Hum. Percept. Perform. **21**, 653–662 (1995)
8. Shapiro, K.L., Caldwell, J., Sorensen, R.E.: Personal names and the attentional blink: A visual "cocktail party" effect. J. Exp. Psychol. Hum. Percept. Perform. **23**, 504–514 (1997)
9. Visser, T.A.W., Bischof, W.F., Di Lollo, V.: Attentional switching in spatial and nonspatial domains: evidence from the attentional blink. Psychol. Bull. **125**, 458–469 (1999)
10. Du, F., Abrams, R.A., Zhang, K.: Spatial distribution of the attentional blink. Front. Cogn. **2**, 360 (2011)
11. Du, F., Qi, Y., Zhang, K.: Spatial distribution of attention during attentional blink is influenced by eye movements. Perception **42**, 907–931 (2013)
12. Du, F., Abrams, R.A.: Onset capture requires attention. Psychon. Bull. Rev. **16**, 537–541 (2009)
13. Du, F., Abrams, R.A.: Endogenous orienting is reduced during the attentional blink. Exp. Brain Res. **205**, 115–121 (2010)
14. Du, F., Yang, J., Yin, Y., Zhang, K., Abrams, R.A.: On the automaticity of contingent capture: disruption caused by the attentional blink. Psychon. Bull. Rev. **20**, 95–944 (2013)
15. Arnegard, R.J., Comstock, J. Jr.: Multi-Attribute Task Battery-Applications in pilot workload and strategic behavior research (1991)

Measuring Trust of Autonomous Vehicles: A Development and Validation Study

David Garcia, Christine Kreutzer(✉), Karla Badillo-Urquiola, and Mustapha Mouloua

Psychology Department, University of Central Florida, Orlando, USA
{david.garcia,mustapha.mouloua}@ucf.edu,
christine_kreutzer@knights.ucf.edu,
kbadillo@ist.ucf.edu

Abstract. Recent advances in technology have improved the ability of vehicles to act autonomously, thereby enabling the implementation of these systems into the lives of the everyday consumer. For example, in the past three years nearly several major vehicle manufacturer, supplier, and technology company have announced projects involving autonomous vehicles (AVs). While the notion of AVs has been popular within the military, the urgency to make them commonplace has gathered pace as companies outside the auto industry have illustrated the feasibility and benefits that AVs offer. However, in order to predict user adoption of these autonomous features, attitudes towards them must be understood. Thus, the purpose of the present in-progress study is to develop and validate a scale to quantify trust towards autonomous vehicles. Upon the completion of data collection, the data will be subjected to a factor analysis. It is hypothesized that the scale ratings will converge to a single underlying dimension. It is also hypothesized that there will be differences in trust among the levels of vehicle autonomy.

Keywords: Autonomous vehicles · Trust · Unmanned vehicles · Robotics

1 Introduction

1.1 Background

As vehicles with autonomous features become standard in today's market, so too does our need to understand the intricate role human trust plays in the operation of these vehicles. Certainly, human trust towards AVs has become a salient issue in human-robot interaction literature. For example, when an autonomous car has anthropomorphized features, humans are more likely to trust the vehicle [1]. However, previous research has indicated that humans are poor at monitoring automated systems [2–5]. Despite numerous advances in technology, autonomous systems still remain prone to automation failures [6, 7]. In addition to technical problems, there are a number of human factors design issues facing AV designers, such as displayed information, situation awareness, level of training and experience, control design, support from backup personnel or systems, data-link delays, and cognitive load limitations [3].

C. Stephanidis (Ed.): HCII 2015 Posters, Part II, CCIS 529, pp. 610–615, 2015.
DOI: 10.1007/978-3-319-21383-5_102

1.2 Levels of Vehicle Automation

The National highway Traffic Safety Administration [8] organizes vehicle autonomy as having 5 different levels. Autonomous.

- No-Automation (Level 0) in this level, there are no autonomous features in this vehicle. The drive is controlling all aspects of the vehicle at all times.
- Function-Specific Automation (Level 1) this level of autonomy includes vehicles with one or more specific control functions. Some examples of this are pre-charged brakes, or cruise control.
- Combined Function Automation (Level 2) vehicles with combined function automation features have at least two principal functions that are designed to work in together in order to relieve the operator of controlling those functions. Level 2 of vehicle automation is where a human begins to lessen their role as an operator and begins to take on the role of a supervisor.
- Limited Self-Driving Automation (Level 3) is defined as a vehicle that can enable the drive to relinquish complete control of functions critical to safety under some conditions. In this level, the driver must still be available for manual control of the vehicle.
- Full Self-Driving Automation (Level 4) implies that the vehicle is designed to monitor roadway conditions and perform functions critical to safety for the duration of a trip.

1.3 The Current Study

Despite the infiltration of autonomous features in the automotive market, and the potential design and safety issues associated with them, researchers have not yet explored attitudes towards these features. For example, how comfortable are humans with a car that can park itself versus a car that can pick you up, and take you to a destination? Our research seeks to bridge this gap and put forth a validated measure to attempt to quantify these new constructs. More specifically, the purpose of this in progress study is to explore the factor structure underlying a novel scale aimed at quantifying trust towards autonomous vehicles. It is hypothesized that scale ratings will converge to a single underlying dimension. It is also hypothesized that trust ratings will differ between each level of autonomy.

2 Methods

2.1 Participants

A total of 400 participants from the University of Central Florida will be recruited for participation in this study. Participants can sign up for this study via SONA, the university's online research participant pool. Extra credit will be awarded in exchange for participation.

2.2 Materials

Vignettes reflecting the five levels of vehicle autonomy as identified by The National highway Traffic Safety Administration [8] will be presented. Each vignette describes the features of the corresponding level of autonomy as follows:

- *Level 0.* The driver is in complete and sole control of the primary vehicle controls (brake, steering, throttle, and motive power) at all times, and is solely responsible for monitoring the roadway and for safe operation of all vehicle controls. This vehicle may have certain driver support/convenience systems but do not have control authority over steering, braking, or throttle. Examples include systems that provide only warnings (e.g., forward collision warning, lane departure warning, blind spot monitoring) as well as systems providing automated secondary controls such as wipers, headlights, turn signals, and hazard lights.
- *Level 1.* Automation at this level involves one or more specific control functions; if multiple functions are automated, they operate independently from each other. The driver has overall control, and is solely responsible for safe operation, but can choose to cede limited authority over a primary control (as in adaptive cruise control), the vehicle can automatically assume limited authority over a primary control (as in electronic stability control), or the automated system can provide added control to aid the driver in certain normal driving or crash-imminent situations (e.g., dynamic brake support in emergencies). The vehicle may have multiple capabilities combining individual driver support and crash avoidance technologies, but does not replace driver vigilance and does not assume driving responsibility from the driver. The vehicle's automated system may assist or augment the driver in operating one of the primary controls – either steering or braking/throttle controls (but not both). As a result, there is no combination of vehicle control systems working in unison that enables the driver to be disengaged from physically operating the vehicle by having his or her hands off the steering wheel AND feet off the pedals at the same time. Examples of function-specific automation systems include: cruise control, automatic braking, and lane keeping.
- *Level 2.* This level involves automation of at least two primary control functions designed to work in unison to relieve the driver of control of those functions. Vehicles at this level of automation can utilize shared authority when the driver cedes active primary control in certain limited driving situations. The driver is still responsible for monitoring the roadway and safe operation and is expected to be available for control at all times and on short notice. The system can relinquish control with no advance warning and the driver must be ready to control the vehicle safely. An example of this would be "smart", or adaptive cruise control as seen with some newly released cars.
- *Level 3.* Vehicles at this level of automation enable the driver to cede full control of all safety-critical functions under certain traffic or environmental conditions and in those conditions to rely heavily on the vehicle to monitor for changes in those conditions requiring transition back to driver control. The driver is expected to be available for occasional control, but with sufficiently comfortable transition time. The vehicle is designed to ensure safe operation during the automated driving

mode. An example would be an automated or self-driving car that can determine when the system is no longer able to support automation, such as from an oncoming construction area, and then signals to the driver to reengage in the driving task, providing the driver with an appropriate amount of transition time to safely regain manual control.

- *Level 4.* The vehicle is designed to perform all safety-critical driving functions and monitor roadway conditions for an entire trip. Such a design anticipates that the driver will provide destination or navigation input, but is not expected to be available for control at any time during the trip. This includes both occupied and unoccupied vehicles. By design, safe operation rests solely on the automated vehicle system. An example of this would be Google's self-driving car, which uses four radars, a laser guidance system, a traffic-light-detecting camera, GPS, an inertial measurement unit, and a wheel encoder (to determine the vehicle's location) to successfully navigate around complex city settings. As is evident by the cost of the equipment used by Google's self-driving car, this may take some time before it becomes affordable enough for consumer use.

Respondents will rate the extent to which they agree with a variety of statements relating to each autonomous level. These items were generated based on the facets of trust identified within the HRI literature [9–12]. Examples from items on this scale include: 'I believe that this type of vehicle would be reliable', 'I believe that my interactions with this type of vehicle would be predictable', and 'I would trust this type of vehicle for my everyday travel'. Responses will be rated on a 5-point Likert scale.

2.3 Design and Procedure

After reading and agreeing to the terms outlined in the informed consent, participants will complete the scale online through Qualtrics. The study will utilize a within-subjects design. All participants will complete each scale corresponding to each vignette. The order in which participants receive each vignette will be randomized. The vignettes will not include the corresponding autonomous level.

3 Expected Results

Upon the completion of data collection, the data will be subjected to a factor analysis to reveal the underlying factor structure of the experimental scale. The goal of factor analysis is to condense a larger set of variables to a smaller set of factors, which account for a sizeable proportion of variability within the items. Thus, it is desirable to have a few factors that account for a large portion of the variance. It is anticipated that scale ratings will converge to support one underlying factor.

A one-way analysis of variance (ANOVA) will also be conducted to examine differences in trust among the five levels of autonomy. It is anticipated that there will be differences in trust depending on the autonomous level. More specifically, we anticipate that trust will attenuate with higher levels of autonomy.

4 Discussion

The aim of the present ongoing investigation is to examine the factor structure of an experimental metric designed to quantify attitudes towards different levels of autonomy in vehicles. In particular, this will allow us to identify the factors underlying trust towards autonomy. In addition, this study will identify differences in trust among the levels of autonomous vehicles.

The technological capacities of vehicles have vastly increased in recent years, leading to the advancement of both the functional capability and autonomy of current systems. With these advancements, autonomous features have become increasingly prevalent within everyday vehicles. This has led to a transition of the human role from an operator to that of a supervising member, assistant, or even bystander. As such, the intricacies of interaction have changed to where consumers must place increasing amounts of trust into these technological features. Thereby, the individual's trust in that system takes a prominent role in the success of any interaction and therefore the future use of the vehicle.

Despite the infiltration of autonomous vehicles faced by consumers, researchers have not examined attitudes towards various autonomous features. This is problematic, as vehicle manufacturers and government agencies responsible for vehicle regulations must understand if consumers are receptive of these recent and ongoing advancements. The deployment of AVs today is less about technological capabilities and more about the ability of stakeholders to implement such vehicles into an everyday environment. One barrier to successful deployment may be a lack of consumer trust. Thus, our study will make the contribution of providing a means to quantifying trust towards autonomous features in vehicles. Additionally, our study seeks to identify how consumers feel about different autonomous features. More specifically, we hope to identify how trusting individuals are of different autonomous features that are gaining popularity. Thus, the results of our study will have implications for vehicle manufacturers, as better understanding their consumers will help them to design more desirable vehicles, thereby increasing profit and user adoption.

We believe that the validation of our measure will also provide fruitful avenues for future research. According to Schaefer [9], individuals' mental models change as trust changes from pre- to post-interaction with a robot. Future work should examine if a similar relationship exists within the context of autonomous vehicles. That is, future research should examine how operating vehicles of varying autonomy changes individuals' degree of trust and thereby, mental models. Moreover, our measure could be utilized to quantify these changes in trust from pre- to post-interaction. An additional avenue for future work is related to trust as it applies to expansion and transition of the human role. The human element is often overlooked or even forgotten during the design and development process [9]. Thus, future work should be conducted to further understand the differences in trust perceptions between individuals as it applies to this process.

References

1. Waytz, A., Heafner, J., Epley, N.: The mind in the machine: anthropomorphism increases trust in an autonomous vehicle. J. Exp. Soc. Psychol. **52**, 113–117 (2014)
2. Hancock, P., Mouloua, M., Gilson, R., Szalma, J., Oron-Gilad, T.: Provocation: is the UAV control ratio the right question? Ergon. Des. **15**(1), 7 (2007)
3. Mouloua, M., Gilson, R., Hancock, P.: Human-centered design of unmanned aerial vehicles. Ergon. Des.: Q. Hum. Factors Appl. **11**(1), 6–11 (2003)
4. Mouloua, M., Parasuraman, R.: Human Performance In Automated Systems: Recent Research And Trends. Erlbaum, Hillsdale, NJ (1994)
5. Parasuraman, R., Riley, V.: Humans and automation: use, misuse, disuse, abuse. Hum. Factors **39**(2), 220–253 (1997)
6. Wiener, E.L., Nagel, D.C. (eds.): Human Factors In Aviation. Gulf Professional Publishing, Houston (1989)
7. Mouloua, M., Koone, J.: Human-Automation Interaction: Research and Practice. Erlbaum, Hillsdale, NJ (1997)
8. National Highway Traffic Safety Administration. Preliminary statement of policy concerning automated vehicles. Washington, DC (2013)
9. Schaefer, K.E.: The perception and measurement of human-robot trust. Doctoral dissertation, University of Central Florida Orlando, Florida (2013)
10. Joosse, M., Sardar, A., Lohse, M., Evers, V.: Behave-ii: the revised set of measures to assess users' attitudinal and behavioral responses to a social robot. Int. J. Soc. Robot. **5**(3), 379–388 (2013)
11. Parasuraman, R., Sheridan, T.B., Wickens, C.D.: A model for types and levels of human interaction with automation. Syst., Man Cybern., Part A: IEEE Trans. Syst. Hum. **30**(3), 286–297 (2000)
12. Yagoda, R.E., Gillan, D.J.: You want me to trust a ROBOT? The development of a human–robot interaction trust scale. Int. J. Soc. Robot. **4**(3), 235–248 (2012)

The Effects of Automation Reliability and Multi-tasking on Trust and Reliance in a Simulated Unmanned System Control Task

Svyatoslav Guznov(✉), Alexander Nelson, Joseph Lyons, and David Dycus

Air Force Research Laboratory, WPAFB, Dayton, USA
{svyatoslav.guznov.ctr,alexander.nelson.2, joseph.lyons.6,david.dycus}@us.af.mil

Abstract. This study examined the effects of automation reliability and multi-tasking on trust and reliance in a simulated unmanned system scenario. Participants performed an insurgent search task with the help of an automated aid that provided information about targets with varying levels of reliability (high, medium, and low). In addition, a multi-tasking condition was implemented in which a radio communication assignment designed to increase cognitive demand was performed. Results indicated that participants were not able to accurately assess the true reliability of the automated aid in any condition, and were unable to discriminate between low and medium reliability. Results from the multi-tasking manipulation show that participants were more reliant upon the automated aid when the secondary task was present. Overall, this study provides insight into the patterns of trust calibration errors that may negatively affect performance in human-machine teams, particularly when additional task pressure is present.

Keywords: Unmanned systems · Automation reliability · Trust · Reliance · Multi-tasking

1 Introduction

In recent years, military systems have become more technologically complex and are incorporating higher levels of automation than ever before. As the function of the operator in these human-machine systems has evolved to more of a supervisory and decision-making role, the importance of understanding the factors that influence trust and reliance has dramatically increased. Most automated systems are not infallible and it is critical that the human partner is able to calibrate their trust for appropriate reliance. When trust is not calibrated correctly, errors in over-reliance and under-reliance can occur, leading to *misuse or disuse* of the automation [12].

The major factor that influences the reliance calibration process is trust [7]. Trust in a system is a belief that the trustee will accomplish a certain objective and the willingness of a trustor to accept vulnerability and uncertainty [6]. Several studies

C. Stephanidis (Ed.): HCII 2015 Posters, Part II, CCIS 529, pp. 616–621, 2015.
DOI: 10.1007/978-3-319-21383-5_103

examined the influence of automation reliability on trust and reliance showing that increased automation reliability increases trust and reliance [1]. However, unmanned systems often incorporate multi-tasking demands where the operator, in addition to the primary task (e.g., target search), needs to communicate with teammates, interact with a control panel, or accomplish other tasks. Such environments might result in overreliance errors and misuse due to the diversion of cognitive resources away from the evaluation of automation performance [11]. These types of overreliance errors can have severe consequences when the automation used to accomplish the task is imperfect [6].

Although previous studies have examined automation reliability and multi-tasking as factors that affect trust and reliance, none of them looked at the joint effects of these two factors. In this study, we examined the effects of three levels of automation reliability and task type on trust and reliance. The participants performed an insurgent search task in the Mixed Initiative eXperimental (MIX) [2] testbed and had an Automated Aid (AA) that provided information about insurgent and other combatant locations on a map. In the multi-task condition, participants were asked to perform a communication task (Coordinate Response Measure (CRM) [3] in addition to the search task.

An interaction was expected between reliability and multi-tasking factors. The participants were expected to calibrate their trust and reliance appropriately to the level of automation reliability when posed with the insurgent search task only. However, the participants were expected to over trust and overrely on low reliability automation when asked to perform the CRM task concurrently with the insurgent search task.

2 Methodology

2.1 Participants

Forty eight participants were recruited for this experiment (28 men and 20 women). Participants ranged in age from 18 to 59 years ($M = 36.67$, $SD = 11.22$). All participants reported normal or corrected-to-normal vision.

2.2 Design

The experiment employed a 3 (Automation Reliability) × 2 (Task Type) mixed design. The Automation Reliability was a between-subjects factor including high reliability (HR), medium reliability (MR), and low reliability (LR) levels with the reliability values of 93 %, 75 %, and 55 % respectively. The Task Type was a within-subjects factor including single task and multi-task levels. The Task Type factor levels were counter-balanced to control for potential carry-over effects. The dependent variables for the study were insurgent search performance and CRM task performance; reliance, trust state, and perceptual accuracy with the regard to the AA; and perceived workload.

2.3 Apparatus and Materials

The experiment was conducted using two computers that ran the MIX testbed and the CRM task. The MIX testbed simulated a UGV task. The MIX interface consisted of a video feed window that showed the UGV camera view and the AA window. In the simulation, the UGV moved along a pre-determined path while the operator monitored the video feed screen searching for insurgents. The AA provided the participants with a map that showed the locations of the combatants. Depending on the condition (i.e., low, medium, or high reliability), the AA made respectively seven, four, or one classification errors. A classification error occurred when the AA marked an insurgent as a non-insurgent or vice versa. Participants were asked to press either *Accept* or *Reject* buttons in the AA interface when they agreed or disagreed with the AA.

The CRM software was used to simulate a military radio communication assignment. Each participant was assigned the call sign "Arrow" and was asked to follow commands associated with their call sign by pressing a color- and number-coded button as quickly as possible on a touch screen monitor. The program logged the accuracy of the selections made by the participants.

In this study, the following metrics were used. The Perceptual Accuracy metric [9] estimated participants' accuracy at evaluating the reliability of the AA. The Trust Scale [8] measured participants' trust state. The NASA-Task Load Index (NASA-TLX) [5] was used to measure participants' perceived workload.

2.4 Procedure

Upon arrival, the participants were trained on how to perform the experimental task in the MIX testbed and the CRM task. Next, the participants performed the experimental task consisting of two phases: single task (insurgent search in the MIX simulator alone) or multi-task (insurgent search and the CRM task). In the single task condition, the participants were asked to search for the insurgents using the AA. The participants were also asked to accept or reject the AA's classification suggestions. The task was paused three times to administer the Trust Scale, Perceptual Accuracy, and NASA-TLX questionnaires. In the multi-task condition, the participants performed the task identical to that of the single task condition, but were also asked to simultaneously perform the CRM task.

3 Results

3.1 Perceived Reliability

Mixed-model ANOVA showed a significant main effect for the Automation Reliability factor, F (2, 33) = 29.85, $p < .001$, partial $\eta^2 = .64$. Post hoc comparisons using the Tukey HSD criterion for significance showed that there was no significant difference between LR and MR levels. However, both LR (M = 59.79, SD = 9.06) and MR (M = 64.44, SD = 9.51) levels had significantly lower perceived reliability ratings when compared to HR (M = 84.31, SD = 8.02) level with $p < .001$ for both comparisons.

3.2 Trust State

Mixed-model ANOVA revealed a significant main effect for the Automation Reliability factor, F (2, 33) = 14.04, $p < .001$, partial $\eta^2 = .46$. Post hoc comparisons using the Tukey HSD criterion for significance showed that there was no significant difference between LR and MR levels. However, both LR ($M = 2.04$, $SD = .7$) and MR ($M = 2.53$, $SD = .68$) levels were significantly lower in trust ratings when compared to HR ($M = 3.68$, $SD = .73$) level with $p < .001$ for both comparisons.

3.3 Reliance

The reliance scores were calculated as a sum of the total number of agreements with the AA. Mixed-model ANOVA revealed a significant interaction between Automation Reliability and Task Type factors, F (2, 33) = 3.48, $p < .04$, partial $\eta^2 = .17$. In addition, there was a significant main effect for Automation Reliability F (2, 33) = 51.89, $p < .001$, partial $\eta^2 = .76$. Post hoc comparisons with the Tukey HSD criterion for significance showed LR Single Task condition ($M = 7.41$, $SD = .97$) produced significantly lower reliance when compared to LR Multi-task condition ($M = 8.45$, $SD = .1.26$), $p < .05$ (Fig. 1).

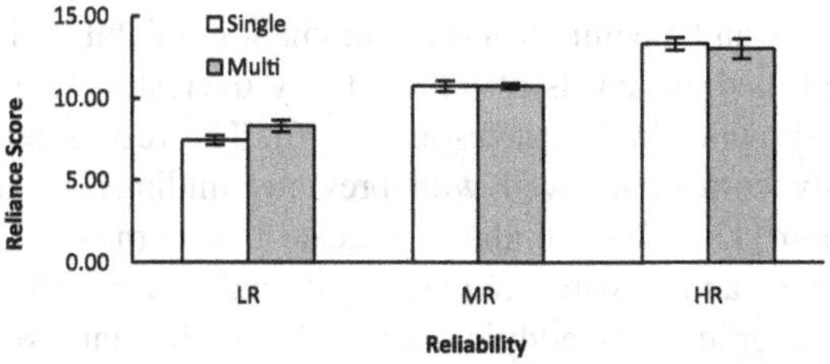

Fig. 1. Reliance across automation reliability conditions. Error bars are standard errors.

3.4 Insurgent Search Task and CRM Task Performance

No significant main effects for the Automation Reliability and Task Type for both the insurgent search and the CRM tasks were observed. In addition, there was also no significant interaction between these two factors for both tasks.

3.5 Global Workload

Mixed-model ANOVA revealed a significant main effect for the Task Type factor, F (1, 44) = 4.88, $p < .05$, partial $\eta^2 = .1$. Participants in the Multi-Task condition ($M = 29.31$, $SD = 16.09$) reported significantly higher workload when compared to the Single Task condition ($M = 26.06$, $SD = 17.27$).

4 Discussion

The main focus of the study was to examine the joint effects of automation reliability and multi-tasking on trust calibration and reliance towards the AA. The overall results confirmed some, but not all, of the original hypotheses. While LR and MR conditions were similar to each other in perceived reliability, each was significantly lower when compared to the HR condition. In addition, the participants in LR condition overestimated the reliability by approximately 6 % and participants in MR and HR conditions underestimated the reliability by approximately 11 %. A similar pattern was observed for the trust state scores: the participants in LR and MR conditions rated their trust to be significantly lower when compared to the HR condition. However, there was no difference between LR and MR conditions showing that the participants were not sensitive to reliability manipulation when the reliability levels are low (50 %–70 %). For the AA reliance, a significant interaction was observed showing that participants relied on the LR automation more when asked to perform the CRM task confirming the original hypothesis that increasing task demand would divert cognitive resources away from evaluating the automation. Finally, participants found the multi-tasking condition more challenging when compared to the single task condition indicating that the CRM task indeed induced additional mental demand.

Generally, the results indicate the complex nature of the interaction between different levels of automation reliability and multi-tasking. Participants were neither accurate in their judgment of automation reliability levels nor were they able to discriminate between low and medium levels of automation reliability. It appears that they "averaged" low and medium levels of reliability by overestimating one and underestimating the other showing low trust resolution [6]. The results related to underestimation of reliability correspond well with previous findings of underestimation of imperfect automation [13]. These findings indicate that human perception of system reliability is not linear and possibly require additional features to help the operators correctly judge its magnitude. In addition, while the participants were not affected by the CRM task in their perceptual accuracy and trust ratings, the behavioral outcome (i.e., reliance) was affected in the low reliability condition. This shows that even if the participants estimated the aid to be equally reliable, they still have a tendency to agree with the automation more, possibly due to a lack of the cognitive resources to adequately interact with the automation as suggested by [10]. Overall, this study provides insight into the patterns of trust calibration errors that may negatively affect performance in human-machine teams, particularly when additional task pressure is present.

There are limitations associated with the experiment that the authors would like to address in future studies. The performance data indicated that the results could have been more dramatic if the insurgent search task and the secondary tasks were higher in difficulty or longer in duration. In addition to addressing these errors, future studies would benefit from the integration of psychophysiological metrics (e.g. EEG, eye-tracking) that give additional information about the participants' trust and workload states.

References

1. Bailey, N.A., Scerbo, M.W.: Automation-induced complacency for monitoring highly reliable systems: the role of task complexity, system experience and operator trust. Theor. Issues Ergon. Sci. **8**, 321–348 (2007)
2. Barber, D., Davis, L., Nicholson, D., Chen, J.Y.C., Finkelstein, N.: The mixed initiative experimental (MIX) testbed for human robot interactions with varied levels of automation. In: Proceedings of the 26th Annual Army Science Conference, December 1–4, ADA505701 (2008)
3. Bolia, R.S., Nelson, W.T., Ericson, M.A., Simpson, B.D.: A speech corpus for multitalker communication research. J. Acoust. Soc. Am. **107**, 1065–1066 (2000)
4. de Visser, E.J., Parasuraman, R., Cosenzo, K.: Effects of imperfect automation on human supervision of multiple uninhabited vehicles. Paper presented at the Annual Meeting of Division 21 of the American Psychological Association, George Mason University, Fairfax, VA, March 2007
5. Hart, S.G., Staveland, L.E.: Development of NASA-TLX (task load index): results of empirical and theoretical research. In: Hancock, P.A., Meshkati, N. (eds.) Human Mental Workload. North Holland Press, Amsterdam (1988)
6. Lee, J.D., See, K.A.: Trust in automation: designing for appropriate reliance. Hum. Factors **46**(1), 50–80 (2004)
7. Lee, J.D., Seppelt, B.D.: Human factors in automation design. In: Nof, S. (ed.) Springer Handbook of Automation, pp. 417–436. Springer, New York (2009)
8. Merritt, S.M., LaChapell, J., Lee, D.: The perfect automation schema: Measure development and validation. Technical report submitted to the Air Force Research Laboratory, Human Effectiveness Directorate, 30 June 2012
9. Merritt, S.M., LaChapell, J., Lee, D.: Continuous calibration of trust in automated systems-phase 2. Technical report submitted to the Air Force Research Laboratory, Human Effectiveness Directorate, 31 May 2013
10. Parasuraman, R., Manzey, D.: Complacency and bias in human use of automation: an attentional integration. Hum. Factors **52**, 381–410 (2010)
11. Parasuraman, R., Molloy, R., Singh, I.L.: Performance consequences of automation-induced "complacency". Int. J. Aviat. Psychol. **3**, 1–23 (1993)
12. Parasuraman, R., Riley, V.: Humans and automation: use, misuse, disuse, abuse. Hum. Factors **39**, 230–253 (1997)
13. Wiegmann, D.: Agreeing with automated diagnostic aids: a study of users' concurrence strategies. Hum. Factors J. Hum. Factors Ergon. Soc. **44**(1), 44–50 (2002)

Enhancement of Performance by Automotive Display Design that Applied Proximity Compatibility Principle (PCP)

Atsuo Murata(✉) and Takaaki Akazawa

Deptartment of Intelligent Mechanical System, Graduate School of Natural Science and Technology Okayama University, Okayama, Japan
murata@iims.sys.okayama-u.ac.jp

Abstract. The aim of this study was to propose an effective method for displaying driving environment and properly transmitting this to drivers. The display was designed by changing two types of proximity, that is, the proximity of the display and the proximity of the task itself. The proximity of the display was controlled as the type of the display or the distance between two displays. The proximity of the task was controlled as the difference of two tasks performed on the two displays. The participants (a total of eight graduate or undergraduate students) were required to carry out simultaneously a main simulated driving task and secondary tasks controlled by the two proximity factors above. The secondary tasks were one of the followings: reaction task to the approach of a following vehicle, lane changing task, reaction task when the distance to a destination is within the predetermined distance, and speed maintaining task. As a result, it has been demonstrated that the performance under the dual task condition does not always obey the predicted result by proximity compatibility principle.

Keywords: Automotive display · Proximity of display · Proximity of task · Proximity compatibility principle (PCP)

1 Introduction

The proximity compatibility principle (PCP) is an approach to display design proposed by Wickens [1–7]. Under the high task proximity between two tasks, we can divide attention to simultaneously conduct two tasks without degrading task performances. In such a case, the display location to perform both tasks has a significant effect on the performance of both tasks. In other words, both performances are enhanced when both displays are located closely, or when both displays are similar. Under the low task proximity between two tasks, we must focus attention to each task in order to simultaneously conduct two tasks without degrading task performances. Even in such a case, the display location to perform both tasks has a significant effect (impact) on the performance of both tasks. Contrary to the high task proximity condition, both performances are enhanced when both displays are located distantly, or when both displays are dissimilar. The explanation above is summarized in Fig. 1. The solid line and

C. Stephanidis (Ed.): HCII 2015 Posters, Part II, CCIS 529, pp. 622–627, 2015.
DOI: 10.1007/978-3-319-21383-5_104

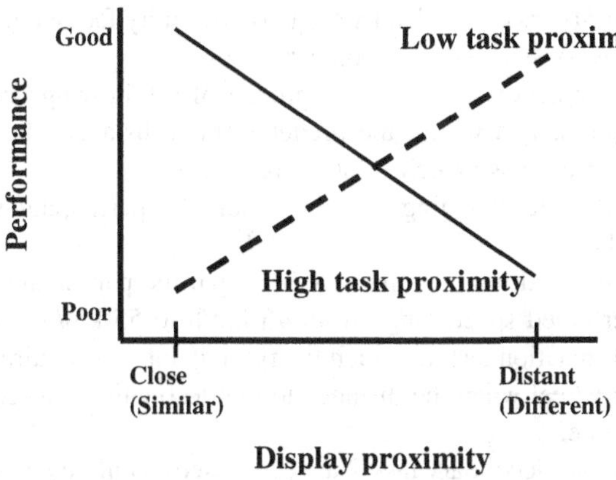

Fig. 1. Schematic explanation of basic concept of PCP (Proximity Compatibility Principle).

the dotted line correspond to high and low task proximity conditions, respectively. The conception is that PCP may be applicable to the design of automotive display.

The aim of this study was to propose an effective method for displaying driving environment and properly transmitting this to drivers using PCP principle. The display was designed by changing two types of proximity, that is, the proximity of the display and the proximity of the task itself. The proximity of the display was controlled as the type of the display or the distance between two displays. The proximity of the task was controlled as the difference of two tasks performed on the two displays. More concretely, the similar proximity of the task was either two analogue tasks or two digital tasks. The different proximity of the task was the mixture of digital and analogue tasks. These two proximities were all within-subject variables.

2 Method

2.1 Participants

Eight healthy male aged from 21 to 24 years took part in the experiment. All had held a driver's license for 2–4 years. The visual acuity of the participants in both young and older groups was matched and more than 20/20. They had no orthopedic or neurological diseases. All signed the informed consent after receiving a brief explanation on the contents and the procedure of the experiment.

2.2 Apparatus and Task

A driving simulator system developed by Murata et al. [6, 7] was used. The participants were required to simultaneously carry out a simulated driving task (main task) using an accelerator and the brake. The participant was required to minimize the deviation from the predetermined line and keep the lane location using a steering wheel.

The following four types controlled by the two proximity factors (display proximity and task proximity) were selected as secondary tasks.

Secondary task 1: reaction task to the approach of a following vehicle. When the following vehicle approached within the predetermined distance, the participant was required to react using a cross switch of steering wheel.

Secondary task 2: lane changing task in which the participant was required to change the running lane.

Secondary task 3: speed maintaining task in which the participant was required to maintain the predetermined speed range from 45 km/h to 55 km/h.

Secondary task 4: reaction task in which the participant was required to react with a cross key of steering wheel when the distance to the destination was equal or less than the predetermined value.

Secondary task 1 and Secondary task 2 are processed mainly by a right hemisphere. Secondary task 3 and Secondary task 4 are processed mainly by a left hemisphere.

Combining the four types of secondary tasks above, the task proximity was determined as follows. Task proximity included four kinds of dual tasks.

High task complexity: Secondary task 1 (Left display) + Secondary task 2 (Right display), Secondary task 3 (Left display) + Secondary task 4 (Right display), and Secondary task 2 (Left display) + Secondary task 1(Right display).

Low task complexity: Secondary task 1 (Left display) + Secondary task 3(Right display), Secondary task 1 + Secondary task 4(Right display), Secondary display 2(Left display) + Secondary task3(Right display), and Secondary display 2 (Right display) + Secondary task4 (Left display).

The display proximity was controlled by the distance between two displays. The distance between displays for the close and the distant displays were 3 cm (visual angle of 2 degrees) and 17 cm (visual angle of 10 degrees), respectively.

2.3 Design and Procedure

The experimental factors were the display proximity (two: levels (close and distant)) and the task proximity (basically, low and high). All were within-subject factors. A total of 16 conditions specified by the task proximity and the display proximity were conducted by each participant. The participant conducted each condition for five minutes. The order of performance of display proximity condition was counterbalanced across the participants. Four participants conducted the low display proximity condition firstly. Other four participants conducted high display proximity condition firstly. For each display proximity condition, the order of performance of eight task proximity conditions was randomized across the participants.

Before starting an experimental session, the participants were allowed practice the experimental task until they were accustomed to the operation. The participants were required to carry out simultaneously a simulated driving task and 16 kinds of dual secondary tasks controlled by two proximity factors above. The performance measures were tracking error in the simulated driving task, the percentage correct and reaction time in the secondary task.

3 Results

3.1 Reaction Time in Secondary Task

As a result of a two-way (task proximity by display proximity) ANOVA was conducted on the reaction time of each of four secondary tasks. As for Secondary task 2, 3, and 4, no significant main effect or interaction were detected. Only for Secondary task 1 in which the participant was required to react using a cross switch of steering wheel when the following vehicle approached within the predetermined distance, a significant task proximity by display proximity interaction was detected ($F(1,7) = 7.250$, $p < 0.05$). In Fig. 2, the reaction time is plotted as a function of display proximity and task proximity in Secondary task 4 (reaction task when the distance to the destination was equal or less than the predetermined value). Figure 3 shows the reaction time as a function of display proximity and task proximity in Secondary task 1(reaction task to the approach of a following vehicle).

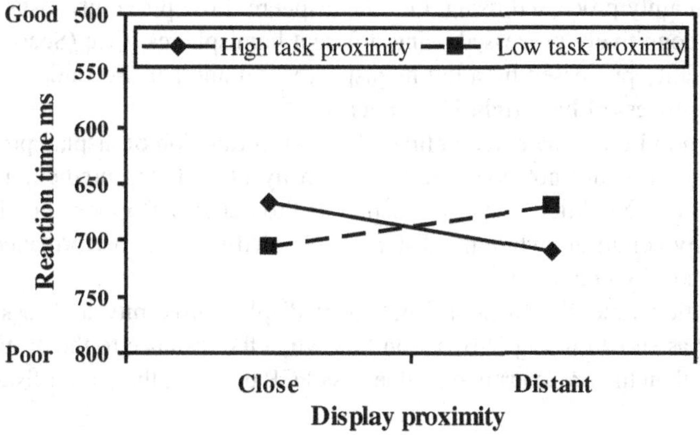

Fig. 2. Reaction time as a function of display proximity and task proximity (reaction task when the distance to the destination was equal or less than the predetermined value).

3.2 Number of Errors in Secondary Task

A similar two-way (task proximity by display proximity) ANOVA conducted on the number of errors in secondary task revealed no significant main effect or interaction for all of four types of secondary tasks.

3.3 Tracking Error in Main Driving Simulator Task

A similar two-way (task proximity by display proximity) ANOVA conducted on the tracking errors in the main driving simulating task revealed no significant main effect or interaction for all of four types of secondary tasks.

4 Discussion

The proximity compatibility principle (PCP) (see Fig. 1) [2–5] is one of the cognitive scientific approaches to the display design. Under the high task proximity between two tasks, this principle predicts that we can divide attention to simultaneously conduct two tasks without degrading task performances. In such a case, the display placement to perform both tasks has a significant effect on the performance of both tasks. In other words, both performances are enhanced when both displays are located closely.

A method for displaying the secondary task and properly transmitting this to drivers using PCP principle was empirically explored. The display was designed by changing two types of proximity, that is, the proximity of the display and the proximity of the task itself. The proximity of the display was controlled as the type of the display or the distance between two displays. The proximity of the task was controlled as the difference of two tasks performed on the two displays. High proximity tasks were those which were cognitively processed with the same hemisphere. In this study, Secondary tasks 1 and 2 were mainly processed using a right hemisphere, while Secondary tasks 3 and 4 were mainly processed using a left hemisphere. Low proximity tasks were those which were cognitively processed using different hemispheres (One (Secondary task 3 or 4) was mainly processed by a left hemisphere, and another (Secondary task 1 or 2) was mainly processed by a right hemisphere).

As shown in Fig. 3, the reaction time plotted as a function of display proximity and task proximity also did not obey the prediction by PCP. If the prediction by PCP is applicable to this condition, the close display led to better performance under the high task proximity condition, while the distant display led to better performance under the low task proximity condition.

The reaction time shown as a function of display proximity and task proximity obeyed PCP as shown in Fig. 2 (reaction task when the distance to the destination was equal or less than the predetermined value). As PCP predicts, the close (distant) display

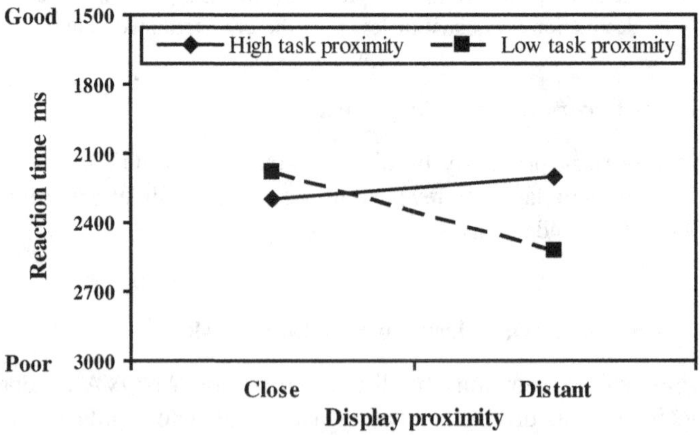

Fig. 3. Reaction time as a function of display proximity and task proximity (reaction task to the approach of a following vehicle).

led to better performance under the high (low) task proximity condition. It has been demonstrated that the performance under the dual task condition does not necessarily obey the prediction by proximity compatibility principle. In other words, in the range of this experiment, it seems that PCP is not necessarily a universally applicable display design guideline.

Future research should continue to explore whether PCP should be universally and effectively applicable to the automotive display design. As far as this study is concerned, the PCP prediction is not robust and does not universally true. Whether PCP is applicable or not seems to depend on the contents of the secondary task. It must be further discussed under what condition of PCP is applicable as Wickens [6, 7] predicted.

References

1. Wickens, C.D., Sandry, D.L., Vidulich, M.: Compatibility and resource competition between modalities of input, central processing, and output. Hum. Factors **25**, 227–248 (1983)
2. Wickens, C.D., Hollands, J.G.: Engineering Psychology and Human Performance. Prentice Hall, Upper Saddle River (2000)
3. Wickens, C.D., Lee, J.D., Liu, Y., Becker, S.E.G.: An Introduction to Human Factors Engineering. Prentice Hall, Upper Saddle River (2004)
4. Wickens, C.D., Carswell, C.M.: The proximity compatibility compatibility principle: Its psychological foundation and relevance to display design. Hum. Factors **37**(3), 473–494 (1995)
5. Wickens, C.D., Andre, A.D.: Proximity compatibility and information display: Effects of color, space, and objectness on information integration. Hum. Factors **32**(1), 61–78 (1990)
6. Murata, A., Kemori, S., Hayami, T., Moriwaka, M.: Basic study on automotive warning presentation to front/rear hazard by vibrotactile stimulation. In: AHFE 2012, pp. 421–430, San Francisco (2012)
7. Murata, A., Kanbayashi, M., Hayami, T.: Effectiveness of automotive warning system presented with multiple sensory modalities. In: Duffy, V.G. (ed.) HCII 2013 and DHM 2013, Part I. LNCS, vol. 8025, pp. 88–97. Springer, Heidelberg (2013)

A Cognitive Systems Engineering Perspective on Fighter Cockpit Design Evaluation

Susanna Nilsson[1(✉)], Britta Levin[1], Staffan Nählinder[1], Jens Alfredson[2], Ulrika Ohlander[2], and Johan Holmberg[2]

[1] Division of Information and Aeronautical Systems, Swedish Defence Research Agency, Stockholm, Sweden
susanna.nilsson@foi.se
[2] Saab Aeronautics, Stockholm, Sweden

Abstract. In this paper a method for evaluating fighter aircraft cockpit design solutions is suggested, taking into account the specific needs and limitations that come from working in the context of developing modern fighter aircraft cockpit design. In this context flight simulators are an essential tool for evaluation. A general problem when using simulators for evaluations is the amount of data generated, and how to approach this data. There is a need to develop methods to manage the data and extract relevant data in order to make it usable in the design and development process. The approaches described also aim at connecting the simulator data to the overall joint goals of the pilot-fighter-aircraft system in accordance with the CSE approach to systems development.

1 Background

The origin of Human Factors as a research domain can be traced back to the early days of modern aviation and cockpit design. Aviation is a safety critical activity, where a human pilot has to interact with a complex technical system, as well as the surrounding world and its physical restrictions. Traditionally this has meant a focus on safety issues relating to human factors on a low level (i.e. interaction with controls and displays), but there is a need to see the pilot-aircraft system from a more holistic perspective that includes organizational as well as systemic issues on a higher level (Harris 2011). Human factors approaches to design and interaction often describe the user and the system, or in this case the pilot and the aircraft, as separate entities exchanging input and output. Improving design of interfaces based on this idea often results in a focus on improving the interaction between user and system. The improvement is often measured in terms of time, amount or frequency of errors or other measurable performance results based on input or measurable user behavior. This approach to design and evaluation has been challenged by more holistic approaches such as cognitive systems engineering, CSE, where focus lies on goals of joint systems (i.e. the joint pilot-aircraft system) rather than on the effectiveness of the interaction between different parts of the joint system (Hollnagel and Woods 1983; 2005).

The speed of systems development cycles has increased in later years as a result of agile and iterative methods being used. Every new design solution has to be tested and a decision must be made whether the design is good enough, or if there is a need to

C. Stephanidis (Ed.): HCII 2015 Posters, Part II, CCIS 529, pp. 628–633, 2015.
DOI: 10.1007/978-3-319-21383-5_105

re-design and eventually re-evaluate. In the context of developing a modern fighter aircraft cockpit design, these evaluations have to be made accurately and efficiently. One of the main reasons for the development of flight simulators was to create environments for training and exercise in order to reduce costs as well as risks. Simulators have, however, also extensively been used in order to evaluate cockpit design options during development, for instance in simulator-based design (Alm 2007). There is a long tradition of evaluating pilot behavior and performance using simulators, measuring everything from the number of interactions with controls to more abstract concepts such as situation awareness (Endsley 1988). Measures might include physiological measures like heart rate as well as other measures like questionnaires, observations and subjective rating of performance and experience.

However, outside the research community, in the industrial development of fighter aircraft, the time resources for extensive simulator research and evaluation may be limited–the demands of short lead time from requirement to delivery through quick development cycles means that the time to actually analyze data obtained through simulators may be constrained. Although the data may be recorded, the main input to the design team can often rely on more subjective measures like questionnaires, interviews and observations. The data recorded in the simulator, including measures such as technical system logs (control stick movements, button presses, menu interactions, flight data such as speed, pitch, elevation etc.) and even psycho-physiological data is more difficult to draw quick conclusions from in order to give meaningful input to the design process.

The main aim of this paper is to describe suggested methods (i.e. work in progress) for analysis of data acquired through simulations in order to determine which measures are of most relevance to the overall design process of fighter aircraft display design. The approaches described aim at connecting the simulator data to the overall joint goals of the pilot-fighter-aircraft system in accordance with the CSE approach to systems development.

2 An Approach for Fighter Cockpit Design Evaluation

The design process for the pilot interface and layout of cockpit features often follows a standard systems development process. The process includes a set of system development phases from requirements through analysis of requirements; design and prototyping to evaluation, implementation and verification of the end product (see Fig. 1)

The evaluation phase in the design and prototyping stage often includes several simulator based trials where test pilots fly the simulators in order to evaluate both functional and design related aspects of the pilot interface. In agile design processes of fighter aircraft, simulations are often used to evaluate aspects of HMI (human machine interface) design in order to determine two things:

- Is the function under evaluation good enough to be implemented?
- How should the function be improved?

During these simulations it is possible to record a large amount of different data. The main input used for evaluation is however often the results of usability tests,

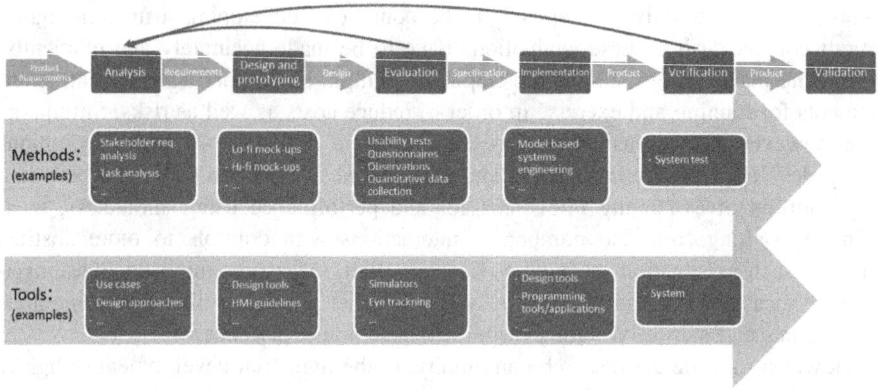

Fig. 1. A schematic view of a generic design process based on standards such as the systems development and life cycle process described in ISO/IEC 15288, and the human-centered design process suggested by ISO 9241-210.

questionnaires and observations by the design team. The main aim of the research project behind this paper is to find methods to identify and extract relevant input from the recorded simulator data, and relate this data to the overall goal of creating efficient pilot-aircraft interaction in order to reach the joint pilot-fighter-aircraft system's mission objectives (i.e. allowing the pilot to perform the mission at hand).

3 Method and Results of Initial Simulation

An initial simulation with a test pilot was conducted where a set of data was recorded. The data was analyzed in order to formulate a set of analysis approaches which are described in this section. The main aim of the analysis of the acquired data was to identify data that indicates for instance a high workload which would have an effect on the pilot's ability to perform and conduct his/her mission.

In the days prior to the simulation, the test pilot received documentation regarding the functionalities and design features in focus for the evaluation. On the day of the simulation the pilot was given a brief instruction before getting in to the simulator. The pilot was also donned with eye tracking equipment. Before the simulated mission was initiated, the pilot was allowed to freely interact with the cockpit user interface and explore the menu features in focus for the simulation. After this the simulated mission commenced and the recording of data began. The simulation lasted for approximately 30 min (ca. 10 min training/exploring and ca. 20 min of recorded data) during which the design team observed and answered questions related to the tasks and interaction.

After the simulation the design team conducted a debriefing where the pilot was asked a set of questions about the features in focus, and about general issues related to the experience. Before leaving the pilot filled out a questionnaire focused on rating the readiness of the functions evaluated. The data logged during the simulation included the following metrics: time, airspeed, altitude, pitch, bank and eye point of gaze data (see Fig. 2).

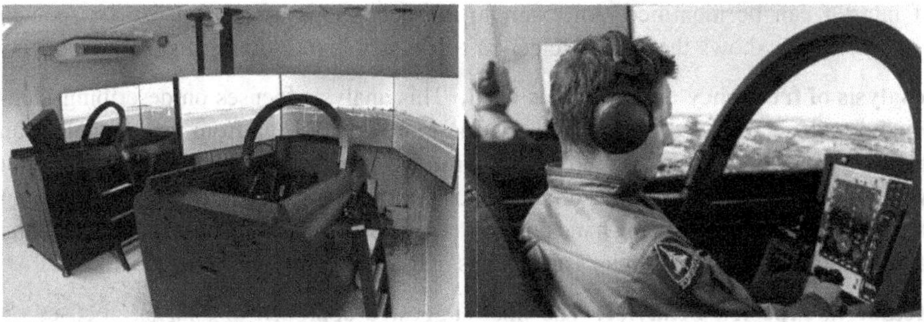

Fig. 2. To the left the simulator setting, to the right a test pilot in the simulator

3.1 Suggested Approaches

Based on the initial simulation data four possible levels of the approach to analysis are suggested: Event detection through anomalies; Frequency analysis; Analysis of frequency and channels used; Actual vs expected behavior. These approaches, described below are the basis for further development of a general method for analyzing simulator data.

Event detection through anomalies in the data. This approach studies data from event logs, flight data recordings, pilot interactions etc. in order to abstract relevant points of interest for further analysis. The main focus of investigation is occurrences of anomalies, for instance in one variable, or in the combination of several parameters (see Fig. 3a). In some cases the correlation of data are of interest, and in other the lack of correlation is the event of interest. The aim of this analysis is mainly to support the evaluator in finding relevant sections of the recorded simulation for further analysis.

Frequency analysis. Analysis of the frequency of certain triggers, for instance display selections, button presses, menu interactions, can give an indication of general work load for the pilot. When looking at the data sets from the simulation recordings, points

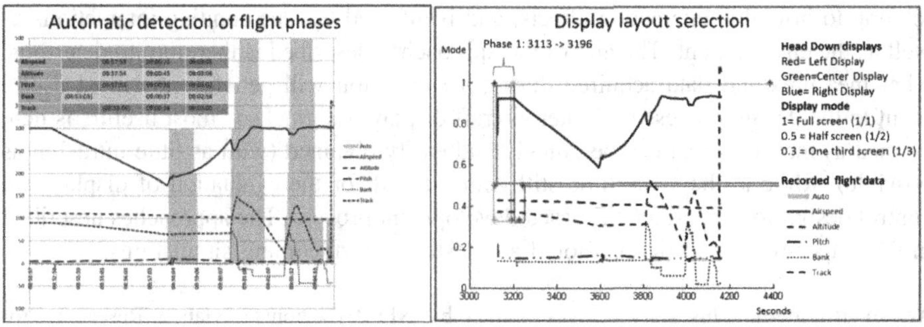

Fig. 3. a. (left) Example data set from simulator trial showing points of interest in recorded flight simulator data. b. (right) Example data set showing change of active display area (selection of display areas) in correlation with flight simulator recorded data.

of interest can be identified. An example of such points of interest can be seen in Fig. 3b, which shows the pilot's selection of display layout during the simulation.

Analysis of frequency and channels used. This analysis focuses on describing identified possible sections of higher workload in more detail. Data from the simulator can describe what modalities are used by the pilot and in what combinations – is the pilot working with the joystick while simultaneously monitoring the HUD, is the pilot using three displays while also using hand controls etc. This gives an indication of how well the layout (and design) of instruments and panels in the cock-pit support the pilots workflow.

Actual vs expected behavior. The final suggested approach of analysis focuses on studying what the pilot is actually doing and comparing this to the expected behavior. This analysis can be based on the sequence of interactions – for instance the number of interactions it takes for the pilot to for change a waypoint in one display, compared to the designer's expected number of interactions. The analysis can also be based on time – the number of interactions may be irrelevant as long as the outcome is the same in the expected time interval. Time is also an essential safety aspect in the often, time critical domain of aviation, making time a relevant measure. From a usability point of view, a large number of interactions is most likely not optimal with regard to the pilots overall workload.

4 Discussion and Future Work

The purpose of the work in progress described in this paper was to develop a set of approaches to using simulator data in the design process of fighter cockpit HMI. The underlying research question for the project is how to make the most use of recorded simulator data in order to answer the design teams main questions – "Are the HMI features good enough for implementation?", and "What should be improved for the next design iteration?".

Simulator data can be used to measure performance of the pilot (or rather the efficiency and effectiveness of the HMI). The CSE approach, however, highlights that these, often small differences in performance on detailed levels may not be the optimal way to ensure that the pilot-fighter aircraft system as a whole reaches its goals (often the mission objectives). There is a need to view the detailed measured improvements in relation to how this interaction affects, and is affected by, surrounding interactions as well as the environment. The aim of the approaches described is therefore to determine what measures and data acquired during a simulation will generate the most useful input to the design process of fighter aircraft display design. The "most useful" is here defined as measures that can be quickly and easily obtained (with as little intrusion as possible), while at the same time still being useful for the evaluation of display and control design to support a CSE based development process. The approaches described in this paper will be further explored and tested in forthcoming simulations.

Acknowledgment. This research was funded by NFFP (National Aviation Research Programme, NFFP6-2013-01201), which is founded by VINNOVA (Swedish Governmental Agency for Innovation Systems), the Swedish Armed Forces and the Swedish Defence Materiel Administration.

References

Alm, T.: Simulator-based design: Methodology and vehicle display applications. Doctoral dissertation (No. 1078). Linköping, Sweden: Linköping University (2007)

Endsley, M. R.: Design and evaluation for situation awareness enhancement. In: Proceedings of the Human Factors Society 32nd Annual Meeting. Human Factors Society, Santa Monica, CA, pp. 97–101 (1988)

Harris, D.: Human Performance on the Flight Deck. Ashgate Publishing Ltd., Farnham (2011)

Hollnagel, E., Woods, D.D.: Cognitive systems engineering: new wine in new bottles. Int. J. Man Mach. Stud. **18**(6), 583–600 (1983)

Hollnagel, E., Woods, D.D.: Joint Cognitive Systems: Foundations of Cognitive Systems Engineering. CRC Press, Taylor & Francis, Boca Raton (2005)

Design and User Studies

Information Assurance Practices in Saudi Arabian Organizations

Abdulaziz Alarifi(✉)

Compuer Science Department, Community College, King Saud University, Riyadh, Saudi Arabia
abdulazizalarifi@ksu.edu.sa

Abstract. While the Web, cell phone 'apps' and cloud computing put a world of information at our fingertips that information is under constant threat from cyber vandals and hackers. Although awareness of information threats is growing in the Western world, in places like Saudi Arabia, information security is very poor. Unlike Western pluralistic democracies, Saudi Arabia is a highly-censored country, with a patriarchal and tribal culture, which may influence its poor information security rating. This paper examines the level of Information Security (InfoSec) practices among the IT departments in organizations in Saudi Arabia, using an online survey, based on instruments produced by specialist organizations on information security such as the Malaysian Cyber Security Organization, the Excellence of Information Assurance Centre, and Alelm organization in Saudi Arabia. The survey attracted 124 respondents and the results indicated that information security in Saudi Arabian organizations is quite low. Several of the areas of weakness in InfoSec appear to be related to the level of censorship or the patriarchal and tribal nature of Saudi culture. This study has clearly indicated that information security in Saudi Arabia faces some serious risks from a range of threat types. There is a need to reduce the risks faced and provide good strategies for further protection from threats quickly. This study has proposed the InfoSec Cultural Adaptation Process model (InfoSec CAP) as a process to inform a culturally appropriate response to this challenge. The vision of this research was to provide a tool that would protect and enhance the InfoSec in Saudi Arabia in the short and long terms. This was provided in the InfoSec CAP model. The use of the model will help to establish a strong information security practice and to provide a further information protection. It will also help embed the identified concepts in information security practice globally.

Keywords: Information security · Information assurance · Information systems · Information security management

1 Introduction

The World Wide Web, mobile computing, and Cloud Computing have changed the world, providing a wide range of information, anytime and anywhere [1]. However, the developments of such technologies also allows new techniques for abusers to misuse or destroy information [2]. These "cyber vandals" can illegally access or destroy online information using techniques such as malware programs (e.g. viruses, Trojans and worms), hacking or denial of service (DoS) attacks [3].

C. Stephanidis (Ed.): HCII 2015 Posters, Part II, CCIS 529, pp. 637–642, 2015.
DOI: 10.1007/978-3-319-21383-5_106

To overcome these threats, it is essential for both information providers and information users to have good information security practices, which can be defined as ensuring the availability, integrity and confidentiality of information [4–6]. However, before Information Security practices become routine, there must be an appropriate level of Information Security Awareness (ISA), which refers to a state in which information users are aware of the information risks and understand the power of both physical and non-physical information security [7, 8]. ISA has become one of the strongest lines of defense against ongoing information threats; it has been demonstrated that a high-level of ISA can reduce information risks and increase the efficiency of information security performance [7].

Although this is generally well-understood, some countries, particularly those which are highly-censored, such as Saudi Arabia, does not appear to have understood either the devastating risks of information security (InfoSec) threats or the importance of ISA. Indeed, Saudi Arabia has among the highest levels of information security risk [9]. This paper aims to understand the relationship between these high risk levels and InfoSec, specifically in the context of Saudi Arabia.

2 Methodology

While our understanding of InfoSec in Saudi Arabia is poor, the concept of InfoSec is well-defined in the literature and several excellent survey instruments exist for assessing InfoSec. Moreover, this study seeks to gather data from as large a sample of the Saudi Arabian organizations as possible, so a survey is an ideal data gathering technique [10, 11]. An online survey is particularly effective over long distances and is well-suited to Saudi culture because women in Saudi Arabia cannot speak to men who are not relatives. Consequently, an online survey can gather a large sample from organizations of both men and women in a short time without any ethical problems.

The survey questions were selected from instruments developed by the Cyber Security Organization in Malaysia the Excellence of Information Assurance Centre and Alelm organization in Saudi Arabia. All of the survey questions from either survey were included unless they would have been inappropriate for the Saudi culture.

The questions in this research were semi-closed ended question that combine the advantages of closed-ended questions and open-ended questions. The survey was translated into the Arabic language because the participants are all from Saudi Arabia. The initial survey was subjected to pilot testing by Saudis who were fluent English speakers to ensure both the validity of the questions and the accuracy of their translation into Arabic. Pilot test participants strongly recommended making all questions optional as they believed that many Saudis would simply stop answering the questions if they encountered a compulsory question that they did not want to answer. The survey questions were then uploaded to Survey Monkey with all questions being optional.

To ensure the high response rate, the researcher distributed an online link to the survey using popular Saudi organizations educational and business websites and IT departments staff emails. This worked well, resulting in 124 responses.

3 Results

Although there were 124 organizational participants from Saudi Arabia in this study, responses in this paper focuses on InfoSec practices in organizations.

This section discusses information assurance tools and measures in the organizations including in two-factor authentications, password practices, firewall system, anti-viruses software and Information security training for employees.

As depicted in Table 1, 82 of the 124 organizations have not implemented two-factor authentication such as smart cards, biometric or one time passwords, whereas the remaining one-third already implements two-factor authentication. Pairing of two basic authentication approaches is very well established among many organizations. However, cautioned that "although use of two-factor authentication increases the overall security by additional layer of complexity, it is important to realize that these systems are not infallible" [12].

Table 1. Implementation of two-factor authentication in organizations

Does your organization implement two factor authentication in your organization (i.e. smart-card, biometric, one time password... etc.)			
		Frequency	Percent
Valid	Yes	42	33.9 %
	No	82	66.1 %
	Total	124	100 %

Data from Table 2 revealed that 31.5 % of the organizations have poor security measures with respect to password setting on the assessment of their respondent-representatives to the present study. Meanwhile, slightly over one-fifth of the organizations have very poor procedures in setting passwords. Only 8.1 % of the organizations have very good password measures, whereas 16.9 % have good password setting security processes. On the other hand, 17.7 % chose to stay neutral regarding the issue and 4 % of the respondents reported that password setting is not practiced in their organizations. It may be observed from the framing of the item that it was the practice,

Table 2. Passwords practices in organizations

How secure is your organization process/practice in setting passwords?							
	Not Exist	Very Poor	Poor	Neutral	Good	Very Good	Total
Frequency	5	27	39	22	21	10	124
Percent	4 %	21.8 %	31.5 %	17.7 %	16.9 %	8.1 %	100 %

not the policy, which was being evaluated. As posited in [13], "password mechanisms and their users form a socio-technical system, whose effectiveness relies strongly on users' willingness to make the extra effort that security conscious behavior requires".

Table 3 revealed that most of the respondents 29.8 % stood on neutral ground with respect to the firewall systems installed in their organizations. About 33.1 % of the organizations reported that their firewall systems are good or very good, whereas 34.7 % of the organizations have poor or very poor firewall systems. Three (2.4 %) organizations do not have security firewall systems. Firewalls are one of the most crucial elements in InfoSec. The secret to the success of firewalls is the formulation and implementation of filtering rules which protect the system from unauthorized access [14].

Table 3. Firewall system in organizations

How secure is your organization Firewall system to protect against undesired access to organization servers from outside the organization?

	Not Exist	Very Poor	Poor	Neutral	Good	Very Good	Total
Frequency	3	14	29	37	25	16	124
Percent	2.4 %	11.3 %	23.4 %	29.8 %	20.2 %	12.9 %	100 %

Table 4 revealed that 43.5 % of the anti-virus software used by the organizations have good or very good performance ratings. Meanwhile 34.7 % of the organizations adopted a neutral stance regarding the anti-virus software issue. On the other hand, 19.4 % of the organizations indicated poor or very poor ratings for their anti-virus software. Anti-virus software is a crucial element of InfoSec because it serves as a solid line of defense capable of detecting and removing viruses before it causes significant harm to the system and the data stored in it [15].

Table 4. The strength of anti-virus software in organizations

How strong is your organization anti-virus software?

	Not Exist	Very Poor	Poor	Neutral	Good	Very Good	Total
Frequency	3	8	16	43	36	18	124
Percent	2.4 %	6.5 %	12.9 %	34.7 %	29 %	14.5 %	100 %

Table 5 indicated that majority of organizations (70.2 %) have not offered special InfoSec training to employees. On the other hand, 29.8 % reported offering special InfoSec training. Adequate InfoSec training for all employees is required as per InfoSec standards. Common training areas include information security awareness, asset classification and control, responding to security-related events, web access and messaging, user access control and responsibilities, legal compliance, as well as business continuity awareness and procedures [16].

Table 5. InfoSec training offered to employees in organizations

Does your organization offer special information security training to employees?			
		Frequency	Percent
Valid	Yes	37	29.8 %
	No	87	70.2 %
	Total	124	100 %

4 Conclusions and Future Research

This paper has suggested that the level of attacks may be due to a lack of Information Security (InfoSec) practices among the Saudi organizations. A survey of 124 organizations in Saudi Arabia has indicated that InfoSec practices are in fact very low and that a number of information security risks may be related to Saudi awareness or culture.

The paper has indicated that a problem exists within the IT practices of many Saudi organizations. The next phase of this research will provide appropriate solutions for the existed weaknesses and recommendation to increase the InfoSec awareness and practices in organizations in Saudi Arabia. This study will proposed the InfoSec Cultural Adaptation Process model (InfoSec CAP) as a process to inform a culturally appropriate response to this challenge.

References

1. Afyouni, H.: Database Security and Auditing: Protecting Data Integrity and Accessibility. Thomson Course, Canada (2006)
2. Bragg, R., Ousley, M., Strassberg, K.: Network Security: The Complete Reference. Coral Ventura, Newbury Park (2004)
3. Easttom, C.: Computer Security Fundamentals. Pearson Prentice Hall, New York (2006)
4. Turban, E., Wetherbe, J., McLean, E.: Information Security Technology for Management: Improving Quality and Productivity, 3rd edn. Wiley, Hoboken (1996)
5. Stallings, W., Brown, L.: Computer Security Principles and Practice. Pearson Education, New York (2008)
6. Whitman, M., Mattord, H.: Management of Information Security. Thomson Course Technology, Canada (2008)
7. Siponen, M.: A conceptual foundation for organizational: information security awareness. Inf. Manage. Comput. Secur. **8**, 31–41 (2000)
8. Kruger, H., Drvein, L., Steyn, T.: A vocabulary test to assess information security awareness. Inf. Manage. Comput. Secur. **18**, 316–327 (2010)
9. Kaspersky Security Bulletin (2011). http://www.kaspersky.com/reading_room?chapter=207716858 Accessed 3 January 2012
10. Creswell, J.: Research design: Qualitative, Quantitative, and Mixed Method Approaches. Sage Publications, California (2003)

11. Hancock, D., Algozzine, B.: Doing Case Study Research. Teachers College Press, New York (2006)
12. Furnell, S., Katsikas, S., Lopez, J., Patel, A. (eds.): Securing Information and Communication Systems: Principles, Technologies, and Applications. Artech House, Norwood (2008)
13. Weirich, D., Sasse, M.A.: Pretty good persuasion: a first step towards effective password security in the real world. In: Raskin, V., Greenwald, S.J., Timmerman, B., Kienzle, D.M. (eds.) NSPW (National Secuirty Paradigms Workshop) Proceedings of the 2001 Workshop on New Security Paradigms. Association for Computing Machinery (ACM), New York (2001). Cloudcroft, New Mexico, 10–13 September 2001
14. Al-Shaer, E.S., Hamed, H.H.: Modeling and management of firewall policies. IEEE Trans. Netw. Serv. Manage. **1**, 2–10 (2004)
15. Ferguson, B.: Network + Fast Pass. SYBEX, Alameda (2005)
16. Calder, A.: Information security training. In: Reuvid, J. (ed.) The Secure Online Business Handbook: A Practical Guide to Risk Management and Business Continuity. Kogan Page, Philadelphia (2006)

User Exploration of Search Space Using Tradeoffs

Zachi Baharav(✉) and David S. Gladstein

Cogswell Polytechnical College, 1175 Bordeaux Drive, Sunnyvale, CA, USA
{zbaharav,dgladstein}@cogswell.edu
http://www.cogswell.edu

Abstract. We describe a system for representing search results as an interactive graph, in contrast to the common static representation as an ordered list. The search terms are represented as Key-Nodes, and the results are represented as connected Record-Nodes. The user can then explore tradeoffs by assigning different importance values to Key-Nodes. We suggest algorithms for placement of Record-Nodes in the graph to ensure both smooth change of the representation in response to changes in user preferences, and clustering of results. The work was implemented using Haskell and a client-side Web interface.

Keywords: Search · Graph · Graph representation · Tradeoff

1 Introduction

With the massive amount of information available on the web, search engines are an instrumental tool in being able to find items in this haystack. The search technology has evolved significantly since the early revolution of Google search methods [Goog98a, Goog98b], yet the way the information is presented has changed very little. The most common method for displaying search results is still a linear, ordered, static list of items that match the query. There have been many suggestions for alternative representatiton methods [UIbo09, Huma11, GLO14, Comp14], but none have prevailed in the general search arena. A few of these methods found their way into specific domains, for example the representation of image search results, the representation of recommendations on specific domains such as movies and shows, related consumer items, or music. In these domain-specific cases, certain key features, such as genre and rating in the case of movies, are used to cluster the search results. Still, these methods assume that users *know* what they are looking for, and can define it well enough using the search terms and mechanism.

In this work we address the cases where users *cannot* specify exactly what they are looking for, but rather have only a vague idea, and would like to explore some results in order to refine the search process. We term these interactions *exploring the search space*, and *exploring tradeoffs*.

C. Stephanidis (Ed.): HCII 2015 Posters, Part II, CCIS 529, pp. 643–647, 2015.
DOI: 10.1007/978-3-319-21383-5_107

Let us use two specific examples to make the above difference clearer. In the first case, a user entered a search query "Napoleon birthday". The user specified well the search terms, and depending on the search engine used, the user may get a 'likely answer' at the very top of the list, followed by an indexed list of plausible references.

In our second example, a user is trying to choose a movie to watch. The user prefers it to be 'not too long', preferably a comedy, and would like it to be 'recent'. The terms used above already indicate that there are tradeoffs to explore. How much time is 'not too long'? Or how long ago is considered 'recent'? And would a 90 minute movie from 2 years ago be preferred over a 140 min movie from last month? And, though the user prefers comedy, what about a short drama (30 min) and was released only yesterday: would that be a better choice?

To address these issues, we introduce a new way to represent the results, which allows the user to interactively explore various tradeoffs in the search space. We describe the concepts, some of the design decisions, and present a working system implemented in Haskell on the Web.

2 Representation as a Network Graph

Network graphs, also referred to as Nodes-and-Link diagrams, have been used in many cases to represent search results [UIbo09]. In these graphs, search terms by the user can be represented as Key-Nodes, and the resulting search records are Record-Nodes connected to these. Clustering of the results is common, in which similarly featured records are displayed in spatially close locations [Stre05, Clas06].

The network graph representation holds, admittedly, a few hurdles to wide adoption. The first is its inability to scale comfortably to large result sets. Once there are too many nodes to display, the user has to investigate deeper to get relevant information. Various methods to deal with this issue have been offered (see [UIbo09], Chap. 10), but all require additional effort on behalf of the user.

Another issue is the connection of the results to the Key-Nodes, or the search terms. In traditional search approaches, each record is naturally connected to each of the Key-Nodes. For example, if one searched for 'Not Too Long' as one of the criteria for selecting a movie, every resultant record would be connected to a 'Movie Length' Key-Node. This does not convey real information. One of the ways to try and mitigate this is by grouping (clustering) of the records according to their length, but this has only limited benefit.

In this work we address these two issues in multiple ways. As for dealing with the possible large number of search records, we limited the number which are presented to the user each time (depending on the size of the screen). Each time the user elects to eliminate one of the records (as not a good fit), the next found record is brought into display. In addition, to avoid overloading of details within the graph, the records are labeled with numbers, and each number is described in more detail in a text box on the side of the screen. More details for a record can be retrieved by double-clicking it. For the second issue, that of all records being connected to all Key-Nodes and thus not conveying any useful information, we presented a natural sub-division of Key-Nodes, or search terms, into sub-Key-Nodes. Thus, for example, a 'Not Too Long' query will translate to one Key-Node labeled as 'Length', with three sub-Key-Nodes labeled 'Short', 'Medium', and 'Long'. Each record will be connected to one of these sub-Key-Nodes. This, together with clustering, affords the user a much faster grasp of the search space.

3 User Interaction

The user may wish to interact with the search query itself, or the results, in multiple ways. When defining the query, the user may wish to define what they mean by 'Not Too Long' of a movie. In various applications, sliders and range-values are used to define such values. These values are then used as filters to remove non-relevant data from the search results. This, in a sense, removes the ability to explore the tradeoff space. In this work, we allow the user to specify similar ranges. However, these specifications are not used as hard-limiting factors to filter the search results, but are rather used to specify the Key-Nodes (and sub-Key-Nodes), and the user can still explore changing these interactively and view their influence on the graph, clustering, and records displayed.

After defining the query, and viewing the results, we allow the user to assign different weights to the various Key-Nodes. Thus, it might be that the length of the movie is more important than the genre for the user. By changing the weight of the different Key-Nodes, the clustering and appearance of the graph (and possibly even the records displayed) would change. This is achieved by clicking on either a Key-Node or a sub-Key-Node.

4 Implemented System

One of the main concerns with the implementation is to ensure that the graph, and the representation, is not changing too dramatically with any user interaction. This is very important to the user's ability to remember the graph results and understand them [Memo12]. To address this, we implemented smooth transition between states of display, so the user has context when things are moving around. In addition, unlike force based methods which are based on running simulation/model to determine the new location of records, in our implementation the location of records (and Key-Nodes) is determined analytically. Thus, we can guarantee continuity of location as a function of, for example, the weight of the various search terms.

The system itself was implemented on various platforms (Matlab, Haskell+Web, d3.js) to experiment in different ways. A demo system will be shared in the talk.

5 Future Directions

As with any user-centered application, the main test is receiving user feedback. To this aim, we are planning to make this system available online for users. The system will initially be tailored to specific domains (movie selection, job search, vacation search, *etc.*), where tailoring the Key-Nodes and settings are easiest.

Another important direction is adapting this concept to small screens. Many of the search interactions today are done on mobile devices with limited screen space. Presenting graphs on small screens presents another challenge.

Figures 1, 2, 3 and 4 are from an earlier version of the interface, but serve to demonstrate the impact of changing the importance (or weight) of Key-Nodes on the layout of the resulting graph.(Video and demo available).

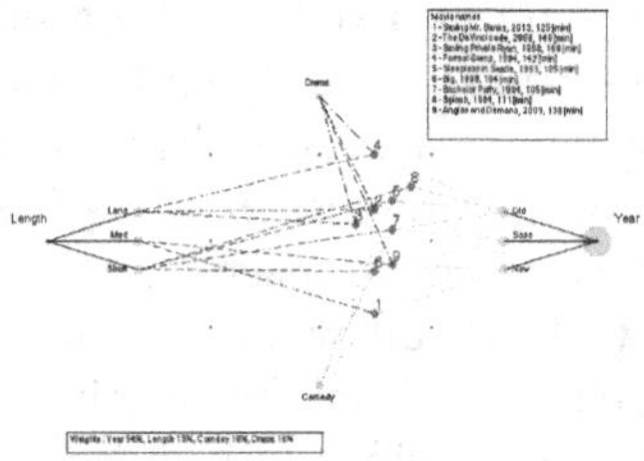

Fig. 1. Year 54 %, Length 13 %

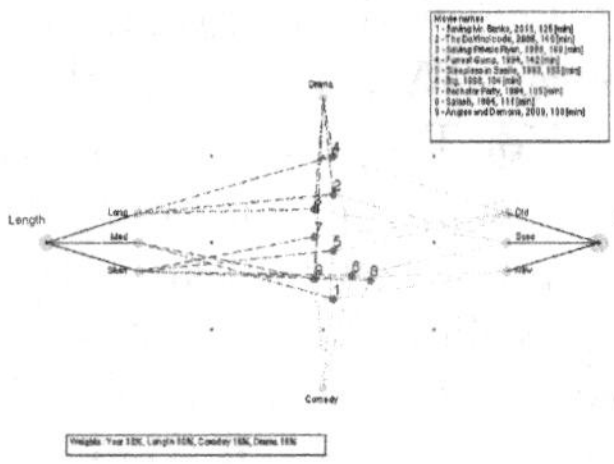

Fig. 2. Year 38 %, Length 30 %

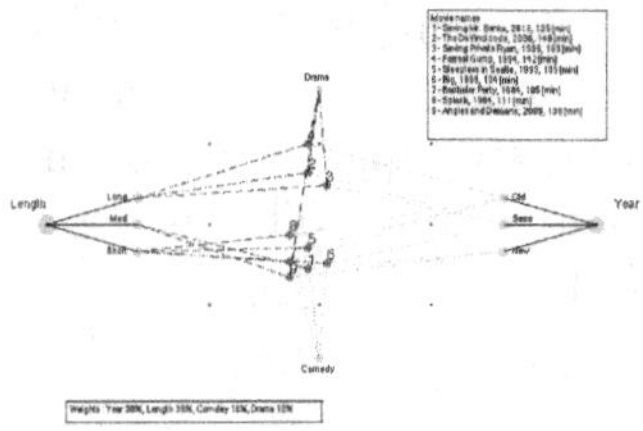

Fig. 3. Year 30 %, Length 38 %

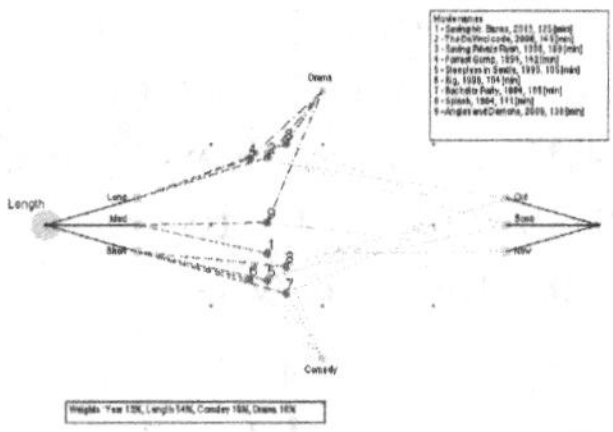

Fig. 4. Year 13 %, Length 54 %

References

[Goog98a] Brin, S., Page, L.: The anatomy of a large-scale hypertextual web search engine. Comput. Netw. ISDN Syst. **30**(1), 107–117 (1998)

[Goog98b] Page, L., Brin, S., Rajeev, M., Terry, W.: The PageRank Citation Ranking: Bringing Order to the Web. Stanford University, Technical report (1998)

[Stre05] Gansner, E.R., Koren, Y., North, S.C.: Graph drawing by stress majorization. In: Pach, J. (ed.) GD 2004. LNCS, vol. 3383, pp. 239–250. Springer, Heidelberg (2005)

[Clas06] Dwyer, T., Koren, Y., Marriott, K.: IPSep-CoLa: an incremental procedure for separation constraint layout of graphs. IEEE Trans. Vis. Comput. Graph. **12**(5), 821–828 (2006)

[UIbo09] Hearst, M.A.: Search User Interfaces. Cambridge University Press, (2009). Also available on the web http://searchuserinterfaces.com/book/

[Huma11] Parameswaran, A., et al.: Human-assisted graph search: it's okay to ask questions. Proc. VLDB Endowment **4**(5), 267–278 (2011)

[Memo12] Marriott, K., Purchase, H., Wybrow, M., Goncu, C.: Memorability of visual features in network diagrams. IEEE Trans. Vis. Comput. Graph. **18**(12), 2477–2485 (2012)

[GLO14] Stolper, C.D., Kahng, M., Lin, Z., Foerster, F., Goel, A., Horng, D.: GLOs: Graph-level operations for exploratory network visualization. In: CHI 2014 Extended Abstracts on Human Factors in Computing Systems, pp. 1375–1380. ACM (2014)

[Comp14] Dwyer, T., Mears, C., Morgan, K., Niven, T., Marriott, K., Wallace, M.: Improved optimal and approximate power graph compression for clearer visualization of dense graphs. In: Pacific Visualization Symposium (PacificVis), pp. 105–112. IEEE (2014)

Usability Evaluation of the Smart TV

Wen-Te Chang[1(✉)], Kuo-Chen Huang[2], and Ching-Chang Chuang[2]

[1] Department of Arts and Design, National Taipei University of Education, Taipei, Taiwan
mimi@mail.mcu.edu.tw
[2] Department of Product Design, Ming-Chuan University, Taipei, Taiwan
{kuochen, ccchuang}@mail.mcu.edu.tw

Abstract. The development of Smart TV creates better quality of life. However, only few previous studies provided the experimental results or suggestions on the usability and satisfaction of the interface designs. There were 72 participants. The subjects were intended-random recruited depending on sex (36 male and 36 female), and age (24 senior and 48 young) factors. The study result indicated that a three-way interactive effect among age, topology and task complexity was found to be significant, especially on the senior and linear topological interface condition (the difference of easy and middle level tasks eliminated). The study result benefit the study related to the interactive effect on the age, topology and task complexity.

Keywords: Smart TV · Interface evaluation

1 Introduction

As numerical and information technology developing progressively, human being are confronting an age of information society. With safety, communication, entertainment, and internet service technology, diversely applications has been extended from individual personal device to family life experience service. Thus the operations system transformed from separately devices to integrated effective and user-centered approach. Take smart home as an example, TV set is no longer a simple visual-audio consumer product, but a key interface for people's daily life (Bull and Rayne 2004; Bin and Gavriel 2009). Nevertheless, smart TV is mainly account on the two critical technologies, namely smart man-computer interactive interface and internet. To provide a simple interface with integrated multiple function network is the goal for all smart TV research and development institute. In this study, we design and evaluate the smart TV interface, hoping to present a preliminary model for the related research and industry.

1.1 Smart TV

As Fig. 1 shows, smart TV not only possesses the internet function which is compatible with PC or touch panel device, but also provides smart control of house-keeping and electrical product including air condition, lighting, washing machine, refrigerator etc.… To support the above multiple functions, a new control device that can shift among

C. Stephanidis (Ed.): HCII 2015 Posters, Part II, CCIS 529, pp. 648–652, 2015.
DOI: 10.1007/978-3-319-21383-5_108

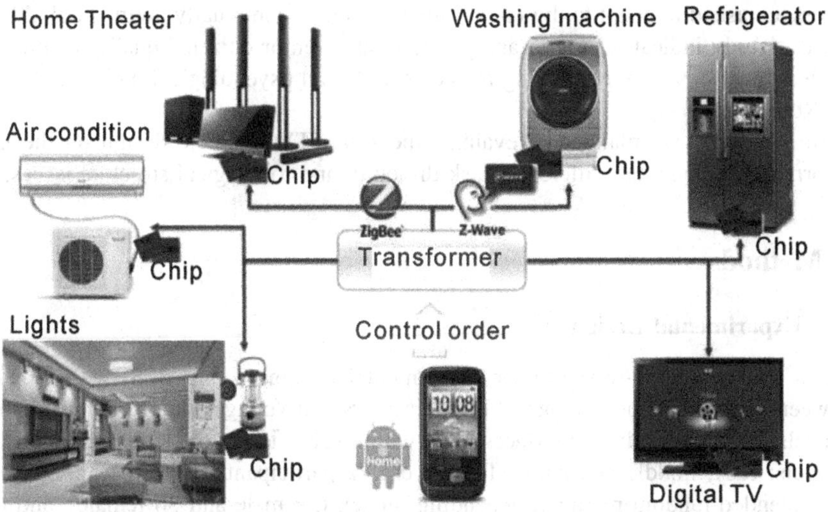

Fig. 1. System devices of the smart TV (source: Institute for Information Industry 2011)

device modes and functions is needed to replace the traditional TV remote control. This new control interface shall have to integrate new function modes such as hot-key, pointing curser, keyboard and monitoring display to enhance the operation effectiveness and efficiency. However, the evaluation of the interface on the usability issues remained to be testified (Sears et al. 2010; Simon et al. 2013).

1.2 Topological Structures

There are two common topological structures in interface layout design, linear and network structures (Chang and Chen 2011). A linear topology is essentially characterized by its linear links where the user can be well guided under such a rigid structure (i.e., less disorientation). In contrast, a network structure provides users with all the functions and layouts on the same user interface, enabling users to visualize them all at one time. Users can "jump" to different functions or units by using hypertext features. Previous studies had attempted to find the best hypertext topology by comparing. These studies were hypothesized based on the theory of spatial metaphor (Chang et al. 2011). It was believed that user behavior in hypertext perusal is similar to the spatial processing in a physical environment. However, they have been divided as to which topological structure is easier to use and best enhances navigation. Chang and Chen (2011) argued that task difficulty and high cognitive load are two major reasons for this uncertainty.

1.3 Individual Difference Effect

Most digital interface is designed to increase convenience and comfort of Human being life, however, it was noted that technological advancement did make the new inventions harder to operate and use by the seniors. As most designs neglected age effects, seniors are asked to adapt to digital consumer products continually (Wirtz et al. 2009). Previous study indicated, due to aging deteriorates senior citizens' quality of life and physical functions were facilitating increased falls and psychological problems (Evans and Rowlands 2004).

In this study we planned to evaluate the smart TV interface design on the task performance among age difference, task difficulty and topological structure issues.

2 Methods

2.1 Experimental Design

In this study, a three-mixed-factor experimental design (2 × 2 × 3) was adopted. Between-subjects factors are age (2 levels: seniors and younger), topological structure (2 levels: linear and mixed-interfaces), and within subject factor is the task complexity (3 levels: easy, middle and hard). There were 72 participants. Note that the subjects were intended-random recruited depending on sex (36 male and 36 female), and age (24 senior and 48 young) factors.

2.2 Topology

Two topological interface designs, namely linear (Fig. 2) and network (Fig. 3) interfaces were proposed with the same modes, function and graphic design after repetitive pilot tests.

2.3 Procedure

All documents were run on ASUS TF101 and were displayed on a 271x176.8x12.98 mm LCD color monitor. The resolution was 1280 × 720 pixels at a frame rate of 85 Hz.

After the participants had become familiar with the interface design, the experiment formally began. Each task was explained on a paper sheet, and the participants followed the list order to complete the navigational tasks. Participants were required to

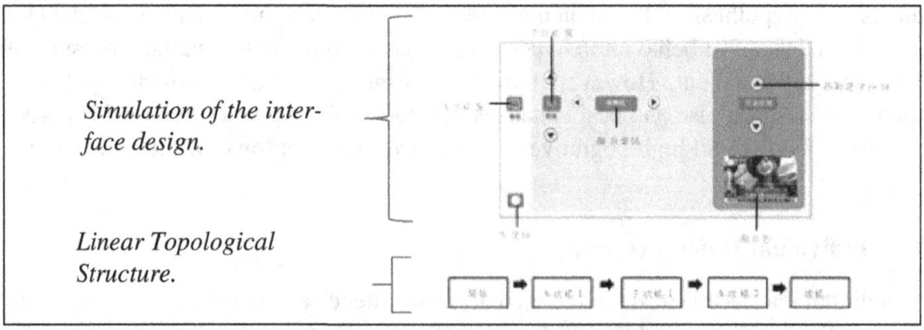

Fig. 2. Linear topological interface design of the smart TV

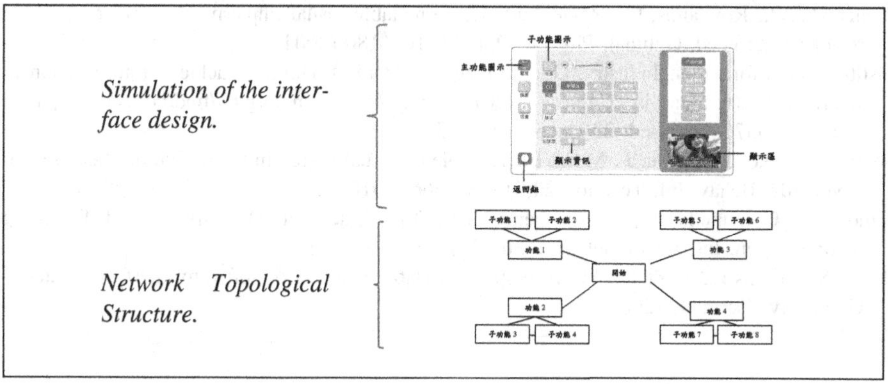

Fig. 3. Network topological interface design of the smart TV

complete all of the interaction tasks. The full experiment lasted approximately 1 h for each of the participant.

3 Result and Conclusion

The result indicated that a three-way interactive effect among age, topology and task complexity was found to be significant, especially on the senior and linear topological interface condition (the difference of easy and middle level tasks eliminated). The study result benefit the study related to the interactive effect on the age, topology and task complexity.

Acknowledgement. Financial support of this research study by National Science Council under the grant MOST 103-2420-H-130-006 -MY2 is gratefully acknowledged. Special thanks to graduated student, Tsung-Wei Chiu, for his assistance on execution of experiment.

References

Bin, Z., Gavriel, S.: Design and evaluation of smart home user interface: effects of age, tasks and intelligence level. Behav. Inf. Technol. **3**(28), 239–249 (2009)

Bull, R.L., Rayne, P.: Pervasive home environment. BT Technol. J. **22**(3), 65–72 (2004)

Cesar, P., Jansen, J.: Leveraging user impact: an architecture for secondary screens usage in interactive television. Multimed. Syst. J. **15**(3), 127–142 (2009)

Chang, W.-T., Chen, C.-H.: The effects of topology and task complexity on digital-speech-desktop interface design and evaluation. J. Soc. Inform. Disp. **19**(10), 700–705 (2011)

Chang, W.-T., Huang, K.-C., Lin, C.-L.: On the factors of the webpage navigational performance. In: Proceedings of the IADIS in International Conference Interfaces and Human Computer Interaction, July 24–26, Organized by IADIS International Association for Development of the Information Society, pp. 447–451 (ISBN: 978-972-8939-52-6) (in Digit file) (2011)

Evans, B.J.W., Rowlands, G.: Review article. correctable visual impairment in older people: a major unmet need. Ophthal. Physiol. Opt. **24**, 161–180 (2004)
Institute for Information Industry. Google using Android @ Home to achieve future vision of smart TV, (written in Chinese) (2011). http://www.find.org.tw/find/home.aspx?page=news&id=6376 Accessed: 23 December 2013
Sears, A., Jacko, J.A., Chu, J., Moro, F.: The role of visual search in the design of effective soft keyboards. Behav. Inf. Technol. **20**(3), 159–166 (2010)
Simon, H., Comunello, E., Wangenheim, A.V.: Enrichment of interactive digital TV using second screen. Int. J. Comput. Appl. **64**(22), 58–64 (2013)
Wirtz, S., Jakobs E.M., Ziefle, M.: Age-specific usability issues of software interfaces. Aachen University, Germany (2009)

Usability of the Submission Process in a Journal System

Ronnie Fagundes de Brito(✉) and Milton Shintaku

Instituto Brasileiro de Informação Em Ciência E Tecnologia,
IBICT, Brasília, Brazil
{ronniebrito, shintaku}@ibict.br

Abstract. Electronic open access journals are adopted by many Brazilian institutions, with over 1600 journals developed with the Open Journal System (OJS) at various universities. In this scenario, the submission process of article's documents in this system becomes focal point for usability analysis, because it is the step that constitutes the initial stage of interaction of various users profiles. Thus, this study aims to measure the level of satisfaction of the authors who submit manuscripts to OJS, with the aim of contributing to studies of this system. Therefore, a survey is presented using the System Usability Scale questionnaire. Satisfaction criteria are evaluated with the submission process by authors of a university journal portal. Results show that OJS appears intuitive, however some difficulties can be identifying in the process, even if the overall evaluation of the system is good. The study contributes to the discussion on the usability of OJS, aimed at improving this system that is widely used in Brazil.

Keywords: System usability survey · Open Journal Systems

1 Usability Analysis of Scientific Publication Systems

Scientific journals with access on the internet require online tools that guarantee performance and satisfaction to its users, especially in tasks associated with publishing scientific papers, as author submission, peer review and publication of digital documents. Some intermediate tasks, restricted to users with defined roles, sometimes present difficulties in implementation.

The submission tasks consist of filling out forms with metadata about the submitted document, sending the file of the paper and any other files with data underlying the conclusions or that were obtained during the research that will be published. However, the author submission task, in some magazines, include steps related to the journal's policies, issues that ensure ethical points and other items that can be misleading.

Large part of current software for automating the publishing process perform in a similar way, especially in the peer review procedures, but can be differentiated into more specific aspects. Given the variety of systems for the publication of scientific journals, this study is restricted to the analysis of the submission process in the Open Journal Systems (OJS) software, due to its wide use in open access journals, as pointed by [1], who considers it as the main software for the implementation of open access journals.

C. Stephanidis (Ed.): HCII 2015 Posters, Part II, CCIS 529, pp. 653–656, 2015.
DOI: 10.1007/978-3-319-21383-5_109

The continuous analysis of processes automated by computerized tools supports software's improvement, even being widely used, this system still can provide better interaction between the author and the article submission task. Usability analysis contributes to developments more contextualized with user's needs.

2 Methods

The study has quantitative and qualitative aspects, and is applied to verify the usability of OJS document submission process. We used the survey technique with a System Usability Scale (SUS) questionnaire, contextualized to the paper submission task. The questionnaire was developed in Google-docs and sent to 350 authors of the University of Brasilia (UNB) journals portal.

The Software Usability Measurement Inventory (SUMI) questionnaire [2] evaluates five aspects of user satisfaction in relation to a system:

- Efficiency: indicates whether the software enables the task to be done quickly, effectively and economically;
- Affection: is the psychological dimension that arises during the interaction, indicating whether the user feel mentally stimulated to use the system.
- Utility: refers to the perception of the user and the system utility;
- Control: indicates how much the user is who controls the system operation flow, not being controlled by the system but controlling the system;
- Learning: the ease with which one can learn to use the system features.

This questionnaire is applied in the analysis of an educational website [3], however, due to the amount of questions (50), we chose to use the SUS with only 10 questions in a likert scale [4]. The SUS survey was developed as part of a usability engineering program of Digital Equipment Co. Ltd, UK. It is recommended that the questionnaire to be applied right after the user interaction with the system, but in this case the questionnaire was sent at a period later of the interaction. At the end of questionnaire a text field was added to allow considerations, bringing wider samples of user's opinions.

3 Results

The SUS questionnaire was answered by 179 OJS authors, returning a score 68, in a 0 to 100 numerical scale. This score, in an adjectival scale, can be analyzed as between OK and good, where values below 25 are 'worst imaginable' and above 85 is excellent [5]. Thus, presents evidence of a good adaption of the OJS submission process and intuitiveness of the steps for users.

The distribution shown in Fig. 1 histogram highlights two user groups, one presenting good interaction (65 to 71.5) and one with less ease of operation (45.5 to 52). However, confirming the general indicator, most authors consider the software easy to use, inasmuch as there is a certain concentration above 65.

Analyzing the responses by applying the Expectation Maximization clustering algorithm over the scores obtained, one can identify two main groups of users: a group

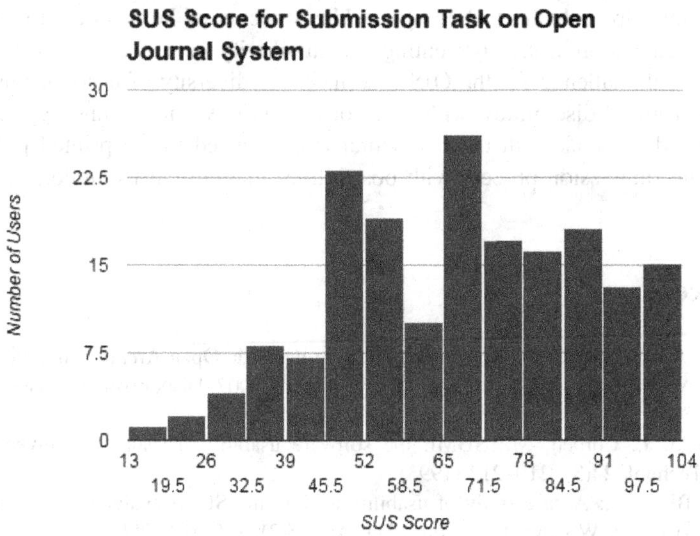

Fig. 1. SUS score histogram

of 142 users, with an average score of 94 and standard deviation of 5, and the other with 37 users with an average of 62 and a standard deviation of 17. This do not indicate consensus among users, but do not have significant evidence to suggest low ratings, only medium and high satisfaction.

Grouping users through k-means algorithm, in turn, led to two groups: a group of 100 users with median score in 53 (good) and another group of 79 users with median score of 87 (best imaginable). it was confirmed the scenario in which most users consider very intuitive OJS of the submission process, but with the possibility of improvement.

The analysis, under more qualitative approach, by the comments obtained presents other perceptions of OJS. This analysis allows to note aspects that quantitative data do not reveal. Initially it was noted that the computing environment in which OJS is made available influences on the system's satisfaction. The same way, some users suggests improvement in the submission process with respect to the interaction between the author and editor, by means of automatic mails.

4 Final Remarks

Journal systems can be analyzed for ergonomic criteria, from which are listed elements that can be improved in new versions of the system [6]. The score hit by OJS and the lack of consensus among users demonstrates that there are elements to be improved in the system through the application of ergonomic criteria to better driving user in the submission task.

For future studies, we suggest analyzing OJS usability according to disciplines categorization of users. It is supposed that more technical disciplines scholars have closer relationship with the technology, while students of humanities use less technology in their research, thus presenting less familiarity.

The current challenge for the OJS is to meet the diversity of users of this system, with users from all disciplines, with more or less affinity with technology. The same way you need to break with the behavioral traces related to the printed publication, adjusting the submission process with possibilities that current technology can offer.

References

1. Baptista, A.A., et al.: Comunicação científica : o papel da Open Archives Initiative no contexto do Acesso Livre. Encontros Bibli n. esp., 1° sem. 2007. Disponível em: . Acesso em: 17 mar. 2013
2. Kirakowski, J., Corbett, M.: SUMI: the software usability measurement inventory. Brit. J. Edu. Technol. **24**(3), 210–212 (1993)
3. Arh, T., Blazic, J.: A case study of usability testing: the SUMI evaluation approach of the EducaNext portal. WSEAS Trans. Info. Sci. App. **5**(2), 175–181 (2008)
4. Borsci, S., Federici, S., Lauriola, M.: On the dimensionality of the system usability scale: a test of alternative measurement models. Cogn. Process. **10**(3), 193–197 (2009). doi:10.1007/s10339-009-0268-9
5. Bangor, A., Kortum, P., Miller, J.: Determining what individual SUS scores mean: adding an adjective rating scale. J. Usability Stud. **4**(3), 114–123 (2009)
6. Oliveria, E.R.: Avaliação Ergonômica de Interfaces da SciELO – Scientific Electronic Library Online. Dissertação (Mestrado em Engenharia de Produção) - Programa de Pós-Graduação em Engenharia de Produção, UFSC, Florianópolis (2001)

Survey on Copyright Infringement of Digital Contents: A Case Study of Japanese University Students

Rieko Inaba(✉) and Remi Yamazaki

Department of Computer Science, Tsuda College, Kodaira, Japan
inaba@tsuda.ac.jp

Abstract. This study clarified the actual use of infringed content for university students in Japan using a survey on the target video and audio contents. In this study, the following became clear. (1) The use of digital content has been pervasive. The demand for music-related content is high. (2) Most users watch and listen to digital contents without consideration for copyright infringement. Indeed, users indicated feeling no guilt and concern for the risks involved when accessing infringed materials. These results show that many users lack a proper understanding of copyright laws.

Keywords: Copyright infringement · Digital contents · Japanese university students

1 Introduction

In recent years, the spread of smartphones and tablet devices has further increased Internet connectivity. Among users in Japan, a major purpose for the Internet is to "obtain and listen to digital content for free", which accounts for 18 % of home Internet use and 10 % of use outside the home. By age, users in their 20s comprise about 25 % of all users, including those at home and outside, and outnumber users from other generations [1].

Given the above, copyright infringement on the Internet has become a major problem in Japan. In fiscal year 2010, the Ministry of Economy, Trade and Industry commissioned a study that aimed to shed light on infringed contents, such as the mass uploading of pirated videos on video-sharing sites [2]. A similar survey conducted in 2012 revealed a list of storage[1] and reach sites[2] [3].

After the revision of the copyright law in 2009, downloading illegally uploaded music and movies became forbidden. However, this law was not sufficient to limit such activity. Thus, in 2012, the government enacted a new copyright law, which criminalized private downloading. According to a survey from the Ministry of Economy, Trade and Industry in 2011, illegal digital contents are uploaded on video-sharing services, such as YouTube[3] and Dailymotion[4]. Further, the spread of the smartphone

[1] Storage sites are websites containing infringed content.
[2] Reach sites direct users to infringed content.
[3] http://www.youtube.com/.
[4] http://www.dailymotion.com/.

C. Stephanidis (Ed.): HCII 2015 Posters, Part II, CCIS 529, pp. 657–660, 2015.
DOI: 10.1007/978-3-319-21383-5_110

has provided users with easier access to digital contents in terms of geographic location.

This study aims to shed light on the end user's situation as regards accessing illegal digital contents. A questionnaire survey is conducted, followed by interviews, targeting university students in Japan.

2 Survey Overview

2.1 Subjects of the Questionnaire

The respondents were university students in Japan. They were chosen for the following reasons. First, university students routinely use digital content. Second, users in their 20s statistically use more free content compared with those from other generations. The Web questionnaire was administered with the help of professors from 10 universities from June to July 2013. The total number of valid responses was 582 (males: 314, females: 268).

2.2 Content of the Questionnaire

This study conducted a survey on actual usage of digital content and awareness of copyright infringement.

(1) Viewing status of digital content
How much is the digital content usage of university students? What types of video and audio content do they use?
(2) Awareness of copyright infringement
Are they aware of the concept of copyright infringement, in which end users watch illegally sourced digital content?

3 Survey Results

3.1 Viewing Status of Digital Content

The results showed that 87.1 % of the subjects accessed video content or audio files on the Internet at the utilization ratio of 72.4 % (435 people) for video content and 45.4 % (264 people) for audio files.

The chi-square test indicated a statistically significant relationship between the type of content and device (Table 1). Indeed, the type of content accessed differed according to the device used. However, both video and audio file types were downloaded at nearly similar rates. The results showed that 42.8 % of the respondents had experienced downloading video content, whereas 49.6 % had downloaded audio files.

As for the content categories, "music promotion videos" were the most common video content accessed regardless of device used (76.0 % of users via the PC and 78.0 % of users via tablet devices). The second most common category was "live movie". Thus, these two types of music-related digital content have a high demand.

Table 1. Content usage by device.

Device	Video content (n = 435)	Audio files (n = 264)
PC	167 (38.4 %)	134 (50.8 %)
Tablet and smartphone	27 (6.2 %)	13 (4.9 %)
Both	241 (55.4 %)	117 (44.3 %)

Similarly, the category "music files" was the most common content type accessed regardless of device used; 93.6 % of users via the PC and 91.5 % of users via tablet devices had downloaded audio files. Therefore, audio files have a high demand compared with other music-related files.

3.2 Awareness of Copyright Infringement

To determine awareness of copyright infringement, this research investigated whether the content accessed by users is provided by an official or informal source. Table 2 shows the results.

Table 2. Awareness of copyright infringement

(a) PC

	Video contents (n=408)	Audio files (n=251)
Official only	83 (20.3%)	62 (24.7%)
Official and informal	196 (48.0%)	118 (47.0%)
Not sure	129 (31.6%)	71 (28.3%)

(b) Mobile device

	Video contents (n=168)	Audio files (n=130)
Official only	63 (23.5%)	37 (28.5%)
Official and informal	123 (45.9%)	55 (42.3%)
Not sure	82 (30.6%)	38 (29.2%)

Regardless of the content type and device, "official and informal" and "not sure" had total usage rates of over 70 %. In other words, many end users use digital content without worrying about copyright infringement.

To delve deeper into the investigation of awareness, the study included interviews with six university students. The results indicated that students tended to bear no guilt and recognition of the risks with respect to the use of infringed content. The following are sample responses:

- I clearly do not understand the copyright law.
- I do not feel the impact of copyright laws; I do not worry about the risks.

4 Discussion

The survey results helped illuminate the awareness of university students regarding content usage on the Internet. The questionnaire investigated students' access to digital content. The search keywords for video content viewing has nine types, namely, "video", "video category", "artist name", "video-sharing site name", "title of content", "story number", "free", "viewing", and "summary". Users search content using a combination of these keywords. Further, "free" is often used as a keyword. For audio files, the keyword "free" is also commonly used. This search behavior indicates the expectation of users to view digital content for free. This aspect was discussed in the interview with six university students. They mentioned the following points:

- We do not want to watch all types of content for free.
- We do not think that should be all types of content are provided for free.

In other words, users consciously select free content (infringed content) and paid content (official content). Nonetheless, they do not hesitate to pay the fee to view a high interest-impressed content. However, for low interest-impressed content, they prefer to view for free through searching for free access on the Internet. This attitude is a significant aspect of the viewing habit for infringed contents.

5 Conclusion

This study clarified the actual use of infringed content for university students in Japan using a survey on the target video and audio contents. In this study, the following became clear.

(1) The use of digital content has been pervasive. The demand for music-related content is high.
(2) Most users watch and listen to digital contents without consideration for copyright infringement. Indeed, users indicated feeling no guilt and concern for the risks involved when accessing infringed materials.

These results show that many users lack a proper understanding of copyright laws. Hence, copyright education is an urgent issue.

Acknowledgments. We are thankful to fruitful discussion with Professor Kashiko Kodate of Photonic System Solutions Inc.

References

1. White paper on Information and Communications in Japan, Ministry of Public Management, Home Affairs, Posts and Telecommunications. http://www.soumu.go.jp/johotsusintokei/whitepaper/h25.html
2. Anti-piracy reinforcement project 2010, Ministry of Economy. http://www.meti.go.jp/meti_lib/report/2010fy01/E000895.pdf (in Japanese)
3. Anti-piracy reinforcement project 2012, Ministry of Economy. http://www.meti.go.jp/meti_lib/report/2012fy/E002243.pdf (in Japanese)

A Branch-Type Slider and its Application

Makio Ishihara[1(✉)], Erika Koriyama[1], and Yukio Ishihara[2]

[1] Fukuoka Institute of Technology, 3-30-1 Wajiro-higashi, Higashi-ku, Fukuoka 811-0295, Japan
m-ishihara@fit.ac.jp
http://www.fit.ac.jp/~mishihara/Lab/

[2] Kyushu University, 3-1-1, Maidashi, Higashi-ku, Fukuoka 812-8582, Japan
iyukio@redoxnavi.med.kyushu-u.ac.jp
http://hyoka.ofc.kyushu-u.ac.jp/search/details/K004222/english.html

Abstract. This manuscript proposes a branch-type slider for indoor navigation and builds a proof-of-concept system, and conducts an experiment in usability. A branch-type slider is a horizontal bar that divides into multiple sub-bars. The result shows that the branch-type slider can be applied to indoor navigation if the user interface is carefully designed.

Keywords: Branch-type sliders · Indoor navigation · Mobile application · Interface design

1 Introduction

Indoor navigation is one of the challenging topics in the field of human computer interaction. Generally, navigation is required to precisely locate the user and navigate him/her through the destination. To locate the user on the earth, the global positioning system or GPS is commonly used. The error ration of GPS is however tremendously large. It is about ~5 meters, so GPS does not work properly for indoor navigation because the scale of corridors and stairs, doors and other things in a building is less than 5 meters. Indoor navigation needs another approach to locate the user.

There are some researches on indoor navigation. For example, Anzai, K. et al.[1] built a system that exploits the number of footsteps of the user, which are tracked by an acceleration sensor, and predicts the distance that the user walks. Nakazato, Y. et al.[2] built a system that uses a handheld camera that is attached on the top of the user's head. The camera captures the ceiling and recognizes the positons of fluorescent lights. Referring to the layout map of fluorescent lights, the system locates the user. The mainstream of those traditional systems or approaches is to figure out what way is effective to locate the user precisely in a building. The main drawback of those approaches is the prediction error caused by sensor noises and camera image noises.

There is another approach to indoor navigation. Google Street View is a good example. In the system, the user can move forward/backward or turn left/right

C. Stephanidis (Ed.): HCII 2015 Posters, Part II, CCIS 529, pp. 661–664, 2015.
DOI: 10.1007/978-3-319-21383-5_111

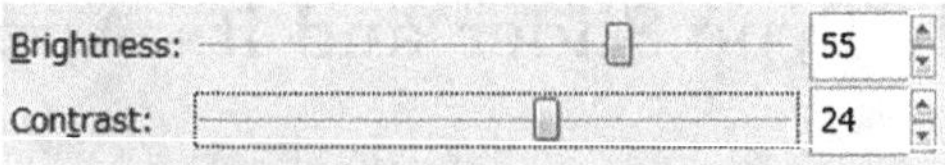

Fig. 1. A common slider.

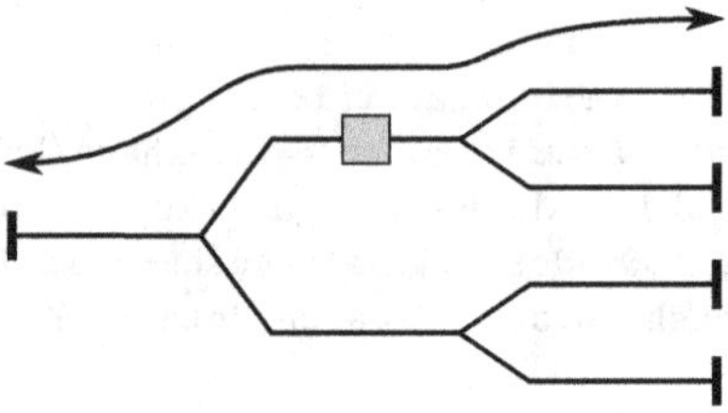

Fig. 2. A branch-type slider.

freely in an augmented virtual world. By doing this, the user is able to build a mental model of the 3D map and picture the way to the destination intuitively. This approach can be easily applied to indoor navigation because it does not need to locate the user in a building. The main drawback of the approach however stems from the style of controls. To move from the start to the destination, the user has to point at the next spot to go. This way hinders the user from learning the progress of navigation from the start to the destination, which plays an important role in picturing the way to the destination in a mental model of the 3D map correctly.

To solve this problem, this manuscript proposes an indoor navigation system with a branch-type slider. A slider has two sides of a start and an end, and the user can move the knob between them. It is expected that the user learns the progress of navigation intuitively from the current position of the knob.

2 A Branch-Type Slider

A slider is a graphical control element with a knob that indicates the current value. The user can move it forward and backward to adjust the value. Sliders are often used to set the level of speaker volume, display brightness, image effects and other things. Figure 1 shows the look of a common slider to set image brightness and image contrast.

A slider is commonly a horizontal bar on which a knob runs. This manuscript proposes a branch-type slider. It is a horizontal bar that divides into multiple sub-bars. Figure 2 shows a branch-type slider that has a single start and four ends, and two forks between them. This manuscript demonstrates an in-campus navigation system using a branch-type slider. Users can choose which path to take at each fork to navigate them.

Figure 3 shows the design of a branch-type slider for our in-campus navigation system that works on a smartphone. This slider starts at the bottom to the

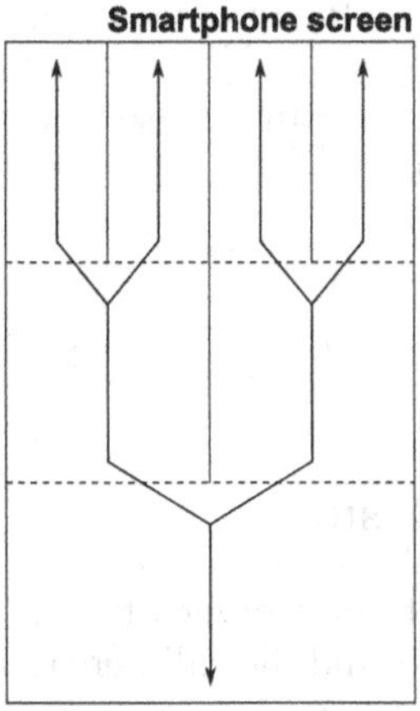

Fig. 3. Design of a branch-type slider for in-campus navigation.

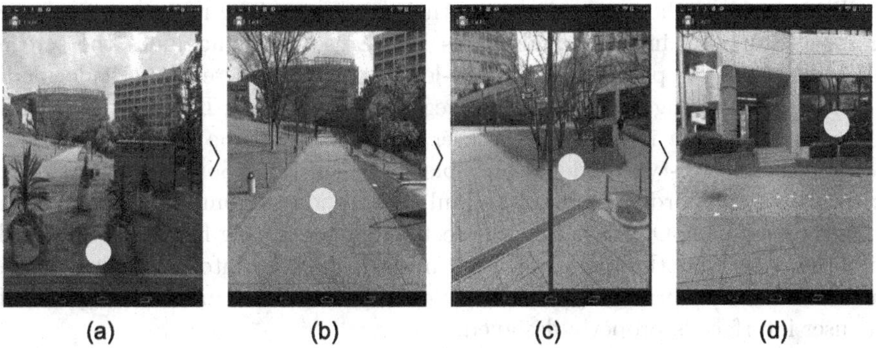

Fig. 4. Demonstrations.

four ends at the top. The screen is divided into seven regions that form the slider. When the user drags his/her fingertip across the dotted line between those regions, the corresponding fork will be selected and the navigation image will be displayed on the screen.

3 Demostrations

Figure 4 is a series of screenshots. The fingertip's position is represented by a gray dot on the screen. The user walks in the university's main gate (a) and takes the main path to the buildings (b), and goes to the right fork to the building C (c, d). When the user meets a fork of the path, a rectangle appears on the screen visually to support the user to choose which fork to take. The position of the rectangle switches between left and right depending on the fingertip's position.

Table 1. Result of the experiment.

Questions	Strongly bad	Bad	Neutral	Yes	Strongly yes
Did you feel your finger hinders you from seeing the screen?	1	1	2	1	1
Was it easy to manipulate?	1	4	1	0	0
Was it easy to take forks?	1	2	0	0	3

4 Experiment and Result

A brief experiment in usability of a branch-type slider for navigation was conducted. There were six subjects and they all were right-handed. Each subject was asked to use our in-campus navigation system for a period of time and answer some questions about usability with a scale with five levels of strongly bad to strongly yes.

Table 1 shows those questions and their responses. The responses from the first question vary in individuals. This is because the hand hides the screen when the subject is pointing at the top-left region of the screen and it does not when he/she is doing at the top-right region of the screen. The responses from the second question imply that the user interface has to be improved. This is because the branch-type slider is invisible to the subjects. Some visual cues like arrows, lines and borders might be helpful. The responses from the third question go into two groups. One says that the rectangle representing forks is helpful and the other says that the rectangle could mislead the user into perceiving it is a button. Overall, a branch-type slider has the potential for indoor navigation if the user interface is properly designed.

5 Conclusions

This manuscript proposed a branch-type slider for indoor navigation and built a proof-of-concept system, and conducted an experiment in usability. A branch-type slider is a horizontal bar that divides into multiple sub-bars. The result showed that the branch-type slider can be applied to indoor navigation if the user interface is carefully designed.

In the future work, we are going to discuss how a branch-type slider is integrated into the screen without any visual feedbacks.

References

1. Anzai, K., Okajima, S. and Tsubokawa, H.: The estimate of the indoor position that used a smartphone and the suggestion of the walk navigation system. Proc. of the DICOMO2011, 921–927 (2011)
2. Nakazato, Y., Kanbara, M. and Yokoya, N.: A quantitative evaluation of wearable AR system using invisible visual markers in real environments. Proc. of the MIRU2005, 1420–1427 (2005)

Airbrush Metaphor and its Application

Makio Ishihara[1(✉)], Yuta Nakazaki[1], and Yukio Ishihara[2]

[1] Fukuoka Institute of Technology, 3-30-1 Wajiro-higashi, Higashi-ku, Fukuoka 811-0295, Japan
m-ishihara@fit.ac.jp,
http://www.fit.ac.jp/~m-ishihara/Lab/

[2] Kyushu University, 3-1-1, Maidashi Higashi-ku, Fukuoka 811-0295, Japan
iyukio@redoxnavi.med.kyushu-u.ac.jp,
http://hyoka.ofc.kyushu-u.ac.jp/search/details/K004222/english.html

Abstract. This manuscript proposes a way of coordinating a schedule with airbrush metaphor and builds a proof-of-concept system. Its design and a brief demonstration are presented, and an experiment in usability is conducted. The result shows that the airbrush metaphor is capable of expressing ambiguity of schedules and effectively applied to a way of coordinating a schedule.

Keywords: Airbrush metaphor · Schedule coordination · Web application · Interface design

1 Introduction

Coordinating a schedule is a task for people often to perform when they are going to arrange meetings, seminars and other things. For example, a secretary asks the members to post their favorite dates and times, and he/she looks for the most overlapped time span between their dates and times. In everyday life, families do the same task when they go on their family trips or even when they go for dinner. It is a very common task.

To facilitate the task, there are various applications available these days. Doodle is a good example of those applications. Figure 1 shows a screenshot of Doodle. It is a web-based application where an organizer can make an event with some candidates of dates and time spans, and the participants can post their favorite dates and time spans by selecting one from three options of **Yes**, **Maybe** and **No** on each of the candidates. After they post, the application will choose the best date and time span to which much more **Yess** and **Maybes** have been posted. Chosei-san and Cho-suke are other good examples. Generally, the procedure of coordinating a schedule using those applications is almost the same. The participants select one of options and post it repeatedly for each of the candidates. In the user interface side, these applications use check-boxes, radio-buttons or hyperlinks as an input method.

One of the improvements to these applications is to increase the variety of options for participants to express ambiguity of their schedules. There are, for

C. Stephanidis (Ed.): HCII 2015 Posters, Part II, CCIS 529, pp. 665–669, 2015.
DOI: 10.1007/978-3-319-21383-5_112

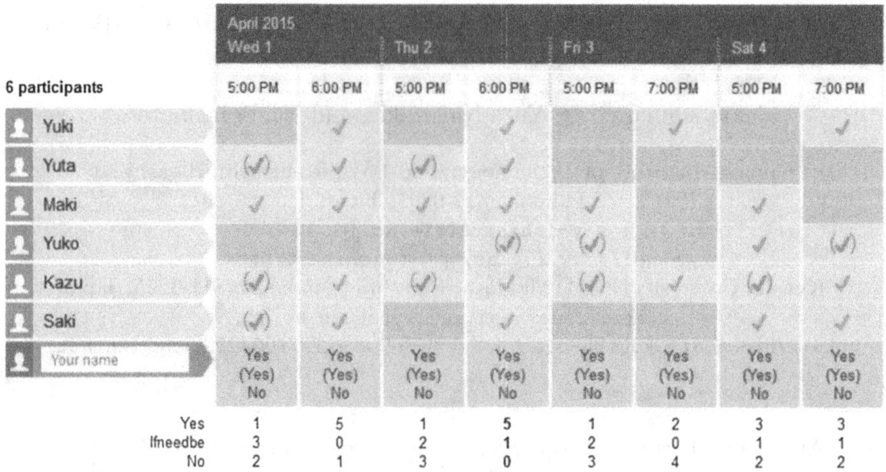

April 2015
Wed 1
Thu 2
Fri 3
Sat 4
6 participants
5:00 PM
6:00 PM
5:00 PM
6:00 PM
5:00 PM
7:00 PM
5:00 PM
7:00 PM
Yuki
Yuta
Maki
Yuko
Kazu
Saki
Your name
Yes
(Yes)
No
Yes 1 5 1 5 1 2 3 3
Ifneedbe 3 0 2 1 2 0 1 1
No 2 1 3 0 3 4 2 2

Fig. 1. A screenshot of Doodle. Six participants posted their favorite dates and time spans, and the application says the most favorite date and time span is 6:00 pm on Tuesday.

example, five levels of options: **Strongly yes**, **Yes**, **Maybe**, **No** and **Strongly No**. The participants will choose **Strongly Yes** if there is no meeting in the evening and they will choose **No** if they are going to give a presentation on the new products in the next morning. They will also choose **Yes** if their favorite date is another date. This way however imposes some stress to them when they struggle to choose which level they are on from **Strongly yes** to **Strongly no**. This manuscript discusses a way of expressing ambiguity of schedules with less effort.

The related work dealing with this problem has not been reported yet. This manuscript focuses on the property of an airbrush and exploits it as a way of expressing ambiguity of schedules, and builds a prototype of coordinating a schedule using an airbrush metaphor.

2 Airbrush Metaphor

An airbrush is a tool for spraying paint onto a canvas, walls and other things. An airbrush metaphor is a computational representation of an real airbrush so that people use it on a computer as if it was real. For example, Microsoft Paint has a variety of brush options such as a pencil, a crayon, a marker pen and an airbrush. They all are metaphors of their real things. One of the good points to apply metaphors to user interface is that people are familiar with those real things, so that they do not need to learn how to use them.

When people spray paint on a canvas once, the color is weak, and the color becomes stronger when they do twice. This is a basic visual effect of an real airbrush, which is applied to expressing the ambiguity of schedules. Figure 2 shows the visual effect of the airbrush created by a GNU Image Manipulation

Program of GIMP. The weak color indicates much ambiguity and the strong one does little ambiguity.

As regards real-world oriented interface, some researches using airbrushes have been done so far. For example, J. Konieczny and G. Meyer [1] built a user interface system for artwork using a real airbrush. In their system, a real airbrush is connected to the host, and the position and orientation of the airbrush is traced in space. When the user pulls the trigger, paint is sprayed onto objects and they are displayed on a computer screen. R. Shilkrot et al. [2] built a computerized airbrush. The airbrush is connected to the host and the host controls the trigger. The position and orientation of the airbrush is traced in space and the host pulls the trigger depending on them so that the specific image appears on a computer screen.

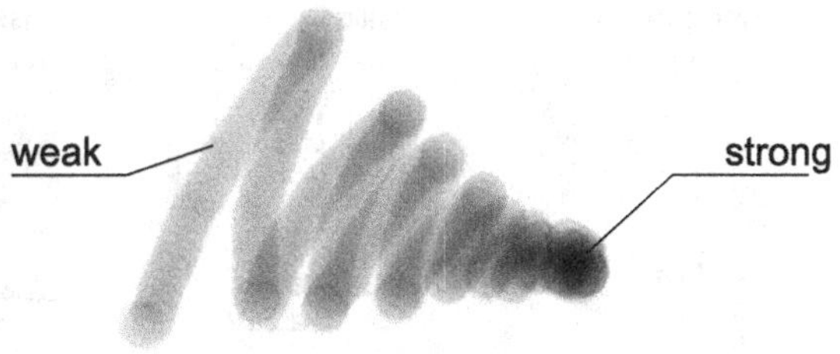

Fig. 2. The visual effect of an airbrush.

3 Schedule Coordination System

Figure 3 represents a schematic diagram of our schedule coordination system. It is a web application and runs on HTML5, CSS3, JavaScript1.7 and PHP5.5. It also

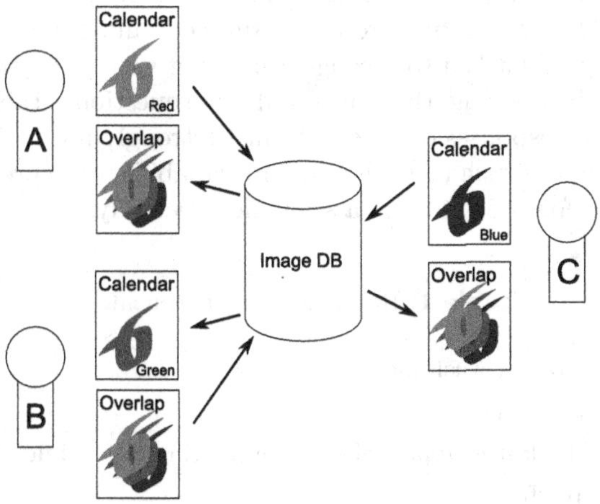

Fig. 3. A schematic diagram of our schedule coordination system.

works for three users. They spray paint on a calendar in the given color and send it to the image database and the system puts these images together and sends back to them. Figure 4 is a series of screenshots of our schedule coordination system. The scenario here is that three users are going to arrange a meeting. The left one shows that one user sprays paint in red on a calendar, where he/she wants to have a meeting. The two middle ones show that the other two users do it in green or blue. The right one shows an overlap between those users' calendars. In this scenario, the 16th or 23rd day in May is a candidate for the meeting.

Fig. 4. Screenshots of our schedule coordination system.

4 Experiment and Its Result

An experiment in usability of the airbrush metaphor for coordinating a schedule was conducted. There were five groups of subjects and three subjects in each group. Each group was asked to arrange a meeting with our system. After they fixed the date for the meeting, they answered some questions. Table 1 shows those questions and their responses on a scale from 1 (strongly no) to 5 (strongly yes). From the table, the airbrush metaphor and its capability of expressing ambiguity have the potential for coordinating a schedule effectively.

Table 1. Result of the experiment.

Questions on airbrush metaphor	Score
Was it easy to use?	4.14
Did you think it is applicable to coordinating a schedule?	4.27
Was it stressful?	1.13
Did you finish coordinating a schedule in a short time?	4.40

5 Conclusions

This manuscript proposed a way of coordinating a schedule with airbrush metaphor and built a proof-of-concept system. Its design and a brief demonstration were presented, and an experiment in usability was conducted. The result showed that the airbrush metaphor is capable of expressing ambiguity of schedules and effectively applied to a way of coordinating a schedule.

References

1. Konieczny, J., Meyer, G.: Airbrush simulation for artwork and computer modeling. In: NPAR 2009 Proceedings of the 7th International Symposium on Non-Photorealistic Animation and Rendering, pp. 61–69 (2009)
2. Shilkrot, R., Maes, P., Zoran, A.: Physical rendering with a digital airbrush. In: ACM SIGGRAPH 2014 Studio, **40**(1) (2014)

Manipulating Animation Speed of Progress Bars to Shorten Time Perception

Yuma Kuroki(✉) and Makio Ishihara

Faculty of Information Engineering, Fukuoka Institute of Technology,
3-30-1, Wajiro-Higashi, Higashi-Ku, Fukuoka 811-0295, Japan
mfml4001@bene.fit.ac.jp, m-ishihara@fit.ac.jp

Abstract. This manuscript introduces the basic idea of how to shorten the perceived time of progress bars' animation. The perceived time is not always proportional to the actual elapsed time. It is affected by a variety of psychological factors, and it is manipulable and distortable under certain circumstances. This manuscript explains how the perceived time is shortened by progress bars' animation, and shows that manipulating animation speed of progress bars has the potential to shorten the time perception.

Keywords: Perceived time · Progress bars · GUIs · Interface design

1 Introduction

CPU performance has been improved recently and the speed of processing tasks has increased. However, the amount of data to process tasks becomes huge so that. We perceive the speed of processing tasks is slow comparatively. The perceived time of progressing tasks affects the psychological stress and it plays an important role in reducing the stress. A progress bar is one of the graphical user interface that is usually used to visualize the progress of download, extraction, installation, etc. By using it, it is possible for users to know intuitively the progress of those computing tasks. They however suffer from a psychological stress so that the speed of the progress looks slower, especially in the case of heavy computing tasks. Figure 1 is a screenshot of a progress bar that shows the completion of 79 percent extracting files from a zip archive. As shown in the figure, the progress is often displayed in percentage. The perceived time is not always proportional to the actual elapsed time. It is affected by a variety of psychological factors, and it is manipulable and distortable under certain circumstances. C. Harrison et al. [1] discussed what visual augmentations have an impact on the percieved duration. Their result showed that visually augmented progress bars can be used to make processes appear faster.

Section 2 introduces the basic idea of manipulating animation speed of progress bars and describes how to shorten the perceived time of progress bars' animation. Section 3 conducts an experiment on perceived time of progress bars' animation and discusses its results, and then shows that manipulating animation speed of progress bars has the potential to shorten the perceived time. Section 4 give the concluding remarks.

C. Stephanidis (Ed.): HCII 2015 Posters, Part II, CCIS 529, pp. 670–673, 2015.
DOI: 10.1007/978-3-319-21383-5_113

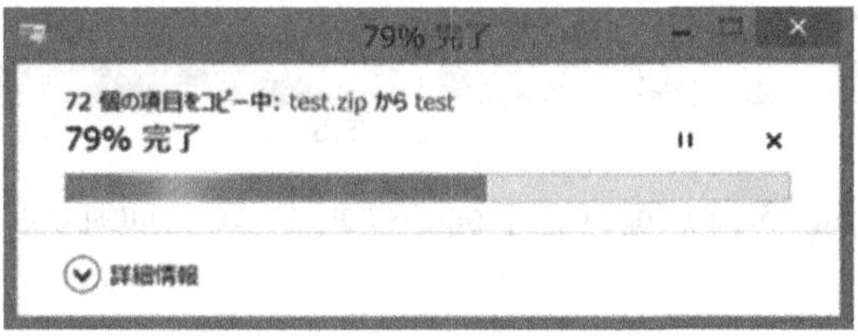

Fig. 1. A common progress bar

2 Manipulating Animation Speed of Progress Bars

This section explains the basic idea of how to shorten the perceived time by altering the animation speed of progress bars. It is based on the Weber-Fechner law shown in Fig. 2. The Weber-Fechner law says that the size of the psychological sense of people is not proportional to the magnitude of the stimulus, but the logarithm of the stimulus. Referring to the Weber-Fechner law, a course of actions to reduce the perceived time is to increase the speed of the progress bar.

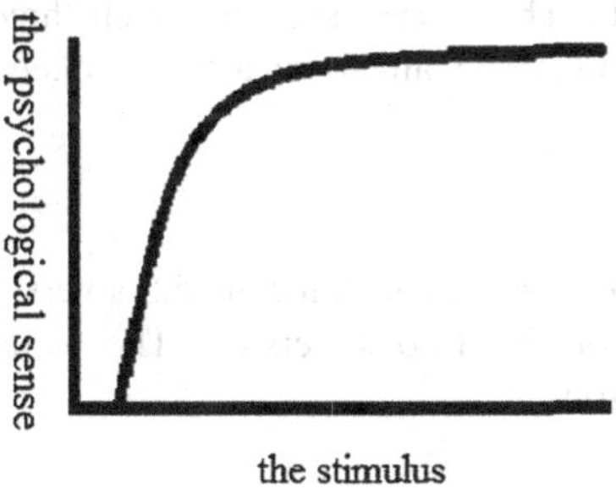

Fig. 2. The Weber-Fechner law

3 Experiment

This section conducts an experiment on the perceived time of progress bars' animation and discusses its results, and then shows that manipulating animation speed of progress bars has the potential to shorten perceived time.

3.1 Design

This manuscript conducts an experiment in three types of animation. The first one is the type of animation where the speed is constant (Fig. 3). It is 18.2 percent per second (pps). The second one is the type of animation where the speed is accelerated from 10 pps to 100 pps (Fig. 4). The third one is type of animation where the speed is decelerated from 100 pps to 10 pps (Fig. 5). All types of animation complete in 5.5 s. There is another version of the progress bar that completes in 11.0 s.

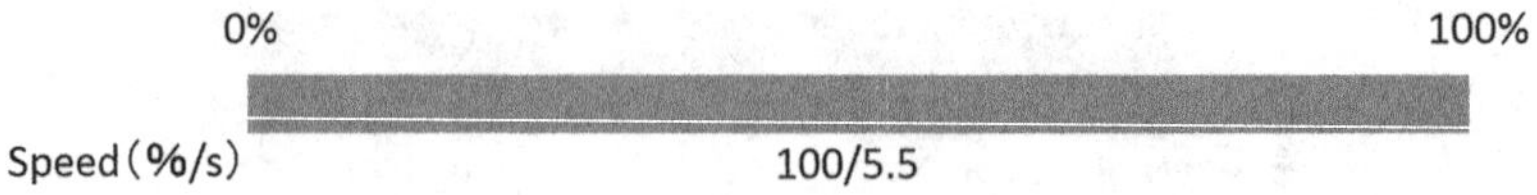

Fig. 3. Settings of a progress bar at a constant speed

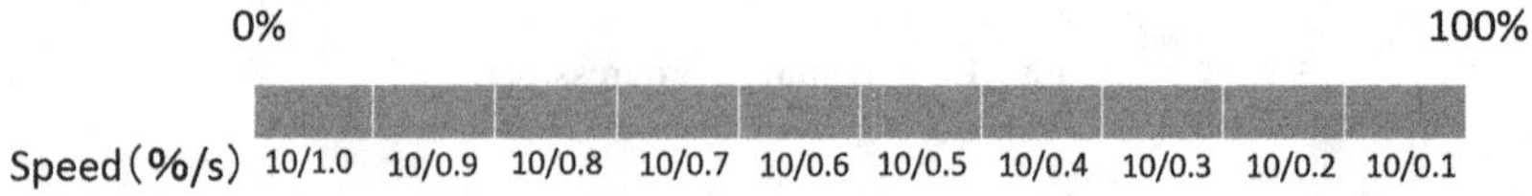

Fig. 4. Settings of a progress bar in speed with constant acceleration

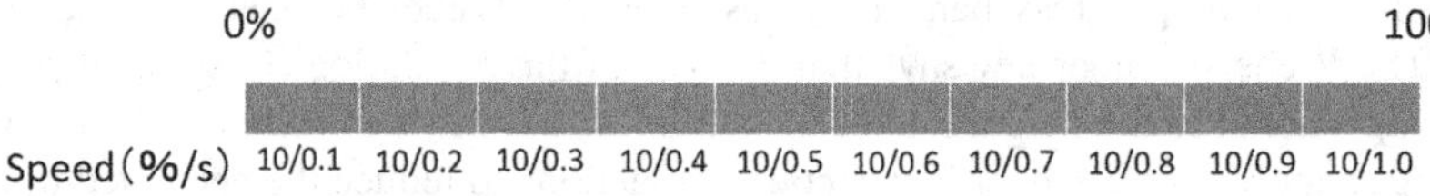

Fig. 5. Settings of a progress bar in speed with constant deceleration

There were 16 subjects. They were asked to watch three types of animation and they answered some questions to evaluate what type looked faster.

3.2 Results

Table 1 shows the result of questionnaires for the 5.5 s version and Table 2 shows the result of questionnaires for the 11.0 s version. The evaluation was done by the Scheffe's Paired Comparison.

Table 1. Result of questionnaires for the 5.5 s version

–	Very fast	Fast	Same	Fast	Very fast	–
Constant speed	0	4	1	3	0	Accelerated speed
Constant speed	0	1	3	3	1	Decelerated speed
Accelerated speed	1	4	1	1	1	Decelerated speed

Table 2. Result of questionnaires for the 11.0 s version

–	Very fast	Fast	Same	Fast	Very fast	–
Constant speed	1	0	1	4	1	Accelerated speed
Constant speed	0	2	2	2	1	Decelerated speed
Accelerated speed	0	3	3	0	1	Decelerated speed

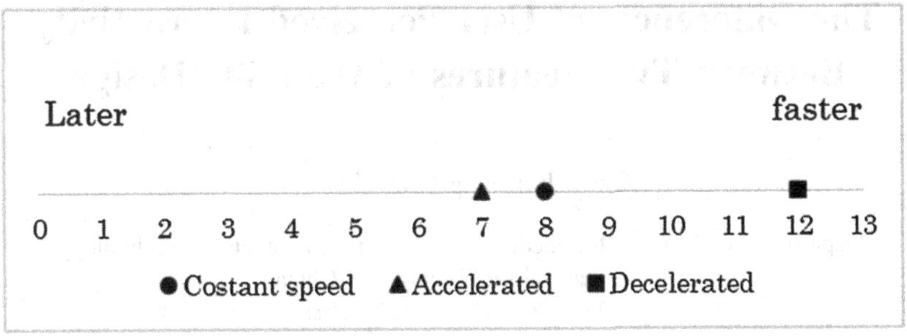

Fig. 6. Result of the Scheffe's Paired Comparison for the 5.5 s version

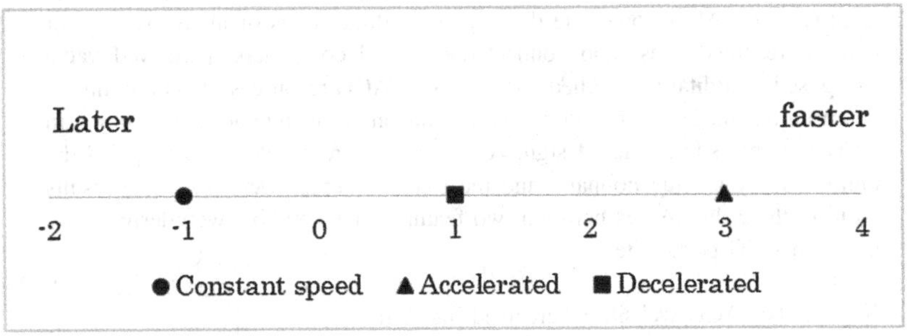

Fig. 7. Result of the Scheffe's Paired Comparison for the 11.0 s version

As a result, the decelerated animation looked faster than the other types for the 5.5 s version and the accelerated animation looked faster than the other types for the 11.0 s version. From the both results, the animation at a constant speed looked comparatively slow (Figs. 6, 7).

4 Conclusions

This manuscript introduced the basic idea of how to shorten the perceived time of progress bars' animation, and then showed that manipulating animation speed of progress bars has the potential to shorten the perceived time. In our future work, we are going to implement other patterns of progress bars' animation and evaluate its performance.

Reference

Harrison, C., Yeo, Z., Hudson, S.E.: Faster progress bars: manipulating perceived duration with visual augmentations. In: Proceedings of the SIGCHI Conference on Human Factors in Computing Systems (CHI 2010), pp. 1545–1548. ACM, New York (2010)

The Differences of User Perceived Interactivity Between Two Features of Web Site Design

Juihsiang Lee(✉)

Department of Digital Multimedia Design, China University of Technology, Taipei, Taiwan Republic of China
leockmail@gmail.com

Abstract. The purpose of this study is to examine the differences between two features of perceived interactivity—interactivity-as-process vs. interactivity-as-product on ACG portal site design. Three dimensions of interactivity (user control, responsiveness and connectedness) and consumers' perceived value composed of utilitarian and hedonic values on ACG resources searching, finally determining the level of overall satisfaction on using interactivity features in ACG portable site service design. A total of 450 respondents participated the online survey by questionnaire and the usable samples were 445. The results indicate three differences between two features of interactive web design —by users on ACG portal site.

Keywords: ACG website · Perceived interactivity

1 Introductory

A portal site is most often one specially designed Web page which brings information together from diverse sources in a uniform way. Japanese manga, anime, games, and related consumer electronic devices which target the younger generation not only attract much more Japanese young male enthusiasts (Sangani, 2008) but are also popular in the overseas markets (Niu et al. 2012), especially the ACG (animation, comic, game) users from Asia, whom would searching information to Japanese platform to get first hand resources aggressively.

In the current investigation we aim to test users' perceived interactivity using two Japanese styles of ACG products sharing platform design, the first one site niconico which designed of media interaction approach in computer mediated environment, the other one is K-island which designed of asynchronized computer mediated interactivity-as-process like. ACG products sharing platform is meant to solicit quick input/opinions and trial/demo reels from a web user, which is typically displayed for viewing by other visitors to the site.

The purpose of this study is to examine the relationships between two features of consumers perceived interactivity—interactivity-as-process vs. interactivity-as-product in three dimensions and perceived value composed of utilitarian and hedonic, finally determining the level of overall satisfaction with two different levels of interactive ACG portal site services. And try to find out if there have differences of users in the information search experiences.

C. Stephanidis (Ed.): HCII 2015 Posters, Part II, CCIS 529, pp. 674–679, 2015.
DOI: 10.1007/978-3-319-21383-5_114

2 Literature Review

The Internet is by definition an interactive medium (Rust & Varki, 1996). An essential part of this interactive ability is the hyperlinks technique (namely, the ability to move from one place to another with a click on the mouse and so reach a new layer of information by a simple movement). Despite the potential for interactivity provided by the Internet, little attention has been paid to how interactivity might be more fully utilized (Johnson et al., 2006).

2.1 Interactivity

Although there have been many studies on interactivity under various contexts and disciplines, researchers still have mixed views on the concept of interactivity (Yadav and Varadarajan, 2005).

Stromer-Galley (2004) arguments that there are two types of computer-mediated interactivity—interactivity-as-process vs. interactivity-as-product. Obtaining from Stromer-Galley's points, while interactivity-as-process emphasizes communication between people via computer, interactivity-as-product underlines people's ability to deliver information by controlling the medium itself. We can see their differences on Table 1.

Table 1. The differences between interactivity-as-process or as-product

Features	Interactivity-as-process	Interactivity-as-product
Research intention	focus on interactivity-as-process	focus on user interactions with technology
Measurement	focus on observed interaction, such as self-disclosure, degree of responsiveness, and coherence of discussion; subjective experience of the interaction; or the effects…	focus on the range of interactive experiences afforded by the medium
Practices	pseudo-synchronous chat or asynchronous message boards	HTML allow for multimedia, such as audio and video downloads,

McMillan (2005) define interactivity more broadly as the perceived direction of communication, control, and time. Previous research by Lee (2005) has particular relevance to the current work. Lee identified (1) user control, (2) responsiveness, (3) personalization, and (4) connectedness as important components to interactivity in a mobile commerce setting. User control refers to the user's ability to control the information display and content. Responsiveness refers to the site as being able to respond to user queries. Personalization concerns the mobile Internet site that enables the purchase of products and services that are tailored to the user and unique desires. Finally, perceived connectedness refers to whether customers share experiences regarding products or services offered with other visitors to the mobile site. We adopt

these three components: user control, responsiveness, connectedness, to fit on the website environment.
Hypothesis 1. Interactivity-as-product of ACG portal site has differences between Interactivity-as-process of ACG portal sites by users' perceived interactivity.

2.2 Consequence of Perceived Interactivity

Users visit websites not only for information, but also for entertainment. We identify utilitarian and hedonic two aspects of Web performance from the definition by Huang (2003, p. 429-430): The utilitarian aspect of Web performance is the evaluation of a website based on the assessment by users regarding the instrumental benefits they derive from its non-sensory attributes. It is related to the performance perception of usefulness, value, and wisdom (Batra and Ahtola, 1990).

The hedonic aspect of Web performance is the evaluation of a website based on the assessment by users regarding the amount of fun, playfulness, and pleasure they experience or anticipate from the site. It reflects a website's entertainment value derived from its sensory attributes, from which users obtain consummatory affective gratification (Batra and Ahtola, 1990, Crowley, Spangenberg, & Hughes, 1992).

Hypothesis 2. Interactivity-as-product of ACG portal site has differences between Interactivity-as-process of ACG portal site in the consequence by user perceived interactivity of utilitarian and hedonic.

2.3 Website Satisfaction

Satisfaction is a post-consumption evaluation based on the comparison between the expected value in the pre-consumption stage and the perceived post-consumption value after the purchase or after the use of services or products (Oliver, 1981; Ravald and Gröroos, 1996). This is especially true for companies selling goods and services on their websites. Customers must be satisfied with their experience with the website or they will not return.
Hypothesis 3. Interactivity-as-product and interactivity-as-product of ACG portal sites have difference between users' perceived satisfaction.

Therefore we propose the research model as Fig. 1, to examine the relationships between the constructs.

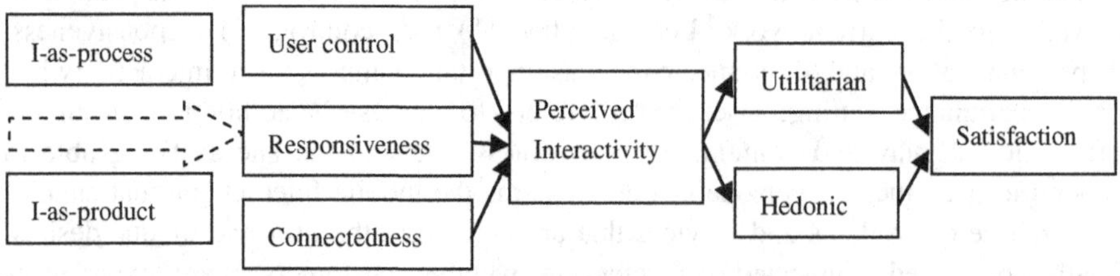

Fig. 1. Proposed model

3 Methodology

3.1 Sample and Data Collection

NICONICO (www.niconico.jp) is a Japanese ACG portal site populated in Asia, K-island is discussing board site. These two ACG portal website offer users the latest news of ACG related publishing, sharing their artificial works with VAT (Video Annotation Tool) functions. A fair and open ranking system was trustworthy for users.

A total of 450 respondents participated the online survey by questionnaire and the usable samples were 445. They were all familiar with the Internet and all have ACG portal site visited experience before.

3.2 Measures

The questionnaire consisted of the following five sections: (1) perceived interactivity, (2) perceived consumption value, (3) satisfaction. Since the population was limited to users who had at least one online ACG searching experience, the first part of the questionnaire was designed to screen out the participants into two different groups.

The questionnaire is designed in Likert 7 point scale and adjusted according to researches on e-commerce. Participants are asked to fill in the questionnaire and indicate their current situation for each variable item (1 = strong disagreement and 7 = strong agreement). The higher score the respondents indicated, the more they agree with these questions. 1 means that the subject disagrees highly with the questions while 7 signifies high agreement.

3.3 Model Evaluation and Modification

Structural equation modeling was conducted using Amos 21.0 to evaluate the fit of the research model (Fig. 1). When conducting SEM, researchers often first evaluate the measurement model (whether the measured variables accurately reflect the desired constructs or factors) before assessing the structural model. As noted by Thompson (2004), it makes little sense to relate constructs within an SEM model if the factors specified as part of the model are not worthy of further attention? (p.110).

Confirmatory factor analysis provided satisfactory support for the six-construct model. The factor loadings associated with each of the six constructs all exceeded 0.50 and were significant at the 0.01 level. And all the value of C.R. in the range of 0.8 ~ 1. All the AVE value in the range 0.538 ~ 0.90. Discriminant validity among the six constructs was assessed by comparing the fit with Hair, et al. (2009), Fornell and Larcker (1981) suggested value (factor loadings > 0.5, C.R > 0.6, AVE > 0.5, SMC > 0.5) all are passed. The second order factor confirmatory analysis is good to fit than examined in first order CFA, see Table 2.

Table 3 shows the value that no one exceed 1 from lower to upper level. Thus, discriminant validity was assessed to ensure that a construct differed from others (see Table 3). Finally the model fit provided satisfactory support for the proposed model of Niconico site and K-island site.

Table 2. The Indicators of Model Fit on K-island and Niconico site

Second order CFA Model	AGFI		CFI		RMSEA	
	Niconico	K	Niconico	K	Niconico	K
1. Null Model	0.156	0.156	0	0	0.294	0.294
2. First order single factor analysis	0.429	0.429	0.668	0.668	0.183	0.183
3. First order three factor analysis uncorrelated	0.832	0.755	0.904	0.842	0.098	0.132
4. First order three factor correlated	0.941	0.928	0.986	0.978	0.038	0.05
5. Second order Factor Confirmatory Analysis	0.941	0.928	0.986	0.978	0.038	0.05
suggest value	> 0.8	> 0.8	> 0.9	> 0.9	< 0.08	< 0.08

Table 3. Discriminant Validity of reflective constructs on Niconico site

Parameter			Estimate		Bias-corrected				Percentile method			
					Lower		Upper		Lower		Upper	
			Niconico	K	Niconico	K	Niconico	K	Niconico	K	Niconico	K
Satisfaction	<->	Interactivity	0.661	0.23	0.559	0.123	0.762	0.335	0.559	0.121	0.762	0.333
Utilitarian	<->	Interactivity	0.599	0.714	0.488	0.615	0.696	0.806	0.493	0.617	0.702	0.809
Utilitarian	<->	Hedonic	0.327	0.538	0.222	0.442	0.422	0.632	0.226	0.442	0.429	0.632
Utilitarian	<->	Satisfaction	0.417	0.205	0.3	0.105	0.513	0.301	0.305	0.102	0.524	0.299
Hedonic	<->	Satisfaction	0.659	0.023	0.577	-0.077	0.74	0.121	0.581	-0.079	0.742	0.118
Hedonic	<->	Interactivity	0.663	0.645	0.546	0.57	0.762	0.721	0.548	0.568	0.763	0.714

4 Results

The results of the structural equation modeling reveal the following three findings. First, There are differences between Interactivity-as-product and Interactivity-as-process environments of user perceived. The order of three dimensions of perceived interactivity in Interactivity-as-product is Connectedness(0.878) > Respon siveness(0.746) > User_control(0.648). And in Interactivity-as-process is User_control (0.876) > Responsiveness(0.783) > Connectedness(0.701), see Table 4.

Table 4. Results of hypotheses tests within two groups

Construct			Standardized estimate		Unstandardized estimate		C.R.		P
			Niconico	K	Niconico	K	Niconico	K	
Utilitarian	<-	Interactivity	0.612	0.783	0.773	0.789	8.574	12.746	***
Hedonic	<-	Interactivity	0.707	0.701	1.085	0.759	9.680	12.106	***
User control	<-	Interactivity	0.648	0.876	1	1			
Responsiveness	<-	Interactivity	0.746	0.831	1.177	0.893	10.305	13.878	***
Connectedness	<-	Interactivity	0.878	0.875	1.065	0.867	10.360	14.249	***
Satisfaction	<-	Utilitarian	0.229	0.522	0.261	0.398	4.7610	8.130	***
Satisfaction	<-	Hedonic	0.624	0.334	0.586	0.237	11.527	5.820	***

Second, the perceived interactivity has positive effect of Hedonic(0.707) than Utilitarian(0.612) in Interactivity-as-product environment. And the outcome is reversed in Interactivity-as-process environment that Utilitarian(0.783) > Hedonic(0.701), see Table 4.

Finally, both perceived utilitarian and hedonic values have a positive effect on satisfaction on the ACG portal site. But in Interactivity-as-product environment the perceived Hedonic(0.624) has more effects than Utilitarian(0.229) for Satisfaction. And the outcome is also reversed in Interactivity-as-process environment that Utilitarian (0.522) has more effects than Hedonic(0.334), see Table 4.

References

Babin, B.J., Darden, W.R., Griffen, M.: Work and/or fun: measuring hedonic and utilitarian shopping value. J. Consum. Behav. **20**, 644–656 (1994)

Bloch, P.H., Richens, M.L.: Shopping without purchase: an investigation of consumer browsing behavior. In: Bagozzi, R.P., Tybout, A.M. (eds.) Advances in Consumer Research, vol. 10, pp. 389–393. Ann Arbor, Association for Consumer Research (1993)

Novak, T.P., Hoffman, D.L., Duhachek, A.: The influence of goal-directed and experiential activities on online flow experiences. J. Consum. Psychol. **13**(1–2), 3–16 (2003)

Fornell and Larcker: Evaluating structural equation models with unobservable variables and measurement error. J. Mark. Res. **18**(February), 39–50 (1981)

Hancock, G.R., Nevitt, J.: Bootstrapping and the identification of exogenous latent variables within structural equation models. Struct. Equ. Model. **6**, 394–399 (1999)

Hirschman, E.: Experience seeking: a subjectivist perspective of consumption. J. Bus. Res. **12**, 115–136 (1984)

Lee, T.: The impact of perceptions of interactivity on customer trust and transaction intentions in mobile commerce. J. Electron. Commer. Res. **6**(3), 165–180 (2005)

McMillan, S.J.: The researchers and the concept: moving beyond a blind examination of interactivity. J. Interact. Advertising 5(1), 1–4 (2005). /http://jiad.org

Oliver, R.L.: Measurement and evaluation of satisfaction process in retail settings. J. Retail. **57** (3), 25–48 (1981)

Niu, H.J., Chiang, Y.S., Tsai, H.T.: An exploratory study of the Otaku adolescent consumer. Psychol. Mark. **29**(10), 712–725 (2012). doi:10.1002/mar.20558

Ravald, A., Gröroos, C.: The value concept and relationship marketing. Eur. J. Mark. **30**(2), 1990 (1996)

Rowley, J.: Product search in e-shopping: a review and research propositions. J. Consum. Mark. **17**(1), 20–35 (2000)

Sangani, K.: Otaku world. Eng. Technol. **3**, 94–95 (2008)

Schlosser, A.E., Kanfer, A.: Interactivity in Commercial Web Sites: Implications for Web Site Effectiveness, Working Paper. Vanderbilt University (1999)

Stromer-Galley, J.: Online interaction and why candidates avoid it. J. Commun. **50**(4), 111–132 (2000)

Stromer-Galley, J.: Interactivity-as-product and interactivity-as-process. Inf. Soc. **20**, 391–394 (2004)

Comparing and Exploring New Text Entry and Edit Methods for Smart TV

Jingtian Li(✉) and Young Mi Choi

School of Industrial Design, Georgia Institute of Technology, Atlanta, USA
{lijingtian1990, christina.choi}@gatech.edu

Abstract. Smart TVs are becoming an increasingly important multimedia device for home entertainment. The need of effective input methods for television text entry or edit is growing as the number of smart TV explodes. In this paper we evaluate and compare four current input methods (traditional remote controller, touchpad, physical keyboard, and smart device virtual keyboard) for smart TV. Based on the result of research, we propose an approach that provides a more effective method of text entry and edit.

Keywords: Smart TV · Text input method · Text edit · User experience

1 Introduction

In these days, Smart TVs are becoming an increasingly important multimedia device for home entertainment (Banerjee et al. 2012). Generally, Smart TV is defined as a medium that provides TV broadcasting, Internet, applications, and intelligent services via the mounting of a CPU and an operating platform on the set-top box or display (Barrero, 2014). Smart TV has its own operating system, so it can provide not only TV channels but also different applications. Unlike traditional TV, people have more interaction needs on smart TV platform, such as playing games, browsing websites, social networking, sharing images/videos and searching information. However, one of the most critical problems of interacting with a Smart TV is that there is not an efficient user interface for entering and editing text (Geleijnse et al. 2009).

The most common interface with a traditional TV is a standard remote control. With it, users can adjust volume, change channels or inputs. Smart TV platform are different in that text input is required to use many features (Geleijnse et al. 2012). For example a user may need to input online account credentials, input key words to search for favorite TV shows, write comments in forums or app stores, or enter text in many other scenarios. Editing and correction of entered text in any of these cases is currently a challenge (Hess et al. 2011).

There are some technologies and new devices to help users input text, but there is no efficient method that allows users to edit text (select, copy, or paste) on a Smart TV. A more efficient method of text entry/edit is needed for interactions with Smart TVs.

C. Stephanidis (Ed.): HCII 2015 Posters, Part II, CCIS 529, pp. 680–683, 2015.
DOI: 10.1007/978-3-319-21383-5_115

2 Specific Aims

The purpose of this research is to evaluate four different text entry/edit methods (traditional remote controller, touchpad, physical keyboard, and smart device virtual keyboard) for smart TV and propose an approach that provides a more effective method of text entry and edit on smart TV. Based on the literature, the critical parameters to be evaluated in the proposed research include:

- Text input efficiency- how much time a subject spends on completing a text input task.
- Text input satisfaction- the rate of satisfaction a subject gives to an input method after completing a text input task.
- Text edit efficiency- how much time a subject spends on completing a text edit task.
- Text edit satisfaction- the rate of satisfaction a subject gives to an input method after completing a text edit task.

3 Research Design

To provide a convincing evaluation of four text entry/edit methods, the study includes both self-report data from subjects and objective measure of time from tester. The independent variables of the test are different text input methods, and the dependent variables are efficiency (time) and user satisfaction. Thus the study combines both qualitative data and quantitative data collection procedures.

3.1 Subjects

The study is conducted at College of Architecture on Georgia Institute of Technology campus with a sample of 20 currently enrolled college students. The subjects are aged 18 or over. Participators should have a minimum of 1 year of using smart phone experience and 1 year of watching TV experience.

3.2 Setting and Materials

The test facility is put in an empty space. The main facility is a television which supports smart TV boxes, like Amazon Fire TV, Google Chromecast.

The four text entry/edit methods are tested as follows:

Input Method 1: Traditional TV remote controller, subjects can use up, down, left, right and OK button to select the letters of the virtual keyboard on TV to input/edit text.

Input Method 2: Touchpad, subjects can move their figure on the touchpad to select the letters of the virtual keyboard on TV to input/edit text.

Input Method 3: Physical TV keyboard, subjects can type/edit text on TV by pressing the letter buttons on the physical keyboard.

Input Method 4: Smartphone virtual keyboard, subjects can use the touchable virtual keyboard on smartphone to type/edit text on TV.

3.3 Procedures

Prior to testing, the participants are asked to fill a pre-test questionnaire about their demographic information—including age, gender, experience of using smart TV and smartphone. Then participants are oriented to the experimental procedures.

The experiment is organized in 2 sessions per participant. The procedures takes approximately 50 min but lasts no longer than 90 min. The order in which the input methods are used in each session is randomly selected, and the purpose is to counterbalance the effects of learning. The participants are asked to sit on a chair about 7 feet in front of the smart TV.

Session 1: The subject is given a sentence which includes letters, numbers and symbols. The sentence is shown on a small screen on the side of subject's seat. The subject is asked to use four different input methods to type the given sentence onto the TV screen. The subject has to correct any typing errors before starting to use next input method. We measure the time the subject spends on typing with each input method. After using each method, the subject is asked to fill a NASA TLX form and a System Usability Scale form.

Session 2: A sentence which includes letters, numbers and symbols is shown on TV, but there are several typing errors in the sentence. The correct sentence is shown on a small screen on the side of subject's seat. The subject is asked to use four different input methods to correct the sentence on TV screen. The subject is not allowed to clear the whole sentence but has to correct certain letters/numbers/symbols in the sentence. The time the subject spends on correcting the sentence with each input method is measured. After using each method, the subject is asked to fill a NASA TLX Form and a System Usability Scale Form.

After the participants finish each session, they are asked to complete a Session Overall Review Form to evaluate four input methods.

4 Discussion

From the research study we mentioned, all the data collected are valuable in this study. The quantitative data is the time subjects spend on using different input methods. By comparing the time of using different input methods, we can find which input method is more effective for typing or editing text on Smart TV. The qualitative data is from the questionnaire filled by subjects. By analyzing the score subjects give to different input methods, we can compare which input method gets the highest score, so we can find which input method has the highest user satisfaction.

From the literature review and field study, we analyze the pros and cons of four input methods as below:

- Traditional remote controller is not suitable to input and edit text on smart TV;
- The interaction like Touchpad is suitable to edit text, but not for text entry;

- Using physical TV keyboard to input text is fast, but it is not very good for edit;
- Virtual keyboard on smart device has the same function as physical TV keyboard, but it is more flexible.

Basing on our research, we found that the virtual keyboard on smart device is more flexible for smart TV text input. User can easily switch different keyboards (number, symbol). However, the biggest problem of current smartphone keyboard apps for smart TV is that users cannot easily move the cursor on smart TV, so it is very hard to correct typos users inputted and it reduces the efficiency of both text entry and edit. We also found that when users use Touchpad to input text on smart TV, it is not effective to type but users have the flexibility to move cursor on smart TV. So we decided to move the advantage of Touchpad to smartphone keyboard app.

We proposed a new input method for smart TV. It is a mobile app on smartphone which can connect to smart TV, and users hold a smartphone and use the mobile app on it to control smart TV. Users can use the virtual keyboards on smartphone to type in text on smart TV. Users can use touch gestures (Slide, tap, press) on the phone screen to control the movement of cursor on smart TV so they can edit the text no matter where the text is, and they can also use touch gestures to select, copy and paste text on smart TV. In the app, subjects can switch different keyboards by using slide gesture on the phone screen.

Our further study will be implementing our new design and doing usability test to evaluate our new design. Our new design combines the advantages of Touchpad and smart phone virtual keyboards, so we expect that it is more effective for users to input and edit text on smart TV. We also expect that our new design is more satisfying than currently smart TV input methods when users input or edit text on smart TV.

References

Banerjee, A., Burstyn, J., Girouard, A., Vertegaal, R.: Multipoint: comparing laser and manual pointing as remote input in large display interactions. Int. J. Hum Comput. Stud. **70**(10), 690–702 (2012)

Barrero, A.D.X.G.G.R.S.: An empirical investigation into text input methods for interactive digital television applications. Int. J. Hum. Comput. Interact. **30**(4), 321–341 (2014). doi:10.1080/10447318.2013.858461

Geleijnse, G., Aliakseyeu, D., Sarroukh, E.: Comparing text entry methods for interactive television applications. In: Proceedings of the Seventh European Conference on European Interactive Television, p. 145 (2009)

Geleijnse, G., Aliakseyeu, D., Sarroukh, E.: Comparing text entry methods for interactive television applications. In: Proceedings of the 10th European Conference on Interactive TV and Video (2012)

Hess, J., Wan, L., Pipek, V., Kuestermann, G.: Using paper and pen to control home-IT. In: Proceddings of the 9th International Interactive Conference on Interactive Television, p. 203 (2011)

Ergonomic Visualization of Logistical Control Parameters for Flexible Production Planning and Control in Future Manufacturing Systems

Jochen Nelles(✉), Sinem Kuz, and Christopher M. Schlick

Institute of Industrial Engineering and Ergonomics of RWTH Aachen University, Aachen, Germany
{j.nelles, s.kuz, c.schlick}@iaw.rwth-aachen.de

Abstract. The research presented in this paper focuses on modeling and visualization of logistical control parameters. In the developed application, the internal logistical control parameters cycle time, timeliness, inventory, and capacity were considered. A novel concept to visualize these parameters was developed on the basis of the well-known funnel model. The original model was enhanced by and compared to a further developed model. Our approach to visualize the internal logistical control parameters is based on a paddle-wheel model. An online survey with both models and different visualizations of the internal logistical control parameters was carried out to compare both models and the different visualizations. Both models are investigated with regard to comprehension and visual learning versus verbal learning. In the poster session, we will present further development of the paddle-wheel model to show the cause-effect relationship between the individual internal logistical control parameters and draw a comparison with the original funnel model.

Keywords: Mental model · Situation awareness · Verbal learner · Visual learner · Production planning and control · Internal logistical control parameters

1 Introduction

One increasing challenge for manufacturing companies is the optimal adaption to global markets. They have to adjust to unforeseen incidents such as problems in the supply chain. Therefore, not only differential characteristics like functionality, quality, or price of the products are important, but also logistical performance gains importance as a competitive factor [12]. Logistical performance indicators have growing influence on the customers' purchasing decisions and thus have an impact on production planning and control in manufacturing companies. Complex and extensive information within manufacturing companies are represented by logistical control parameters, which are the basis for production planning and control [7]. According to the model of production control by Lödding [5], the fundamental internal logistical control parameters are cycle time, timeliness, inventory and capacity. Due to a variety of interaction effects and conflicts of objectives, it is not only necessary to measure logistical control parameters, but also to understand the production system and cause-effect-relationship between the parameters for specific regulation of the logistical control parameters.

C. Stephanidis (Ed.): HCII 2015 Posters, Part II, CCIS 529, pp. 684–689, 2015.
DOI: 10.1007/978-3-319-21383-5_116

The aim of this research is the comprehensive and transparent modelling and visualization of the four fundamental internal logistical control parameters of production control and logistical performance. In this context, it should be considered how mental models and situational awareness emerge from visual and textual models [3, 10].

Mental models are individually created stabile structures of knowledge regarding a segment of reality. They are used to understand environmental circumstances and support action planning and control. Mental models simulate environmental circumstances in a dynamic way [9]. They are based on heuristic analogies, and hence are incomplete, robust, and steady [2]. Content and structure of a mental model depend on individual experiences and knowledge [4]. According to the integrated theory of text and picture comprehension [10], mental models emerge from visual perception. The visualizer-verbalizer hypothesis states that some people can process visual content more easy, while others prefer verbal content [6]. This hypothesis plays an important role in the development of multimedia training and visualization.

Besides the modelling and visualization of the relationship between the four fundamental internal logistical control parameters, this study aims at the evaluation of the models regarding their comprehension. One hypothesis is that visual learners have a better comprehension than verbal learners with the help of the graphical models. On the other side, verbal learners perform textual information better than visual learners [6]. A high comprehension of the cause-effect-relationship between the logistical control parameters and an ergonomic visualization of the parameters lead to a higher transparency in production planning and control. Therefore, the aim of this study is to develop a good representation form to visualize the logistical control parameters. In this study, we concentrate on the comparison of two models. The first model is the so-called funnel model developed by Wiendahl by the Institute of Production Systems and Logistics (IFA) at Leibniz University Hannover [12]. The second one, the so-called paddle-wheel model, was self-developed.

2 Modelling Internal Logistical Control Parameters

A basic approach to model logistical parameters is a funnel model. Thus, the internal logistical control parameters cycle time, inventory, capacity and – in combination with the input/output diagram – timeliness, can be presented systematically (Fig. 1, left side). Based on a draft by Bechtle, the standard funnel model visualizes the order processing in a production plant like a funnel. The incoming orders (represented as circles), which are measured in hours of work content, form the inventory and leave the funnel after processing. The diameter of the outlet can be described as the capacity of the work system, which depends on the current performance. The capacity is measured in hours of work content per shop calendar day [1, 5, 12]. The cycle time for incoming orders changes with the work systems inventory and the capacity. These interdependencies between cycle time (here: mean range, mr [scd]), capacity (here: mean performance, mper [h/scd]) and inventory (here: mean work-in-process $mwip_{work}$ [h], are stated through the funnel formula as follows [11].

$$mwip_{work} = mper * mr$$

The research project ProSense (production control based on cybernetic support systems and intelligent sensors) focuses on the company intern logistical control parameters – especially on cycle time, inventory, capacity, and timeliness – on the basis of the model of production control by Lödding [5]. For this purpose, the Hanoverian funnel model was modified. The internal logistical control parameters, including timeliness, were transferred to the standard funnel model (Fig. 1, right side).

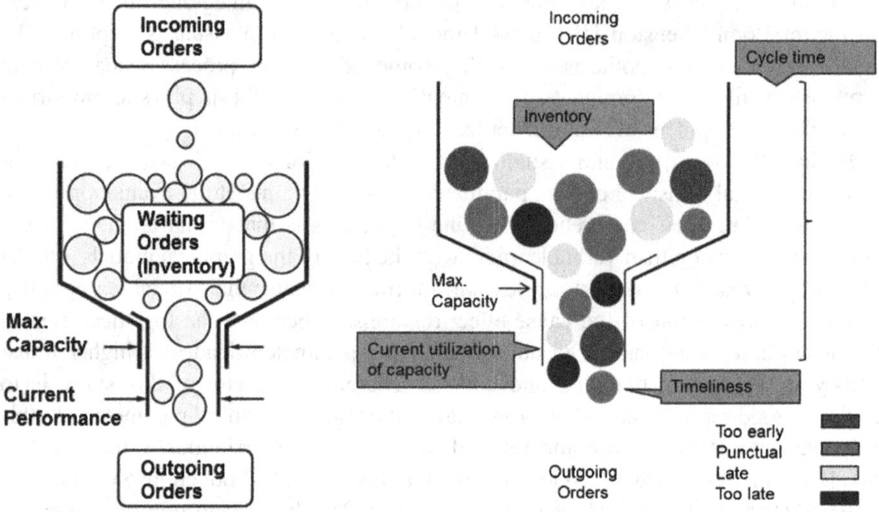

Fig. 1. Funnel model as a description model für logistical processes. Left: Standard funnel model of the Institute of Production Systems and Logistics (IFA) at Leibniz University Hannover; right: modified funnel model.

A further approach to visualize the cause-effect relationship between the logistical control parameters is the dynamic paddle-wheel model (Fig. 2), which was developed at the Institute of Industrial Engineering and Ergonomics of RWTH Aachen University in this project. This analogy model shows the relationship of the four logistical control parameters cycle time, inventory, capacity, and timeliness schematically by means of a paddle-wheel model. The paddle-wheel principle is also used in natural science and describes, for example, cation movements. Within the context of production planning and control the inventory of incoming orders are represented as a circle; the area of the circle is equivalent to the order process time. The status of timeliness is colored according to the expected delivery time and analog to the degree of ripeness of fruits – too early, punctual, late, or too late. The capacity of the production respectively of the paddle-wheel is the ratio of the circle area and the paddle-wheel container area. The cycle time is analog to the paddle-wheel angular velocity. The advantage of the paddle-wheel model compared with the (modified) funnel model is the dynamic modeling of cycle time in the form of a physical parameter. Moreover, individual orders can be assigned to specific production capacities and to a specific expected delivery time.

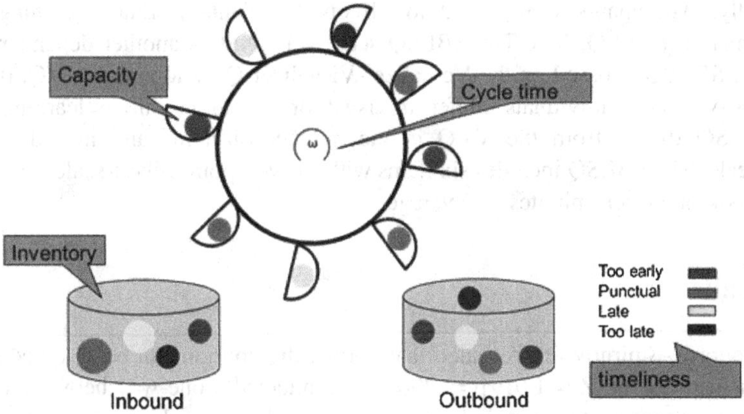

Fig. 2. Dynamic paddle-wheel model describing the internal logistical control parameters

3 Methods

For the purpose of this study, we carried out an online survey using the software Enterprise Feedback Suite 10.5 by QuestBack GmbH. In a between-subject design, we used the presentation of the logistical control parameter models as a three level independent variable (funnel model, paddle-wheel model, textual description). The dependent variable was the score in a questionnaire about the four logistical control parameters.

In the study 64 participants (35 females, $M_{AGE} = 23.98$, $SD = 3.49$, range = 17) attended. 84.4 per cent of the participants are highly educated and hold the german general qualification for university entrance or a higher diploma. Twelve participants had experience in manufacturing companies.

At the beginning, participants were informed about the aim of the study. Additionally, we provided general information about logistical control parameters and their importance. Then, participants were faced either with one of the models, or with the textual description. Participants were divided at the online survey randomly in three different groups. One group was faced the funnel model (16 participants), while the other was faced the paddle-wheel model (25 participants). A third group (23 participants) received a text (112 words) describing the funnel model. This group served as a control group. Participants were instructed to understand the model or the text. After the presentation, participants had to take part at a questionnaire comprised of eleven statements. This questionnaire was created for the online survey and asked about the interrelationships between the logistic control parameters (e.g., "Timeliness is dependent on circle time."). The task was to evaluate each statement whether it was true or false. Based on the statements a comprehension-score was calculated. Additionally, the option "no statement" was provided. Beside the questionnaire, participants had to evaluate the difficulty of the questionnaire and the comprehensibleness of the model on a five-point Likert-scale.

Finally, participants were asked to fill out the Santa Barbara Learning Style Questionnaire (SBLSQ, [6]). The SBLSQ score was used as another dependent variable. The SBLSQ is based on the Verbalizer-Visualizer-Questionnaire (VVQ, [8]) and measures whether individuals prefer a visual or verbal cognitive learning style. The SBLSQ differs from the VVQ in the number of items and in order to the Likert-scale. The SBLSQ includes six items with a seven-point Likert-scale. The online survey took about ten minutes on average.

4 Results

A Kolmogorov-Smirnov-test revealed that normal distribution can be assumed for the comprehension-score, $Z = 1.01$, $p = .206$. We conducted a one-way between subjects ANOVA to compare the comprehension-score in the control group, paddle-wheel group, and funnel group. There was a significant effect of the presented model on the comprehension-score at the $p < .05$ level, $F(2, 61) = 3.20$, $p = .048$. Post Hoc comparisons using LSD test revealed that the comprehension-score for the funnel condition ($M = 7.31$, $SD = 1.40$) was significantly higher than in the paddle-wheel condition ($M = 6.04$, $SD = 1.65$). However, the control group ($M = 6.96$, $SD = 1.92$) did not differ significantly from the other groups. In summary, these results suggest that participants could understand the relationship between the logistical internal parameters better with the help of the funnel model. Furthermore, a Pearson product-moment correlation coefficient was computed to assess the relationship between the comprehension-score and SBLSQ score only for the model groups. Therefore, the control group was excluded for this analysis. We found no correlation between the two scores, $r = -.137$, $n = 41$, $p = .393$. Up-to-date results, discussion and conclusion are presented at the conference in the poster session.

Acknowledgements. The presented project ProSense (production control based on cybernetic support systems and intelligent sensors) is supported by financial resources (02PJ2490) of the Federal Ministry of Education and Research (BMBF) within the frame concept "Research for the production of tomorrow" and support initiative "Intelligent networking in production – a contribution to industry 4.0". It is supervised by the research center of Karlsruhe (PTKA).

References

1. Bechte, W.: Steuerung der Durchlaufzeit durch belastungsorientierte Auftragsfreigabe bei Werkstattfertigung. Diss. Universität Hannover 1980, Nachdruck veröffentlicht in: Fortschritt-Berichte der VDI-Zeitschriften, Reihe 2, Nr. 70, VDI-Verlag, Düsseldorf (in German) (1984)
2. Dutke, S.: Mentale Modelle: Konstrukte des Wissens und Verstehens. Kognitionspsychologische Grundlagen für die Software-Ergonomie. Verlag für Angewandte Psychologie (in German) (1994)
3. Endsley, M.R., Kiris, E.O.: The out-of-the-loop performance problem and level of control in automation. Hum. Factors J. Hum. Factors Ergon. Soc. **37**(2), 381–394 (1995)

4. Hanke, U.: Externale Modellbildung als Hilfe bei der Informationsverarbeitung und beim Lernen. Diss. Universitätsbibliothek Freiburg (in German) (2006)
5. Lödding, H.: Verfahren der Fertigungssteuerun 2. Auflage. Springer (in German) (2008)
6. Mayer, R.E., Massa, L.J.: Three facets of visual and verbal learners: cognitive ability, cognitive style, and learning preference. J. Educ. Psychol. **95**(4), 833 (2003)
7. Nyhuis, P., Seitz, K.F.: Steigerung der logistischen Leistungsfähigkeit durch die Entwicklung eines kybernetischen Systemdenkens. In: Schuh, G., Stich, V. (eds.) Enterprise-Integration, pp. 77–89. Springer, Berlin Heidelberg (in German) (2014)
8. Richardson, A.: Verbalizer-visualizer: a cognitive style dimension. J. Ment. Imagery **1**, 109–125 (1977)
9. Schlick, C., Bruder, R., Luczak, H.: Arbeitswissenschaft. Springer, Berlin (in German) (2010)
10. Schnotz, W., Kürschner, C.: External and internal representations in the acquisition and use of knowledge: visualization effects on mental model construction. Instr. Sci. **36**(3), 175–190 (2008)
11. Wiendahl, H.-P., Breithaupt, J.W.: Automatic production control applying control theory. Int. J. Prod. Econ. **63**(1), 33–46 (2000)
12. Wiendahl, H.-P.: Auftragsmanagement in der industriellen Produktion Grundlagen, Konfiguration, Einführung. Springer (in German) (2012)

Can You Judge a Video Game by Its Cover?

An Exploration of Subjective Impressions and Viewing Patterns

Mikki H. Phan(✉), Jibo He, and Barbara S. Chaparro

Wichita State University, Wichita, KS, USA
{mhphan, jibo.he, barbara.chaparro}@wichita.edu

Abstract. Studies have shown that first impressions of websites can lead to lasting opinions regarding usability and trustworthiness. However, little research has been conducted concerning first impressions of video games. In this study, 20 college-age students were asked to view and rate images of 48 game box covers after a brief exposure while their eye movement patterns were recorded. Results revealed that participants can reliably form different impressions (e.g., fun vs. boring) about certain video games based on a brief viewing of the game box cover. Analysis of eye tracking data revealed that participants viewed the front image, side title strip, and front game title the most. Relationships among the different subjective attributes (e.g., design quality, entertainment value) are reported.

Keywords: Video games · Box cover · Game quality · Subjective ratings · Eye tracking · Eye movement pattern · First impressions

1 Introduction

Conventional wisdom tells us that first impressions matter, especially when we are meeting someone new or deciding whether we should try or buy an unfamiliar product. A substantial body of academic literature exists about the topic of first impressions. Specifically, many studies have focused on first impressions in relation to person perception and social cognition [1]. For instance, Willis and Todorov [2] showed that in as little as 100-ms exposure participants were able to make specific trait judgments about a person (e.g., likeability, trustworthiness, and competence) just by viewing his/her face.

In the Human-Computer Interaction (HCI) domain, there are a growing number of studies examining first impressions in relation to user interface and product design. In particular, researchers found strong relationships between user's initial impressions of interface aesthetics and their a priori and post facto evaluations of system usability [3–5]. Additionally, researchers have found that users may form an impression of a website in as little as 50 ms [6, 7]. Lindgaard and colleagues [6] also found that first impressions not only influenced the visual appeal of a website, but also its perceived trustworthiness and usability.

C. Stephanidis (Ed.): HCII 2015 Posters, Part II, CCIS 529, pp. 690–696, 2015.
DOI: 10.1007/978-3-319-21383-5_117

2 Purpose

While there has been a large focus on first impressions in the context of websites, there has been very little research about first impressions of video games. First impressions of video games may occur at a gaming store in which game boxes are displayed or online where images of the boxes may appear. The main goal of this study was to explore people's first impressions about game quality and content based on images of video game covers. Specifically, this study aimed to answer the following questions:

- Q1. Are people able to form first impressions about a video game from a brief exposure to the game box cover?
- Q2. What portions of the game box cover do people view to form first impressions?
- Q3. How do the perceived attributes of game box covers relate to one another?

3 Method

3.1 Participants

Twenty native English-speaking undergraduate students (Age: M = 21.45 years, SD = 4.24 years) participated in the study in exchange for course credit. All participants reported to have 20/20 or corrected-to-normal vision, and normal color vision. Eleven of the participants were females, and all but one reported that they were video game players. Of the 19 game players, 2 self-identified as "Newbie/Novice", 11 as "Casual", 5 as "Core/Midcore", and 1 as "Hardcore/Expert" gamer. In addition, 13 gamers reported going to video game stores (e.g., GameStop) at least once a year to purchase video games. None of the participants had previous experience with playing any of the video games that they viewed in the study.

3.2 Materials and Apparatus

Fifty-two Xbox 360 game covers were presented in the study (four covers were used in practice trials). Forty-eight of the covers were from less popular game titles. Prior to the selection of the game covers, two video game experts heavily involved in the business of selling games were asked to evaluate a list of 139 less popular video games on a 7-point Likert scale (1 = Not Popular; 7 = Very Popular). The 48 game covers selected were rated 3.5 or less on the popularity scale. Four covers were selected for each of the 11 major game genres (see Table 1).

A computer with Intel Core 2 Duo 2.53 GHz processor running Mac OS X (Version 10.6.8) and a ThinkVision C220p 22.0-inch CRT monitor were used to present the game cover images at a resolution of 1920 × 1080. The EyeLink 1000 was used to track participants' eye movements, and a chin rest was used to keep participants' head stable throughout the experiment. Fixations were automatically defined in the system as the periods between saccades (velocities > 30°/sec and accelerations > 8000°/sec^2) that

Table 1. List of 48 less popular game titles per genre

Genre	Game Titles
Action	*Blades of Time, Fairytale Fights, Kung Fu High Impact, Splatterhouse*
Adventure	*Deadly Premonition, Rise of Nightmares, Vampire Rain, Knights Contract*
Driving	*Autobahn Polizei, Ben 10: Galactic Racing, Nail'd, PocketBike Racer*
Fighting	*Battle Fantasia, Lucha Libre AAA: Heroes Del Ring, TNA Impact!, WarTech: Senko no Ronde*
Fitness	*Jillian Michael's Fitness Adventure, The Biggest Loser: Ultimate Workout, UFC Personal Trainer: The Ultimate Fitness System, Your Shape Fitness Evolved*
Music/Dance	*Dance Masters, Disney Sing It, Rock of the Dead, Rocksmith*
Other	*Culdcept Saga* (Card Battle), *Kinectimals* (Virtual Life), *Motion Explosion!* (Party), *Rabbids: Alive & Kicking* (Party)
Role-Playing	*Enchanted Arms, Infinite Undiscovery, Kingdom Under Fire: Circle of Doom, Venetica*
Shooter	*Bullet Witch, Hour of Victory, Velvet Assassin, Wanted: Weapons of Fate*
Simulation	*Air Conflicts: Secret Wars, DarkStar One, Heroes Over Europe, Naval Assault: The Killing Tide*
Sports	*Adrenalin Misfits, Blood Bowl, Motion Sports, Stoked*
Strategy	*Record of Agarest War, Stormrise, Thrillville, Warhammer: Battle March*

are not blinks [8]. All images presented were 3000 × 2000 in pixels. A keyboard and mouse were used to record participants' responses.

3.3 Procedure

Participants were seated approximately 70 cm in front of the computer. After a consent form was signed and general instructions were given, participants' eyes were calibrated on the EyeLink 1000. Each trial began with a fixation screen, followed by a screen, which displayed a cover image for 20 s, and ended with the response screens.

All 52 game covers were presented in a random order to every participant. After each cover was viewed, participants were asked to complete seven subjective ratings about the game on a 9-point Likert scale similar to what Lindgaard and colleagues [6, 7] used. Only one attribute rating targeted the game covers (i.e., visual complexity), the remaining five attributes (excluding game familiarity) asked participants to evaluate the games themselves based on what they saw from the covers (see Table 2).

The first four game covers that participants saw were presented as practice trials to allow participants to be familiarized with the general procedure of the study. Excluding the practice trials, participants were offered a 5-minute resting period for every 16 trials they completed. Participants took about 60 min to complete the study.

Table 2. List of subjective ratings according to the order in which they were asked (top = asked first; bottom = asked last).

Attribute	Scale Anchors
Design Quality of the Game	1 = Poorly Designed; 9 = Well Designed
Challenge Level of the Game	1 = Easy; 9 = Difficult
Visual Complexity of the Cover	1 = Simple; 9 = Complex
Entertainment Value of the Game	1 = Boring; 9 = Fun
Violence Level of the Game	1 = Not Violent; 9 = Very Violent
Purchase Likelihood: Imagine that you're in a game store, what is the likelihood that you would buy this game?	1 = Very Unlikely; 9 = Very Likely
Familiarity: How familiar are you with this game (i.e., seen it, heard of it, or play it before)?	1 = Not Familiar; 9 = Very Familiar

4 Results

Data from the four practice trials were excluded from final analyses. The mean game familiarity ratings across the 48 game titles were very low ($M = 1.78$, $SD = 1.78$ out of 9), which confirmed that participants were not familiar with the game titles.

4.1 Q1. Subjective Rating Differences Among Game Box Covers

Six dependent samples *t* tests were conducted comparing the highest- and lowest-rated game covers in order to assess whether first impressions about a game can be formed based on a brief exposure of the cover. Bonferroni correction method was implemented to control for family-wise type I error. Results revealed that there was a significant difference between the highest- and lowest-rated game covers per subjective attribute rating (see Table 3). This indicated that participants reliably perceived certain video games as better designed or more fun based on a 20-second viewing of the game covers.

4.2 Q2. Viewing Patterns Across Game Box Covers

Eye tracking data were analyzed in order to examine how people viewed the video game covers. Each game cover was divided into nine natural segments (front image, side title, front title, back image, front Entertainment Software Rating Board (ESRB) label, back ESRB label, back other info, Xbox 360 header; company logo), which are commonly referred as areas of interest (AOI).

The first three AOIs that participants typically fixated on were the: front image, side title strip; front game title. The three AOIs that tended to be visited last were the: the other info area on the back, Xbox 360 header; game publisher's logo. After accounting

Table 3. Comparison of the highest- and lowest-rate game covers ($N = 20$; $df = 19$)

Attribute	Game Cover Pair (Mean; SD)	*t* Statistics & Effect Size
Cover Visual Complexity (9 = Complex)	*Kingdom Under Fire* (7.40; 1.23) vs. *PocketBike Racer* (3.60; 1.93)	*t* value = 6.90, $p < .001$ *Cohen's d* = 2.35
Game Design Quality (9 = Well Designed)	*Kingdom Under Fire* (6.65; 1.42) vs. *PocketBike Racer* (3.65, 2.08)	*t* value = 5.58, $p < .001$ *Cohen's d* = 1.68
Game Challenge Level (9 = Difficult)	*Stormrise* (7.20; 1.64) vs. *Kinectimals* (2.90, 2.10)	*t* value = 9.36, $p < .001$ *Cohen's d* = 2.10
Game Entertainment Value (9 = Fun)	*Motion Sports* (6.70; 2.52) vs. *Splatterhouse* (3.90; 1.86)	*t* value = 3.70, $p = .002$ *Cohen's d* = 1.26
Game Violence Level (9 = Very Violent)	*Splatterhouse* (8.60, 0.82) vs. *Sing It* (1.00; 0.00)	*t* value = 41.40, $p < .001$ *Cohen's d* = 13.11
Game Purchase Likelihood (9 = Very Likely)	*The Biggest Loser* (4.65; 2.44) vs. *Lucha Libre* (1.85; 2.08)	*t* value = 4.80, $p < .001$ *Cohen's d* = 1.14

for the different sizes of AOIs, results revealed that participants are more likely to look at the main images on the front and back covers, and were less likely to look at the game publisher's logo, Xbox 360 header, and front ESRB label (see Table 4).

Table 4. Areas of interest (AOI) data across 48 game covers

Mean Fixation Order	Areas of Interest	Mean (*SD*) Dwell Time in seconds	Adjusted Mean (*SD*) Dwell Time in seconds
1	Front Image	3.95 (*2.52*)	2.88 (*1.84*)
2	Side Title	0.80 (*0.76*)	2.47 (*2.32*)
3	Front Title	1.22 (*1.43*)	2.40 (2.82)
4	Back Image	4.58 (*2.77*)	2.49 (*1.51*)
5	Front ESRB Label	0.01 (*0.09*)	0.12 (*1.16*)
6	Back ESRB Label	0.27 (*0.78*)	2.14 (*6.27*)
7	Back Other Info	0.83 (*1.35*)	1.27 (*2.06*)
8	Xbox 360 Header	0.01 (*0.05*)	0.01 (*0.14*)
9	Company Logo	0.00 (*0.01*)	0.00 (*0.13*)

Note: Adjusted Dwell Time = (AOI's Dwell Time /AOI's Area)*1000

Table 5. Spearman's correlations between attributes ($df = 958$)

	Visual complexity	Design quality	Challenge level	Entertainment value	Violence Llevel	Purchase likelihood
VC	1.00					
DQ	0.57	1.00				
CL	0.52	0.66	1.00			
EV	0.45	0.70	0.52	1.00		
VL	0.31	0.13	0.38	$p > .05$	1.00	
PL	0.28	0.59	0.46	0.78	-0.07*	1.00

*The only case where $p = .03$, the rest had $p < .001$.

4.3 Q3. Relationship Between Subjective Attribute Ratings

A series of two-tailed Spearman's rank-order correlations were conducted in order to examine whether the subjective attributes were related to one another. The strongest relationships were found to be between game purchase likelihood and game entertainment value; game entertainment value and game design quality (see Table 5).

5 Discussion

To the best of the authors' knowledge, this is the first study that investigated first impressions of video game box covers. Overall, findings in this study support the notion that first impressions of a video game can be formed by simply viewing the game cover for a short duration. Specifically, participants were able to develop general impressions about the quality and content of the games (e.g., design quality, violence level).

Interestingly, visual complexity of the covers had strong positive relationships with design quality and challenge level of the games. This suggests that a game cover with a complex rather than simple appearance can lead people to perceive that the game itself is challenging and well designed, which in turn can influence their purchasing decision.

Eye tracking data suggests that the front image area of the cover was viewed first and the longest, and may possibly be the most influential to first impressions. Overall, these results suggest that careful thought and care should be given to the overall design of game covers as there are strong positive correlations among game design quality, entertainment value, and purchase likelihood. A limitation of this study is that we only assessed people's subjective impressions of video games based on the game box cover, and did not assess the validity of these impressions. Future studies should examine how these perceptions might change after participants played the games, as well as uncover specific design elements on game covers (e.g., contrast, color scheme, text density) that contribute to both positive and negative first impressions of video games.

References

1. Ambady, N., Skowronski, J.J. (eds.): First impressions. Guilford Press, New York (2008)
2. Willis, J., Todorov, A.: First impressions making up your mind after a 100-ms exposure to a face. Psychol. Sci. **17**(7), 592–598 (2006)
3. Kurosu, M., Kashimura, K.: Apparent usability vs. inherent usability: experimental analysis on the determinants of the apparent usability. In: Conference Companion on Human Factors in Computing Systems, pp. 292–293. ACM, May 1995
4. Tractinsky, N.: Aesthetics and apparent usability: empirically assessing cultural and methodological issues. In: Proceedings of the ACM SIGCHI Conference on Human Factors in Computing Systems, pp.115–122. ACM, March 1997
5. Tractinsky, N., Katz, A.S., Ikar, D.: What is beautiful is usable. Interact. Comput. **13**(2), 127–145 (2000)
6. Lindgaard, G., Dudek, C., Sen, D., Sumegi, L., Noonan, P.: An exploration of relations between visual appeal, trustworthiness and perceived usability of homepages. ACM Trans. Comput. Hum. Interact. (TOCHI) **18**(1), 1–30 (2011)
7. Lindgaard, G., Fernandes, G., Dudek, C., Brown, J.: Attention web designers: you have 50 milliseconds to make a good first impression! Behav. Inf. Technol. **25**(2), 115–126 (2006)
8. Nguyen, D., Owens, J., Chaparro, A., Chaparro, B., Palmer, E.: Gaze pattern differences between subjective and objective search of e-commerce Web pages. In: Proceedings of the 56th Annual Human Factors and Ergonomic Society Meeting, pp. 1619–1623, October 2012

Questionnaire for User Habits of Compute Clusters (QUHCC)

Johanna Renker[1](✉), Stephan Schlagkamp[2], and Gerhard Rinkenauer[1]

[1] Leibniz Research Centre for Working Environment and Human Factors, Dortmund, Germany
{renker,rinkenauer}@ifado.de

[2] Robotics Research Institute, TU Dortmund University, Dortmund, Germany
stephan.schlagkamp@udo.edu

Abstract. There is an increased interest to improve existing schedulers of compute clusters. Trace data are used to analyze the performance of compute clusters and to develop improved algorithms, but the interaction of the user and the compute cluster is not considered yet. Therefore, the current study investigates user behavior and satisfaction with regard to compute clusters. The resulting data are used to model users and to run a scheduler simulation with these modeled users. A new questionnaire for User Habits of Compute Clusters (QUHCC) with 7 scales and 53 questions was developed for this purpose. Results indicate that there is considerable potential to improve the performance of computer systems, viz. users satisfaction is limited, because different kinds of user strategies are necessary to improve the performance of the system. Future work includes the further validation and improvement of the questionnaire.

Keywords: Questionnaire · High performance computing · User strategies · User satisfaction

1 Introduction

Workload traces can be used to evaluate the performance of computing systems [1], but they represent only one instantiation of the interaction process. The interaction of the user with the computing system is often disregarded. Users submit jobs and receive responses from the computing system, so that a mutual influence occurs. In the current study this mutual influence is investigated by focusing exemplarily on user satisfaction and user strategies with regard to computing systems. To assess the interaction patterns a questionnaire was developed and employed for data collection. Those data provide insights into the dynamic process of users and computing systems and allow to model user behavior in a simulation to test different scheduler algorithms, which might improve the performance of computing systems [2]. Several questionnaires regarding user experience and satisfaction already exist [3–5], but they are not usable in the context of High Performance Computing (HPC), because the interaction with compute

C. Stephanidis (Ed.): HCII 2015 Posters, Part II, CCIS 529, pp. 697–702, 2015.
DOI: 10.1007/978-3-319-21383-5_118

clusters is rather abstract and the handling specific. Therefore, a need emerged to develop a new questionnaire, which is adapted to the different characteristics of compute clusters. In order to gain deeper insights into the interaction between users and compute clusters, we consulted a focus group with administrators of a compute cluster.

2 Method

The used research method is twofold. First, we interviewed a focus group to get an overview of interaction patterns between users and compute clusters. Based on these information, a questionnaire is developed to get more detailed insights into the interaction process from a larger sample of compute cluster users.

2.1 Focus Group

The employment of a focus group is a common research method to get qualitative information about a certain topic during a moderated discussion. This technique involves in-depth group interviews with a sample of a specific population. Group interviews are resource-efficient and support the dynamic social interaction, so that the achieved data are often richer than from one-to-one interviews [6]. In the current study we used this method in the first explorative phase to gain insights into users interaction with compute clusters and to detect the main issues, which are investigated in the second phase by means of the questionnaire. Our focus group comprises administrators of a compute cluster at TU Dortmund University. We discussed issues concerning user habits, user satisfaction and needs of users with these experts. Finally, the following main research questions resulted from the discussions:

- Which factors determine user satisfaction?
- Which strategies are used to gain results faster?
- What waiting times are acceptable by users?
- How do sparse resources affect users working habits?
- How can different job types be categorized?

During the group interviews, we received information about the work environment and working habits of users of computing systems, e.g., we were informed that users of smaller clusters, like the Linux compute cluster of the Faculty for Physics at the TU Dortmund, often ask for assistance in case that urgent results are needed. Together with the administrators we categorized jobs of compute clusters into small, medium, and large jobs as well as interactive work. Then, we determined definitions: Interactive work is the submission of very short jobs, which are immediately processed to allow continuous work; small jobs last up to four hours, mediums jobs last one to three days and large jobs last longer than three days. This categorization helps to consider user behavior in terms of job submissions in a differentiated way. All information gathered from the focus group are considered in our further work.

2.2 Item Design

To answer the research questions concerning the focus group results we developed a questionnaire - Questionnaire for User Habits of Compute Clusters (QUHCC). We derived seven scales from the questions: Level of Experience, Job Perception, User Behavior, User Strategies, User Satisfaction and Acceptance of Waiting Times (see Table 1).

The scale User Strategies is divided into five subscales to investigate different kinds of strategies: strategies which deal with working time, usage of strategies, general job adjustment, ego job adjustment and job cancelation. After defining these scales, several items in the context of compute clusters are developed. The Big-Five-Inventory-10 [7] as well as questions about the work environment

Table 1. Overview of the seven scales of QUHCC.

Scale name	Main subject	Amount of items
Level of Experience (LE)	- Total work experience with the compute cluster (objective measurement) - Confidence while working with compute clusters (subjective measurement) Example: I feel confident in working with Super-/HP-/Cloud-Computing.	2 (objective) 4 (subjective)*
Job Length Perception (JLP)	- Categorization of different job types (interactive work, small, medium and large jobs) - Perception of the length of these job type Example: How long do you consider a small job to take on average?	3
User Behavior (UB)	- Frequency of job submissions per job type on average Example: How often do you submit small jobs?	7
Waiting for Jobs (WJ)	- Estimated waiting times for responses according to the different job types Example: To continue work, I have to wait for results of small jobs.	3
User Strategies (US)	- Usage of strategies to accelerate the computing process Example: I often submit bag-of-tasks (=lots of single jobs) to exploit the promised capacities.	23*
User Satisfaction (USF)	- Satisfaction with the working time of the compute cluster Example: I am often frustrated if I have to wait longer than expected for a result.	4*
Acceptance of Waiting Times (AWT)	- Willingness to wait for results depending on the submitted job type Example: Imagine you submit a job you expect to run for 10 minutes. How long are you willing to wait for the result on top of the 10 minutes?	7

* Items were rated on a 6 point scale from "strongly disagree" to "strongly agree"

(e.g., the name of the compute cluster), personal information (e.g., age) and the comprehensibleness of the items are added to the whole survey.

2.3 Participants

In total, 24 users of three different compute clusters at the TU Dortmund University took part in the study (*mean age* = 33 years; *SD* = 9.52). They work in the fields of mathematics, statistics, chemistry, physics or computer science. On average 34 % of the participants working times deals with HPC. Generally, results from the subjective LE scale show that participants feel quite confident while working with compute cluster (*mean* = 4.92; *SD* = 0.88).

3 Results

In the following we present some exemplary results for the first two main research questions, viz. users satisfaction and usage of strategies. Results from the USF scale show that users satisfaction with the waiting times of their submitted jobs is limited (*mean* = 3.82, *SD* = 0.95). Furthermore, the level of user experience (t = 2.59, p = .02) and working outside the usual working hours (r = -2.59, p = .02) were shown to be statistically significant predictors of user satisfaction (see Table 2).

Regarding the user strategies, most of the users (63 %) submit bags of tasks (=lots of single jobs) to exploit the promised capacities and/or switch to other cluster which are less utilized (42 %). Overall, only 5 out of the 24 participants do not use one of the four mentioned strategies at all (see Table 3).

Table 2. Regression model with User Satisfaction as the criterion variable.

	Unstandardized coefficients	Standardized coefficients	t	Sig
Constant	2.30			
Level of Experience	0.48	0.44	2.59	.017
Strategy Working Time	-0.41	-0.44	-2.59	.017

Adjusted R^2 = 32.9 per cent; $F(2, 21) = 6.64$; $p < .01$

Table 3. Item statistics of subscale "Usage of Strategies (US)".

	Yes	No
I submit bags of tasks (=lots of single jobs)	63 % (15)	37 % (9)
I prioritize jobs by urgency	13 %(3)	87 % (21)
I switch to other clusters, which are less utilized	42 % (10)	58 %(14)
I consult and agree with other users	33 % (8)	67 % (16)
None of the above applies	21 % (5)	79 % (19)

4 Discussion

Purpose of the current study was to elucidate user satisfaction and strategies during the interaction with HPC. For this a questionnaire (QUHCC) was designed. QUHCC seems to be suitable to identify the main factors influencing user satisfaction. Furthermore, QUHCC allows identifying user strategies. Exemplary results are presented for the main topics users satisfaction and strategies. Users satisfaction with HPC seems to be limited and is modulated by users experience and the amount of work outside of the usual working hours. The more experienced the users are and the less they are working outside usual work hours the more satisfied users are with the waiting time of their compute cluster (see also Schlagkamp and Renker [8]). Thus, there seems to be still potential to increase users satisfaction by improving schedulers of compute clusters. Regarding users' strategies, O'Donnell and Draper [9] already showed that users use multiple alternative methods to deal with response delays. In accordance with those authors, we also found that users employ a quantity of strategies to avoid long waiting times. They mostly submit bags of tasks or switch to other clusters, which are less utilized to gain faster responses.

In addition, the information derived from the QUHCC will allow to model relevant aspects of user behavior in scheduler simulations. This may help to get deeper insights in specific patterns of the trace data, so that crucial time intervals can be detected and schedulers improved. However, modeling could be still improved by changing data characteristics. For example the definition of job types is a crucial issue, because every user has another mental representation of short, medium and long jobs. The findings of our study suggests that job types should be not defined as a time interval, but rather as a distribution of points of time to gain more precise data for the modeling.

A limitation of the current study is the small number of participants, which makes it challenging to validate the current data set. Therefore, besides of the improvement of the questionnaire in future studies larger samples will be tested.

Acknowledgments. We thank the administrators of the compute clusters at TU Dortmund University and all participants for their support.

References

1. Feitelson, D.G.: Workload Modeling for Computer System Performance Evaluation. Cambridge University Press (in press)
2. Fischer, G.: User modeling in humancomputer interaction. User Model. User Adap. Inter. **11**(1–2), 65–86 (2001)
3. Chin, J.P., Diehl, V.A., Norman, K.L.: Development of an instrument measuring user satisfaction of the human-computer interface. In: Proceedings of SIGCHI, pp. 213–218 (1988)
4. Kirakowski, J., Corbett, M.: Sumi: the software usability measurement inventory. Br. J. Educ. Technol. **24**, 210–212 (1993)

5. Laugwitz, B., Held, T., Schrepp, M.: Construction and Evaluation of a User Experience Questionnaire. Springer, Berlin Heidelberg (2008)
6. Rabiee, F.: Focus-group interview and data analysis. Proc. Nutr. Soc. **63**, 655–660 (2004)
7. Rammstedt, B., John, O.P.: Measuring personality in one minute or less: a 10-item short version of the big five inventory in english and german. J. Res. Pers. **41**, 203–212 (2007)
8. Schlagkamp, S., Renker, J.: Acceptance of waiting times in high performance computing. In: HCI International 2015 - Posters' Extended Abstracts. Springer, Berlin Heidelberg (in press)
9. O'Donnell, P., Draper, S.W.: How machine delays change user strategies. SIGCHI Bull. **28**(2), 39–42 (1996)

Usability Assessment of a Suicide Intervention-Prevention Mini-Game

Joan M. Savage[1,2(✉)]

[1] Florida Institute of Technology (FIT) Human-Centered Design Institute, Florida, USA
savagej2014@my.fit.edu
[2] Indiana University (IU) School of Informatics, Indiana, USA

Abstract. Video games are growing in popularity and are fulfilling genuine human needs that the real world is currently unable to satisfy. Games teach, inspire and engage us in ways that reality is not. This study evaluated a video game designed to educate players concerning suicide prevention. It is aimed at educating on how to identify and address someone who might be contemplating suicide. Six veterans with varied demographics played Suicide Intervention- Prevention Mini-Game (SIP-M) and showed improvement in knowledge concerning suicide intervention-prevention. Participants found the game entertaining, informative and felt better equipped to identify and handle someone who might be contemplating suicide. SIP-M is discussed in the larger context of a virtual environment where veterans can participate in activities and receive information about a variety of mental and physical disorders.

Keywords: Design: human centered design and user centered design · Entertainment: gamification · Technology: graphical user interface · Technology: interaction in virtual and augmented reality environments

1 Introduction

Suicide Intervention-Prevention Mini-Game (SIP-M) is a video game designed to educate players on suicide intervention-prevention through an interactive simulation (game) which utilizes our cognitive functions to allow visual thinking. Visual thinking can provide potential solutions to support the learning about suicide prevention through Tangible Interactive Objects (TIO's) [2]. Players control an avatar and collect facts on defensiveness. Defensiveness plays an important role in suicidal behavior and learning to properly cope with a defensive person can be pivotal in helping to intervene and/or prevent suicide. SIP-M is part of a project completed for a grant under The Solutions Center Venture Fund during the summer of 2011. The project was called *Suicide Intervention–Prevention: A Health Education Simulation* (SIP).

Through playing SIP-M, a veteran (regardless of age) should show improvement in learning about suicide. This is vital because suicide and the well-being of military personnel is a topic of growing concern in public health [3].

C. Stephanidis (Ed.): HCII 2015 Posters, Part II, CCIS 529, pp. 703–708, 2015.
DOI: 10.1007/978-3-319-21383-5_119

It is estimated that 22 veterans commit suicide a day [4] and recently a press release was issued stating that mental health of veterans is now the highest priority for the Department of Veterans Affairs (VA) [5]. Recent research on veterans exposed to combat indicates that they are at an increased risk for mental health disorders (especially post-traumatic stress disorder (PTSD) and major depression) which can lead to suicide [6] or a Crisis in Belief.[1] Although there are successful treatments for full-blown PTSD, early interventions are lacking. An early intervention method that has shown to help is using visuospatial computer games which research has shown will interfere with and reduce flashbacks [7].

Developing games for mental health can be crucial for veterans who are struggling with mental health issues and who cannot or will not receive treatment from VA health care facilities.

There are three main problems that affect veterans concerning receiving treatment - Eligibility: Not all veterans are eligible for VA health care services. Enrollment: Not all eligible veterans enroll in VA health care services. Use: Not all enrolled veterans actually use VA health care services [8]. SIP-M was developed as a means to provide for veterans who fall under one of these three main problems. It was designed to help veterans better understand and recognize defensiveness. It is expected that a veteran will show improvement in learning about defensiveness for suicide intervention–prevention and that the veteran will rate the usability of SIP-M favorably.

1.1 Suicide Intervention-Prevention Mini-Game

Prototype: SIP-M is an interactive simulation (game) played in the third person to challenge a "Player" to complete it within three minutes.

Knowledge is conveyed, reinforced, and tested as veterans play the mini-game. This approach was selected in an effort to help the player learn the content while being entertained through personal challenge (e.g., meeting an attainable, but difficult, goal) [9]. To complete the game or attain the goal, the player must actively collect three facts about defensiveness. Data shows that those who commit suicide are more defensive and guarded; evaluations reveal an escalation of adverse mental conditions such as defensiveness [10]. Each fact on defensiveness presented in the mini-game was researched [11] and confirmed with clinical psychologist, Dr. Kevin Rand, Associate Professor at IUPUI.

The software used for developing SIP-M was Thinking Worlds by Caspian Learning. Sound Forge by Sony was used for voice-overs & some sound effects. Soundbooth by Adobe was used for voice-overs, sound effects & background music. Soundsnap by Tera Media was used for sound effects and Word by Microsoft was used for the script.

---

[1] *A Veteran's Guide to Civilian Living* is a book that I wrote to discuss several Crises that a veteran might be suffering from; including, a Crisis in Belief where a veteran stops believing that he or she can actually get better or improve.

2 Methods

The design process began with a field study consisting of interviews with experts in the area of suicide prevention, military sexual trauma and homelessness. Next a literature review was completed from the latest literature on veteran issues, trends, preferences and current online gaming preferences because the popularity of online gaming is only increasing [12]. A needs analysis was completed using this information and SIP-M was given IRB approval for this project.

Strong patterns emerged from this analysis and mental health – specifically suicide - emerged as the top priority. The term "suicide" was defined and the symptom "defensiveness" [13] was chosen as the mini-game's central theme. Identical multiple choice pre-test and post-test were created with the answers specifically addressed in the game. If the veteran did not complete the game within the three minutes (completion results when all facts are found within the game) then the game automatically came to a stop and the facts about defensiveness were displayed. The post-test and survey immediately followed game completion.

All participants were veterans currently living in the Indianapolis, Indiana area. The ages ranged from 28–60 years old and consisted of three males and three females. Very little background was known about the veterans in an effort to respect privacy, with the exception of their age, location and "veteran" status.

3 Results

All users with the exception of user five showed improvement in learning about suicide intervention-prevention or scored the same after the post-test; however, user five was not accustomed to playing this type of interactive video game. After completing the post-test and survey, user five immediately played the game a second time and showed substantial improvement learning the facts. Again, only the initial results were used with each participant. User three scored the same but user's one, two, four and six showed improvement. Playing SIP-M resulted in successfully informing veterans about suicide intervention-prevention as indicated by the results from the post-test (Fig. 1).

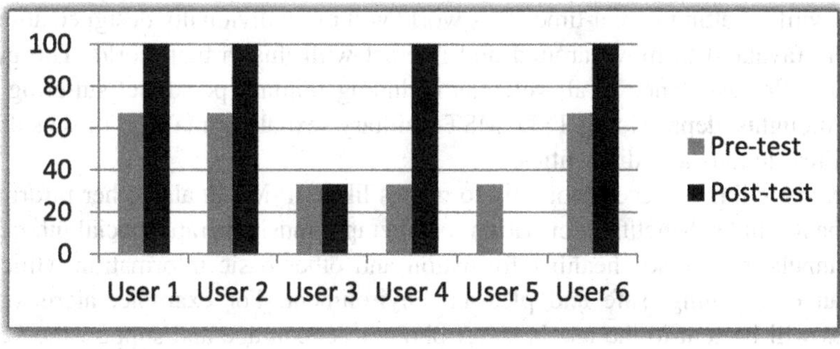

Fig. 1. Percent of knowledge learned pre and post-test. Note that user five scored a zero on the post-test

Following the post-test, a survey was given using a Likert-type scale. The survey asked users to rate the game on four factors; informative, better equipped to talk with someone who might be suicidal, entertaining, and character maneuverability. Participants rated each factor on a scale of one to ten with ten being "excellent" and one being "poor." Users felt they were better informed about suicide and found the game entertaining; all users with the exception of user four scored the game six and above on entertaining. User four found the character difficult to maneuver, therefore, did not find the game as entertaining but still gave an average score of five. However, user four felt informed and better equipped to handle someone who is defensive. Overall, users rated SIP-M "Good" to "Excellent".

Suicide Intervention-Prevention Mini-Game was successfully designed to help veterans identify suicidal tendencies using a video game. Suicide intervention-prevention information was provided in the form of an entertaining game with the thought that veterans will want to play more health games and as they play, continue to learn about issues that affect them.

4 Conclusion

Restating the two study hypotheses: (1) veterans would show an improvement in learning about defensiveness for suicide intervention-prevention and (2) veterans would rate the usability of the SIP-M favorably. The first hypothesis is supported by the results of the pre and post-test (Fig. 1). The second hypothesis is supported by the user ratings for 'informative', 'better equipped' (to talk with someone who might be defensive), 'entertaining', and 'character maneuverability', as well as the overall usability ratings as "Good" to "Excellent". Therefore, results support that SIP-M is successful in helping veterans become better equipped to cope with someone who is suicidal through an entertaining game. These results satisfy objectives 2:3 and 2.4 of the Surgeon General's *2012 National Strategy for Suicide Prevention* by supporting increasing knowledge of warning signs for suicide using innovative applications like virtual worlds and gaming [14].

SIP-M will be one of many games within a larger project called SavageWorld (SW). SW is a virtual collective online shared space where veterans can explore, meet other veterans, socialize, play games and participate in activities as a group or individually while chatting in real-time. This world will use individually designed animated characters (avatars) to move around and interact with this virtual world. The project intends to offer assistance to all veterans including military personnel suffering from suicidal thoughts, depression, PTSD, MST (military sexual trauma) and those suffering physical restrictions and disabilities.

Veterans will have access not only to games like SIP-M but also other informative games, health links, benefits information, pet therapy, music therapy, social interaction, help channels, help links, health information and other basic information while providing an entertaining, safe and pleasant environment. For example; alerts or text messages will be sent to the user's smart phone to encourage and support the veteran throughout the day. The message will be indicative of what the veteran prefers, i.e. Christians will receive a motivating scripture, etc. These messages can also invite the veteran to fulfill their responsibilities like a Twelve Step Program and the need to complete step nine, etc. Also, if the veteran is caring for a virtual pet, the animal will periodically need feeding, walking and loving. This will come as an alert and an invitation to socialize in SW. Caring for a pet has been shown to be very therapeutic [15].

The underpinning principle behind these alerts and invitations is to be a constant reminder that SW is a safe-always available place a veteran can go for help and support. The Office of the Inspector General expressed concerns that veterans may not be able to access the mental health care they need in a timely manner [16]. SW would always be available; day or night, from any PC and/or mobile device.

Acknowledgements. Special thanks to Dr. Jason Saleem, for editing and helping to organize *Usability Assessment of a Suicide Intervention–Prevention Mini-Game.* This material is based upon an unfunded course project led by Ms. Savage. SIP-M is part of a project completed for a grant under The Solutions Center Venture Fund during the summer of 2011. The project is called *Suicide Intervention–Prevention: Health Education Simulation* (SIP) and was completed with Dr. Joseph Defazio, IUPUI Director of Media Arts & Science, Dr. Kevin Rand, Clinical Psychologist and Jay Hardin, IUPUI Associate Professor.

References

1. McGonigal, J.: Reality Is Broken: Why Games Make Us Better and How They Can Change the World. Penguin, London (2011)
2. Boy, G.: From automation to tangible interactive objects. Annu. Rev. Control **38**, 1–11 (2014)
3. Kramarow, E., Pastor, P.: The Health of Male Veterans and Nonveterans Aged 25–64: United States, (2007–2010). NCHS Data Brief; [Internet] 2012 [cited 2012 Apr 24]. http://www.cdc.gov/nchs/data/databriefs/db101.pdf
4. Kemp, J., Bossarte, R.: Suicide Data Report. Department of Veterans Affairs, Mental Health Services, Suicide Prevention Program (2012). http://www.va.gov/opa/docs/Suicide-Data-Report-2012-final.pdf
5. Shinseki, E.: President Obama Signs Executive Order to Improve Access to Mental Health Services for Veterans, Service Members, and Military Families [News Release], August 31, 2012
6. Sundararaman, R., Panangala, S., Lister, S.: CRS Report for Congress; Suicide Prevention Among Veterans. Domestic Social Policy Division (US); [Internet] 2008 [cited 2012 May 04]. Order Code RL34471. http://www.fas.org/sgp/crs/misc/RL34471.pdf
7. Holmes, E., James, E., Coode-Bate, T., Deeprose, C.: Can playing the computer game "Tetris" reduce the build-up of flashbacks for trauma? Cognitive science; [Internet] 2009 [cited 2012 Apr 24]. http://www.plosone.org/article/info:doi/10.1371/journal.pone.0004153
8. Bagalman, E.: Suicide Prevention Efforts of the Veterans Health Administration Congressional Research Service (US). Report No.: R42340, February 2012
9. Thompson, D., Baranowski, T., Buday, R.: Conceptual model for the design of a serious video game promoting self management among youth with type 1 diabetes. J. Diab. Sci. Technol. **4**(3), 744–749 (2010)
10. Sheehan, D., Warren, J.: Law Enforcement suicide: psychological autopsies and psychometric traces. Suicide and Law Enforcement, 223–233 (2001)

11. Smith, M., Segal, J., Robinson, L.: Suicide Prevention: spotting the signs and helping a suicidal person. HelpGuide.org; [Internet] 2012 [cited 2012 Dec 18]. http://www.helpguide.org/mental/suicide_prevention.htm
12. Chen, K., Huang, P., Lei, C.: How sensitive are online gamers to network quality? Commun. ACM **49**(11), 34–38 (2006)
13. Smith, M., Segal, J., Robinson, L.: Suicide prevention: spotting the signs and helping a suicidal person. HelpGuide.org; [Internet] 2012 [cited 2012 Dec 18]. http://www.helpguide.org/mental/suicide_prevention.htm
14. U.S. Department of Health and Human Services. Office of the Surgeon General and National Action Alliance for Suicide Prevention. National Strategy for Suicide Prevention: Goals and Objectives for Action (2012)
15. Robinson, L., Segal, J.: The Therapeutic Benefits of Pets, How Caring for a Pet can Make You Happier and Healthier; [Internet] 2012 [cited 2012 Dec 18]. http://www.helpguide.org/life/pets.htm
16. Office of Inspector General. Veterans Health Administration Review of Veterans' Access to Mental Health Care; [Internet] 2012 [cited 2012 Dec 04]. http://www.va.gov/oig/pubs/VAOIG-12-00900-168.pdf

Acceptance of Waiting Times in High Performance Computing

Stephan Schlagkamp[1(✉)] and Johanna Renker[2]

[1] Robotics Research Institute, TU Dortmund University, Dortmund, Germany
stephan.schlagkamp@udo.edu
[2] Leibniz Research Centre for Working Environment and Human Factors, Dortmund, Germany
renker@ifado.de

Abstract. In high performance computing, users submit computing jobs to a parallel computing infrastructure. Ressources for jobs must be allocated according to the job's requirements. At times of high workload, waiting times are unavoidable. Hence, we investigate user acceptance of waiting times in high performance computing. We analyze data provided by Questionnaire for User Habits of Compute Clusters (QUHCC) among high performance computing users ($n = 24$). On the one hand, the results indicate that increasing processing times of jobs lead to greater acceptance of waiting times. On the other hand, the percental difference between processing times and waiting times decreases for increasing job lengths. We suggest that scheduling strategies should respect our findings.

Keywords: User satisfaction · Service levels · High performance computing · Waiting times

1 Introduction

In high performance computing (HPC), different users submit jobs to a parallel computing infrastructure. A job j is characterized by many different properties. This work considers its length r_j (the running time on the HPC environment) and its waiting time w_j. Waiting time incurs in a situation of high workload, when users submit more work than the system can process at a time. In such situation, the HPC system needs strategies to decide which job among all submitted jobs will be processed next. Literature discusses different optimization goals for HPC environments, e.g., cost optimality according to energy consumption [1]. Since human users submit jobs to a certain HPC environment, we consider their satisfaction with waiting times in detail. Therefore, we focus on user satisfaction in high performance computing according to waiting times. Two different questions occur: what is a good criterion to optimize user satisfaction according to waiting times and how does this criterion influence user satisfaction. Hence, we want to find an *acceptable* way to schedule jobs in situations of high workload.

The structure of this work is as follows. The methodology of this study is in Sect. 2. Furthermore, Sect. 3 presents results a conducted survey, where we also

C. Stephanidis (Ed.): HCII 2015 Posters, Part II, CCIS 529, pp. 709–714, 2015.
DOI: 10.1007/978-3-319-21383-5_120

argue for slowdown as an approriate metric. In Sect. 4, we discuss the correlation between user satisfaction and slowdown. This work ends with a brief conclusion in Sect. 5.

2 Methodology

In this study, we analyze the answers provided by 24 participants, who answered QUHCC [2]. Beside other methods, Pruyn and Smith use such methodology in their research on customer's reaction to waiting times as well [3]. We perform statistical analyses in form of boxplots and empirical cumulative distribution functions (CDF) to argue for an increasing acceptance of waiting times according to job lengths. We show that acceptences of waiting times in HPC environments are exponantially distributed. Therefore, we analyze the *slowdown* of jobs and rate the quality of different slowdown values.

3 Acceptence of Waiting Times

Questionnaire QUHCC contains six questions asking participants for their acceptance of waiting times for jobs of different lengths (cf. scale Acceptance of Waiting Times (AWT)). We analyze the answers given in a survey among different HPC users and call them *observations.*

Definition 1 (Observation). *An observation* $o = (p_j, w_j)$ *represents the accepted waiting time* w_j *for a job length* p_j*. It is based on an answer provided by a participant.*

We cluster the observations according to the different questions into six sets and sort them according to the assumed job lengths:

- INT: interactive jobs
- 10M: ten minutes
- SHO: short jobs (up to four hours)
- 180M: 180 min.
- MED: medium (one to three days)
- LAR: large (longer than three days)

For sets SHO and MED, we chose the average job length of 120 min and two days, which is equal to 2,880 min, minutes as reference. Figure 1 visualizes all observations as boxplots, Table 1 presents means and medians. The figure reveals an increasing acceptance of waiting times for increasing job lengths. The medians increase from 12.5 min to 10,080 min, and the means increase monotonically from 61.2 min to 9,516.5 min.

Based on this observation, we conclude that growing job lengths cause a greater acceptance of delayed results, which we can exploit in terms of user satisfying scheduling in HPC.

We continue the analysis by introducing slowdown, e.g., [4]. Slowdown describes the relative factor between an optimal response time with zero waiting time and the actual response time as the sum of processing and waiting time.

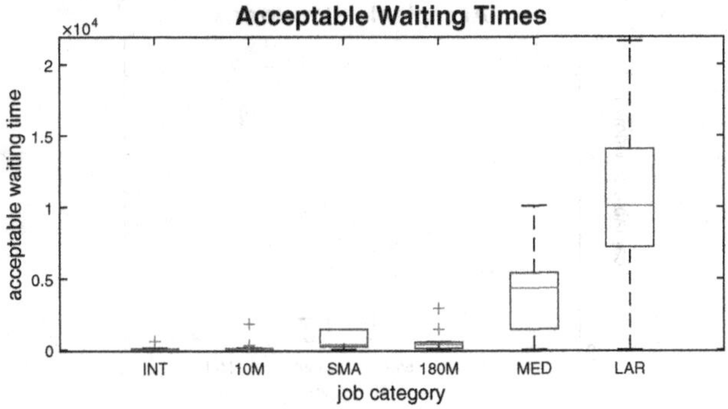

Fig. 1. Acceptable waiting times for six different sets.

Table 1. Mean and median values of acceptable waiting times for six different sets.

	INT	10M	SHO	180M	MED	LAR
median	12.5	30.0	360.0	360.0	4320.0	10,080.0
mean	61.2	171.9	636.7	553.8	3,863.5	9,516.5

Definition 2 (Slowdown). *The slowdown of job j with processing time $p_j > 0$ and waiting time $w_j \geq 0$ is* $\mathrm{SD}(j) = \frac{p_j + w_j}{p_j}$.

Therefore, slowdown allows rating the quality of a schedule independent of specific jobs' lengths and waiting times. Figure 2 depicts the slowdowns for observation sets 10M, SHO, 180M, and LAR as boxplots. Table 2 presents means and medians of slowdowns of each set. We do not consider INT and LAR because of the unspecified exact job lengths disallowing calculation of slowdown. While the acceptance of waiting times increases for larger jobs, the according slowdown decreases. Due to the comparability of observation sets using slowdown, we use this metric to rate the quality of service in the next section.

Table 2. Mean and median values of observations in 10M, SMA, MED, and 180M.

	10M	SMA	180M	MED
mean	18.1938	6.3062	4.0764	2.3415
median	4.0000	4.0000	3.0000	2.5000

4 Quality of Service Regarding Slowdown

By means of *acceptability of slowdown* $A(s, O)$, we calculate the percentage share of observations applying to that slowdown.

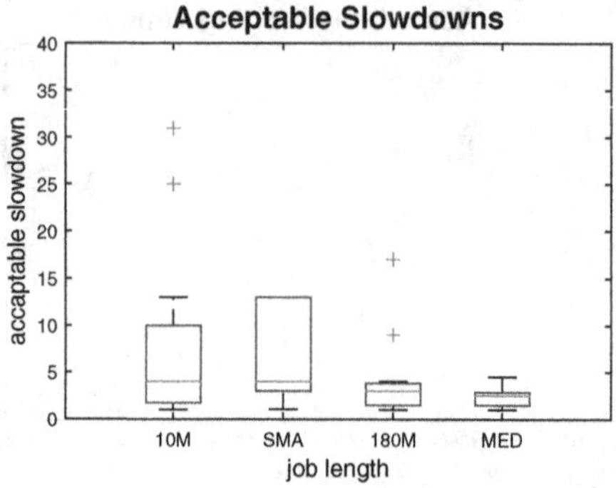

Fig. 2. Acceptable slowdowns for categories 10M, SMA, MED, and 180M.

Definition 3 (Acceptability of Slowdown). *Given a set of observations* $O = \{(p_j, w_j)\}$, *the acceptability of slowdown* s *is the amount of observations meeting the slowdown, i.e.,*

$$A(s, O) = \frac{|\{\mathrm{SD}(o) \leq s \mid o \in O\}|}{|O|}. \tag{1}$$

Figure 3 depicts the acceptability of slowdowns for all observations as an empirical CDF, as well as an exponential CDF fit, according to an exponential probability density function

$$f(x|\mu) = \frac{1}{\mu} e^{\frac{-1}{\mu}}. \tag{2}$$

To find a suitable fit, we shift the slowdowns by minus one. This calculation is necessary because a minimal value of slowdown is one, while it is zero for a distribution function. Applying least squares, we obtain a parameter of $\mu = 3.85$. We then shift the exponential CDF by one again (cf. Fig. 3). Note that slowdowns greater than 20 are adjusted to 20, since these observations strongly influence the fitting and are not suitable as an optimization objective in practical application.

Beside that, Table 3 presents the acceptability of slowdowns for all sets ranging from 1.0 to 4.0. Set ALL is the union of all sets considered. Based on these plots and analyses, we discuss two different forms of service-levels for HPC environments.

4.1 Single Service Level

To treat all users and jobs equally, we pay special attention to the data of set ALL. Defining a single service quality, we suggest to allow a slowdown between 1.5 and 2.0. For ALL, the amount of satisfied users lays between 74.4 % and 85.9 %, meaning that almost 3/4 of acceptability is met for 2.0 and less than

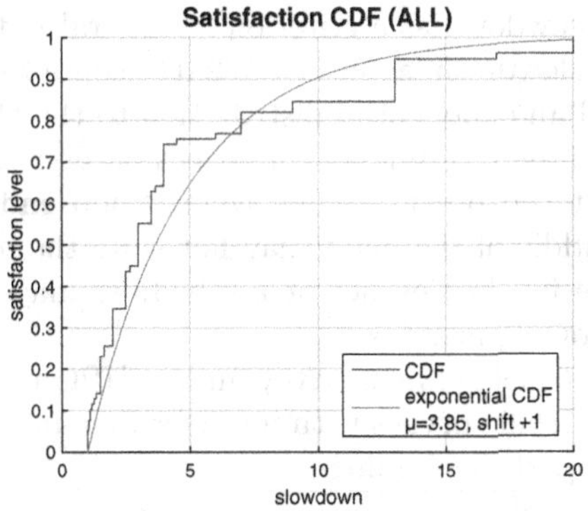

Fig. 3. Acceptibility of slowdowns in observations from 10M, SMA, MED, and 180M combined.

Table 3. Satisfaction-Levels in 10M, SMA, MED, and 180M according to different slowdowns.

	1.0	1.5	2.0	2.5	3.0	3.5	4.0
ALL	100 %	85.9 %	74.4 %	65.4 %	55.1 %	44.9 %	35.9 %
10M	100 %	87.5 %	75.0 %	62.5 %	62.5 %	62.5 %	62.5 %
SMA	100 %	95.7 %	87.0 %	78.3 %	78.3 %	69.6 %	52.2 %
180M	100 %	75.0 %	62.5 %	62.5 %	56.3 %	31.3 %	25.0 %
MED	100 %	82.6 %	69.6 %	56.5 %	26.1 %	17.4 %	8.7 %

1/8 of acceptibility are not met for a slowdown of 1.5. Nearly the same holds for the fitted exponantial CDF with acceptance values between 72.2 % and 85.0 %. Nevertheless, considering set 180M only gains acceptability between 62.5 % to 75.0 %, which is not in the demanded interval. Therefore, we consider multiple service levels next.

4.2 Multiple Service Levels

Beside a single criterion, a scheduling strategy could also pay respect to different job lengths. As analyzed in Sect. 3, the accepted slowdown decreases for increasing job lengths. Therefore, we suggest usage of function (2) to rate acceptibility represents a monotonically increasing way to penalize slowdown.

5 Conclusion and Future Work

In this study, we analyzed the data provided by QUHCC asking users for their acceptance of waiting times. The data indicates a growing acceptance of waiting times according to jobs' length, although the relative acceptable waiting time decreases. Regarding slowdown as a criterion to generalize the accepted waiting times, we argued for a slowdown factor of 1.5–2.0 to suit a tolerable level of users. Additionally, we fitted an exponential distribution to the CDF of slowdowns.

Future work should analyze further influences on user satisfaction, e.g., this work does not respect the point in time when a job ends. Jobs finishing on weekends or in the middle of the night may not suite the users working habits. Such jobs should have finished earlier or a scheduler may exploit, that results are needed on the following monday.

Since the data was collected in a survey among HPC users at TU Dortmund University ($n = 24$), further surveys with more participants at other universities or institutes could support our findings.

References

1. Tang, Q., Gupta, S.K.S., Varsamopoulos, G.: Energy-efficient thermal-aware task scheduling for homogeneous high-performance computing data centers: a cyber-physical approach. IEEE Trans. Parallel Distrib. Syst. **19**(11), 1458–1472 (2008)
2. Renker, J., Schlagkamp, S.: QUHCC: questionnaire for user habits of compute clusters. In: HCI International 2015 - Posters' Extended Abstracts (in press)
3. Pruyn, A., Smidts, A.: Effects of waiting on the satisfaction with the service: beyond objective time measures. Int. J. Res. Mark. **15**(4), 321–334 (1998)
4. Feitelson, D.G.: Metrics for parallel job scheduling and their convergence. In: Feitelson, D.G., Rudolph, L. (eds.) JSSPP 2001. LNCS, vol. 2221, p. 188. Springer, Heidelberg (2001)

Analysis on the Influencing Factors of the Comprehensibility of Graphical Symbols

Chuan-Yu Zou[1(✉)], Fan Zhang[2], and Huimin Hu[3]

[1] Research Group of Graphical Symbols and Way Guidance, China National Institute of Standardization, Beijing, China
zouchy@cnis.gov.cn
[2] Center for Quality and Statistics, China National Institute of Standardization, Beijing, China
[3] Ergonomics Laboratory, China National Institute of Standardization, Beijing, China

Abstract. With the development of modernization and urbanization in China, more and more buildings develop into a huge collection group with massive functions. People often have to face difficulties and anxieties in locating their destinations. As a non-verbal presentation of information, graphical symbols are often used to help people in wayfinding. It's comprehensibility that determines the effect of information transmission of graphical symbols. This research collected comprehension data of thirty-two symbols in China. To explore statistically significant relationships between symbol comprehension and influencing factors, Pearson's Chi-square tests, logistic regression analysis, and correspondence analysis were conducted. From the test results of two different variants of rental bicycle, it shows that concrete symbols are more likely to be understood correctly than abstract symbols. Furthermore, the respondents with higher education level have less difficulty than those with lower education level in comprehending graphical symbols.

Keywords: Graphical symbol · Comprehension test · Wayfinding

1 Background

Graphical symbols are visually perceptible figures with particular meanings used to transmit information independently of language [1, 2]. In modern society, in order to meet the demands of transiting information quickly, barrier freely and aesthetically, graphical symbols are widely used in various field, for example, the wayfinding systems in street blocks and public facilities, the emergency evacuation systems and early warning systems, the interfaces of devices and apparatuses for operating and instructing, the interfaces of family appliances and personal electronic devices for operating and controlling, the instructions of geometrical features and manufacturing process in technical product documents. Among the above fields, graphical symbols used in wayfinding systems are the most popular and important ones that are close related with our ordinary life.

Comprehensibility is "extent to which a graphical symbol is likely to be interpreted with the intended meaning" [3], graphical symbols with good comprehensibility can be

C. Stephanidis (Ed.): HCII 2015 Posters, Part II, CCIS 529, pp. 715–721, 2015.
DOI: 10.1007/978-3-319-21383-5_121

used as non-verbal presentation of information in public places to help people finding their destinations, while graphical symbols with poor comprehensibility cannot convey the intended meaning independently and must be used with local languages.

With rapid urbanization and modernization development in China, more and more buildings develop into a huge collection group with massive functions [4]. It is common that some people have difficulties in locating their destinations [5]. The comprehension test [3] plays a key role in ensuring the graphical symbol to be understood by its intended users, it's also a vital process in the standardization of graphical symbols. Using comprehension test, experts have done plenty of research to analysis possible factors which influencing graphical symbol comprehensibility. Foster and Afzalnia [6] found the criterion of acceptability of the comprehension test and the importance of gathering cross-cultural data. Lee and Dazikir's [7] research demonstrated that symbol comprehension can be varied significantly in different countries. Previous researches mainly focus on the criterion of acceptability of comprehensibility test result and age, culture related differences in the comprehension of graphical symbols. While there is little research on other factors that will influence the comprehensibility, e.g. symbol design and education level.

Based on the comprehension test result of graphical symbols, this paper focuses on the possible factors that may influence symbol comprehensibility without the consideration of cultural differences.

2 Method

This study tested thirty-two graphical symbols (see Fig. 1) using the comprehension test method in ISO 9186-1:2007 [8], among which, eleven graphical symbols (including two "Rental bicycle" variants were developed by Keiichi Koyama from i Design company, Japan. The other twenty-one graphical symbols are selected from Chinese national standards [9] or practical applications in China wayfinding systems.

Fig. 1. Graphical symbols used in the comprehension test

According to ISO 9186-1:2007 [8], there are three age groups, two sex groups and three educational groups in the sample. The three age groups are: 15-30, 31–50, and over 50. The two sex groups are: Male and Female. The three educational levels are: "Left school at normal school-leaving age", "Post-school qualification which is not a degree", "Degree or degree equivalent". This research tested the comprehension of graphical symbols in 2010 and 2013. Altogether the sample added up to 450 respondents.

The test material includes: the instruction page, the respondent detail page, the sample page and test pages. Random orders are used in test pages.

In order to calculate the comprehensibility of each individual variant, all the results were categorized as "Correct", "Almost correct", "Wrong", "Wrong and opposite", "Don't know", and "No response". Before the test, a list of all possible responses and relative categories was prepared.

To explore statistically significant relationships between symbol comprehension and influencing factors, Pearson's Chi-square tests, logistic regression analysis, and correspondence analysis were conducted.

3 Test Results and Analysis

3.1 Relationship of Graphical Symbol Element and Comprehensibility

Among the 32 symbols, "rental bicycle" is the only one tested twice but with different variants (see Fig. 2). It was interesting that the correct rate of comprehensibility in 2010 and 2013 is very different, i.e. 28.0 % and 64.2 %, respectively. For all interviewees are random selected, a possible influencing factor could be the different graphical symbol element. The "rental bicycle" symbol of 2010 is more abstract than that of 2013. Now we use Pearson's Chi-square test to reveal whether there exists a relationship with the symbol type and comprehensibility. The Chi-square is 27.494 and p-value is 0.000, which implies the symbol comprehensibility has a relationship with symbol type and the concrete symbols are easier to be understood than abstract ones.

3.2 Relationship of Education Levels and Comprehensibility

In this test of China, education level question was added for respondents. Number of answers with combination of education levels and comprehension categories are listed in crosstables. Pearson's Chi-square test is used to reveal the relationship of symbol comprehensibility and education level. For more than 20 % expected frequency values in Chi-square test are less than 5, the result is not so reliable. So Fisher exact test is introduced. Tables 1 and 2 show the test result.

Fig. 2. Two "rental bicycle" symbols

Table 1. Pearson's Chi-square test result for symbol comprehension test 2010

	Baggage delivery service	Automatic vending machine	Rental bicycle	Convenience store	WLAN	Barber	Garage	Underpass
χ^2	21.314	27.939	20.448	4.470	42.272	14.636	14.618	17.972
p	0.002	0.000	0.009	0.613	0.000	0.023	0.006	0.021
Fisher	19.606	28.313	18.799	3.570	49.553	12.702	11.389	15.111
p	0.002	0.000	0.003	0.798	0.000	0.014	0.002	0.009
	Cinema	Safety check	Overpass	Lecture hall	Snack	Ancient pagoda	Luggage store	Baggage check
χ^2	10.857	19.355	10.717	28.536	29.710	12.479	29.762	20.946
p	0.093	0.004	0.098	0.000	0.000	0.052	0.000	0.007
Fisher	9.893	18.269	10.048	26.797	24.198	12.320	25.467	19.652
p	0.090	0.002	0.055	0.000	0.000	0.031	0.000	0.004

Table 2. Pearson's Chi-square test result for symbol comprehension test 2013

	Lost children	Meeting point	Rental bicycle	Park & ride	Group gathering point	Toilet Paper	Tissue	Toilet Seat Covers
χ^2	6.826	8.460	10.031	10.221	17.111	10.075	3.442	7.634
p	0.145	0.393	0.040	0.106	0.002	0.039	0.487	0.266
Fisher	6.661	7.128	9.028	9.230	17.208	9.201	3.627	8.183
p	0.150	0.505	0.042	0.129	0.001	0.031	0.461	0.196
	Automatic Sensor Faucet	Hand Lotion	Hand Dryer	No fireworks	No leaning on	No corrosive and toxic material	No radioactive and magnetic material	Warning; Mind gaps
χ^2	32.072	8.647	18.865	15.251	33.000	29.679	22.321	27.196
p	0.000	0.194	0.004	0.018	0.000	0.000	0.001	0.000
Fisher	27.666	8.073	15.416	12.891	23.456	27.162	24.692	28.012
p	0.000	0.203	0.008	0.023	0.000	0.000	0.000	0.000

From the test result 23 out of 32 symbols have *p*-values smaller than the significance level 0.05, which shows these symbols have significant statistical relationship with education level.

- **Symbols significantly related with comprehensibility:** baggage delivery service, automatic vending machine, rental bicycle (2010), barber, garage, underpass, safety check, overpass, lecture hall, snack, ancient pagoda, luggage store, baggage check, rental bicycle (2013), group gathering point, toilet paper, automatic sensor faucet, hand dryer, no fireworks, no leaning on, no corrosive and toxic material, no radioactive and magnetic material, warning mind gaps.
- **Symbols not related with comprehensibility:** convenience store, WLAN, cinema, lost children, meeting point, park & ride, tissue, toilet seat covers, hand lotion.

For the symbols have significant relationship with education level, we further use logistic regression to explore which education level influencing more to comprehensibility. We find that for most symbols Logit 3 (1a/3) the coefficient of education level 3 has a p-value less than 0.05, and the coefficient of education level 3 is larger than zero, which shows that people with education level 3 are more inclined to have correct answers comparing to answer "Don't know".

Now we use correspondence analysis to show pictures how education levels related to comprehensibility degrees. We take symbol "Baggage delivery service" as an example.

According to the Fig. 3, coordinate 1 can explain 70.47 % of the relationship between education level and comprehensibility. People with high education level more likely to have correct answers, and low education level people usually don't know the exact meaning. From the correspondence plot of other symbols, similar conclusions can be received either.

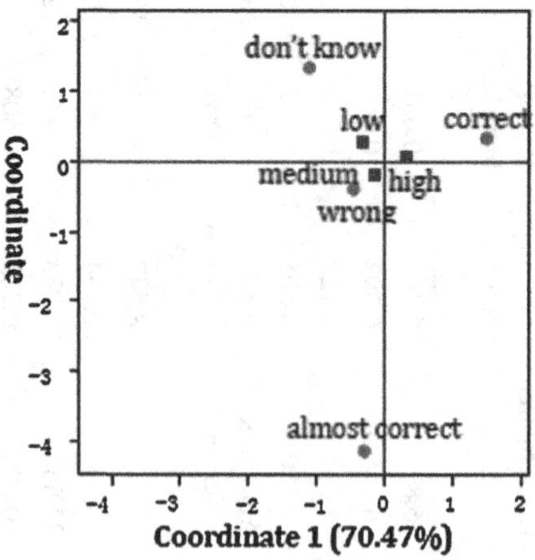

Fig. 3. Correspondence plot for symbol "Baggage delivery service"

4 Conclusion

The test results showed that concrete symbol is easier to be understood than abstract symbol. According to test results of two different variants of the same meaning, it shows that concrete symbols are more likely to be understood correctly than abstract symbols. It was also found that 23 symbols among 32 tested have significant relationship with education level. The respondents with higher education level have less difficulty than those with lower education level in comprehending graphical symbols.

Results of this study demonstrate that symbol comprehension can be influenced significantly by the design and respondents' education level.

Acknowledgement. This research was supported by China National Institute of Standardization through the "special funds for the basic R&D undertakings by welfare research institutions" (522014Y-3344) and the National Key Technology R&D Program (2012BAK28B03, 2014BAK01B01).

References

1. GB/T 15565.1—2008, Graphical symbols-Terms-Part 1: General, 图形符号 术语 第1部分: 通用. Standardization Administration of the People's Republic of China (SAC). 01.080.10 (2008)
2. ISO 17724:2003, Graphical symbols – Vocabulary. International Organization for Standardization (ISO). 01.080.10 (2003)
3. ISO 9186-1:2014, Graphical symbols – Test methods – Part 1: Method for testing comprehensibility. International Organization for Standardization (ISO). 01.080.10 (2014)
4. Li, T.: Design of high-rise buildings– A tend of cluster and large-scale, 高层建筑设计的一种倾向——大规模高层建筑的集群化和城市化. Chin. Overseas Archit. **05**, 10–12 (2003)
5. Tam, M.L.: An optimization model for wayfinding problems in terminal building. J. Air Transp. Manage. **17**(2), 74–79 (2011)
6. Foster, J.J., Afzalnia, M.R.: International assessment of judged symbol comprehensibility. Int. J. Psychol. **40**(3), 169–175 (2005)
7. Lee, S., Dazkir, S.S., Paik, H.S., Coskun, A.: Comprehensibility of universal healthcare symbols for wayfinding in healthcare facilities. Appl. Ergonomics. **45**(4), 878–885 (2014)
8. ISO 9186-1:2007, Graphical symbols – Test methods – Part 1: Methods for testing comprehensibility. International Organization for Standardization (ISO). 01.080.10 (2007)
9. GB/T 10001(all parts), Public information graphical symbols, 公共信息图形符号. Standardization Administration of the People's Republic of China (SAC). 01.080.10 (2012)

Author Index

Printed in the United States
By Bookmasters